War without End

D0817710

In order to properly comprehend the events of September 11 it is necessary to trace them from the roots. In the case of 9/11, this requires an elementary knowledge of Islam followed by an understanding of Islamic fundamentalism as an ideology both of resistance (as in Egypt) and of governance (as in Saudi Arabia). However, in Afghanistan, fundamentalism emerged as the prime force of opposition and resistance in the 1980s, and eventually defeated the Moscow-backed regime to become the state ideology.

It is against this setting that Dilip Hiro narrates the devastating attacks on the two American embassies in East Africa in 1998 – a prelude to the attacks on the World Trade Center and the Pentagon.

The result is a timely and topical book that enlightens the reader on such basics as the cardinal principles of Islam, as well as lays bare several Islamist ideologies and groups simply yet fully, and provides a multi-faceted narrative of America's short, sharp campaign against the Taliban in Afghanistan in which hi-tech weaponry played a crucial role.

Dilip Hiro is a specialist on the Middle East, Islam, Central Asia and South Asia, and the author of more than twenty books, including *Neighbors, not Friends: Iraq and Iran after the Gulf Wars* (Routledge, 2001). A frequent commentator on the above subjects on CNN, BBC Television, Sky Television, and various American and British radio channels, he has published articles in most of the major newspapers in the US and the UK.

By the same author

Non-fiction
Neighbors, Not Friends: Iraq and Iran after the Gulf Wars (2001)
Sharing the Promised Land: A Tale of Israelis and Palestinians
  (1999)
Dictionary of the Middle East (1996)
The Middle East (1996)
Between Marx and Muhammad: The Changing Face of Central Asia
  (1995)
Lebanon, Fire and Embers: A History of the Lebanese Civil War
  (1993)
Desert Shield to Desert Storm: The Second Gulf War (1992)
Black British, White British: A History of Race Relations in
  Britain (1991)
The Longest War: The Iran–Iraq Military Conflict (1991)
Holy Wars: The Rise of Islamic Fundamentalism (1989)
Iran: The Revolution Within (1988)
Iran under the Ayatollahs (1985)
Inside the Middle East (1982)
Inside India Today (1977)
The Untouchables of India (1975)
Black British, White British (1973)
The Indian Family in Britain (1969)

Fiction
Three Plays (1985)
Interior, Exchange, Exterior (Poems, 1980)
Apply, Apply, No Reply and *A Clean Break* (Two Plays, 1978)
To Anchor a Cloud (Play, 1972)
A Triangular View (Novel, 1969)

War without End

The rise of Islamist terrorism and global response

Dilip Hiro

London and New York

Revised edition 2002 by Routledge
11 New Fetter Lane, London EC4P 4EE

Simultaneously published in the USA and Canada
by Routledge
29 West 35th Street, New York NY 10001

Reprinted 2003

Routledge is an imprint of the Taylor & Francis Group

Typeset in Times by BC Typesetting, Bristol
Printed and bound in Great Britain by
TJ International Ltd, Padstow, Cornwall

British Library Cataloguing in Publication Data
A catalogue record for this book is available from the British Library

Library of Congress Cataloging in Publicaiton Data
A catalog record for this book has been requested

ISBN 0–415–28801–0 (hbk)
ISBN 0–415–28802–9 (pbk)

Contents

PART III
Islamist terrorism and global response 265

Illustrations

Osama bin Laden, leader of Al Qaida, and Ayman Zawahiri, leader of Al Jihad.

Al Shifa Pharmaceutical factory, Khartoum, destroyed by US missiles on 20–21 August 1998.
Reuters/Aladin Adbel Naby

The World Trade Center Towers, Manhattan, hit by two hijacked planes on September 11.
AP Photo/Chao Soi Cheong

New Yorkers fleeing from the burning WTC Towers.
AP Photo/Amy Sancetta

The damaged Pentagon on September 11, with the dome of the Capitol in the background.
AP Photo/Stephen J. Boitano

Mugshots of the 19 hijackers on September 11: Khalid al Midhar; Majid Moqed; Nawaq al Hamzi; Salem al Hamzi; Hani Hanjour; Ahmad al Haznawi; Ahmad al Nami; Ziad Samir Jarrah; Saeed al Ghamdi; Marwan Yusuf al Shehhi; Fayez Rahsid al Qadi Bani Hammad; Mohald al Shahri; Hamza al Ghamdi; Ahmad al Ghamdi; Satam al Suqami; Muhammad al Amir Awad al Sayyid Atta; Abdul Aziz al Omari; Waleed al Shahri; Wail al Shahri.

The War Cabinet of President George W. Bush, third on the left: (anti-clockwise, from left) Attorney-General John Ashcroft; Vice President Dick Cheney; Secretary of State Colin Powell; Secretary of Defense Donald Rumsfeld; Deputy Secretary of Defense Paul Wolfowitz; FBI Director Robert Mueller; Secretary of the Treasury Paul O'Neill; CIA Director George J. Tenet; White House Chief of Staff Andy Card; National Security Advisor Condoleezza Rice and Chairman of Joint Chiefs of Staff General Henry H. Shelton.
AP Photo/J. Scott Applewhite

Mullah Muhammad Omar, Supreme Leader of the Taliban, Afghanistan.
AP Photo/HO

The Pentagon's poster and leaflet showing Mullah Omar as a wanted fugitive, October 2001.
AP Photo

Chokar Karez hamlet, Afghanistan, hit by the American bombing on 22–23 October 2001.
Reuters/Mian Khursheed

Two dead Kashmiri terrorists on the steps of the Indian Parliament, New Delhi, 13 December 2001.
Reuters/Reuters TV

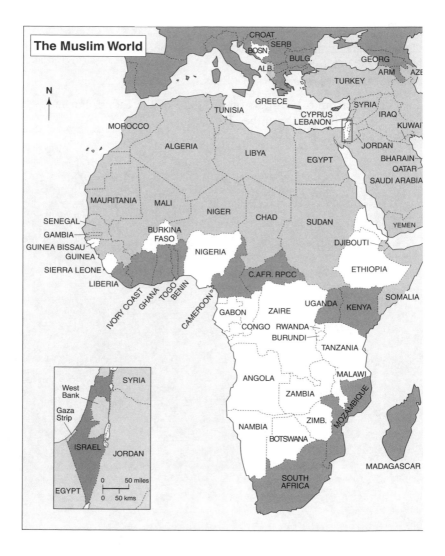

The Muslim World

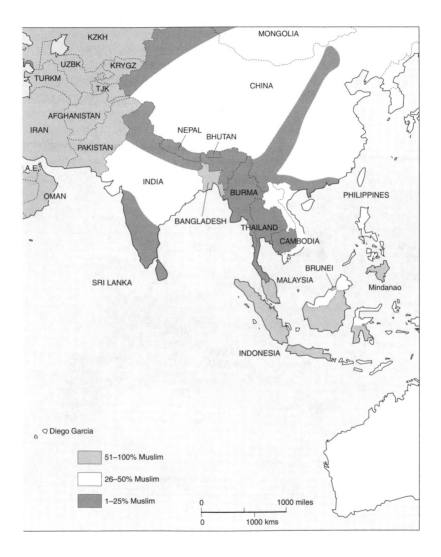

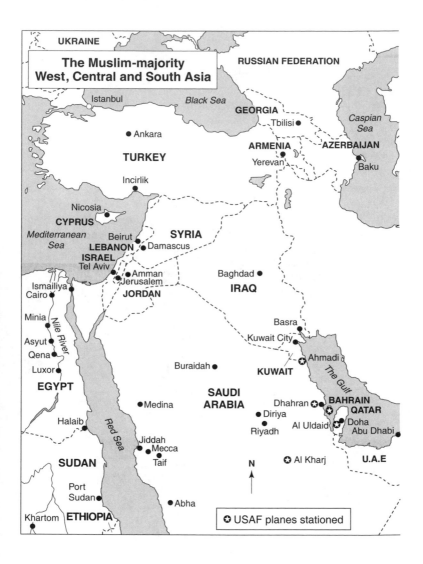

The Muslim-majority West, Central and South Asia

USAF planes stationed

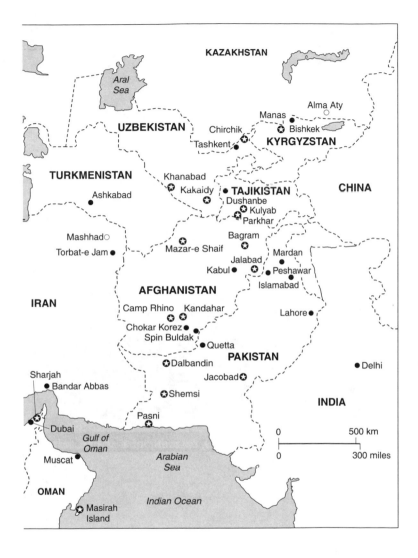

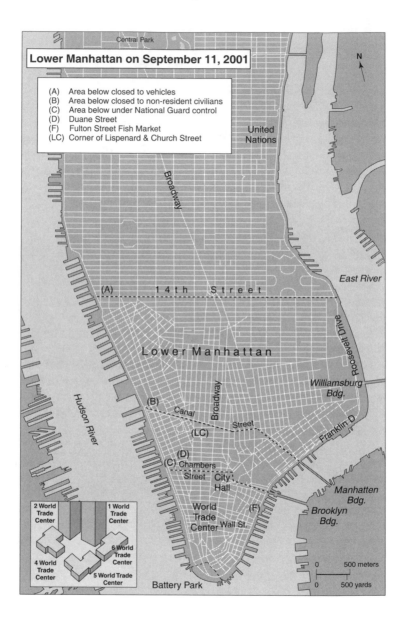

Lower Manhattan on September 11, 2001

(A)   Area below closed to vehicles
(B)   Area below closed to non-resident civilians
(C)   Area below under National Guard control
(D)   Duane Street
(F)   Fulton Street Fish Market
(LC) Corner of Lispenard & Church Street

Central Park

N

Broadway

United Nations

East River

(A)   1 4 t h   S t r e e t

L o w e r   M a n h a t t a n

Roosevelt Drive

Hudson River

(B)

Canal

Broadway

Street

Williamsburg Bdg.

(LC)

Franklin D

(D)
(C) Chambers

Street   City
           Hall

World
Trade
Center   Wall St.

(F)

Manhatten Bdg.

Brooklyn Bdg.

2 World
Trade
Center

1 World
Trade
Center

6 World
Trade
Center

4 World
Trade
Center

5 World Trade
Center

Battery Park

0   500 meters

0   500 yards

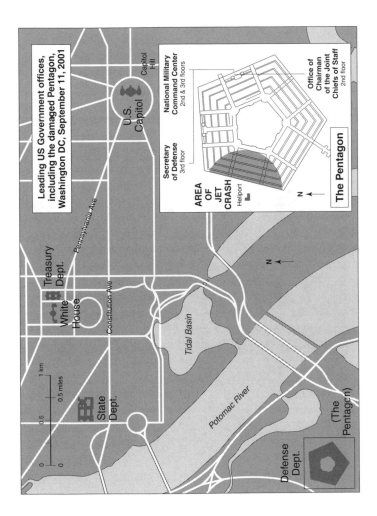

Leading US Government offices, including the damaged Pentagon, Washington DC, September 11, 2001

Pennsylvania Ave

Capitol Hill

U.S. Capitol

Treasury Dept.

White House

Constitution Ave

Tidal Basin

State Dept.

1 km

0.5 miles

0.5

0

0

Potomac River

N

Defense Dept.

(The Pentagon)

N

AREA OF JET CRASH

Heliport

Secretary of Defense
3rd floor

National Military Command Center
2nd & 3rd floors

Office of Chairman of the Joint Chiefs of Staff
2nd floor

The Pentagon

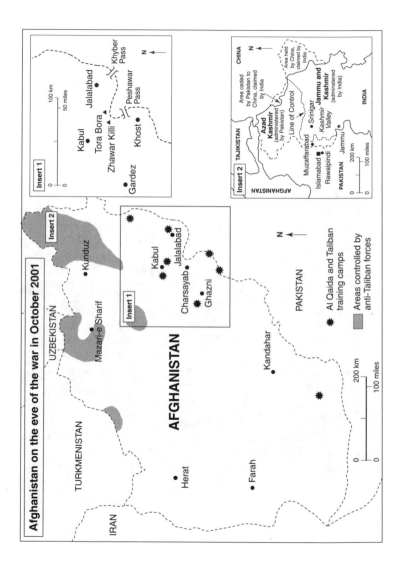

Afghanistan on the eve of the war in October 2001

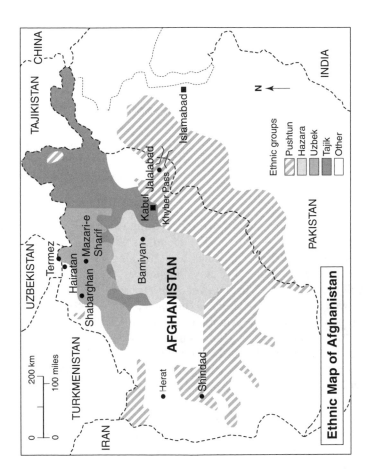

Ethnic Map of Afghanistan

Prologue

If it had been gray or foggy or overcast, there is no way those
bastards could have crashed those planes.

Richard Picciotto, a New York firefighter[1]

A perfect, late summer morning in Manhattan with the temperature set to rise to 27°C/80°F – cloudless sky, clear horizon with
visibility stretching for miles and no hint of the horror that
awaits the islanders. Tuesday, September 11, 2001, a date that
will enter as "9/11" in the *American Heritage College Dictionary*
as well as the *Oxford English Dictionary, and* top the annual poll
on new words by the American Dialect Society.

As on other days, Ian Williams, a tall, bearded, broad-
shouldered journalist in his late thirties, finds the Fulton Street
fish market below his apartment on South Street Sea Port, stocked
with millions of dollars worth of seafood, humming with activity
in the early morning.

At 08.44 hours EST, Jules Naudet, a slim, handsome film-
maker in his late twenties with a luxuriant black thatch of hair,
accompanying a fire engine battalion of the Duane Street fire
station, is shooting a documentary on New York firefighters at
the junction of Lispenard Street and Church Street, several
blocks north of the World Trade Center (WTC), a 16 acre
(6.5 hectare) complex of seven buildings with Twin Towers as
its sentinels, symbols of the economic might of the world's sole

superpower, each word – World – Trade – Center charged with profound meaning, all together signifying more than the sum of its parts. His elder brother Gedeon, endowed equally with abundant raven black hair, is at the Duane Street fire station, the subject of the brothers' television documentary.

At 08.45 hours, when Jules Naudet sees an aircraft vanish behind a tall building, he follows it with his camera. He sees it smash into the 110-story North Tower (aka Tower One) and hears a delayed crash. His fire engine battalion races to the WTC, and he notices a gaping wound in the world's second tallest building. The Tower is spewing flames, black smoke billowing out from the floors above and below the 87th–92nd floors.

At George's Lunch, a block away from the WTC, Lucy Torres, a rotund Hispanic woman in her early thirties, snub-nosed and short-haired, is serving breakfast to her regular customers, some of whom are employed at the WTC. "They jumped out of their seats [when they heard the crash] and went outside," she recalls:

> I followed them and saw smoke coming out of Tower One. Everyone thought it was an accident, but when we heard the noise of the second plane coming towards the building, we knew it wasn't. The side of the building seemed to explode and people ran down the street away from it. My boss's daughter was in a panic, trembling, because she had seen people jumping out of the building.

While the diner owner's daughter views the jumpers from the outside, Jules Naudet has a perspective from the opposite side. As an associate of a firefighting team that has entered Tower One through the shattered windows of the ground-floor lobby, he has a rare view from the inside: desperate, distraught men and women leaping from such heights that they disintegrate on hitting the ground outside the lobby windows. He is already shaken by what he has encountered inside the lobby in the aftermath of a fireball created by the jet fuel pouring down the elevator shafts – marble tiles ripped off the walls, broken windows, and two persons burning on the floor.[2]

Despite the mad rush, the chief of 20th Firefighting Battalion, Richard Picciotto, a tall, muscular man in his mid thirtiess, takes in the ghost-town aura of the 16th floor: "Computer screens were still on, chairs were kicked away from desks, half-sipped coffee and half-eaten muffins sat on almost every surface. Family photos smiled out into empty rooms."[3]

On hearing a boom, and finding the Fulton Street fish porters, crowded in Peck Slip Square, staring up, westwards, into the sky filling with smoke, Ian Williams rushes down with his cell phone, camera, binoculars and tape recorder to join them. He proceeds to probe the police line. Finding it impenetrable, he makes a detour, past Battery Park and the new bicycle path by the Hudson River, to get close to the WTC.

Soon after 09.30 hours Jules Naudet flees Tower One through a glass-enclosed walkway and reaches the street, but is still near enough to the Tower to get hurt by its collapse. Around 10.00 hours he hears a man near him shouting "It's coming down!" He runs like hell, shelters between a television news van and a car, and covers his nose and mouth with his T-shirt.

"I could see flames through the window and I went outside to take a look," remembers Lucy Torres. "The building fell, and that's when I broke down. A huge cloud of white dust was rolling towards me, and my legs wouldn't move. A big guy standing next to me yelled, 'Move! It's coming this way.' I thought, 'Oh, my God, I'm going to die.' He pushed me into the diner, and it went black for 10 minutes."

At the Duane Street fire station, Gedeon Naudet, armed with a camera, and three firefighters jump into a pickup truck and race toward the WTC as everybody else is running in the opposite direction. "After four minutes I look up and see Tower Two collapsing literally above my head," he recalls. "I jumped into the belly of the fire truck. Every thing is falling down and falling hard. I could hear pieces of steel crashing . . . I remember the truck windows shattering." All along, he keeps his camera running with its focus on Tower Two.

The collapse of the Twin Towers takes a heavy toll of the fire-fighters. Ian Williams lends his cell phone to a group of them, all caked in ash and sweat, to check on their families. "We lost 300 of our guys when they [the Towers] collapsed," says one, fiddling with his large, lit cheroot. "I don't want to offend any one, but we just gotta go in and nuke the whole fucking Middle East now."[4]

At Manhattan's central mortuary, there have been only two autopsy cases until 09.00 hours, according to Oliver Monfredi, a young, sprightly British medic from Leeds University. A medical technician, nicknamed Practical Joker, breezes into the theater, and says, "A plane has hit the World Trade Center." At first, none of his colleagues takes him seriously. Finally, when they do, they say, "It is going to be light plane, a two-seater," recalls Monfredi. "We concluded the first examinations [of the corpses] in 15 eerie minutes. I thought they were going to arrive with a truck full of victims but they never did. There were four victims, then two, then two." Then firefighters started arriving, carrying dead colleagues. "That is when I felt like a foreign intruder."[5]

It is a long while before Lucy Torres recovers her wits. Outside her diner, she sees people "running down the street, with debris under their feet; rubbish, paper, and lots of shoes." She finds her own shoes full of dirt as she trudges home over the Brooklyn Bridge as part of a column, among many, of refugees, all covered in ash, as Lower Manhattan is evacuated. She reaches home, sits on a couch and cries.

By the time Williams returns to his apartment, electricity and telephones are down. Sitting at his desk in the dark, he sees the first convoys of armored cars and troops arriving along Franklin D. Roosevelt Drive, lights flashing. The troops will occupy the zone below Canal Street, barring it to all civilians, and placing the area below Chambers Street under National Guard control, with civilian traffic brought to a standstill. By the end of the day the Coast Guard has managed to evacuate one million people from Manhattan, an impressive figure when compared with the 186,000 passengers that are transported daily to and from the island. "Manhattan is in a virtual lockdown state," says a Coast Guard spokesman.

Along with the other wings of the US armed forces, the Coast Guard is put on the highest alert by the Department of Defense within minutes of a hijacked plane slamming into the Pentagon building on the outskirts of Washington, DC at 09.36 hours. Within the next half an hour, the White House, the State Department and the Treasury are evacuated, with the White House manned only by the Secret Service and the staff of the National Security Council. President George Walker Bush (1946– ; r. 2001–), visiting an elementary school in Sarasota, Florida, is hustled to his jet, Air Force One, and starts a zigzag journey back to Washington. The Federal Aviation Authority closes all airports, ordering the planes in the air to land at the nearest airport, while the Coast Guard shuts down all 12 major seaports. The FAA goes on to ban private planes from flying below 18,000 ft (5,630 m) and within 11.5 miles (18 km) of 86 nuclear power plants.[6]

The moment the Secret Service learns that one, possibly two, hijacked planes are heading for the capital, Vice President Dick Cheney (1941–) is literally lifted from his seat in the White House and taken to an underground bunker.

In the White House Situations Room, gripped by the thought that the White House could be hit by suicide hijackers, Frank Miller, director for military affairs, instructs an aide to e-mail a list of all those present to several addresses so that "when and if we died, someone would know who was in there." Reports and rumors are flowing in fast: a car bomb at the State Department; the National Mall in flames; the Pentagon up in smoke; hijacked jets zeroing in on Washington. Recalling the warnings about terrorists striking on American soil, Richard Clarke, the counter-terrorism chief at the White House, mutters: "This is Al Qaida."[7]

The drama at the federal capital is duplicated at all state capitals where government buildings and court houses are evacuated and sealed off for several days.

Stars and Stripes appear everywhere, with street vendors in Manhattan selling flags, a dollar each. The star-spangled banner is seen outside homes, on car and taxi aerials, pinned to lapels, fluttering above offices, factories and gas stations, and streaming from the back of motorcycles and trucks. Enthusiasts start downloading images of the flag from the Internet. Its electronic versions shine from display boards beside the interstate highways. It is draped over the skyscrapers surrounding the shattered WTC and over the ruined gap in the Pentagon. Thousands of rescue workers at these sites adorn their helmets with miniflags. Americans have taken to flag-waving en masse to demonstrate national solidarity, sympathy for the victims and defiance of the terrorists.

At the Valley Forge flag factory in Womelsdorf, Pennsylvania, they have produced 1.2 million flags on small sticks in a fortnight – a *hundred-fold* increase. It is the most dramatic outburst of demand in the company's 74-year history – bigger than Pearl Harbor, World War II, the Korean War (1950–3), the John Kennedy assassination (1963) and the Gulf War (1991), says the factory's general manager.[8]

Whitney Houston's re-released version of *The Star Spangled Banner* is the best-selling single, followed by Lee Greenwood's *God Bless the USA*. The freshly released compilation entitled *God Bless America: Songs of Hope, Freedom and Inspiration* has become Number One in the album charts. Radio stations are having a field day playing these records.

Flags and patriotic songs are antidotes to the depression that has descended on the nation. Immediately after the ghastly flying bombs, a national survey shows 70 percent of the respondents feeling depressed, 50 percent having difficulty concentrating at work, and 33 percent having trouble sleeping at night; and 75 percent think there will be further attacks.[9]

As a security measure, the New York City authorities require hot-dog sellers to post their names and pictures on the stalls. Many of them are Pakistanis and Bangladeshis with Muslim names. Hot-dogs sales plummet by 40 percent.

Most people below Chambers Street in Manhattan go about wearing masks. "It is the smell . . . that emanates from the tangled wreckage of the World Trade Center," reports N.R. Klienfield in the *New York Times*:

> [During] the first days . . . it was so pungent that shifting winds transported it for miles, all the way to the upper reaches of Manhattan. They carried it over into Brooklyn and Queens across the East River, deposited it in New Jersey across the Hudson to the west. Everybody seemed to smell the horror of death . . . A man peddling American flags said, "It is the smell of souls being disturbed."[10]

Because Osama bin Laden (1957–), named by President Bush as the suspected mastermind behind the terrorist atrocities, wears a turban, male Sikhs – required by their faith not to cut their hair and who therefore cover it with a turban – are assaulted. A Sikh religious organization logs 200 incidents of Sikhs being targeted in a fortnight, with one of them, Balbir Singh Sodhi, a storekeeper in Arizona, shot dead.

The Arab-American Anti-Discrimination Committee collects 300 nationwide reports of violent incidents, including three murders. With airports opening gradually, Arab-Americans discover that TWA, "Traveling while Arab," has become almost a federal offense. Oddly, their resulting depression is shared by a substantial body of mainstream Americans, albeit for different reasons.

On the eve of the American air strikes against Afghanistan on 7 October, 40 percent of the respondents are still feeling depressed, 25 percent are having difficulty concentrating at work, and 16 percent are having trouble sleeping at night. And the percentage of those who forecast further attacks has risen from 75 to 83.[11]

Amidst fears of retaliation, thousands of additional armed police and National Guard troops patrol New York and other cities. Fighter jets frequently scramble over Washington on homeland defense missions. Security remains tight at all government buildings and at sporting events. The cases of anthrax in

Florida and New York have raised national anxiety further. The sales of firearms have risen by up to 30 percent in some states, and the sales of ammunition, bullet-proof jackets, gas masks and antibiotics to fight anthrax and smallpox are brisk.

The Federal Bureau of Investigation (FBI) has arrested 600 suspects, and eavesdropped on client–attorney conversations, thus depriving the suspects of protection accorded by the Sixth Amendment of the US Constitution, but none of the detainees has been found to be a key player. The FBI has received 100,000 tips on possible hijackers.

When, as a result of the collapse of the Twin Towers, the 47-story building at 7 World Trade Center falls, it reveals a clandestine station of the Central Intelligence Agency which is, by law, banned from operating on American soil. Its embarrassed headquarters at Langley, Virginia, dispatches a team to retrieve documents. In the immediate aftermath of the devastating attacks, at President Bush's behest, US Congress increases the CIA's annual budget of $3.5 billion by a hefty $1 billion.[12] This and increased spending on defense will result in a budget deficit, reversing the healthy surpluses of recent years.

The commercial gloom has spread from airlines and travel – hotels, car rentals, aircraft manufacture, theme parks – to car sales to home building to high-tech industry and departmental stores. The US economy, barely afloat before 9/11, sinks rapidly. For the first time in 11 years, 60 percent say recession has arrived. Consumer confidence falls more sharply than at any time since the 1973 Arab oil embargo and the 1990 Iraqi invasion of Kuwait. The federal financial year ends on 30 September with a $110 billion surplus, down from $236 billion for the previous year. For the next 12 months, Washington will be lucky to break even – with the anticipated surplus of $304 billion disappearing in thin air. The nervous Federal Reserve Board will cut interest rates down to 2 percent, the lowest in 40 years.

In a single month New York has lost 79,000 jobs compared with the forecasts of 80,000–115,000 over several months.

Lower Manhattan is still plagued by a strange odor. "[A] stubborn reminder," says a report in the *New York Times*:

On certain days people as far away as the Greenwich Village say they can sniff it. The other day it was particularly potent in the crowded Wall Street. Some workers in the financial district went home early on Friday because they found the smell so repugnant . . . It is like burning plastic, or what a burning computer might smell like . . . A few people tie handkerchiefs around their faces, bandit style. Others pinch their noses . . . Ann Hoch, when she was able to enter Battery Park City where she lives, on 23 September, said, "It was the smell of rotting food in people's apartments and in the grocery stores. It was enough to make you gag. When it was overcast, it was stronger. It made your lips tingle."[13]

In the nearby, affluent Tribeca residential neighborhood, tests show that dust from an air vent in George Tabb's building's hallway has 555 times the acceptable level of asbestos, and the samples from his bathroom vent indicate dangerous levels of fiberglass.[14]

An acrid pall still hangs over downtown Manhattan when a memorial service is held on 28 October at Ground Zero, where 7,000 rescue workers have been toiling over the site for more than six weeks. The initial estimate of 10,000 fatalities has mercifully been reduced to 5,422 from 65 countries. So far only 425 bodies have been identified, and about 8,000 body parts recovered. The next day the FBI issues its second general warning: attacks may be carried out during the next week on US targets at home or abroad. On 30 October firefighters excavate $200 million of gold bullion from the WTC's underground network of tunnels and roads. Two days later the New York City authorities decide to reduce the number of firefighters from 60 to 24. Incensed firefighters protest, and a dozen are arrested.

A dramatic turnaround – both in the national mood and financial markets – comes only when the Taliban evacuate Kabul on the night of 12–13 November. Stock exchanges, allergic to uncertainty, are relieved that the fighting is almost over and are buoyed by a swift American victory. The subsequent news of the 7.1 percent upturn in retail sales in October, wiping out the 2.2 percent drop in September, acts as a tonic.[15]

A sign of New York getting back to normal. After two months of returning home to his Greenwich Village stoop, festooned with the Stars and Stripes – a sight that nourishes his patriotism – Graydon Carter, editor of *Vanity Fair*, finds the flag gone, stolen. Photographs of firefighters and police officers that replaced the celebrity pictures in the tabloids and on the covers of glossy magazines like *Vanity Fair* are gone. So too is the chatter about cultural sea change in the aftermath of 9/11.

As Thanksgiving approaches on 22 November, the official total of the dead at the WTC is set at 3,900 – down from the previous 5,422. The unofficial estimates vary between 2,600 and 2,950.[16] To this must be added 126 Defense Department employees and another 109 who perished in the two plane crashes at the Pentagon and in Pennsylvania.

On 7 December, the sixtieth commemoration of the Japanese assault on the Pearl Harbor Naval Base in Hawaii has a special meaning for Americans. In that strike 2,403 people died or went missing.

The statistics for gun sales for the three months following 9/11 show a rise of 9 to 22 percent in different states, peaking in October with a little over one million sales. Many of the customers are serious first-time buyers. "September 11, like other catastrophes . . . makes people want to protect themselves and their families against the enemy who, in this case is hard to identify," says James Fox, professor of criminal justice at Northeastern University in Boston. Students at Holyoke College, Massachusetts, will form the first collegiate chapter of Second Amendment Sisters, a national women's pro-gun group.

On the one hundredth day after the tragic suicide strikes, while the Federal September 11 Victim Compensation Fund announces that the average payment to the families of the dead will be $1.65 million, including any insurance, the first tourist boat arrives at Liberty Island as the Statue of Liberty is reopened. In post-Taliban Afghanistan, people await the inauguration of an interim government, backed solidly by Washington.

An *International Herald Tribune*/Pew Research Center for the People and the Press survey of 275 opinion leaders in 24 countries shows that 79 percent of non-US respondents consider the terrorist attacks a "new chapter in world history" – the same percentage as among the US opinion leaders. But 70 percent of the non-US opinion leaders believe that "It is good that Americans now know what it is like to be vulnerable".[17] Seventy-five percent of non-US opinion leaders like America because it is "a land of opportunity."

The year ends with an Arab-American secret service agent, Walied Shater, being barred from traveling on an American Airlines jet from Baltimore to Washington International airport.[18]

The year 2002 begins with the FBI extending warning of terrorist threats until 11 March by sending out e-mails to 18,000 law enforcement agencies, but not publicizing the alert.

Of the 1.4 million tons of rubble to be removed, 962,725 tons of debris and steel have been lifted, the next phase being the digging out of the debris compressed into the basement levels. Plans are afoot to create an archive, a memorial: bicycles still locked to a metal rack; directional signs for the subways and trade center towers; computer keyboards; pages from calendars; clocks stopped at the moment of the strike; a file cabinet; and dozens of other items valuable by virtue of their link to cultural history.

On 11 March 2002, the six-month anniversary of the collective trauma inflicted on New York, at 08.46 hours New Yorkers observe a minute's silence, and at night two towering streams of light arise at the spots where the Twin Towers stood. The civilian deaths caused by US military strikes in Afghanistan total 3,608.[19]

That day, in Venice, Florida, Huffman Aviation International, a flight school, is notified by the Immigration and Naturalization Service that the August 2000 applications of its two students, Muhammad Atta and Marwan al Shehhi, for a change over of their tourist visas to student visas have been granted. Atta and Shehhi flew the jets that sliced into the WTC six months earlier.

Meanwhile, at the University of California in Los Angeles, an honors seminar in "Perspectives on September 11" has aroused trans-Atlantic interest. The courses include: "Beyond Tears: Evidence, Fact and Crisis"; "Navigating between Blithesome Optimism and Cultural Despair"; "What the US Should Do To Be Popular in the Third World"; and "Understanding the Unthinkable and Incomprehensible."[20]

What follows is a modest attempt to understand "the incomprehensible."

Preface

The purpose of my book is threefold: to provide a history of Islam; to examine the cases of Egypt, Saudi Arabia and Afghanistan, the countries at the center of Islamist terrorism that emerged in the late 1970s; and to describe and analyze the response to this phenomenon by America and the rest of the world, a narrative which takes up nearly two-fifths of the text.

Until the late 1990s popular belief in the West associated Islamic fundamentalism with the Iranian revolution of 1979, and viewed it as a movement of fanatic mullahs bent on harming Western interests. Yet Saudi Arabia, the oldest Islamic fundamentalist state of our times – run strictly according to the Islamic law, Sharia, since its inception in 1932 – has always been firmly allied with the West. And Western arms and funds bolstered the Afghan fundamentalist camp in its war against the Moscow-backed Marxist regime in Afghanistan to the extent that it won. Later it was pro-Western Pakistan and Saudi Arabia that helped, materially and militarily, the insignificant Taliban movement to capture 95 percent of Afghanistan.

One of the salient features of Islamic history is that it offers many examples of revivalist movements. It is in the nature of any major religion to revitalize itself periodically. But Islam is special. It is more than a religion; it is a complete socio-political system. That is, it has both cultural-ethical and political aspects. In this book, the term "Islamic" applies to Islam as a whole whereas "Islamist" applies to political Islam. Thus "Islamist terrorism" means terrorism perpetrated by those Muslims who stress Islam as a political ideology.

A comprehensive system like Islam sets standards and norms for its followers in every aspect of life. Being human, they fail to live up to these stringent, all-pervasive standards. And every so often an extraordinarily pious leader rises and calls for an end to back-sliding.

Fundamentalism is the term used for the effort to define the fundamentals of a religious system and adhere to them. One of the cardinal tenets of Islamic fundamentalism is to protect the purity of Islamic precepts from the adulteration of speculative exercises. Related to fundamentalism is Islamic revival, a renewed interest in Islam. Behind all this is a drive to purify it. In medieval times this drive meant ridding Islam of superstition and/or scholastic legalism. That is, the fundamentalist response was purely internal. Today the response is both internal and external: to release Islam from its scholastic cobwebs as well as to rid it of ideas imbibed from the West.

The founder of Islam, Muhammad ibn Abdullah, was not only a messenger of God's word and a prophet but also an administrator, judge and military commander. Islamic law, Sharia, consists of the Quran and the Hadiths (the Sayings and Doings of Prophet Muhammad). It is therefore essential to offer an outline of Muhammad's life, and that is what I do in chapter 1.

After Prophet Muhammad's death in 632, Islam expanded widely and rapidly, to the east and west of the Arabian Peninsula, and was adopted by peoples who had their own long-established traditions and religions. It was through the rise of Sufism that Islam was often able to absorb the pre-Islamic beliefs and practices of the new converts. Thus Islam adapted itself to widely differing cultures and, after the first generation of Arab military conquerors, Sufi leaders frequently became its most effective missionaries. In the process, however, Islam became diluted. This in turn led to the emergence of revivalist movements, concentrating on either injecting orthodoxy into Sufism or purifying Muslim practices. This forms the gist of chapter 2.

The next chapter deals with Islam in modern times when the Muslim world found itself on the defensive wherever it came into contact with Christian power, political or commercial. This was as true of the Ottoman Turkish empire in Istanbul *vis-à-vis* European powers as it was of the Mogul empire in Delhi in its dealings with the British East India Company. A multifarious response to the rising dominance of Western powers in the Islamic world was articulated by the pan-Islamist Jamaluddin Afghani (1838–97): a defensive call to arms, a concerted attempt to learn the secrets of Western strength, and adoption of Western modes of thought within Islam. Muhammad Abdu (1849–1905), Afghani's most renowned disciple, became an eminent Islamic reformer of Egypt, and was followed by his brilliant acolyte, Muhammad Rashid Rida (1865–1935).

It is against this background that I present the case studies of Egypt, Saudi Arabia and Afghanistan. Each of these is different. In Egypt, the birth-place of the Muslim Brotherhood, Islamic fundamentalism has been a feature of the political landscape since the 1930s. At different times it has been wooed, co-opted or suppressed by the regime. With the advent of Muhammad Anwar Sadat (1918–81; r. 1970–81), the moderate segments of the fundamentalist movement were briefly co-opted into the political–religious establishment while its radical offshoots resorted to armed resistance and assassinations, including that of Sadat himself. After a brief respite, President Hosni Mubarak (1928– ; r. 1981–) followed a policy of relentless repression of militant and moderate Islamists, which continues.

Saudi Arabia is a monarchical autocracy without a fully fledged constitution or partially or fully elected parliament. In a modern re-enactment of the events of Arabia in the days of Prophet Muhammad in the 620s, Abdul Aziz ibn Saud (1879–1953; r. 1932–53), acting as a fervent Islamist, subdued and unified the feuding Arabian tribes, nomadic and sedentary, to forge the kingdom of Saudi Arabia in 1932.

Afghanistan is a case unto itself. An independent country, which escaped European domination, political or economic, its religious establishment played a major role in the overthrow of King Amanullah (r. 1919–29) when he tried to accelerate the tardy processes of modernization and secularization. In the Afghanistan of 1979-92, ruled by a leftist regime, Islam emerged as an ideology of armed resistance. Later when the fundamentalist Mujahedin Alliance seized power, traditional ethnic differences proved so strong that a civil war along ethnic lines ensued which paved the way for the emergence of an ultra-radical version of Islamic fundamentalism, represented by the Taliban, as the predominant authority. Among other things Afghanistan became a haven for Islamist terrorist groups such as Al Qaida led by Osama bin Laden, a renegade Saudi militant.

In Part III, I deal with the bombing of the American embassies in the Kenyan and Tanzanian capitals in August 1998 as a precursor of the September 11 attacks on New York and Washington in 2001. The events of that fateful day, and the responses of both America and the United Nations, constitute chapter 8. In the next chapter I examine where the United States-led war on terrorism is headed.

A summary of the text and conclusions ends with a note of caution against sweeping so much under the umbrella of terrorism, indiscriminately, that the world community finds itself waging a war without end.

At the first mention of an important person, I provide in parentheses his/her birth-date or birth- and death-dates, followed by, if appropriate, the years when he/she was in office.

The British practice of stating the day and then the month and year has the advantages of being logical and visually balanced (with the letters of the month preceded and followed by a number) while avoiding the juxtaposition of two numbers, requiring separation by a space or comma – as is the case with American dating. I have therefore opted for the British model, except when using such commonly used numerical abbreviations as 9/11.

A word about place names, and the spellings of Arabic, Persian, Pushtu and Urdu words. A foreign word, written in italics at the first mention, later appears in roman. While I have referred to "the Gulf" that divides Iran from the Arabian Peninsula, I have listed the two other names in common use – the Persian Gulf and the Arabian Gulf – in the index. There is no standard way of transliterating Arabic, Persian, Pushtu and Urdu names. In each case I have chosen one of the most widely used spellings in the English-language print media – except when the spelling of the book author is different from mine. There I have merely reproduced the published spelling in quoted material. While looking up an index, a particular difficulty arises when different spellings of a proper noun, or an object, begin with a different letter – as in Koran/Quran or Kandahar/Qandahar. I have solved this problem by using one spelling in the text but including others as well in the index.

Wherever appropriate, after the English translation of the name of an organization or concept I give the original title in Arabic, Persian, Pushtu or Urdu in parentheses.

Since many of the Arabic and Persian words used in the text are also part of the Urdu vocabulary, I have prepared a combined glossary of Arabic, Persian, Pushtu and Urdu words.

The following terms signify religious or secular titles: ayatollah, hajji, imam, maulana, maulavi, mullah, qazi, shaikh and sultan.

The epilogue is not indexed.

Dilip Hiro
London
May 2002

Part I

Islam

1 The rise of Islam

Sunnis and Shias

Islam emerged out of a rudimentary beduin society in Arabia in the first quarter of the seventh century, and created from scratch an entire social order. How this came about, and how Islam developed after the death of its founder, Prophet Muhammad, form an important body of learning for the believers. The events of early Islam offered precedents upon which subsequent Muslim societies strove to organize themselves. It is to this seminal period of Islam that contemporary Muslims return for answers to such basic questions as those pertaining to a political-administrative entity as power, legitimacy, relations between the ruler and ruled, law and order, and social harmony.

Islam, in Arabic, means "state of submission"; and a Muslim is one who has submitted – to Allah, the one and only God. By putting all believers on an equal footing – submission to Allah – Islam created a confraternity above the traditional bonds of clan and tribe. The faithful were united in their belief in Allah and his precepts, as conveyed through Muhammad (literally, praise-worthy), his messenger.

Muhammad was born on 22 April AD 570 (or AD 571) to Amina bint Wahb and her husband, Abdullah, of the Hashimi clan of the merchant tribe of Quraish in Mecca. A trading post of some 5,000 people in western Arabia, Mecca was a place of pilgrimage for the worshippers of idols at the sanctuary of Kaaba, a small square temple containing the sacred Black Stone, which was probably a fallen meteorite. Over many centuries the

animistic beliefs of Arabia's nomadic tribes had developed into
the worship of idols often placed around a rock or tree regarded
as sacred, the Black Stone at Kaaba being a prominent example
of this. Muhammad grew up to be a sturdy man of average
height with a curved nose, large eyes, sensuous mouth and thick,
slightly curly hair. He was a quiet man, serious, reflective, given to
speaking briefly and pointedly. When he was about forty his
introverted, religious nature drove him to retreat periodically to
a cave in the hills near Mecca to engage in solitary contemplation.
During one such period of prayer and meditation he became
aware of a "Presence" telling him, "Muhammad, thou art the
Messenger of Allah." In the course of a subsequent retreat,
according to Muslim tradition, the first divine revelation "came
down" to Muhammad on the night of 26–27 Ramadan, the
ninth month of the Islamic calendar.[1] Over the next 20 years or
so, these revelations, delivered in rhythmic prose, continued. They
were taken down by Muhammad's followers on palm leaves,
camel bones or patches of leather, and compiled into 114 *suras*
(chapters) of varying lengths to form a book of some 6,616
verses, called the Quran (lit. recitation or discourse), which took
a definitive form a few years after Muhammad's death.

In 613 Muhammad ibn Abdullah began to preach the divine
revelations to a small body of relatives and friends. His message
to his followers was: abandon all forms of idolatrous worship and
surrender yourself completely to the omniscient and omnipotent,
yet compassionate, Allah. He warned the wealthy that considering the accumulation of riches as an end in itself and being
niggardly would lead them to catastrophe. Since Muhammad's
monotheistic teachings were antithetical to the polytheistic idol
worship practiced at Kaaba, he angered the Meccan merchants
who profited by the arrival of the pilgrims. Also, by demanding
unequivocal acceptance of one God, Muhammad created a loyalty
which went beyond traditional allegiance to the clan, and this
upset powerful clan leaders who also resented Muhammad's strictures against their unshared riches.

By 619 hostility towards Muhammad and his small band of
followers – forty men and twenty women – had reached a point

where they were often harassed and attacked. In 620 during their visit to Kaaba some members of the Khazraj tribal federation from the oasis of Yathrib, known in Aramaic as Medinta, or City (later to be called Medinat al Nabi, City of the Prophet, or simply, Medina), about 200 miles (320 km) north-east of Mecca, embraced Islam. On their return to Medina they won more converts, and the following year they brought to Mecca some of the new converts, including two members of the Aus tribal federation, which had maintained a long feud with the Khazraj. In June 622 a secret meeting of 75 Medinese Muslims promised to protect the Muslims of Mecca if the latter decided to migrate to Medina. During the next several weeks the Muslims of Mecca quietly slipped out of the town and headed for Medina, with Muhammad and his companion Abu Bakr being the last to leave.

In Medina the feuding Aus and Khazraj tribal federations welcomed Muhammad as an arbiter. Their subsequent acceptance of Islam brought an end to their conflict: they were now all believers, Muslims. Gradually Muhammad assumed the authority of a civil and military governor of Medina.

Divine revelations continued to "come down" to Muhammad, but they were now full of legal and moral guidelines. These were well suited to the need of the time for a framework for an orderly and pious existence within society. Thus the Medinese section of the Quran is concerned with commenting on current affairs and providing a corpus of law. Firstly, it deals with the external and internal security of the Islamic *umma* (community). The task of protecting the umma from external threats lies with the whole community. The best way to assure the security of the person and property of individuals at home is seen to lie with the old tribal custom of retribution, set down in the Quranic verse: "A life for a life, an eye for an eye; a nose for a nose, an ear for an ear; a tooth for a tooth, and for wounds retaliation."[2] The only modification is that in the case of an unintended murder the aggrieved party must accept the blood price. Secondly, family life is regulated. Women are given the right to own and inherit property, an improvement on the situation then prevailing in Arabia. They are also awarded the same rights in marriage and divorce as men. The obligations of the husband are defined; and a man is allowed a maximum of four wives with the proviso that "if you fear you will not be equitable [to them], then [take] only one [wife]."[3] Thirdly, the Quran lays down ethical and legal injunctions. It forbids intoxicants, flesh of swine, games of chance and hoarding. It condemns fraud, slander, perjury, hypocrisy, corruption, extravagance and arrogance. It prescribes punishments for, among others, stealing, murder and adultery. Cutting off of hands is the penalty for thieving. If adultery is proved for married women through the testimony of four witnesses, then "detain them in their houses until death takes them or God appoints for them a way." Furthermore, "And when two of them commit indecency, punish them both."[4]

In Medina Muhammad laid the foundations of the Islamic umma and Dar al Islam, Realm of Islam. A written document issued by him, most probably in 627 and later called The Constitution of Medina, is enlightening. It can be summarized as follows. First, the believers and their dependants form a single community, umma. Secondly, each clan or subdivision of the umma is responsible for blood money and ransoms on behalf of its members. Thirdly, the members of the umma must show solidarity against crime, and must not support a criminal where the crime is against another member of the community even when he is a near kinsman. Fourthly, they must maintain solidarity against unbelievers in war and peace. Finally, in case of a dispute arising between members of the community, it should be referred to "God and to Muhammad for a decision."[5]

Following a series of victories on the battlefield, Muhammad expanded his domain, and defeated the Quraish in Mecca. In January 630, at the head of an army 10,000 strong, he entered Mecca. He had the 360 stone idols at the Kaaba overturned from their pedestals, and the pagan Quraish were forced to march past him in homage. He touched the Black Stone with his stick and shouted, "Allahu Akbar!" (God is Great!), the battle-cry of Islam.

The ranks of Muhammad's followers swelled, with the poly-theist nomads converting to Islam in droves. Delegation after delegation from various parts of the Arabian Peninsula, the land of Arabs, arrived in Medina imploring the Prophet to include them in the Islamic umma. Muhammad welcomed them, aware that the nascent state of Medina needed all the protection he could muster in order to survive his death.

Islam thus evolved differently from Judaism and Christianity, the other monotheistic faiths which existed in Arabia and the surrounding lands and which were mentioned many times in the divine revelations to Prophet Muhammad. According to historian Bernard Lewis, in the case of Islam, religion was the state – with its Prophet acting as the military commander, making war and peace, collecting taxes, laying down the law and dispensing justice. In contrast, Christ made a distinction between what belonged to God and what belonged to Caesar at the very outset. Since then Christianity has recognized two separate authorities – church and state – existing sometimes in harmony and sometimes in conflict. As for Judaism, the situation is unclear: classical, rabbinical Judaism emerged only after the Hebrew state had ceased to exist. Judaism, therefore, falls un-easily between Islam and Christianity as far as relations between the state and religion are concerned.[6]

Muhammad realized that the best way to ensure the survival of the Islamic umma was by inculcating the new converts with a sense of solidarity which transcended traditional loyalties, and which was so ritualized that it impinged on everyday life. Out of this emerged the five pillars of Islam, a compendium of indi-vidual and social obligations, prescribed by Prophet Muhammad in a *hadith* (saying): *shahada* (literally, act of religious witness; figuratively, central precept); *salat* (prayer); *zakat* (literally, puri-fication; figuratively, obligatory charity); *sawm* (annual fast of Ramadan); and the *hajj* (pilgrimage to Mecca).[7]

A Muslim is enjoined to recite the shahada, the central pre-cept of Islam: "*la ilaha illallah, muhammadur rasulullah*" (There is no god but Allah, Muhammad is the messenger of Allah).

To embrace Islam it is enough to say the shahada before witnesses. After the public ritual it is left to the individual to decide the frequency with which he or she wishes to practice it in private. The prayer is performed both individually and collectively. Its public performance on Fridays and religious days strengthens group solidarity. The specific bodily movements – standing, bowing, kneeling, prostrating – that the faithful undergo in the course of the prayer in the congregation engender discipline in the same way as does a troop drill. By specifying that the believer must cease all other activity and turn to prayers at least three times daily, Muhammad wanted to remind his followers that Allah's claims were uppermost. The practice of all Muslims standing together at the same level in a mosque or on a prayer ground, irrespective of their social status, underlined the equality of all before Allah. Mosques are remarkable for their simplicity and provision of a single-level floor for prayers. The sermon that follows the Friday prayer has an important social and religious purpose, for it deals with not only some religious aspects of the faith but also the current socio-political situation. Today in the Islamic Republic of Iran, for instance, the Friday sermon is the prime vehicle by which the leaders educate and inform the populace on current affairs, internal and external.

The requirement for zakat, mentioned in the Quran as "the freewill offerings" for "the poor and needy . . . the ransoming of slaves, debtors, in God's way, and the traveller," was refined later as obligatory charity amounting annually to 2.5 percent of the believer's wealth.[8] The underlying principle is that Muslims should purify their wealth by paying their dues to the umma, which spends the resources on aiding the indigent.

Fasting during Ramadan, the ninth month of the Islamic (lunar) calendar, requires that the believer must abstain from food, drink and sex between sunrise and sunset. By so doing a Muslim learns to exercise control over his or her physical requirements. This ascetic practice by individual Muslims helps transform the Islamic umma into a self-disciplined community.

The hajj is enjoined upon those who can afford it. The pilgrimage is undertaken in Dhu al Hijja, the final month of the Islamic calendar. It begins with circumambulating the Kaaba in Mecca and ends with sacrificing an animal in Mina, 10 miles (16 km) away, with prayers offered at Arafat and Muzdilfa in between. The hajj rituals, which can be completed in five days, are derived from the practices already common among the inhabitants of Arabia before Prophet Muhammad's days. By incorporating pagan traditions the hajj helped to solidify the newly emergent Muslim community; and by undertaking the hajj the umma became conscious of its own existence as a powerful social force. In modern times the gathering of over 2 million Muslims from all over the world sharpens the sense of Islam's universality.

Prophet Muhammad himself prescribed the hajj rituals after his last pilgrimage to Mecca in early 632. He was then at the zenith of his power, the most powerful man in Arabia, and a highly respected religious figure at home and abroad. The numerous Arabian tribes, which had hitherto spent much of their energy in bloody feuding, were now united under his leadership. But Muhammad knew that this unity was tenuous, and that the only means by which he could ensure the survival of the Medinese nucleus of the Dar al Islam after his death was by keeping up an expansionary drive – a strategy which also appealed to his beduin followers eager to appropriate the (legitimate) booty from successful campaigns.

After his return to Medina from the hajj Muhammad prepared to attack Syria. But, following a sudden and severe illness, he died on 8 June 632, leaving behind no male child. Had Muhammad left a worthy son behind, it is likely that the umma would have chosen him the successor, thus setting a precedent, and sparing subsequent Muslim generations the internecine conflicts which centered round succession, the single most contentious issue in Islamic history.

The custom in Arabia was that when a tribal chief died he was succeeded by the best-qualified person in the leading family or the tribe, and the decision was taken by a meeting of all adult males

of the family or tribe. There are several versions of events during
Muhammad's illness and after his death, culled from written and
oral historical records. The description offered here is what passes
for the "standard account" of the accession of the next three
successors to Prophet Muhammad.

During Muhammad's fortnight-long illness intense rivalry
broke out between his close aides. The main contenders for
the succession were Abu Bakr, father of Aisha, the Prophet's
youngest (and favorite) wife; and Ali ibn Abu Talib, the Prophet's
cousin married to his daughter Fatima. Whereas Abu Bakr led
the public prayers during Muhammad's illness, the Prophet
chose Ali, then aged 33, to wash his body, a singular honor.

While Ali and other Muslims were busy mourning the
Prophet's death and burying him, the Medinese followers of the
Prophet, known as *ansars* (lit. helpers), held a meeting at Saada
banu Saqifa. Hearing this, Abu Bakr and Omar ibn Khattab –
father of Hafsa, the Prophet's other wife – rushed to the Saqifa
assembly. They forestalled a move by the assembly to have a
Medinese Muslim, an ansar, succeed the Prophet. They argued
that only someone who was a Meccan from the Quraish tribe,
to which Prophet Muhammad belonged, would be acceptable
as the leader to the nomadic tribes. They won the argument.
The assembly chose Abu Bakr as the leader, and conferred on
him the title *Khalifa* (caliph, or successor) of the Messenger of
Allah. The oldest among the contenders for the caliphate, Abu
Bakr, a merchant, was one of the early converts to Islam, the
companion of the Prophet during the latter's migration from
Mecca to Medina, and the leader of the hajj of 631.

Abu Bakr died two years later in 634. But before his death he
nominated Omar ibn Khattab as his successor. Still, before
assuming the high office, Omar sought and secured the community leaders' approval. This disappointed Ali, who largely
withdrew from public life, devoting himself to teaching and
compiling an authoritative version of the Quran.

In 636 Omar's troops defeated the Byzantine forces in Syria,
and the following year they inflicted defeat on the Sassanids at
Qadisiya on the banks of the Euphrates, seizing (present-day)

Iraq and part of Iran. Four years later Omar's forces conquered Egypt. The sustained expansion of the Dar al Islam through the waging of *jihad* (holy war) helped Omar to hold together the coalition of Arabian tribes under his leadership. He combined the expansionist drive with a well-designed plan to maintain a large standing army and inculcate it with Islamic teachings and practices. He forbade the conquering soldiers to colonize the captured territories. He levied land tax on the landowners in the seized territories as well as a poll tax on the inhabitants. He compiled a register of the men in the armies, all of them belonging to the tribes of Arabia, and paid them fixed stipends derived from the taxes on the conquered peoples. He maintained the troops in garrison towns which he furnished with mosques and reciters of the Quran in order to indoctrinate the soldiery. In other words, he intensified the holy struggle while strengthening the ideological basis of Islam.

Omar was equally relentless at home, and his harshness aroused more fear than affection. Following the practice of Prophet Muhammad and Abu Bakr, he acted as the chief judge. He was conscientious, yet not all his judgments were flawless. Every so often Ali would point out the drawbacks in his verdicts. One such judgment so infuriated the plaintiff, named Firuz, an Iranian slave of an Arab resident of Medina, that he murdered Omar in November 644.

On his death-bed Omar nominated an electoral college of six to choose the successor, the college including Ali ibn Abu Talib and Uthman ibn Affan, a member of the Ummayyad clan (of the Quraish tribe), who was married to Ruqaiya and Umm Kulthum, daughters of Prophet Muhammad. Thus Omar was less arbitrary than Abu Bakr. The caliphate was offered to Ali but on two conditions: he was required to rule according to the Quran and the Prophet's Practice, *Sunna*, and to accept the (recorded) precedents set by the previous caliphs. Ali rejected the second condition. He had in the past publicly criticized some of the actions of Abu Bakr and Omar; and being a man of integrity, he refused to compromise his principled stance by concurring with all their decisions. The caliphate was then offered to Uthman on the same conditions. He accepted without hesitation.

This choice sowed the seeds of dissension in the Dar al Islam. Ali became the focus of opposition which grew as Uthman began favouring fellow Ummayyads brazenly. Ali's Islamic credentials were unmatched. He had adopted Islam when he was a boy; he was steeped in the Quran. An extremely pious man who never failed to observe Islamic rituals and practices, he had emerged as an uncompromising idealist, the conscience of Islam, a believer who had let the opportunity to become the caliph pass because of one unacceptable condition. Along with his piety and idealism went striking looks: a stocky, broad-shouldered man, he wore a long beard.

Uthman relaxed his predecessor's policy of banning the Arabians from colonizing the conquered territories, particularly in the fertile region of Mesopotamia, present-day Iraq. The subsequent rise of an affluent, absentee landlord class in Mecca, Medina and Taif caused much resentment. Many Quranic reciters objected strongly to the growing Ummayyad monopoly of top administrative posts. The soldiers complained bitterly against paltry stipends and demanded a return to the customary booty of successful campaigns. The simmering discontent boiled over in open conflict between the Muslims of Arabia, civilian and military, and the local inhabitants in the Iraqi garrison towns of Kufa and Basra.

Matters came to a head in mid-656 when rebel troops from Egypt combined with dissidents from Basra and Kufa and surrounded Uthman's house in Medina, demanding his abdication. Ali interceded on the mutineers' behalf, but failed to resolve the crisis. In June a group of rebel soldiers attacked Uthman's house and killed him. Ali condemned the assassination, but made no effort to apprehend the murderers.

Calling Ali the "First among the Muslims," the rebels and most of the adult male Medinese elected him the caliph, thus recovering for the community at large the right to choose the caliph – a right which had been usurped earlier by both a living caliph (Abu Bakr) and a college appointed by the living caliph (Omar). So, after a lapse of 24 years, the highest office in Islam was offered, unconditionally, to Ali. He accepted it. But by now the conflict within the Dar al Islam had proliferated to such an extent that he was compelled to channel most of his time and energy into subduing the opposition.

Muwaiya ibn Abu Sufian, the Ummayyad governor of Syria and a brother-in-law of Prophet Muhammad, and Aisha, the surviving wife of the Prophet, refused to acknowledge Ali as the caliph, and demanded that Uthman's murder be avenged. The assassins sought refuge in the argument that since Uthman had not ruled according to the edicts of the Quran, and had therefore ceased to be a member of the Islamic umma, murdering him was a legitimate act. Throughout the centuries assassins and armed insurgents in Muslim societies have offered this rationale for their actions: the ruler, having disobeyed the Word of God, the Quran, has ceased to be Islamic. A recent example was the assassination in 1981 of President Sadat of Egypt by fundamentalist soldiers.

When Ali refused to concede the demand of Aisha to punish Uthman's assassins, she rushed to Basra to raise a force against the new caliph. Ali withdrew to Kufa, a stronghold of his supporters. In the ensuing battle near Basra in December 656 Ali vanquished Aisha's partisans, but was courteous to the Prophet's widow. Most military governors now swore allegiance to Ali.

In 658 the armies of Ali and Muwaiya clashed at Siffin on the banks of the Euphrates, a battle in which Ali's forces soon established their superiority. Then Muwaiya's men induced intervention by the Quran – literally – by sticking pages of the holy book on their lances. This led to a ceasefire.

After several months of negotiations Ali and Muwaiya agreed to refer their dispute and the issue of the caliphate to two arbiters, one appointed by each side. The arbitration that ensued has become the most tangled tale in Islamic history due to the partisan descriptions offered by various interested parties of the course of events and the motivation of the participants.

To start with, several hundred of Ali's militant followers, arguing that there was no provision for arbitration in the Quran, abandoned Ali and set up a camp near Baghdad. They came to be called Kharajis, Outsiders or Seceders. Ali defeated them in July 658. Yet enough survived to continue the Kharaji movement, which believed among other things that any pious Muslim was worthy of becoming caliph. (In this they differed from Shiat Ali – Partisans of Ali – who insisted on the sanctity of the lineage of Prophet Muhammad through his daughter Fatima and her husband Ali as a prerequisite for the caliphate.)

One version of the arbitration has it that the arbiters agreed that both the contenders be deposed and that a new caliph be elected by an assembly of notables. Ali's representative, being senior in age, was the first to speak before such a gathering. He declared the deposition of both rivals. Then Muwaiya's representative rose but, instead of inviting nominations for the caliphate, he announced that Muwaiya was the rightful caliph. The meeting broke up in pandemonium. Ali stuck firmly to his office. The treachery of Muwaiya's representative has been much condemned by Shiat Ali – or, simply, Shias – and left a deep mark on them. This continues. The consistent refusal of Ayatollah Ruhollah Khomeini (1902–89; r. 1979–89), a Shia, to accept mediation in the Iran–Iraq War stemmed from a deep mistrust of mediators rooted in Ali's experience after the Battle of Siffin.

The surviving Kharajis were out to avenge the deaths of their comrades by Ali's forces. Ali was therefore high on their hit list. One of them, named Ibn Mujlam, fatally stabbed Ali on 19 Ramadan 40 AH (10 January 661) as he was praying in his mosque in Kufa. Ali's assassination was a great blow to those who had supported him all along in his claims to the caliphate. In another context his departure marked the end of the 30-year-long rule by four "Rightly Guided" caliphs based in Medina.

Muwaiya was proclaimed caliph in Jerusalem, and Hassan, the oldest son of Ali, in Kufa. But this duality did not last long. Muwaiya, a scion of the Ummayyad clan, part of the long-established upper class of Arabian society, enjoyed greater prestige and military power than Hassan. His emissaries persuaded Hassan to retire to Medina on a comfortable pension with the promise that after Muwaiya's death the caliphate would return to the Hashimi clan, whose stature had risen sharply due to the popular acceptance of one of its sons, Muhammad, as the Messenger of Allah, and the involvement of the clan members in promoting the new, vigorous religion of Islam. Hassan died of poisoning in 669. Muwaiya reneged on his promise, and nominated his son, Yazid, as caliph during his lifetime. He thus set up a dynasty, something that had not happened so far in the Dar al Islam. This practice undercut the tradition of choosing the most able and pious Muslim from among the Hashimi or Ummayyad clan as the leader of the Islamic umma. Dynastic rule continues to be opposed by many present-day Islamic thinkers on ideological grounds.

By the time Muwaiya died in 680 the Ummayyads had consolidated their power. Yet Shias were still adamant in their argument that because Ali had been the divinely appointed successor to Prophet Muhammad, and because Allah's message had been clearly received by Ali and his family, only the descendants of the first truly Muslim family were fit to rule the Dar al Islam.

From this arose the concept of Imamat; that is, that only those who were in the lineage of Prophet Muhammad – and thus of Fatima and Ali – can govern Muslims on behalf of Allah, and that the imams, religious leaders, being divinely inspired, are infallible. This view is not shared by Sunnis – or, more specifically, Ahl al Sunna, People of the Sunna, the Beaten Path or Tradition – who regard caliphs as fallible interpreters of the Quran, the Word of Allah. Unsurprisingly, Sunnis revere the Prophet and the four "Rightly Guided" caliphs, whereas Shias venerate only the Prophet and Imam Ali, and Ali's descendants. Sunnis believe in three basic concepts: monotheism, that is, there is only one God; prophethood, which is a means of communication between God and humankind; and resurrection, that is, souls of dead human beings will be raised by God on the Day of Judgment and their deeds on earth judged.[9] Shias believe in these as well as in Imamate and social justice. However, in the late seventh century, Shiaism was more a school of thought than a well-defined sect.

Following Muwaiya's death Yazid became the caliph. Hussein, the oldest surviving son of Ali, then living in Medina, staked his claim to the caliphate on the grounds that it belonged to the House of the Prophet, of which he was the most senior male member, and that Yazid was a usurper. His stance won him swift and fervent messages of support from Kufa, a stronghold of Ali's supporters, coupled with exhortations to claim the caliphate and rekindle the glory that had visited the Dar al Islam during Imam Ali's reign. The news of this reached Yazid. He rushed a trusted aide, Ubaidullah ibn Ziyad, to Kufa. Ibn Ziyad employed the age-old tactics of co-option and repression, and neutralized the anti-Yazid forces. By then the unsuspecting Hussein, acompanied only by his family and 72 retainers – 40 horsemen and 32 footmen – was well advanced in his march to southern Iraq.

On 1 Muharram 61 AH (May 681), Hussein's entourage was intercepted near Karbala, some 30 miles (48 km) from Kufa, by Yazid's soldiers. For the next eight days their commander tried to obtain Hussein's unconditional surrender through negotiations. He got nowhere. Hussein's belief in his right to the caliphate was total. He refused to budge even when he knew that his forces were no match for Yazid's, and that defeat and death were inevitable. This disregard for pragmatism, which demands the sacrifice of exalted principles on the altar of realism, was a manifestation of the idealism that fired Hussein, and made him the most revered martyr in Islam, particularly among Shias. Rather than surrender or retreat, he resolved to battle and perish in the cause of justice, which he felt had been denied to him, as well as in the belief that his martyrdom would revitalize the claim of the House of the Prophet to the caliphate. On the morning of 10 Muharram, Friday, Hussein led his small band of warriors to confront Yazid's 4,000 heavily armed troops, mounted and infantry. To match the occasion he donned the sacred mantle of his grandfather, Prophet Muhammad. Hopelessly outnumbered, Hussein's partisans fell one by one. The last was Hussein. He was decapitated, and his severed head was presented to Yazid.

A narrative of the dramatic events of these ten days of Muharram is recited annually, wherever Shias live, by professional readers in mosques and meeting halls, and mounted as the second act of the most celebrated passion play of Islam, accompanied by frenzied grief and tears, wailing and self-flagellation, an annual ritual which sets Shias firmly apart from Sunnis. This popular ritual revives the memory of Imam Hussein and brings to life the early history of Islam, offering current Shia leaders the opportunity to draw lessons from the heroic tragedy of a man of charisma and extraordinary piety – the chief one being that the true believer should not shy away from challenging the established order, with arms if necessary, if it has become unjust and oppressive, even if the chances of overthrowing it are slender. No wonder, then, that those rulers who wish to lead their citizens away from the Islamic path attempt to suppress the ritual. In 1939 the Iranian Shah, Reza Pahlavi (r. 1925–41), banned self-flagellation in public on 10 Muharram, and tried to stop the public performance of Shia passion plays preceding the mourning.

At Yazid's court in 681 the fact that Imam Hussein was a direct descendant of Prophet Muhammad weighed heavily on the ruler. Yazid allowed a safe passage to Medina to all the surviving women of the Hussein family as well as to Ali Zain al Abidin, Hussein's seriously wounded son, considered dead by Yazid's troops, and an infant grandson, Muhammad al Baqir. Zainab, Imam Hussein's sister, upheld the Shia cause until Zain al Abidin had fully recovered. From then on Shias attracted dissident and revolutionary elements in the Dar al Islam.

Imam Hussein's martyrdom was an important milestone in Islamic history and not merely in terms of the final defeat of the Hashimi clan by the Ummayyads. The clash between the corrupt, cynical Yazid and the self-righteous, pious Hussein was part of the same dialectic which had earlier pitted the pragmatist Uthman against the idealist Ali: the dialectic of an ideology which had succeeded. The basic question, in the words of Malise Ruthven, a historian of Islam, was: "Could the new solidarity of the umma, based on the common observance of the Quran and the Prophet's Sunna, be the ideological base for a new Islamic order, or would the order first have to establish itself on the basis of Quraishi – and specifically Ummayyad – power?"[10] The real life answer was, as is often the case, a compromise between the two polarities. But the dialectic continued, and remains unresolved. "The problem of finding a balance between the ideal and the real, the perfection of Islam and the human and material facts of life, became the stuff of Islamic history from the Prophet's time down to the present."[11]

Within the opposition Shia camp itself a conflict developed. While Zain al Abidin accepted the Ummayyad rule, Muhammad ibn al Hanafiya, a son of Ali by a Hanafi woman, revolted against the Ummayyads in 687. The revolt failed, but social conditions for dissidence remained fertile. Under the Ummayyads society had become stratified: Ummayyad aristocrats at the top, and the conquered non-Arab peoples, called *mawalis* (clients) at the bottom – with Arab ansars and nomadic tribes in between. The discrimination practiced against non-Arab Muslims by the Ummayyads ran counter to the teachings of the Quran, and was a source of much disaffection among the mawalis, who were attracted to the Shia camp.

In line with the Shia tradition, Ali Zain al Abidin named his son Muhammad al Baqir as his spiritual heir before his death in 712. Since Baqir continued the quietist stance of his father, activist Shias lent their support to his younger half-brother, Zaid ibn Ali. Zaid raised a banner of revolt in 740, but was struck down. Later, in 743, his son, Yahya ibn Zaid, revolted in Khurasan, the easternmost province of the Dar al Islam which now included all of Iran, but was defeated.

These failures did not arrest the sharpening of the contradictions within the system. The pious were scandalized by the corruption and luxury of the Ummayyads, whose empire now spanned Spain in the west and Sind in the east. In Damascus, the capital, much of the administration was in the hands of the Christian clerical families who had run the country under the Byzantine emperors, a situation which the Islamic scholars found intolerable. The Damascus of the 730s was a far cry from the simple egalitarianism of Medina a century before.

Little wonder that the garrison towns in Iraq and Khurasan seethed with discontent. Increasingly in the 730s and 740s intellectual energy was channeled into the subject of the right to rebel against an unjust ruler.

It was against this backcloth that in the late 740s a second series of revolts was launched under the leadership of Abu Muslim who, interestingly enough, was a former slave of Ibrahim, the Imam of Hashimis and a descendant of Abbas, uncle of Prophet Muhammad. These revolts were joined by the garrison tribes of Khurasan and backed by urban Islamic intellectuals who were bitterly critical of the Ummayyads' worldly ways. Abu Muslim won the support of Shias by declaring that the Ummayyad caliph would be replaced by a member of the House of the Prophet. Thus the Hashimi rivalry with the Ummayyads, the ideological revulsion against the corrupt rulers who had deviated from Islam, and the Shia yearning for the return of the caliphate to the House of the Prophet coalesced to produce a formidable force. The insurgency gathered momentum and succeeded in overthrowing the Ummayyads in 750.

What followed the Ummayyads was called the Abbasid caliphate, named after Abbas, the Prophet's uncle. The Abbasid revolution was hailed by both religious intellectuals and non-Arab Muslim masses. It was the first victory of fundamentalism in Islamic history. The Ummayyads had deviated from the true ways of the Quran and Sunna, and were overthrown. Those who replaced them, the Abbasids, pledged to stick strictly to the Quran and Sunna. They also promised to treat mawalis, non-Arab Muslims, on a par with Arabs, and choose judges from among those who had studied the Quran and the Prophet's practices.

Since Abbas al Hashimi was one generation older than Prophet Muhammad, the Abbasid claim of belonging to the House of the Prophet was invalid. Still Jaafar al Sadiq, the sixth Shia Imam, acquiesced in Abbasid power. In return the Abbasid caliph honored Sadiq while keeping him under discreet surveillance. This was the beginning of an uneasy cooperation between the Shia Imam's followers and the Sunni state.

But not all Shias followed Jaafar al Sadiq. Within a few decades of seizing power the Abbasids imitated the dictatorial style of the Sassanids whom they had overthrown, and let the administration fall into the hands of the bureaucrats who had served the Sassanid emperors. The Islamic militants, who had been fervent supporters of the Abbasids, felt betrayed. In 786 Shias revolted in Hijaz, the region which includes Mecca and Medina. They were suppressed by the Abbasid caliph.

Over the next several generations three branches of Shiaism crystallized: Zaidis or Fivers, Ismailis or Seveners, and Imamis or Twelvers. Zaidis share the first four Imams with Twelvers[12] and follow a different line beginning with Zaid, son of Zain al Abidin. Ismailis share the first six Imams with Twelvers[13] and then follow a different line beginning with Ismail, the older, militant son of Jaafar al Sadiq, who pre-deceased his father. Those who followed Musa al Kazim, the younger, moderate son of Jaafar al Sadiq, came to be known as Jaafaris – and later as Twelvers.[14] They believe that Muhammad al Muntazar (literally, the Awaited Muhammad), the infant son of the Eleventh Imam, went into occultation in 873, thus acquiring the title of Hidden Imam, leaving behind four special assistants.

By then the effective power of the Abbasid caliph had declined, with the Dar al Islam's eastern region being increasingly usurped by semi-independent Iranian dynasties. Indeed, in 932 Baghdad fell into the hands of Ahmed Muizz al Dawla, a Buyid king, who was a Twelver Shia. But neither he nor his descendants attempted to institute Shiaism at the caliph's court or abolish the Abbasid caliphate. Thus a division of power came about – the Buyid king exercising political authority, and the Abbasid caliph spiritual.

Such an arrangement was contrary to true Islam and was disapproved of by the Ismailis, the most militant of the Shias. They too challenged the Abbasids but with a view to overthrowing them. They succeeded in Tunisia. There, led by Ubaidullah al Mahdi and aided by Berbers, they seized power in 909, and established themselves as the Fatimid (derivative of Fatima, wife of

Ali) caliphate. This signified a successful Shia fundamentalist challenge to Sunni Abbasid rule which was considered by the Fatimids as unjust. Its importance rose when in 969 the Fatimids captured Egypt and became rivals to the Abbasids. In the new palace city of Al Qahira (Cairo) they founded the mosque and theological college of Al Azhar which became the leading centre of Shia learning.

During the Buyid hegemony in Baghdad (932–1055) four collections of Shia *hadiths* – "Sayings and Doings of Shia Imams" – were codified. In legal terms this put Shias on a par with the already existing four Sunni codes of the *Sharia* (canon law): Hanafi, Maliki, Shafii and Hanbali. The Buyids were overthrown by the Seljuks from central Asia, who were Sunni.

The loss of Jerusalem, the third holiest city of Islam, to Christians in the First Crusade (1095–9) created a crisis in the Islamic world. To the extent that it gave impetus to revivalist impulses among Muslims it initially aided the Fatimids and their vision of Islam more than the others. The Fatimids were bent on bringing all Muslim lands under the sway of their imams. They made much headway. At its peak the Fatimid domain extended from Tunisia to Sind, including Egypt, Syria, Hijaz, Yemen and Oman – leaving only Iraq and Iran under Abbasid control.

It was from this base that Salahuddin Ayubi, also known as (aka) Saladin, a Kurdish general who had risen from the ranks of the Seljuk army, mounted his attack on the Fatimids in 1171, and ended their Shia rule. With this Sunnism once again became the dominant force in Islam. Today Shias are no more than 12 to 15 percent of the global Muslim population of some 1.25 billion.

Summary

Muhammad was born in a feuding, polytheistic tribal society. In order to forge a unified monotheistic community under his leadership he prescribed a comprehensive set of rituals and practices, a meticulous code of moral-ethical behaviour and strict ground-rules for the running of a political state. His revelations of the Word of God, the Quran, and his personal practices, Sunna, became the foundations for the ordering of the Islamic umma. By advocating strict adherence to the Quran and Sunna, Ali came to represent the idealist polarity in Islam. The pragmatist polarity was represented by those who succeeded Prophet Muhammad as caliphs. Indeed the third caliph, Uthman, stretched pragmatism so far as to trigger off a determined campaign by groups of militant soldiers against him, ending in his assassination. With this, Shiat Ali, Partisans of Ali, became the first fundamentalists in Islamic history. Ali's son Hussein took up arms against Yazid, an unjust ruler, even though the odds against him were desperately high. He thus turned the concept of martyrdom into a tactic to achieve an ideal Islamic order.

Shias, the early fundamentalists, drew the bulk of their support from pious Muslims and non-Arab Muslim clients, who felt discriminated against by Arab Muslims. Though the times have changed, the fundamentalists' constituencies have not. Today the alienated class of recent migrants to cities from villages provides the popular backing for the fundamentalist movement which is led mainly by low- and medium-ranking clerics and pious professionals and traders.

Shias were an important part of the coalition which engineered the Abbasid revolution against the Ummayyad caliphs who had deviated widely from the true Islamic path, thus scoring the first fundamentalist triumph in Islam. But it was not long before the Sunni Abbasid caliphs too began slipping away from the Quran and Sunna, thus allowing Shias to become the sole repositories of the vision of ideal Islam. This role, coupled with the martyr complex inspired by Imam Hussein, turned Shias into valiant soldiers. The consequences were the subjugation of the Sunni caliph in Baghdad by a Twelver Shia king in 932, and the emergence of an Ismaili Shia caliphate, the Fatimids, in Cairo in 969. Shia domination lasted many generations, losing its grip first in Baghdad in 1055, and then in Cairo in 1171.

But, oddly enough, Salahuddin Ayubi, the Sunni general who defeated the Shia caliphate in Cairo, was riding the wave of Islamic revivalism which swept the Muslim lands in the wake of the loss of Jerusalem to Christians in 1099.

2 Orthodox Islam and Sufism

In a general sense, while the Ummayyad era (661–750) was a period of expansion for Islam, the Abbasid age was a period of consolidation. The early Ummayyads were committed to keeping the Arab conquerors separate from the conquered peoples. They confined their soldiers to garrison towns and forbade sexual liaisons between them and non-Arab women. They provided protection to the non-Muslim population on payment of a poll tax, a practice initiated by Prophet Muhammad after his victory at Khaibar, an oasis populated largely by Jewish tribes. They were lukewarm to the idea of converting native populations to Islam.

In time, however, lured by the advantages, financial and otherwise, which stemmed from embracing Islam, the conquered peoples opted for Islam in large numbers, and came to be known as mawalis. With this, social distinctions between Arab Muslims and non-Arab Muslims diminished. The tribal habits and simple rules of the Arabs intermingled with the more complex rules and regulations of the agrarian societies of Mesopotamia and Iran. The Ummayyad caliphs took the easy way out by adopting the legal and administrative practices of the Byzantine and Sassanids emperors they had overthrown. This went down badly with pious Muslims. They wanted specifically Islamic solutions to the problems thrown up by the conquest of vast non-Arab lands and peoples. With the later Ummayyads encouraging mass conversions in the conquered territories, Islam spread to villages among non-Arab peasants, and this made the need for an Islamic legal and administrative system more urgent. The Ummayyads failed to meet this need. So the religious intellectuals sided with the Abbasid revolutionary forces as they rebelled against the Ummayyads.

The early Abbasids concentrated on developing Islam as a social system and thus consolidating the empire. It was a complex and demanding task which took Islamic intellectuals nearly two centuries to accomplish. They found that of the 6,616 verses in the Quran only 80 concerned legal issues, and these were mainly about women, marriage, family and inheritance. But since Prophet Muhammad had ruled a political entity there was an oral record of what he had said and done as judge and administrator. After his death elaborate means had been employed to collect his sayings and doings, called the Prophet's Practice, or Sunna. Later, in the mid-ninth century, some 2,700 sayings and doings of the Prophet were to be codified, and published in six canonical collections, called *Hadiths* (Reports), the most famous collections being by Muhammad al Bukhari (810–70). In short, the Quran is the Word of Allah, and the Hadiths explain the Quran.

Among the first to codify the Quran and Sunna was Abu Hanifa al Numan (699–767), an Iranian merchant resident in Kufa. His *madhhab* (legal school) was adopted by the Abbasids. Later another canonical school was pioneered by Malik ibn Anas (714–96), a lawyer in Medina. The environments in which these scholars worked are reflected in the characters of the documents they produced. The Hanafi code is liberal and oriented towards urban society whereas the Maliki is conservative and suitable for pastoral communities.

But the *alim* (the religious-legal scholar, pl. *ulama*) who was to make the greatest impression on the legal-administrative apparatus of the Abbasid empire was Muhammad ibn Idris al Shafii (767–820), a student of Malik ibn Anas in Medina, who later settled in Cairo. He founded the science of *fiqh* (religious jurisprudence) on four pillars: the Quran, the Prophet's Sunna as recorded in the Hadiths, the consensus (*ijma*) of the community, and analogical reasoning (*qiyas*). Until then, ijma had been construed as consensus of *ahl al hall zeal aqd* (those who loose and bind), a term which embraces various types of representatives of the community, including religious intellectuals, but Shafii enlarged it to include the whole community. Analogical reasoning allowed the community to incorporate new situations into the system of the Sharia (Islamic law), without disturbing the primacy of the Quran and Sunna. It also permitted individual opinions and differences, something sanctioned by the hadith: "The differences of opinion among the learned within my community are [a sign of] God's grace."[1] By pursuing this method the ulama could merge Prophet Muhammad's teachings, Arab traditions and non-Arab traditions into a single canonical system applicable to the life of all Muslims, Arab and non-Arab. Thus Shafii's systematization of the Sharia provided the foundation upon which a common identity of Muslims scattered around the world could be built.

The other school which has survived is that of Ahmad ibn Hanbal (780–855). He was against a legal superstructure built upon the Quran and Sunna, and argued that a legal decision must be reached by referring directly to the Quran and Sunna instead of a body of religious jurisprudence derived from them. According to him, the Quran and Sunna were the law itself, not merely the source of it. His fundamentalist approach proved unpopular in the sophisticated societies of the Fertile Crescent – comprising present-day Iraq, Syria, Jordan, Lebanon and Egypt – but found its followers among the nomadic tribes of the Najd region of Arabia.

Over the next several generations most of the Sunni ulama in the Dar al Islam settled for one of these four schools which set the boundaries of the Sharia, from the fundamentalist Hanbali code to the liberal Hanafi. In order not to upset the consensus thus arrived at with some new radical innovations, the ulama from the tenth century onwards declared that the doors of *ijtihad* (creative interpretation) in Islam had been shut. The cumulative effect of this stance was to prove detrimental to Islam. It became rigid and reflected the status quo, and declined perceptibly in the latter centuries of the second (Christian) millennium as the pace of technological development in the West quickened and rivalry between the Ottoman caliphate and European powers sharpened.

Hanafi's school, adopted by the Abbasids, became established in West Asia. The Maliki school, native to Medina, spread to North and Central Africa. The Shafii school, originating in Egypt, reached southern Arabia, and from there spread along the monsoon route to East Africa and South-East Asia. The Hanbali school, on the other hand, remained confined to the Najd.

The Sharia governs the life of a Muslim completely. Religious jurisprudents, called *faqihs*, studied all human actions and categorized them as obligatory, recommended, allowed, unspecified, undesirable or prohibited. From this they graduated to prescribing exactly how the obligatory, recommended and allowed acts were to be performed. They began to ascribe profound meanings to certain obligatory acts. The simple edict by Prophet Muhammad that a believer must undertake ritual ablution with water (or sand) before prayers became enmeshed into a profound debate on the purity and pollution of the human body. Religious jurisprudents conducted minute examinations of all bodily functions – eating, drinking, breathing, washing, urinating, defecating, farting, copulating, vomiting, bleeding, shaving – and prescribed how these were to be performed, the main stress being on keeping the body "pure." Along with this went a code of social behaviour which too was all-encompassing. The twin codes were *so* demanding that, even with the best will in the world, a believer could not abide by them all the time. On the other hand it was the introduction of these codes into the lives of those who had embraced Islam that led to common behavioural patterns among Muslims whether they lived in the Mauritanian desert or the Indonesian archipelago.

The speed with which this process took root varied from region to region. In general, the farther away a territory was from the Islamic heartland in West Asia the longer was the period before Islamization took firm root. It also depended on how Islam was brought to a region: whether by armed conquest or economic contacts with Arab traders arriving either overland or by sea.

For instance, in sub-Saharan Africa Islam spread through the trade routes serviced by the Arabs from the north. Here, often an African tribal chieftain would embrace Islam to raise his social and political status by joining a superior, larger civilization with a written scripture. He would start by accepting an amulet or costume, graduate to offering prayers, and then replace the local taboos with Islamic ones in his personal life. His example would be emulated by his followers. Only after Islamic culture had thus become established in the tribe would the fiqh be applied.

The same process was at work in the major Indonesian islands of Java and Sumatra. These were under Hindu or Buddhist influence when Arab traders arrived in the thirteenth century. Islam percolated from the coast into the interior through the trade network. The Islamization process, which began seriously in the fourteenth century, has yet to be completed. In Java and other major islands the hill people in the hinterland are either animist or Christian or "nominal Muslims" called *abangan* (whereas orthodox Muslims on the coast are known as *santri*). In the interior Islamic practices and worship exist alongside those rooted in animism, Hinduism or Buddhism.

The fiqh is less a system of law, with a developed apparatus of procedure and enforcement, than a process of socialization and acculturation which progressively transforms human societies in a more or less autonomous manner, notes Malise Ruthven. In time the process of Islamization takes root, imposing a degree of cultural homogeneity. Observance of the Divine Law becomes a social factor functioning more or less independently of the state.[2]

Islam spread among those societies where existing religious faith involved either idol worship or a personality cult. This was as true of the Arabia of the seventh century as of the Java of the thirteenth. As a result, those who adopted Islam, for whatever reasons, missed the psychic satisfaction they had derived from worshipping idols, or objects of nature, or even some superior human being, practices strictly forbidden by the Quran. Furthermore, the Allah portrayed in the Quran was a severe entity who aroused awe and reverence among the believers rather than love or affection. To the bulk of new converts Islam came across as a creed concerned primarily with precise and overt observance of the Quranic edicts, and pursuing of political power. Strict obedience to Allah's commandments and meticulous observance of religious rituals left many believers spiritually and psychologically unfulfilled. The debates about the finer points of the Quran and Sunna, which deeply engaged the ulama, left the largely illiterate body of the faithful cold and bewildered. At the very least the Muslim masses needed a humane, charismatic Islamic leader whose words and actions would infuse their new faith with warmth. In the early days of Islam the tragic figure of the idealist, uncompromising Ali became the personality from whom many of the fresh converts drew living inspiration. Later Imam Hussein and his martyrdom provided the spiritual sustenance to this body of believers. After Hussein's death in 681 no equivalent figure emerged to satisfy the spiritual needs of such Muslims.

Some Muslims sought solace in undertaking ascetic exercises and arduous spiritual practices, believing that such means would bring them closer to the Deity. They were inspired by the example of Prophet Muhammad who used to withdraw into a cave and undertake nightly vigils, and by the practices of Christian hermits. Like the adherents of the Eastern Orthodox Church they came to believe that Allah, or the Ultimate Reality, could be apprehended only by direct personal experience. They therefore stressed meditation and contemplation of the Deity, and regarded direct involvement in worldly affairs, or pursuit of political power, as a distraction from the path of seeking Allah within. Through their practices they injected warmth, piety and altruistic love into Islam. They came to be known as *Sufis* – from the term *suf* (woo), linked to the woollen garments the pioneers among them wore as a sign of asceticism. Hassan al Basri (d. 728), who adopted the path of simple asceticism, was the first known Sufi personality.

In time two kinds of Sufis emerged: ecstatic and sober. The ecstatic Al Hussein ibn Mansur al Hallaj (857–922) declared

"I am the Truth," and was executed as a heretic. Among sober Sufis Abu Hamid Muhammad al Ghazali (1058–1111) was the most prominent. His personal experience led him to conclude that mysticism was a meaningful way of perceiving the Ultimate Reality, even though it did not enable the believer to learn anything about Allah, or the Ultimate Reality, over and above what was already in the Quran. He thus tried to fit the mystical experience within the limits of the Sharia. His greatest contribution to Islam was to write *Ihya Ulum al Din* (Revival of the Religious Sciences), a manual for everyday existence which blended institutional religion with individual virtue.

While Shafii had built a legal superstructure on the foundation of the Quran and Sunna, Ghazali tried to integrate the whole legal system with a spiritual infrastructure originating in Prophet Muhammad's mystic consciousness. In *Ihya Ulum al Din* Ghazali urged the faithful to be aware of God's presence while undertaking not only prayers and fasting but also such mundane actions as eating, washing and sleeping. His work became the living document for the Sufi orders which sprang up soon after his death.

The first Sufi brotherhood was Qadiriya, founded by Abdul Qadir al Gailani (1077–1166), who was based in Baghdad. It was later to spread as far as West Africa and South-East Asia. It is a more orthodox order than the subsequent ones and stresses piety and humanitarianism.

In the absence of any social organization outside the fold of the extended family, Sufi orders provided the only platform for social solidarity. A brotherhood consisted of aspirants (*murids*) or mendicants (*dervishes*) who took an oath of allegiance to the guide, known as *shaikh*, *pir* or *murshid*. (Women were admitted as associate aspirants.) The shaikh headed a hierarchy within the order which was linked by a chain of inherited sanctity (*baraka*) or kinship to the founding saint. This chain went back to the early Sufi founders, such as Hassan al Basri, and through them to the House of the Prophet or Prophet Muhammad himself. It was a common practice for a Sufi brotherhood to establish its own convents.

As long as the Shia Buyid monarchy flourished in Baghdad and the Fatimid caliphate in Cairo, a great deal of the ideological-spiritual energy of the Islamic world was channeled into the Sunni–Shia feud. But once the Buyids had been replaced by the Sunni Seljuks in 1055, and the Fatimids by Salahuddin Ayubi in 1171, and the supremacy of Sunnism had been re-established, sectarian disputes virtually ended. Since sufi orders were generally free of sectarian influences they became the recipients of the intellectual energy which had been previously expended in Sunni–Shia disputation. This gave a fillip to sufism.

The overthrow of the Sunni Abbasids in 1258 by the invading Mongols led by Hulagu Khan created an ideological and intellectual vacuum in which sufism thrived; and so did Shiaism. During this period of rapid expansion sufi orders took on board both orthodox and dissident ideologies.

An example of a dissident order was Bektashi in Turkey. Its excessive respect for the House of Ali bordered on Shiaism, and not surprisingly many of its followers belonged to the Alevi (a variation of Shia) sect. An example of a mainstream brotherhood was Naqshbandi, established by Yusuf al Hamadani (d. 1140) but named after Bahauddin Naqshband (1318–89), a mystic born in Tajikistan and buried near Bukhara. Naqshbandis believed that there was no *tariqa* (road) outside the Sharia, and followed the maxim, "The exterior is for the world, the interior for Allah." Believing that piety was best expressed through social activity, they opposed withdrawal from the world. That the Naqshbandi order was free of the Sunni–Shia divide was obvious from its genealogy: Abu Bakr, Ali, Salman al Farsi (a companion of the Prophet), Jaafar al Sadiq and Abu Yazid al Bistani. Naqshbandis are noted for their silent remembrance (*dhikr*) in mosques undertaken to induce a state of collective ecstasy.

From about the mid-twelfth century onwards sufism became so prevalent as to be indistinguishable from mainstream Islam. Sufis ceased to be apolitical, and became involved in political-military campaigns. For instance, in 1453 Sufi dervishes participated in the successful seizure of Constantinople by the Ottoman Turks.

In 1501 the sufi order of Safavi, based in Ardebil, captured Tabriz and laid the foundation of the Safavid dynasty in Iran.

There was all along a certain tension between the ulama – steeped in scriptures and conscious of their role as the only qualified spiritual guides – and sufi shaikhs, who invariably invoked a call by Allah or the Prophet in a dream or vision to take up the mantle of spiritual leadership (without the rigorous book learning of the conventional ulama). Sufi shaikhs were frequently credited with miraculous powers, and it was widely believed that their inherited sanctity, which survived their death, stayed on around their tombs. This turned their tombs into shrines where saint-worship was practiced, much to the chagrin of the ulama. While saint-worship was heretical in Islam it appealed to most of the new converts from the societies which were steeped in this tradition. Thus sufism became a bridge between pre-Islamic creeds and Islam, helping to win converts to Islam and retain them.

Also, while the conventional ulama, in their capacity as religious jurisprudents or judges, could not provide a model for social behaviour to the faithful or encourage more devotional forms of worship, the sufi shaikhs were not so inhibited. They bent rules to suit local customs.

Whereas Islamic rituals were by and large austere, sufi orders provided a framework within which rich and colorful liturgical practices were spawned in the form of the devotional rituals of novices. The ecstatic sufi orders were particularly suitable for this purpose. The Rifaiiya brotherhood, originating in Iraq, was a case in point. Its followers went into frenzies during which they would ride dangerous animals, walk into fires, ravage venomous reptiles, or mutilate themselves by placing iron rings in their ears, necks or hands – to demonstrate the supremacy of mind over matter. Given the frequent appearance of devils and angels in the Quran it required no major dispensation to let African pagan cults coexist with Islamic rituals. Sufi silent prayers were conducted with the dual purpose of remembering Allah and propitiating savage pagan gods and goddesses.

Sufism grew rapidly between 1250 and 1500 when the caliphate was based in Cairo under Mamluk sultans, and when Islam penetrated central and western Africa, and southern India and South-East Asia, along the land and sea routes used by Arab traders. Islam came into contact not only with paganism in Africa but also with the advanced religions and civilizations of Hinduism and Buddhism in Asia.

In fact the first encounter between Islam and Hinduism had occurred in 711 when Islamic forces from Arabia had arrived in Sind by sea. Their rule lasted until 828. A later Islamic incursion occurred through the Khyber pass along the Afghanistan–Indian border when the invader Mahmud of Ghazni (an Afghan city) incorporated Punjab into his realm. But it was only in 1206 that Qutbuddin Aibak, a Turko-Afghan, established a Turko-Afghan sultanate in northern India.

Islam's egalitarianism proved particularly attractive to lower-caste Hindus and outcastes. But a bridge between polytheistic Hinduism and monotheistic Islam was needed to win converts to the new faith. It was provided by such sufi orders as Qadiriya, Chisti and Naqshbandi. The Qadiriya brotherhood, having originated in Baghdad, had spread to India and from there to eastern Afghanistan. The Naqshbandi order, having grown up in Tajikistan, had found its way through proselytized Tartars into Turkey (where Ottoman sultans were to base the caliphate from 1517 onwards), and also into India through its Turko-Afghan and Mogul invaders. Theologically, these brotherhoods subscribed to the "unity of being" thesis articulated by Muhyiuddin al Arabi (1165–1240). According to Arabi, there was no duality between Allah and his universe. Instead, Allah and his creation were part of a continuum, or "unity of being," composed of different grades of reality. Man was the microcosmic being through whom Allah contemplated himself. Thus divinity and humanity were two distinctive aspects which found expression at every level of creation – divinity corresponding to the covert side of reality and humanity to the overt.

Sufi shaikhs in India extended Arabi's thesis by arguing that since Allah was the only reality, all physical objects were mere "appearances" (an idea remarkably similar to the Hindu concept of the world being an illusion, *maya*), which could be revered as manifestations of the divine will. From this the acceptance of Hindu pantheism was only one short step. It was thus that sufi shaikhs built a theological bridge which enabled disaffected Hindus to cross over to Islam and synthesize some of the pre-Islamic practices with the Islamic ones.

The process of synthesis between Islam and Hinduism found its apogee during the reign of Jalaluddin Muhammad Akbar (1556–1605), a grandson of Zahiruddin Muhammad Babar, who founded the Mogul dynasty in India in 1526. Akbar cultivated sufi shaikhs, and was close to the Chisti brotherhood which was renowned for its universalist outlook. He tried to overcome the differences between Hinduism and Islam by treating his Hindu and Muslim subjects as equals, something which was not sanctified by the Sharia, and which had not been attempted by any of the previous Muslim rulers. Akbar got around the problem by declaring himself to be the chief and absolute *mujtahid* (practitioner of ijtihad), thus inadvertently ending the virtual ban on ijtihad that the ulama had maintained since the tenth century. He then changed those parts of the Sharia which discriminated against his non-Muslim subjects. He abolished the poll tax, and declared that Hindu women did not have to embrace Islam when marrying Muslims. His actions amounted to a gross deviation from Islam, and caused consternation among orthodox ulama.

In 1581 Akbar went so far as to launch his own faith, Din Illahi (Divine Faith), by synthesizing Islam with other religions. It was founded on the twin pillars of reason and asceticism. It praised the sufi attributes of devotion, piety, kindness and yearning for Allah, and condemned imitation and blind application of Islamic jurisprudence, which were the hallmarks of the Islamic establishment in India and elsewhere. Din Illahi had the full backing of the crown. Yet it failed to catch the popular imagination. It was adopted mainly by courtiers who treated the Emperor Akbar as their religious guide.

Orthodox Islamic circles considered Din Illahi heretical, for it implicitly challenged the claim of Islam to be the final and most authentic faith bestowed upon humanity by Allah. A fundamentalist reaction was bound to follow, and it did. But, interestingly enough, it was led by a Naqshbandi shaikh, Khwaja Abu al Muayyid Radiuddin Baqibillah (1563–1603). He won recruits to his order from among Akbar's courtiers. However, an open attack on the dilution of Islam and the ingression of esoteric practices into sufi orders had to wait until after Akbar's rule had given way to that of Nuruddin Salim Jahangir (r. 1605–27). It was mounted by Shaikh Ahmad Sirhindi, a disciple of Baqibillah. He blamed Arabi's "unity of being" doctrine for opening the floodgates of Hinduism into Islam and dissolving the monotheistic faith of Prophet Muhammad into the polymorphous structure of Hindu society. He reiterated the Naqshbandi position: the only way to perceive the Deity was through the Sharia, and (as elaborated earlier by Abu Hamid al Ghazali) the believer's mystical experiences had to be adapted to the Sharia and its external forms so as to avoid a relapse into heterodoxy or getting lost in individualistic eccentricities. He countered Arabi's "unity of being" doctrine with his "unity of witness" thesis. It differentiated absolutely between Allah and his creation, and rejected the concept of continuum. While Arabi had argued that reality was the mirror through which Allah contemplated himself, Sirhindi reasoned that reality was a reflection of Allah but was at the same time quite apart from him. In short, in Sirhindi's view, the Sharia was supreme both in the believer's inner mystical experiences and in his outward practices. Such an uncompromising stance precluded any chance of reconciliation between Islam and Hinduism. Sirhindi was called the Mujaddid Alf-e Thani, Reformer of the Second (Islamic) Millennium.

By arresting the synthetic tendencies in the Indian Muslim community, Sirhindi placed a stamp of rigid orthodoxy on Islam in India, and sowed the seeds of Muslim communalism which resulted three-and-a-half centuries later in the creation of Pakistan, a homeland for the Muslims of the Indian subcontinent.

The heyday of Sirhindi and the Naqshbandi order came during the rule of Muhyiuddin Aurangzeb (1658–1707), a grandson of Jahangir. Inspired by Sirhindi's ideology, Aurangzeb set out to purify the Muslim community by strictly implementing the Sharia. He actively pursued the Quranic edict of suppressing evil and enjoining virtue. He appointed censors to check alcoholism and sexual vices. He banned prostitution and hashish cultivation, and actively discouraged music. He strictly prohibited the construction of roofs over saints' graves and the use of such tombs as places of pilgrimage, a fairly common practice among Indian Muslims. He provided free kitchens, inns and subsistence allowances to indigent Muslims and withdrew taxes not sanctioned by the Sharia. He reintroduced the poll tax on Hindus, thus ending the equal treatment accorded to them since the days of Akbar. He replaced the Hindu solar calendar with the Muslim lunar calendar.

Aurangzeb's policies helped to rid Indian Islam of the heterodoxy and superstition that had crept into it since the early thirteenth century. They also enabled the Islamic state to reassert its authority over its non-Muslim citizens. In the process, however, the state lost much of the goodwill that Akbar's policies had engendered among the Hindus – who constituted three-quarters of the total population. The result was a series of revolts by Hindus and Sikhs (followers of a monotheistic faith which originated as a Hindu reform movement in the late fifteenth century), which debilitated the Mogul empire and, after Aurangzeb's death in 1707, showed to the Muslims that they were a vulnerable minority.

Faced with the prospect of a declining Mogul empire, Shah Waliullah of Delhi (1703–64), an eminent Naqshbandi shaikh educated in Mecca and Medina, argued that what Aurangzeb had achieved was insufficient, and that since Islam had been weakened by the infusion of Hindu customs and beliefs the only solution lay in further intensifying Islamic reform. He believed that the essence of Islam was eternal, but not its detailed practices. Hence there was a need for perpetual ijtihad, a stance totally at variance with the religious establishment. He proposed that the conclusions of the four (Sunni) legal schools be sifted with the texts of the Quran and Hadiths – a fundamentalist position. To help this process, and bring ordinary educated Muslims (totally dependent on their local mullahs for guidance) into direct contact with the Quran, he translated the holy book into Persian, the language of the literate Muslims, an unprecedented step. More importantly, he argued that with the Islamic umma enlarging and progressing there was constant need for ijtihad to cope with the new problems arising. He was probably the first Islamic thinker to articulate that religious thought had to interact with changing social conditions.

But the disintegration of the Mogul empire continued. It was under attack by Hindu and Sikh kings as well as by British East India Company forces. With this the reformism preached by Waliullah turned into militancy under the leadership of Ahmad Barelvi (d. 1831), a disciple of Waliullah's son Abdul Aziz. He broadened the base of the reformist movement by attracting supporters from the three leading sufi orders – Naqshbandi, Qadiriya and Chisti – and harnessing them within the framework of renewed Sharia orthodoxy. Thus was born the Tariq-e Muhammadiya (Way of Muhammad), an order which coupled sufi discipline with Sharia orthodoxy. Since the Sikh rulers had taken to persecuting Muslims, Barelvi declared a jihad against them in 1826. Later he led his followers to the Indo-Afghan border region with a view to founding an Islamic state on a "liberated territory," thus emulating the example of the *hijra* (migration) of Prophet Muhammad from Mecca to Medina.

His venture met with initial success. But when he attempted to impose Sharia taxes on the resident Pushtun tribesmen of the region, they abandoned his camp. The Sikh army battled with Barelvi's forces and defeated them in 1831. Barelvi was executed. But Tariq-e Muhammadiya survived as a militant movement and played a substantial role in the major Indian rebellion of 1857 against the British. This was an instance where a reformist

movement in Islam proved to be double-edged: against adulteration of Islamic practices among Muslims as well as against
Western Christian forces.

It was not only the periphery of the Dar al Islam which experienced moral and scriptural back-sliding, but also the Islamic
heartland. Those who attacked this tendency vociferously were
often the followers of Ahmad ibn Hanbal, the founder of the
Hanbali legal school. In so far as the Hanbalis referred directly
to the Quran and Sunna to reach legal decisions they stood
apart from the other three schools which had codified the
Sharia into a comprehensive jurisprudential system. In the late
fourteenth century Taqiuddin ibn Taimiya emerged as an
eminent Hanbali reformer. Though he started as a member of
the Qadiriya sufi brotherhood he later severely condemned the
practices of saint-worship and tomb cult. He opposed the contemporary ulama's assertion that the doors of ijtihad had been
closed. In jurisprudence he placed the Quran and Sunna far
above ijma (the community's consensus) and stressed loyalty to
salaf (ancestors) rather than to any specific legal school. The
salafi concept was later to become the foundation of the fundamentalist movement among Sunnis. His views found a positive
response among the Mamluk sultans in Cairo, the base of the
caliphate from 1250 to 1517.

The situation changed when the Ottoman Turks became the
leading power in the Dar al Islam: they were followers of the
Hanafi school. The Ottoman empire was founded by Osman I
(1259–1326), a leader of Osmanli Turks. When Muhammad II
seized Constantinople/Istanbul in 1453 he became heir to the
Byzantine empire. Under Selim I (r. 1512–20) the Ottoman
empire acquired Islamic primacy by usurping the caliphate
from the Mamluks. The expansion continued under his successor,
Suleiman the Magnificent (r. 1520–66), when the empire included
Algeria, Libya, Egypt, most of Greece and Hungary, much of
Persia and Arabia, and Syria. Transylvania, Wallachia and Mol-
davia were its tributary principalities. The growth and consolidation lasted until 1683 when the Ottomans reached, but failed to
conquer, Vienna. By now the Ottoman empire spanned Africa,

Europe and Asia, and had Muslim, Christian and Jewish subjects. The emperor was the protector of the Muslim holy cities of Mecca and Medina, which were also thriving centers of Islamic learning.

It was in Mecca and Medina, for instance, that Shah Waliullah had acquired his knowledge of Islam. Among his contemporaries was Muhammad ibn Abdul Wahhab (1703–87), a native of Najd, a Hanbali stronghold. Born into a religious family in Uyaina, Abdul Wahhab was inspired as much by Hanbal as by Taimiya. After his education in Mecca and Medina he returned to his home town. He was appalled by the prevalence of superstition, adultery and tribalism in his community, which had grown lax in its observance of Islamic rites and practices. He called for the discarding of all the medieval superstitions which had collected around the pristine teachings of Islam, and for the exercise of ijtihad. He opposed the codification of the Sharia into a comprehensive system of jurisprudence. He and his followers resorted to destroying the sacred trees and tombs of the saints. This upset the local community so much that its members drove out Abdul Wahhab and his supporters in 1744, an action reminiscent of that of the Meccans in the early days of Islam. They took refuge in the principality of Diriya where Abdul Wahhab made an alliance with the ruler, Muhammad ibn Saud. The followers of Abdul Wahhab, called Wahhabis, armed themselves and mounted a campaign against idolatry, the association of others with Allah, injustice, corruption and adultery. Regarding themselves as the true believers, the Wahhabis launched a jihad against all others whom they described as apostates – a practice which had many precedents in Islamic history. But what was unprecedented was the degree of puritanism they wanted to impose on the community. Claiming authority from the Hadiths, they banned music, dancing and even poetry which had always been an integral part of Arab life. They prohibited the use of silk, gold, ornaments and jewellery. Parallels with early Islam were unmistakable. Yet there were important differences too. While Prophet Muhammad had wielded the sword himself, Abdul Wahhab let his principal ally, Muhammad ibn Saud, wage battles and govern the community of muwahhidin (unitarians), believers in the unity of Allah. Muhammad ibn Saud called himself Imam and each Imam chose his own successor, with the descendants of Abdul Wahhab, known as Aal Shaikh, providing the leading ulama to the government. As in the seventh century, so now: the zealot members of rejuvenated Islam expanded their domain rapidly.

But here too there were essential differences. For instance, when in 1802 Saud ibn Abdul Aziz, grandson of the founder of the Saudi dynasty, invaded Karbala and destroyed the shrine of Imam Hussein, robbing it of all finery, he ordered the killing of all the Karbala residents since, according to him, they were apostates.

The following year the Wahhabis seized Mecca and demolished all the domes over the graves of the leading figures of early Islam. In 1805, finding themselves besieged by the Wahhabis, the local Medinese destroyed the domes over all the tombs in their city. These events signaled the victory of fundamentalist forces, and the emergence of a unified Arabia, including Mecca and Medina, ruled by its own imam.

However, unlike the unified community under Prophet Muhammad, Muslims in the early nineteenth century were divided among various sects. The hegemony of Wahhabis, an extremist sect, over Mecca and Medina created unease among the pilgrims whose loyalties were spread over a whole range of orthodox sects and sufi orders. What was more, the Ottomans' loss of Mecca and Medina threatened the security and well-being of Damascus and Baghdad, which were intimately tied up with the pilgrimage trade. So the Ottoman sultan could not let Wahhabi actions go unchallenged. In 1812 Sultan Mahmud II (r. 1808–39) dispatched Muhammad Ali Pasha, governor of Egypt, to defeat the Wahhabis. He succeeded. By 1819 he had crushed the Wahhabis, destroyed Diriya, and taken the ruler Abdullah ibn Saud to Istanbul where he was executed. Thus ended a vigorous fundamentalist movement.

The logic of their convictions and geographical location had left the Wahhabis no choice but to march on Mecca and Medina and impose their vision of Islam, hoping thus to win converts to their camp. But since these settlements were part of the Ottoman empire a clash between Wahhabis and the Ottoman empire became inevitable; and so did the defeat of the Wahhabis. It is likely that had the Wahhabis by their example induced a similar movement in a key part of the Ottoman empire such as Egypt, Syria or Iraq, they would have set in motion forces that the Ottomans would have found difficult, if not impossible, to overcome. But they did not.

To be sure, Sultan Mahmud II was beset with intractable problems, unable to modernize the administration and military as he wished, and caught up in the shifting balance of forces within the ruling elite – not to mention the challenge of administering a large non-Muslim population in the empire. The issues were complex and overwhelming, and defied the simplistic solutions offered by Wahhabi fundamentalism.

Increasingly, as the Islamic heartland fell under Western influence, the nature of the threats and dangers that Islam faced changed. Dilution and corruption of Islam began to occur not so much because of the ingression of the pre-Islamic practices of native populations as because of the infiltration of Western secular ideas, practices and political models, into the body politic of Islam. The Ottoman empire straddling Europe, Asia and Africa lay at the hub of this process.

3   Islam in modern times

Islam entered the modern age under the leadership of Ottoman Turks, with Istanbul as the capital of the caliphate. It is therefore crucial to study major developments within the Islamic empire as well as its relations with European powers.

Once the Ottomans failed to annex Vienna in 1683 they found themselves on the defensive *vis-à-vis* the empires of the Habsburgs and Tsars. The Treaty of Kuchuk Kainarji of 1774 allowed the Russian Tsar to aid the Muslim Tartars, who were scattered from the Polish border to the Caspian Sea, including Crimea, to establish a semi-independent state under his tutelage. A decade later the Tsar annexed this state. In 1791 the Habsburgs formalized their annexation of Belgrade. Clearly the Ottoman military was proving unequal to the task of fending off its European rivals.

Selim III (r. 1789–1807) realized the need to modernize the army. He established a new militia and military schools with French instructors and training manuals. This upset the 50,000 professional soldiers and officers, called Janissaries, who had been the traditional armed force of the caliphate since 1259. The Janissaries allied with the ulama in arousing popular passions against military modernization, and deposed Selim III. The bureaucratic elite, the third center of power which had been growing steadily, was not strong enough to alter the course of events. Selim III's successor, Mahmoud II (r. 1808–39), ended military reform.

What had struck a severe blow to Selim III's prestige was the occupation in 1798 of Egypt, a Muslim territory of his empire, by Napoleon Bonaparte. Later, in 1830 France occupied another Muslim territory of the Ottoman empire, Algeria. It was apparent that Christian Europe, helped by striking advances in technology and administration, was forging ahead at the expense of the Ottomans. That Europe's rising supremacy stemmed from the rapid growth of capitalism, largely due to the discovery and development of the Americas, did not detract from the fact that the Ottoman power was on the decline.

There was a growing awareness in intellectual circles in the Ottoman empire of political and social malaise. The degree of stagnation of official Islam can be judged by the *fatwa* (verdict) issued by the *mufti* (religious-legal jurist) of Cairo's Al Azhar early in the nineteenth century. "The four orthodox schools are the best results, the finest extraction of all schools, because they count among their partisans many men dedicated to the search for truth and blessed with vast knowledge," stated the mufti. "Deviation from these four schools shows the desire to live in error." It was therefore obligatory to follow one of the four orthodox schools. He unequivocally rejected the claim to ijtihad, in interpreting the sacred texts: "No one denies the fact that the dignity of ijtihad has long disappeared and that at the present time no man has attained this degree of learning. He who believes himself to be mujtahid would be under the influence of his hallucinations and of the devil."[1]

The reason for the suppression of independent thinking lay in the way that exercise of power had evolved in the Islamic world. The successors to the four Rightly Guided caliphs came to rely increasingly on sheer force to secure power and retain it. Yet they felt a periodic need for doctrinal legitimation. The only way to ensure this was by undermining independent thought on the doctrine. Time and again independent-minded thinkers were forced to retreat in the face of rigid official dogma sanctified by venal ulama whose sole argument was that opposition to the ruler would lead to chaos, which had to be avoided at all costs.

In the early nineteenth century, faced with unmistakable decline, the Ottoman intellectuals pondered the reasons for the growing strength of Christian European powers. Either Europeans had devised a system better than Islam or the Muslim community had failed to follow true Islam. Since none of them was prepared to concede the inferiority of Islam to any other social system the inevitable conclusion was that Muslims had deviated from the true path. So the stage was set for Islamic reform. Yet, this time, the reform had less to do with theological or spiritual arguments and more to do with political power and policies. The numerous solutions offered boiled down to exhortations to Muslims all over the world to unite against European encroachment and/or to devise a strategy to study the sources of European power with a view to tapping them.

In the specific field of shoring up Ottoman military power, Mahmoud II aligned more with the bureaucratic elite, committed to modernization, than with the coalition of the Janissaries and the ulama. The Janissaries suffered a severe setback in 1821 when they failed to curb a rebellion by the Greek subjects of the empire. It was a painful reminder to the sultan that the Islamic empire could no longer maintain its hold over its non-Muslim subjects. The standing of the Janissaries sank so low that when Mahmoud II disbanded them in June 1826 the ulama uttered not a word of protest. This signaled victory for the state bureaucrats and their strategy of learning from the Europeans abroad while making administrative and military reforms at home. Thus began the process of *Tanzimat* (lit. reorganization). Feudal tenure was abrogated and religious trusts reformed in 1827. Schools were opened in 1838 to train civil servants, doctors and military officers. Mahmoud II prescribed the wearing of the fez instead of the assorted headgear used by various sections of Ottoman society. This signified symbolic equality for all Ottoman citizens, Muslim or non-Muslim, a concept which went down badly with Muslims at large. But these measures failed to appease the European powers. After annexing Bessarabia in 1812, Russia took over the Ottoman possessions in the Caucasus region in 1829.

Tanzimat gathered momentum under Abdul Majid (r. 1839–61). He laid down the doctrine of equality for all Ottoman citizens, irrespective of their religion, and the provision of security of life and property for all the inhabitants of the empire. In 1847 he founded military schools. Commercial and criminal codes, based on the Code Napoléon, were drafted in 1859. This meant limiting the Sharia to personal affairs. Control of education by the ulama was reduced when a ministry of education, formed in 1857, promulgated regulations for public instruction three years later. With the growing popularity of Western dress in urban areas the ulama became differentiated from bureaucrats and military officers with whom hitherto they had been associated. Gradually the ulama came to be seen as diehard conservatives opposed to all innovations. Among the inventions they had (unsuccessfully) opposed was the printing press. Also the ulama came to be viewed as being concerned only with family matters and not with the believer's entire life.

European powers favoured Tanzimat, but that did not deter them from attacking the Ottoman empire. Tsarist Russia was the most aggressive, determined to act as the militant protector of 12 million Eastern Orthodox Christians under the Ottomans. It was at the same time consolidating and expanding its territories in Central Asia inhabited by Muslims.

Taking their cue from Russian aspirations towards the Christians of the Ottoman empire, the leaders of the Central Asian Muslims appealed to Sultan Abdul Aziz (r. 1861–76) to establish himself as the guardian of the Muslims in Tsarist Russia. Abdul Aziz also became the recipient of appeals from the Muslims of India. There, after the failure of the 1857 uprising against the British – in which Muslim princes and kings played a leading role – depression had spread among Muslims as they pondered their fate as British subjects after having been the ruling caste for nearly seven centuries. To both the Indian and Central Asian Muslims the Ottoman empire – containing the holy cities of Mecca, Medina and Jerusalem as well as the leading Islamic cultural centers of Cairo, Damascus and Baghdad – was the prime embodiment of Islamic civilization and power.

But Abdul Aziz could do little. He was an extravagant ruler, heavily indebted to the European powers, and had no leverage over them. His impotence became embarrassingly obvious when in the last years of his reign, at Russia's behest, Bulgaria, Bosnia, Serbia and Montenegro rebelled against Istanbul. This caused such a tidal wave of disaffection that, following a fatwa against Abdul Aziz by the Shaikh al Islam (Wise Man of Islam) the supreme legal authority, Abdul Aziz was overthrown by Midhat Pasha, the leader of the Young Ottomans, a powerful group formed in 1859 with the main objective of securing an elected assembly for the umma of believers as a true application of the Sharia.

Midhat Pasha produced a constitution, an unprecedented development in Islam. Among other things it formalized the religious status of the Ottoman sultan. "His Majesty the Sultan is, in his capacity as the Supreme Caliph, the protector of the Muslim religion," it stated. The constitution, which included a Bill of Rights and stipulated an elected chamber, was promulgated by Abdul Aziz's successor, Abdul Hamid II (r. 1876–1909) in December 1876.

In April 1877 the Russian army crossed the Ottoman borders with the objective of winning freedom for Slavs, and reached Istanbul. The sultan had to sign the humiliating Treaty of San Stefano in March 1878, which was revised in July by the Treaty of Berlin. According to the treaty Cyprus was ceded to Britain, and Tunisia to France. Furthermore, the sultan was obliged to engage financial and military advisors from Germany to implement reform, and allow judicial inspectors from European nations to travel through the empire to redress grievances.

The continued loss of territory coupled with growing intrusion by Europeans into the internal affairs of the Ottoman empire convinced Abdul Hamid II that the 50-year-old Tanzimat program had failed to reassure either the European powers or his Christian subjects. It was therefore time to change direction.

In February 1878 he suspended the constitution and dissolved parliament. He arrested Midhat Pasha and banished the Young Ottomans to different parts of the empire. He repudiated Islamic modernism and turned to traditional Islamic values and thought. But, interestingly enough, he continued to import Western technology and methods. As it was, the ulama had no objection to the import of sewing-machines or railroads. At the same time they insisted that Islam had nothing spiritual to learn from the West – a position they still maintain.

Abdul Hamid II adopted the argument and policies first advocated by Ahmad Cevdet Pasha, who condemned Tanzimat leaders for destroying the cohesion of Ottoman society by implementing secular reform of the judicial system, and proposed that while the technological apparatus should be modernized, Islam in its traditional form should be maintained as the central system of Ottoman society. Indeed, Abdul Hamid II went one step further. He tried to regenerate cohesion in Ottoman society by activating the popular masses on a religious platform round the Islamic banner and harnessing their energies. In order to succeed in the venture he activated sufi brotherhoods and used them as channels of communication to reach the masses. His strategy worked since there had all along been a widespread current of Islamic feeling among the humbler subjects of the Ottoman empire.

He also tried to engender a pan-Islamic movement. In this he had the active backing of, among others, Jamaluddin Afghani, a religious personality of varied talents: a scholar, philosopher, teacher, journalist and politician. He was born of Shia parents in Asadabad near Hamadan in western Iran, but claimed that his birthplace was Asadabad near Konar in eastern Afghanistan, and that his parents were Sunni.[2] By claiming a Sunni background he could reach a wide audience. However, he did spend his childhood and adolescence in Kabul where he studied Islam and philosophy. At 18 he left Kabul for pilgrimage to Mecca as well as Karbala and Najaf. Then he spent a year in India at a time when, following the failure of the 1857 Indian uprising against the British, there was strong anti-British feeling among Muslims. This left a deep mark on him.

On his return to Afghanistan in 1861 he became entangled in local politics. When his patron, Muhammad Azam, was ousted in 1869 by his half-brother, Sher Ali, Afghani was expelled from the country. He arrived in Istanbul, then in the throes of Tanzimat, and was well received by Sultan Abdul Aziz. Afghani, who favored educational reform and scientific thought, was appointed to the Council of Education. In one of his lectures he referred to the esoteric meaning of the Quran, a concept regarded as heretical by Sunnis. This offended the ulama headed by the Shaikh al Islam, Hassan Fahmi, who was jealous of Afghani's scholarship and popularity. Afghani considered it prudent to leave Istanbul.

Soon after his arrival in Cairo in 1871 he was given a generous allowance by the ruler, Khedive Ismail. Among his students were Muhammad Abdu and Said Zaghlul Pasha; the former was to become the Grand Mufti of Egypt, and the latter a founder of the nationalist Wafd Party. Afghani encouraged patriotic resistance to growing British and French interference in Egypt's affairs, attacked Khedive Ismail for his extravagance, and proposed a parliamentary system of government which he saw as being in line with Islamic precepts. He thus proved to be an innovator in offering Islamic responses and solutions to contemporary problems.

When Tawfik succeeded his father, Khedive Ismail, in early 1879, the British advised him to expel Afghani. In September Afghani was deported to Hyderabad, India, and then to Calcutta, and kept under British surveillance. Here he attacked the Islamic modernist Sayyid Ahmad Khan for being servile towards the British and adopting a Western lifestyle. He also condemned Ahmad Khan for persuading Indian Muslims to acquire British education and trying to offer a rationalist interpretation of the Quran. He advocated Hindu–Muslim unity in order to resist British rule. In Egypt, where Afghani had backed the nationalist movement led by Ahmad Urabi Pasha, anti-British feelings spilled over in an armed uprising in 1881–2 which was crushed. This marked the beginning of the British occupation of Egypt which continued until 1954.

Afghani turned up in Paris in January 1883. Four months later he published an article in the *Journal des Débats* in which he repudiated Joseph-Ernest Renan's arguments, delivered in an earlier lecture, that Islam and science were incompatible. While agreeing that, like other religions, Islam had been a barrier to scientific progress, he repudiated Renan's thesis that Islam was in this respect worse than other religions. Elsewhere he insisted that it was wrong to describe scientific study as antithetical to Islam, that it was indeed an integral part of Islamic civilization and that its loss was chiefly responsible for the decay that had set in in the Islamic umma.

He and his disciple Muhammad Abdu published a journal in Arabic, *Al Urwat al Wuthqa* (The Indissoluble Link). In it they supported Sultan Abdul Hamid II's pan-Islamist proclivities and elaborated their reformist ideas.

Following an invitation in 1886 by Iran's Nasiruddin Shah, Afghani went to live in Tehran. But his popularity there disconcerted the Shah. The next year Afghani left for the Uzbekistan region of the Tsarist empire. There he engaged in propaganda against the British in India, and this pleased the Tsar. Later, in St. Petersburg, he persuaded Tsar Alexander II to allow the publication of the Quran and other Islamic literature for the first time in Tsarist history.

In 1889, on his way to the Paris World Exhibition, he met Nasiruddin Shah in Munich. Accepting the Shah's invitation, he returned to Tehran. However, his plan to reform the judiciary aroused the Shah's suspicion, and Afghani retired to a religious sanctuary near the capital. In early 1891, following his arrest, he was expelled to Turkey.

Afghani made his way to Basra. From there he attacked the Shah for giving the tobacco concession to a British company. His disciple Mirza Hassan Shirazi decreed that the faithful should stop smoking until the Shah had withdrawn his tobacco concession. This was the first time in modern history that a religious leader had openly challenged the ruler in Iran. The popular response to Shirazi's call was so overwhelming that the Shah canceled the tobacco concession in early 1892. Again this was the first instance of public opinion in a Muslim country impinging directly on royal decision-making.

From Basra, Afghani went to London where he carried out a sustained campaign against the dictatorial rule of the Shah, chiefly through *Diyal al Khafikyan* (Radiance of the Two Hemispheres), a monthly journal published in Persian and English. He thus helped to build a political reformist movement in Iran under the leadership of the ulama which was dedicated to the Shah's overthrow – a precursor of the events of the late 1970s.

When Sultan Abdul Hamid II invited Afghani to Istanbul, he went. The sultan was liberal in his allowances to Afghani, and tried to persuade him to cease his anti-Shah propaganda. Afghani refused and sought, in vain, to leave. In March 1896 the Shah of Iran was murdered by a merchant who had once been a student of Afghani. About a year later Afghani died of cancer.

Afghani was outstanding in more ways than one. He was the first – and the last – Islamic figure who played an active part in the religious-political life of the people in all the important Islamic regions: Ottoman Turkey, Egypt, Iran, India and Central Asia. This gave him a truly pan-Islamic perspective, and made him realize that all of the Islamic umma was threatened by European powers. Not surprisingly, as Wilfred Cantwell Smith, an expert on Islam, points out, Afghani was the first to use "the concepts 'Islam' and 'the West' as connoting correlative – and of course antagonistic – historical phenomena."[3]

He was perceptive enough to realize that, of Britain and Russia, Britain was the bigger threat to the Islamic world. The British economic system was more advanced along capitalist lines than the Russian, and it was Britain which ruled both India and Egypt.

Afghani was both a militant reformist of Islam and a vehement anti-imperialist. He wanted to goad the Muslim masses and rulers into active resistance against European imperialism. While he used traditional Islamic language and constantly called on the dynamism and militancy of *salaf al salih* (the pious ancestors) to unite and resist the growing domination of the Islamic world by unbelievers, he also called on Muslims to revive scientific thought and reform their educational system – that is, to learn from the West.

Arguing for ijtihad, Afghani stated that each believer had the right and responsibility to interpret the Quran and Sunna for himself. He wanted the people to help themselves, and often quoted the Quranic verse: "Verily, Allah does not change the state of a people until they change themselves inwardly."

His influence was seminal in the creation of pan-Islamic nationalism and the reformist salafiya movement. In the dialect of Islam versus the West his position combined (in the words of Edward Mortimer) "three types of Muslim responses to the West: the defensive call to arms, the eager attempt to learn the secret of Western strength, and the internalization of Western secular modes of thought."[4]

Afghani was a genuine Islamic thinker. While he took an interest in certain Western concepts, he never allowed Western ideology to be the font of his inspiration. He remained rooted firmly in his Islamic heritage even though he spent some years in France, Britain and Russia.

In retrospect Afghani emerges as the modern progenitor of Islamic reform. His disciple Muhammad Abdu applied his general principles and guidelines to the specific task of law-making; and Muhammad Rashid Rida, one of Abdu's disciples, went on to offer a blueprint of an Islamic state suitable for the present day and age.

Muhammad Abdu, born into an Egyptian peasant family, came under Afghani's influence in the 1870s. When Egypt was occupied by the British in 1882, Abdu left for Paris where he assisted Afghani in publishing an Islamic journal, *Al Urwat at Wuthqa*. He parted with Afghani on the question of resisting the West. The militant Afghani believed in rousing Muslim rulers and their subjects to fight the European forces, whereas Abdu argued that Muslims must initially concentrate on educational and religious reform, and inculcate those aspects of Western civilization which were in line with Islam.

Arguing that Islam was not incompatible with the basics of Western thought, Abdu interpreted the Islamic concept of *shura* (consultation) as parliamentary democracy, *ijma* (consensus) as public opinion, and *maslah* (choosing that ruling or interpretation of the Sharia from which greatest good will ensue) as utilitarianism.

He returned to Egypt in 1888, and concentrated on educational and legal reform. After he had become the Grand Mufti he extended the concept of maslah to drafting laws based on the general principle of public morality. He even went so far as to state that if a particular Islamic ruling had become a source of harm – which it had not caused before – then it must be changed to suit contemporary conditions. He extended the concept of *talfiq* (choosing an interpretation from a legal school other than one's own) to produce a synthesis of different rulings and go beyond these to the original sources of the Sharia: the Quran, the Hadith and salaf al salih principles. While Afghani stressed the general militancy of the salaf of early Islam, Abdu focused on their impact on the shaping of the Sharia and their rationalism. Later, Abdu's approach to law-making was to be adopted by many Muslim states in the drafting of personal law.

Muhammad Rashid Rida, the best known of Abdu's disciples, carried the salafi principles further by researching what Prophet Muhammad and the salaf had done and said in order to apply it to contemporary conditions. In legal matters he preferred to follow the ideas of the salaf rather than formal legal schools. Like Ahmad ibn Hanbal he believed that the Quran and the Hadith were paramount because God could only be described by what he had done in the Quran, and Prophet Muhammad by what he had done in the Sunna. Also, when specific injunctions were found to be in contradiction, the best way that the believer could solve the problem was by turning to the first principles as outlined in the Quran and the Hadith. He was thus a supporter of the practice of ijtihad which he defined as "independent reasoning from first principles." He outlined this and many other ideas in *Al Manar* (The Lighthouse), the journal he published in Cairo after his arrival there in 1897 from his native Tripoli, north Lebanon, where he had first met Abdu three years earlier.

While Egypt was occupied by Britain it was nominally part of the Ottoman empire. By the early twentieth century Abdul

Hamid II's populist approach to Islam at home and espousing of pan-Islamism abroad had proved inadequate to revitalize the disintegrating empire. In 1908 the army officers of the empire's European territories compelled Abdul Hamid II to reinstate the 1876 constitution. The next year they deposed him, hoping that this would improve the health of the empire. It did not. The basic problem was that while the traditional idea of an Islamic umma governed by a strong and pious ruler had become outmoded, the concept of securing equal loyalty for the empire from different religious groups was too new and untested.

The war of 1912–13, which led to the loss of the remaining European territories, as well as Libya, once again underlined the weakness of the Ottoman empire. However, it could also be said that following the latest setback the reduced empire had become religiously more homogeneous. It was against this background that the Kaiser's Germany encouraged the military leaders in Istanbul – known as the Young Turks – to liberate fellow Turks from Russian bondage and extend their empire eastwards to Central Asia. It was thus that Turkey joined Germany in World War I in October 1914. The war ended four years later with the Ottomans conceding defeat, an event which signified the end of the last Islamic empire, a traumatic experience for the world Muslim community.

For the next several years the situation in Turkey, the heartland of the old Ottoman empire, remained turbulent. In Istanbul Sultan Mehmet VI cooperated with the occupation forces of the victorious Allies whereas the nationalist Turks, led by Mustafa Kemal, opposed them, and set up the Grand National Assembly in Ankara. Kemal's prestige rose sharply when he succeeded in expelling the occupying Greek forces from Turkey in August 1921. At his behest, in November 1922, the Grand National Assembly abolished the sultanate but retained the caliphate as a religious office. To justify this action Kemal referred to the precedent in the Abbasid period when the caliphs had lost all political authority and become symbolic figures of Islamic unity. This time around, however, the arrangement was to prove a stop-gap. In March 1924 Kemal asked the Grand

National Assembly to "cleanse and elevate the Islamic faith by rescuing it from the position of a political instrument, to which it has been accustomed for centuries." The caliph was deposed, and the caliphate abolished, thus ending a 1,292-year-old tradition. This created a spiritual crisis in the Muslim world outside Turkey, which was to follow a militantly secular path under Kemal's leadership.

Muhammad Rashid Rida, a native of Greater Syria, was directly involved in the events that followed the dissolution of the Ottoman empire. In 1920 he became president of the Syrian National Congress which chose Prince Faisal ibn Hussein as king of Syria. Three years later he compiled his series of articles on the caliphate in *Al Manar* into a book entitled *The Caliphate or the Supreme Imamate*. This work established him as the founding theoretician of the Islamic state in its modern sense. In it he outlined the origins of the caliphate and examined the gulf that existed between the theory and practice of the caliphate, and went on to offer a blueprint for an Islamic state.[5]

The affairs of the Islamic state must be conducted within the framework of a constitution that is inspired by the Quran, the Hadith and the experiences of the Rightly Guided caliphs, Rida stated. Creative reasoning (ijtihad) must be employed to interpret these sources in drafting measures to promote public welfare. The head of the Islamic state – to be called the caliph or supreme imam – must be a mujtahid. In his juridical role he is to be assisted by *ahl al hall wal aqd* (the people who loose and bind) a term which embraces various types of representatives of the community, including the ulama. They are to be the protectors of the Islamic character of the state. The caliph must consult them; and it is this consultation which makes his decisions religiously binding. Traditionally, "the people who loose and bind" have been the community's representatives and electors of the caliphs. But nowadays they must also exercise the power to legislate, to find rational and systematic solutions to emerging problems. The Sharia is the dominant authority in legislation but, over the centuries, it has been complemented by a corpus of "positive law" (*qanun*), which is subordinate to it. In the final analysis the "positive law" too must be in line with broad Islamic principles. A temporal authority must be established to conduct a system of sanctions and punishments to the law-breakers. (However, Rida was silent on the link between this authority and the caliph/supreme imam.)

The caliph/supreme imam must be chosen by the representatives of all Muslim sects (Sunni, Shia and Kharaji) from among a group of highly trained jurisconsults of unimpeachable renown. Rida's stress on jurisprudence stems from the fact that in modern times legislation is a crucial element of the state, and that the caliph is expected to be the prime force behind the legislative process. As the head of state the caliph is the leader of all Muslims, and must as such recognize the pluralism of the Islamic doctrine. The believers must obey the caliph to the degree that his actions are in line with Islamic precepts and serve the public interest. When his decisions are perceived to contravene Islamic principles or public welfare, the community's representatives have the right to challenge them.

In Rida's view a Muslim is entitled to gain understanding of the Quran and the Hadith without the aid of any intermediary, past or present. Women should be treated on a par with men except in heading households or leading prayers or holding the office of the caliph or supreme imam.

A systematic study of the theory and practice of the caliphate coupled with updating of the caliphate concept in the light of contemporary conditions was an important milestone in the history of Islamic reform, and a symptom of the innovative energy of Muslim thinkers in the first quarter of the twentieth century. It is noteworthy that the reformist line etched by Afghani–Abdu–Rida was double-edged, poised as much against the scholastic tradition of the fossilized jurisconsults, whom the reformers blamed for Islam's decay, as it was against the Western or Westernized detractors of Islam.

Rida was sufficiently realistic to regard the attainment of the Islamic state of his vision as a long-term objective, and quite willing meanwhile to settle for a "caliphate of necessity." His pragmatic approach was also reflected in the implicit acceptance in his blueprint of the coexistence of religious and political states, the Sharia and the "positive law."

However, various factors brought about an end to this duality, with the political aspect ceding its place to the religious. First, the reformers gradually accepted the view current among the ulama that the West's assault on Islam was not only political but also ideological, and that Western secular ideas had penetrated Islamic thinking and debilitated it. Second, from the 1920s onwards it became increasingly clear that the salafiya or any other reformist idea could be realized only if it acquired the support of the Muslim masses; and when the salafiya concept was exposed to popular mobilization its religious dimension emerged as the supreme element. Finally, with the abolition of the caliphate in 1924, an acute crisis developed in the Islamic world, and it pushed the religious aspect of Muslim life to the fore.

While the reformers increasingly stressed confronting the West, politically and culturally, they did not soft-pedal the need for Islamic reform. Indeed, they felt an urge to cleanse Islam of its non-Islamic accretions, and thus enable Muslims to reclaim the glory of the faith. In other words, they led a movement which was two-tracked, where the emphasis came to be "less on cleansing Islam from medieval sufism or scholastic legalism and more on cleansing it from new heresies, Western secular ideas that had crept in under the guise of modernism; less on acquiring (or repossessing) for Islam the sources of Western strength, and more on ridding Islam of the seeds of Western decadence."[6]

Unsurprisingly, the first country to spawn a popular Islamic revivalist movement was Egypt, politically and culturally the most important state in the Arab world, the historic nucleus of Islam. Before the Ottomans it had been the heart of the Islamic caliphate for two and a half centuries. As a protectorate of the British since 1882, however, it was subjected to ever-increasing waves of Western thought and culture. The Islamist movement which grew and thrived on its soil was called Ikhwan al Muslimin, the Muslim Brotherhood.

Part II

Islamic ideologies and fundamentalist states

4 The Muslim Brotherhood in Egypt and its offshoots

Among the regular readers of Rashid Rida's *Al Manar* was Hassan al Banna (1904–49), a primary school teacher in Ismailiya, capital of the British-occupied Suez Canal Zone. He came from a pious family in the Nile Delta town of Muhammadiya; his father, Ahmad al Banna, a graduate of Al Azhar University, the most important authority on Sunni Islam, and author of books on the Hadiths and Islamic jurisprudence, was a religious teacher who led prayers at the local mosque.

Banna grew up during particularly turbulent times. Following World War I (during which Britain declared Egypt to be its protectorate) Egyptians revolted on a massive scale and won semi-independence in 1922. The first parliamentary election of 1923 saw the nationalist Wafd Party beat the Liberal Constitutionalists. In Turkey secular republican forces, led by Mustafa Kemal Ataturk, abolished the caliphate in 1924, an event which created a crisis in the Islamic world. Banna attributed the upheaval to the discord between the Wafd and the Liberal Constitutionalists, and "the vociferous political debating" which had erupted after the 1919 revolution; to "the orientations to apostasy and nihilism" then engulfing the Muslim world; to the attacks on tradition and orthodoxy, emboldened by "the Kemalist Revolt" in Turkey, which had graduated into a movement for the intellectual and social emancipation of Egypt; and to the non-Islamic, secularist and libertarian trends which had pervaded the academic and intellectual circles of Egypt. As a result of this turbulence, Banna argued, Egyptian youths were inheriting a "corrupted religion'; and imbued with "doubt and perplexity" they were tempted by apostasy.[1]

He responded to the prevailing conditions in moralistic and didactic terms. He sponsored discussions in public places, and went on to establish in 1928 the Muslim Brotherhood as a youth club with its main stress on moral and social reform through communication, information and propaganda. In retrospect the birth of the Muslim Brotherhood in Ismailiya seems logical. As the headquarters of the Suez Canal Company and the British troops in Egypt, Ismailiya was a powerful outpost of the West as well as a multi-dimensional threat to Egypt's political, economic and cultural identity.

It was only after Egyptians had mounted militant resistance to the 1936 Anglo-Egyptian Treaty, and Palestinian Arabs had launched an armed uprising in Palestine against the British Mandate and Zionist colonization in 1936–7, that the Muslim Brotherhood formally transformed itself into a political entity. This happened in 1939, and illustrated the thesis that radicalism thrives under the threat of an external enemy. Now the Muslim Brotherhood declared that: "(a) Islam is a comprehensive, self-evolving system; it is the ultimate path of life in all its spheres; (b) Islam emanates from, and is based on, two fundamental sources, the Quran, and the Prophetic Tradition; and (c) Islam is applicable to all times and places."[2] In short, Islam was a total ideology, offering an all-powerful system to regulate every detail of the political, economic, social and cultural life of the believers.

The Muslim Brotherhood too was presented as an all-encompassing entity. Describing his movement as the inheritor and catalyst of the most active elements in Sunni traditionalist and reformist thinking, Banna stated that it was "a Salafiya message, a Sunni way, a Sufi truth, a political organization, an athletic group, a scientific and cultural union, an economic enterprise and a social idea."

Along with this went a rapid expansion of the movement, headquartered since 1933 in Cairo. In 1940 the Brotherhood had 500 branches, each one having its own center, a mosque, a school and a club or home industry. Its schools ran religious classes, and imparted physical education (later military training) to its young members in order to prepare them for a jihad. The jihad was to be mounted to liberate not merely Egypt from alien control but also the whole of "the Islamic homeland." In this homeland was to be instituted "a free Islamic government, practicing the principles of Islam, applying its social system, propounding its solid fundamentals and transmitting its wise call to the people."[3] The objective was similar to what Afghani had propounded several decades earlier. But he had lacked a vehicle to bring it about: a popular party of the believers.

The Brotherhood's growth occurred at a time when Egyptians were being humiliatingly made aware of their servitude to an alien power. In February 1942, while German troops were marching towards Egypt from Libya and King Farouq (r. 1936–52) was considering appointing a new prime minister known to be anti-British, the British ambassador in Cairo ordered British tanks (normally stationed in the Suez Canal Zone) to surround the royal palace, and then gave Farouq the choice of abdicating or appointing the pro-British Wafd leader, Nahas Pasha, as prime minister. Farouq invited Nahas Pasha to form the government. While this secured the Allies' position in Egypt for the rest of World War II, it destroyed the monarch's prestige among his subjects.

Such events swelled the ranks of the Brotherhood, which drew its popular support from students, civil servants, artisans, petty traders and middling peasants. Brothers met for congregational prayers where they were exhorted by their leaders to observe religious duties and Islamize their personal lives. They were organized into cells of five called families – and then upwards into clans, groups and battalions. Later the leadership was to set up secret cells.

After World War II the anti-British struggle escalated, and political violence became endemic in Egypt. King Farouq's popular standing suffered a further setback when, following the British withdrawal from Palestine in May 1948, the Egyptian army joined the Arab war effort against the newly formed state of Israel. It did badly, mainly due to the incompetence and corruption of its senior officers, the obsolescence of its (British-supplied) arms, and irregular and inadequate supplies of food and medicine. Muslim Brotherhood volunteers fought in the Arab–Israeli War and came into contact with nationalist Egyptian officers. While many officers picked up Brotherhood ideology, the Brothers underwent military training under the officers' supervision. Brotherhood leaders shared with the nationalist officers – functioning as the Free Officers' Organization – their frustrated anger at the injustice and decadence prevalent in Egypt, their disapproval of secular ideologies, particularly Marxism, which divided the nation, and their impatience with electoral politics. The recruitment of military officers into its ranks further strengthened the Brotherhood, which in 1946 claimed 500,000 active members and 500,000 sympathizers organized in 5,000 branches. It had by then coined a highly attractive slogan: "The Quran is our constitution; the Prophet is our Guide; Death for the glory of Allah is our greatest ambition."

The Brotherhood also benefited from the fact that the religious establishment, represented by Al Azhar University and its rector, sided firmly with the monarch. Al Azhar ulama considered any action against the ruler, indigenous or alien, as *fitna* (sedition), which contributed to creating chaos in society, a situation which had to be avoided at all costs. So acute was their fear of chaos that in the past they had condoned foreign occupation. In 1798 Al Azhar ulama urged their followers to obey the French occupiers: "It is incumbent on you not to provoke *fitan* [plural of *fitna*], not to obey trouble-makers, or listen to hypocrites or pursue evil."[4] In 1914, following the declaration of martial law by the British occupiers, Al Azhar ulama stated: "Praise be to God who cautioned the believers to avoid all *fitan* . . . Thus it is our duty to remain tranquil and silent and to advise others to do so, to avoid interfering in things which do not concern you."[5] So the ulama's current servility to King Farouq was in line with their past behavior. They showed no sign of distancing themselves from the ruler in the wake of the Egyptian defeat in the 1948 Arab–Israeli War.

By contrast the Muslim Brotherhood held the Egyptian political establishment solely responsible for the Arab debacle in the war with Israel. It resorted to terroristic and subversive activities. Prime Minister Mahmoud Fahmi Nokrashi Pasha retaliated by promulgating martial law and banning the Muslim Brotherhood in December 1948. Three weeks later he was assassinated by a Brother. This led to further repression of the organization by the state. Banna argued that since the Brotherhood had been disbanded the assassin could not be described as its member. On 12 February 1949 Banna was killed by Egyptian secret service agents outside his office in Cairo.

Ideologically Banna was firmly in line with Afghani, Abdu and Rashid Rida's salafiya reformism. He was against *taqlid* (imitation of the ulama) and favored *maslah* (choosing that ruling or interpretation which ensures greatest good) and ijtihad, to be employed so that Islam could face the problems of the modern world. Where he differed from his reformist predecessors was on the means used to achieve an Islamic state. Afghani had limited himself in his pamphleteering to appealing to Muslim rulers and intellectuals to unite against the unbelievers, Abdu had focused his attention on religious reform and issuing fatwas, and Rashid Rida had used *Al Manar* to expound and propagate the salafiya ideology, and combined this with resorting to popular social and political actions to re-create the Islamic state. But it was Banna who had established a mass political party. He argued that the goal of re-creating the Islamic state could be realized within the existing constitutional framework. What the present regime had to do was to recognize the Sharia as the supreme source of law and replace the imported European codes which, by their rejection of the Sharia, had undermined the very foundations of the Islamic order.

These ideas were elucidated by Muhammad Ghazali, a Muslim Brotherhood ideologue, in his book *Our Beginning in Wisdom*, published in 1948. Ghazali argued that, like the French and Russian revolutionaries, true Muslims cannot separate their moral values from politics without depriving themselves of the possibility of promoting moral values. He insisted that the Sharia had to be the source of law in all aspects of life – be they social, political or economic. This was mandatory on the Islamic authority, because only then could the (social) Quranic injunctions on jihad, *qisas* (retribution) and *zakat* (alms) be enforced along with the (private) injunctions about prayers, fasting and pilgrimage. Ayatollah Ruhollah Khomeini was later to advance the same argument in his exhortations towards the creation of an Islamic state in Iran.

On the punishments prescribed in the Sharia, Ghazali agreed with Rashid Rida that amputation of thieves' hands and flogging of adulterers had to wait until a proper Islamic society had been established. He was critical of such practices in Saudi Arabia. "We do not dispute that these prohibitions are part of Islam, but we find it strange that they are considered to be the whole of it," he wrote. "We wish to see the punishments enforced so that the rights and the security and the virtues may be preserved, but not that the hand of a petty thief be cut off while those punishments are waived . . . in the case of those who embezzle fantastic sums from the state treasury."[6] On women Ghazali took the traditional Islamic stance. He was for outlawing seductive clothing and appearance in women and their unchaperoned presence at picnics and outings. He favored women's education as long as it was geared strictly towards preparing them for raising families.

When martial law was lifted in 1950 the ban on the Brotherhood was removed and it was allowed to function as a religious body. However, after the election to the head of the Brotherhood a year later of Hassan Islam al Hudaybi – a senior judge who was opposed to violence and terrorism – the Brotherhood returned to the political arena. Responding to popular anti-British feelings, the government pressed Britain to withdraw its troops immediately from Egypt. When London stonewalled, Cairo unilaterally abrogated the 1936 Anglo-Egyptian Treaty (valid until 1956) in October 1951. The Brotherhood publicly offered its support to the Egyptian government, and declared a jihad against the British occupiers. With the Brothers now being trained and armed by their sympathizers in the army, the Brotherhood's leadership fell into militant hands. The organization played a significant role in the January 1952 riots in Cairo, an event which shook the monarchy and paved the way for an army coup six months later.

In their preparations for a coup against King Farouq the Free Officers assigned their Muslim Brotherhood cohorts back-up tasks. But these proved unnecessary: the coup on 23 July 1952 met with no resistance. When the officers, led by Brigadier Muhammad Neguib and Colonel Gamal Abdul Nasser (1918–70, r. 1953–70), banned all political parties they exempted the Muslim Brotherhood on the grounds that it was a religious body. Of the 18 members of the Revolutionary Command Council (RCC) which had assumed power, four had been close to the Brotherhood's hierarchy. These included Muhammad Anwar Sadat (1918–81, r. 1970–81). One of the early acts of Neguib, the supreme military leader, was to visit Banna's tomb to pay his respects. The RCC offered the Brotherhood three seats in the cabinet, but Hudaybi declined the offer. When Nasser, a young, charismatic leader, eased out the older Neguib and assumed supreme authority in late 1953, the military leaders began implementing land reform. The Brotherhood opposed the reform, and a gulf developed between it and the regime. It dawned on the Brothers that the military rulers were by and large modernizers more interested in spreading secular education, giving equal rights to women and reforming landownership patterns than in applying the Sharia to all spheres of life. Militant Brothers revived the secret cells, also known as the Spiritual Order, to carry out assassinations and subversive acts. On 23 October 1954 Abdul Munim Abdul Rauf, an extremist Brother, attempted to assassinate Nasser at a public rally in Alexandria. He failed. He and five other Brothers were executed, and more than 4,000 Brotherhood activists jailed. Several thousand Brothers went into self-imposed exile in Syria, Saudi Arabia, Jordan and Lebanon. To satisfy the prevalent religious feelings among Muslims, Nasser set up a radio station devoted exclusively to the recitation of the Quran and the broadcasting of the commentaries on it. He also ordered the separation of Muslim and Coptic students in classrooms.[7]

Two years later Nasser overcame the crisis caused by an invasion of Egypt by Israel, Britain and France in a masterly fashion. His star rose, and the Brotherhood lost ground rapidly. Following the long-established tradition of backing the ruler, Al Azhar ulama offered whatever fatwas were sought by Nasser's regime (which nationalized the institution in 1960), whether on land redistribution or nationalization of internal and external trade, or seizure of the property of political exiles.

In 1964, as part of a general amnesty, Nasser released the Brotherhood members with a view to co-opting them into a reformed political set-up as a counterforce to the Communists who were also freed. But reconciliation between Nasser and the Brotherhood proved temporary. Many of its leaders were reportedly implicated in three plots to assassinate him, allegedly inspired and financed by the Saudi monarch then engaged in a battle with Nasser for supremacy in North Yemen (following a republican coup there in September 1962) and elsewhere in the Arab East. As a result, following the arrest of 1,000 Brothers and the trial of 365, the top leaders were executed in August 1966. Among them was Sayyid Qutb (1906–66), a life-long bachelor, who was to emerge as the leading ideologue of radical Islamists in the Muslim world.

Born into a poor, but notable, family near Asyut, Sayyid Qutb trained as a teacher in Cairo, and became a school inspector with the Ministry of Education. He was a prolific writer, as much at ease with essays and literary criticism as with fiction. In 1948 the ministry sent him to a university in Colorado, USA, for further studies. His three years in America convinced him that society was racist and sexually depraved, and he concluded that the West was "in a civilizational decline similar to the fall of the Roman empire." He became interested in his Islamic roots and Islam. On his return to Egypt in 1951, the Education Ministry found his anti-American views so objectionable that it asked him to resign. Later in his *Islam and the Problem of Civilization*, he wrote, "What should be our verdict on this synthetic [Western] civilization? What should be done about America and the West, given their overwhelming danger to humanity . . . ? Should we not issue a sentence of death? Is it not the verdict most appropriate to the nature of the crime?"[8] Decades later, such views would be expressed by Osama bin Laden and his intellectual mentor, Ayman Zawahiri (b. 1950; aka Abu Muhammad and Muhammad Ibrahim), an Egyptian.

Sayyid Qutb joined the Muslim Brotherhood and soon became one of its eminent members. Following the ban on the Brotherhood in 1954, he was arrested and held in a concentration camp. Here he wrote his classic *Maalim fi al Tariq* (Signposts on the Road Milestones), which is the primer for Islamic activists worldwide. It was smuggled out, and published in 1964, the year Qutb, along with other Brotherhood detainees, was released. In his book, Qutb divided social systems into two categories: the Order of Islam and the Order of *Jahiliya* (ignorance). The latter was decadent and ignorant, the type of order which had existed in Arabia before Prophet Muhammad had received the Word of God, when men revered not God but other men disguised as deities. He argued that the Nasserist regime was a modern version of jahiliya. This earned Qutb the approval and respect of young Brothers and the opprobrium of the political and religious establishment.

The militant members of the (still clandestine) Muslim Brotherhood drafted Qutb into the leadership. They wanted among other things to avenge the persecution of the Brotherhood in the mid-1950s. Qutb, by inclination a thinker, wished to avoid violence. But when his radical followers pressed for a jihad to be waged against the social order he had himself labeled jahiliya because of its betrayal of Islamic precepts, Qutb could find no way out.

During his trial he did not contest the official charge of sedition, and instead tried to explain his position ideologically. "The bonds of ideology and belief are sturdier than those of patriotism based upon region, and this false distinction among Muslims on a regional basis is but one expression of crusading and Zionist imperialism which must be eradicated," he argued.[9] In other words, *watan* (homeland) was not a land but the community of believers (*umma*). He argued that once the Brothers had declared someone to be *jahil* (infidel), they had the right to attack his person or property, a right granted in Islam. If in the process of performing this religious duty of waging a jihad against unbelievers, a Brother found himself on the path of sedition, so be it. The responsibility for creating such a situation lay with those who through their policies had created such circumstances in the first place.

Within a year of Qutb's execution, which, in the eyes of his followers, turned him into a martyr, his thesis acquired a wider acceptance in the Arab world. This had to do with the Arab–Israeli Six-Day War of June 1967. The humiliating defeat that the Israelis inflicted on Egypt, totally destroying its air force and seizing the Sinai Peninsula, dealt a grievous blow to the semi-secular Arab socialism of Nasser, and created an environment conducive to the acceptance of the Brotherhood view that traditional Islamic beliefs had been neglected or suppressed by the Nasserist regime. A general belief prevailed among the populace that the Arabs had met defeat because they had turned away from the will of God. Even the monthly *Majallat al Azhar* (The Azhar Review), the mouthpiece of the revered university, which had been obsequious to Nasser, as it had been to rulers before him, stated that Egypt's humiliation had resulted from the fact that Muslims had discarded their glorious past and allowed themselves to be enticed by fleeting, superficial and exotic concepts. Arguing that the Arab-Israeli War was a conflict between Islam and Judaism, it called for intensified Islamic education of the masses as the most effective way of fighting Israel.[10] A common explanation for the Israeli victory was that it was due to Jews being truer to their faith than were Arabs, who had been obsessed with building an Arab nation based on common language with equal rights for citizens of all religions. The defeat by Israel put secular pan-Arabists on the defensive and revived the confidence of the fundamentalists.

So severe was the shock of the defeat among the people that they badly needed solace, and they found it in religion. The government sensed this. The state-guided media reminded their readers and listeners of the great achievements and adversities of Islam and the actions of Prophet Muhammad and his companions. The military ranks were soon provided with a publication which set out the meaning and significance of jihad, and described the battles fought by Prophet Muhammad. Nasser's regime was quick to co-opt popular Islamic sensibility and identify it with Egypt's national interest and well-being. Not surprisingly, in April 1968 Nasser released several hundreds of the thousand Brothers he had imprisoned nearly three years earlier.

The tidal wave of religiosity was given further impetus by the Israeli annexation of (Arab) East Jerusalem (which, with its Al Aqsa Mosque and the Dome of the Rock, is the third holiest place in Islam) and the arson in July 1969 at Al Aqsa Mosque.

Nasser's death in September 1970, followed by the accession to the presidency of Muhammad Anwar Sadat, raised the spirits of the Brotherhood. Sadat had first met Hassan al Banna in 1940, and attended several weekly lessons given by him at the Brotherhood headquarters in Cairo. He had maintained contacts with Brotherhood leaders during the 1940s. It was only after the Brothers had attempted to kill Nasser in 1954 that he had turned against their party. Sadat was well known for his personal piety, and Nasser often used him to project an Islamic image of the regime. For instance, Sadat was chosen as the general secretary of the Islamic Congress, established in 1965 to rally Muslim opinion abroad behind Egypt.

On assuming the presidency, Sadat came up with the slogan "Faith and Science." He instructed the state-run radio and television to broadcast prayers five times a day. Promising that the Sharia would be the chief inspiration of future legislation, he released all Brotherhood prisoners, including Hudaybi. He deliberately cultivated the image of "The Believer President."

In May 1971 Sadat carried out a "corrective" coup against the left-leaning Ali Sabri group in the ruling Arab Socialist Union, and actively encouraged Islamic sentiment and groups as a counterweight to the leftist influence. He directed Gen. Abdul Munim Amin to establish about a thousand Islamic Groups in universities and factories with the aim of combating atheistic Marxism, with these entities later becoming centralized under the title of Al Gamaa/Gamaat at Islamiya (The Islamic Group). He was keen to see that young Egyptians in search of an ideology turned to Islam rather than Marxism. Muslim Brotherhood exiles in Saudi Arabia and elsewhere began returning to Egypt, and strengthened Islamic forces at home.

The October 1973 Arab–Israeli War did much to improve Sadat's popular standing. He stressed the Islamic elements of the warfare: it was mounted in the holy month of Ramadan, and was codenamed "Badr" after Prophet Muhammad's first victory over pagan Meccans. The Egyptians gave their best performance on the battlefield so far. They crossed the Suez Canal and, despite repeated attempts by the Israelis, heavily armed with weapons airlifted from America, held on to most of their gains in the three-week-long conflict. Although in military terms the final outcome was a stand-off, the political payoff for Sadat was enormous. His regime painted the result as a victory for Egypt and the Arabs. There is little doubt that the 1973 war, initiated by Egypt and Syria, helped restore Arab and Egyptian self-respect. Many Egyptians felt that Allah had accepted their collective penitence offered after the 1967 defeat and rewarded them with victory in the latest war.

The freedom allowed to the fundamentalists after long suppression spawned the birth of groups more radical than the Muslim Brotherhood. One such body was the Islamic Liberation Group. In June 1974 its leader, army cadet Salah Sirri, mounted an armed attack on the Technical Military Academy in a Cairo suburb to capture its armory before marching to the ruling party's headquarters in central Cairo – where Sadat was scheduled to give a speech – to overthrow the regime and establish an Islamic state. The attempt failed. But this attack, which killed 30 soldiers, was a sharp reminder to the government that Islamic militants functioning outside the Brotherhood's fold were active underground.

Sadat's declaration of a general amnesty in 1975, coupled with his decision a year later to allow a return to the multi-party system of the monarchical era, enabled the Brotherhood to reorganize its forces and reintegrate itself into Al Azhar University, the official center of Islam, which had been purged of the Brotherhood elements by the Nasserist regime. But, because

Sadat was apprehensive of the popular appeal of the Muslim Brotherhood, he frustrated its leaders' plan to have the organization recognized as a distinct "tribune" by the authorities on the eve of the 1976 parliamentary poll. The Brothers therefore had no choice but to stand either as independents or as members of the ruling Arab Socialist Union (ASU). This suited Sadat, who was intent on dividing the Brotherhood and co-opting its moderate section into the political establishment.

The six Brothers elected to parliament on the ruling party's ticket, led by Salih Abu Rokait, were treated favorably by the government, and allowed to publish a monthly journal called *Al Daawa* (The Call). It was edited by Omar al Talmasani, an elderly lawyer who, as a veteran Brotherhood leader, had been given a long sentence in 1954 and was later allowed to emigrate to Saudi Arabia. Though the Daawa group shared Sadat's anti-Communist and anti-Nasserist views, it opposed his policy of leading Egypt into the American camp and subscribing totally to the American-sponsored peace plan for the Middle East. The nine independent Brothers in parliament, led by Said Ramadan, enjoyed much wider popular support and were more radical than the Daawa group. They offered to cooperate with the government only on the basis of their program of Islamic action.

Sadat's success in co-opting many of the Brotherhood leaders into the political system resulted in many militant Brothers leaving the organization to establish radical groups clandestinely. Prominent among these were Mukfirtiya (Denouncers of the Infidel); Jund Allah (Soldiers of God); Munnazamat al Jihad (The Jihad Organization), popularly known as Al Jihad and sometimes called the Islamic Jihad; and Al Takfir wa al Hijra (The Denunciation/Repentence of Infidels and the Migration). All of them were violently opposed to the regime.

The members of Al Takfir wa al Hijra played a leading role in ransacking and burning the nightclubs along Cairo's "golden strip" during three days of widespread rioting in mid-January 1977 caused by the withdrawal of governmental subsidies on daily necessities. It was led by Shukri Ahmad Mustafa, an agricultural engineer, who was arrested in 1965 as a Brotherhood activist. In jail he became disillusioned with the older Brothers whom he found fractious and weak.

After his release from prison, Mustafa began recruiting members for his group. Though they called themselves Jamaat al Muslimin (The Muslim Society), the authorities were later to confer the title of Al Takfir wa al Hijra on them to sum up their ideology and tactics. In his manuscript entitled *Al Tawassumat* (The Searching Looks) (which he refused to have printed to avoid the blasphemy of printing) Shukri Mustafa called on the faithful to escape the danger of *shirk* (ascribing another divinity to Allah) and avoid being tortured by infidels. Then they must spread "the knowledge" throughout the land. Finally they must wage a jihad to establish an Islamic state. Mustafa argued that the destruction of atheists and their state could not be achieved while the faithful were living among them. Furthermore, he added, Prophet Muhammad required the believers to leave the blasphemous land. Only then would Allah's retribution fall upon the infidels. Since Mustafa considered Egyptian society infidel, it was incumbent upon his followers to migrate and form a pure community along the lines of the Medinese polity of the Prophet.[11] Actually, many of Mustafa's followers took to living in the caves and mountains of Minia in Upper Egypt where, among other things, they underwent arms training. They were discovered by the security forces in September 1973, only to be pardoned by Sadat after the October War.

Since Mustafa's followers considered religious functionaries as infidel they boycotted prayers led by them, and prayed together in their own homes. They married among themselves, withdrew their children from state schools and refused to be drafted into the military.

Some of the secret cells through which the organization functioned were assigned the task of attacking nightclubs, cinemas and bars. And that is what they did during the January 1977 rioting. The security forces picked up 60 members of the party. This incensed the younger adherents who demanded that those arrested should be either tried or released. When this did not happen, they forced the issue by kidnapping, on 3 July, Shaikh Muhammad Hussein al Dhahabi, a former minister of religious endowments and Al Azhar, for writing a newspaper article against their party. The government refused their demand, and they killed Dhahabi. The subsequent hunt by the security forces discovered Al Takfir wa al Hijra members throughout the republic; 620 were arrested and 465 tried by military courts. Five, including Mustafa, were executed. Official investigations revealed that the organization had between 3,000 and 5,000 members belonging to all social classes and scattered throughout the country.

As it happened, in July 1977 a congress of Islamic associations and groups was held under the auspices of the Al Azhar rector, Shaikh Abdul Halim Mahmoud, in Cairo. The congress issued a comprehensive declaration:

> All legislation and all judgment contrary to Islam is considered false . . . The faith of Muslims is only effective when submitted to the Divine Law [i.e. Sharia] and that alone. To demand the application of the Sharia is the duty of all Muslims. We accept no advice concerning moderation or delay in this matter. To postpone the application of Sharia is a sin and disobedience of God and his Prophet. The legislature must proceed with the ratification of bills proposed to it.

Finally, the congress was "pleased to note the President's declaration that he intends to purge the administration of all atheistic elements."[12]

Soon after this congress Sadat ordered that those clauses of Egyptian law which were based on the Napoleonic Code be replaced with appropriate clauses from the Sharia. The State Council announced that a bill to punish those found drinking or committing adultery was being studied, and that a presidential decree specifying the death penalty for those who renounced Islam was to be submitted to parliament for approval.[13] On 10 August *Al Ahram* (The Pyramids), the official newspaper, said that a bill permitting amputation of a thief's hand was being drafted.

These statements pacified the Islamic groups, but upset the Copts, Egyptian Christians, who formed about 10 percent of the population. They felt that the apostasy bill was directed against them since they often converted to Islam to secure a quick divorce and then reverted back to Christianity. Led by their church the Copts undertook a four-day protest in early September 1977 and declared that they would not submit to the apostasy law if passed. Faced with such opposition Sadat dropped the idea.

Sadat was now caught between two contradictory forces in Egypt: orthodox Muslims attacked him for reneging on Islamizing legislation and liberal Muslims for encouraging traditional Islam. He tried to juggle his way out by offering contradictory concessions.

In his 9 November speech before parliament he combined his public offer to appear before the Israeli parliament in his search for Middle East peace with a blistering attack on the atheists whom he blamed for the riots of 18–19 January 1977. "I will not permit any group . . . to spread atheism among our faithful people – our people in whose veins the faith flows," he warned.[14] The warning was misdirected: it was radical fundamentalists who were the major force behind these riots.

From then on Sadat busied himself with negotiating peace with Israel. Since such actions ran counter to Islamic sentiment at home and abroad it widened the gulf between his regime and the Islamic groups. This helped the Islamic movement as a whole to capitalize on the prevailing discontent and widen its base. "The history of the Arab world is one of Islamic revival movements which appear in the aftermath of what is considered to be a great failure of the existing regime," stated Saad Eddin Ibrahim, sociology professor at Cairo University. "The present cycle began in 1974–5. Students looked with alarm at the apparent rapprochement with Israel, and generally with the West. There were also the socio-economic dislocation of society, the frustrations of the lower and middle classes."[15]

An important manifestation of this phenomenon was the support gained by Islamic elements on university campuses. In the spring 1978 elections for the university student union officials, Al Gamaat al Islamiya won 60 percent of the posts. By then the Muslim Brotherhood and its offshoots had gained control of most of the 1,000 Al Gamaat al Islamiya branches established at Sadat's behest in the early 1970s.

The majority of university students came from rural, petty-bourgeois families who had been the traditional backbone of the Muslim Brotherhood. Alienated by Sadat's recognition of Israel, and disgusted by the rising corruption, material and spiritual, engendered by the regime's open-door economic policy to attract foreign capital and give a boost to private enterprise, this section of society turned against the government. Sadat's economic policies widened the gap between the poor and the rich by causing sharp increases in food prices and rents, and by delivering a grievous blow to local industry with the imports of cheap foreign goods. Between 1964–5 and 1976 the share of the Gross Domestic Product (GDP) of the middle 30 percent of the Egyptian population halved: from 40.2 percent to 21.52 percent. The corresponding figures for the lowest 60 percent were 28.7 percent and 19.93 percent. In contrast the top 10 percent nearly doubled their income: from 31.9 percent to 58.55 percent.[16] The new rich flaunted their affluence. Cairo and Alexandria became the fleshpots of the Middle East, filling the vacuum left by war-ravaged Beirut. Along with Western goods came Western values of consumerism which scandalized the believers.

The impending signing of a peace treaty between Egypt and Israel in March 1979 so angered the Islamic students that they mounted anti-government demonstrations at Alexandria and Asyut universities: a daring step, since it made the demonstrators liable to life imprisonment. Their slogans summed up their grievances and aspirations: "No peace with Israel'; "No privilege for the rich"; "An end to moral decadence"; and "No separation between Islam and state." They had been cheered by the victory of Islamic forces in Iran about a month earlier.

Sadat was quick to respond to the downfall of Muhammad Reza Pahlavi (1919–80; r. 1941–79), the Shah of Iran, who was his personal friend. He urged the local Islamic leaders to reform the (official) Daawa group and increase the number of preachers on its staff. The Ministry of Higher Education ordered the universities to make religious instruction compulsory, and the parliament's speaker promised that legislation based on the Sharia, which had been kept in abeyance since July 1977, would be passed and strictly enforced.

Al Daawa monthly, enjoying a healthy circulation of 80,000, echoed the feelings of the protesting university students on the Egyptian–Israeli treaty. It greeted the accord with the headline: "It is impossible to live at peace with the Jews." The article drew heavily from the experiences of the Prophet, the Quran and Islamic history to illustrate its theme. Even the moderate Brothers, who published and read the journal, were disappointed by the failure of the Egyptian–Israeli treaty to resolve the crucial Palestinian problem. In contrast, under Sadat's prodding, Al Azhar produced a fatwa in May 1979 to sanctify the president's act. "The ulama of Al Azhar believe that the Egyptian–Israeli treaty is in harmony with the Islamic law," it stated. "It was concluded from a position of strength after the battle of jihad and the victory realized by Egypt on 10th Ramadan 1393 AH [6 October 1973]." The statement then referred to the Hudabiya Treaty signed by Prophet Muhammad with the Quraish of Mecca in 628,[17] ignoring the fact that that treaty was a step towards Muhammad taking control of Mecca.

From then on the moderate Brotherhood, as represented by *Al Daawa*, began opposing Sadat on many other important issues. Its early support for his open-door policies that were meant to benefit private enterprise and attract foreign investment – seen as a welcome antidote to Nasser's propensity for nationalization and a strong public sector – turned into calls for state intervention in the management of the economy and redistribution of wealth. The Brotherhood denounced Sadat for selling Egypt's independence to America just as in the past it had attacked Nasser for kowtowing to the Soviets. It went on to argue that the so-called "Communist threat" was concocted by Western imperialism to keep the Third World countries tied to the West after they had acquired political independence. It continued to attack the government's economic policies, which had fostered a growing class of corrupt rentiers, property speculators, middlemen and importers of Western goods. "Who is protecting corruption in Egypt, the heart of Arabism and lighthouse of Islam?" asked *Al Daawa* in its July 1981 editorial. "The stench is spreading and an explosion is feared."[18]

Al Daawa's reference to corruption in high places was all the more apt since it appeared in the holy month of Ramadan. During that period Israel mounted several air raids on Palestinian targets in south Lebanon and central Beirut which left 386 Lebanese and Palestinians dead. All Arab states, except Egypt, rallied to the Palestinian–Lebanese side. Beyond voicing public disapproval of the Israeli raids, and letting some Egyptian doctors fly to Beirut to tend the wounded, Sadat did nothing. This severely undermined his popular standing. On Eid al Fitr (1 August), encouraged by the Islamic groups, over 100,000 faithful gathered for prayers in Abidin Square, outside the presidential palace in Cairo, and shouted anti-Sadat slogans. The criticism of the Egyptian–Israeli peace treaty became more vocal than before.

In late August Israeli Prime Minister Menachem Begin reportedly warned Sadat that Israel would not honour its commitment in the treaty to vacate the Sinai Peninsula in April 1982 if open criticism of the treaty was tolerated in Egypt. On 3 September Sadat clamped down on the opposition, jailing nearly 2,000 dissidents, most of them Islamic fundamentalists (including Omar Talmasani), and shutting down *Al Daawa*. He purged the military of 200 officers suspected of being pro-Brotherhood, and ordered that all independent religious societies as well as preachers must register themselves with the Ministry of Religious Endowments. He also enjoined the 40,000 privately run mosques to register with the ministry. This meant the state extending its power over all preachers and mosques, and exercising full control over them, for the 1911 law, which established the Supreme Council of Al Azhar, had turned all ulama into state employees.

The new Act authorized the government to dismiss an alim and even remove his name from Al Azhar records, thus rendering him ineligible for any job, religious or secular.

Sadat set up new disciplinary councils for students and civil servants. He swiftly quashed sporadic protest attempts made mainly by Islamic militants. He did all this at a time when the vast majority of believing Muslims held him and his regime in low esteem.

On 6 October, four soldiers armed with automatic weapons and hand grenades attacked the review stand at the military parade in a Cairo suburb to celebrate the Egyptian performance in the October 1973 war. They killed Sadat and seven others. They were led by 24-year-old Lieutenant Khalid Ahmad Shawki Islambouli, who, having fatally machine-gunned Sadat, declared, "I have killed the Pharaoh, and I don't fear death."[19] His elder brother, Muhammad, was one of the 469 members of Al Takfir wa al Hijra arrested in early September. (On his release, Muhammad Islambouli left for Afghanistan where he fought the Soviets alongside Afghan Mujahedin. He was sentenced to death in absentia in Egypt in 1992.) Islambouli and his three colleagues belonged to Al Jihad – or Al Jihad Organization, to use its full title. Founded in 1974, in the wake of a failed coup at the Military Technical Academy in Heliopolis, Cairo, its leaders included Muhammad Abdul Salam Faraj, an electrical engineer who was an Islamic thinker; Abbud Abdul Latif Zumur, a colonel in military intelligence; and Ayman Zawahiri, then a student at Cairo University's medical school, born into a highly prestigious family – his father being pharmacology professor at that university and his grandfather, Rabiaa Zawahiri, the Grand Shaikh of Al Azhar University – who would graduate as a surgeon in 1978, and then become the leader of Al Jihad after its leader, Ismail Tantawi, had departed for West Germany.[20] Their spiritual guide was Shaikh Omar Abdul Rahman (b. 1938), a burly professor of Islamic studies at Asyut University, who was closely associated with Al Gamaat al Islamiya.

Faraj, the chief theoretician of Al Jihad, was the author of two books: *Al Jihad: The Forgotten Pillar*, and *The Absent Obligation*.

In these he outlined his theory and plan of action. His basic premises were that every true Muslim is obliged by his faith to struggle for the revival of the Islamic umma, and that the Muslim groups or leaders who have turned away from the Sharia are apostates. It is therefore sinful for a genuine Muslim to cooperate with an infidel ruler. Those who want to end the Order of Jahiliya and revive the Islamic umma are obliged to wage a jihad against the infidel state. The only acceptable form of jihad is the armed struggle; anything less implies cowardice or foolishness. A true Muslim must first confront the internal infidel (i.e. the Egyptian state) and then the external infidel (i.e. the non-Muslim world at large). Straying from the course of jihad has led to the current sorry state of the Muslim world: divided, degraded and disdained. But this condition is destined to end as God has foreordained the history of Islam: the era of the Prophet followed by the eras of the caliphs, kings and dictators and finally the replacement of dictators by a system similar to the one prevalent in the days of Prophet Muhammad. Leadership of the Islamic umma must be given to the strongest among the believers who also fears Allah. He must be chosen collectively and must then be obeyed.

Two concepts in Faraj's writing were new: jihad as the sixth obligation of a Muslim, and jihad as a perpetual movement to transform the non-Muslim world into the Islamic umma, something akin to Leon Trotsky's idea of permanent Marxist revolution. These concepts made Faraj the most radical fundamentalist thinker so far.

As for Shaikh Abdul Rahman, he was qualified to issue fatwas, and these were considered essential to confer religious legitimacy on the actions and policies of Al Jihad and Al Gamaat al Islamiya. Sometime in late 1980 he allegedly issued a fatwa that it was lawful to shed the blood of a ruler who did not enforce the divine law as contained in the Sharia. This was construed as conferring legitimacy on assassinating President Sadat. In January–February 1981 Faraj and Zumur, head of the operational wing of the organization, set out to implement the plan to assassinate Sadat. It was Zumur who ensured that, unlike all others participating in the military parade on 6 October, Islambouli and his associates were equipped with live ammunition in their weapons.

Al Jihad leaders had visualized Sadat's assassination acting as a catalyst to transform Egyptian Muslims' simmering hatred of infidel Sadat's corrupt, oppressive rule into an uprising against the regime paving the way for engineering an Islamic revolution. In the event, ordinary Egyptians demonstrated their passive approval of the assassins' act by refraining from public mourning at the loss of their president;[21] nothing more. This disappointed Al Jihad leaders. However, armed confrontations occurred between Islamic militants – chiefly Al Gamaat al Islamiya partisans – and Egyptian security forces, most prominently in Asyut in Upper Egypt. There Islamic extremists stormed the local broadcasting station, several police stations and the headquarters of the security forces. Two days of fighting left 188 dead, including 54 security personnel. On 25 October *Al Ahram* reported that the Islamist groups had planned "a bloody terrorist plot to impose a Khomeini-style regime in Egypt," and that this was to have been executed on 13 October, the day presidential elections were to be held.

Though Al Gamaat al Islamiya and Al Jihad shared the common objective of establishing an Islamic state in Egypt, their strategies were different as were their recruits. Al Jihad focused on infiltrating military and security officer corps in order to replicate Nasser's successful "Free Officers" movement, albeit with an Islamist agenda. Its recruits came mainly from urban professional classes. Gamaat, on the other hand, believed in a protracted armed struggle against the secularist regime, aiming to raise the religious consciousness of the masses as a prelude to a popular insurrection. Its recruiting grounds were in city slums and poor villages – especially among students from these areas. Little wonder that Al Jihad functioned very secretly whereas Al Gamaat al Islamiya's existence was semi-clandestine: it collected donations in mosques and engaged in charitable activities.

The authorities had first discovered the existence of Al Jihad in 1978 during Muslim–Copt riots – four years after its formation.

Following Sadat's assassination, Al Jihad and Al Gamaat al Islamiya reportedly came together, a process helped by the fact that both operated in self-contained cells, each led by an *emir* (lit. commander), with a collective of these emirs forming an informal *majlis al shura* (consultative council).

Vice President Hosni Mubarak, who had been sworn in as president on Sadat's death and had immediately promulgated emergency laws, was confirmed in office by popular vote. By late October he had imprisoned over 3,000 Islamic extremists belonging chiefly to Al Jihad, Al Gamaat al Islamiya and Al Takfir wa al Hijra.

During his trial Islambouli outlined his reasons for killing Sadat: the Egyptian president had made peace with Israel; he had persecuted "the sons of Islam" by his wholesale arrest of them in early September; and the current laws of Egypt, being incompatible with the Sharia, imposed suffering on believing Muslims.

The 11-year rule of Sadat was an important period in the history of Islamic fundamentalism in Egypt. It ceased to be a relentlessly persecuted movement as it had been during the Nasserite regime. While denying the Muslim Brotherhood a license to function as a political party, Sadat provided it with an environment in which its moderate wing could function in comparative freedom, acting as a reluctant ally of the government or at worst as its loyal opposition. On the other hand, the main thrust of Sadat's political, diplomatic and economic policies after the October 1973 war was so contrary to the core fundamentalist ideology and policies that, by cooperating with the government, albeit conditionally, the moderate fundamentalists lost much ground to their radical rivals.

Mubarak's presidency: the first term (1981–7)

Once Mubarak had overcome the immediate challenge to his regime he released the secular dissidents jailed by Sadat and established dialogue with them. In contrast he intensified the drive to repress Islamic militants and their agitation. He was well served in this by the interior minister, Maj.-Gen. Hassan Abu Bhasha. Overriding appeals from various quarters to spare the lives of Khalid Islambouli and his associates, Mubarak went ahead with their executions. He became the target of an un-successful assassination attempt by Islamic extremists. This led to the arrest of 140 of them, who were accused of conspiring to install an Islamist regime. The government intensified its infil-tration of the fundamentalist groups, including Al Gamaat al Islamiya which, guided by Shaikh Muhammad Abu Nasr, an elderly cleric, would turn increasingly to social welfare work – running health clinics and providing religious education – while Al Jihad became almost extinct.

At the popular level the measured, lackluster style of Mubarak's leadership contrasted well with the flamboyance of Sadat, who had been much given to theatricality. On the other hand, Mubarak made only cosmetic changes to his predecessor's open-door economic policy, alignment with the West and com-mitment to the Camp David peace process: the policies which had proved to be a breeding ground for Islamic militants.

Mubarak used Al Azhar ulama not only to win legitimacy for his regime but also to re-educate the Islamist prisoners. These ulama tried to convince the extremists that their interpretation of Islam was wrong. Accepting this view and repenting for their past actions were deemed sufficient by the government to allow the imprisoned militants to go free. And many did.

To widen his popular base Mubarak allowed secular opposi-tion an unprecedented degree of freedom. He let the conservative New Wafd Party contest the May 1984 parliamentary election, a privilege denied to it by Sadat. Since the New Wafd was for private enterprise, Mubarak's National Democratic Party pre-sented itself as the defender of "the socialist gains made by workers and peasants." No mention was made of Sadat in the election campaign. As before, poll results were forged. Still, the New Wafd won 15 percent of the vote and 58 seats in a house of 560 (with 450 elected seats), and replaced the Socialist Liberal Party as the major right-of-center opposition group. Since the Election Law of June 1983, like its predecessor, disallowed parties based on religion or (Marxist) atheism, the Muslim Brotherhood was barred from contesting elections. In desperation it had allied with the New Wafd on the ground that both of them had been opposed to the July 1952 Nasserist revolution. The New Wafd accommodated the Brotherhood by demanding that the Sharia should become the principal source of legislation. But it adopted only 18 of the 70 candidates the Brotherhood offered. Of these, eight won. So, in essence, the strength of independent fundamentalists in parliament was about the same as in Sadat's days. Radical Islamic groups boycotted the elections as they had done in the past.

Yet there were differences. The protest against election rigging was so vociferous that Hassan Abu Bhasha, the interior minister in charge of the poll, was transferred to another ministry. Also, so fervent was Islamic sentiment at large that the opposition in parliament and the Islamic elements outside combined to demand full and immediate implementation of the Sharia. The movement gathered momentum in the spring of 1985, and was checked only by a court ban on pro-Sharia marches and demonstrations. The government found itself on the defensive. In public it argued that Egyptian law was 90 percent Islamic, and that the Sharia was the basis for the Egyptian constitution. In private, however, it was unwilling to adopt the Sharia in full. First, it felt that such a step by the regimes in Sudan and Iran had led to unhealthy developments in those countries. Second, it was reluctant to alienate the Coptic minority. Finally, and most importantly, it feared that Western investors and aid donors would be reluctant to do business with an Egypt functioning on strictly Islamic lines. When pressured by opposition, the government promised to "purify" Egypt's law of its non-Islamic elements.

Egyptian fundamentalists accused the government of playing for time. In June 1985 Shaikh Hafiz Salaama, an eminent Islamist leader, called for a pro-Sharia march from his mosque in Cairo. Mubarak responded by having the mosque surrounded by a large contingent of the Central Security Forces (CSF), commonly called security police. Soon the authorities banned religious stickers on vehicles the numbers of which had mushroomed over the past year and which, along with the sight of veiled women in the streets, were taken to be a visual and dramatic index of the rise of Islamic fundamentalism.

At universities Mubarak's efforts to contain the fundamentalists' power by curtailing students' organizing rights and implanting secret police on the campuses failed. By early 1986 Islamic fundamentalists had gained control over all university student unions and were actively pressuring university authorities to bring the curricula and textbooks into line with Islamic precepts and to enforce sexual segregation.

Elsewhere, allied to the New Wafd, the Brotherhood had succeeded in dominating the ruling bodies of the influential syndicates of journalists, lawyers, doctors and engineers. Islamist journalists had established influence over two of the four opposition magazines which, among other things, published laudatory accounts of life in the Islamic Republic of Iran. Many construction and consumer goods firms owned by seven large Islamic holding companies with vast assets, financed by over a million Egyptians working in the Arabian Peninsula, had become popular with small fundamentalist investors; they offered a share of profits in line with Islamic precepts, and not a fixed rate of return. These companies were said to be funding Islamist organizations. The emergence of an independent economic base to sustain Islamist groups was a new and important development in the history of fundamentalism in Egypt.

In February 1986 some 17,000 conscripts of the CSF – formed after the January 1977 riots – in five provinces, including Cairo, rioted. The scale and diversity of rioting by one of the chief organs of state security jolted the regime. It took the army five days to quell the rebellion during which 115 people, including CSF personnel, were killed. In a move reminiscent of the acts of Al Takfir wa al Hijra adherents during the January 1977 rioting, the mutineers destroyed bars, nightclubs, expensive hotels and apartment blocks – symbols of corruption and luxury – worth US$500 million. To the alarm of the authorities, half of the rioters absconded with their weapons.

Islamic fervor seemed to be spreading among military cadets as well as non-commissioned and lower- and middle-ranking officers. Instead of watching films or playing games during their leisure the military cadets had taken to praying or discussing Islamic literature.

A study of 303 Al Jihad members, jailed before Sadat's assassination, revealed that 4 percent of them were military, police or intelligence officers.[22] This was not surprising. Given the traditional extended family system prevalent in Egypt, the members of the fundamentalist groups were bound to recruit some blood relatives employed in security or intelligence services into their organizations. A fresh reminder that Al Jihad continued to be active in the military came in December 1986, when the cabinet was headed by Atef Sidqi (1930– ; r. 1986–96). Thirty Al Jihad members, including two majors, one captain and one lieutenant, were arrested for setting up combat training centers with a view to overthrowing the government.[23]

The CSF rioting erupted at a time when Egypt was entering a period of acute economic crisis. All major sources of foreign income – oil, tourism and remittances of Egyptian expatriates – were in decline. Oil prices had fallen by two-thirds in three months. Tourism was down by 40 percent. The 3 million Egyptian workers in the Gulf states and Iraq, who in the past had contributed US$4 billion a year to Egypt's foreign revenue, were returning home in droves. The national debt stood at a staggering US$32 billion.

This created an environment in which a growing number of ordinary citizens, suffering from falling living standards due to high inflation, became receptive to the fundamentalists' argument: since the capitalism of Sadat and Mubarak had failed in the way Nasser's socialism had, it was time to try the Islamic model. Once Egypt had ended its dependence on the non-Muslim West and introduced an economic system based on Islam – reasoned the fundamentalists – it would solve the worsening socio-economic ills of society, including corruption. Being out of power, Islamic radicals had the advantage of making extravagant promises and painting a rosy picture of the model they offered.

This was in contrast to President Mubarak's position. He presided over a sinking economy; he had undertaken half-hearted political liberalization; he had failed to offer any socio-economic ideology of his own; and his lack of strong direction had created a leadership vacuum at the top. He was in a quandary. Were he to suppress the fundamentalists violently (as Sadat had done towards the end of his rule), he would be accused of persecuting the sons of Islam and become a hate figure like his predecessor; on the other hand, were he to give them free rein, they would gain further ground and pose a real threat to his regime.

Meanwhile, his government kept a watchful eye on Shaikh Abdul Rahman after he had been cleared of the charges of complicity in Sadat's assassination due to lack of evidence. In the coming years the blind shaikh would loom large not only in the Arab world but also in America. Born into a poor peasant family in Gamaliya village, Daqaliya district, in the Nile delta in 1938, he went blind in infancy as a result of diabetes. He established his piety at 11 when he memorized the Quran in braille. After his education in local religious schools he joined Al Azhar University in 1955 where he obtained a doctorate in Islamic jurisprudence in 1965. He became a lecturer in Islamic studies at Al Azhar's branch at Fahyum in the Nile delta. As the prayer leader of the mosque in the nearby village of Fedmeen, the shaikh delivered sermons that were critical of the government of President Nasser and its ideology of Arab socialism. Following Egypt's defeat in the June 1967 Arab–Israeli War, he became more daring in his attacks. He was arrested in 1968 and expelled from Al Azhar. On his release he criticized the official policies on religious trusts and Islam. After Nasser's death in 1970, he was arrested for calling on the faithful not to pray for the soul of Nasser, whom he considered an atheist. He was released as part of the general amnesty President Sadat granted following his "corrective" coup against leftist Ali Sabri in May 1971. The shaikh taught in Minia province and, in 1973, became a lecturer on Islamic affairs at the University of Asyut in southern Egypt, a bastion of Islamists. Here he started interpreting the works of Sayyid Qutb. Then he moved to Muhammad bin Saud Islamic University in Riyadh, but stayed in touch with Islamist activists in Egypt during his annual holidays there. On his return home in 1979, he became a professor of Islamic studies at Asyut University. He attacked President Sadat for the Camp David Accords with Israel and economic liberalization which, according to him, had led to moral and material corruption. He encouraged his young followers to join the anti-Soviet jihad that was being waged by Afghan Islamists in Afghanistan, ruled by Moscow-backed Communists since 1978.

Shaikh Abdul Rahman was one of the 24 suspects arrested for complicity in Sadat's assassination, charged with issuing a fatwa for Sadat's killing. When released due to lack of evidence, Rahman was denied reinstatement as professor at Asyut University, and he settled at Fahyum and continued his attacks on the regime, now headed by Mubarak. He toured the country giving speeches which inspired Islamic militants, and which were sold as audiocassettes. He was preaching in an Egypt where over the past decade millions of men had during their short-term contractual employment in Saudi Arabia, been exposed to conservative Islamic views on women's role ("They should stay home and serve men"), limits of artistic expression ("Art must keep away from religion"), relations between Muslims and Christians ("to be treated as second-class citizens"), and the West's impact on Islamic civilization ("Political or social innovations coming from the West are incompatible with Islamic values"). The government arrested him in 1984 for delivering a subversive sermon but failed to win a conviction. It then put him under house arrest and banned him from speaking in public.[24]

In that year Ayman Zawahiri, a thick-set man wearing thick glasses, was released from jail after serving a three-year sentence for his participation in the plot to assassinate Sadat. He quietly revived Al Jihad which issued its first manifesto, *The Philosophy of Confrontation*. It coincided with the issuance of a manifesto by Al Gamaat entitled *The Program for Islamic Action*, thus underscoring the separate identities of the two organizations. The next year Al Gamaat resumed its violent activities in a low key. By the mid-1980s, some of the Egyptian volunteers in the anti-Soviet jihad in Afghanistan had begun returning home while many more were headed in the opposite direction. Among the latter was Ayman Zawahiri, who went to Pakistan via Saudi Arabia in 1986, and joined the medical corps in the Pakistani city of Peshawar serving the Mujahedin. He established a branch of Al Jihad and a monthly magazine, *Al Ghazu* (The Conquest).[25] He had been preceded three years earlier by a 6ft 4in (1.93 m) tall Egyptian police officer named Muhammad Atef (aka Tayseer Abdullah, Abu Hafs al Misry, and Abu Khadiha), as militantly Islamist as Zawahiri but not as well educated. Another Egyptian militant of importance in Afghanistan was Muhammad Shawki Islambouli.

The parliamentary election of April 1987 demonstrated the growing strength of the fundamentalists. This time the Muslim Brotherhood allied with the opposition Liberal Socialist Party and the Socialist Labor Party to form the Labor Islamic Alliance (LSA). The Alliance adopted a simplistic slogan: "Islam – that is the solution." As before, the election was rigged: 750 opposition supporters, chiefly fundamentalists, were arrested, ballot boxes were stuffed with the votes of the dead, absent and under-age for the ruling National Democratic Party, and the polling stations in many villages were closed several hours ahead of schedule to prevent legitimate voters from exercising their right. Yet the Brotherhood-led Alliance gained 17 percent of the popular vote and 60 parliamentary seats, displacing the New Wafd as the main opposition party.

With 36 of its members in the new chamber, the Muslim Brotherhood planned to dominate the Alliance's parliamentary activity, and reiterate its demands for the immediate application of the Sharia, the promotion of Islamic investment companies at the expense of conventional banks (which are seen as violating the Quran's injunction against usury), the termination of Egypt's strategic and economic links with the US, and the abrogation of the Camp David peace process. This would amount to questioning the very basis of the secular government.

In May 1987 Hassan Abu Bhasha, former interior minister responsible for repressing Islamist activists, was wounded in an assassination attempt. Following this terrorist act, and a series of Muslim–Copt clashes in the spring of 1987, the government arrested 500 radical Islamists.

It was against this backdrop that Mubarak was nominated the sole presidential candidate by two-thirds majority of parliament, and in October he was duly confirmed by 97 percent of the voters. His nerves would be tested in his next term in office, during the later years of which he would adopt a two-track policy of suppressing Islamic extremists and excluding Muslim fundamentalists from the political arena, while promoting religious-cultural Islam in government-run broadcasting media and state-supervised textbooks to accommodate the rising religiosity of Egyptians.

Mubarak's second term (1987–93)

In the late 1980s Al Gamaat's leadership shifted towards those Egyptians who were engaged in the anti-Soviet jihad in Afghanistan conducted by the seven-party Islamic Alliance of Afghan Mujahedin (IAAM) from Peshawar, with funds, arms and training provided by the American CIA, Pakistani Inter Services Intelligence (ISI) Directorate, and Saudi intelligence (*Istikhabarat*). Among the IAAM's constituents, *Ittihad-e Islami* (Islamic Alliance) was popular with the Egyptians. Its leader was Abdul Rasul Sayyaf, an Arabic-speaking graduate of Al Azhar and Medina Islamic University, who, as an adherent of Wahhabism – a Sunni sub-sect to which the Saudi royal family belonged – had the first priority over Saudi funds allocated for the Afghani jihad and became very influential. As a result, the Peshawar-based Muhammad Shawki Islambouli (a brother of Khalid Ahmad Islambouli, Sadat's assassin) and Talat Fuad Qasim (1957–98), who associated with Sayyaf, became the pre-eminent leaders of Al Gamaat. They were the ones who hosted Shaikh Abdul Rahman when he first arrived in Peshawar in 1988, a visit which resulted in his two sons, Ahmad, 22, and Assad, 16, joining the jihad,[26] and which indicated a covert link with the CIA – one of the leading agencies to feel triumphant at the Soviet troop withdrawal from Afghanistan in February 1989. A few months later, on the eve of the annual hajj, the blind shaikh left Egypt. But instead of arriving in Jiddah on his way to Mecca, he landed in Khartoum, the capital of Sudan, where a pro-Islamic military junta had seized power on 30 June. There, in late 1989, he received a tourist visa from the US embassy even though he was on the prohibited list.[27]

In Cairo, the interior minister, Maj.-Gen. Zaki Badr, narrowly escaped assassination in December 1989. The reason why Islamic extremists targeted interior ministers was that they were the ones assigned the task of crushing their movement. Also as the head of three security forces – the black-uniformed CSF, the much-feared State Security Investigation (SSI), popularly known as *Mubahas* (Investigation), and the Tourist Police – as well as tens of thousands of informants, the interior minister controlled 300,000 men, two-thirds as numerous as military troops.[28] In October 1990 Al Gamaat assassinated a top official – parliamentary speaker Rifaat Mahjoub – together with his four bodyguards, in retaliation for the unprovoked murder of Al Gamaat spokesman Alaa Muhyiuddin (presumably by the Interior Ministry's secret agents) at a time when many hoped radical groups would be co-opted into the political system.[29] This was a setback for the government which was now focused on defusing the crisis caused by Iraq's invasion and occupation of Kuwait two months earlier. During the run-up to the Gulf War in January 1991, there was an exodus of Egyptian and other non-Iraqi workers from Iraq and Kuwait. Though the war ended successfully for America and its allies, with the Iraqis expelled from Kuwait, it led to recession in the US and elsewhere, and a drop in oil prices, which depressed the economies of the oil-rich Gulf states and resulted in even more Egyptian workers returning home. This caused a worsening of the already dire economic situation in Egypt, burdened with the problems of population explosion, land hunger and high joblessness, with 3 million unemployed university and high school graduates. The proportion of Egyptians living below the officially defined poverty line rose from 42 to 54 percent during the decade starting in 1984,[30] with impoverishment driving more and more Egyptians to seek solace in religion. Also the manner in which the US behaved in the run-up to the Gulf War – rejecting all proposals for negotiations with Iraq – and its bombing of the retreating Iraqi soldiers engendered anti-American, and pro-Islamic, sentiment in the Arab world, including Egypt.

With the break-up of the Soviet Union in December 1991, the future of the leftist regime of Muhammad Najibullah in Kabul became uncertain. It collapsed in April 1992, enabling the Afghan and non-Afghan Mujahedin to claim victory in their jihad against a superpower. With this, the presence in the region of non-Afghan Mujahedin – now called jihadis, meaning supporters of jihad, or "Afghanis" – became superfluous, and the nearly 6,000 Egyptian jihadis as well as other Arab jihadis began returning home as veterans of urban guerrilla warfare and experts at bomb-making and assassinations. During the next year or so, between 800 and 2,000 Afghani Egyptians returned home (as did hundreds of Afghani Algerians, who would help intensify the armed struggle against the military regime after Front du Islamique Salvation (FIS) had been deprived of its impending victory in the parliamentary poll in late December 1991). As a result there was a spurt in the terrorist activities of Islamic extremists, especially Al Gamaat, which went on to target foreign tourists from October onwards on the ground that tourism, centered around the statuary of pre-Islamic Egypt, was un-Islamic.

The following events sum up the situation between May and December 1992, when Mubarak vowed to "crush" the militant Islamic groups – with an estimated 10,000 hard-core members – through mass arrests, brutal interrogation techniques and blanket policing of militant strongholds, with the year seeing 322 violent deaths of policemen and extremists:

14 May: Islamic militants kill 13 Copts in two villages near Asyut; the worst sectarian violence for a decade.

9 June: Extremists kill Faraj Foda, an academic and columnist, and an outspoken critic of Islamic fundamentalists.

1 October: Militants fire on a Nile cruiser carrying 140 Germans near Asyut, and kill a tourist.

21 October: An attack on a tourist bus near Dayrut leaves one British woman dead.

12 November: Extremists shoot and injure five German tourists and two Egyptians in Qena.

Late autumn: Islamist extremists plant mines at the air strip near Sid Barrani along the Egyptian–Libyan border shortly before the arrival of Mubarak on his way to Libya. One officer and eight conscripts are arrested.

December: In a dragnet operation in Cairo's Imbaba district, police arrest 1,500 Islamist suspects.

"As night falls like charcoal dust on the teeming streets of the Cairo suburb of Imbaba, the outlines of the buildings become blurred and the smells get sharper," reported Patrick Bishop of the *Daily Telegraph*.

As the stalls pack up, the market is awash with odors, from the scent of melons to the stench of old fish. Through the hot dusk comes a bronchitic splutter of static as a loud speaker comes to life and the muezzin begins chanting his call to evening prayer. This particular muezzin has a throbbing, melodramatic delivery that sounds menacing. The impression is deceptive. He is an employee of the state, as are all the clerics in this squalid Cairo suburb where the police moved in late last year [1992] to smash the Islamic fundamentalist network that had taken root in the district, arresting hundreds and closing their mosques. . . . Imbaba, packed with poverty stricken émigrés from the bleak countryside of southern Egypt, is not a relaxed place . . .

The churned up streets of Imbaba, where workmen are installing a much needed new sewerage and water system, are evidence of a government initiative to ameliorate the conditions that have created a fertile ground for the fundamentalist message.[31]

In January 1993, the government introduced fast-track military courts to deal with Islamic extremists as it found the Emergency High Court, appointed to try cases of political violence, too slow. But there was no let-up in terrorist operations. The attacks on tourist haunts and buses continued. On 26 February, when a blast inside the basement of the World Trade Center in New York led to six deaths, a bomb in a coffee house in central Cairo killed three foreigners.

March 1993, coinciding roughly with the holy month of Ramadan, started badly for the government as newspapers headlined the sex scandal involving Lucy Artine, 28-year-old niece of an Armenian actress, and Field Marshal Muhammad Abdul Halim Abu Ghazala, 63, presidential advisor and a former defense minister, who resigned over allegations (backed by tape recordings) that he interceded with a judge over increased alimony to Lucy Artine, divorced from the son of a rich tobacco factory owner. Lucy had also secured the help of Gen. Hilmi al Fikri, director of public security, and Gen. Fadi Hebashi, head of investigations focusing on Islamic terrorism. "We need a government that is not corrupt, that is more efficient, and that would try to redress the grievous social and political problems and become an alternative to the fundamentalists," said Hussein Amin, a former Egyptian ambassador to Algeria. "If there was a free election today, the Islamicists would win. Not because people want Egypt to become an Islamic republic, but simply as a reaction."[32] The Artine scam was a tip of the iceberg of the proliferating corruption of the regime, its bureaucracy and its ruling National Democratic Party and of the ostentatious wealth of an increasingly unsavory amalgam of the old- and new-rich, as later scandals would reveal. Not long after, in parliament, Maj.-Gen. Zaki Badr, a former interior minister, accused his successor, Abdul Halim Mousa, "of complicity in heroin smuggling, siphoning off police benevolent funds, and bribing journalists." In return Mousa accused Badr of corruption.[33]

When, against this background, Al Gamaat tried to levy *zakat* (religious tax) in its strongholds – Cairo's slums, Aswan and Asyut – the government despatched special forces with orders to shoot to kill. Three major clashes during 9–17 March in these areas – including one in Aswan where the CSF attacked a mosque during evening prayers – left 28 militants, 11 police and 3 civilians dead. In retaliation for the Aswan assault, Al Gamaat activists set off a bomb under the luggage compartment of an empty tourist bus outside Cairo's Antiquities Museum, the city's most popular tourist attraction. It thus struck a heavy blow to the industry which, by attracting 3 million tourists annually, earned Egypt $4 billion in foreign exchange (the largest such contribution) and benefited 2 million Egyptian families directly or indirectly, and which was also the main recipient of direct Western investment.[34]

In a gesture of defiance, Mubarak prayed at Al Azhar Mosque on 19 March, the last Friday of Ramadan, as swarms of black-uniformed CFS troops sealed off roads, blue-helmeted presidential guards stood vigil inside the mosque and, in the nearby, teeming bazaar, almost every other bystander was a secret police-man with a pistol hidden under his vest.[35]

The next month, when the interior minister, Abdul Halim Mousa, publicly acknowledged that he had met the ulama trying to mediate between the government and Islamic militants, Mubarak was so upset that he sacked him. His replacement, Gen. Hassan Muhammad Alfi, 57, immediately reasserted an uncompromising stance on Islamic militancy.

Radical Islamists were not intimidated, confident in the knowledge that an Islamic tide was sweeping the country. Appearing before an isolated military court on the outskirts of Cairo in March 1993, 40 white-robed Al Gamaat members, charged with attacks on tourists and facing life or capital punishment, defiantly shouted Islamic slogans and complained loudly of torture. On the streets in Cairo and elsewhere, veils and beards were far more numerous than a few years before; the attendance at mosque prayers was on the rise, and so too was the readership of Islamic literature. An increasing number of zealot men addressed foreign women with their backs turned while heavily veiled Egyptian women shielded the photos on their identity cards from prying male eyes. Scores of well-known belly dancers and actresses made a very public display of their freshly adopted Islamic modesty. For Hala Safi, one of the most famous Egyptian belly dancers, renowned for her sensuality on stage and screen, her days of diamante bras and ruby red lipstick were over for ever: she had taken to propagating Islam. Addressing some 60 women in an affluent Cairo suburb, she said, "In my former life everybody stared at me. I could feel the contempt in their eyes." She broke down and began sobbing. "The Prophet came to me in a dream. He covered me, and from that moment I knew I would never feel naked again." [36]

President Mubarak could not be impervious to such facts on the ground. Nor could he ignore the intelligence reports that even mainstream intellectuals were debating the pros and cons of a moderate Islamic political structure. Indeed, in off-the-record remarks during an interview with Judith Miller of the *New York Times*, he conceded that he could not stand against the strong Islamic tide in the country, and that he could not say publicly that he would reduce the amount of religious programming on television or take other steps to weaken the Islamic current in Egypt, thus letting the fundamentalists accuse him of being anti-Islamic. Having put the fundamentalists on the run by now, he added, he would jeopardize that momentum by making statements that could be twisted to mean he was attacking Islam. [37]

As it was, Mubarak's policy of promoting religio-cultural Islam had gone beyond increased religious programs on state-run television and radio. It had impinged on school and university curriculums to a degree that many liberal, Westernized Egyptians found unacceptable. "Eighty percent of the material in my daughter's Arabic-language text book in her private, secular school is from the Quran!" said Baha Eddin Hassan, the legal advisor to the Egyptian Organization for Human Rights (EOHR). "More and more men refuse to swim in integrated swimming pools. Islamic pressure to ban 'un-Islamic' books and movies is growing."[38] Unknown to Hassan, however, Mubarak had planned on reversing the trend during his third and final term in office, as he assured *New York Times'* Miller in his interview.

His third term was contingent on his surviving periodic assassination plots. One such was foiled in May 1993 when the authorities arrested 19 Islamist conspirators, including two uniformed officers – one of them a member of the presidential security guard – who were caught with detailed drawings of the houses of the president and his neighbors in a quiet street of Nasser City, a Cairo suburb. The plan was to kill Mubarak by firing rocket-propelled grenades at the presidential residence.[39] Further arrests followed.

Assaults on police stations and tourists, interspersed with assassination attempts on high officials, continued. On 18 August 1993, an Al Jihad team of seven exploded a bomb by remote control near the entrance to the interior ministry building in central Cairo and forced the cars of the minister, Gen. Alfi, and his bodyguards to stop. Then the attackers raked the official cars with bullets, wounding the minister. In the ensuing melee, four people died, including two attackers, bringing the aggregate violent deaths since April 1992 to 175.

The suspects were brought before military courts whose judges, more interested in delivering quick verdicts than dispensing justice, seemed unfamiliar with basic courtroom procedures and rules of evidence – such as the inadmissibility of audio- or video-tapes as primary evidence (in law, their role is corroborative). These courts gave defense attorneys limited access to the defendants and insufficient time to draft responses to often long and detailed charges. They denied the accused the right to appeal, and were too prone to handing out capital punishment. Within eight months of their existence they had chalked up 22 hangings. A remark by Mubarak's close advisor – "People would respect the President more if a few more Islamic fanatics were hanged"[40] – indicated the political nature of the justice these courts were dispensing.

By contrast, in some instances civilian judges showed independent-mindedness. In August 1993, acquitting the 24 defendants in the case of Speaker Mahjoub's murder, the head of the Emergency High Court, Wahid Mahmoud Ibrahim, accused the CSF of "attempting to bend justice" after failing to provide evidence in support of the charges. Censuring the security forces for their failure to catch the real culprits, he accused them of forcing confessions through torture. Dismissing the prosecutor's attempt to charge the defendants for possessing banned publications advocating the implementation of the Sharia, he said, "This court does not try ideas . . . Calls for enforcement of the Sharia were consistent with the provisions in the constitution."[41] The torture, mentioned by Judge Ibrahim, included beating detainees with coiled wire on their bodies and soles of their feet while being held in painful contortions, electric shocks to genitals, sexual molestation, dousing with cold water while standing naked outdoors, and threatening to beat and rape wives and children of male suspects.[42]

The unease expressed by Judge Ibrahim was shared by the US embassy – housed in a massive citadel-style complex towering over the center of Cairo – funneling $2.3 billion of aid annually to Egypt, three-fifths of it in sophisticated weaponry. Despairing of the cycle of Islamist violence and state repression – widespread police raids, mass arrests, torture of suspects, and military trials and executions – and keen to secure Mubarak's survival, regarded as crucial to the Middle East peace process started by the Madrid Conference in October 1991, the American envoy urged Mubarak to reach accommodation with the moderate Muslim Brotherhood and initiate social reform to deprive the hardline fundamentalists of a political platform. If the Brotherhood were co-opted into the political system, that would disperse the responsibility for Egypt's current state of affairs on to the Brotherhood, and that would divide the Islamist movement, now almost unanimously favoring violence over peaceful participation in politics, into moderates and hardliners, the US ambassador reportedly argued. Mubarak spurned the advice. The embassy's political section then made discreet contact with the Brotherhood. When the news leaked that the American embassy had been talking with the opposition groups – religious as well as secular – the semi-official press, reflecting the president's views, declared that such talks verged on "treason."[43] Mubarak persisted in his refusal to consider legalizing the Brotherhood as a political party, arguing that it would then provide a cover for radical Islamists to infiltrate the regime to undermine it. According to Gen. Alfi, the Muslim Brotherhood, Al Gamaat and Al Jihad were "all one" anyway: "Those [such as the Brotherhood] who incite are more dangerous than those who shoot . . . These are entire organizations trying to seize power by any means."[44] As far as peaceful means were concerned, Alfi, the interior minister charged with conducting elections, had publicly declared that he would never allow an Islamist victory at the ballot box.[45]

Drawing on the expertise in vote-rigging that it had accumulated over the past few decades, the Interior Ministry announced 84 percent turn-out in a referendum for the presidency on 4 October 1993, with 96.3 percent voting for the sole candidate, Hosni Mubarak. The actual turn-out was probably no more than a third of the official figure.

Mubarak's third term (1993–9)

Following his re-election, President Mubarak retained Atef Sidqi as the prime minister, despite repeated calls for his replacement by the semi-official press, which could not help ridiculing his ineptitude. In a way, Sidqi mattered little since the cabinet was not a coherent body, its individual members competing with one another for power by gaining the attention of the president, who in effect ran the important defense, foreign and interior ministries.

Nonetheless, a failed attempt to assassinate Sidqi in November – the third assault on a top official in seven months – set alarm bells ringing in the regime. A 25 lb (11 kg) bomb placed under an abandoned parked car 500 yards (450 m) from Sidqi's residence near a girls' school in the heavily guarded Cairo suburb of Heliopolis was detonated by remote control as the prime minister's motorcade passed by. It damaged eight vehicles and killed a pupil. Sidqi, riding an armor-plated car, was unhurt. A fax sent by Al Jihad to an international news agency, saying the attack was "a revenge for the blood of the martyrs," vowed to continue "the path of the Jihad until Egypt is free from the American and Jewish occupation."[46]

The attack goaded Mubarak to pursue his suppression of Islamist extremists more vigorously and reverse his policy of promoting the religio-cultural aspect of Islam – as he had revealed to Judith Miller earlier. The immediate result was the arrest of hundreds of Islamic radicals. Yet one of the alleged prime suspects – Yasser Tawfiq al Sirri – was not one of them. But then al Sirri – a taciturn, balding man in his late 30s, with a straggly beard – later surfacing in Britain, would insist that he was "no longer in Egypt" at the time of the attack on Sidqi. Given temporary permission to stay while his asylum application was processed, he would run the Islamic Observatory Center from his apartment in London as "a humanitarian and media platform" as Britain's MI5 (Military Intelligence 5, title of domestic intelligence) and Special Branch kept him under surveillance[47] – until his arrest in late 2001 after the 11 September attacks on the US.

Egypt's security forces now resorted to taking hostage family members of the suspected Al Gamaat and Al Jihad activists, as well as threatening to rape female members, to secure the surrender of the wanted militants. The government began challenging Al Azhar's right to censor publications it deemed religiously offensive, and warned its professors not to endorse fatwas that could encourage "fanatics." It actively encouraged writers who upheld separation between state and mosque to disseminate their viewpoint while denying space in the government-controlled press to even moderate Islamists.[48]

The Ministry of Information and Culture turned state-run television into an anti-terrorist instrument. In the spring of 1994 it broadcast the militants' confessions, apparently obtained under torture, in which they said they killed for profit. On the creative side, the ministry got high ratings for its television serial *Al Irhabi* (The Terrorist): it showed a young man – played by a celebrated actor, Adil Imam – joining Islamist guerrillas, who terrorize foreign tourists, Copts and police, realizing his wrongs and making peace with secular Egyptian society, only to be murdered by his former comrades. Given the oral orientation of popular Egyptian culture, the impact of television outweighed that of the printed word.[49]

With the approach of Ramadan (in February 1994), Al Gamaat "implored [foreign] tourists and investors" to leave the country by 22 February "as the next operations will be extremely ferocious," explaining that "We are forced to do this in order to defend our faith and ourselves in the face of the lack of law and human rights which the dictatorial Mubarak regime embodies."[50]

The run-up to the deadline saw Al Gamaat activists fire at a cruise boat, attack a Cairo–Luxor tourist train in southern Egypt and plant explosives outside four banks in Cairo, while the government arrested nearly a thousand suspected militants. In early March Al Gamaat gave the deadline of 22 March (end of the Islamic month of Shawal) to Egyptians to withdraw their deposits from the banks, "these usurious monuments," thus signaling the next phase in their jihad directed at eliminating usury which is banned in Islam. It is worth noting that Al Gamaat and Al Jihad militants had initially funded their terrorist acts by robbing banks and Coptic jewelers.

A typical example of the official response was a security police raid in Cairo's Zawiya al Hamra slum which led to the deaths of seven suspected extremists. Torture of the detainees was so routine and severe that in May there was the death in police custody of Abdul Harith Madani, a lawyer who defended fundamentalists, and who was abducted from his office on 26 April by SSI agents. Protesting attorneys marched on the presidential palace, and were dispersed by the police firing tear gas canisters.[51]

In September, the hosting in Cairo of a week-long United Nations International Conference on Population and Development, attended by over 10,000 delegates from 156 countries, highlighted the differences between Mubarak and Al Azhar whose rector, Grand Shaikh Jad al Haq, branded the gathering un-Islamic because of its advocacy of "homosexuality, abortion and pre-marital sex." The event brought together Al Azhar, an official institution, and the opposition Brotherhood, both of them opposed to birth control. Discomfited by this development, in his inaugural speech to the conference, Mubarak stressed the need

> to preserve the principles of divine laws as demarcation lines between good and evil, right and wrong, what is lawful and what is unlawful . . . We deeply believe that there are no discrepancies between religion and science . . . We have been quite keen to make our population programs conform to established religious values.

In the end, the Brotherhood commended the government for ensuring that the final declaration by the conference did not offend Islamic values.[52] The holding of a successful international conference raised Egypt's profile abroad, especially in the West, and marginally improved its chance of attracting Western capital investment. By contrast, Al Gamaat assailants' stabbing of Neguib Mahfouz (1911–) – the winner of the Nobel Prize for Literature and the most renowned and respected writer in the Arab world – in mid-October was an act that alienated even many Islamist intellectuals.

The cumulative effect of the government's hard line and the extremists' increasingly desperate acts caused a dramatic drop in the number of violent deaths – down from 1,116 in 1993 to 305 in 1994, partly as a result of the successful infiltration of Al Gamaat cells by Interior Ministry agents. On the macro-economic front too, there was improvement. The government had succeeded in reducing inflation as well as budget deficit (down to a respectable 1.4 percent of the GNP) and subsidies on food and other necessities, down by three-quarters, while raising the annual GDP growth to 4 percent.[53] But, with the benefits being mal-distributed, the gap between the rich and the poor widened, and more Egyptians fell below the poverty line. That in turn meant a greater need for privately funded networks of mosque-centered social services, traditionally provided by the Muslim Brotherhood, with Al Gamaat as a late-comer. The services, funded by Islamic charities registered in Egypt (about 2,000 in 1994), Saudi Arabia and other Gulf monarchies, Western Europe and North America, included free educational classes and low-cost health clinics as well as social welfare centers and youth clubs. They benefited some 6 million people, or about one-fifth of the 30 millions Egyptians surviving below the poverty line. A typical beneficiary was Umm Ahmad, a mother of two, abandoned by her husband, and living in a tiny, bare brick tenement flat in Cairo's Talbia neighborhood. She received almost free medical care, cheap meat from the local butcher, and in case of acute need, some cash from the Muslim Brotherhood.[54]

Little wonder that, in 1995, Mubarak concentrated on suppressing the Brotherhood, and pursued the aim with added vigor after an assassination attempt on him by Al Gamaat activists on 26 June 1995 in Addis Ababa, Ethiopia, where he was attending a summit conference of the Organization of African Unity (OAU). The attack created a groundswell of sympathy for him at home.

Mubarak was on his way to the summit venue from the airport when a truck obstructed his motorcade. A group of men fired a volley of shots at his car, which was bullet-proof. The ensuing gun battle claimed the lives of two bodyguards and three attackers whose remaining two companions escaped. Unhurt, Mubarak returned immediately to Cairo to a hero's welcome. He accused Sudan of involvement, especially Hassan al Turabi, the leader of the National Islamic Front, the main force behind the Islamist military regime of Gen. Omar Hassan al Bashir. While the state-run media pilloried Turabi and al Bashir, calling for their overthrow, the Egyptian troops seized the disputed 6,500 square mile (17,000 km) border area of Halaib on the Red Sea.

By focusing on Sudan, Mubarak diverted attention away from domestic enemies. The rallies and meetings he held with the public and professional syndicates boosted his popularity.

Egyptians stopped referring to him as *la vache qui rit* (the cow that laughs), a sobriquet applied to him due to his perceived resemblance to the laughing cow on a brand of processed cheese. Now he acquired an aura of invincibility. Following Sadat's footsteps, he encouraged a personality cult, with the state television broadcasting the video footage of him after the assassination attempt for six consecutive days. He intensified his campaign for greater international coordination to counter Islamic terrorism.

In July and August 1995 the police arrested over 200 Brotherhood leaders after searching their homes. Unprecedenedly, the government brought 49 of them to trial before one of the military courts, which had been established to try only civilians charged with political violence. The charge against them of attempting to reconstitute a banned political party was hardly an example of political violence. While the list of the accused did not include any of the Brotherhood's Supreme Guidance Council members, it contained Muhammad Habib, an MP from Asyut, and Issam al Aryan, deputy head of the Doctors' Syndicate. Apparently, the government wanted to intimidate the leaders with grassroots support to cripple the Brotherhood as a mass movement, while sparing the formal leadership to encourage its reluctance to challenge the state by launching a civil disobedience campaign that it had been considering.

The case began on 1 October, and a fortnight later the prosecutor added a further 32 defendants, most of them Brotherhood candidates for the parliamentary poll on 29 November. The main charge against them remained directing an illegal organization with plans to impede the law and constitution. For evidence the prosecution produced a videotape of people entering a building to attend a meeting, but they were shown only from behind, and identified only by one State Security Investigation officer. The meeting discussed nothing more seditious than how to increase the Brotherhood's representation in the professional syndicates and in parliament. This was considered enough for the judge to convict 54 defendants and sentence most of them to three years in jail with or without hard labor a week before the parliamentary election.[55] The government closed the Brotherhood's headquarters in Cairo, thus ending the quarter century of tolerance of the organization accorded it by Sadat, and placed the pro-Brotherhood governing council of the Lawyers' Syndicate under its direct control.[56]

'Isn't this a clear signal to millions of zealots that moderation is futile, talk of democracy in Egypt nothing but a mockery?' asked the London-based Liberty for the Muslim World group. "The only means available to anyone who wants to express his opinion or participate in correcting the deteriorating situation – due to corruption, mismanagement and poverty – is to resort to violence."[57] The London group of moderate Muslims could have easily added "sham elections" to the list. The parliamentary poll conducted in November–December 1995 was the most fraudulent yet, with the opposition winning a mere 13 (and the Muslim Brotherhood, none) of the 444 elected seats. It was the most violent election as well, with 51 people killed, 28 by the police. The list of irregularities prepared by six human rights organizations included early arrival of the ballot boxes filled with ballots, police denying opposition monitors entry to polling stations, presiding officers permitting National Democratic Party supporters to vote many times and without voting cards, and police cars transporting ballot boxes to the counting centers going missing for hours and arriving stuffed with votes for the NDP.[58] Little wonder that disgruntled Brotherhood members began establishing contacts with militants.

However, Islamic extremists too continued to be pressured. As a result, many fled to Yemen, Saudi Arabia, the United Arab Emirates and Sudan, where Egyptian intelligence agents, working in cooperation with their respective counterparts, tried to track them down. Others joined the civil war in the Balkans, fighting alongside the Muslims of Bosnia. Still others sought a haven in the Muslim-majority, post-Communist Albania.

Those who remained in Egypt had shifted their operations from Cairo and Asyut to Qena and Minia provinces, where sugar-cane fields and caves provided good hiding places. These activists resorted to donning police uniforms, setting up road blocks and searching buses for their quarry, such as official policemen in civilian dress. The raids by the CSF became so bloody that they were accused of acting as "policemen, judges and executioners, all in one." In a single day in June they killed nine people in one incident. In early November, 1,500 of them stormed Maghaga village in Minia province, looking for terrorists, and killed 13 villagers.

With this, Islamist extremists targeted Egyptian targets abroad. On 13 November 1995 Al Gamaat's international affiliate, called *Al Gamaat al Adila al Alamiya* (The International Justice Group [IJG]), assassinated Egypt's trade representative in Geneva who, according to the IJG, was an armed agent of the Egyptian Interior Ministry. Six days later, the truck bombing of the Egyptian embassy in Islamabad by the IJG left 18 dead – some of them Interior Ministry agents working under diplomatic cover. Cairo held Ayman Zawahiri, then based in Khartoum along with Osama bin Laden, the Saudi fugitive, responsible for the bombing.

Claiming responsibility for the explosion, the IJG demanded the release of Shaikh Abdul Rahman, jailed in the US, and Talat Fuad Qasim, held in Egypt. After arriving in the US in 1989, the blind shaikh had been in touch with Al Khifa (lit. The Struggle) Refugee Center, run by the Afghan Refugee Services Incorporated in Brooklyn, New York, to recruit volunteers for the jihad in Afghanistan,[59] and had run a mosque in Brooklyn, popular with Egyptian, Sudanese and Yemeni immigrants. After obtaining an immigrant visa he moved to the adjoining state of New Jersey. From there his followers sent thousands of tapes of his sermons to Egypt. Following the bombing of the World Trade Center in New York in February 1993, and the aborting of a plan to bomb the United Nations and other targets some weeks later, he was arrested as a suspect. Egypt demanded his extradition which was rejected by the US. After a lengthy trial, he was found guilty in October 1995, and sentenced to life imprisonment the following January.

As for Talat Qasim, while his family in Denmark claimed that he had left for Croatia to research a book, he had only gone there on his way to fight alongside Muslims in Bosnia, where a civil war was raging. However, the Croatian government arrested him in Zagreb on 12 September 1995 and expelled him a week later. He was then abducted by the agents of the Foreign Operations Section of the SSI of the Egyptian Interior Ministry, and taken to Cairo. Some months earlier the ministry had dispatched 100 security policemen – 40 of them armed – to different embassies in Europe to conduct an anti-terrorist campaign. It was particularly interested in London, believed to be the base of half a dozen Al Gamaat and Al Jihad leaders. Following the tip-offs from its agents in London, the ministry arrested 36 Al Jihad militants in mid-November 1995, and reportedly thwarted attacks on ministers, journalists and tourist sites, including the popular Khan al Khalili market in Cairo.[60] "Britain has become the land of asylum for the leading figures of fundamentalist terrorists," declared the semi-official *Al Ahram* (The Pyramids) on 27 November 1995, a statement that would acquire especial significance six years later in the aftermath of the September 11 tragedy.

However, if the government had concluded that it had finally ended Islamist terrorism, it received a rude shock when in April 1996 four Al Gamaat gunmen killed 17 Greek tourists outside a hotel in Cairo in the mistaken belief that they were Israelis. Their action was in retaliation for the Israeli Operation "Grapes of Wrath', ordered on 11 April by Prime Minister Shimon Peres, against Lebanon to punish the Lebanese Hizbollah (Party of God), which resulted in the deaths of 210 people, including 160 civilians.[61] This was a reminder once more of the linkage between Islamist violence and the state of the Middle East peace process – especially with regard to the Israeli–Palestinian conflict. This point had been made three years earlier by *Al Ahram*. "Israel and the US want to make the fight against terrorism, instead of the pursuit of a just basis for peace, the region's priority," it wrote on 29 March 1993. "Israel, the product of ethnic and religious cleansing on a massive scale, continues to try to uproot

Palestinians from their land through transfer, deportation, repression, economic siege and Jewish settlement. This is what fuels the fundamentalists' ideology – this and the Arab governments' failure to get Washington to stop it."[62] Nearly a decade on, with the final Israeli–Palestinian settlement still eluding the contending parties, this analysis held.

Instead of a steady trickle of low-level violence, Al Gamaat leadership inside Egypt decided on a dramatic operation. When, in September 1997, a military court tried 97 Islamic extremists for subversion, many of them in absentia, handing out four capital and eight life sentences,[63] Al Gamaat activists responded in kind. Three of them, armed with guns and petrol bombs, attacked tourist buses outside the Antiquities Museum in Cairo, killing ten people, including six German tourists. "This is not a political or terrorist act, but a criminal one by a mentally deranged person and his brother," said the tourism minister, Mahmoud al Beltaji,[64] while the interior minister banned reports to the contrary in the local media.

But the government could not put the same gloss on what happened on 17 November 1997 at the Temple of Queen Hatshepsut at Luxor in southern Egypt. That sunny morning, as scores of British, French, Japanese, Spanish and Swiss tourists disembarked from their buses about 500 yards (450 m) from the newly restored 34-centuries old pharaonic temple, six Al Gamaat extremists, led by Midhat Muhammad Abdul Rahman, an Afghani, wearing the black uniforms of the CSF and carrying automatic weapons, rushed towards them, firing. Screaming tourists fell over one another in panic and fear. Forcing the tourists to kneel, the attackers started shooting. Then they went around the wounded, finishing them off, sometimes with their knives, cutting their throats or disemboweling them. After the 45-minute killing spree, which left 58 tourists dead and another 20 wounded, they tried to hijack a bus to flee, but failed. They were chased into the surrounding hills by the CSF, and killed after a three-hour battle.[65]

In retrospect, the grisly attack could be seen as a retaliation for the government-sponsored open-air performance on 12 October of Verdi's *Aida* (commissioned originally by Egypt's ruler, Khedive Ismail, to commemorate the opening of the Suez Canal in 1869), attended by an audience of Western celebrities, paying $200–350 a seat, five times the average monthly salary of an Egyptian civil servant. As seen by Al Gamaat militants, the Mubarak government had compounded its un-Islamic behavior of promoting pharaonic statuary by staging a Western opera for the benefit primarily of a Western elite. It came at a time of growing frustration in the Arab world at the near collapse of the US-led peace process in the Middle East caused by the hawkish policies of Israeli Premier Binyamin Netanyahu. But the indiscriminate shooting of innocent tourists, followed by gory throat-cutting and disembowelment of the injured victims, created widespread revulsion among Egyptians, a generally mild people. Al Gamaat's exiled leadership condemned the Luxor massacre, which also ran counter to the growing consensus among the organization's jailed leaders to cease armed operations. Swiss security officials would allege in May 1999 that the massacre had been organized and funded by Osama bin Laden, then based in Afghanistan.[66] In the immediate aftermath of the Luxor attack, tour operators canceled trips to Egypt, and foreign embassies advised their nationals to leave the country. Egypt's tourist industry remained in shock for almost a year.

As expected, the authorities intensified their anti-Islamist campaign through large-scale arrests and trials, with Mubarak replacing Gen. Alfi as interior minister with Habib Ibrahim Adli, then head of the State Security Services and infamous for his ruthlessness. At the same time, responding to conciliatory gestures by the jailed Al Gamaat leadership, the government released 5,000 Al Gamaat prisoners in 1998 after they had pledged to renounce violence.

In February 1998 Al Jihad, led by Ayman Zawahiri, allied with the Al Qaida (The Base) network of Osama bin Laden to form the World Islamic Front for Jihad against Crusaders and Jews, with its members concentrating on forging documents, transferring money and arranging communications. As before Al Jihad members continued to translate US army manuals and topographical maps into Arabic for terrorist training in Afghanistan. Al Jihad's funding came from the members donating 10 percent of salaries as well as trading in sugar and raising sheep in Albania.[67]

It was in Albania that Egyptian agents, working in conjunction with CIA operatives, smashed an Al Jihad cell in 1998, and apprehended Ahmad Ibrahim Sayyid Najjar, who had earlier been active in Yemen, and had been sentenced to death in absentia in 1997 for plotting to explode a bomb in Cairo's Khan al Khalili bazaar in 1996. After his extradition from Albania to Egypt in June 1998, his jailers blindfolded him and held him in a Cairo prison cell filled with water up to his knees for 35 days to extract a confession. Other Al Jihad suspects suffered flogging, electric shock and hanging from the ceiling.[68]

In early 1999, based primarily on the testimony of Najjar, the government put on trial 107 Al Jihad suspects, 60 of them in absentia, then believed to be in Afghanistan, Albania, Azerbaijan, Bulgaria and the UAE. Several accused referred to bin Laden as their financier, and revealed that his network maintained accounts in Albania, Britain, Germany and Poland. According to Najjar, bin Laden believed that the attacks by his followers would force America and its allies to change their policies in the Middle East and the Muslim world, and that would fulfill the ultimate objectives of the World Islamic Front for Jihad of establishing fundamentalist regimes in all Muslim-majority countries, and re-creating the Islamic umma under the caliph, and demonstrate the weakness of the present Arab and Muslim leaders. In April, the military judge acquitted 20. Of the rest, 78, including Yasser al Sirri, received one year to life imprisonment, and nine capital punishment, raising the total of death sentences so far in Egypt to 118, a third of these imposed in absentia. The latter included Najjar, Ayman Zawahiri and his younger brother, Muhammad, an engineer.[69]

A month earlier, Al Gamaat's unilateral ceasefire had been endorsed by Shaikh Abdul Rahman from his jail in America as well as by the exiled leadership and its clandestine Egypt-based

Shura (Consultative Council). Whether the leader of the group's military wing, Abu Yasser Rifia Ahmad Taha, based in Afghanistan, had done so remained unclear. During the first nine months of the year, the government freed 5,000 Islamists; but that still left 15,000 detainees behind bars, two-thirds of them Islamists, and most of them without charges or trial.[70] During the same period the authorities arrested 200 Brotherhood members and tried them for belonging to a proscribed organization.

Mubarak's fourth term (1999–)

In February 2000, four months after being elected president for the fourth time, Hosni Mubarak appointed his son Gamal, a businessman, to the secretariat of the ruling National Democratic Party, fueling rumors that he was grooming him as a successor. That month Al Jihad leaders announced a cessation of military operations in order to focus on liberating the Al Aqsa Mosque in Jerusalem, a reference to the Palestinian struggle to end the Israeli occupation. The next month the authorities released 800 Al Gamaat and Al Jihad members. And, following the imprisoned Al Jihad military leaders' endorsement of the ceasefire in July, the government freed a further 500 militants after they had renounced violence.

Having driven the Brotherhood underground, Mubarak began squeezing the leading secular opposition group, the 24–year-old Socialist Labor Party. In January 2000 the state-controlled Political Parties Committee suspended it and its weekly paper *Al Shaab* (The People) for "exceeding its political mandate."

Al Shaab had been pre-eminent in exposing corruption in high places. For instance, it alleged venal links between Zakaria Azmi, head of the presidential office, and Fawzi al Sayyid, a property tycoon owning 89 luxury tower blocks, who, it alleged, had grossly violated building codes by constructing buildings 20 stories higher than the official limit, and got away with massive tax evasions. It alleged that Azmi and his former wives had benefited from their links with al Sayyid, who threatened to reveal all. It asked how Azmi, who in 1978 was a modest local government official, had since then acquired substantial property assets. Its exposé became credible when the tax fraud squad acknowledged that 452 building contractors nationwide had illegally gained 2.5 billion Egyptian pounds (US$750 million) in the past five years. Samir Abdul Qadir, a columnist in the quasi-government *Akhbar Al Yom* (The Daily News), wrote: "Will the authorities put the corrupt on trial, and allow them to unravel hideous secrets about their high connections, or will they just wink at the whole matter and let it pass?"[71] Of course the authorities ignored the scam. That enhanced the corrosive cynicism with which a growing number of young well-educated Egyptians viewed the socio-political system, where a third of the workforce was employed in government jobs paying an average of $70 a month, and a lawyer earned less than half that amount. Among them was Muhamamd al Amir Awad al Sayyid Atta (1968–2001), a qualified architect and urban planner in Cairo who, despite his post-graduate education and experience in Germany, found the remuneration so poor that he traveled back to Germany in 1996 to pursue his studies further. In his conversations with his classmates at Hamburg University – Volker Hauth and Ralph Bodenstein – he spoke bitterly of "the autocratic government of President Mubarak and the small coterie of former army officers and rich Egyptians gathered around him," calling them "the Fat Cats" and denouncing their close ties to America. As an architect he was appalled by the restoration project around Cairo's old city gates, Bab al Basr and Bab al Futuh, which involved demolishing the homes and workshops of the poor, and turning the neighborhood into "a Disney World."[72]

Like many of his colleagues in the engineering faculty of Cairo University, after graduating with an architecture degree in 1990, he had joined the Engineers' Syndicate dominated by the Muslim Brotherhood. In 1992 his father, Muhammad al Amir Atta, sent him to Hamburg Technical University for a master's degree in town planning. Between then and September 11, 2001, the young Atta would intermittently study, work, and shuttle half way around the world, and end up as the crucial link between four different cells of Al Qaida to stage the most lethal attack on mainland America in history. In a sense, his role would underline the significance of Egypt in Islamic politics, dating back to Hassan al Banna eight decades before.

For now, however, President Mubarak had ample reason to feel smug, having brought the domestic political scene absolutely under his control. But then, to his discomfiture, the Supreme Constitutional Court ruled in July that magistrates, not police officers, should oversee casting and counting of votes, thus depriving the government of the means of rigging the result by stuffing ballot boxes and fraudulent counting.

His civil servants, however, contrived other means of rigging. In the parliamentary poll to be held in three stages in October–November 2000, they deprived opposition candidates of the voters' list. Unlike them the official candidates had full access to the list. And, having determined those voters who were dead or out of town, these candidates filled out cards in their names. The government singled out the Brotherhood by disqualifying its most effective organizers from running, disrupting its campaign, and arresting its election monitors, who had to register three days ahead of the poll. To avoid confrontation, the Brotherhood contested only 77 seats. The state pursued the strategy of keeping the Brotherhood voters away by surrounding polling stations with police who barred all except those getting off the official candidates' mini-buses – in the process using tear gas and live ammunition against the protesting voters, and killing 10 of them. Despite this the Brotherhood won 17 seats, nearly three times as many as the second largest opposition party, New Wafd. Of the 388 MPs that the National Democratic Party claimed, 212 were independent NDP who, having defeated the official candidates, returned to the NDP fold in the now familiar pattern.[73]

Though elections in Egypt were a charade, at least the regime felt compelled to go through them, thus underscoring the fact that in theory at least power rested with the public as the official title of the country, Arab Republic of Egypt, implied. There was no such pretension in the case of Saudi Arabia, a royal autocracy.

5   Saudi Arabia

The oldest fundamentalist state

The collapse of the Ottoman empire followed by the abolition of the caliphate by Mustafa Kemal Ataturk in March 1924 created a leadership vacuum in the world Muslim community. Among those who tried to fill it was Sharif Hussein ibn Ali al Hashim of the Hashimi dynasty which had governed Hijaz, containing Mecca and Medina, since the tenth century and which claimed lineage from Prophet Muhammad. During World War I the British had successfully encouraged Sharif Hussein to rebel against his Ottoman overlords, and after the war placed his two sons on the thrones of Iraq and Transjordan. The Hashimi–British alliance was regarded as anti-Islamic by non-Arab Muslims as well as by many Arab leaders. Sharif Hussein's claim to the caliphate therefore received scant support outside Hijaz. In certain cases it even aroused outright hostility. Among those who took umbrage at Sharif Hussein's declaration was Abdul Aziz ibn Abdul Rahman al Saud – a colorful man of enormous libido, imposing in appearance, father of 269 children, and fiercely ambitious, popularly known as Ibn Saud – whose forces controlled the territories surrounding Hijaz.

Abdul Aziz symbolized a high point in the varying fortunes of the House of Saud. After its defeat by the Ottomans in 1819 it had recaptured Riyadh only to be sent into exile in 1891 by the Rashidi tribal chief, Muhammad ibn Rashid, acting as a client of the Ottomans. In 1902 Abdul Aziz had ventured out of Kuwait and regained Riyadh. From there he had mounted a series of campaigns to gain control of the central Arabian region of Najd and defeat Muhammad ibn Rashid. He then extended his domain to the eastern territory of Hasa, inhabited by Shia tribes, in 1913. But his plans to attack Sharif Hussein's Hijaz were disrupted by the outbreak of World War I.

Najd was sparsely inhabited, with half of its population being nomadic tribes who were none the less related to those settled in villages and towns. Though nominally Muslim, these tribes had resorted to resolving their disputes through customary tribal law rather than the Sharia, and reverted to performing pre-Islamic rituals. The tribes had also taken to distinguishing themselves as noble, inferior or despicable. (The Saudi family belonged to the Musalikh branch of the Ruwalla tribe, considered noble.) Abdul Aziz resolved to transform the fractured, hierarchical Najdi community into a unified Islamic umma by replacing loyalty to the tribe with loyalty to Islam and its leader, the Imam: a replay of what had occurred in Arabia during the days of Prophet Muhammad. Abdul Aziz used Wahhabism as his ideological tool to achieve this end. At the same time, by reiterating the Arab and Islamic heritage of the Saudi dynasty and its frequent intermarriage with the descendants of the much-revered Muhammad ibn Abdul Wahhab, he justified its assumption of the Imamate.

Unitarianism and socio-religious equality of the believers were the hallmarks of Wahhabism, and as a Wahhabi leader Abdul Aziz stressed these. He abolished the protection tax which the inferior and despised tribes used to pay to the noble ones, thereby underlining the egalitarian nature of Wahhabism and winning fierce loyalty from the lower tribes. Having done this, Abdul Aziz decreed that all tribes must pay him zakat, the Islamic tax – an order which firmly established him as the Imam even though the nominal title stayed with his father, Abdul Rahman, until the latter's death in 1928.

Considering themselves as "the truly guided Islamic community," Wahhabis set out to attack polytheists, unbelievers and hypocrites (i.e. those who claimed to be Muslim but whose behavior was un-Islamic). Any deviation from the Sharia was labeled by them as innovation, and therefore un-Islamic. Any Muslim who disagreed with the Wahhabi interpretation of Islam was regarded by them as an unbelieving apostate who deserved severe punishment.

Wahhabis believed in the division of the world into Dar al Islam and its counterpart, Dar al Harb (The Realm of War [between believers and non-believers]), and in the concept of hijra. They viewed the departure of Muhammad ibn Abdul Wahhab in 1744 from Uyaina to Diriya in the same light as they did Prophet Muhammad's migration from Mecca to Medina – and called it Al Hijra.

Abdul Aziz sponsored the fresh converts' "hijra" to Wahhabism which was both physical and religio-spiritual. It meant having to give up nomadic life and "migrating" from customary tribal law to the Sharia and from the traditional tribal bonds to membership in the Islamic Brotherhood, called the Ikhwan.

He set up Ikhwan colonies, called *hijar*, soon after his conquest of Hasa in 1913. Each settlement included agricultural land, grazing pastures and reliable water supplies. Yet most of them failed to become self-sufficient and had to be subsidized by Abdul Aziz. In due course they became the religious, political, military, administrative and educational centers of Wahhabism, and enabled Abdul Aziz to achieve something that no other power or leader had so far done: impose a centralized rule over the 40 major tribes inhabiting Najd. In order to lessen inter-tribal conflict Abdul Aziz ordered that no tribe should leave its territory without his permission. He kept many tribal chiefs in the capital, Riyadh, under surveillance under the guise of educating them in Wahhabism.

Life in an Ikhwan colony, with an average population of 2,000, was highly organized and centered round the mosque. The ulama played an important role as did the *muttawin* (lit. enforcers), religious police who were trained at religious colleges in Riyadh. (Originally muttawin missionaries were sent by Abdul Aziz into the beduin communities in the Najd to encourage them to abandon their nomadic existence and settle down in religious Wahhabi communities.) The tasks of the religious police were to impart the Wahhabi doctrine to the faithful and punish those found smoking, singing or dancing, wearing gold or silk, or failing to perform the Islamic rituals. An Ikhwan colony was run jointly by an emir and a governor. The emir, elected by the local consultative council, was responsible to the Imam in Riyadh. The governor, who dealt with the Sharia, was responsible to the Shaikh al Islam, the head of the ulama, also based in Riyadh.

Abdul Aziz combined ideological zeal with pragmatism. He made a point of marrying into the family of the subjugated tribal chief, thus consolidating his control of the conquered territory without in any way undermining the internal structure of the defeated tribe. In the process he acquired 17 wives and sired 54 sons and 215 daughters, thus integrating most of the kingdom's tribes – Ajman, Awazim, Balt, Bani Hajir, Bani Khalid, Dawasir, Ghamid, Huwaitat, Jahadila, Juhaina, Manasir, Munjaha, Quraish, Rashid, Shahram and Yam – as well as the tribal confederations: Anaza, Harb, Murrah, Mutair, Qahtan, Shammar and Utaiba. Thus the religious unity of the new and expanding Dar al Islam – now encompassing 200 Ikhwan settlements with many thousands of soldiers – was reinforced with filial connections.

Like the first converts to Islam in the mid-seventh century, the Ikhwan were fired with crusading zeal to spread the Wahhabi version of Islam to the farthest corners of the Arabian Peninsula and beyond. By 1920 their colonies had become the primary source of soldiery to Abdul Aziz. They proved to be excellent fighters. They were highly mobile and, being members of nomadic tribes, they were extraordinarily tenacious and hardy. On top of this, they were motivated by religious fervor. While fighting they used such Islamic war cries as "The Riders of Unity!" "The People of Unity!" and "The Winds of Paradise have blown/ Where are you, the Dissenter?!" If they won and lived, they felt proud to have been instruments in effecting a victory of virtue over sin. If they met death, they believed it transformed them into martyrs and thus guaranteed them a place in paradise. After all, Taqi al Din ibn Taimiya (1268–1328), one of the major inspirers of Abdul Wahhab, had stated: "Death of the martyr for the unification of all people in the cause of His word is the happiest, best, easiest and most virtuous of all deaths."[1] Finally, since the Ikhwan were engaged in Islamic jihad, they were religiously entitled to four-fifths of the booty, with only one-fifth going to the state.

In 1920 Abdul Aziz conquered Asir province south of Hijaz, a fertile region. The next year he dealt a final blow to his rival, Muhammad ibn Rashid, captured Hail, and proclaimed himself Sultan (Commander), a secular title. After he had added more territories to his domain in 1922, he became Sultan of Najd and its Dependencies. He couched every campaign in Islamic terms, as a struggle to punish either religious dissenters or those who had strayed from true Islam. Only then could his forces appropriate the booty as their legitimate reward.

Abdul Aziz wanted to seize Hijaz in order to control the lucrative traffic of Muslim pilgrims to Mecca and Medina. At the same time he was intent on clothing his actions in Islamic terms. By declaring himself caliph, Sharif Hussein provided Abdul Aziz with the kind of pretext he was looking for. At about the same time the British decided to punish Sharif Hussein for his continued refusal to sign an Anglo-Hijazi treaty by cutting off their subsidies to him: a development which emboldened Abdul Aziz to implement his plans. He condemned Sharif Hussein for the sacrilegious act of claiming to be the caliph, for the corrupt ways in which he managed Mecca and Medina, and for the desecration he caused to the holy places by letting Christians enter them. During the 1924 hajj season Abdul Aziz sponsored a conference of the ulama and lay notables, which was presided over by his father, Abdul Rahman, the nominal Imam. It called on the (Wahhabi) Ikhwan to act on behalf of the Islamic umma and overthrow the false caliph, Sharif Hussein. Messages to this effect were sent to the leaders of Muslim communities throughout the world for their endorsement. Given the trepidation which most foreign Muslim leaders felt about the prospect of Wahhabis gaining administrative control of Mecca and Medina, very few responded. But the exercise served Abdul Aziz's purpose. He had created an Islamic aura around his impending military action, and by so doing actively discouraged the British, the ultimate underwriters of Sharif Hussein's power, from siding with him. In early October the Ikhwan led by Abdul Aziz laid siege around Mecca. To avoid bloodshed and destruction, the local ulama and traders prevailed upon Sharif Hussein to abdicate in favour of his son, Ali, and leave Mecca. For his part Abdul Aziz promised that there would be no repetition of the violent 1803 takeover of Mecca by the Wahhabis. Ali fled. Abdul Aziz occupied Mecca. A year later Medina surrendered to the Ikhwan.

"I have no wish to be the master of Hijaz," Abdul Aziz wrote to the heads of various governments in Muslim countries. "It is a mandate that has been entrusted to me until the Hijazis have chosen a governor who can consider himself servant of the Muslim world and who will work under the watchful eye of the Muslim people."[2] Obviously, Abdul Aziz had learned from the experience of his forefathers that, unlike other parts of the Arabian Peninsula, the fate of Hijaz mattered enormously to the leaders of foreign Muslims, and that it would be foolhardy to ignore this fact. At the same time there was no doubt in his mind as to whom Hijazis would "choose" as their governor.

In early 1926 Abdul Aziz proclaimed himself King of Hijaz, the title used earlier by Sharif Hussein; it was intended to reassure foreign Muslims who would have protested vehemently had Abdul Aziz declared himself Imam of Hijaz. He was aware of the need to reassure foreign Muslim communities that Mecca and Medina would remain open to all Muslim sects. In order to impress the pilgrims with the welcome changes he had implemented, he prescribed capital punishment for any Hijazi trying to swindle pilgrims or extort protection money from them – a common practice during the Hashimi rule. He allowed Hijazi courts to follow the Hanafi school of law, as they had done before his conquest, and not the Hanbali school which prevailed elsewhere in Abdul Aziz's domain.

While these steps went some way to reassure local Hijazis and foreign pilgrims, they caused a rift between Abdul Aziz and his

Ikhwan followers who, now settled in 222 colonies, numbered more than 150,000 men.[3]

The fast growth of Ikhwan settlements, in both number and size, meant a greater demand on the treasury of Abdul Aziz. Only the booty gained from a succession of victorious campaigns in the early 1920s allowed Abdul Aziz to overcome the problem. Administering Hijaz was an expensive business, and a tax on tobacco had been a major contributor to the state revenue during the Hashimi rule. Abdul Aziz's decision to continue the tobacco tax met with stiff opposition from Wahhabi ulama. They argued that since smoking tobacco was un-Islamic (and punishable in Najd) levying tax on it was also un-Islamic. Abdul Aziz reluctantly accepted their ruling. But, soon, pleading insufficient funds, he refused to pay salaries or give gifts to the Ikhwan. This created disaffection among them.

In late 1926 two militant Ikhwan leaders – Faisal al Dawish of Artawiya colony (and Mutair tribal federation) and Ibn Humaid Sultan ibn Bijad of Ghatghat colony (and Utaiba tribal federation) – convened a conference. It criticized Abdul Aziz for levying un-Islamic taxes, failing to impose the Wahhabi doctrine on the Shias of Hasa, and using telephones, telegraphs, cars and planes in whose working magic, and therefore the devil, was involved.

Abdul Aziz responded by convening a conference in January 1927. He abolished all the non-Islamic laws of Hijaz, and ordered that all Shias attend classes in Wahhabism and stop celebrating publicly their festival of mourning – Ashura. The ulama attending the conference ruled that levying un-Islamic taxes was not sufficient ground for the faithful to disobey the Imam.

These moves only postponed a confrontation between Abdul Aziz and the Ikhwan, which seemed inevitable, and which had many precedents in Islamic history – replete with examples of temporal and spiritual forces allying to achieve certain aims and then parting bitterly, with the temporal force emerging victorious.

In practical terms, having conquered 80 percent of the over 1 million square miles (2.59 million km^2) of the Arabian Peninsula with a population of 1.3 million, there was virtually no more territory left for Abdul Aziz to capture. So he had little use for a militant force of 150,000 Ikhwan fanatically committed to the tenets of Wahhabism. Having declared himself King of Najd and its Dependencies in January 1927, Abdul Aziz sought international recognition. He was keen to secure it from Britain, the single most important foreign power in the peninsula. The result was the 1927 Treaty of Jiddah. London recognized Abdul Aziz as King of Hijaz and Najd and its Dependencies. In return Abdul Aziz accepted Britain as the "protector" of the Arab principalities in the Gulf and Oman, and the integrity of Transjordan and Iraq under British mandate. This meant having to rein in the Ikhwan to whom fixed, Western-style borders were meaningless, and whose fervor to spread the Wahhabi creed to the rest of the world remained undiminished.

Their continued raids on the territories outside Abdul Aziz's domain strained relations between the Ikhwan and their ruler. When the British insisted on restitution for the Ikhwan raids, Abdul Aziz resorted to confiscating the booty that the Ikhwan were entitled to on such occasions (provided their actions been sanctified by the imam or ulama). In early 1929, after failing to cross into British-controlled Iraq, the Ikhwan spent their aggressive energies on the mainly Shia tribes on their side of the border. This enraged Abdul Aziz. He ordered the disbanding of the Ikhwan. His decree was ignored. He secured a ruling from the ulama that attacking the Ikhwan was now legitimate, and began to enlarge his army with recruits from the tribes and townsmen. He led an army of 30,000, equipped with motorized weapons supplied by the British, to confront 8,000 Ikhwan headed by Faisal al Dawish and Sultan ibn Bijad at Sabila in March 1929, and defeated them.

However, the Ikhwans' final demise did not occur until December. They found themselves sandwiched between the advancing forces of Abdul Aziz and the British contingents in Kuwait. Large-scale desertions reduced their ranks. Finally they surrendered to the British, who passed them on to Abdul Aziz. He punished them mercilessly to ensure that no such revolt would ever occur again.

So, what finally destroyed the Ikhwan was the acceptance by Abdul Aziz – the one-time Imam of the Islamic umma – of fixed, Western-style frontiers, and his crushing attack on them with the active assistance of the Christian British. Between waging an eternal jihad against Dar al Harb, the non-Muslim world, and building a power base in one country, Abdul Aziz chose the latter.

In September 1932 Abdul Aziz combined his two domains into one and named it the Kingdom of Saudi Arabia, proclaiming himself its king. The national flag carrying the Islamic *shahada* (central precept) and the crossed swords respectively of Muhammad ibn Abdul Wahhab and the House of Saud aptly symbolized the new political entity.

Having established a state (in the modern sense of the word), the House of Saud has used Islam to legitimize its dynastic rule. Saudi Arabia is unique. Created out of a series of Islamic campaigns in modern times, its character as a fundamentalist polity has remained unchanged since its inception in 1932. It is thus the oldest politically independent Islamic fundamentalist state in the world. And given its history steeped in Islam during the era of Prophet Muhammad and in more recent times, it is the most revered country in the Muslim world.

Fundamental Islam and the modern state

Strictly speaking, kingship and hereditary power have no Islamic sanction. This is obvious from the early history of Islam. The caliph was chosen by consultation among either traditional community elders or an electoral college appointed by the reigning caliph. Contrary to this practice, the Imams of the House of Saud had taken to naming their successors, and establishing dynastic rule.

Faced with criticism on this ground, Abdul Aziz and his successors replied that the Quran was the constitution of Saudi Arabia, and since the king was as much subject to Quranic dictates as any other believer, monarchy was legitimate in Islam.

There was yet another Islamic principle which was flouted by the House of Saud: consultation with the subjects in running the state. A verse in the Quran says: "So pardon them [believers], and pray forgiveness for them, and take counsel with them in the affair; and when thou art resolved, put thy trust in God" (3:153).[4] To be sure, when Abdul Aziz acquired the title of King of Hijaz, he announced the establishment of a 24-member consultative council, consisting of ulama, lay notables and merchants. It played an insignificant role for a while, and then disappeared unceremoniously. Sixty-seven years would pass before his fourth successor, King Fahd ibn Abdul Aziz (1921– ; r. 1982–), would appoint a fully nominated consultative council.

The possession of Mecca and Medina enabled Abdul Aziz to emphasize his role as the Custodian of the Holy Places and the Patron of Hajj, and paint the House of Saud in deeply Islamic colours. Actually Abdul Aziz's status was far more complex and weighty. Not only was he the head of state, commander in chief and head of the royal family but he was also the leader of all tribal chiefs (*shaikh al mashaikh*). And as the Custodian of the Holy Places, he acquired the status of the Protector of the Faith.

However, Abdul Aziz founded his kingdom at a time of economic crisis caused by a severe drop in the number of pilgrims (because of a worldwide depression) and therefore in the pilgrimage tax payable to his government. It was against this backdrop that he granted an oil concession to Standard Oil Company of California (Socal) in 1933 for £50,000, paid in gold, as advance against future royalties on actual oil production. Exploration began immediately in Hasa, and modest commercial extraction followed five years later.

World War II interrupted oil production. But, once the war was over in 1945, output jumped from 50,000 barrels per day (bpd) in 1946 to 900,000 bpd five years later. Two years later came the establishment of Arabian American Oil Company (Aramco), a consortium of Socal (later Chevron), Texaco, Mobil Oil and Standard Oil Company of New Jersey (later Esso, then Exxon). The 1951–3 crisis caused by oil nationalization in Iran caused a spurt in the demand for Saudi petroleum. The subsequent boom in the economy overstretched the rudimentary institutions of the state supervised by Abdul Aziz and some of his close relatives. Yet it was not until October 1953 – a month before his death – that King Abdul Aziz issued a decree establishing a council of ministers as an advisory body.

Five more years passed before the new ruler, King Saud ibn Abdul Aziz (1902–69; r. 1953–64), gave executive and legislative powers to the ministers. He did so only because by then the country's administration, lacking any budget or even an accounting system, had come to a virtual halt, and Crown Prince Faisal ibn Abdul Aziz (1904–75; r. 1964–75) had been put in overall charge of state affairs.

In 1960 a draft constitution, declaring Islam to be the state religion, describing private property and capital as "fundamental values of natural wealth," and specifying the creation of a National Assembly of 90 to 120 members – two-thirds elected and the rest nominated by the monarch – was presented to King Saud for approval. He rejected the document, stating blithely, "The Quran is the oldest and the most efficient of the world's constitutions."[5]

But the overthrow of religious monarchy in neighboring North Yemen on 27 September 1962 made the Saudi royal family anxious. On 6 November Crown Prince Faisal issued a 10-point program covering the constitutional, religious, judicial, social and economic aspects of the state. It declared its commitment to the improvement of "the lot of the average citizen" through intensified economic development and the implementation of "social legislation." It promised the issuance of a "Basic Law" (i.e. constitution), based on the Quran and the Hadiths, which would provide a citizen with his fundamental rights, including "the right to freely express his opinion within the limits of Islamic belief and public policy." It also pledged to reform the existing Committees for Propagating Virtue and Preventing Vice (*Hayat al Amr bil Maruf wal Nahyan al Munkar*) in accordance with the Sharia, and establish a Supreme Judicial Council of 20 members to reconcile the legal problems of modern society with the Sharia. (Forty years on, the kingdom still lacks a written constitution.

And it was not until 1975 that the promised Supreme Judicial Council was formed.)

In the kingdom, religious hierarchy is interwoven with secular authority at all levels. Locally, the religious establishment – the imam, the ulama and the *qadi* (religious judge) – works in conjunction with the government administrator along the lines followed earlier in Ikhwan colonies. The muttawin (religious police) execute the local imam's decisions. They ensure that Islamic practices are observed, that businesses close during prayer times, that women in the street are clad in modest, Islamic dresses, that no alcohol is consumed, and that during Ramadan there is no infringement of the ban on food and drink between sunrise and sunset. They also instruct the faithful at educational institutions, and outside, on the observance of Islamic edicts. At the national level the king is assisted in religious and judicial matters by the minister of religion/justice, traditionally a descendant of Muhammad ibn Abdul Wahhab, and the chief qadi.

In 1970, following the death of Shaikh Muhammad bin Ibrahim al Aal Shaikh, King Faisal replaced the Office of the Grand Mufti (also called Shaikh al Islam), the head of Sharia courts, with the Ministry of Justice, making sure that it was headed by a respected alim from the family of Abdul Wahhab, known as Aal Shaikh. Whereas the Grand Mufti had been an independent religious authority, the justice minister, being a member of the cabinet, was required to follow the monarch's instructions. This change put the final seal on the subordination of the ulama to the political authority of the Saudi king, a situation reminiscent of the Ottoman court. In the mid-eighteenth century, though, the founders of the Saudi dynasty and the Wahhabi doctrine were equally dependent on each other. The balance had shifted perceptibly in favor of the House of Saud during the rule of Abdul Aziz. Indeed, once Abdul Aziz had gradually replaced Hanafi jurists in Hijaz with Hanbalis, the ulama as a body came to rely exclusively on the state for their livelihood and status. With this, Saudi Arabia fell in line with most other Sunni countries where the ulama are dependent on the state for their livelihood.

In Saudi Arabia, however, the ulama enjoy more power and prestige than in any other Sunni state. They are the key element bestowing legitimacy on the Saudi regime. This became clear during the crisis caused by King Saud's scandalous extravagance and mismanagement of public funds which led to an open split in the royal family, with the monarch appointing a new cabinet and handing over premiership, his prerogative, to Crown Prince Faisal ibn Abdul Aziz, well-known for his fiscal responsibility. This lasted until late 1960 when the monarch reasserted his executive authority and demoted Faisal to deputy prime minister. In that capacity, Faisal, son of an Aal Shaikh mother, Tarlah, and renowned for his piety and asceticism, established in 1963 the Supreme Council of Religious Judges (SCRJ, *Al Majlis al Ali lil Qada*) and the Institute for Fatwas and Study and Supervision of Religion (*Dar al Ifta wal Ishraf 'ala'l Shuaun al Diniyya*). In late March 1964 a dozen members of the SCRJ issued a ruling that while Saud should remain king, Crown Prince Faisal should supervise all internal and external affairs without consulting the monarch. The next day 70 senior princes, representing all six branches of the House of Saud, endorsed the SCRJ's ruling. But Saud refused to act as a figurehead, and called on the SCRJ to reconsider its decision. On 29 October 1964 a conclave of all senior ulama, including the members of the SCRJ, invoked the Sharia principle of "public interest," and ruled that King Saud should step down and that Faisal should assume the highest office. About 100 senior princes backed the senior ulama.

Faced with a formidable alliance of the religious establishment and an overwhelming majority of the royal household, Saud prepared to use his military power. He mobilized his well-trained, well-armed, elite 2,700-strong Royal Guard, by deploying them around his pink palace in Riyadh, ready to confront the National Guard – the successor to the White Guard established by Abdul Aziz in 1932 with a sprinkling of former Ikhwan fighters, now consisting of 10,000 lightly armed tribal levies – loyal to Faisal, with the regular army staying neutral. The impasse ended when, in the middle of the night, National Guard officers arrived in a fleet of taxis at the house of the Royal Guard commander and arrested him.[6] Saud abdicated on 2 November, and left the country – to die in Athens a little over four years later, leaving behind 52 sons and 55 daughters. Faisal ruled until March 1975, when he was shot dead by an American-educated, disgruntled junior prince.

One of the important functions of senior ulama is to advise on the drafting of royal orders, called *nizams*, which regulate Saudi society in those areas where fiqh is either absent or insufficient or radically out of tune with the modern age. The Saudi government views the issuing of such regulations as part of its administrative effort to implement the Sharia rather than expanding or altering it. Such a legislative practice is firmly rooted in the history of Islam, and goes back at least nine centuries. The Ottomans had a distinct term for such laws: *qanun*. The earliest example of qanun in the Saudi kingdom was the Commercial Code decreed by Abdul Aziz in 1931. During King Saud's rule came a revision of the Commercial Code along the lines of the Western-influenced Ottoman Commercial Code – and the promulgation of the laws on nationality, forgery, bribery and mining. In 1961 he promulgated the State Security Act prescribing the death penalty or 25 years' imprisonment for anybody convicted of "an aggressive act" against the state or the royal family. Among the important laws King Faisal decreed were those on labor and workmen, social insurance and civil service.

Such actions are permitted in the Hanbali school of Islamic law. While it demands strict application of the Quran and the Hadiths, it is quite flexible in the areas not covered by these scriptures. Also Hanbali jurists never closed their doors to ijtihad (independent reasoning) for those areas where the Quran and the Hadiths are vague. Furthermore, jurists are allowed to choose a ruling from other recognized schools where their own school is silent or confused on a particular subject. Finally, the Hanbali school accepts the general Islamic principle of "public interest" or "welfare of society" which, for instance, was invoked by the ulama to demand the deposition of King Saud.

When it comes to coping with the day-to-day problems of staying within what is legitimate in Islam in the face of new situations and modern inventions, Saudi rulers apply the general criterion of "welfare of society." It was on this basis that Abdul Aziz found telephones, telegraph, cars and airplanes acceptable. But most Ikhwan leaders held different views: they saw these contraptions as the works of the devil. Yielding to their pressure, Abdul Aziz postponed using these inventions, but not for long.

However, Ikhwan leaders were not the only ones to oppose modern technology. Certain senior ulama did too. When it came to radio, Shaikh Abdullah ibn Hussein al Aal Shaikh, the chief qadi of Hijaz, believed that since it was Satan who carried messages through the air the operators at the kingdom's radio stations were guilty of being Satan worshippers. Abdul Aziz arranged for the Quran to be read at Riyadh radio station for Shaikh Abdullah ibn Hussein to hear it in Mecca, thus proving that Satan was not involved: it was unthinkable that Satan would carry the Word of God even a single inch forward. From then on radio became Allah's own miracle.

As petroleum exploration and extraction got going there was an increasing presence of American and other Western oil technicians in the kingdom. Abu Bahz, a former Ikhwan leader, criticized King Abdul Aziz for this and argued that the monarch was helping non-believers to gain profit from Muslims. Abdul Aziz called Abu Bahz and a group of leading ulama to his court in Riyadh. He showed himself to be well versed in the life and traditions of Prophet Muhammad, and referred to several instances where the Prophet had engaged non-Muslims, singly or jointly, for specific jobs. "Am I right or wrong?" he reportedly asked. Those present replied that he was right. "Am I breaking the Sharia, therefore, when I follow in the footsteps of the Prophet, and employ foreign experts to work for me . . . under my direction to increase the material resources of the land, and to extract for our benefit the metals, oil and water placed by Allah beneath our land intended for our use?" Abdul Aziz inquired. The unanimous view was that the monarch had not broken the Sharia.[7] Elsewhere he argued that as Christians the Americans and British were People of the Book, and therefore preferable to idolaters and back-sliders.

Abdul Aziz took issue with the ulama on photography. Islam forbids man's intervention in creating human forms, and thereby all graphic arts which involve human shapes and forms. Abdul Aziz argued that photography, being merely juxtaposition of light and shade, both created by Allah, was quite distinct from the pictorial arts. So photography was allowed in Saudi Arabia. It was on this foundation that King Faisal tried to introduce television in 1965. He faced stiff opposition from conservative ulama. So he introduced it stealthily, always insisting that television broadcasts – consisting exclusively of prayers, readings of the Quran and religious discussions – were being "tested" to assess the virtues and vices of the medium.

While Abdul Aziz and his successors had periodically to cajole the ulama to accept modern technology and rapid economic development, they fully agreed with the ulama that Saudi Arabians should not abandon their traditional ways of living and thinking for Western ones. This was particularly true of Abdul Aziz, who did not consider Europeans or Americans more civilized than Saudi Arabians. Since Saudi Arabia had undergone neither Western colonization nor governance by a local Westernized elite, which regarded the West as being the pace-setter in all endeavors of life, Saudi monarchs genuinely believed that as a social-moral system Islam was superior to any other.

As the oil industry expanded, and with it the size of the foreign population – Muslim and non-Muslim – and as Saudis themselves traveled abroad increasingly or pursued higher education at Western universities, Saudi Arabia began to lose something of its rigid, austere face. This worried the ulama and the monarch. In the autumn of 1967 King Faisal issued a proclamation which warned the country's youth against laxity in behavior and dress, and ordered that civil servants must stop working at prayer times and congregate for prayers on the premises, that school children must be segregated sexually at nine, and that all females aged nine or more must wear a veil. The proclamation had the enthusiastic backing of the ulama.

The ulama were well paid and well respected. They stayed in touch with the community by acting as counselors on personal problems, mediating in disputes and helping citizens in their dealings with the bureaucracy. They ran the judicial system where the Sharia's *hadd* punishments were in force: flogging for drinking alcohol, cutting off hands for stealing, and death by stoning for adultery committed by married adults. The Sharia courts, presided over by the ulama, were generally considered fair by the public. The ulama managed the affluent religious trusts which included not only numerous hostels endowed for use by poor pilgrims but also religious colleges in Riyadh, to be amalgamated into the Imam Muhammad ibn Saud Islamic University in 1974, to become the prime center of Wahhabism, producing religious teachers and jurists, coordinating all religious education, supervising the National Guard schools, and running retraining programs for the muttawin. They were in charge of organizing the hajj, a five-day ritual, which in the mid-1960s attracted up to a million Muslims from home and abroad. They ran the Committees for Propagating Virtue and Preventing Vice and their executive arm, the muttawin. As employees of the censorship department, the muttawin went through imported magazines blackening the photographs of improperly clothed women and adverts for alcohol. In the streets, armed with metal-tipped bamboo switches, they ensured that shops and offices closed for half an hour at prayer times when the muezzin called from the nearest mosque; that no alcoholic drinks or drugs were stored or consumed anywhere; and that women in the street wore an abaaya – a long black cloak with large sleeves that rests on the head and shoulders, anchoring the veil, often made of heavy gauzelike fabric that completely covers the face – at the top of the head, whose hair is covered by a tightly tied scarf.

In Saudi Arabia the role of women is defined strictly, according to the Quran, and these restrictions apply to all women, whether Muslim or not. The position of women derives from the premise that the family is the cornerstone of Muslim society, and that an Islamic state must create an environment where men are not tempted to indulge in extra-marital sex and thus undermine the foundation of family life. From this stems the prohibition on women driving motor vehicles or traveling alone or working alongside men to whom they are not related. A general view prevails among the ulama and others that Islam upgraded the position of women in the Arabia of the seventh century by conferring upon them the rights of marriage, divorce and inheritance. Since men are, broadly speaking, emotionally stable and intellectually superior – so the argument runs – they are entitled to lead society in general and the family in particular. A woman's primary role is as wife and mother, and so her education should be directed mainly along these lines.

There was resistance from the ulama to women's education *per se* in Saudi Arabia. Faisal and his (one and only) wife, Iffat bint Ahmad al Thunayan, introduced girls' education in 1960. The Quran, argued Faisal, enjoins learning on every believing Muslim, whether male or female. Despite this it took a few years before the idea of female education was formally accepted by the ulama.

Faisal enjoyed high standing among the ulama before and after he became king. Through his mother he claimed lineage from Abdul Wahhab, the progenitor of Wahhabism. He lived a spartan life, and his piety was legendary. He increased the salaries of the ulama and at the same time strengthened state control over them. Following the death of the Grand Mufti, Shaikh Muhammad bin Ibrahim al Aal Shaikh, in 1969, he did not appoint his successor. Two years later he established the Council of Committee of Senior Ulama (*Al Majlis Hayat Kibar al Ulama*) – better known as the Council of Senior Ulama (COSU) – whose membership has varied between 17 and 22. It included the heads of the Supreme Council of Religious Judges and the Institute for Fatwas and Study and Supervision of Religion as well as the justice minister. But unlike the Grand Mufti, who was free to issue fatwas on subjects he regarded as important, the COSU was required to give its opinion only on the subjects referred to it by the ruler. By so doing Faisal put a final seal on the subordination of the Wahhabi religious establishment to the House of

Saud. Concerning the balance of power between the ruler and the ruled, ignoring his 10-point program of November 1962, promising inter alia constitutional reform, he had on ascending the throne two years later repeated his predecessor's statement: "Saudi Arabia has no need for a constitution because it has the Quran, which is the oldest and most efficient constitution in the world."[8] Within the House of Saud, he met the princes' demand for a share in the kingdom's rising oil income through largesse from the public funds by the ingenious device of allocating them vast areas of arid, desert land. In the aftermath of the oil price hike in 1973–4, the real estate value would explode, with a hectare of land, worth $3 in the 1960s, selling for $6,000 in 1980 to meet the fast-rising demand for highways, housing, factories and airports.[9] Faisal raised his popularity among his subjects by introducing price controls, and authorizing generous grants for educational and health facilities.

The October 1973 Arab–Israeli War added further to Faisal's prestige. By dispatching several thousand troops to Jordan and Syria, and agreeing with Arab oil ministers' decision to embargo oil exports to Israel's backers, and cutting Saudi output by 25 percent,[10] he scored a double hit. He showed that he was an Arab nationalist and simultaneously helped to secure a quadrupling of the oil price, from $2.65 a barrel to $11. In 1974, the kingdom's oil revenue reached $22.57 billion, a 36-fold increase in a decade.[11] Little wonder that at $142 billion, the Second Five Year Plan was 18 times the size of the First Plan. More than 80 percent of the First Plan funds were earmarked for building or expanding the infrastructure of roads, communications and power plants. These ambitious projects could only be realized by importing a vast pool of foreign workers from other Arab countries and elsewhere. The presence of a large number of single, unmarried men created a host of social and other problems.

Saudi society itself underwent profound social change. The oil boom led to a rapid and dramatic expansion of urban centers, and an equally rapid disappearance of villages and nomadic tribes. In the mid-1970s nomads formed only 10 percent of the indigenous national population of 4.3 million. Urbanization and commercialization undermined tribal loyalties, a process which had been accelerated by such governmental actions as the nationalization of water supplies and active discouragement of tribal attachment to specific grazing lands and certain water wells.

On the other hand, the oil boom acted as cement to hold the vastly inflated royal family together. There were now over 4,000 princes, one half of them direct descendants of Abdul Aziz, and the other half those of his five brothers and first cousins. Between them they held most of the top civilian and military positions, and ran leading commercial companies. In a sense the inflated royal family paralleled the single ruling party in many secular Third World countries, held together by blood rather than any particular social ideology.

Yet there were always some malcontents. One senior prince, Talal, had in August 1962 defected to Egypt, then led by Nasser, an enemy of King Faisal, and formed the Liberation Front of Arabia. Later, after he had relented, he was welcomed back into the royal fold. In August 1965 another prince, Khalid ibn Musaid, led his followers in an attack on Riyadh television station. He and his close associates were killed by the security police. It transpired later that Prince Khalid ibn Musaid was the leader of the revived Ikhwan movement and that he had opposed Faisal's modernization plans in private before mounting his dramatic assault on the television station. Some ten years later, on 25 March 1975, his younger brother, Faisal ibn Musaid, assassinated King Faisal. The 28-year-old prince had personal and political reasons for his action. There was the killing of his brother to be avenged. There was also the element of inter-tribal feuding since the mother of these two princes was from Rashidi tribe, a traditional rival of the Anza tribal confederation to which the royal house belonged. Faisal ibn Musaid was engaged to a daughter of King Saud, in whose deposition Crown Prince Faisal had played a crucial role. The later discovery that the young prince had received military training at one of the Palestinian camps in Lebanon meant that he was a political radical of some kind.

Beyond the portals of royalty there existed opposition to the monarch from secular quarters: Arab nationalists operating either as Nasserists or Baathists (members of the Arab Baath Socialist Party that ruled Syria and Iraq), and Marxists. In March 1955 and again in September 1956 the government thwarted coup plots by Arab nationalist military officers and civilians.[12] In the 1970s the secular opposition groups, functioning clandestinely, declined partly due to the success the Saudi government had in buying off expatriate opponents. Their place was taken by radical Islamist groups. The revival of the Ikhwan was part of that process. It was to mature in the late 1970s in the form of a dramatic assault on the legitimacy of the Saudi monarchy.

The accession in March 1975 of Crown Prince Khalid ibn Abdul Aziz (1913–82; r. 1975–82) came at a time when the Saudi economy was entering a period of boom. The overheated economy and the concomitant socio-religious problems caused differences within the ruling elite. One group led by King Khalid and Prince Abdullah, head of the National Guard, advocated a slower pace of industrialization and closer adherence to the Wahhabi doctrine. Born in Riyadh and educated in the Quran by a palace tutor, Khalid was rooted in traditional values. Like his father, Abdul Aziz, he received his subjects daily, listening to their complaints and appeals for money. A pious man, he drank camel's milk and mixed with tribal chiefs during his long hunting expeditions, thus underlining his accessibility and nurturing emotional ties between the governor and the governed. Though born in the royal household, Abdullah, a superb horseman with limited education, untutored in English, was beduin at heart, and possessed the qualities required of a tribal chief – courage, generosity, piety and leadership – which endeared him to the National Guard soldiers. The opposing group, led by Crown Prince Fahd and Prince Sultan (1923–), in charge of the Ministry of Defense and Aviation since its inception in 1964, wanted a faster pace of industrialization accompanied by greater religio-cultural liberalization and closer ties with America. Given his widely known propensity

for pursuing the joys of the flesh – drinking, gambling and fornication – his mastery of English, and his US-educated sons, Fahd
was a point of departure among the ruling royals, more of a tech-
nocrat than a tribal shaikh. The conflict between the two camps
was building up and would have most likely led to a showdown
– but for the Mecca uprising in late 1979 which made the royals
close ranks for their survival.

Meanwhile, Saudi Arabia was generous in its purchase of
US treasury bonds to prop up the ailing American dollar. It
reinforced its intelligence and military links with Washington.
Saudi contacts with the West had grown to the extent that the
number of Saudi students at universities in the West, particularly
in America, was far higher than the 14,500 at home. The vigorous
implementation of the economic and military plans – including
the construction of three military cities – led to a rapid rise
in the American presence in the kingdom. In early 1977 the
number of American civilian and military personnel was
30,000: five times the figure in 1971.[13] In their day-to-day business
they often dealt with Saudi ministers and top civil servants who
were themselves US-educated and enamored of the American
lifestyle.

The rapid spending of billions of dollars had its own logic.
Corruption and kickbacks on contracts in the public and private
sectors reached unprecedented proportions, and fostered billion-
aire princes. "For every purchase the government makes, the
princes who negotiate the contract receive their cut," reported
Sandra Mackey, an American journalist. "In ministry after
ministry, purchases are often determined not by need but by
who is on the receiving end of the commission." Also princes
became the legally required Saudi partners of foreign construction and service corporations operating in the kingdom, secured
contracts from ministries and enriched themselves on a percentage of the profits. One such deal involved $100 million in
agent's fees.[14] Along with this went a decline in public morality.
The un-Islamic behavior of many princes and their close associates as well as prospering businessmen within the privacy of their
palaces – involving drinking, gambling and fornication – became

grist to the gossip mills at home and abroad. There were also growing mutterings against the excessive presence of Americans in the oil industry, military and the National Guard.

Soon after his accession King Khalid considered establishing a consultative council, but nothing came of it. In mid-1978 Crown Prince Fahd opposed the notion of representative government on the ground that elections would not confer leadership on the country's most qualified people: the young Saudis who had received university education at home or in the West. "We have invested heavily in educating these young men, and now we want to collect a dividend on our investment," he told *Time* magazine. "But if we were to have elections . . . the winners would be rich businessmen."[15]

But the overthrow of the dictatorial Muhammad Reza Pahlavi of Iran by a popular Islamic republican movement led by Ayatollah Ruhollah Khomeini in February 1979 alarmed the Saudi royal family. The Iranian media, particularly radio, often attacked the decadent lifestyle of many members of the House of Saud. King Khalid responded by decreeing that no prince should vacation abroad during Ramadan, a device frequently used by the royals and their families to avoid the rigor of fasting between sunrise and sunset for a whole month. The revitalized Committees for Propagating Virtue and Preventing Vice closed all beauty parlors and hairdressing salons and forbade women to try on garments on the premises of clothing stores. Yielding to their pressure the government banned all non-Islamic services, including confirmation classes at foreign schools in the kingdom. The sale of crosses, even as jewelry, was prohibited. Ever since the rule of Abdul Aziz there had existed a ban on the building of any church or temple of a non-Islamic faith. This was in accordance with the words of Prophet Muhammad on his death-bed: "Let there be no two religions in Arabia."

During the hajj season in October–November the Saudi authorities awaited with trepidation the arrival of the Iranian pilgrims, imbued with revolutionary fervor. But the hajj passed off peacefully. It was on 1 Muharram (20 November 1979), the New Year's Day – which also marked the beginning of Islam's fifteenth century – that the House of Saud was severely shaken. At 05.20 hours on that day some 400 well-armed Islamic militants, calling themselves the Ikhwan, took over Islam's holiest shrine, the Grand Mosque in Mecca. Their military leader was 40-year-old Juhaiman ibn Saif al Utaiba, and their religious leader 27-year-old Muhammad ibn Abdullah al Qahtani, brother-in-law of Juhaiman.

Juhaiman was born around 1939 in the Utaiba colony of Sajir in the west-central province of Qasim, and was a grandson of an Ikhwan militant who died in the battle of Sabila in 1929 fighting Abdul Aziz. He grew up when the memory of that battle was still fresh among the Arabian tribes. In his late teens he joined the National Guard, and rose to become a corporal. However, military discipline seemed to frustrate his fierce piety and his vocal opposition to the presence of non-Muslim Westerners in the kingdom's institutions (including the National Guard) and elsewhere. In 1972 he left the force after 15 years' service. He enrolled at the Islamic University of Medina, an institution set up in 1961 by leading Egyptian Muslim Brothers after they had convinced the Saudi monarch that President Nasser was misusing Al Azhar and that an alternative center of Islamic learning was sorely needed. At this university Juhaiman became a student of Shaikh Abdul Aziz ibn Abdullah al Baz (1911–99), the rector since 1969. Shaikh al Baz advocated a return to the letter of the Quran and the Hadiths, and decried innovation of any kind. Juhaiman imbibed al Baz's teachings and applied them to the actions of the Saudi dynasty only to conclude that the Saudi rulers had deviated from the true path of Islam. Juhaiman's uncompromising stance towards the House of Saud created friction between him and al Baz, and led to his expulsion in 1974.

Accompanied by 10 of his followers, Juhaiman retired to his native Qasim and began preaching along the lines of Shaikh Abdul Wahhab in the mid-eighteenth century. Juhaiman was a charismatic figure, courageous and a natural leader. He was also a popular poet and writer on Islam. He set up cells in numerous beduin settlements in Qasim. His followers were inspired by militant piety, a recurring theme in Islam through the centuries.

In 1976 he and his close followers moved to Riyadh. There he published a pamphlet, *Rules of Allegiance and Obedience: The Misconduct of Rulers*. In it he attacked the Saudi rulers for their deviation from the Sharia, their greed and corruption, misuse of the laws for their personal benefit, and for mixing with atheists and unbelievers.

In that year Saudi Arabia became the top oil supplier to the US. In December, Patrick Seale of the *Observer* reported that Riyadh and Washington had struck a secret deal whereby America was assured of Saudi oil in exchange for "far reaching protection of the Saudi regime."[16] The tightening of links between the two countries was reflected in the increased number of Americans, civilian and military, in the kingdom during 1971–6, from 6,000 to 30,000.[17]

In the summer of 1978 the government arrested Juhaiman and 98 of his followers in Riyadh. Shaikh al Baz, then head of the Council for the Committee of Senior Ulama, was called from Medina to interview them. He concluded that what they had been propagating was not treasonable. Their six-week-long detention ended when they promised not to undertake subversive actions or propaganda.

They were kept under surveillance. But Juhaiman and his close associates gave the intelligence agents the slip. Juhaiman took to clandestine preaching and developed the idea of *mahdi* (the one guided by God) which he allied to the traditional Wahhabi doctrine. The concept of mahdi, one who will restore the faith and usher in a golden age while claiming divine sanction, is not as sharply defined in Sunni tradition as it is in Judaism, Christianity and Shia Islam. Among Sunnis the prevalent concept is that of *mujaddid* (renewer of faith). The idea is rooted in the hadith revealed by Abu Huraira, a companion of Prophet Muhammad, and recorded by Abu Daoud.[18] As a renewer of the faith, the mujaddid appears every (Islamic) century to defend the sunna from *bida* (innovation). So the belief goes. A mujaddid is not a messiah, a mahdi; and he may be recognized only after his death. For instance, many Muslims regard Hassan al Banna as a mujaddid. In contrast, a mahdi claims divine sanction and is recognized by the people as a messiah during his lifetime. One of the earliest references to al Mahdi al Muntazir, the Awaited Messiah, appears in *Muqqadimina* by Abdul Rahman ibn Khaldun (1332–1406), an eminent Arab historian.

> There will arise a difference at the death of a caliph, and a man of Medina will go forth, fleeing to Mecca. Then some of the people of Mecca will come to him, and make him go out against his will, and they will swear allegiance between the rukn [courtyard of the Grand Mosque] and the maqam Ibrahim [building beside the Kaaba containing a stone with Prophet Abraham's footprint]. And an army will be sent against him from Syria, but [it] will be swallowed up in the earth in the desert between Mecca and Medina.[19]

What Juhaiman al Utaiba did was to study the traditions about the mahdi meticulously and publish them in August 1979 in his pamphlet, *The Call of the Ikhwan*. In his brother-in-law, Muhammad ibn Abdullah al Qahtani, a former student of Imam Muhammad ibn Saud Islamic University in Riyadh, he had found the mahdi with the name of the Prophet, and a surname which was a derivative of Qahtan, the legendary ancestor of Arabs. To this fact he attached the notion, widely held among Sunnis, that a mujaddid appears once every century. The new Islamic century was to begin on 1 Muharram (20 November), and on that day he and his close aides expected King Khalid to be present at the Grand Mosque in Mecca to offer his dawn prayers. Given his military expertise, his wish to avenge the death of his Ikhwan grandfather, his fierce piety, his charisma and the tradition of tribal retribution, Juhaiman al Utaiba was an ideal figure to lead an insurrection against the House of Saud.

During the hajj season he sent messages to his followers in the country to converge on the Grand Mosque in Mecca on the eve of the New Year's Day. They did so, having earlier smuggled and hidden arms in the labyrinthine cellars and retreats of the vast mosque.

On the fateful day, they were disappointed by the non-arrival of King Khalid at the Grand Mosque for dawn prayers (he was down with a severe cold, it was revealed later). None the less, Juhaiman al Utaiba and Muhammad al Qahtani went ahead with their plans. After their followers had closed all 48 gates of the mosque, Juhaiman delivered a speech in which he set out his ideology. It was mandatory for true Muslims to follow Prophet Muhammad's example of revelation, propagation and military struggle, he began. In the present circumstances genuine Muslims must overthrow their present Saudi rulers: they were deficient in Islamic attributes and had been forced upon the populace; and in any case in Islam there was no place for kings or dynasties. A legitimate Muslim ruler must govern according to the Sharia, must be a devout Muslim, originate from the Quraish tribe, and must be chosen by the Islamic umma. None of these attributes applied to Saudi monarchs. Islam must be grounded in the Quran and the Hadiths, and not on *taqlid* (imitation) of the interpretations offered by the ulama, as was the practice in contemporary Arabia. Believers must detach themselves from the present system by rejecting all official positions, he urged. The mahdi would come from the House of the Prophet, through the lineage of Imam Hussein ibn Ali, to counter impiety and taqlid, and to bring peace and justice to the believers. It was the duty of all true Muslims to establish an umma which protects Islam from unbelievers and refrains from courting non-Muslim aliens.[20] In short, Juhaiman issued a call for the overthrow of the Saudi monarchy and severance of ties with the unbelieving West. As for Qahtani, Juhaiman claimed mahdiship on his behalf, and referred to the tradition: "The mahdi and his men will seek shelter and protection in the Holy Mosque because they are persecuted everywhere until they have no recourse but the Holy Mosque." The gathering of many thousands of worshippers was stunned by this event and by the speed with which the armed militants had taken charge of the enormous mosque with a courtyard that could hold 250,000 worshippers.

It was significant that the revived Ikhwan led by Juhaiman al Utaiba and Qahtani challenged the deviation of King Khalid from true Islam and his alliance with the Americans just as the original Ikhwan had fought King Abdul Aziz for straying from the true faith and allying himself with the British.

King Khalid contacted the Council of the Senior Ulama to seek its ruling on the storming of the Grand Mosque. It was quick to point to the Quranic verse: "Do not fight them near the Holy Mosque until they fight you inside it, and if they fight you [inside], you must kill them for that is the punishment of the unbelievers."[21]

Recapture of the Grand Mosque proved to be a tortuous and bloody operation for the government. It had to deploy 10,000 security personnel of its own as well as thousands of Pakistani troops and a contingent of French anti-terrorist experts (who had to be given special dispensation to enter Mecca, closed to non-Muslims), and wage a fortnight-long battle to restore order. In the process 127 troops were killed, as were 25 worshippers and 117 Ikhwan members, including Qahtani. Of the 170 militants arrested, 67, including 26 non-Saudi Arabs, were beheaded. The uprising in the Grand Mosque and its bloody end severely damaged the prestige of the House of Saud, the custodians of Islam's foremost holy shrine. Distrustful of the loyalty of his armed forces, King Khalid would hire three Pakistani brigades, wearing Saudi military uniforms – including infantry, armored and anti-aircraft units – to safeguard the royal palaces and other sensitive sites, an arrangement that would last six years.[22]

For now, there was a news blackout of the event in Saudi Arabia as long as the crisis lasted. Later, however, the government made it a point to decapitate the 67 culprits in the public squares of different cities to impress on the people the severity of their crime and its determination to carry out the capital punishment. A study of the demographic and tribal backgrounds of the Saudi Ikhwan militants had disturbing implications for the authorities. In the main the radicals came from Najd, the power base of the Saudi dynasty. Many of the militants were Utaibas, members of the tribal confederation that included Sultan ibn Bijad, an Ikhwan leader who in 1929 confronted King Abdul Aziz. Tribal loyalties ran deep, and so did inter-tribal feuding.

The Ikhwan ranks also contained a substantial number of theological students, both Saudi and non-Saudi, the latter including Muslim Brothers from Egypt, Ansars from Sudan, and members of the Society of Social Reform in Kuwait. It was hard for observers inside Saudi Arabia or outside to gauge the feelings of ordinary Saudis about the uprising. Later, as the severity of the crisis became known, considerable sympathy for the rebels was detected among students, junior ulama and the lower- and middle-middle classes in cities and towns, and among those tribal chiefs who were opposed to the governmental policies of settling nomads and centralizing authority.

Undoubtedly the Mecca uprising was the severest shock that the Saudi dynasty had received in the half century since the 1929 Ikhwan rebellion. It was accustomed to attacks from the proponents of such alien ideologies as Western liberalism, nationalism and Marxism, and knew how to tackle them. But a frontal and bloody assault from the followers of orthodox Islam, on which the Saudi dynasty based its own legitimacy, was novel and carried extraordinarily dangerous implications. To placate traditional sensibilities, the government immediately removed women broadcasters from the Arabic-language television – albeit not from the English-language channel – and instructed the print media to stop publishing photographs of women. On the ideological front, it denounced the insurgents as Kharajis, the anarchic irridentists of early Islam, notorious for their terrorist tactics, which led to the death among others of Imam Ali. Its political-administrative response contained the usual mix of repression and reform, or at least a promise of the latter. It arrested about 7,000 sympathizers of the Ikhwan, and imposed stricter controls on the freedom of movement of expatriate workers. The size of the Interior Ministry would nearly double from its present strength of 64,000 employees (two-thirds of them engaged in fieldwork) in the next six years.[23] King Khalid reshuffled the top 17 military and civilian posts. And his government whittled down its rhetoric about rapid economic and technological development being the most effective way of safeguarding Islam. The following March it would appoint an eight-member committee to draft a constitution – a task which, 22 years on, would remained unaccomplished.

Among the young, university-educated Saudis who were pro-foundly affected by the Mecca uprising was a 22-year-old Osama bin Muhammad bin Awad bin Laden, a fresh civil engineering graduate of King Abdul Aziz University, Jiddah, where he had also studied business administration. "He was inspired by them [the Mecca insurgents]," a close friend of bin Laden informed the *Observer* many years later. "He told me these men were true Muslims and had followed a true path."[24]

Osama bin Laden had just started working for the family's Jiddah-based Saudi Binladin Group (SBG), founded by his father, Muhammad Awad bin Laden. An illiterate bricklayer from the Hadramaut region of Yemen, Muhammad had arrived in the Saudi kingdom's Hijaz region in 1925 when he was about 25, and worked on construction sites. In the late 1940s, he came to the notice of King Abdul Aziz when he suggested to the monarch an easy way to get around in his wheelchair to inspect his new palace. With the ruler's encouragement, he soon set up his own construction company which maintained close links with the royal family. In the early 1960s it was given the con-tract to rebuild the Grand Mosque in Mecca and the Prophet's Mosque in Medina. Muhammad was killed in 1968 when his private jet crashed into mountains in southern Saudi Arabia. Of the 54 children he sired by 11 wives, Osama – named after one of Prophet Muhammad's companions – was the only one of his 24 sons to be born to his youngest wife, Hamida Alia Ghanoum, from Syria. The bin Laden family was so close to the royal house that following Muhammad bin Laden's death, King Faisal told his sons, "I am going to be your father now." The monarch issued a royal decree to keep the bin Laden family and fortune together.[25] In 1974 after finishing his second-ary education at an elite Jiddah high school where, despite his shyness, he stood out because of his unusual height, Osama enrolled at King Abdul Aziz University. Though not an Islamic institution, the university offered many courses in religion, and Osama took advantage of that. As one of only three sons of

Muhammad bin Laden who did *not* study abroad, Osama was not exposed to life in the West at first hand.

About a month after the Mecca uprising, Moscow sent its troops into Afghanistan to bolster the Marxist government there. This angered Osama bin Laden. In the spring of 1980 he went to Peshawar, and stayed for a month. On his return to Jiddah, he successfully lobbied his brothers, relatives and friends to support the anti-Soviet struggle in Afghanistan. Some months later, he returned to Pakistan with the hefty donations he had collected in Saudi Arabia, and several Afghan and Pakistani employees of Saudi Binladin Group, to set up an office to support non-Afghan mujahedin. His activities dovetailed with the official Saudi policy.

Saudi Arabia's Islamic foreign policy

It has been a cardinal policy of Saudi monarchs to stress their roles as the custodians of the holy places, patrons of the hajj and supporters of Islamic causes throughout the world.

Due to the absence of European imperial rule in Arabia the idea of nationalism never took root there. The partition by the British and the French of the Arab part of the Ottoman empire left the Arabian Peninsula virtually untouched. The people and territories that Abdul Aziz brought under his control did not cohere as a nation-state. It was only under Faisal's leadership – exercised first during King Saud's reign – that the infrastructure of a modern state began to emerge. In general a state's foreign policy is based on the notion of national interest. But, by constantly stressing Islam, a universalist ideology, Saudi Arabia tended to de-emphasize nationalism.

In any case, during the days of Saud and Faisal the concept of an "Arab nation" – one Arab nation divided into 22 states – was being fostered by Nasser. In so far as Prophet Muhammad was an Arab from Arabia and it was through him, and in Arabic, that the Word of Allah was revealed to humanity in the form of the Quran, King Faisal and his followers took pride in being Arab. But to them, articulating and fostering the idea of the Arab nation as a separate entity, apart from the Islamic umma, was unacceptable. Faisal expressed this view forcefully to counter Nasser's attacks on him and his kingdom, as being corrupt and reactionary. Faisal contended that Arab nationalism was a Trojan horse to smuggle into the Arab world alien doctrines like socialism. To meet the ideological challenge of pan-Arabism, Faisal, in consultation with the Wahhabi religious establishment, chose to raise the regime's religious credentials by stressing Islam further in the educational system. This decision would over the coming decades result in the Saudi kingdom becoming a rich source of young men ready to martyr themselves in the name of Islam.

As it happened, in May 1962 Nasser transformed the National Union, Egypt's ruling party, into the Arab Socialist Union with a national charter that adopted Arab socialism as its doctrine. This was the time of the hajj. At Faisal's behest a group of senior ulama in Saudi Arabia issued a statement condemning socialism as being inimical to Islam. "We believe neither in socialism nor in communism, nor in any doctrine outside Islam," it declared. "We only believe in Islam."[26]

Soon Faisal set up the World Muslim League (WML) in Geneva. Its function was to hold seminars and conferences on Islam, and act as a mouthpiece of Saudi Arabia in its interpretation of Islam. "The Islamic world forms one collectivity united by Islamic doctrines," stated the WML charter. "In order for the collectivity to be a reality, it is necessary that allegiance will be to the Islamic doctrine and the interests of the Muslim umma in its totality above the allegiance to nationalism or other isms."[27] Faisal employed many exiled Muslim Brothers at the WML headquarters.

Although this was a move in the right direction by Faisal, it had little impact on the Arab heartland of Islam. Here Nasser's pan-Arabist socialist ideology continued to engage popular imagination and following. In late 1965 King Faisal tried to launch an official trans-Islamic body, to be named the Islamic Alliance, with the backing of Muhammad Reza Shah Pahlavi of Iran and King Hussein of Jordan. The project failed to get off the ground.

However, the defeat of Nasser's Egypt in the June 1967 Arab–Israeli War – and the loss to Israel of Arab Jerusalem containing Al Aqsa Mosque, Islam's third holiest shrine – changed the scene dramatically. Many Arabs believed that they had been defeated because of their deviation from their faith. The secular states of Egypt and Syria, humiliated by the setback, accepted subsidies from Saudi Arabia and other oil-rich Islamic monarchies to rebuild their armed forces and economies. Yet this was not enough to enable King Faisal to realize the Islamic Alliance he had mooted earlier.

Oddly, the action of an Australian Christian fundamentalist, Michael Rohan, came to his rescue. In July 1969 Rohan tried to set fire to Al Aqsa. He failed. But the arson attempt sent shock waves throughout the Muslim world. At Faisal's behest an Islamic summit conference, attended by 25 Muslim-majority countries, was convened in Rabat, Morocco, in September. Faisal declared a jihad against Israel and vowed to liberate Al Aqsa from the Israelis. Nasser sent his vice president, Anwar Sadat, to the conference. It was decided to set up a permanent secretariat. Out of this emerged the Islamic Conference Organization (ICO, aka Organization of Islamic Conference), the first official pan-Islamic institution of inter-governmental cooperation among Muslim states, with its headquarters in Jiddah: a body funded mainly by Saudi Arabia. Since then there has been a proliferation of trans-national Islamic organizations financed chiefly by Saudi Arabia: the Islamic Development Bank, the International Islamic News Agency, the International Center for Research in Islamic Economics, and the Institute for Muslim Minority Affairs. All of these are based in Saudi Arabia.

As Saudi oil revenue rocketed in the 1970s Riyadh's influence rose sharply in the Muslim world. It became one of the leading aid donors. But it limited its financial assistance to Muslim countries, and that too to those which accepted its policies. First and foremost, the recipient country had to wage a struggle against Marxism and the Soviet Union since atheistic Marxism was, according to Riyadh, the deadliest enemy of Islam. Second, the recipient Muslim state had to join the jihad against Israel and Zionism. Indeed, these two points were seen at least by King Faisal as interrelated: he genuinely believed that Zionism had been propped up by Communists as part of their world wide conspiracy. Third, the Muslim state had to agree to enforce in full the Sharia, howsoever gradually, along the lines already being pursued in Saudi Arabia.

The early years of Sadat's presidency in Egypt fitted the Saudi prescription well. Sadat received generous funds from King Faisal. But later when he acted independently, and signed a separate peace treaty with Israel in March 1979, thus violating one of the cardinal preconditions for Riyadh's aid, he was stigmatized by the Saudi regime.

In any event there was an inherent contradiction in the Saudi alliance with the US, which was (and remains) Israel's strategic partner and principal underwriter, economic and political. This exposed the regime to attacks from secular leftists and radical Islamists who argued that the Saudi-led jihad against Israel and Zionism was an exercise in hypocrisy.

The November 1979 American hostage crisis in Iran and the Soviet military intervention in Afghanistan in December raised tensions in the region and brought pressure on Riyadh from Washington to lease military bases to the Pentagon. Aware that such an overt alliance with the US would damage Saudi standing in the Muslim world, King Khalid professed non-alignment in international affairs. Addressing the third ICO summit in Taif, Saudi Arabia, in January 1981, he said, "Our loyalty must be neither to an eastern bloc nor to a western bloc. The security of the Islamic nation will not be assured by joining a military alliance, nor by taking refuge under the umbrella of a super-power."[28] There was nothing original in this. Indeed, Sayyid Qutb had expressed similar sentiments a generation before. "There are two huge blocs: the Communist bloc in the East and the capitalist bloc in the West," he wrote. "Each disseminates deceptive propaganda throughout the world claiming that there are only two alternative views in the world, Communism and capitalism, and that other nations have no alternative but to ally themselves with one bloc or the other."[29] The only difference was that while Qutb never held power Khalid did. But Khalid's declaration of non-alignment was rhetorical. His country was too closely tied to the West, especially America – militarily, economically, diplomatically and intelligence-wise – to envisage a truly non-aligned stance for itself.

In any event Saudi Arabia was a crucial partner of the US, particularly its Central Intelligence Agency (CIA), in its policy of overthrowing pro-Moscow leftist regimes. Its intelligence agency, Istikhabarat, working closely with the CIA and free of any restrictions that normally apply on intelligence agencies in democratic countries, was generous with its cash for anti-Marxist groups when the CIA's hands were tied. Its huge financial backing to the Afghan guerrillas fighting the Marxist regime in Kabul is universally known. What is not known widely is its cash subsidies to right-wing groups in Bangladesh, Malaysia, Indonesia and the Maldive islands. For many years it financed the Eritrean insurgents against the Marxist regime in Ethiopia. And in non-Arab Africa Saudi funds went to Cameroon, Chad, Gabon, Mali, Niger, Nigeria and Uganda. In Central America, it funded the anti-leftist Contra guerrillas in Nicaragua.

In the Muslim world Riyadh was the major financial backer of the Muslim Brotherhood in various countries as well as the Jamaat-e Islami in Pakistan. In addition Saudi Arabia channeled moneys through its ministries for such diverse activities as sponsoring foreign scholars to study at Saudi universities, production of radio and television programs on Islam, the teaching of Arabic in non-Arab states, and building of mosques and Islamic schools and colleges abroad. Saudi Arabia also funded conferences and seminars on Islam and Islamic subjects, and distribution of Islamic materials.

For a decade – from the founding of the Islamic Conference Organization in 1969 to the Iranian revolution in early 1979 – Saudi Arabia had a clear run in its campaign to project itself as the leader of the Muslim world, and present its capitalist policies at home and friendship with America abroad as the desirable Islamic model for Muslim-majority countries to emulate.

But after 1979 both its leadership role and the model it offered were seriously challenged by the Iranian fundamentalist, republican regime of Ayatollah Ruhollah Khomeini. This took some of the shine off Riyadh and put it on the defensive. Overall, though, Iran failed to displace Saudi Arabia from its leading position. The main reason was sectarian: Iran is an overwhelmingly Shia country whereas the Muslim world at large is 85 percent Sunni.

Saudi Arabia: from Mecca uprising to 1990 Kuwait crisis

While the emergence of a revolutionary Muslim fundamentalist regime in Iran, inimical to the US, posed a danger to the conservative Islamic monarchy of Saudi Arabia, the immediate economic effect on Riyadh was uplifting. The disappearance of Iran's 3 million barrels per day (bpd) petroleum exports from the market due to the year-long revolutionary turmoil, raised the price from $13 to $28 a barrel, and doubled Saudi oil revenue to $106 billion in 1980.

Having nationalized Aramco in 1978 while assuring its former American constituents of ample supplies of crude oil, the Saudi government stood to benefit from the price bonanza in more ways than one. The royals now had additional opportunities to enrich themselves especially when the upward price continued. For instance, David Ignatius reported in the *Wall Street Journal* that the Saudi government ordered one of the constituents of the former Aramco to sell oil at $32 a barrel to "Petromonde," a Japanese company, which then sold it to a Japanese refinery at $34.63, with $2.63 a barrel going to Petromonde as commission. On investigation, Petromonde turned out to be a London-based company with the same phone and telex numbers as Al Bilad, owned by Prince Muhammad ibn Fahd, son of the then Crown Prince.[30]

Admittedly, only the most senior princes had access to such a privilege. At the lower level, princes benefited from the ruler's land grants. The usual practice was for the monarch to allocate land – secretly earmarked for residential or industrial development – to a prince, who then sold it to the government at a grossly inflated price, and pocketed the profit.[31] The wealth so garnered was preposterous, a fact brought home to an American journalist when a servant at one such household gave her a towel and a liter bottle of Chanel No. 5 to wash her hands.[32]

Such goings-on provided grist to the revolutionary mills in Iran – more specifically to the Qom-based World Organization of the Islamic Liberation Movements, led by Ayatollah Hussein Ali Montazeri. Among the groups it aided was the Islamic Revolutionary Organization of the Arabian Peninsula, with secret cells in Saudi Arabia, especially in its oil-rich Hasa province, where most of the kingdom's half a million Shias lived. Along with other similar groups in the Arabian Peninsula, it accepted Khomeini's religious interpretation that hereditary power had no sanction in Islam. "Islam is fundamentally opposed to the whole notion of monarchy," he had written in 1971. "Anyone who studies the manner in which the Prophet established the government of Islam knows that Islam came in to destroy tyranny. Monarchy is one of the most shameful and disgraceful reactionary manifestations."[33] It also endorsed his condemnation of the Gulf monarchs as corrupt men who fostered what Khomeini labeled "American Islam" or "Islam of gold." He was scathing about their policy of depleting the valuable oil resources of their countries to satisfy the ever-growing demands of America, which he called the Great Satan, the prime source of corruption on earth, and denying their subjects any role in the decision-making processes of the state. The creation of a representative system in Iran, with a popularly elected president and parliament, made his arguments for republicanism attractive to many in the Gulf kingdoms.

With the seizure of American hostages in Tehran in November 1979, political tensions in the region sharpened. It was against this background that the information ministers of the Gulf states met in Riyadh and decided on guidelines for the state-controlled or -guided media regarding the Iranian revolution. These stressed "playing down the news from Tehran" and demoting "the Iranian revolution from the status of an all-Muslim one to a purely Shia one, and then to downgrade it to a purely Iranian Shia one."[34]

Saudi Arabia was the main force behind this conference. It had just experienced pro-Khomeini demonstrations and riots by its Shia citizens in Hasa at the time of their festival of mourning, Ashura, on 29 November 1979, resulting in the deaths of 57 security personnel and 99 Shias,[35] not to mention the seizure of the Grand Mosque in Mecca by militant Islamists. This had made its leaders extremely security-conscious and led them to seek internal security pacts not only with other monarchs of the Gulf but also with President Saddam Hussein of Iraq, a Shia-majority state, whose secular regime too felt threatened by revolutionary Iran.

Indeed, by the following summer, having tired of trying to placate Tehran, Saudi and Kuwaiti rulers encouraged Saddam to act against Iran. On 5 August 1980 Saddam visited Riyadh to discuss "the current situation in the Gulf region" with the Saudi monarch. On 12 August Saudi Arabia and Kuwait signed secret agreements with Baghdad to raise their oil outputs by 1 million bpd and 800,000 bpd respectively, and contribute the revenue to Iraq's war chest.[36] Ten days later Saddam invaded Iran, starting a war that would last eight years. The outbreak of the First Gulf War pushed the oil price to a peak of $41 a barrel, raising the Saudi annual petroleum income to a record $110 billion in 1981.

The armed conflict gave urgency to the issue of the Gulf monarchies' security. The Saudis were advised by Britain and France to create a supra-national body of the Gulf states which could call on the West for military assistance in case of serious internal or external threat to one or more of its members. As a result, the Gulf Cooperation Council (GCC), led by Saudi Arabia, came into being in May 1981 with the objectives of co-ordinating internal security, procurement of arms and the national economies of the six member-states: Bahrain, Kuwait, Oman, Qatar, Saudi Arabia and the UAE.

Anti-Tehran feeling reached a peak in the region in January 1982 when the Bahraini government arrested 60 people on charges of plotting a coup, and linked them with the exiled Sayyid Hadi al Moderasi, leader of the Islamic Liberation Front of Bahrain based in Iran. Prince Nayif, the Saudi interior minister, rushed to the Bahraini capital, Manama, and offered to send Saudi troops. "The sabotage plot was engineered by the Iranian government and was directed against Saudi Arabia," he said.[37] Threatened by Iran's revolutionary fervor, Gulf monarchs drew closer together, and resolved not to share sovereignty with their subjects in the belief that any such move would be seen as weakness, and would lead to further demands for democratization.

Led by Riyadh, they bankrolled Iraq's war against Iran as a way of keeping the Islamic revolutionary regime busy fighting and refrain from exporting its revolution. The accession of Fahd as Saudi king, following the death of Khalid in June 1982, left the Gulf states' policy undisturbed. By 1983 Riyadh had provided Iraq over $15 billion in cash and oil sales, and funded Baghdad's purchase of advanced warplanes. Equally importantly, having based its newly purchased US-made AWACS (Airborne Warning and Control Systems), piloted by Americans, at Dhahran since October 1980, Saudi Arabia began relaying intelligence on Iran to Baghdad. This would later be confirmed by Saddam Hussein.[38] On the ideological front, it assisted Saddam to convene the First Popular Islamic Conference in Baghdad in April 1983 to counter Iran's Islamist propaganda. Riyadh seconded Marouf Dawalbi, a religious aide to King Fahd, to help organize the conference. He drew on the Saudi network of Islamic affiliations, and representatives from 50 countries turned up.[39] However, after having backed Saddam's stance on the war, when the conference leaders tried to mediate between the warring parties, they were rebuffed by Iran.

This was one of the several instances of Iranian intransigence that angered the Saudi kingdom. "Ever since the Iranian and Islamic peoples were afflicted by the Khomeini regime, this regime has failed to render any noteworthy service to Islam, and to Muslims," said *Al Medina*, a semi-official Saudi daily, in July 1983. "This regime has tried to create schism among

Muslims, not only in their politics but also in their mosques. The Khomeini regime sends its agents everywhere to foment discord."[40]

Here were two fundamentalist states, deriving their inspiration from Islamic scriptures and basing their legitimacy on Islam, exchanging diatribes – the newer one, Iran, accusing the older of deviation from the faith, and the established, conservative polity of Saudi Arabia condemning the revolutionary upstart for trying to create chaos in Muslim countries in the name of furthering the cause of Islam.

In theological terms, their differences had crystallized along the rituals of the hajj. They disagreed on the right of pilgrims to shout slogans against the enemies of Islam – America, the Soviet Union and Israel – as part of "the disavowal of the infidels," one of the main pillars of monotheism, which the believer is enjoined by Prophet Muhammad to practice. The Saudi authorities insisted that using hajj for political purposes contravened Prophet Muhammad's injunction to refrain from ill-temper, bad manners and violence during the holy pilgrimage. After protracted discussions, and repeated violence between protesting Iranian pilgrims and Saudi security forces, the matter was resolved in 1983: Riyadh allowed Iranian pilgrims to raise slogans against the enemies of Islam at certain fixed venues in Mecca and Medina.

This arrangement held for four years. It seemed that the two Islamic regimes were learning to coexist – partly because they had found a common cause in actively opposing the Soviet military intervention in Afghanistan. Yet they pursued the objective in separate ways. While Saudi Arabia operated in alliance with America and Pakistan, making sure to aid only Sunni Afghan fundamentalists, Iran, sharing a common frontier with Afghanistan, backed Shia Afghan partisans while sheltering about 2 million Afghan refugees within its borders. Saudi Arabia became one of the early suppliers of arms to Pakistan-based Afghan parties fighting the Marxist regime in Afghanistan. Among the Islamic Afghan groups then in existence, it particularly favored the Islamic Alliance (Ittihad-e Islami) of Afghanistan headed by Prof. Abdul Rasul Sayyaf who was a Wahhabi. Saudi Arabia encouraged its citizens as well as others from fellow Arab countries to join the anti-Soviet jihad and became a staging post for the non-Saudi Arab volunteers on their way to Peshawar, Pakistan, where they were encouraged to join Sayyaf's Islamic Alliance. Once Washington authorized financial aid to the seven-party Islamic Alliance of Afghan Mujahedin in 1983, Riyadh offered to match the publicly acknowledged American aid. Within four years the annual figure reached $640 million each from the US and the Saudi kingdom.[41] Riyadh's official grants were supplemented by private donations made by affluent citizens of Saudi Arabia and other Gulf monarchies, many of them collected personally by Osama bin Laden, who commuted between Pakistan and the Gulf during 1980–2. Since banking in Peshawar was not geared to handling large sums of foreign currencies, he would arrive with cash in US dollars. The anti-Soviet activities in Pakistan along the eastern border of Afghanistan were quite separate from what happened along Afghanistan's frontier with Iran.

On the other hand, in an effort to reverse the downward trend in their petroleum revenues, Iran agreed with Saudi Arabia in the autumn of 1986 to reduce oil output within the framework of the Organization of Petroleum Exporting Countries (OPEC) to raise the price to $18 a barrel from the mid-teens. Tehran had also reacted favorably to King Fahd's recent decree that instead of "His Majesty," he should be addressed as "The Custodian of the Two Holy Mosques," the mosques being the ones in Mecca and Medina.

However, improved relations with republican Iran, which held parliamentary and presidential elections regularly, were not reflected in any moves by King Fahd to share power with his subjects. Indeed, the regime became even more sensitive to criticism as Fahd put his imprint on it. Lacking the widespread support that ascetic-looking Faisal enjoyed or the rapport that avuncular Khalid had with his subjects, the unprepossessing and obese Fahd centralized authority, blocked fresh advice reaching him, and came to rely on compulsion as a means of securing loyalty. His extended absences abroad and his decision to spend long stretches of time away from Riyadh to avoid the prying eyes of the ulama, and on his luxurious yacht, the size of a luxury liner, off the coast of Jiddah where he could live his dissolute lifestyle unobserved, made his subjects view him as "a high level captive of the West," deride him as a "hypocrite, a rogue masquerading as a pious Muslim," and prone to believe him to be "a heavy drinker and fond of foreign women."[42] While King Fahd built a series of luxurious palaces at home and abroad – in Marbella, Spain; Geneva; a $3 billion Al Salem Palace in Jiddah with a white beach imported from Greece;[43] in Taif; and between Riyadh and Diriya – the governmental reserves built up earlier were going down. Falling oil prices, causing a recession in the kingdom, forced the Finance Ministry to dip into its reserves of $150 billion to cover the recurring budget deficits, and as popular disaffection rose, Fahd got rough with dissidents. The customary penalty of the loss of livelihood and exile for dissidence escalated to include flogging, torture and even disappearance while the authorities widened the scope of the death penalty to include apostasy, conspiracy, robbery with violence, sabotage and corruption. Executions were carried out with a sword often in a public square. (The number of executions tripled in 1989 from the previous year's 22.) While repressing dissidents, by and large militant Islamists, the government had failed to co-opt, institutionally, the members of the rising technocracy into the decision-making apparatus of the state: its repeated promises of producing a written constitution and appointing a consultative council remained unfulfilled.

In the region, the Riyadh–Tehran rapprochement came under strain when the US increased its naval presence in the Gulf in the summer of 1987 to protect Kuwaiti oil tankers being threatened by Iran. Tension in the region escalated. A few days before the hajj, Khomeini issued guidelines to the pilgrims, and combined his political message of "Islamic unity against the superpowers" with the religious theme of "disavowal of the infidels," listing the enemies of Islam: America, the Great Satan; the Soviet Union for its occupation of Afghanistan; and Israel for its occupation of Palestine. (A decade later, with the Soviet Union gone,

Osama bin Laden too would name the US and Israel as the prime foes of Islam, calling them respectively the Crusaders and the Jews.)

On 31 July about 100,000 Iranians and non-Iranians in Mecca started marching peacefully. But when the vanguard of the procession was about 500 yards (450 m) from the previously agreed termination point 1 mile (1.5 km) from the Grand Mosque – they were blocked by the police. Tempers flared and rioting broke out. During the hour-long riot, the marchers were subjected to electrified batons, tear gas, rubber bullets and live ammunition. As a result of the police action and the stampede caused by it, 402 people, mostly pilgrims, died.[44] This enraged the Iranian government and people.

The Mecca killings ended the rapprochement between Riyadh and Tehran. The two fundamentalist regimes were now back in an adversarial mode, openly competing for the leadership of the faithful in the Muslim world. Between them, Iran felt the more self-righteous, and more of a model for the people in other Muslim countries which had been colonies of Europe until a few decades ago. It was in their country, Iranian leaders argued, that the faithful had struggled in their millions to overthrow a corrupt, un-Islamic regime of pro-American Muhammad Reza Shah Pahlavi, and institute a government of God. Iran therefore provided a model for people in other Muslim countries to follow.

When in March 1988 Riyadh announced a quota of one pilgrim per 1,000 Muslims, thus allowing Iran only 45,000 pilgrims instead of the usual 150,000, Tehran rejected the offer. Saudi Arabia severed diplomatic links with Iran, and Tehran boycotted the hajj for the next three years. During that period the Iran–Iraq War – also called the First Gulf War – ended in a draw and Khomeini died in 1989, with Saudi Arabia failing to send condolences to Tehran. It would take the Second Gulf War in 1991, when Saudi Arabia allied with the US to liberate Kuwait from its occupation by Iraq, its close ally in the First Gulf War, before the two Islamic regimes would resume diplomatic ties but only after Riyadh had agreed to double the quota of hajj pilgrims for Iran and accepted their right to demonstrate peace-fully in Mecca.[45]

Meanwhile Saudi Arabia as well as Iran was pleased to see the Soviet troops leave Afghanistan in early 1989. To their dis-appointment, though, the leftist regime of President Najibullah (1946–96; r. 1986–92) in Kabul did not collapse. Nonetheless, the departure of the Soviets from Afghanistan deprived the non-Afghan Mujahedin of a rationale to participate in what now became a purely Afghan issue. Such stalwarts as bin Laden returned home. As the only Saudi born into luxury who had abandoned his privileged life for the rigors of the caves and mountains of arid Afghanistan for the better part of a decade, he was held in high esteem, especially by young Saudis. (The fellow-Saudis who joined him in the jihad for a year or two were almost invariably from humbler families, often being semi-skilled workers.) Those who returned from Afghanistan came back with an exalted sense of religious purpose and a fanatical commitment to the Islamist cause, possessing guerrilla and conventional war experience in arduous conditions as well as an unshakable belief that God was on their side, and proud to call themselves "al Afghani." Their time in Afghanistan, where besides weapons training they had undergone political education which emphasized Islam and nationalism as antidotes to Soviet imperialism, had heightened their political consciousness. Aware of the nature of imperialism, as practiced by the Soviets in Afghanistan, many of them on their return to their home-lands would see the hand of American imperialism behind their domestic regimes, and would set out to undermine it by the only means they knew – terrorism. Though comparatively small in numbers, they would emerge as a force to be reckoned with for the traditional, pro-Western regimes in the Middle East. Yet there were still others who stayed behind in Afghanistan or Pakistan, apprehensive about their return, fearing arrest by the local authorities, or worse. In any event, the new US administra-tion of President George Herbert Walker Bush (b. 1924; 1989–92) did not think the anti-Soviet struggle was finally over. It pledged to supply weapons to the Afghan Mujahedin to the tune of

$500 million a year, with Saudi Arabia matching the publicly acknowledged US aid.[46] Both states would continue the funding until 1991 when the war against Iraq would radically divert both their attention and funds.

1990 Kuwait crisis and after

Iraq's invasion and occupation of Kuwait on 2 August 1990 created a crisis that King Fahd, a slothful ruler, was not equipped to handle speedily. President George Bush realized that it was imperative for the Pentagon to secure land bases next to occupied Kuwait if (as seemed most likely) it were required to expel the Iraqis by force. Such bases were only available in Saudi Arabia. So how to persuade King Fahd to invite US troops to his kingdom became the most urgent issue. The Saudi monarch had to be convinced that he needed American military presence and that could be the case only if it could be shown that Saddam Hussein intended to attack Saudi Arabia. That is when the White House produced satellite pictures on 3 August and showed them to the Saudi ambassador in Washington since 1983, Prince Bandar, the flamboyant son of Prince Sultan ibn Abdul Aziz, Saudi defense minister. While Sultan was in favor of inviting the Americans, Crown Prince Abdullah was not.

When on 5 August Bush told Fahd that Iraq had massed troops along the Saudi border, Fahd replied politely that while they needed some US assistance with their air force they did not need the army.[47] Indeed, until 1967 the US Air Force (USAF) had a lease on Dhahran air base – the site where the first US Air Force training mission was posted in 1950, four years after an American military advisory delegation arrived in Riyadh to reorganize King Abdul Aziz's regular army. The monarch had wanted a defense pact with Washington, but the latter was unwilling. In 1951, however, the US signed a limited five-year military cooperation agreement whereby the Pentagon leased Dhahran air base. Sensitive to the rising Arab nationalist tide in the region and his country, King Saud let the agreement expire in 1956, and took to renewing it on a monthly basis.

When US President Eisenhower (r. 1953–60) opposed the Anglo-French-Israeli invasion of Egypt in November 1956, King Saud warmed towards the US. During his visit to Washington in February 1957, he signed a new military cooperation agreement. It renewed the US lease on Dhahran for five years and committed the Pentagon to help double the Saudi army to 15,000 – and add navy and air force to the kingdom's defense establishment.[48] When during his power struggle with Faisal, King Saud appointed a liberal cabinet, with commoners forming a majority, in December 1960, pro-Nasser sentiment came to the surface, and the US lease of Dhahran began to embarrass Saud, who faced angry demonstrations during his tour of the Eastern Province in early 1961. He declared that he would not renew the Dhahran arrangement on its expiry in April 1962. But he did renew it. Indeed the American lease of Dhahran continued into the rule of King Faisal, ending only in 1967 after the Six Day Arab–Israeli War, when Saudi Arabia and other Arab states cut off oil supplies to America and Britain.[49] After that the kingdom remained free of any Western military presence – until the fall of the Shah of Iran in February 1979. Then US President Jimmy Carter (r. 1977–80) dispatched a squadron of F-15 warplanes to Dhahran. Furthermore, in a secret meeting between Hermann Eilts, former US ambassador to Saudi Arabia, and Crown Prince Fahd in Rome in May, it was agreed that the Pentagon would come to the military aid of the kingdom in the event of a direct threat to it, and that in the autumn the Carter administration would pressure Israel to make concessions on the Palestinian issue.[50] The next year when Saudi Arabia obtained American-piloted AWACS, it based them at Dhahran. In short, there had been a history of USAF presence in the Saudi kingdom.

But the prospect of US army troops being stationed in Saudi Arabia under their own flag was an altogether different matter. This was more than a military or political issue. It was tied up with a cardinal religious principle that the Saudi kingdom had enforced since its inception, resulting in barring non-Muslim places of worship. "This injunction is the result of an Islamic concept which holds the whole of the kingdom of Saudi Arabia to be considered within Islam a mosque, where two religions cannot exist," explained a professor of propagation of Islam at the Islamic University of Medina.[51] The concept was derivative of Prophet Muhammad's last injunction about there being no two religions in Arabia. It also explained why Christians, wearing the cross, were not allowed to show it.

It was therefore imperative for Fahd to consult leading theologians, including the members of the Council of Senior Ulama. While he did so, the official and semi-official media withheld news about the Iraqi aggression. By the time Prince Bandar arrived in Jiddah from Washington on 6 August, Saudi scouts had failed to spot Iraqi troops along the Saudi–Iraq or Saudi–Kuwait border. But Bandar said he had earlier seen contrary evidence on the US satellite pictures. By now, however, the Americans had upped the ante by claiming that their latest pictures showed that Iraq had positioned surface-to-surface missiles in Kuwait aimed at Saudi targets. This was not something Saudi army scouts could check with binoculars from their side of the border. US defense secretary Dick Cheney left Washington with the satellite pictures. The same day Saddam Hussein assured Jospeh Wilson, the top US diplomat in Baghdad, that he had no intention of attacking Saudi Arabia, with which Iraq had signed a non-aggression pact in February 1989. Iran, which had been the victim of Saddam's aggression a decade earlier, watched with uncommon interest. "There is suspicion in Iran that the Saudi acceptance of the American military aid has more to do with the Al Saud royal family seeking to safeguard its own power and interests than to protect the country's borders," reported Celia Hall of the *Independent* from Tehran.[52] This was also the conclusion bin Laden would reach later.

Taking into account the concerns senior ulama and others expressed about the large-scale presence of US army troops in the kingdom, Fahd attached conditions to his invitation. These were to be revealed by Cheney when he telephoned Bush at 23.00 hours local time on 6 August to say that Fahd had agreed to invite American forces on three conditions: a written promise by the US administration that it would leave Saudi

Arabia once the threat from Iraq was over; that it would obtain Saudi approval before taking any military action against Iraq; and that it would keep the Saudi invitation secret until the first American troops had arrived in the kingdom (so that Saudis would accept their presence as a *fait accompli*). Apparently Fahd saw as a real possibility the US troops in the kingdom acting as an independent force to achieve their anti-Iraq objective without much thought to the impact of their actions on Saudi interests or sovereignty.

While the matter of US troops was being feverishly discussed, albeit privately, at the highest level, bin Laden, well connected with the royal family, had a meeting with inter alia Prince Sultan to explain his plan of repelling any aggression by Saddam Hussein: by complementing the kingdom's military with 30,000 battle-hardened Afghani Arabs, about half of them Saudi nationals, who had participated in the successful anti-Soviet jihad. Sultan reportedly listened politely but rejected the proposal.[53] Instead, he successfully pressed on the king, his blood brother, his strong recommendation to invite the American troops, who arrived in the kingdom late on the night of 7 August.

This was a seminal event. It would set in train the bin Laden Phenomenon that would lead first to the bombing of American embassies in East Africa on the eighth anniversary of the arrival of the US troops on Saudi soil and culminate three years later in the first ever attack on mainland America, taking a toll higher than the 2,405 dead or missing caused by the Japanese attack on Pearl Harbor naval base, Hawaii, in 1941.

Bin Laden was not alone in opposing King Fahd's decision. The Council of Senior Ulama was divided. It held meetings with the monarch and senior princes, and agonized for days, aware that it was being asked to sanction soliciting military protection from those whom Wahhabi literature traditionally called "infidels," "Crusaders" and "enemies of Islam." On 9 August, the day the Saudi government belatedly publicly acknowledged the presence of US troops, it published the opinions of several lesser known members of the 17-strong COSU, supporting the official decision, with television repeating their endorsement several times for the next 48 hours. Significantly, though, Abdul Aziz al Baz was not among them nor was Muhammad ibn Salih ibn Uthaimin, COSU's second best known member.[54]

As reports poured in of the round-the-clock airlifting of US troops of both sexes – the total eventually reaching 550,000 – unease in the kingdom mounted. It was first expressed in a sermon on 17 August at a Riyadh mosque by Shaikh Safar al Hawali (1950–), dean of Islamic studies at Mecca's Umm al Qura University, a religious intellectual who, while being popular among theological students, was also in close touch with the old ulama. He declared that there was a Western-Crusader conspiracy to enslave Muslims of the Arabian Peninsula and control all oil-producing countries in the region as a first step towards implementing a more ambitious Western design to dominate the entire Arab and Muslim world. Ridiculing the idea of the US defending Saudi Arabia, he asked: "Can 30,000 immoral American women protect the sons of Prophet Muhammad?" A week later Shaikh Fahd Salman al Audah (1952–), a charismatic preacher from Bureidah, too spoke out. Decrying the moral and material corruption that had afflicted Saudi society, he accused the government of placing "its trust in the President of America rather than in God," and criticized the COSU members for "signing on behalf of God what He had forbidden and what God had allowed." Both of them based their argument on the writings of Muhammad ibn Abdul Wahhab, the founder of Wahhabism. Within a month, about 100,000 audiotapes of these lectures were sold, and the debate was joined by junior ulama, most of them graduates of the kingdom's three Islamic universities in Mecca, Medina and Riyadh.[55] In late October came a meeting of the protesting ulama at Al Jawhara Mosque in Riyadh to discuss "the state of the nation," followed soon by another such gathering. In December, while the armed forces of the US and its Western and Muslim allies were readying themselves for an offensive against Iraq, 200 prominent personalities, mostly religious – including bin Laden – forwarded an advisory document in the form of a private letter to King Fahd. Its contents remained secret.

Lacking theological credentials, bin Laden cited Shaikhs Hawali and Audah, who rooted their arguments in the writings of Muhammad ibn Abdul Wahhab, in his criticism of the government that he began expressing stridently. This led to a ban on his travel outside Jiddah, where an enlarged body of muttawin – many of them transferred from the Eastern Province now saturated with 880,000 troops, 70 percent of them Western – had begun aggressively enforcing Islamic injunctions.

By the time the war ended on 28 February 1991, it had cost Saudi Arabia, directly and indirectly, $45 billion, or 57 percent of its annual GDP. So depleted were the national coffers that the government took the unprecedented step of borrowing money from foreign banks to balance its budget. Its cash reserves were down to $15 billion from the peak of $150 billion only a decade before. The personal fortunes of the royals, though, were unaffected. Angry at the Western media reports during the run-up to the Gulf War that his assets were worth $18 billion, King Fahd told a delegation of US businessmen and former diplomats meeting him after the conflict: "Eighteen billion! If anyone can prove I'm worth more than $9 billion, I'll share it with them." [56]

Those Saudis who expected a swift and complete withdrawal of US and other Western troops from the kingdom after the war were disappointed. They took to protesting. The known example of it was in Bureidah, a bastion of Wahhabism. On 17 May 1991 the governor of the province, Prince Abdul Ilah, banned Shaikhs Audah and Abdullah Jallali from delivering their Friday sermons. Two days later thousands of their supporters, led by local ulama and muttawin, staged a noisy demonstration which was broken up by the security forces. Shaikh al Baz addressed a letter of support to the dissident shaikhs. On 24 May it was revealed that a week earlier, during his meeting with King Fahd, al Baz had passed on to him a single-page document, signed by 400 leading ulama, judges and academics, entitled "Letter of [Ten] Demands." With the signatories releasing it to news agencies, its contents became public. Its crisp, business-like style indicated that it had been drafted by youngish Islamic intellectuals who had succeeded in getting the older ulama to sign it even though it did not contain any specific demands of the ulama. The letter demanded a consultative council to debate and decide "all domestic and foreign affairs"; Islamization of all social, economic, administrative and educational institutions; Islamization of the military; reform of the judicial system; ensuring "equality for all citizens without any exception or exclusion"; punishing all those who had enriched themselves illegally; reform of the press and media; assuring freedom of expression within the Sharia; preserving the interests and purity of the Islamic umma by keeping it out of non-Islamic pacts and treaties; and a thorough reform of the Saudi embassies according to the Sharia.[57] Fahd expressed his disapproval to COSU, which condemned the publication of the letter as un-Islamic, saying that advice to the ruler had to remain secret. Significantly, though, it did not pass judgment on the text of the letter.

The revelation in September 1991 that 37,000 US troops remained in the kingdom in "a non-military capacity"[58] kept popular disquiet simmering – even though bin Laden had departed five months earlier for Pakistan, ostensibly to tidy up some loose ends there, never to return home and, instead, set up an ostensibly commercial base in Khartoum under the benign eyes of an Islamist regime where Hassan al Turabi, an Islamic thinker, wielded much power. It would be another year before the Saudi-based American armed forces would find a military assignment to perform – to monitor the "no-fly" zone in southern Iraq that President Bush and his British and French counterparts would impose on Saddam Hussein – which would provide an ostensible reason for the US warplanes and troops to remain on Saudi soil.

Major wars accelerate social change; and Saudi Arabia did not escape the socio-political consequences of the Gulf conflict. "The war brought into focus so many things: it raised our consciousness and gave us an opportunity for soul searching," said Khalid Maeena, editor of the semi-official *Arab News*. "All sections of society are having this experience."[59]

This was the backdrop against which, in March 1992, King Fahd promised a fully nominated 60-member Shura (consultative) council "within six months" and adherence to the rule of law in administering the country. At the same time he ruled out any move toward representative government. "Western democratic practices are not suited to traditional Arab societies of the Arabian Peninsula," he declared.[60] His statement would be countered a year later by the successful parliamentary elections, based on universal suffrage, in Yemen, very much part of the Arabian Peninsula.

Encouraged by the first chink in the armor of monarchical autocracy, protesting theologians expanded the 10 points in the "Letter of Demands" into 10 chapters. The new document, entitled "Memorandum of Advice" and signed by 92 ulama, was submitted to the monarch in July 1992, and published simultaneously. This time COSU immediately dismissed the memorandum as "unbalanced" and criticized its publication. Its authors responded by indirectly accusing COSU of not performing its duty of monitoring the conduct of the political leadership.[61]

But this was not the end of the matter. Encouraged by the holding of the multi-party general election in Yemen in April 1993, six signatories of the Memorandum of Advice established the Committee for the Defense of Legitimate Rights (CDLR). It was headed by Shaikh Abdullah al Masaari, former chief justice at the high court, and included his son, Muhammad al Masaari, 50, a physics professor, and two lawyers. It demanded regular elections, male and female suffrage, press and trade union freedoms within the Sharia, independent judiciary, redistribution of wealth and expulsion of the American troops. Having secured an edict against the CDLR from COSU in May, the governor of Riyadh, Prince Salman, dissolved the organization, jailed its founders and confiscated their passports. "It is the duty of Muslims to obey their sovereign and the ulama," Shaikh al Baz told the London-based, Saudi-owned *Asharq al Awsat* (The Middle East) on 24 May 1993. "Criticism that leads to destabilization of society constitutes 'revolt' and is unacceptable in Islam. The only situation when disobedience is allowed is when the sovereign takes a decision which is evil in the eyes of God. Then the people should gently advise him, and pray that the sovereign will change his mind." Following the standard procedure, the US embassy in Riyadh had monitored the situation and, between the establishment and dissolution of the CDLR, its political section had held meetings with some of its founders.

In September the government arrested 10 intellectuals, including 6 academics at the King Saud University in Riyadh, and Shaikhs Audah and Hawali. Such actions stemmed from the view held by King Fahd and most senior princes that if they gave ground even slightly they would end up ceding everything. This is what, in their view, had happened in Iran in the late 1970s when the Shah began making concessions to his opponents. They were determined to avoid the fate of Muhammad Reza Shah of Iran at all cost.

Riyadh's anti-CDLR acts angered such traditional, low-profile groups in the kingdom as the Muslim Brotherhood and Salafis, members of the Sunni Islamic movement which advocates following the concepts of salaf al salihin, the pious ancestors (of Muslims), rather than one of the later four Sunni legal schools.[62] In protest they discontinued their monthly meetings with the five-member subcommittee of COSU, chaired by al Baz, to discuss matters of mutual interest. "The official ulama lost control over the [Islamic] activists long time ago," said a Brotherhood leader. "But now the lines are being drawn between those ulama who support the government in everything and those who do not."[63] This was the first open sign of a split in the Wahhabi religious establishment between the top religious figures appointed by the monarch and those below them, which would widen over coming years. This disturbed the top policymakers in Washington to the extent that the National Security Agency based at Fort Meade, Maryland was ordered to monitor the telephone conversations of the monarch and crown prince as well as the senior-most princes,[64] Saudi Arabia being a bulwark against Iraq and a counterweight to Iran.

From his office in McNimr Street, Khartoum, bin Laden kept up his attacks on the continued presence of infidel soldiers on the holy soil of Arabia and the regime that allowed it. He used the freedom that residence in Sudan gave him to set up several businesses under the banner of Wadi al Aqiq (Valley of the Brown Gem), including Al Themar al Mubarak (The Blessed Fruit), which owned farms that also provided useful sites for military training, Ladin International Company, specializing in import-export with a near monopoly on the exports of sesame seed and products, Taba Investment, trading in foreign currencies, and Al Hijra for Construction and Development Company Limited, a joint venture with the Sudanese government, commissioned to build the 700 mile (1,100 km) road from Khartoum to Port Sudan, for which bin Laden employed 600 people, most of them Afghani Arabs. Along with this went his undeclared plan to strengthen Al Qaida (The Base), which originated as an organization to provide social welfare to the widows and orphans of the non-Afghan Mujahedin that had been initiated by the Maktab al Khidmat (Bureau of Service [to the Mujahedin]), established in 1984 in Peshawar by bin Laden's mentor, Abdullah Azzam (1941–89). Now the political and commercial aims of bin Laden became intertwined – both subservient to his overarching objective of waging jihad against the US by either financing directly Al Qaida's terrorist actions or sponsoring like-minded groups worldwide, with their activists coming to Sudan for weapons training and bomb-making instructions to participate in jihads where Muslims are being persecuted or to replace un-Islamic regimes in Muslim-majority countries with truly Islamist ones. It was during his five-years stay in Sudan that bin Laden combined his business acumen with his political–religious philosophy to shape Al Qaida as an umbrella organization specializing in conducting jihad through violent means. At the top was a Shura Council of 12, which formulated policies that were implemented by four executive committees. The military committee conducted training and bought weapons; the business committee ran the Wadi al Aqiq companies; the fatwa and Islamic studies committee dealt with religious matters; and the media committee published a weekly newsletter on Islam and jihad. Al Qaida established associate relationship with like-minded groups in Algeria,

Chechnya, Egypt, Ethiopia, Lebanon, Libya, Philippines, Syria and Yemen, and maintained guest houses in different countries.[65] It would emerge later that bin Laden's business activities in Sudan proved unprofitable, greatly diminishing his wealth, particularly when, according to him, the Sudanese government failed to pay his Al Hijra for Construction and Development for the 1994 road project.[66]

Bin Laden's activities were being closely monitored by the intelligence operatives attached to the Saudi embassy in Khartoum. Inside the Saudi kingdom, the authorities invoked the intervention of Osama's elder brothers to silence him, or at least to persuade him not to strike targets in Saudi Arabia. "They sent my mother, my uncle, and my brothers in almost nine visits to Khartoum asking me to stop and return to Arabia to apologize to King Fahd," said bin Laden. "I refused to go back."[67] As a consequence, the Saudi government quietly revoked his citizenship and froze his assets – estimated by his brother Yeslam to be $20–25 million – in February 1994. But it was not until 7 April that an official statement explained that the measure was taken due to bin Laden's behavior that "contradicts the Kingdom's interests and risks harming its relations with fraternal countries" and "for refusal to obey instructions issued to him." Four months later, Osama's eldest brother, Bakr, the head of the Saudi Binladin Group, expressed his family's "regret, denunciation and condemnation" of Osama's "extremist activities."[68] Soon thereafter a group of men carrying Kalashnikov assault rifles opened fire at bin Laden's house in Khartoum – an act probably engineered by the Saudi authorities.

On 11 July 1994 bin Laden signed a document describing the Committee for Advice and Reform (CAR) as "an all-encompassing organization that aims at applying the teachings of God to all aspects of life" in general and promoting "peaceful and constructive reform" in the governance of "Arabia" – deliberately omitting the qualifying "Saudi" – and establishing its office in London, with Khalid al Fawwaz (b. 1957) its director. A richly bearded man dressed invariably in traditional Arab robe and headdress, Fawwaz was a civil engineering graduate of King

Fahd University in Dhahran, who joined the anti-Soviet jihad in the early 1980s in Afghanistan where he met bin Laden. When the latter moved to Sudan in 1991, Fawwaz followed. From there he went to Nairobi where he set up an import-export company. In early 1994 he went to Britain, lived in north-west London, and took up an English language course at a local college. CAR's specific objectives were to eliminate all forms of jahiliya (pre-Islamic) rule and all aspects of injustice, to reform the political system of (Saudi) Arabia by ridding it of corruption and injustice, and to revive the Islamic tradition of *hesba* (lit. accountability), which entitles citizens to bring charges against government officials.[69] "Fawwaz was collecting all the media publications, video tapes and newspaper cuttings [available in Britain]," said Muhammad Masaari. "He had a full office working on that and supplying bin Laden with this information. That is his main function, as a channel of communication."[70]

Intent on proving that he was serious about political reform in the kingdom, King Fahd named Shaikh Muhammad ibn Ibrahim ibn Jubair, former justice minister, as president of the promised consultative council in September 1992. He appointed al Baz the Grand Mufti, a job that had been vacant for 23 years, but only after transferring many of the Mufti's functions to the Ministry of Justice directly under monarchical control.

Having made some concessions in the political and religious spheres, Fahd moved to repress further the dissident Islamic ulama at home and block financial assistance to Islamist militants overseas. Abroad, he tightened ties with Washington still further while the latter's dependence on Saudi petroleum grew. A quarter of America's oil imports now originated in Saudi Arabia, which had purchased $25 billion worth of US arms between August 1990 and December 1992 – by which date, according to *The Economist*, a "less formalized defense agreement" between Riyadh and Washington was "in place."[71]

In May 1993 the Saudi Interior Ministry ordered that all private donations by Saudis to foreign Muslim charities,[72] running at $1 billion a year, must be channeled through a new fund to be managed by Riyadh's governor, Prince Salman ibn Abdul Azia. It acted after Egypt had complained that some of the funds, meant for charity, were being used by fundamentalists for violent purposes. Until then, private donations had financed such organizations as the Muslim Brotherhood, generally classified as a religious body in the Middle East, and the Palestinian Islamic Resistance Movement (*Harkat al Muqawama al Islami*, Hamas). After the Saudi government stopped bankrolling the Afghan Mujahedin groups in 1991, private citizens continued their donations to them.

In August 1993, a year behind schedule, Fahd finally announced the names of the members of the consultative council (first promised in 1960!), who would serve for four years as full-time state employees. About a third were present or past civil servants, and the rest retired military, police or security officers, academics, businessmen, mainstream ulama and professionals, including six writers and journalists. Only one of them was an adherent of the Shia sect, to which 9 percent of Saudi citizens belonged. Eleven years into the rule of Fahd, the limits of freedom for citizens had actually contracted. "We actually used to have more freedom [in the early years of Fahd]," a pro-Western, liberal critic told the visiting reporter from the London-based *Guardian* in August 1993. "We could choose the heads of university departments . . . Now we couldn't even set up a neighborhood committee for dealing with stray dogs."[73]

On the eve of the inauguration of the council in December, US President Bill Clinton (b. 1947; r. 1993–2000) wrote a letter to King Fahd in which he called the council "an important step to widen popular participation" – a naively inaccurate statement since the unelected council lacked legislative powers and had no control over the budget. The monarch himself hardly elicited the respect or admiration of his subjects, a point made by Tony Horowitz of the *Wall Street Journal*, one of the select few Western journalists allowed to visit the kingdom briefly. Alluding to "lots of political jokes" – which sprout luxuriantly in authoritarian soils – Horowitz reported that most depicted Fahd as "a witless despot surrounded by yes men."[74] Certainly his message to the inaugural session of the Consultative Council was vintage Fahd. "We are a country that follows the Book of God [Quran] and will not deviate from that in any way. So we are not bothered in any way by those who object and say 'Why not have elections?'"[75]

His government's crackdown on dissidents continued into the next year, bringing the total of their jailed ilk to 200. Its foreign policy continued to converge with Washington's in Middle Eastern affairs especially when the signing of the Oslo Accord between Israel and the Palestine Liberation Organization (PLO) in September 1993 eased tensions in the region. Riyadh ended its boycott of foreign companies trading with Israel, and decided to admit foreigners who had previously visited Israel. There were also repeated reports of American Jewish delegations secretly visiting Saudi Arabia for talks at the highest level, arranged by the Saudi ambassador in Washington, Prince Bandar, who had represented his country since 1983.[76]

In December 1994 and the following month, Grand Mufti al Baz came out with a radically revised opinion on what Allah and Prophet Muhammad had said about the Jews, Palestine and peace with Israel. Stating that "A truce with the enemies, be it absolute [i.e. permanent] or temporary is permissible if the Ruler perceives an interest in it," he alluded to the Quranic verse: "If they incline to peace, do thou likewise, and trust in God, for He heareth and knoweth." Any Muslim state was free to "buy and sell, or exchange ambassadors," with the Jews, he added; and Muslim pilgrims could visit their holy shrines in Jerusalem. He then qualified his interpretation. "Peace with the Jews – or any other infidels – did not require any lessening of 'hostility or hatred' towards them, and – once the balance of power had changed – Muslims were required to 'drive them out of Muslim lands by force' and 'convert them to Islam or make them pay the jizya [tribute], they having been brought low.'" This caveat did not soften the hostility with which a large majority of Wahhabi ulama reacted to al Baz's fatwa (religious opinion). They weighed in with their sermons against what they called the Grand Mufti's heretical aberrations.

"As if it were not enough for you [al Baz] to open up the Land of the Two Noble Sanctuaries to the occupying armies of the Jews and Crusaders, you are now bringing calamity on The Third Sanctuary [in Jerusalem] by legitimizing the surrender deeds of the Arab traitors, despots and cowards," said Khalid al Fawwaz of CAR in London. "The Jewish enemy is the corrupter of Heaven and Earth, and the Muslim's highest duty, after professing the Faith, is to get rid of him."[77]

By now al Fawwaz had been complemented in London by Muhammad al Masaari of the CDLR. After escaping from al Hayir jail near Riyadh, he had traveled to Yemen, and from there to the United Kingdom in early 1994 to seek asylum. He was lucky. The other co-founders of the CDLR would receive long-term jail sentences in August 1995, and one of them, Abdullah al Hudhaif, would be publicly beheaded for allegedly throwing acid in the face of a police torturer, though it was said that Hudhaif was tortured to death in detention and that the beheading was a sham, the head of the corpse being severed in public.[78] To counter the perceived threat of radical Islam, King Fahd replaced more than half of the Council of Senior Ulama, making sure the new appointees would be servile.[79]

Settling in London, Masaari started a monthly newsletter which he faxed to 700 people in the kingdom. It was a curious mixture of academic research, gossip and invective, with a regular column, "Prince of the Month," detailing the prince's misdeeds. It encouraged readers to convey unflattering information about the Saudi regime on toll-free telephone lines.[80] The newsletter could fairly be described as scurrilous and sometimes hasty in exposing the regime's various sins: ineptitude, wastefulness, oppression, corruption and decadence. On the other hand it was the only publication which offered structured information and insight into the darker side of the desert kingdom which, possessing a quarter of the world's known petroleum reserves, was the second largest oil producer in the world. In any case, it deeply worried the Saudi royals. Following King Fahd's complaint to British Prime Minister John Major (r. 1990–7), the two sides began conferring on how to handle the Masaari problem.

By late 1995 the Major government had realized that Britain's commercial interests would be hurt if there was no end to his activities. Since 1987 British aerospace, defense and construction companies had been engaged in fulfilling – in stages – $25 billion worth of arms and military construction contracts between them and the Saudi Ministry of Defense and Aviation, called Al Yamamah: the largest deals of its kind in Western history and the largest too in kickbacks to the Saudi royals, a subject on which Judith Miller had written in the *New York Times*.[81] But when the British authorities informed Masaari in December that he would be deported to the Caribbean island of Dominica (which had agreed to take him in exchange for the quadrupling of its annual grant of $3 million), he appealed to the Immigration Tribunal, arguing that his life would be endangered in Dominica from where he could easily be abducted by Saudi security agents who had done so in several other cases. He won.

In the midst of the Masaari controversy, the Saudi government's attention was diverted by a bomb explosion in the capital. On 13 November 1995 a 220 lb (100 kg) car bomb exploded in the car park of the National Guard training center in Riyadh, a building leased by the Pentagon for military contractors training the Saudi National Guard – the first such explosion in the kingdom. Five American officers and two Indian civilians died, and 60 others, mainly American, were injured. One of the two groups claiming responsibility had warned earlier that US and UK military personnel would become "legitimate targets" if they did not leave the kingdom by June 1995. Two elements were particularly worrisome to the authorities: the attackers' audacity in targeting the capital, where security had always been very tight; and the specific site, the training center of the National Guard, the regime's single most reliable armed force.

The authorities immediately claimed that the terrorists were foreigners – either Iranians or Iraqis. But when they arrested four suspects – Riyadh al Haja, Abdul Aziz al Mitham, Khalid al Said and Muslih al Shamrani – the following April, they all turned out to be young Saudi citizens in their mid- to late 20s, with three of them being Afghan veterans. In late May they

were decapitated after they had confessed their guilt on television. One of them referred to his knowledge of explosives and
assembling of bombs as a participant in the Afghan jihad.[82]
Another, al Shamrani, turned out to be a former member of
bin Laden's Farouq Brigade in Afghanistan.[83] The third admitted
being a student of the writings of bin Laden as well as Al Gamaat
al Islamiya and Al Jihad. The government tried to portray them
as an inconsequential group of zealots who had imbibed fanatical
concepts during their years with the Afghan Mujahedin, and
suggest that its terrorist act was an isolated incident, and not
the start of a bloody process such as the one currently in train
in Algeria. When there was an unpublicized threat of retribution
by a clandestine group if the four defendants were beheaded,
Prince Sultan publicly dismissed it as "childish."[84]

Over the past two decades, despite widespread corruption,
wastage and ineptitude, the economic development of the kingdom had been impressive. This was particularly noticeable to
those foreigners who had visited the country in the mid-1970s
at the start of the oil boom. Between 1976 and 1995 Riyadh
had changed, with freeways and fly-overs, with a million date
palm trees, dozens of fancy shopping malls, with "armies of
Asian workers in bright orange uniforms collecting garbage and
litter" – with "the wealthy [Saudis] hiding their good fortune
behind high beige-toned cement walls – compounds that included
acres of homes, all marble and coolness, indoor and outdoor
swimming pools, clay tennis courts, and family mosques,"
noted American journalist Sandra Mackey during her second
residence in the kingdom as the wife of a US professional.
"Within those walls we could swim, drink whisky, watch
banned videos."[85] It was this lifestyle of the affluent that the
Saudi regime was keen to see maintained, and the rich Saudis
as well as the authorities were disturbed to infer the hand of
bin Laden behind the bombing.

Riyadh's intelligence agency, Istikhabarat, had been increasingly alert in monitoring bin Laden. It had also diligently monitored the Popular Arab and Islamic Congress, sponsored by
Hassan Turabi's National Islamic Front, in March 1995 in

Khartoum, which had drawn delegates from the Lebanese Hizbollah – well versed in exploding lethal bombs – and the Algerian Group Islamique Armée (GIA, Armed Islamic Group), who had conferred with bin Laden and his aides. So too had the CIA been monitoring bin Laden. By early 1996, while considering naming bin Laden a most dangerous terrorist in the light of the law passed by the US Congress in the aftermath of the bomb in Oklahoma City on 19 April 1995, which killed 168 people, directing the president to use all necessary means "including covert action and military force" to disrupt, dismantle and destroy international infrastructure by international terrorists,[86] the US State Department was also planning to close down its embassy in Khartoum. At a dinner party hosted by him, Sudanese foreign minister, Ali Othman Taha, asked American diplomats what his country needed to do to get rid of the terrorist nation label applied to it in 1993. On 8 March 1996 the State Department listed six conditions, one of them being furnishing of details of the Mujahedin that bin Laden had brought into Sudan. In the bargaining that ensued, Sudan agreed to put bin Laden under surveillance. But that was not enough. The State Department wanted him to be handed over to "a responsible external authority." The Sudanese were prepared to deliver him to Riyadh on the ground that earlier that year he had issued a fatwa denouncing the House of Saud as corrupt. But the Saudi government refused to have him, partly because it had no evidence of his involvement in the November 1995 Riyadh bombing,[87] and partly because it feared a severe backlash if it imprisoned or beheaded him. The State Department did not want him for itself as it did not then hold him responsible for killing Americans. So it said to the Sudanese, "Let him go anywhere but Somalia." On 15 May both sides dropped the idea of handing him over to an agreed third party. Three days later he and his entourage left for Afghanistan in a cargo plane.[88] Bin Laden would claim later that, by then, Al Qaida was supporting about 5,000 mainly Arab fighters in the Balkans where a civil war had raged in Bosnia during 1992–5, and that its aid covered Albania, Britain, two Gulf states, Iraq, Lebanon, Malaysia, Netherlands,

Pakistan, Romania, Russia and Turkey.[89] The two unnamed Gulf states probably included Saudi Arabia.

In any case, what happened in Saudi Arabia five weeks later – on 25 June 1996 – was anything but "childish," to quote the term used by Prince Sultan. That night two suspects exploded 4,500 lb (2,000 kg) of explosives planted in a fuel tanker parked outside the perimeter of a guarded and fortified compound of an eight-story residential block in Khobar, called Khobar Tower – part of a vast complex used by US service personnel stationed at Dhahran air base, and then escaped in a car as a security patrol approached them. Creating a 35 ft (11 m) crater, and sending sound waves that traveled 40 miles (65 km) to Bahrain, it tore the front off the Khobar Tower, killing 19 servicemen and injuring 400. The casualties would have been higher had not the security men begun a frantic evacuation of the building a few minutes before the blast. One of the two groups which claimed responsibility was named after Abdullah al Hudhaif, the decapitated CDLR activist. Washington rushed 70 FBI agents to Saudi Arabia.[90]

Following the explosion, for the first time the Pentagon officially acknowledged that 6,000 US service personnel were based on Saudi soil. But, taking into account the American military officers in uniform and civilian clothes attached to Saudi defense offices and facilities in Riyadh, Dhahran, Jiddah and the military cities of Tabuk, Hafar al Batin and Khamis Mushayit – as well as those assigned as training officers to the Defense Ministry and the National Guard – the total was in the range of 12,000 to 15,000.[91] Later, 4,000 of them would be moved to the sprawling Prince Sultan air base near Al Kharj, 70 miles (110 km) south-east of Riyadh, and accommodated in a complex standing in the middle of nowhere, and therefore safe. On their arrival at the new location, US military personnel would be greeted by a huge billboard: "SECURITY UPGRADED BY SAUDI BINLADIN GROUP."[92] Less dramatically, Saudi Binladin Group would get a $150 million contract to rebuild the Khobar Complex. But then SBG was a conglomerate with an annual turnover of $5 billion a year and offices in a dozen countries.[93]

The perpetrators of the Khobar explosion, Washington claimed, were trained in Iran – a statement not taken seriously by Riyadh. Over the coming months and years Saudi Arabia would repeat that no foreigners were involved in the Khobar bombing, and finally its defense minister, Prince Sultan, would say categorically in late 1998 that the investigations so far had showed no Iranian link.[94]

The immediate effect of the explosion was an attempt by the Saudi kingdom to downplay its military links with the Pentagon. In early September 1996 when, following the military assistance Saddam Hussein provided to the Kurdistan Democratic Party in its fight with the rival Patriotic Union of Kurdistan in the Kurdish region, the Pentagon struck targets in Iraq, Riyadh opposed the strikes, and refused permission to US warplanes to take off from Saudi air bases to hit Iraq. This was in contrast to what had happened in January 1993 when American aircraft had flown from Saudi air bases to bomb targets in Iraq.[95] The major domestic difference between January 1993 and September 1996 was that King Fahd had passed on his powers to Crown Prince Abdullah after suffering a stroke which left him speechless, in late November 1995, and after Abdullah had successfully rebuffed a serious challenge to his position by Prince Sultan, a blood brother of Fahd.[96] Though Fahd formally retrieved these powers three months later, there was less and less of his imprint on the regime in the coming years as Abdullah became the *de facto* ruler. At the same time Abdullah remained commander of the National Guard, with his second son, Prince Mitab, trained at the British military academy in Sandhurst, as the deputy commander.

Abdullah as *de facto* ruler

Rooted firmly in the Saudi soil and tribal way of life, Abdullah focused on defusing internal tensions by conciliating political and religious dissidents at home and abroad. Yet he failed to address the long-running issue of the presence of American soldiers on Saudi soil. That the subject remained high on the agenda even of senior ulama became apparent in June 1998 when, in his Friday sermon, Shaikh Ali al Hudaybi, the imam of Prophet Muhammad's Mosque in Medina, the second holiest shrine in Islam, called for the withdrawal of US troops.[97]

Abdullah's efforts to build bridges with Iran, however, bore fruit quickly. In this endeavor he was helped by the election of Muhammad Khatami (1943– ; r. 1997–), a moderate cleric, as president by a large majority in August 1997. A public manifestation of Saudi–Iranian rapprochement came in December when Iran hosted the Islamic Conference Organization summit in Tehran, the first Shia country to do so. By delivering a moderate, erudite speech, President Khatami impressed the audience. "Islamic and Western civilizations are not necessarily in conflict and contradiction," he declared. Citing the Greek and Roman roots of the West, he said, "We should never be oblivious to the careful acquisition of the positive accomplishments of the Western civil society."[98] The summit ended with the adoption of the Tehran Declaration. Denouncing Israel for its occupation of the Arab land, its expansionist polices and its state terrorism, it resolved to regain Al Quds (i.e. Jerusalem) and the Al Aqsa Mosque and restore "the inalienable national rights" of the Palestinians. It condemned terrorism "while distinguishing terrorism from the struggle of peoples against colonial or alien domination or foreign occupation." Declaring that killing of innocents was forbidden in Islam, it urged the international community to "deny asylum to terrorists and assist in bringing them to justice."[99]

Breaking with protocol, Khatami had two private meetings with Crown Prince Abdullah, when the latter reportedly advised his host that Iran must convince Washington that it was no longer a threat to the Gulf monarchies. After nearly two decades of rivalry and conflict, the two Islamic fundamentalist neighbors had finally decided to coexist in peace while pursuing different models of governance, with Tehran firmly committed to its republicanism, whereby power lay ultimately with the public, and Riyadh clinging to its monarchical autocracy with a few cosmetic concessions such as the hand-picked Consultative Council.

In February 1998, as the Clinton administration in Washington prepared to strike Iraq for its refusal to cooperate unconditionally with UN weapons inspectors, it dispatched Secretary of State Madeleine Albright to the Gulf region to win support for the American policy. She drew a blank in Riyadh. "There are those in Saudi Arabia who would grant the US use of Saudi facilities; there are also those who would refuse; and still others who want to see all Americans leave the kingdom," Abdullah reportedly told her. "Since I represent all these people, I am obliged to say 'no' to the use of Saudi facilities for attacks on Iraq." He also asked why Washington was preparing to use force against Iraq for failing to implement a few Security Council resolutions while Israel not only violated with impunity many Council resolutions but also refused to honor its internationally guaranteed treaty commitments to the Palestinians. "Saudi Arabia will not allow any strikes against Iraq under any circumstances from its soil due to the sensitivity of the issue in the Arab and Muslim world," said the official communiqué after the meeting.[100]

While such statements by Riyadh pleased Tehran, the two capitals continued to be in competition in Afghanistan, with Saudi Arabia cooperating actively with Pakistan to ensure that the Taliban, which had captured Kabul in September 1996, extended its jurisdiction to all of Afghanistan, a prospect that depressed Tehran, given the hostility Taliban manifested towards Shias at home and Iran next door.

6   Afghanistan

Fundamentalism victorious, with American backing

Special geographical and historical circumstances shaped Afghanistan into a landlocked society which clung to medieval Islam and tenaciously resisted modernization well into the last quarter of the twentieth century. The present state of Afghanistan, the Land of Afghans, was created out of numerous tribal fiefdoms in the mid-nineteenth century as a buffer between Russia, British India and Iran by imperial Britain and Tsarist Russia.

As for historic Afghanistan, it became part of Dar al Islam with the rise of the Abbasid caliphate in 750. The weakening of the caliphate, which followed a century later, led to the emergence of semi-independent dynasties which ruled Iran, Afghanistan and parts of Central Asia. The most prominent of these was the Ghori dynasty (1000–1215), which ruled present-day Pakistan, much of Afghanistan and eastern Iran. In the first quarter of the sixteenth century Zahiruddin Muhammad Babur (1483–1530), a descendant of Jenghiz Khan (aka Genghis Khan, Chingiz Khan; 1162–1227) and Timur Lang (aka Tamerlane; 1337–1405), seized a territory in Afghanistan and governed it from Kabul. In 1525 he ventured out to India and established the Mogul dynasty. From then on the Mogul and Safavid empires competed for control of Afghanistan. In 1729 Nadir Shah Afshar, having expelled the Afghan tribes from Iran, went on to subdue Kandahar (also Qandahar) in southern Afghanistan. He was assassinated in 1747 by Abdali Afghans, centered around Kandahar, who chose Ahmad Shah Abdali as their leader. On assuming power he took the title of Durr-e Durran (Pearl of the Age), which became transformed into Durrani. He seized parts of the decadent Safavid and Mogul empires, and added to them bits of Tajik territory in the north. In 1776 the capital was moved from Kandahar to Kabul. The new political entity was shaken by a civil war which lasted from 1818 to 1826.

Later, rivalry between Britain and Tsarist Russia led to two wars between Afghanistan and British India: in 1839–42 and 1878–80. The occupation of eastern Afghanistan, which followed the First Anglo-Afghan War, was resisted by the Afghans. In the wake of the second war the British left, but kept control of Afghanistan's foreign relations. The overall result of these conflicts was to engender a sense of Afghan identity as well as to isolate Afghanistan politically and diplomatically. Furthermore, the bloody experience made the traditional tribal and Islamic leaders view all reform and modernization as Western innovations which had to be resisted.

It was against this background that Abdur Rahman (1830–1901; r. 1880–1901) assumed power in 1880. Starting with firm control of Kabul and its environs, he staged several campaigns to subdue the Pushtun tribes in the south and south-east, and then the Uzbek and Turkmen tribes in the north. In 1888, when Shia Hazaras[1] (speakers of Persian), pushed into the inhospitable Hazarajat mountains over the centuries, rebelled, Abdur Rahman rallied Pushtun (speakers of Pushtu/Pashto), Uzbek (speakers of the Uzbek language) and Turkmen (speakers of the Turkmen language) under the banner of Sunni Islam, and subdued the Hazaras in 1891. Four years later he seized Kafiristan, Land of the Infidel, to the east of Kabul, dotted with Christian missions, and converted its pagan inhabitants to Sunni Islam, renaming the area Nuristan, Land of Light. This made Afghanistan 99 percent Muslim: 80 percent Sunni of the Hanafi school, and the rest Shia of the Jaafari school, mostly ethnic Hazaras.

Islam in Afghanistan was a mixture of orthodoxy and Sufism. In cities and towns there were properly trained ulama. But in most of the 26,000 villages, where 85 percent of Afghans lived, the locally appointed mullahs were often semi-trained, having been educated by an alim at a local *madressa*, a religious high school. There were very few Islamic seminaries of repute in Afghanistan. For proper training in Sunni Islam an aspiring alim had to go to either Al Azhar in Cairo or Dar al Ulum, the seminary in Deoband, 60 miles (100 km) north of Delhi, India, established in 1866 and still going strong,[2] specializing in the Hanafi legal system, which, while opposing the cult of saints, was tolerant of such orthodox Sufi orders as Naqshbandi. For the Shia, advanced theological education came either in Mashhad in eastern Iran or in Najaf in Iraq.

A typical village mullah was an integral part of the rural elite by either marriage or birth, often himself being a substantial landlord. Besides performing religious rites he imparted elementary religious and other education to village children, and was also a folk healer.

While Afghan tribes had embraced Islam they had not totally discarded their pre-Islamic, traditional law and values. An example among Pushtun tribes, who formed nearly half of the Afghan population, was Pushtunwali, or Nang-e Pushtun, the Way of Pushtun. Pushtunwali is both an ideology and a corpus of common law with its own institutions and sanctions. Some of the major features of the Pushtunwali are:

> To avenge blood; to fight to death for a person who has taken refuge with me no matter what his lineage; to defend to the last any property entrusted to me; to be hospitable and provide for the safety of the person and property of guests; to pardon an offense (other than murder) on the intercession of a woman of the offender's lineage, a sayyid or a mullah; to punish all adulterers with death; to refrain from killing a man who has entered a mosque or the shrine of a holy man.[3]

There are many instances where the provisions of the Pushtunwali and the Sharia are at odds. The Sharia requires four witnesses to adultery; in the Pushtunwali mere hearsay is enough. Divorce is easy in the Sharia, particularly for the husband, but almost impossible in the Pushtunwali. Women are entitled to inheritance in the Sharia but not in the Pushtunwali. Retribution is total in the Sharia but limited in the Pushtunwali. On the one hand the Pushtunwali has perpetuated feuding among tribes; on the other it has proved adequate in providing a semblance of law and order among warrior tribes.

The dominant Sufi orders are Qadiriya and Naqshbandi. Qadiriya had reached Pushtun tribes in eastern Afghanistan from India where it had become established in the sixteenth century. After World War I Naqib Gailani arrived in the Pushtun area from Baghdad, the original source of the Qadiriya, to gain greater control over the brotherhoods. In contrast, the Naqsh-bandi order had permeated Afghanistan in the course of its expansion from Bukhara (now in Uzbekistan), the city of its founder, and encompassed both Pushtun and non-Pushtun tribes. In the late 1800s descendants of Shaikh Ahmad Sirhindi, an eminent Naqshbandi leader, called the Mujaddid Alf-e Thani, arrived from India to settle in Kabul's Shor Bazaar district. In due course the patriarch of the Mujaddidi family came to be called the Hazrat of Shor Bazaar, the first one being Qayum Jahan. These two Sufi orders had the whole gamut of supreme guides (pirs), aspirants (murids) and lay members, a string of lodges and holy shrines, coupled with the practice of pilgrimage to these shrines where the faithful called for the inter-cession of the saint. The fact that orthodox ulama considered such practices heretical had no impact on their continued popularity.

It was in this milieu that Abdur Rahman exercised power which, according to traditional Afghan thinking, he derived from the tribal *jirga* (assembly). While not disputing this view, he asserted that only "divine guidance" could ensure that the people would choose a true and legitimate ruler. The throne, he argued, was the property of Allah who appointed kings as shep-herds to guard his flock. Thus kings were vice-regents of Allah who derived their duties and responsibilities from His will. Among the duties and responsibilities he saw himself performing were championing the cause of Islam and freeing Afghan soil from the domination of infidel and foreign forces. It was in the name of Islam that he subdued ethnically heterogeneous tribes and founded a centralized state, a strategy which Abdul Aziz ibn Saud was to use later in Najd. Abdur Rahman set up an Executive Council and a *Loya Jirga* (National General Assembly), consisting of aristocrats from the royal family or clan, village notables and landlords, and ulama. Since he had no intention of sharing power these bodies were purely advisory.

Among the ministerial departments he established were those of justice and education, which had so far been the monopolies of the ulama. He thus came into direct conflict with the religious establishment. He resolved this by assuming the dual role of the Leader of the Islamic community and the sole interpreter of the Sharia, something Emperor Akbar (1542–1605; r. 1556–1605) had done in Mogul India in the late sixteenth century. He attacked the ulama for disseminating strange doctrines which were never part of the teachings of Prophet Muhammad. He deprived them of the right to declare jihad which, he asserted, could be waged only under the orders of a ruler. As a self-proclaimed mujtahid, he published various pamphlets on the foundations of Islam, jihad and religious advice. To underline his status as the leader of the umma, he took over the religious trusts, thus destroying the economic self-sufficiency of the ulama. He reduced them to the status of government bureaucrats. He ordered that they should undergo formal examination to prove their suitability as state officials. By depriving the ulama of their right to interpret the Sharia, turning them into state employees dependent on his treasury, and controlling their numbers by introducing a formal examination, Abdur Rahman severely undermined their position. He rationalized the legal system by dividing it into the Sharia, qanun (administrative and civil law), and tribal law. He assigned the judgment of business disputes to boards of commerce. He appointed himself the supreme judge.

Such concentration of power was bound to elicit counter-vailing demands. These arose during the reign of his successor, Habibullah (r. 1901–19). However, the calls for a constitutional monarchy came not from the ulama but from liberal secularists who were inspired by the 1907–11 Constitutional Revolution in

Iran. They got short shrift from the ruler: he executed some of their leaders and jailed many more.

Habibullah pursued the idea of the Triple Alliance of the Ottoman empire, Iran and Afghanistan as a barrier to Russian expansion in the Middle East that had been conceived by his predecessor. From 1911 onwards Afghanistan experienced a surge of pan-Islamism which was actively encouraged by Habibullah. He found in it a useful concept to unite his ethnically divided subjects and consolidate national independence. Pan-Islamism appealed to both traditionalists and modernists. The latter saw in it an opportunity to rationalize reform and innovation as a means of reinforcing monarchy and defending Afghanistan and Islam. During World War I Habibullah failed to side with Ottoman Turkey which was ranged against Britain that still controlled Afghanistan's external affairs. This led to his assassination in 1919.

His successor, Amanullah (r. 1919–29), set out as a fervent pan-Islamist. He waged a jihad against the British along the border with India to recover the Pushtun land Britain had annexed and retrieve the right to conduct his country's external relations, thereby strengthening Islamic bonds between him and the border tribes. His campaign was a military failure but a political success: he gained the right to conduct Afghanistan's foreign affairs. In March 1921 he concluded a treaty with Turkey whereby Afghanistan recognized Turkey as the guide of Islam and custodian of the caliphate. Three months later he signed a treaty with Iran, thus moving towards Islamic solidarity along the lines first mooted by Jamaluddin Afghani some decades earlier. Amanullah's actions united the ulama and modernists behind him.

However, he was aware that his landlocked country, lacking financial resources of its own, needed to normalize relations with its powerful non-Muslim neighbors: British India and Bolshevik Russia. He signed a treaty with Britain in November 1921, having concluded a comprehensive treaty with Soviet Russia nine months earlier.

At home he could not sustain the simultaneous support of modernists and the ulama. When he opened government schools to train future administrators and professionals, and liberalized women's position by banning child marriage and transferring the regulation of family affairs from the ulama to the state, he ran into stiff opposition from the religious establishment. The first sign of disaffection came with a tribal rebellion in the east in March 1924. Amanullah successfully crushed it, but his hiring of German and Russian pilots for the aircraft used in the campaign incensed the traditionalists: they found the intrusion of infidels into the internal feuds of Muslims intolerable. Amanullah capped his victory with a ban on contacts between the armed forces and mullahs, and the enrollment of military personnel in Sufi brotherhoods. He thus enlarged his power at the expense of the ulama.

He formalized the situation by offering the nation a written constitution in 1923 along the lines of the Iranian constitution of 1906–7. In it he declared Islam to be the official religion of Afghanistan, where the name of the ruler had to be mentioned in religious sermons.

Having thus consolidated his position, Amanullah, dapper in his well-cut Western suits, undertook a nine-month-long tour (from October 1927 to July 1928) of India, the Middle East and Europe, a sojourn which laid the seeds of his deposition. At receptions in Europe his wife, Soraya, a doe-eyed beauty, appeared unveiled, and photographs of such appearances began circulating in Kabul. Amanullah returned home via Turkey, then in the midst of militant secularism, and Iran, then undergoing rapid modernization under Reza Pahlavi Shah (1878–1944; r. 1925–41).

The special Loya Jirga that Amanullah convened on his return went along with his proposal for a representative government based on votes for all, and military conscription for men. But it opposed modern education for girls and age limits for marriage. When he tried to implement legal and financial reform the ulama responded with the argument that the Sharia, having been derived from Allah, was enough, and needed no elaboration.

But Amanullah was not to be stopped. He issued decrees outlawing polygamy among civil servants, permitting women to discard the veil, and requiring all Afghans residing in or visiting Kabul to wear Western dress complete with a European hat from March 1929 onwards. Clerics regarded the dress order as blasphemous, particularly the insistence on the European hat as it interfered with the Islamic way of praying which required the believer to touch the ground with his forehead in the course of the prayer. The king forbade theological students from enrolling at Deoband seminary and banned foreign-trained ulama from teaching. To crown it all, in October 1928 a hundred women led by Queen Soraya appeared unveiled at an official function in Kabul. For the religious and traditional establishments this was the limit. The ulama's attitude was summed up by a cleric's quip: "When reforms come in, Islam goes out.'

When Fazl Muhammad Mujaddidi, the Hazrat of Shor Bazaar, began collecting signatures against the reforms, King Amanullah arrested him. Violent rioting broke out in Kabul. In November Shinwaris in the east joined other Pushtun tribes in a revolt against the king. Amanullah dispatched royal forces, but they defected to the other side. Disaffection within monarchist forces stemmed from the ruler's secular reformist actions as well as his employment of European military advisors.

In early January 1929 forces led by Bacha-e Saqqao (lit. Son of a Water-Carrier), a Tajik highwayman based in the Shomali plain north of Kabul, a stronghold of fundamentalism, laid siege to the capital. He had the active support of the ulama, who in turn had popular opinion on their side. Under pressure from Bacha-e Saqqao, Amanullah agreed to close girls' schools, withdraw permission for women to discard the veil, cancel the Western dress order, allow religious students to join Deoband seminary, and rescind the requirement of a teaching certificate for a cleric imposed by Abdur Rahman. He promised to appoint *muhtasibs* (religious supervisors) in provinces to ensure that Islamic precepts were being observed. Most importantly, he agreed to abide by the Sharia as interpreted by orthodox ulama, and rule in consultation with a council of 50 religious and tribal leaders.

But all this proved inadequate to save Amanullah his throne. On 14 January, aided by defectors from the royal troops, Bacha-e Saqqao captured Kabul and promised to establish the rule of the Sharia. On assuming power he confirmed all the cancellations of Amanullah, and went on to dissolve the education and justice ministries and hand over the task of running courts and schools to the ulama.

While Bacha-e Saqqao performed the job of deposing Amanullah, the inspiration for his actions, and the crucial popular backing they received, stemmed from the ulama. In short, clerics were the main agents who brought about the downfall of the monarch in Afghanistan, a Sunni country – an achievement they were to repeat 50 years later in Shia Iran. The event was all the more remarkable because most of the ulama were state employees. Only Sufi leaders and their followers formed an independent Islamic force. It was not accidental that it was the Mujaddidi family in Kabul who took the lead in expressing and mobilizing Islamic sentiment against the monarch. Unlike Reza Pahlavi Shah in Iran, who rose to power as a military leader and built up a strong army before challenging the ulama, Amanullah lacked a strong, secular force in the form of a properly trained, disciplined and, above all, loyal army. It would not be until 1953 that the army would come into its own in Afghanistan when, led by Muhammad Daoud Khan (1917–78; r. 1973–78), it would become the primary power center.

Bacha-e Saqqao failed to consolidate his position. Political anarchy and severe economic crisis overwhelmed him. In October 1929 he was overthrown by Muhammad Nadir Khan – a third cousin of Amanullah and a brother of King Habibullah's second wife – with the aid of Fazl Umar Mujaddidi in Kabul and Sher Agha Naguib, a religious leader in the eastern city of Jalalabad.

The brief reign of King Nadir Shah marked the zenith of Islamic fundamentalism in Afghanistan. Obligated to religious luminaries for his position, he set out to found a fully fledged Islamic state. He established the Jamaat-e Ulama (Group of the

Ulama) and authorized it to interpret the Sharia and vet all government laws and regulations in its light. One of the Jamaat's interpretations held that women were not entitled to vote. The Ministry of Justice, placed under Fazl Umar Mujaddidi, was given the task of enforcing the Sharia. Nadir Shah ordered that all civil and criminal laws should be based entirely on the Sharia. He set up the department of *ihtisab* (religious observance) to supervise adherence to Islam with instructions to enforce strictly the Islamic dietary restrictions, particularly on alcohol. He consulted the ulama on all important social, educational and political issues. So beholden was he to the ulama that when they opposed his plan of establishing a central bank on the ground that it would amount to creating an instrument of usury, he dropped the idea. Never before in modern times had the ulama enjoyed such power and prestige, with the Hazrat of Shor Bazaar acting as a close advisor to the monarch. Islam and tradition were the two pillars which firmly supported Nadir Shah's regime.

In the constitution of 1931 Nadir Shah formalized the role of religion and religious leaders. The first four articles described Islam of the Hanafi school as the official religion, required that the king be a Hanafi Muslim and that his name be mentioned in Friday sermons, and barred non-Muslims from becoming government ministers. Other articles institutionalized the powers that Nadir Shah had conferred on the ulama and Sharia courts, and recognized the supremacy and orthodoxy of the Hanafi school. Still another provision authorized Afghan citizens the right to impart "Islamic scholastic or moral sciences" either in private or in public. This confirmed the right of the ulama to educate Muslim children. With this primary-school teaching reverted to the mullahs, and religious instruction became the central preoccupation of the educational system.

The constitution incorporated the Quranic injunctions on popular consultation – "Take counsel with them in the affairs" (3:153) and "Their affairs are by consultation among them" (42:38) – by prescribing a consultative council based on votes for all male Afghans.

The first parliament assembled in 1931, but Nadir Shah did not live to see the second parliament three years later: he was assassinated in November 1933. The throne went to his son Muhammad Zahir Shah (1914– ; r. 1933–73), a youth of 19. Power was exercised in his name by his three uncles, one of whom, Muhammad Hashim Khan, became prime minister, and held the position until 1946.

During these years much intellectual energy was spent in diagnosing the reasons for the backwardness of Afghanistan and the poor condition of Muslims at large. The traditionalist thinkers blamed the present sorry state on Muslim leaders' deviation from the true path of Islam and the Sharia. But nationalist modernists disagreed. They said that there was no inherent contradiction between Islam and progress. In fact Islam enjoined upon the believers to seek knowledge. Social welfare and national defense demanded knowledge and science. They argued furthermore that the Sharia offered guidance towards public well-being, progress and justice, and that such principles could be learned and applied by reason which could be cultivated only through education and learning. In other words they called for ijtihad (creative interpretation), dormant in the Sunni world for many centuries, except in the Hanbali school.

Every so often even *Al Falah* (The Good Path), the journal of the Jamaat-e Ulama (Society of Ulama), would publish an article in this vein. One author argued that the ethical precepts of Islam and the Quran were sources of inspiration for social reform. Another, Abdul Razak Khan Tulimsher, argued that in modern times Muslims could preserve their societies and spiritual legacy through military power which could be achieved only through knowledge. The sword was essential, he wrote, but Islam also needed knowledge and progress to defend itself.[4]

However, these were the views of a tiny minority among the ulama, the vast majority holding modernization to be antithetical to Islamic and traditional values. Tribal chiefs shared this belief. With these two important centers of power – the ulama and tribal leaders – wedded to the status quo, the monarchical regime became static.

World War II, in which Afghanistan remained neutral, underlined the importance of science and technology. It made the ruling dynasty realize the pressing need for rapid reform and modernization in order to preserve itself and Afghan independence as well as tackle the rising socio-economic problems.

Modern education grew, but at a very slow pace. Kabul University, founded in 1932, with a Faculty of Medicine affiliated to Lyons University in France, acquired Faculties of Science, and Law and Political Science, during the next decade.

Religious education continued to have priority. Curricula in primary and secondary schools, designed in the main by the ulama, laid heavy emphasis on Islam, Islamic history, moral lessons, Islamic precepts and law, and Persian classics. In 1944 the government established a School for Instruction in the Sharia, and upgraded it six years later to a Faculty of Theology at Kabul University in conjunction with Al Azhar in Cairo. Thus the monarchical regime established a state-run system through which an Afghan could become an alim without leaving the country: a breeding ground for a new type of religious scholar.

Overall, nationalist modernists seemed to be gaining ground at the expense of traditional and religious leaders. One symptom of it was the emergence in 1947 of the Awakened Youth movement of intellectuals who demanded constitutional reform. Prime Minister Shah Mahmoud allowed comparative freedom to voters in parliamentary elections whose results in the past had been predetermined by the royal family. Of the 120 members of the Seventh Parliament (1949–52), between 40 and 45 were considered liberal. They were instrumental in allowing a degree of freedom to the press. With this the differences between the traditional-religious and nationalist-reformist camps sharpened. The liberals' demands for further extension of freedom of speech and the press, and the formation of political parties, were rebuffed by the palace. This made them virulent. Students at Kabul University, a stronghold of nationalist-reformists, formed a union and began discussing such blasphemous subjects as Communism and atheism. The three opposition magazines became strident and attacked religious luminaries, including the

Hazrat of Shor Bazaar, for their fanaticism and conservatism. An example of their conservative interpretation of Islam was their opposition until 1949 to smoking tobacco, which they regarded as a narcotic. Radical students staged plays which ridiculed the royal family and religious leaders. Premier Mahmoud found these developments intolerable. He banned the Students' Union in 1951, and then the Awakened Youth. He arrested top opposition leaders before the 1952 parliamentary poll.

Clearly the royal family, the ultimate arbiter of power, found Islamic and tribal leaders unrealistically conservative and a continued barrier to modernization. At the same time they saw in the rival group of constitutional modernizers a threat to their unchallenged supremacy in politics. Fortunately for royalists, the mounting hostility between the competing forces of religious tradition and secular modernization had left them both weak. Thus the time was ripe for the palace to inject into the political drama its own active player: the military.

In September 1953 Muhammad Daoud Khan, commander of the Central Forces in Kabul, and a cousin of King Zahir Shah, mounted a coup against Premier Mahmoud with the active consent of the palace, and became the prime minister. His first priority was to modernize and strengthen the military. For this he relied heavily on the Soviet Union – a neighbor with which Kabul had built up a special relationship after the 1917 Bolshevik Revolution – for historical and contemporary reasons. By concluding a treaty with Soviet Russia in early February 1921 Afghanistan under Amanullah became the first country to recognize the Russian revolutionary regime. Following two serious border incidents in 1925, the two countries signed a Treaty of Neutrality and Non-aggression which was reiterated and strengthened five years later. Good relations between the two neighbors were undisturbed by World War II due to the neutrality that Afghanistan maintained in the conflict. Oddly, the creation of Pakistan, a Muslim state, in August 1947 was badly received by Kabul. Britain's departure from the Indian subcontinent led to the revival of Afghan irredentist claims on the Pushtun lands in Pakistan, which had been kept in abeyance since 1893 when Abdur Rahman had signed an agreement with British India to delimit the border, which divided various Pushtun tribes in the region. Now Afghanistan sponsored a movement for an independent Pushtunistan consisting of Pushtun tribes living east of its pre-1947 border with British India. Pakistan vehemently opposed the Pushtunistan movement. Relations between the two countries worsened. As Pakistan drifted towards the Western camp, formalizing its links with the US with a Mutual Security Pact in 1954, Kabul tilted towards Moscow. In order not to upset its Pakistani ally, America refused to sell arms to Afghanistan. In response, Daoud Khan began attaching Soviet advisors to the Afghan military academies and dispatching military officers to the Soviet Union for further training. At the same time, intent on developing Afghanistan economically, he successfully solicited funds and experts from America and other Western nations for economic projects.

An autocrat, Daoud Khan wanted to centralize state authority through the military, and implement socio-economic progress through executive decrees rather than democratic debate and consensus. He was intolerant of such independent power centers as the Jamaat-e Ulama and deprived it of the powers vested in it by Nadir Shah. He began supplanting orthodox ulama by fresh graduates of Kabul University's Faculty of Theology in the justice and education ministries. Also he tried, quietly, to effect women's emancipation. In 1957 Kabul Radio introduced female singers and announcers. Mild protest followed but did not linger. The following year the government sent a woman delegate to the United Nations in New York, an unprecedented step. The state-owned Ariana Afghan Airlines employed female receptionists and hostesses, and they went about their job without a veil. Also unveiled women were employed as telephone operators. At the independence day celebrations, on 25 August 1959, wives and daughters of senior government officials appeared unveiled on the review stand: an act which reminded senior traditionalists of what had occurred under Amanullah 31 years earlier. As before, the ulama protested vehemently. Daoud Khan replied that if they could find indisputable evidence for the all-embracing shroud, called *burqa*, in the Sharia he would impose it. The appropriate verse in the Quran states, "And say to the believing women, that they cast down their eyes and guard their private parts . . . and let them cast their veils over their bosoms, and not reveal their adornment save to their husbands, or their fathers, or their husbands' fathers, or their sons, or their sisters' sons, or their women . . . or their children who have not yet attained knowledge of women's private parts."[5] This could not be interpreted to mean wearing a burqa. Yet the ulama refused to accept the discarding of the burqa.

Soon they began to preach against the regime, arguing that Daoud Khan was an anti-Islamic leader who among other things was letting atheistic Communists and Western Christians undermine the Islamic way of life. They were particularly upset about the presence of Russian advisors, military and civilian, in Afghanistan, apprehensive that the Russians would steer Afghans away from Islam, something they had done to the Muslim inhabitants of the Central Asian republics of the Soviet Union: Kazakhstan, Kyrgyzstan, Tajikistan, Turkmenistan and Uzbekistan. The government arrested 50 clerical leaders on charges of treason and heresy. The severity of the charges dampened the spirits of the ulama, who were well aware of the iron fist with which Daoud Khan ruled the country. The chastened ulama were released after a week. The protest against the unveiling of women died down. This was in marked contrast to what had happened under Amanullah. The major difference between then and now was that Daoud Khan controlled a loyal, well-disciplined and modern army, which was not the case with Amanullah.

Daoud Khan's continued commitment to establish the independent state of Pushtunistan brought him into open conflict with Pakistan in September 1961. The two countries severed diplomatic links. Pakistan closed its frontier with the landlocked Afghanistan, causing high inflation and an acute fuel shortage there. King Zahir Shah tried to conciliate Pakistan by getting Daoud Khan to resign in March 1963 and replacing him with

Muhammad Hashim Maiwandwal. Two months later Pakistan reopened its border with Afghanistan.

The exit of Daoud Khan from the premiership did not alter the fact that the military was the single most important center of power and that it was ultimately loyal to the monarch. This reassured King Zahir Shah, who had so far been overshadowed first by his uncles and then by his cousin, Daoud Khan. Now he decided to assert his authority.

Realizing the need for political reform, he promulgated in October 1964 a liberal constitution, which inaugurated constitutional monarchy, better known in Afghanistan as "New Democracy," and which proved to be the last chapter in the long history of monarchy in the country. This period witnessed an important change in the composition of Islamic forces. As before, the new constitution assigned Islam a prime place in society. Article 1 stated that Islam was the sacred religion of Afghanistan and that the king had to be a Hanafi Muslim. The official language was Dari (derivative of *darbar*, court), the specific name given to the Persian language as used at the royal court, in order chiefly to distance Afghanistan culturally from Iran. Article 64 ruled out any law "repugnant to the basic principles of the sacred religion of Islam." Another article stated that where no law existed the provisions of the Hanafi school of the Sharia would apply. (As in the past the National Center of Legislation at the Ministry of Justice was to continue to examine whether the existing laws were unconstitutional or un-Islamic.)

The 1964 constitution provided for a parliament composed of a fully elected Wolesi Jirga (Assembly of the People) and a partly elected Meshrano Jirga (Assembly of Nobles). The first Wolesi Jirga which met in October 1965 consisted of three main groups: clerics led by the Mujaddidi family; nationalist centrists, represented partly by the Musavat (Unity) party under Muhammad Hashim Maiwandwal, who looked to the king to implement progressive policies under constitutional monarchy; and Marxists.

For the ulama, parliament provided a national platform, an improvement on the past when they had functioned on a regional basis. But they were now losing power since they were being supplanted by the graduates of Kabul University's Faculty of Theology who had been given important administrative and religious jobs during Daoud Khan's premiership. Also, like the freshly established parliament, Kabul University had been fostering inter-tribal and inter-regional contacts: half of the university's 3,000 students (in 1962) were from the provinces.

The 12-year-old Faculty of Theology was headed by Professor Ghulam Muhammad Niyazi, who during his education at Al Azhar had come under the influence of the Muslim Brotherhood. At certain times two Egyptian professors, and one Indian – a follower of the Islamic thinker Sayyid Abul Ala Maududi (1903–79) – taught at the faculty. Through them and a local cultural group, led by Sibghatullah Mujaddidi, the Persian translations of the works of Sayyid Qutb and Maududi became available to theological students and others. These books presented Islam as a modern ideology – not an obscurantist faith associated with traditional ulama and village mullahs. *Majale-ye Shariat* (Review of the Sharia), published by the Faculty of Theology, proved to be a fruitful channel for discussion for the new breed of Islamic fundamentalists.

By 1965 the expanding body of Islamist students felt confident enough to mount a demonstration and distribute a pamphlet entitled *A Tract of the Jihad*. The Organization of Young Muslims was the public face of Islamic fundamentalists who functioned secretly under the guidance of a council headed by Professor Niyazi. In 1970 the council decided to branch out of the university campus and establish cells in the army. Two years later they shifted their focus from spiritual revival of the community to acquiring political power. Following the adoption of a constitution, the fundamentalists elected Professor Burhanuddin Rabbani (1940– ; r. 1992–6), an ethnic Tajik, as president and Professor Abdul Rasul Sayyaf as his deputy.

Gahiz (Morning), a pro-Islamic, anti-Marxist publication established in October 1968, provided a popular platform for the Organization of Young Muslims and other fundamentalists. This was a consequence of the press legislation passed by parliament in 1965 and endorsed by King Zahir Shah. However, when parliament passed a bill on political parties the monarch refused his assent. He did the same to the legislation establishing provincial and local councils. So the much-flaunted "New Democracy" proved stillborn.

By the late 1960s secondary education had expanded so rapidly that only a minority of applicants to Kabul University were able to gain entry. Student protest at teaching and other facilities often took a political turn, and the university became a hotbed of Marxists and Islamic fundamentalists. The latter were as much opposed to the autocracy and corruption of the royal family as they were to the rising tide of Marxism. In secondary schools, teacher-training colleges and technical institutes too dissent grew, with a large body of students and rising numbers of unemployed graduates blaming the corrupt monarchy for their problems and backing the radical solutions offered by Marxists or Islamic fundamentalists.

The palace found Marxists particularly threatening since leftist students had taken to allying with industrial workers and their periodic strikes. It ensured the defeat of all Marxist candidates in the 1969 parliamentary poll. In April 1970 the publication in the *Parcham* (Flag), a Marxist magazine, of a poem on Lenin's birthday entitled *Dorud Bar Lenin* (Long Live Lenin), a benediction normally reserved for Prophet Muhammad, provided the government with an opportunity to apply popular pressure against the Marxists. It encouraged the ulama and their followers to demonstrate against the leftist magazine, which they did. But they did not stop there. They went on to attack the regime's steady drift towards secularization and the growing presence of female students in secondary and higher educational institutions during the premiership of Maiwandwal. They argued that injecting large doses of non-traditional education into the system was fast eroding the morals of the youth and undermining traditional social values. What reinforced, for them, a sense of general moral decadence was the presence of thousands of young Western men and women and their licentious behavior in Kabul, which was then on the trail that Western hippies followed from Europe to India.[6] In 1972 the Kabul-based press reported famine in the provinces due to the failure of rains for two consecutive years, which claimed about 100,000 lives. Islamists staged demonstrations against foodgrain hoarders and called for limits on personal wealth. All in all, therefore, in the early 1970s there was a general sense of drift, decadence and turmoil in the country; and Islamists held the royal family responsible for it.

On 17 July 1973, while King Zahir Shah was in Italy for medical treatment, Muhammad Daoud Khan seized power. This time he abolished the monarchy and set up a republic. He declared that he had assumed power in order to return Afghanistan to Islamic principles. But instead of ordering the immediate and total application of the Sharia he announced land ceilings of 20 and 40 hectares respectively for irrigated and unirrigated land. Through this measure he expected to win popularity in rural Afghanistan. To enlarge his support, particularly in urban areas, he secured the cooperation of the Parchami group which had split with its radical rival, the Khalqi faction, in 1966 – a year after the formal founding of the (Marxist) People's Democratic Party of Afghanistan (PDPA) in January 1965. Parchamis regarded Daoud's republic as an improvement over the corrupt, autocratic monarchy whereas Khalqis did not.

As before, Daoud Khan tried to monopolize authority. With Parchami Marxists supporting his regime and the Musavat crippled by the execution of Maiwandwal, the only party which hindered his path to total power was that of the Islamic fundamentalists, who had established themselves at Kabul University as the dominant force. In 1972 the Organization of Young Muslims, led by Gulbuddin Hikmatyar (b. 1946–), a civil engineering graduate, had secured a majority of seats on the Students' Council. Young Muslims drew most of their support from rural high school graduates, who felt frustrated at every step: university admission, jobs and career advancement. By and large they were more pious than their Kabul counterparts. As for the parent body of the Young Muslims, popularly called Ikhwan (Muslim Brothers), it was winning recruits among military officers.

While senior fundamentalist leaders kept in touch with the traditional ulama, the Young Muslims were dismissive of them, regarding them as conservative compromisers. Consequently, no united front of old and new fundamentalists emerged. This helped Daoud Khan as he increased pressure on the Islamists. In one swoop in June 1974 his government arrested 200 Islamic fundamentalists in Kabul as they gathered to discuss a blueprint of an Islamic republic where the Sharia would be applied in its totality. Hikmatyar fled to Pakistan. But Niyazi and Rabbani made one more attempt to persuade Daoud Khan to break with Parchamis. They failed. Rabbani then escaped to Pakistan, and Niyazi was subsequently imprisoned.

In exile, Rabbani proposed a long-term strategy of infiltrating the military and seizing power through a coup in Kabul. By contrast, Hikmatyar was for immediate armed struggle. This suited Pakistan's prime minister, Zulfikar Ali Bhutto (1928– ; r. 1972–7). He wanted to strike at Daoud Khan, who had once again revived the contentious issue of Pushtunistan. Bhutto readily agreed to aid Hikmatyar and his followers with arms and training. July 1975 was chosen as the date for a national uprising. But very little happened except in the north-east. Daoud Khan used the trouble caused by the armed fundamentalists to tighten his grip on power. He banned all privately owned publications. He set up his own political party called the National Revolutionary Party (NRP). Much to the chagrin of the ulama, he secularized commercial and civil laws, thus undoing the work of King Nadir Shah and contradicting his earlier claim that he had seized power to revive Islam.

Following the failure of their uprising, the Islamists took refuge in Peshawar, Pakistan. Here the split between Rabbani and Hikmatyar became final in 1976, and that marked the final demise of the Ikhwan and Organization of Young Muslims. Due to his lack of classical religious education, Hikmatyar failed to win the respect or support of the ulama. He was, however, a charismatic figure and an outstanding organizer who had spent years in student politics. He formed Hizb-e Islami (Islamic Party), which believed inter alia that the piety of a believer should be judged primarily on the basis of his political actions and only secondarily on his religious behavior and expertise. Rabbani, a graduate of Al Azhar and a literary critic, was much respected by orthodox ulama as well as leaders of the Sufi orders. Rabbani named his party Jamiat-e Islami (lit. Islamic Society) of Afghanistan. Its ideology was based on the writings of Maududi, who had founded the Jamaat-e Islami (Islamic Group) in India in 1941, followed six years later by the Jamaat-e Islami in the newly created Pakistan, where he received the death sentence in 1953 for inciting violence against the heterodox Ahmadiya sect,[7] although this was later commuted. Maududi and his party were well known in Kabul's Islamic circles, and through *Gahiz* magazine efforts had been made in the early 1970s by Afghan Islamists to establish formal links with the Pakistani party. By then Maududi had emerged as the most important non-Arab Islamic theorist and propagandist in the Sunni world: his books in Urdu had been translated into Arabic, Persian and English.

Born in Jabalpur, India, in 1903 in a religious family, Abul Ala Maududi started his working life as editor of a religious journal. He believed that the character of a social order flowed from the top to the bottom, and therefore to change society one had first to change the theoretical thinking of its leaders. He founded the Jamaat-e Islami to produce a cadre of sincere and disciplined Muslims capable of bringing about the victory of Islam in India. When India was partitioned in August 1947 he moved to Pakistan.

The author of 60 books, Maududi developed Islam through ijtihad and literal exposition into a modern ideology with answers for all individual and social problems. Unlike traditional ulama who spent their energies in tackling arcane and largely irrelevant matters, Maududi faced modern life armed with the Sharia. Like Abdul Wahhab he attacked orthodox ulama for confusing the fundamentals of Islam with the details of its application, and diluting Islam by attaching their own rules to the injunctions of the Sharia. He advocated ijtihad but only in accordance with the spirit of the Sharia's commandments.

What made Maududi particularly attractive to young urban pious Afghans – caught in the web of Western cultural influences and Soviet military and commercial links – was his argument that Islam was self-sufficient and quite separate from, and indeed opposed to, both Western and socialist ways of life. Describing the West as morally decadent and corrupt, he stated, "Islam and Western civilization are poles apart in their objectives as well as in their principles of social organization."[8] He wanted Muslims to acquire scientific knowledge – which he seemed to regard as finite – for the benefit of Islam.

While regarding the government under Prophet Muhammad and the First Four (Rightly Guided) Caliphs as the model, Maududi gave it a democratic interpretation. He prescribed that the leader of an Islamic state today – heading the legislative, judiciary and executive organs – must be elected by the faithful; so must the consultative council. Its members should be able to judge whether or not the leader was following Islamic policies. Maududi had no objection to candidates contesting elections on party tickets, but ruled that once they had been elected they must give up party labels and owe allegiance only to the Islamic state, and vote on issues according to their individual judgment.

Maududi's innovation, however, failed when it came to tackling social and family issues. Here he followed an ultra-orthodox line. He favored sexual segregation and the veil for women. He insisted that a woman must cover her face when she leaves home. Arguing that since the objective of the Sharia is to curb indecency and obscenity, "nothing can be more unreasonable than to close all the minor ways to indecency but to fling the main gate [i.e. face] wide open."[9]

But the merit of Maududi's blueprint was that rejection of some of its elements left the whole edifice still intact and self-sufficient. More specifically, Maududi's thesis provided a modern interpretation of Islam as an alternative to the secular and atheistic ideologies that were being disseminated in Afghanistan.

While sharing Maudidi's thesis, Rabbani diverged from him on the nature of the party to be established. He wanted Jamiat-e Islami to be a mass organization. But since the structure of a modern political party was unsuited to the social conditions prevailing in the predominantly tribal society of Afghanistan, he wanted to adapt the Jamiat to tribal institutions.

In a different context President Daoud Khan proved himself to be equally flexible. Having crushed the rebellion in the north-east, he put the Pushtunistan issue on a back-burner, thus upsetting the Afghan Millat (Nation) group, led by Abdul Haq Ahadi, which stressed Pushtun nationalism. In domestic affairs too he modified his stance. He purged the Parchamis from his administration. Then he resorted to persecuting them as well as the Khalqis. Under this pressure the two Marxist groups merged in July 1977 to re-establish the People's Democratic Party of Afghanistan. Daoud Khan continued his earlier policies of enhancing his powers, and persecuting Islamic fundamentalists as well as secular nationalists. The new constitution he promulgated in January 1977 provided for a strong president and a weak legislature. It gave equal rights to men and women, and gave Islam only a passive role. In December, following the confession of the assassin of the planning minister, Ahmad Ali Khorram, the government arrested 54 fundamentalists on charges of plotting to assassinate President Daoud Khan and his cabinet. Meanwhile, the persecution of the Marxists had taken the form of murders of their leaders by government agents. This aroused much disquiet in leftist ranks who did not know how to react to this tactic.

However, the assassination of Mir Akbar Khyber, a respected trade union leader and a former editor of *Parcham,* on 17 April 1978 changed the situation. The PDPA leadership organized massive anti-government demonstrations in Kabul. Daoud Khan ordered the imprisonment of all PDPA leaders. But Nur Muhammad Taraki (1917–79; r. 1978–9), the party chief, escaped arrest. He activated the Marxist network in the military that had been built up over two decades. The result was a coup by leftist military officers on 27 April 1978, an event officially described as the Saur (April) Revolution. Daoud Khan was killed in the fighting at the presidential palace, and his official positions of president and prime minister went to Taraki.

The coup was the culmination of the Marxists' efforts to recruit military officers over the past many years, and of Kabul government policy, initiated by Daoud Khan in the mid-1950s, of sending its officers to the Soviet Union for further training. Since they were trained at military academies in the Central Asian republics of the Soviet Union, they felt racially and culturally at home. At the same time they could not avoid comparing the economic, social and educational progress of the predominantly Muslim inhabitants of these regions with the backwardness of Afghans. These experiences made them pro-Soviet and a suitable quarry for recruitment into the military network of Afghan Marxists.

Marxist regime, phase one: 1978–9

Once in power, the differences between the PDPA's two components came to the surface. The Khalqi faction led by Taraki and Hafizullah Amin (1937–79; r. 1979) wanted rapid changes, describing the revolution not as socialist but as "national democratic," based on an alliance of workers, peasants and national bourgeoisie in conflict with feudal lords and comprador bourgeoisie subservient to foreign capital; the Parchami wing, led by Babrak Karmal (1929–96; r. 1979–86), advocated a gradualist approach. However, conscious of national history and popular culture, the revolutionary leaders reiterated their faith in Islam and all their public utterances began with *"Bismillah al Rahman al Rahim"* (In the name of Allah, the Merciful, the Compassionate). So too did all official statements, and radio and television broadcasts. Taraki and other PDPA leaders repeatedly assured the public that all reforms would be in accordance with the Sharia.

The motive behind the reform package they offered was promotion of the socio-economic welfare of the vast majority of the people, which was in line with Islam. Nonetheless, there was opposition to it from various quarters, all of whom rationalized their stance in Islamic terms.

In May the government declared a "jihad" against illiteracy, male and female. The extent of female education had been exceedingly low. Only 5 percent of girls were then attending school versus 30 percent of boys.[10] The campaign went well in urban areas, but not in rural, where 80 percent of Afghans lived. Here opposition to the mixing of the sexes, particularly in adult education, was very strong. What made the situation even more tense was the fact that due to the paucity of female teachers the task of teaching adult women fell on male teachers who had arrived from towns, considered by rural folk as hotbeds of licentiousness. The textbooks, portraying the urban lifestyle favorably, were tinged with Marxism. By completing the expulsion of mullahs from the educational system, the literacy campaign swelled the ranks of anti-government clerics. The result was periodic murders of secular, revolutionary teachers by fundamentalists. The literacy campaign in villages reached a peak in early 1979 and then declined rapidly.

Decree 6 issued in early July abolished all pre-1973 mortgages and debts, and drastically reduced the excessive interest (often 100 percent a year) on later loans, thus potentially benefiting four out of five peasant families. In practice, however, in the absence of a socially committed bureaucracy, the beneficial impact of the decree on rural life was dulled because many village mullahs, often related to landlord-moneylenders, ruled that cancellation of debts amounted to stealing, and was therefore un-Islamic. (In reply the pro-regime minority among clerics cited the Quranic verse against riba [usury].) The authorities started dismissing or arresting rebellious mullahs. In September, encouraged by the ruling issued by a group of pro-regime ulama in Kabul and elsewhere, the government mounted a jihad against the Ikhwan, the generic term used for Islamic fundamentalists.

By then the conflict within the ruling PDPA had been resolved in favor of the radical Khalqis. So the pace of reform and secularization quickened. In mid-October the government replaced the national tricolor – black, red and green – with a red flag, flagrantly similar to the standards of the Soviet Central Asian republics. The disappearance of the Islamic green from the national flag aroused popular suspicion that the state had taken the path of atheism. This view was reinforced when the practice of invoking Allah, "In the name of Allah . . . ," at the beginning of broadcasting programs or governmental statements was dropped by the official media as well as political leaders. These steps undid all that had been achieved by months of state propaganda that the new regime wanted to uphold Islam.

They also virtually neutralized the impact of Decree 7 concerning marriage and family relations which was issued at about the same time. Women were granted equal rights, forced marriage was banned, and the minimum age for marriage prescribed: 16 for females and 18 for males. The decree fixed the bride price at $7, its going rate then being $1,000. This provision was meant to help poor prospective bridegrooms, but it was extremely hard to enforce in villages.

Finally, in late November 1978, came the reform in the ownership of land, the primary source of income in a predominantly agrarian Afghanistan. Forty percent of the peasants were landless, and another 40 percent possessed only 1.5 to 6 acres each. In contrast, the top 2.2 percent of the landowners, holding 30 acres or more each, owned 42 percent of the total of 25 to 29 million acres.[11] Decree 8 divided land into three categories, and fixed ceilings of 30 acres for first-class, perennially irrigated land to 300 acres of dry land. The government expected to secure 2.5 to 3 million acres of excess land for distribution to landless peasants. To implement the reform it set up land committees composed mainly of urban-based PDPA members. From January 1979 onward, these committees, backed by radicalized, well-paid police, began visiting villages to give the title deeds to the landless. This was a bold move by the revolutionary regime to break the power of the traditional-religious elite which had effectively ruled rural society for many centuries. Rich landlords protested while their religious allies, local mullahs, issued verdicts that taking somebody's land was tantamount to robbery, a crime, and that those receiving such property would be transgressing the Sharia. This, and the fear of violent reprisals from the landlords, discouraged many landless villagers from accepting the title deeds offered to them by the visiting land committees.

Nonetheless, by March 1979, the government claimed to have distributed 512,000 acres to 104,000 families.[12]

Abroad, the Marxist regime strengthened its ties with the Soviet Union by signing a Treaty of Friendship and Cooperation in December 1978. The treaty, modeled on the ones Moscow had earlier concluded with Ethiopia, Angola and Vietnam, specified close military, political and economic links between the two neighbors. Article 4 of the treaty stated that the signatories "shall consult with each other and take, by agreement, appropriate measures to ensure the security, independence and territorial integrity of the two countries."[13] This provision would later be invoked by Kabul to invite in Soviet troops.

The aggregate effect of these developments was to polarize society, with opposition becoming more vociferous and gaining more supporters. Such Islamic luminaries as Muhammad Ibrahim Mujaddidi condemned the reforms as un-Islamic and preached against the government. After some hesitation the authorities moved against the religious opposition in January 1979. They seized the offices of Mujaddidi, arresting all adult male members of the family. They executed some religious figures, but did not make this public. Religious circles were alarmed. Many Islamic and Sufi leaders fled the country, and joined the resistance groups based in Peshawar.

Resistance against the Marxist regime hardened during the winter of 1978–9, with the (seasonally) inaccessible Nuristan slipping out of its control and falling into the hands of the (Islamic) Nuristan Front. A similar situation prevailed in the Hazarajat highlands, with the Revolutionary Council of the Islamic Union of Afghanistan taking charge.

But the event which caused a shift in the balance of forces within the PDPA was the uprising in Herat in mid-March 1979. Some of the several dozen Afghan fundamentalists, returning to the city from Iran in the wake of the Islamic revolution there in early February, established contacts with pro-Islamic officers in the local garrison while others mobilized the faithful in the surrounding villages on the issue of male teachers imparting education to women. On Friday 16 March, the demonstrating villagers murdered government teachers and then converged on Herat in a series of armed marches. Their ranks were bolstered by disaffected townsmen and defectors from the local garrison led by Captain Ismail Khan (b. 1946), a small, cheerful-looking Persian-speaking Tajik from a middle-class family in Shindad, who disobeyed orders to fire at the anti-government demonstrators. Together the insurgents turned on the PDPA cadres and military officers as well as their Soviet military advisors and their families, killing 350 Soviet citizens. They took over Herat.

A few days later when they found a column of armored cars approaching from the direction of Kandahar, waving a green flag and a copy of the Quran, they thought that they were being joined by fellow-insurgents, and let the column pass. These were in fact government troops. Once they had entered Herat, and received air cover, they attacked the rebels and recaptured the city, a campaign in which 300 tanks dispatched from Soviet Turkmenistan participated. The five-day-long insurrection caused some 5,000 deaths, including several hundred loyalist troops and PDPA functionaries.[14] Ismail Khan and his partisans fled to Iran. Kabul blamed Islamic Tehran for the insurgency. To meet the rising danger of counter-revolution, a government of "national deliverance" was formed on 1 April, with Amin as the prime minister. An uncompromising hardliner, Amin began purging the administration of the Parchamis, much to the chagrin of President Taraki. A power struggle ensued.

Washington, which had been rattled by the downfall of Muhammad Reza Pahlavi, the Shah of Iran, kept a keen eye on the unfolding drama in neighboring Afghanistan. Losing Iran, which shared a long border with the Soviet Union, was bad enough. On top of that, to see a pro-Moscow regime consolidate its position in the hitherto neutral Afghanistan, adjoining the Soviet Union, verged on a disaster. So the administration of US President Jimmy Carter was pleased to notice the emergence of active resistance to the pro-Moscow regime in Kabul. On 3 July 1979 Carter signed a Presidential Finding on covert assistance to anti-Marxist Afghan insurgents.

In Kabul, Premier Amin gained ground, and took over the Defense Ministry – and counter-insurgency operations. In mid-September there was a shoot-out between the aides of Amin and Taraki, a prelude to further violence, which ended with the official announcement on 6 October that President Taraki had died after a "serious illness." In reality he died of suffocation when a pillow was pressed over his face by unknown assassins.

Soviet leaders, who had provided refuge in Moscow to such leading Parchamis as Karmal, advised Amin to take conciliatory steps to allay public hostility toward the regime. Aware of Kabul's dependence on the Kremlin's aid, economic and military, Amin accepted the counsel. He released several thousand political prisoners. He reintroduced the invocation of Allah in official statements and broadcasts, and ordered the repairing of mosques at state expense. He promised "complete freedom of religion, and profound respect for and wide scale support to Islam."[15] He tried to woo Sufi leaders, and instructed the committee drafting the new constitution to "pay special attention to Islam'.

Proclaiming an amnesty to refugees, now numbering a quarter million, he invited them to return. This was a futile gesture. Anti-government sentiment was running high among the refugees in Pakistan where the Hizb-e Islami was active. It had started assassinating PDPA leaders in Kabul. Amin called on the Soviets to help him fight the rebels in the Paktiya province adjoining Pakistan, ruled by pro-American General Muhamamd Zia al Haq, who had seized power in a military coup against the elected prime minister, Zulfikar Ali Bhutto in 1977. The joint Afghan–Soviet campaign was successful. Marshal Ivan Pavlovsky, commander of the Soviet ground forces, toured Afghanistan to prepare overall plans for countering insurgency. This was the beginning of a process which would culminate in the arrival of tens of thousands of Soviet troops.

From late October 1979 onward Soviet Central Asian contingents – ethnically indistinguishable from Afghans – began taking over guard duties from Afghan troops in order to relieve the latter to fight the rebels. In mid-December two Soviet battalions arrived at Bagram air base 35 miles (55 km) north of Kabul, which came increasingly under Soviet control. By 24 December there were about 8,000 Soviet troops and another 4,000 military and other advisors in Afghanistan.

Three days later Soviet forces seized military installations in Kabul, and attacked the presidential palace. Amin was killed. Babrak Karmal, who had been in exile in Moscow for over a year, arrived to lead the new regime. Soon there were 50,000 Soviet troops in Afghanistan compared with 80,000 Afghan military personnel. This showed that the local Marxist regime had alienated large sections of society, and that its leaders had failed to calibrate the pace and nature of reform according to the mood of the people.

On assuming power Karmal proclaimed the release of all political prisoners, abolition of "all anti-democratic, antihuman regulations, and all arrests, arbitrary persecutions, house searches and inquisitions," respect for "the sacred principles of Islam," protection of family life, and observance of "legal and lawful private ownership."[16] Relegating the red flag to the PDPA, he restored the national tricolor. His attempt to undo the damage done by Amin's excesses had the wholehearted backing of the Kremlin whose dispatching of Soviet troops to Afghanistan, stemming from Article 4 of the year-old Afghan–Soviet Friendship Treaty, was described by Karmal as ushering in the "second phase" of the Saur Revolution.

Washington had little time for such sophistry. "The Soviet invasion of Afghanistan is the greatest threat to peace since the Second World War," President Carter reportedly said. "It is a sharp escalation in the aggressive history of the Soviet Union."[17] In public he pledged to defend "the Persian Gulf region" which, according to his national security advisor, Zbigniew Brzezinski, included Baluchistan, the Pakistani province between Afghanistan and the Arabian Sea.

Afghanistan would soon turn into the hottest front in the Cold War between Moscow and Washington that had started in 1946, where CIA-supplied weapons would be used unprecedentedly to kill Soviet troops, a prospect so alarmingly provocative that the Carter administration decided to work through a proxy – Pakistan's Inter-Services Intelligence (ISI) Directorate – to be able to exercise "plausible deniability."

Marxist regime, phase two: 1980–9

Moscow's military intervention led thousands of nationalist-minded professional men to leave their urban homes to join the resistance activity in the countryside or enroll with the anti-Marxist parties based in Pakistan or Iran, religious and secular. There were six Pakistan-based (Sunni) Islamic parties of Afghans. They had a vested interest in remaining independent entities: the Pakistani government had decided to channel Islamic charity to Afghan refugees through them rather than its own bureaucracy, requiring the refugees to register with one of them. Three of them were fundamentalist: the Hizb-e Islami (led by Hikmatyar), the Jamiat-e Islami (headed by Rabbani) and the breakaway Hizb-e Islami (led by Maulavi Yunus Khalis, a Deoband-trained cleric, who split with Hikmatyar by participating in the insurgency in Paktiya, which Hikmatyar considered premature). The rest were traditional religious parties, committed to returning Afghanistan to the pre-1973 set-up, with King Zahir Shah as the constitutional monarch; and they drew their support from village mullahs, tribal chiefs, landlords and Sufi leaders. The National Islamic Front of Afghanistan (NIFA) was headed by Sayyid Ahmad Gailani; the National Liberation Front of Afghanistan (NLFA) by Sibghatullah Mujaddidi, and the Islamic Revolutionary Movement (IRM) by Maulavi Muhammad Nabi Muhammadi. Besides the religious groups there were the nationalist, secular factions: the Musavat, now led by Bahauddin Majrooh, an academic; the Afghan Millat, headed by Abdul Haq Ahadi; and the remnants of the National Revolutionary Party originally set up by Daoud. They were completely ignored by Gen. Zia al Haq, who was keen to create a popular base for his own regime by inducting Islam into Pakistani politics. Indeed, the ISI and its cohorts in the Hizb-e Islami (Hikmatyar) went on to harass and even eliminate the leaders of these groups.[18]

Zia al Haq's strategy ran parallel to that of Brzezinski. In the debate that followed at the White House in the aftermath of the Soviet military intervention in Afghanistan, the hawkish national security advisor, Brzezinski (1928–), a Polish-American of aristocratic background, who was virulently anti-Communist as well as anti-Russian, got his way at the expense of Cyrus Vance, Secretary of State, who advocated a measured response to Moscow. Had Vance's viewpoint prevailed at the White House, the US would have then encouraged the three traditionalist Islamic groups to ally with the nationalist, secular Musavat, Afghan Millat and the remnants of the National Revolutionary Party to forge an anti-Marxist, anti-Moscow coalition, and sidelined the Islamic fundamentalist groups, thus aborting a process that would culminate 21 years later in the horrific attacks by suicide bombers directed by the Afghanistan-based Osama bin Laden. Now, though, having won the argument, Brzezinski reasoned that it was not enough to expel the Soviet tanks from Afghanistan. This was a great opportunity to export a composite ideology of nationalism and Islam to the Muslim-majority Central Asian republics with a view to destroying the Soviet system. As he famously put it, "It is time to finally sow shit in their [Soviet] backyard."[19] The fact that this backyard was 80 percent mountains, and thus ideal for guerrilla warfare, was a plus. Brzezinski created the Washington–Islamabad–Riyadh alliance whereby the US, the overall coordinator, became the sole supplier of arms to be channeled exclusively through Pakistan, the staging post for Afghan guerrillas, with Saudi Arabia putting as much money into the kitty as America would acknowledge publicly – plus making further direct contributions as well as later acting as a recruiter of jihadis (i.e. supporters of jihad) from all over the Muslim world.

Gen. Zia al Haq assigned the task of arming, training and funding the Afghan insurgency to the Inter-Services Intelligence Directorate, housed in a drab, unmarked red-brick building behind high stone walls on Khiyaban-e Suhrawardy in Islamabad. A sinister, shadowy organization, it combined the functions of the American FBI and CIA. Conceived in the mid-1950s by

Gen. Ayub Khan, the military chief of staff, as an agency to keep watch on increasingly querulous politicians, its authority grew when he seized power in 1958, becoming in effect the military's political arm. Later, Prime Minister Z. A. Bhutto used it to harass his political adversaries, and it became the source of smear campaigns against opposition politicians and journalists. Nonetheless, its director, Lt.-Gen. Ghulam Jilani, conspired with the army chief of staff, Gen. Zia al Haq, to overthrow Bhutto. Gen. Zia al Haq replaced Jilani with Gen. Akhtar Abdul Rahman Khan as director of the ISI, which had about 100 military officers maintaining an internal and external intelligence network of thousands of agents and freelance spies. With the new, ambitious assignment and a vastly increased budget, the ISI would expand its staff and agents, engaging Pakistanis fluent in Persian and Pashto/Pushtu as well as hundreds of Afghans with promises of money and domicile for their families in Pakistan, pushing the total number of ISI employees, full- and part-time, to 100,000.[20]

With Ronald Reagan (1910– ; r. 1981–8) – well known for his vehement anti-Communism, expressed succinctly in his description of the Soviet Union as the "evil empire" – becoming US president in 1981, and appointing as the CIA director William Casey, who had started his working life with the CIA's predecessor, Office of Strategic Surveys (OSS) established during World War II, the Afghan insurgency picked up. Personal rapport quickly developed between Casey, Gen. Akhtar Khan and Prince Turki ibn Faisal, head of the Saudi Istikhabrat. With this, Islamic fundamentalism in Afghanistan, with a patchy record until the turmoil of the April 1978–December 1979 period, would become the pre-eminent part of the Afghan political-military scene and, quite uniquely, get sucked into the balance of power equation of the two superpowers.

In 1981 the active cadres of the six Afghan Islamic parties numbered 75,000, with the fundamentalists accounting for two-thirds of the total, the contingent of Hikmatyar's Hizb-e Islami being by far the largest. In contrast the three traditional religious parties were even in strength.[21]

To Hikmatyar, returning Afghanistan to the true path of Islam meant having to reform the religious establishment, eradicate Sufi orders and implement the Sharia in its totality. The last requirement could only be achieved by abrogating such traditional laws as the Pushtunwali. Also it would mean imposing the veil on women in rural Afghanistan where it was not the norm.

While Hikmatyar, running a tightly knit party, was unwilling to adjust its structure to accommodate the peculiarly Afghan social reality of tribes, Sufi brotherhoods and traditional rural elites, Rabbani swiftly abandoned the elitist nature of his Jamiat to integrate supporters who were not fully committed to the party ideology inspired by Maududi and Sayyid Qutb. Also, alone among Sunni leaders, he conceded the Shia demand that the Jaafari school of law be applied to them. His weakness was that he was an ethnic Tajik, and not a Pushtun like Hikmatyar. Tajiks (speakers of the Tajik language, a dialect of Persian), forming only about a quarter of the total Afghan population of 19 million, were only half as numerous as Pushtuns.

While both Rabbani and Hikmatyar were committed to full implementation of the Sharia in a future Islamic state, Rabbani envisaged a multi-party system, as expounded by Maududi, which was not the case with Hikmatyar. Arrogant and authoritarian, he was for a single-party Islamic state. He vehemently attacked his rivals, describing them variously as monarchists, religiously corrupt or deviant, or pro-Western. His party, he stressed, was a contrast to theirs: it was republican, religiously pure and committed to the "Neither East nor West" policy. Whereas the aim of other parties was to bring about the withdrawal of the Soviet troops from Afghanistan and restore Afghan independence, the Hizb-e Islami talked of carrying the guerrilla raids beyond the Oxus River into Soviet Central Asia and rolling back Communism from there. Hikmatyar's dogmatic ambition and exceptional organizational ability made the Hizb-e Islami by far the strongest party with a command structure stretching as far as Herat, with a network of recruitment centers, training camps, medical facilities, warehouses and offices. His party claimed to have set up parallel government in the areas it controlled inside Afghanistan. In Rabbani's case, his ally Ahmad Shah Masoud (1953–2001), a wiry Tajik with an ascetic face, based in the Panjshir (lit. Five Lions) valley near Kabul, had proved to be one of the ablest guerrilla commanders, acquiring the honorific of the "Lion of Panjshir." While successfully resisting central control he had established a parallel political-administrative infrastructure in the valley. This bolstered the prestige and credibility of the Jamaat-e Islami.

Additionally, there were territories in the central Hazarajat highlands ruled by Shia organizations which maintained offices in Iranian cities as well as Quetta, Pakistan. The Revolutionary Council of the Islamic Union of Afghanistan, which set up its administration in the Hazarajat region in September 1979, consisted of moderate and radical Shia Islamists. In the spring of 1984, however, a coalition of the pro-Iranian Sazman-e Nasr (Organization of Victory) and the Sejah-e Pasdaran (Army of the Guards) overthrew the Revolutionary Council and assumed control of the region, thus strengthening Tehran's role in Afghani politics.

Fundamentalist parties drew their recruits mainly from young college-educated men with rural or small-town backgrounds from the families of civil servants, teachers or traders. They were often radical, dogmatic and intolerant, mirror images of the young cadres of the PDPA.

In the traditional Islamic camp, the NFLA leader, Sibghatullah Mujaddidi, a graduate of Al Azhar and an Islamic teacher, was a nephew of the Hazrat of Shor Bazaar. Due to the cosy relations between the Mujaddidi family and the king, the NFLA attracted many monarchists. Ahmad Gailani, leader of the NIFA and head of the Qadiriya (Sufi) order, was related to the former monarch, Zahir Shah, through marriage and had been his close advisor during his rule. The least religious of the leaders, and a realist, he advised coexistence with the Soviet Union. As heads of largely Westernized families, Gailani and Mujaddidi came in handy to the CIA and its public relations department when they visited the US, which they did at least twice a year. Muhammadi, the IRM leader, was a cleric, a former head of an Islamic college in

Logar, and a leading figure in the Qadiriya order. His party contained both traditional mullahs and young men with modern education. At ease with religious and secular figures, modern or traditional, he was a bridge between the traditionalist and fundamentalist camps.

Islam played a crucial role in providing a sense of purpose to the constituents of both camps. Yet it proved insufficient to bring them under one umbrella and one leader.

Attempts made at the Islamic Conference Organization foreign ministers' meetings in January and May 1980 to forge a united front of the exile parties failed. However, Hikmatyar and Rabbani succeeded in soliciting funds from the oil-rich Gulf states. Thus strengthened, Hikmatyar's Hizb-e Islami tried to penetrate into the regions where other parties and tribes were dominant. The worsened inter-party relations brought some 300 mullahs from Afghanistan to Peshawar in April 1981 to foster unity. Gailani, Mujaddidi and Muhammadi set up a joint council. The three fundamentalist parties formed an umbrella organization – the Islamic Alliance of Afghanistan – under the chairmanship of Professor Abdul Rasul Sayyaf. The establishment of these coalitions helped to coordinate the distribution of arms and ammunition bought by the CIA mainly from Egypt, Saudi Arabia and America which in the summer of 1981 were arriving at the rate of two planeloads a week – and which were distributed by the ISI to the Afghan parties according to the number of refugees registered with them. Sayyaf used his exalted position to win over many floating Afghan factions with money supplied generously by his patron, Saudi Arabia, and transformed the Islamic Alliance of Afghanistan into a party of his own – carrying the same name, Ittihad-e Islami – a development which revived inter-party discord.

However, this did not discourage Riyadh from pressuring the Islamic parties to unite. In early 1983, fearing that they would be excluded from the negotiations in progress under the United Nations aegis between Kabul, Moscow, Islamabad and Tehran to solve the Afghanistan problem, the Islamic parties tried hard to create an umbrella organization. The result was the formation of the seven-party Islamic Alliance of Afghan Mujahedin (IAAM) – popularly known as Afghan Mujahedin – in May 1983 under the chairmanship of Sayyaf with Mujaddidi as his deputy and its headquarters in Peshawar.

To see a fellow Wahhabi installed as the head of the Afghan Mujahedin pleased Osama bin Laden, who had based himself since 1982 in the University Town suburb of Peshawar, a city bulging at the seams with an influx of refugees, exiles, arms merchants, drug dealers, spooks, diplomats and journalists. Here, bin Laden had teamed up with Abdullah Azzam, a prominent Islamic thinker and charismatic preacher of Palestinian origin. Born in Jenin, Palestine, his parents became refugees in Jordan after the creation of Israel in 1948. After graduating in Islamic theology from Damascus University in 1966, he fought in the Six Day Arab–Israeli War in 1967. He then pursued further education at Al Azhar and obtained a doctorate in fiqh (Islamic jurisprudence) in 1973. After teaching the Sharia briefly at Jordan University, Amman, he moved to Saudi Arabia to lecture at the King Abdul Aziz University in Jiddah. His taped lectures became popular among young pious Saudis such as bin Laden. Like the Egyptian Muhammad Abdul Salam Faraj before him, Azzam held that jihad was compulsory for a true Muslim[22] – "To stand one hour in the battle line in the cause of Allah is better than 60 years of night prayer" – and added that only by engaging in jihad would the faithful be able to revive the Islamic umma under a caliph (khalifa), as a prelude to restoring the glory of Islam. A well-built man with a thick beard and a booming voice, he had great presence. Like bin Laden he was attracted by the anti-Soviet jihad in Afghanistan, and traveled to Pakistan where he became a lecturer in Islamic studies at Islamic University in Islamabad.

In Peshawar, bin Laden had by now initiated a scheme of recruiting volunteers from the Arab world to join the anti-Soviet jihad, an enterprise in which he had the active backing of the Saudi intelligence chief, Prince Turki. This program was then extended to the non-Arab Muslim world. By the time the Afhgan Mujahedin captured Kabul in 1992, an estimated 35,000

Islamists from 43 countries had participated in the jihad,[23] nearly two-thirds of them from Arab states, with the Saudi kingdom contributing 15,000 – according to Saudi foreign minister, Saud al Faisal[24] – followed by Yemen, Algeria and Egypt.

In Kabul, the Marxist regime ignored the traditional Islamic groups among the Afghan Mujahedin, and directed its attacks at the fundamentalist ones. It projected itself as a guardian of Islam. President Karmal prayed in public regularly, and began his statements with an invocation to Allah. His audience responded to his public speeches with intermittent cries of "Allahu Akbar" (God is Great). He instituted the Office of Islamic Teachings under his direct control, and radio and television reintroduced recitations of the Quran. He gave a higher profile to the Ministry of Religious Affairs and Trusts, and had its activities widely reported in the media. The ministry awarded hefty salary increases to the ulama and gave them enhanced importance. In return the clergy became more willing to explain official policies and reforms to their congregations. The ministry initiated a widely publicized program of building new mosques and madressas, and began exchanging Islamic delegations with the Soviet Central Asian republics. Radio broadcasts from these republics in Persian, Azeri, Tajiki, Uzbek and Turkmen languages stressed that Islam was safe in the Soviet system and that danger to it came from America, Britain, China and Israel.

This was partly the Kabul regime's response to the anti-Soviet propaganda, broadcast by the US-funded Radio Liberty and Radio Free Europe, directed specifically at the Muslim populations in Central Asia and Azerbaijan to arouse and heighten Islamic consciousness and ethnic nationalism in the region to undermine the Moscow-directed Soviet system – with its lead followed swiftly by Saudi Arabia, which combined propaganda broadcasts with courses on the Quran and Sharia, and later by Egypt, Qatar and Kuwait.[25]

On the ground, the government acted to block the cross-border movement of the guerrillas by offering money, weapons and promises of regional autonomy to tribes along the Afghan-Pakistan frontier. In this, an active role was played by Khad

(Khidmat-e Amniyat-e Dawlati, or State Security Service), working in close cooperation with the Soviet KGB (Komitet Gosudarstevenoy Bezopasnosti, or Committee for State Security) contingent, based in a large KGB enclave in Kabul. Since relations between the fundamentalist parties, lacking leaders with traditional status, and the border tribes had been tenuous, the regime met with some success. Those tribals who opted for loyalty to Kabul began harassing the Mujahedin.

To expand its popular base, the Karmal government founded the National Fatherland Front in early 1981, with due consideration to the composition and characteristics of various nationalities, tribes and clans that inhabited the country. Among the Front's components were the Jamaat-e Ulama and numerous tribal jirgas (assemblies). The Front's major task was to publicize and explain official policies to the people. By March, the Front claimed to have 100,000 members affiliated to 400 local councils. The number of full and candidate members of the PDPA was officially put at 90,000.[26] But the activities of both organizations were limited mainly to urban centers since large parts of the countryside had slipped out of the control of the central authority.

How extensive the resistance's actions had been could be judged by the official statements in early 1983 that the counter-revolutionaries had destroyed or damaged nearly half of the schools and hospitals (1,814 and 31 respectively), 111 basic health centers, three-quarters of communications lines, 800 heavy transport vehicles and 906 peasant cooperatives.[27]

Human casualties were mounting too. By early 1984 the number of dead or injured Afghan troops was put at 17,000 and guerrilla casualties at 30,000. The estimates of Soviet casualties varied between 13,500 and 30,000, including 6,000 to 8,000 fatalities.[28]

From then on, the Mujahedin movement, fueled by American and Saudi money and weapons, accelerated. "From 1984 to 1986, over 80,000 Mujahedin went through our training camps," said Brig. Muhammad Yousaf, head of the Afghan Bureau of the Pakistani ISI. "Hundreds of thousands of tons of weapons and ammunition were distributed, and active operations were planned and carried out in all of Afghanistan's provinces."[29]

In 1984 Abdullah Azzam left his job in Islamabad and joined bin Laden in Peshawar where they rented a house-cum-office, and named it Beit al Ansar (House of Helpers). In Peshawar, Azzam devoted himself to running the Maktab al Khidmat (Bureau of Service), set up to look after the welfare of the non-Afghan Mujahedin and their families, periodically touring the Muslim world to solicit cash and recruits for the jihad. The Maktab's primary funding came from the Saudi Istikhabrat, Saudi Red Crescent, the Saudi-financed World Muslim League headed by Grand Mufti Abdul Aziz al Baz, and contributions by affluent Saudis as well as mosques. The total would rise to $240 million a year in 1986.[30]

"To counter these atheist Russians, the Saudis chose me as their representative in Afghanistan," bin Laden would tell the Agence France-Presse in August 1998:

> I settled in Pakistan in the Afghan border region. There I received volunteers who came from the Saudi kingdom and from all over the Arab and Muslim countries. I set up my first camp where these volunteers were trained by Pakistani and American officers. The weapons were supplied by the Americans, and the money by the Saudis.[31]

Besides vetting non-Afghan volunteers, and sending them to one of the constituents of the Afghan Mujahedin Alliance – preferring Sayyaf's Islamic Alliance or Hikmatyar's Hizb-e Islami – bin Laden supervised the construction of roads and refurbishing of caves for storing weapons in the Mujahedin-controlled areas.

At the training camps established on both sides of the Afghan–Pakistan frontier, the volunteers underwent military training – based on the manuals used by the Pentagon and the CIA and translated into Persian and, later, Arabic and Urdu – as well as political education. The training involved learning the most effective ways to strangle and stab; handling explosives, fuses, timers and remote-control devices; carrying out industrial and other sabotage; operating small arms as well as anti-tank and anti-aircraft missiles. US Marine training manuals, translated into Persian, Arabic and Urdu, were found to be particularly good in teaching the recruits how to make booby traps and break down weapons. In the political classes the Mujahedin, whether Afghan or not, were given a strong dose of nationalism and Islam. The fact that Soviets were foreign and atheistic made them doubly despicable. The end purpose was to fire up militant Muslims to fight Soviet imperialism vigorously.

By the mid-1980s firm lines were drawn between the Mujahedin and the Marxist regime. The Karmal government, heavily dependent on 115,000 Soviet troops and generous military aid from Moscow, was resolved to subdue the resistance in rural Afghanistan, while maintaining control over cities and major towns, the national highway that ringed the country, and airports. In its anti-insurgency campaign, the Afghan government deployed KGB-trained guerrilla units masquerading as anti-Soviet Mujahedin to wrong-foot the opposition, draw out the real Mujahedin and attack them. By 1983 nearly 90 units were in the field, provoking clashes between different genuine Mujahedin groups, and occasionally "surrendering" to the authorities in order to boost the general morale of those siding with the Kabul regime.[32] On the other side, the Mujahedin, receiving arms and cash from America and Saudi Arabia and other Gulf monarchies to the tune of $500 million a year – twice the Afghan budget, including foreign aid, in 1980[33] – were equally determined to bring about the Soviets' expulsion and collapse of the infidel regime.

It was against this background that the UN-sponsored talks between various parties proceeded, centered around the timetable for Soviet withdrawal, the cessation of foreign arms aid to the Afghan Mujahedin, and the return of the refugees. The Afghan parties wanted an immediate and unconditional Soviet withdrawal whereas the Moscow–Kabul axis proposed staged Soviet withdrawal over four years after the termination of foreign military assistance to the Mujahedin.

After Mikhail Gorbachev became secretary-general of the Communist Party of the Soviet Union in March 1985, the Kremlin curtailed the period of Soviet withdrawal to 18 months. When he realized that the Mujahedin would not deal with Karmal, Gorbachev worked behind the scenes to ease him out. In May 1986 Karmal was replaced by Muhammad Najibullah, a barrel-chested physician, nicknamed "the ox" because of his strong constitution.[34] By announcing shortly afterward that it would withdraw 6,000 Soviet troops in October, Moscow underlined its intent to settle the Afghanistan crisis.

The Mujahedin–Islamabad–Washington coalition tried to raise the cost of Soviet presence in Afghanistan. To neutralize Kabul's air superiority, based on an extensive deployment of helicopter gunships, Washington decided to arm the guerrillas with British-manufactured Blowpipe and US-made shoulder-held Stinger anti-aircraft missiles. It airlifted about 150 Stingers to Pakistan in late spring 1986 followed by 300 Blowpipes several months later. The Mujahedin started firing them extensively in the autumn, downing 60 helicopters before the year-end,[35] thus finding them to be more effective than the Soviet-designed SAM-7s (surface-to-air missiles), clandestinely procured from Egypt and China by the CIA, which they had used before.

To counter Kabul's strategy of cutting off the Mujahedin's supply lines from Pakistan, sharing a 1,500 mile (2,400 km) porous border with Afghanistan, the CIA–ISI–Istikhabrat trio decided in 1986 to construct a tunnel complex at Zhawar Killi in the vicinity of Khost near the Pakistani border, to house a training center, weapons store and medical facility with electricity, piped water and a jail for prisoners of war – an ambitious project to be overseen by bin Laden.[36] The new underground base was to be an addition to the already existing nearby cave complex at Tora Bora, which had proved impervious to Soviet-Afghan assaults. (Another area that had escaped control by the Kabul regime, despite repeated attempts, was the Panjshir valley under the command of Ahmad Shah Masoud, the right-hand man of Burhanuddin Rabbani.) Once the Zhawar Killi project was completed, bin Laden set up his own training camp, named Al Ansar (The Helper), nearby. It saved him the chore of having to dispatch non-Afghan volunteers to different Mujahedin factions.

To help its Afghan ally, Moscow began using crack units, Spetsnaz, instead of regular troops to shut off rebel supply lines from Pakistan. In a joint operation in November 1986 Afghan and Soviet forces seized Kama Dakka, a vital staging post for delivering weapons to the Mujahedin from Pakistan. They also continued to exhort and bribe the border tribes to impede the passage of arms and guerrillas from Pakistan.

Having established a secure base at Zhawar Killi, the ISI-directed Mujahedin tried to challenge the joint Soviet–Afghan front line in the area, resulting in periodic skirmishes. In one such encounter in April 1987, involving 50 Afghan and non-Afghan Mujahedin, bin Laden played a commanding role. Basing themselves in the caves in the heights around the village of Jaji near the governmental front line they tried to dislodge the enemy. In response, on 17 April, some 200 Soviet troops, including crack units, launched an offensive. Despite heavy fire for a week, the bin Laden contingent stayed put. The Peshawar-based Arab reporters filed glowing accounts of the resistance offered by bin Laden and company, which made head-lines in the Middle Eastern media and attracted new recruits for the Mujahedin. In the euphoria created by the battle, Arab jour-nalists overlooked the fact that bin Laden lost a quarter of his force, an unacceptably high figure.[37] One of those who survived, Mia Muhammad Agha, a Mujahedin commander at the time, would later describe bin Laden's performance thus: "Bin Laden was right in the thick of it. I watched him with his Kalashnikov in his hand under fire from mortars and multiple-barreled rocket launchers." Such behavior, combined with his modesty and accessibility, and readiness to share, made bin Laden popular with fellow combatants. "You never knew he was so rich or the commander of everyone," recalled a former member of the Mujahedin. "We used to sit down and eat like friends."[38] These tales added to his fame especially among his fellow Saudis. Aware of his super-affluent background, they could not help but admire him for abandoning the luxuries of life in Jiddah for the rigors of caves in Afghanistan. His mentor, Abdullah Azzam, meanwhile, toured the world, collecting funds and recruiting volunteers for the jihad, visiting Al Khifa Refugee Center in Brooklyn soon after its establishment in 1987.

In April of that year, Hikmatyar, a favorite of both bin Laden and the ISI, too made a mark. After crossing the Oxus River, small units of his Hizb-e Islami had fired rockets at a frontier guard post near Piyanj in Soviet Tajikistan,[39] thus signaling that a future Islamic State of Afghanistan would become a springboard for exporting Islamic revolution to the Soviet Central Asian republics – a sign quietly welcomed by the Reagan administration in Washington.

It was noteworthy that the battle of Jaji occurred during the six-month unilateral ceasefire Najibullah had declared in January 1987. The Mujahedin were as dismissive of this move by Najibullah as they were of his decision to establish the Commission for National Reconciliation (CNR), with hundreds of branches in the country, to encourage the opposition to abandon its resistance and participate in normal political life, after getting his presidency endorsed by a Loya Jirga (Grand Assembly). Instead of calling guerrillas "bandits" or "counter-revolutionaries," the official media described them as "misguided brothers." The Mujahedin responded by assassinating provincial leaders of the CNR. By the end of the ceasefire in July 1987, the government claimed that 44,000 refugees had returned and that 21,000 "misguided brothers" had given up arms. Given that, by official accounts, there were 2 million refugees in Pakistan and 250,000 (intermittently active) guerrillas,[40] the results of the unilateral ceasefire were unimpressive.

Najibullah tried to lure the three traditionalist groups within the Mujahedin to share power with him, but failed. Neither Kabul nor Moscow was prepared to cede the dominant position that the PDPA visualized for itself in any future coalition government. During its nine years of rule it had engendered its own constituencies: the peasants who had secured land; the emancipated women who dreaded the prospect of being returned to the four walls of home and the veil; and all those who had benefited, materially and otherwise, from the literacy campaign.

On the opposite side the traditional Islamic factions, which had their heyday in the 1930s and 1940s, had merely managed to maintain the networks their leaders had headed before the April 1978 revolution. It was the four fundamentalist parties which, like the PDPA, had created new constituencies both inside and outside Afghanistan. Being the main beneficiaries of the aid by foreign powers – running in 1987 at a publicly acknowledged $640 million from the US, matched by an equal amount from Riyadh – [41] they had the means to sustain the vastly enlarged networks to promote the fundamentalist cause.

In sum, the Marxist revolution, and the resources and facilities provided by Pakistan, Iran, the Gulf states, Egypt and America, had caused an upsurge in Islamic fundamentalism in a society which, unlike Egypt, was ethnically heterogeneous and economically underdeveloped. Until the April 1978 revolution the state had made minimal inroads into the individual or social life of Afghans. In a sense the resistance by rural Afghans to the Kabul government was as much a rebellion against rapid socio-economic reform as it was against the central state itself. While the PDPA, as well as Islamic fundamentalists, was convinced that its revolution would change the stagnant Afghan society, moored to centuries-old feudalism, through the instrument of a strong state, neither had a blueprint for creating that state and funding its expanded role. In the event, therefore, each ended up depending on foreign assistance in its struggle

The result of the parliamentary poll in April 1988 – held under the new constitution adopted four months earlier, declaring Islam to be the state religion and allowing a multi-party system – showed the PDPA securing only 27 percent of the seats and the National Front, an umbrella body, 28 percent, with the rest going to such popular organizations as the Peasants Justice Party, Islamic Party and the Workers Revolutionary Party.

Alluding to the election results, Najibullah urged a conference of PDPA delegates not to underestimate the role of Islam and the importance of the ulama, and reminded them that the objectives of the Afghan revolution should not be realized by military means.[42]

Najibullah's reminder was apt since Moscow was poised to undertake the first stage of its troop withdrawal on 15 May 1988 according to one of the four agreements it signed with Washington and Islamabad under the UN aegis in Geneva in February. Another agreement required Pakistan not to interfere in Afghan affairs – that is, to stop transporting military supplies into Afghanistan and close down training camps for Afghan rebels on its soil. In the event, to the chagrin of Kabul and Moscow, Islamabad openly breached this agreement. And since the two superpowers exchanged secret letters that allowed them to continue military supplies to their allies, peace proved elusive.

With the Soviet troops reduced by half to about 60,000, by August, the Najibullah government vacated many border posts and garrisons to consolidate its strategic position. It raised its budget for the Ministry of Religious Affairs and Trusts to the extent that it amounted to three times that of the Foreign Ministry.

The death of Gen. Zia al Haq and his military chief of staff, Gen. Akhtar Khan (formerly of the ISI), in a mid-air explosion of his helicopter in August made no difference to Pakistan's Afghan policy. Gen. Hamid Gul, who had been ISI director since 1987, was even more committed to the Mujahedin cause than his predecessor, and was quite close to Hikmatyar.

As 15 February 1989, the final date of Soviet withdrawal, approached, there were predictions that with the disappearance of the cement that held the Afghan Mujahedin together – the Soviet military presence – the coalition would disintegrate. But it did not. The chief reason was that America, under the new administration of President George Bush, pledged to supply weapons to the Afghan Mujahedin to the tune of $500 million a year (as acknowledged publicly), with Riyadh matching the US dollar for dollar. Any faction splitting from the Mujahedin would have lost its share of arms – and thus its followers in the field whose loyalty rested largely on a steady supply of cash and weapons. Yet their coexistence was uneasy, with personal and ethnic rivalries – especially between Pushtuns and Tajiks – which had been suppressed to fight the common foe, coming to the fore. Little wonder that they failed to form an interim government.

Equally, on the other side, lacking a political settlement leading to a coalition government in Kabul, the Kremlin handed over its vast military stores to the Afghans, airlifted more arms and ammunition, and promised to honor its December 1978 Afghan–Soviet Treaty of Friendship, which specified mutual consultations about ensuring "the security, independence and territorial integrity of the two countries," and which had resulted in the loss of some 14,500 Soviet soldiers during the 1980s.

After the Soviet withdrawal

On the eve of the Soviet pull-back from Afghanistan, cajoled and bribed by the Pakistani ISI and Saudi Istikhabrat, 439 delegates of the Islamic Alliance of Afghan Mujahedin met in Rawalpindi, Pakistan. After much deliberation and horse-trading, coupled with cash deals funded by the Saudis, they elected an interim government on 19 February 1989, with Sibghatullah Mujaddidi and Abdul Rasul Sayyaf as respective chairman and deputy chairman, with Gulbuddin Hikmatyar, Yunus Khalis and Burhanuddin Rabbani respectively as foreign, defense and interior ministers.

About a week earlier, the authorities in Kabul discovered unauthorized arms and explosives which they viewed as part of the Mujahedin plan to infiltrate the capital with men and weapons before besieging it. President Muhammad Najibullah declared a state of emergency and set up military courts to try those charged with breaking the law. He appointed a new 22-member Supreme Council for the Defense of the Homeland, and reshuffled the cabinet, increasing the PDPA share. The new government recalled thousands of Afghans in Soviet schools and military academies. It handed out 30,000 Kalashnikov assault rifles to the young Defenders of the Revolution, thus partially mobilizing PDPA members. It replaced the departed Soviet troops by raising 45,000-strong Special Guard Corps, to be posted in Kabul and the capitals of the remaining 30 provinces. Additionally, there were 20–25,000 paramilitary troops of the Interior Ministry, and another 15–20,000 working for Khad (State Security Service). The Kabul regime regarded these forces, totaling 80–90,000, out of the grand total of 140–150,000 regular troops and paramilitary personnel, as its hard core, ready to fight to the bitter end against the 70,000 full-time combatants in the enemy camp, which lacked a central military command.[43]

A test of this came in March when the Mujahedin's interim government made a determined effort to capture Jalalabad – a city of 200,000 situated 45 miles (70 km) from the Pakistani border on the road to Kabul – to establish a secretariat there. The Najibullah regime's 15,000 troops, aided by the air force, successfully defended the city against an onslaught by 8,000 armed Mujahedin in which about 1,000 of them were killed.[44] The Mujahedin's failure to set up a secretariat inside Afghanistan discouraged America and Pakistan – now ruled by elected Prime Minister Benazir Bhutto (1953– ; r. December 1988–August 1990, June 1993–Novemebr 1996), daughter of Zulfikar Ali Bhutto – from recognizing its interim government Their morale fell, and heated recrimination ensued among the constituent groups about the military debacle at Jalalabad.

But that did not result in a formal split between the moderate and hardline factions within the Mujahedin Alliance, with the moderates opting to share power with Najibullah in Kabul with the tacit agreement of the US, as the Kremlin would have liked to see. In the debate among the American policymakers between ideologue "bleeders," determined to exploit Afghanistan to humiliate the Soviet Union, and pragmatic "dealers," keen to sideline Islamic fundamentalists, the former had won, with President Bush committing publicly acknowledged military aid of half a billion US dollars to the Mujahedin Alliance for the next financial year.

As spring gave way to summer, the simmering tension between the Hizb-e Islami of Hikmatyar and Jamiat-e Islami of Ahmad Shah Masoud boiled over, with the former killing 30 of Masoud's key lieutenants in northern Afghanistan, a Tajik stronghold, in July. In return, Masoud's partisans sabotaged three attempts by Hikmatyar's fighters to attack Kabul in summer and early autumn.

The internecine violence, centered around ethnicity among Afghan Mujahedin, angered and frustrated bin Laden, the nominal head of the non-Afghan jihadis. "He used to tell them that they had defeated the Soviet empire because they were united and Allah had blessed them," recalled Jamal Nazimuddin, a former Afghan mujahid. "If they are not united, he said, they could not do Allah's will."[45] But since ethnic animosities among Afghans had long roots they could not be overcome by bin Laden's repeated assertions that all believers were equal in Islam, irrespective of their color, race or ethnicity.

In late November 1989, a car bomb in Peshawar killed Abdullah Azzam and his two sons as they were entering their mosque for the Friday prayer. No one claimed responsibility. Bin Laden was shattered by the loss of his mentor. But he resolved to continue running Azzam's Maktab al Khidmat (Bureau of Service) under the new title of Al Qaida but with a more ambitious aim of creating an international network of jihadis, those who had participated in the anti-Soviet jihad. As mentioned before, during his exile in Sudan in 1991–6, Al Qaida would be run along corporate lines – with the policy-making shura council of 12 served by four executive committees: military, business, fatwa and Islamic studies, and media and public relations, the last one headed by a journalist-writer with the nom de guerre of Abu Masad Reuters, and producing inter alia promotional videos to gain recruits. Disappointed by the continued inter-ethnic violence among the Afghan Mujahedin, bin Laden packed his bags in the spring of 1990 and returned to Jiddah where he found himself much in demand as a speaker and where his taped speeches became best-sellers.

In Afghanistan, though the Najibullah government had repelled the Mujahedin onslaught on Jalalabad and was well supplied with arms, fuel and food ferried from the Soviet Union at the daily rate of 25 Ilyushin transport planes, each carrying

20 tons, and though the PDPA had, at Najibullah's behest, changed its name to Watan (i.e. Homeland) Party in January 1990, and distanced itself from its Marxist past, the regime had its internal problems.

On 5 March 1990, the day after the opening of the trial of military officers arrested three months earlier for plotting a coup, Gen. Shah Nawaz Tanai, the defense minister, made a more serious attempt to overthrow the regime. The rebels bombed the presidential palace as well as the defense and interior ministries, and briefly captured the Bagram and Shindad military air bases. Among those who were implicated in the plot were the interior minister, the air force chief, many generals and hundreds of other military officers and senior civil servants. Their intention was to replace the present government in order to facilitate reconciliation with Mujahedin leaders.

What drove Tanai, a member of the Pushtun tribe of the same name, to rebel was personal rivalry. His tribe came from the same Paktiya province as did Najibullah's, a member of the Ahmadzai tribal federation. He was a brilliant soldier. A graduate of a Soviet military academy, he became the commander of an elite commando unit in 1983. He rose fast to become chief of the army general staff, the position he held when Najibullah, lacking field experience, was promoted to the presidency in 1986 by the Kremlin. Gorbachev preferred Najibullah, then head of Khad, thinking that he would be more flexible in the political negotiations that lay ahead. Tanai's elevation to defense minister in August 1988 did not satisfy him. But so long as the Soviets were in Afghanistan, he could not move against Najibullah. Once they had left, he began plotting against the president by presenting himself as an Afghan nationalist.

In the Mujahedin camp, Hikmatyar had resigned his post as foreign minister, and his partisans had begun assaulting the fighters of Jamiat and other groups to compel them to join his plan to attack Kabul. The latter refused, arguing that such an action would cause untold misery to civilians. Indeed, fed up with Hikmatyar's arm-twisting, most of the commanders not belonging to his party decided to form the Islamic Jihad Council

(IJC) with Ahmad Shah Masoud as its chairman. In early 1990 it would start receiving aid from the US.

On his part, Najibullah gave autonomy first to Hazaras, forming 15–17 percent of the population, and then to Uzbeks, who constituted 9–12 percent of the total. This won him the backing of the north-west-based, 10,000 strong Uzbek militia, led by Gen. Abdul Rashid Dostum (1954–), who defected from the Mujahedin camp. Najibullah had the continued backing of the Kremlin which realized that the only alternative to him and his Watan Party was a regime dominated by Islamic fundamentalists. The annual cost of bolstering his government with arms, food and 900,000 tons of oil was far less than the $250 million estimated by Western sources: a lot of the military goods were surplus from the Soviet stores being closed in Eastern Europe.

But the foundations on which the Soviet bloc rested were sinking as the fast-moving events in Eastern Europe after the demolition of the Berlin Wall in November 1989 showed. So Najibullah tried to strike a deal with the monarchist-Islamist opposition. He offered to step down in favor of a broad-based government. The hardliners in the Mujahedin camp dismissed the offer but Washington took it seriously. This enabled the UN to offer a peace plan in May 1991 to be implemented by an "interim authority" created to facilitate dialogue among all Afghan parties to install a broad-based government.

That, however, did not stop Masoud's Jamiat-e Islami fighters extending their control in the north. Indeed, they and other Mujahedin groups, including the Hizb-e Islami, began crossing the fluvial borders between Afghanistan and Tajikistan and Uzbekistan to incite anti-Communist feeling among Soviet Tajiks and Uzbeks.

As the end of 1991 approached, the Najibullah government found three-quarters of the countryside slipping away and falling under the control of assorted elements of the opposition, leaving it with the full jurisdiction only over major cities along the (roughly circular) national highway linking Mazar-e Sharif with Kabul, Jalalabad, Kandahar and Herat. There was no sign of relief from the UN since its efforts to create a broad-based government had become bogged down.

The formal break-up of the Soviet Union on 31 December 1991 brought about sharp policy shifts in Islamabad and Kabul. Pakistan decided to develop trade with the newly independent Central Asian states, and this necessitated a truce in Afghanistan. It therefore backed the UN peace plan. With economic aid from Moscow drying up, Najibullah turned to his newly independent Central Asian counterparts for assistance. They supplied him with 6 million barrels of oil and 500,000 tons of wheat to survive the winter.[46] They did not want his regime supplanted by Islamic fundamentalists, fearing they would destabilize their regimes.

However, Najibullah's Watan Party began to split between those who wanted to maintain the status quo and those who urged political liberalization. Deprived of the Soviet largesse, Najibullah also had difficulty maintaining the loyalty of some 80,000 tribal militia men, most of whom had earlier abandoned the Mujahedin camp owing to large grants of money, arms and food from his government.

These developments encouraged Benon Sevan, UN special envoy, to bring about a ceasefire. In his four long meetings with Najibullah in March 1992, he told the president that there would be no UN aid for Afghanistan so long as he remained in office. On 18 March Najibullah informed Sevan that he would hand over power to "an interim government" of 15 neutral Afghans, to be proposed by the UN, to establish a forerunner to a transitional, broad-based administration. The next day in a broadcast he made public his decision.[47] He did so without consulting any of his 50 military generals or other leading civilian backers, a blunder that nearly cost him his life.

Najibullah's statement confused and demoralized his supporters in the military and militia officer corps. To save their lives, the commanders of garrisons and militias began striking deals with local Mujahedin leaders. Prominent among them were Generals Dostum, Abdul Momen, a Tajik, and Mansour Naderi, an Ismaili Shia. They cut deals with local Mujahedin units, under the overall command of Masoud, as well as pro-Iranian Shia groups.

Together they attacked Mazar-e Sharif – the site of the Blue Mosque containing the tomb of Imam Ali – 30 miles (50 km) from the Uzbek border, defended by the Afghan army's 18th division. They won after fierce street combat. By the end of March, the city was under the control of the rebel military council. From here the rebel council extended its authority to the adjoining provinces as the Uzbek militia, led by Dostum, began advancing toward Kabul. Nine-and-a-half years later, in the autumn of 2001, history would repeat itself, with the Taliban-ruled Mazar being the first city to fall to the opposition, presaging the Taliban's loss of the capital.

By the time Najibullah called on the assembled military leaders in Kabul, on 12 April, to stand by him, it was too late. The response was poor. On 15 April, when he tried to escape via Kabul airport to join his family in Delhi, India, he was prevented from leaving by Dostum's militia, who controlled the airport. He then put himself into the hands of the UN mission in Kabul. It tried to get him out of Afghanistan, but in vain.

The Mujahedin leadership, meeting in Peshawar on 15 April, decided to have the current chairman, Sibghatullah Mujaddidi, as president of Afghanistan for two months on arrival in Kabul on a rotating basis, and established a Leadership Council of 51 members, including the chairman and deputy chairman (Rabbani), divided equally among the seven constituents. Afghanistan's vice president, Rahim Hatif, negotiated the entries of the forces of Masoud and Dostum into the capital while ignoring the partisans of much-hated Hikmatyar.

President Mujaddidi's arrival in Kabul, now under the military control of Masoud and Dostum, marked the end of the 14-year conflict between Afghan Marxists and Islamists that started in April 1978, and escalated two years later. Once Moscow intervened militarily in December 1979, the civil conflict escalated into a battle between the two antagonistic superpowers. Washington's rising commitment to Afghan Islamists could be judged by the financial aid it provided them: up from the publicly acknowledged $20 million (a fraction of the actual figure, which included much covert aid) in 1980 to $700 million in 1988, the last year of Ronald Reagan's presidency as well as of the Soviet military presence in Afghanistan.[48] The estimates of Soviet military aid to the Kabul regime varied from $1 million to $4 million a day for roughly 10 years – $3.5 to $14 billion – plus economic aid, comprising food and fuel; but part of this was offset by the Afghan natural gas that Moscow bought at a giveaway price.[49] The estimated human loss of one million – or 110,000 a year – included deaths caused directly or indirectly by the conflict, the direct category covering those killed either in combat between the warring camps or among the various constituents of each camp, or owing to the acts of sabotage or widespread drug trafficking in Afghanistan and Pakistan; and the indirect category consisting largely of infants whose deaths could be linked to malnutrition or breakdown of the health services caused by the hostilities, and those blown up by the tens of thousands of mines scattered throughout the countryside.[50]

The withdrawal of Soviet troops from Afghanistan in early 1989 loosened Moscow's ties with that country, but did not end them. So Afghanistan's fate continued to be linked with the state of play in the Cold War. The fall of the Berlin Wall in late 1989 foreshadowed Soviet defeat which materialized in the break-up of the Soviet Union two years later. Though the combination of Afghan nationalism and Islam adopted by the Mujahedin was a powerful force with which to confront the secular, leftist regime in Kabul, it was not enough to destroy it. In the final analysis, it was the lure of American and Saudi money and weapons that held together the seven recognized factions within the Mujahedin Alliance. Thus Washington emerged as the crucial player in bringing about the victory of Islamists over Marxists in Afghanistan – an unpalatable fact to be conceded by such Muslim fundamentalist leaders as Hikmatyar and bin Laden, who persisted in their unsupported assertion that the Mujahedin had won their anti-Soviet jihad strictly on their own. Equally, Washington was loath to admit that it achieved its Islamist victory in Afghanistan while busily decrying Islamic fundamentalism in neighboring Iran, and that it became willy-nilly a midwife – along with Pakistan and Saudi Arabia – of the latest Muslim fundamentalist state.

The Mujahedin in Kabul: the second civil war (1992–6)

The new regime changed the country's name from the Republic of Afghanistan to the Islamic State of Afghanistan. Its other decrees included banning alcohol, gambling and nightclubs, enjoining the veil for women, transforming co-educational schools and colleges into single-sex institutions, and declaring the Sharia to be sole source of Afghan law. But their actual impact on the lives of urban dwellers was minimal as the government in Kabul soon became embroiled in a deadly civil conflict and lacked both the resources and single-mindedness to impose these rules. As a result of a decade and a half of nationwide fighting, many people had migrated from villages to cities, including Kabul, swelling its population to nearly 2 million, – about a third of them Hazaras, housed chiefly in the poor western sector and loyal to the pro-Iranian Hizb-e Wahdat-e Islami (Islamic Unity Party), popularly called Wahadat, headed by Ayatollah Abdul Ali Mazari.

With the common enemy finally gone for good, long-standing rivalries between factional leaders and the four major ethnic groups re-emerged. Having enjoyed autonomy, stemming from access to large quantities of weapons and money, in their decade-long struggle against the leftist regime, the non-Pushtun minorities were not prepared to let the Pushtun hegemony, stretching back to 1747, re-assert itself. With Kabul now controlled by Tajik, Uzbek and Hazara fighters, and with the Defense Ministry run by Masoud, the ethnic minorities were in a strong position to frustrate Pushtuns' attempts to become the ruling group – as was the intent of Hizb-e Islami's Hikmatyar.

To enlarge his base, President Mujaddidi, head of the small National Liberation Front of Afghanistan, promoted Dostum to a four-star general before stepping down in late June. He was followed by Burhanuddin Rabbani, a Tajik, whose party included Masoud. This concentration of power in Tajik hands angered Hikmatyar, who began stressing Pushtun nationalism more than Islamic fundamentalism.

Based in Charasayab, 20 miles (32 km) south of Kabul, Hikmatyar orchestrated a punishing barrage of shells and mortars aimed at Kabul in early August. Wahadat's Mazari sided with Rabbani and Dostum to defend the city. By the time a cease-fire was agreed in late August, 2,500 people were dead and 500,000 were displaced. Ironically, it was under an Islamic regime that civil war finally caught up with the residents of Kabul, which had hitherto remained comparatively peaceful.

The continuing inroads that Islamists made in Tajikistan, capped by the resignation of President Rahman Nabiyev, a neo-Communist, in September 1992, encouraged Hikmatyar to shore up his assistance to the Islamist forces there. He did so partly for ideological reasons and partly to keep the civil conflict in Tajikistan going, thus diminishing any chance of ethnic Tajiks in Tajikistan and Afghanistan uniting.

When Rabbani's four-month presidential tenure finished in late October, he managed to get an extension of two months by cajoling the Leadership Council, by now a reduced, fractured body. An angry Hikmatyar unleashed his shells and mortars on Kabul. But Rabbani was obdurate. Indeed, he went on to summon a jirga, packed with his supporters, on 28 December, and had it extend his tenure by two years.

Hikmatyar's complaint that Rabbani had hijacked the presidency was shared by a few other constituents of the Mujahedin Alliance as well as the Wahadat, which had boycotted the Rabbani-sponsored jirga. The Wahadat joined Hikmatyar in his attacks on Kabul's Tajik-majority neighborhoods, situated in the northern sector and controlled by Rabbani. Having pulled out of the city, but retaining its civilian airport as well as its north-eastern suburbs, Dostum remained neutral in the latest fighting which continued for weeks. "In the south and west of the city, pounded mercilessly for weeks at a time, entire suburbs have been reduced to rubble," reported Gerald Bourke of the

Guardian from Kabul in late February 1993. "Hundreds of thousands have fled to the provinces or to Pakistan . . . The destitutes tell harrowing tales of murder, mutilation, abduction or rape at the hands of defense ministry or rebel forces. Their stories suggest not just breakdown of law and order, but disintegration of society."[51] The inter-ethnic atrocities committed by both sides left such an imprint on the psyche of Kabulis that nine years later they shuddered at the thought of the Jamiat-e Islami's Tajik forces re-entering the city as latter-day victors. Luckily for them, history did not repeat itself.

The deplorable state of affairs persuaded Afghan leaders to accept the mediation offer by Pakistani Prime Minister Muhammad Nawaz Sharif (1943– : r. October 1990–April 1993, February 1997–October 1999). Meeting in Islamabad in March, the eight negotiating parties (seven members of the Mujahedin Alliance and Wahadat) signed an accord which gave the premiership to Hikmatyar and presidency to Rabbani for 18 months starting on 28 December 1992, by the end of which time parliamentary elections would have been held under a new constitution. At Hikmatyar's insistence, Dostum – described by him as "an unreconstructed Communist" – was denied any role in the cabinet or the Leadership Council or the 40-member Constitutional Committee set up to draft the constitution.

Accompanied by Hikmatyar and Rabbani, Nawaz Sharif traveled to Mecca for a joint *umra* (short hajj) and a meeting with King Fahd, who co-signed the Islamabad agreement. The three leaders then traveled to Tehran where President Ali Akbar Hasehmi Rafsanjani too co-signed the document. The one prominent Saudi commoner who would have been greatly interested in the document – Osama bin Laden – was no longer in the desert kingdom.

Had he been there and met the four leaders, bin Laden would most likely have presented them each with a copy of the recently published *Encyclopedia of the Afghan Jihad* (in Arabic), a project financed by his Al Qaida. It was a record of both political and military aspects of the jihad – the 1,050 pages of military text not only providing detailed information on the range and operation of the whole array of arms and ammunition, including the Stinger anti-aircraft missiles supplied by the CIA – an organization which went unmentioned – but also explaining how to mount terrorist and paramilitary attacks as had been taught to the Mujahedin by the ISI working in conjunction with the CIA. Another Al Qaida-sponsored publication was *Military Studies in the Jihad against the Tyrants*, a 180-page manual in Arabic, with a chapter on suicide bombings.[52]

By 1993, working in close collaboration with Sudan's Islamist regime, and particularly its chief ideologue, Hassan al Turabi of the National Islamic Front, bin Laden helped capitalize a new interest-free bank, Al Shamal Islamic Bank, and established 10 companies with varied interests – from modest tannery and bakery to agro-industry, processing the produce from reportedly one million acres of land near Khartoum and in eastern Sudan growing corn, peanuts and sesame oil – under the umbrella of Wadi al Aqiq. With the group including four trading, investment and transport companies, and maintaining bank accounts abroad – from London to Hong Kong via Nicosia and Dubai – bin Laden had created ideal covers for Al Qaida's clandestine activities worldwide.[53] Furthermore, Wadi al Aqiq's multifarious commercial activity enabled bin Laden to employ hundreds of Afghan Arabs whose return home was barred by their governments. As jihad veterans, they also provided a suitable recruiting pool for Al Qaida, which by now probably had at least a thousand members, including those based in Pakistan and Afghanistan.

The war-ravaged Afghanistan was now divided, with Dostum – calling himself "President of the Northern Alliance" – controlling six provinces, extending from the Central Asian borders to the outskirts of Kabul, including the gas fields near Shebarghan, developed by the Soviets, and a large chemical plant near Mazar-e Sharif, the capital of the "Northern Alliance," covering Jozjan, Faryab, Baghis, Ghor and Baghlan provinces. His region had its own tax- and customs-collecting bureaucracy. The efficiency with which he ran Mazar (estimated population now 500,000, twice the normal), ensuring that it had electricity, drinking water and public transport, contrasted sharply with the bleak disorder and desolation prevailing in Kabul whose population had shrunk by three-quarters to below 500,000. Dostum's military was the most powerful in Afghanistan, equipped with several hundred Soviet-made tanks, and about 100 fighter aircraft, helicopter gunships and transport planes. While manned chiefly by Uzbeks, Tajiks and Turkmens, it also contained former Communist Pushtun officers. The name of the party he headed – National Islamic Movement (NIM) – was misleading. "With Afghanistan's almost entire population being Muslim, it cannot be a non-Muslim state," he explained. "We also want democracy which the fundamentalists are opposed to. Further Islamic laws cannot be implemented. If the fundamentalists implemented these laws, nobody will be able to live in Afghanistan."[54]

To Dostum's delight, the Constitutional Committee in Kabul became embroiled in the controversy about giving the Shia Jaafari code the same status in the constitution as the Sunni Hanafi, with Sayyaf of the Islamic Alliance opposing it vehemently and Mazari of the Wahadat insisting on it. This threw into disarray the timetable for elections following the adoption of the constitution. It also led to fighting between Wahadat and Islamic Alliance militias in Kabul in October. The next month there were clashes between the forces of Rabbani and Hikmatyar, now entrenched in the south-eastern suburbs of Kabul. Dostum remained neutral. But, when the warring sides agreed a truce to replenish their ammunition in late December, Dostum attacked Rabbani's men in central Kabul on 1 January 1994. Suddenly, doing an opportunistic U-turn – typical of Afghan politics – Hikmatyar joined Dostum, whom he had until then described as a mortal enemy, and Mazari. "At four o'clock in the morning on 1 January, the bombardment started," noted Latifa, the young daughter of an upper-middle-class businessman in Kabul:

It lasted without respite for a week. With our neighbors we huddled in the cellar. Water and electricity had been cut off throughout the city. Then the opposing sides decided on some kind of truce that allowed foreign diplomats to leave. We made use of this, too, to seek refuge in the [Tajik] north of the city. On the way we met thousands of people, entire families, who had had to leave their homes.[55]

During the almost non-stop two-month-long hostilities, hospitals were hit by rockets, electric supplies interrupted frequently and bakeries left unattended. Half of the city's residents lost their homes.[56]

Dostum and Hikmatyar formalized their alliance by forming the Supreme Coordination Council (SCC) under the latter's chairmanship. When Rabbani refused to step down on 28 June 1994 according to the Islamabad agreement, civil war intensified. Rabbani's Tajik fighters performed well. They routed Hikmatyar's in south-eastern Kabul and seized control of Kabul airport from Dostum's partisans.

Unlike in the past, the efforts of neither regional powers nor the UN had any success in ending the violence. The Afghan factions, originally fostered by foreign powers, had become autonomous. At the UN, Russia and America were content to see Afghans continue their internecine violence since they visualized, correctly, that a stable Islamic Afghanistan would actively aid Islamist forces in Tajikistan and elsewhere in Central Asia and damage their interests.

It was in this vacuum that many Pushtun mullahs in southern Afghanistan, veterans of the past anti-Marxist jihad but now unattached to the currently feuding parties, held conclaves to end the civil war – an aim shared actively by Pakistan, determined as it was to buy the much-needed raw cotton for its textile mills from Turkmenistan and Uzbekistan.

A consensus grew among the concerned mullahs in the Pushtun region around a three-point program: restoration of peace, disarming of civilians and full application of the Sharia. Being current or former students of madressas, mostly based in Pakistan, where they had grown up in refugee camps, they decided to call their organization Taliban, plural of Talib (one who pursues religious learning). As Mullah Muhammad Omar Akhund

(1959– ; r. 1996–2001), the Taliban's spiritual leader, put it: "We took up arms to achieve the [real] aims of the Afghan jihad and save our people from further suffering at the hands of the so-called Mujahedin."[57]

As a member of the Hizb-e Islami of Yunus Khalis, Mullah Omar (the name by which he was widely known) had participated in the jihad against the Najibullah regime during 1989–92, and suffered injuries four times, including when a rocket exploded near him, blinding him in the right eye. Born in the Hotak tribe of the Ghilzai branch of Pushtuns to a landless peasant in Nodeh, a village near Kandahar, he studied at a madressa in the city even when the family migrated to Tarin Kot, Uruzgan. His family was so poor that he wore his first shoes when he was 13. Following his father's death in the mid-1980s, he became the sole breadwinner. He settled in the Singesar village in Kandahar province as the local mullah and opened a madressa there, an enterprise that did not deter him from engaging in guerrilla actions against the Marxist government. He was noted more for his piety than for his charisma. Later he would be remembered for issuing his handwritten orders on small pieces of paper, called "chits," and maintaining a treasury in the form of a tin trunk, filled with local currency, to be subsequently supplemented by another containing US dollar bills. Given his reclusiveness, and his strict ban on photography and representation of the human body, his appearance remains almost undocumented. During the first three years of the founding of the Taliban, he gave only two interviews, both to Rahimullah Yusufzai, a Pushtun Pakistani journalist freelancing for the British Broadcasting Corporation (BBC), with his producer, David Loyn, kept outside the room in the former governor's residence in Kandahar. "I was rewarded at the end with a glimpse of a tall [bearded] man with only one eye but an otherwise distinguished appearance, a fair complexion and a Grecian nose," reported Loyn in the *Observer*.[58]

Soon after being elected the Taliban leader in spring 1994, Mullah Omar heard a complaint from the residents of Singesar that a commander of the nearby military camp had abducted two teenage girls and taken them to the base where they had been raped. Leading a contingent of 30 local Taliban, Omar attacked the camp, set the girls free, seized arms and ammunition, and hanged the offending commander from the barrel of a tank, a common practice.[59] Omar's fame grew. In July he intervened in a public fracas between two commanders in Kandahar over an attractive young boy whom they wanted as a homosexual partner – an act deserving capital punishment according to the Sharia – and freed the boy. This event in Kandahar, southern Afghanistan's regional capital with a population then of over 300,000, was later taken to signal the formal founding of the Taliban, who adopted a black turban as their uniform and a white flag as their emblem.

Omar's effective strong-arm tactics brought him to the notice of Pakistani truckers whose business had suffered due to some 200 road blocks that local warlords had erected along the highway from the Pakistani city of Quetta to Iran via Herat as customs collecting points. They offered money to Omar to clear the highway. He started at the border crossing at the Afghan village of Spin Baldak, where Hikmatyar's Hizb-e Islami had its garrison. In mid-October, leading a force of 200 Taliban, Omar captured the garrison – and with it 18,000 Kalashnikovs, dozens of artillery guns, ammunition and many military vehicles.

Meanwhile, the earlier contacts that many Taliban had had with the pre-eminent Pakistani fundamentalist leader, Maulana Fazlur Rahman of the Jamiat-e Ulama-e Islami (JUI), came in handy in securing the assistance of Pakistan, then governed by Prime Minister Benazir Bhutto in association with the JUI. The timing was right. Seeing no end in sight for the fighting in northern Afghanistan, which provided the shortest distance between Pakistan and Central Asia, Islamabad had recently opted for the southern route for trade with Turkmenistan and Uzbekistan. Thus the interests of the ISI, JIU, Pakistani truckers and newly emerged Taliban converged: to clear the passage from Quetta to Ashqabad via Herat, with the Quetta–Herat road blocked by nearly 200 checkpoints erected by local war lords.

As a dry run, in late October 1994 the Pakistani government sent a convoy of 30 trucks loaded with medicine. When it reached the outskirts of Kandahar, a local warlord, Mansour Achakzai, stopped it. After heavily bribing the most important warlord inside Kandahar, the ISI called Mullah Omar for assistance. As heavily armed militia appeared on the horizon, Achakzai's men fled, assuming them to be Pakistani soldiers. The Taliban's subsequent capture of Kandahar increased their arsenal by half a dozen MiG-21 fighters and scores of tanks and armored vehicles, not to mention an abundant supply of small weapons.[60] With this, the Taliban was in business, both politically and commercially, a fact hailed by its midwives, the JUI and the Pakistani government, with its interior minister, Gen. Naseerullah Babur, an ethnic Pushtun – having set up the Afghan Trade Development Cell as a back door to funnel money to the fledgling organization – quietly describing the Taliban as "our boys." They swiftly swept away all road blocks to Herat, enabling the Pakistani trucks to proceed to Turkmenistan unhindered, and introduced a one-toll system. With Afghan madressa students in Afghanistan and Pakistan joining in droves, the Taliban's militia was now 12,000 strong, the size of an infantry division in a regular army.

Settling down in Kandahar, Mullah Omar lost no time in disarming civilians and irregular militias and imposing his exceedingly puritanical version of the Sharia. He required women to wear the head-to-toe shrouds, burqas, and men to don long shirts, loose trousers and turbans, and grow bushy beards by not cutting or shaving facial hair – in effect preventing clean-shaven men from shaving for at least six weeks – while banning long hair in order to "prevent British and American hairstyles."[61] He shut down all girls' schools and forbade women from working outside the home. His blanket ban on music (which included even beating a music drum) and television resulted in the destruction of audio- and video-tapes as well as television sets. With this, streamers of audio-tapes from seized cassettes fluttering from police stations would become a common site in the Taliban-controlled towns and cities. The reason for prohibiting music, singing and dancing was that, in the view of Mullah Omar and fellow clerics, they aroused lust and led to fornication, thus undermining marital fidelity and the stable family structure which were the foundations of a truly Islamic social order. The ban on jewelry stemmed from the reasoning that it was a dangerous temptation to idolatry. Mullah Omar also prohibited such leisure activities as chess, football and kite flying as well as keeping birds as pets. To prevent idolatry, he ordered the tearing up of all pictures and portraits, and prohibited photography. He outlawed gambling as well as charging interest on loans. Finally, he prescribed compulsory prayer, and banned all transport during the prayer times. These edicts were to be enforced by the Department of Propagating Virtue and Preventing Vice.

For the next three months the Taliban forged ahead, capturing province after province, often by bribing local warlords with the funds supplied by the Pakistani ISI and later by the Saudi intelligence agency, and opening up roads, which lowered food prices and gained them immediate popularity. By disarming all irregular militias, punishing corrupt officials and warlords, and restoring law and order, the Taliban expanded their popular base among a people who had grown weary of incessant violence and corruption. In February 1995 the Taliban captured Charasyab, the headquarters of Hikmatyar, who fled without fighting to Sarobi, 45 miles (70 km) east of Kabul. This led to his losing the presidency of the Supreme Coordination Council – now also encompassing the Wahadat and the NFLA – to Sibghatullah Mujaddidi. However, Hikmatyar felt consoled when the Taliban's advance stalled in the face of heavy air and artillery bombardment by Rabbani's forces, thereby losing the momentum which had gained them a third of Afghanistan.

The arrest in February 1995 in Islamabad of Ramzi Ahmad Yousef, accused of involvement in the bombing of the World Trade Center (WTC) in New York two years earlier, highlighted for the first time the centrality of Afghanistan/Pakistan in global terrorism, a fact which would be impressed on the Western psyche with greater force and horror six-and-a-half years later, with the self-same WTC becoming the prime target. The Pakistani authorities promptly extradited Yousef to America.

Speaking to the US media representatives in Islamabad on 21 March, Pakistan's Prime Minister Benazir Bhutto alluded to the presence of "terrorist gangs and Muslim militants on the Pakistani soil," pointing out that most of them were Afghan refugees with a sprinkling of Pakistanis and Arabs. With more than one million Afghan refugees, "and with most men in refugee camps being well armed and with battle experience during the Afghan war," her government lacked resources to deal with them.[62]

Around that time hundreds of delegates from the Muslim world were on their way to attend the Popular Arab and Islamic Congress in Khartoum, sponsored by Hassan Turabi's NIF. One of the subjects debated was how far jihad for an Islamic state should include armed struggle. Attending the conference was Osama bin Laden and his associate Dr. Ayman Zawahiri, who had left Pakistan a year earlier to join him. At the congress they met delegates from the Group Islamique Armée (GIA, Armed Islamic Group), then engaged in an armed struggle against the secularist military regime in Algeria, and the Lebanese Hizbollah, which had experience not only of assembling and exploding big bombs – having killed 259 US Marines in Beirut in October 1983 with one such device – but also in suicide bombing. (Three years later Al Qaida too would detonate large bombs at two US embassies in East Africa, with the bombers sacrificing their lives.) The activities of bin Laden and Zawahiri were being monitored closely by the Sudanese, Saudi and American intelligence agencies – especially after Washington had suspected bin Laden's involvement in the deaths of 18 US soldiers on a UN peacekeeping mission in a confrontation in Mogadishu, the capital of the war-ravaged Somalia, in October 1993, in which at least 500 Somalis were also killed.

Bizarrely, at the end of the congress in Khartoum on 27 March 1995, Sudanese President Omar al Bashir held a joint press conference with Jimmy Carter, former US president, whose Global 2000 project had sponsored a program to end river blindness in

Africa. In appreciation of Carter's effort, Bashir announced a two-month ceasefire in the long-running Sudanese civil war between the predominantly Muslim north and largely Christian south.[63]

With the internecine war in Afghanistan among the erstwhile Mujahedin factions entering its fourth year, Saudi Arabia, a major player in the anti-Soviet jihad, felt frustrated. To assess the situation on the ground, Prince Turki met President Rabbani in Kabul, Mullah Omar in Kandahar and Hikmatyar in Jalalabad in early June, and announced a plan to hold a meeting of all factions in Jiddah. Nothing came of it. But his meeting with Mullah Omar would blossom into an alliance three months later when the Taliban, having mobilized 25,000 militia men, would capture Herat, a city of 400,000, as well as the Shindad military base along with its 41 aircraft and helicopters, thus ending the three-year rule of Gen. Ismail Khan, who had joined Rabbani's Jamiat-e Islami.

Following the defeat of pro-Iranian Ismail Khan in Herat by the Taliban, which held Shia Muslims in low esteem, Tehran turned strongly anti-Taliban. It increased its assistance to President Rabbani, and advised him to patch up his differences with the non-Taliban factions. In early 1996 his personal envoy met Hikmatyar in Sarobi, Dostum in Mazar, and pro-Tehran Karim Khalili, an ethnic Hazara, in Bamiyan. Together they set up a 10-member committee to devise a plan to overcome the Taliban threat and end the violence, which in less than three years had claimed 25,000 lives in Kabul alone.[64]

While maintaining its siege of Kabul from the south, the Taliban moved to consolidate its political-religious standing. On the eve of the Afghan New Year (Nawruz), starting on the spring equinox, about 1,200 Sunni clerics and tribal leaders from all over Afghanistan, except the north, gathered in Kandahar to deliberate on the future of the Taliban and Mullah Omar. On 4 April 1996, they decided to accept Omar as their *Emir al Mumineen* (Commander of the Faithful). They collectively swore their fealty to him by repeatedly shouting "*Emir al Muminin!*" as Mullah Omar presented himself on the roof of a tall building in central Kandahar, covered in the *Khirqa* (lit. used cloth; fig. cloak) of Prophet Muhammad – brought to Kandahar in 1761 and preserved in a local shrine – now taken out for the occasion. "The oath of allegiance, or 'bayat', was a procedure similar to when Caliph Omar was confirmed as leader of the Muslim community in Arabia after the death of Prophet Muhammad," explained Ahmed Rashid, a Pakistani specialist on Central Asia. "It was a political masterstroke, for by cloaking himself in the Prophet's mantle, Mullah Omar had assumed the right to lead not just all Afghans but all Muslims."[65] Among those who accepted this interpretation of the religious ritual was Osama bin Laden after he had taken refuge in Afghanistan later that year, initially in an area outside the Taliban's control.

A few weeks after this historic ritual, Mullah Omar's aides received Robin Raphel, US assistant secretary of state, in Kandahar during her tour of the region – a meeting which, to the satisfaction of Islamabad, recognized the Taliban as a crucial element in the Afghan imbroglio. Determined to frustrate Iran's strategy of cementing a powerful anti-Taliban alliance, Pakistan increased its material support for the Taliban after having repaired the infrastructure of electricity and roads in the south. Besides keeping up its steady supply of food, fuel and ammunition to the Taliban, Pakistan improved Kandahar airport, furnished the Taliban with a telephone and wireless network, and provided military and intelligence personnel to direct the Taliban's military activities against their enemies. At the same time Riyadh was generous with fuel and cash as well as pick-up trucks used extensively in fighting.[66] The Taliban made good use of the Saudi-supplied dollars, making sure to pay its newly hired helicopter and fighter pilots, tank operators and military technicians – often picked from among Afghan exiles or refugees in Pakistan – in much sought-after dollars. In a gesture designed to please Arabs in general and the Saudis in particular, Mullah Omar named the Taliban intelligence agency Istikhabarat, an Arabic term, thus deviating from the Afghan policy of using Persian titles for all official agencies. Publicly, both Saudi Arabia and Pakistan professed neutrality and non-interference in Afghan affairs while Washington declared that it had no favorites in Afghanistan. None of this fooled the emerging anti-Taliban alliance. In May 1996 a thousand troops of Hikmatyar arrived in Kabul to defend the city from the continuing Taliban rocketing.

That month bin Laden arrived at Jalalabad airport in a chartered cargo plane, which also carried three of his four wives (the oldest one and their son, Abdullah, preferring to return to Jiddah), at least six of his children and about 100 Afghan Arab fighters, to live in Afghanistan after being asked to leave by the Sudanese government, mainly due to pressure from Washington which had been building up since late 1995.[67] Following the failed attempt on Egyptian President Mubarak's life in Addis Ababa in mid-1995, blamed on Khartoum by Cairo, Sudan was also urged by Egypt and Saudi Arabia to expel bin Laden.

American officials would have liked bin Laden to be repatriated – or even hijacked – to the Saudi kingdom to be prosecuted there. But the last thing Riyadh wanted was bin Laden's presence in Saudi Arabia. In Khartoum, Hassan al Turabi resolved the problem by contacting Atiya Badawi, Sudan's ambassador to Pakistan and Afghanistan. As a veteran of the Afghan jihad, Badawi was well connected to the Mujahedin commanders. He succeeded in persuading three of them based in the Jalalabad area to accept bin Laden as their "guest." They traveled to Khartoum to assure him of their protection.[68]

Pressure on Sudan had mounted after the US State Department in February 1996 described bin Laden as "the most significant financial sponsor of Islamic extremist activities in the world today," while the CIA's Counter-terrorism Center – the clearing house for intelligence on international terrorists – had named him as its leading target after setting up a special operations unit – Bin Laden Station – to concentrate on his network, Al Qaida, thus focusing on not a country or regime, but a non-governmental organization (NGO), an unprecedented step. Soon afterwards, President Clinton signed a secret presidential covert action order that authorized US intelligence agencies to plan and implement covert operations that might lead to deaths, thus legalizing the "inadvertent" killing of bin Laden in a military action against his Al Qaida network.[69] To track bin Laden's activities the National Security Agency used its eavesdropping satellites to listen in on conversations of his Al Qaida activists worldwide, and its spy satellites to take photographs from space to search for any signs of him reactivating the Afghan training camps used in the past against the Soviets. But the Bin Laden Station's important break came in early spring of that year when Jamal Ahmad al Fadl (b. 1963), a Sudanese who had been a middle-level courier and general fixer for bin Laden and his companies in Sudan, defected and placed himself into the hands of the CIA station chief at an (unnamed) American embassy in an African country whose name remains classified.[70]

Soon after bin Laden had based himself in Jalalabad in May 1996, local intelligence agents informed Maulavi Yunus Khalis, the de facto governor of the Paktia province, that strangers, carrying pictures of bin Laden, had been making inquiries about his whereabouts. So, on Khalis's advice, bin Laden and his entourage moved to the Tora Bora cave complex.

For the most part, though, his Afghan hosts were absorbed in the events at home – such as Hikmatyar arriving in Kabul on 26 June at the head of a procession of his fighters and followers to be welcomed by his erstwhile enemy, President Rabbani, to take up the prime ministerial office, followed by Dostum lifting the siege of the capital from the north – and (unknown to the rest of the world) Taliban leaders secretly discussing with the visiting Saudi intelligence chief, Prince Turki, the Pakistani ISI plan to capture Kabul before winter.

Sheltering in a cave did not stop bin Laden from keeping in touch with news and issuing periodic statements, often responding to events. His reaction to the Al Khobar bombing in Saudi Arabia on 25 June 1996 came on 23 August. Under the title "Declaration of the Jihad Against the Americans Occupying the Land of the Two Sacred Mosques," it read: "The Muslims have realized they are the main target of the aggression of the coalition of the Jews and the Crusaders . . . The latest of these assaults [by them] – that is the occupation of the Land of the Two Sacred Mosques, the home ground of Islam – is the greatest disaster since the death of Prophet Muhammad (Peace be upon him)." It referred to the words of the Prophet on his death-bed – "If Allah wills and I live, Allah willing, I will expel the Jews and the Christians from Arabia" – and appealed to "our Muslim brothers throughout the world" to join fellow Muslims in "the Land of the Two Holy Mosqures and in Palestine" and "participate with them against their enemies, also your enemies – the Israelis and the Americans – by causing them as much harm as can be possibly achieved." It concluded: "The presence of the American Crusader forces in Muslim Gulf states . . . is the greatest danger and [poses] the most serious harm, threatening the world's largest oil reserves. Expelling this American occupying enemy is the most important duty [of Muslims] after the duty of belief in God." [71] While this declaration of jihad by bin Laden got worldwide publicity, it went largely unnoticed in Afghanistan where people and politicians were too absorbed in their civil war to pay attention to anything else.

On 25 August the Taliban attacked Jalalabad from the south and east. However, their siege, lasting a fortnight, ended in victory only after a promise of safe passage to Pakistan and a $10 million bribe to Hajji Abdul Qadir, the local senior-most commander, had resulted in his sudden exit. [72] During the next 10 days the Taliban overran Nangarhar, Laghman and Kunar provinces, ruled hitherto by the Eastern Shura Council (independent of the government in Kabul) which had hitherto dealt with bin Laden. On 24 September the Taliban seized Sarobi, the stronghold of Hikmatyar.

Soon two mobile columns of the Taliban militia, packed into Toyota pick-up trucks, converged on Kabul from the east and the south as another column rushed north to cut off the Bagram military air base from the capital. At nightfall on 26 September the Taliban forces drove into the capital a few hours after Gen. Ahmad Shah Masoud had ordered an evacuation, taking most of the artillery and tanks with him to the north.

'Every building along the road to the Afghan capital [from Jalalabad] bears the scars of heavy fighting," reported David Loyn in the *Observer*. "Lorry containers are used as warehouses; shops and houses lie burst open by shell fire on the sand. It is like an archaeological site layered with the evidence of nearly two decades of war. Mounds of shell cases lie at the side of the road, but the tanks which fired them have gone."[73] Unlike the previous takeover of Kabul by the Mujahedin, which was accompanied by looting by the victorious soldiers, this time there was no looting or breakdown of law and order.

The lightning speed with which the Taliban captured Kabul dazed not just them and their domestic enemies but also the neighboring states, except, of course, Pakistan. For an organization that had barely registered on the political radar of Afghanistan two years earlier, this was an astounding achievement. Nobody could have guessed then that history would repeat itself five years hence, with the Taliban withdrawing overnight from Kabul.

Taliban in power

Around 01.00 hours. on 27 September, a special Taliban unit forced its way into the United Nations compound in Kabul, and seized Muhammad Najibullah and his brother Shahpur Ahmadzai. After castrating Najibullah, and dragging him behind a jeep a few times around the nearby presidential palace, the Taliban militia shot him in the head. At first light they hung his blood-soaked corpse from a traffic control post just outside the palace in the Ariana Square, the site of several public rallies that Najibullah had addressed as president.[74] They hung his murdered brother by his side. The Taliban went on to pass death sentences on Dostum, Rabbani and Masoud, but not Hikmatyar, a fellow-Pushtun.

Mullah Omar appointed a six-man shura council, headed by Mullah Muhammad Rabbani (1958–2001), a Pushtun from the Uruzgan province and no relative of President Burhanuddin Rabbani, as the prime minister of the interim government.[75]

At 11.00 hours on Saturday 28 September, Radio Shariat (a variant of Sharia) – the renamed Radio Kabul – broadcast the following decrees issued by the government of Mullah Rabbani in accordance with the Sharia:

> Any person with a firearm must deposit it at a military post or the nearest mosque. Girls and women are not allowed to work outside home. All women who have to leave their homes must be accompanied by a *mahrim* (male blood relative). Public transport will be segregated, with separate buses for men and women. Men must grow beards. Men must wear a turban or white beret. Suits and ties are forbidden; traditional Afghani dress must be worn. Women and girls must wear the burqa. They are forbidden to wear brightly colored clothes under the burqa. Nail polish, lipstick and make-up are forbidden. All Muslims must say their prayers at the specified times and at the place where they find themselves.

The decrees issued in the following days included:

> Displaying photos of animals or humans is forbidden. No male doctor is permitted to touch the body of a woman under the pretext of consultation. A woman may not go to a men's tailor. A young woman must not converse with a young man. Muslim families may not listen to music even during a wedding. Muslim families are prohibited from taking photos or making videos even during a marriage ceremony. No merchant may sell alcohol or women's underwear. All non-Muslims – that is, Hindus, Sikhs and Jews – must wear something yellow, and point out their abode by flying a yellow flag.

The ban on music was extended to "whistling kettles."[76] And the ban on high heels for women was later accompanied by the edict: "Women are duty bound to behave with dignity, to walk calmly and refrain from hitting their shoes on the ground, which makes noise."[77] The social injunctions imposed by the Taliban were an amalgam of an extremist interpretation of the Hanbali school of Sunni Islam and Wahhabi practices.

By disarming civilians and non-Taliban militias, the new regime brought peace and tranquillity to Kabul where some 50,000 people had died in the civil conflict that erupted after the fall of the Najibullah regime. This consideration weighed so heavily that many non-Taliban politicians, including Hamid Karzai (1957– ; r. 2001–), who had briefly been deputy foreign minister in the Burhanuddin Rabbani government, backed the Taliban.

The Taliban's dramatic triumph went down badly in Iran as well as Russia and Central Asia. In contrast, Pakistan was quietly jubilant for having trounced Tehran's plans and placed its protégé in Kabul. This was to be expected. But what was not expected was Washington's reaction. Instead of raising alarm at the victory of the most diehard Islamic fundamentalist party, the US State Department spokesman, Glyn Davies, said there was "nothing objectionable" about the domestic policies pursued by the Taliban.[78]

Ironically, while the ruling Iranian clerics were quick to condemn especially the Taliban's ban on women's education, describing it as contrary to the Quranic verse which enjoins upon all believers, irrespective of their sex, to acquire knowledge, the US State Department remained silent on the subject for several weeks during which it announced the dispatch of an envoy to Kabul to confer with the Taliban regime. The Taliban were impervious to what the Islamic Republic of Iran in particular, or the international community in general, thought of them. What mattered to them was how their policies were viewed by their most active constituency, young Afghan males, those who had grown up in refugee camps in Pakistan, where life was even more conservative than in Afghan villages, and who had flocked to fight for their ultra-orthodox movement.

Lacking a well-defined Afghan policy of its own in the post-Najibullah period, the US stance on Afghanistan became derivative of Pakistani policy. Islamabad stressed the Taliban's anti-Russian disposition which suited the Clinton administration, determined to counter Moscow's renewed attempts to regain influence in Afghanistan. One of the advantages of a strong, uncorrupt Taliban government in Kabul would be better control over the growing of poppies, used for producing heroin (most of it destined for the US), which had thrived in the chaotic conditions prevailing after April 1992, Islamabad assured the Clinton administration, which was keen to curb the use of hard drugs in America. Since Turkey, Iran and Pakistan enforced drug control laws during 1972–80, severely restricting cultivation of heroin-yielding poppies, the war-torn Afghanistan became a leading producer of opium, its output rising five-fold to 500 metric tons during 1979–86, or about a third of global production. The figure rose to 1,200 metric tons at the time of Soviet withdrawal in 1989, and then peaked at 3,200 metric tons in 1994, amounting to more than half of the world total.[79] By the mid-1990s the opium–heroin trade had become such an integral part of the economies of Afghanistan and Pakistan that Islamabad's estimation proved wishful thinking. Another advantage stemming from the new set-up in Kabul would be the realization of a natural gas pipeline running from gas-rich Turkmenistan to Pakistan via Afghanistan, an enterprise in which Unocal, the twelfth largest American oil corporation, was deeply interested. "We regard the Taliban's victory as very positive," said Chris Taggart, a vice president of Unocal.[80] This tied in neatly with America's Iranophobia, which was sustained strongly by US secretary of state, Warren Christopher who, as deputy secretary of state under President Carter, had felt personally humiliated by Iran's refusal to release 52 American diplomats taken hostage in Tehran in 1979. This had led Washington to urge Turkmenistan to look east toward Pakistan for its gas exports rather than west toward Iran as a transit link for Turkey and Europe. The fact that the Taliban had adopted an anti-Iran stance was another point that pleased Washington. "Between 1994 and 1996 the US supported the Taliban politically through its allies Pakistan and Saudi Arabia, essentially because Washington viewed the

Taliban as anti-Iranian, anti-Shia and pro-Western," noted Ahmed Rashid. "The US conveniently ignored the Taliban's own Islamic fundamentalist agenda, its suppression of women and the consternation they created in Central Asia."[81]

The Taliban's swift victory alarmed the five Central Asian republics – especially after a declaration by their commander, Muhammad Shoiab: "We are going into the Panjshir Valley and then into Badakhshan [province]. After that we will move into Uzbekistan, Tajikistan and all other countries where the Communists are."[82] Central Asian leaders met hastily in Alma Aty, Kazakhstan, on 4–5 October, to review the latest development. They were joined by Viktor Chernomyrdin, the prime minister of Russia, which, after signing a mutual security pact with Tajikistan in May 1993, had posted 15,000 border guards along the Tajik–Afghan border.[83] The emergence of the Taliban as the predominant force in Afghanistan divided the region into two camps: Pakistan and Saudi Arabia on one side; and Iran, Central Asia and Russia on the other.

Later in October, instructed by Mullah Omar in Kandahar, his deputy in Kabul, Mullah Muhammad Rabbani, invited bin Laden for talks. The Taliban leaders had known him to be close to Hikmatyar and Abdul Rasul Sayyaf during the anti-Soviet jihad, and not Yunus Khalis, their favorite, and so it was essential for them to find out where exactly his present loyalties lay. Little wonder that the first meeting between bin Laden and Mullah Rabbani in Kabul was, by most accounts, in the "getting-to-know-each-other" mode.[84] It took further talks and praise of the Taliban's aims and achievements by bin Laden, combined with his *bayat* (allegiance) for Mullah Omar, whom he recognized as Commander of the Faithful, before the Taliban's supreme leader offered him the protection of the Taliban regime.

The outside world got its first insight into bin Laden's life in the inhospitable caves of north Afghanistan after his interview with Abdel Bari Atwan, editor of the London-based *Al Quds al Arabi* (The Arab Holy Jerusalem), in November. Atwan met bin Laden at an Afghan Arab base consisting of many caves at an altitude of 10,000 ft (3,000 m). Bin Laden's 20 × 13 ft (6 × 4 m) cave contained a library full of books on Islam as well as five wooden platforms serving as beds at night, with the walls hung with Kalashnikov rifles. During their conversation, there was sudden shouting outside, accompanied by artillery and rocket firing. Bin Laden left, and returned shortly, explaining that "mobilization" occurred periodically to maintain the highest level of alert. Atwan noticed 20 to 30 people around him – Egyptians, Saudis, Yemenis and Afghanis – all deferential to "this millionaire, who sacrificed all those millions," sitting with them in a cave, "sharing their dinner, in a very, very humble way." Dinner consisted of "chips soaked in cottonseed oil, a plate of fried eggs . . . salty cheese . . . and bread that must have been kneaded with sand." The mattress of the bed allocated to Atwan was "featureless and gray after so much use and lack of cleaning', and under the bed lay "boxes of grenades." The cave was heated by "a water tank and a wooden stove," with the outside temperature around 12 °F (−20 °C). At 04.00 hours. came the call to prayer, requiring the mandatory ablution, carried out with lukewarm water. The base was equipped with a power generator, computers, communications equipment – and an archive which included clippings from the Arab and foreign press. It was protected by anti-aircraft guns, tanks and armored vehicles along the approach roads. "He talked to me about the days he spent in Sudan and Somalia, the attempts made on his life, and the financial rewards he was promised [by the Saudi government] if he would give up his mission and jihad," Atwan wrote. More specifically, bin Laden told Atwan that the Saudi government had offered him $400 million if he declared that the Saudi regime was an Islamic one.[85]

Atwan found his host using a cane to walk due to the injury to his foot that he suffered during a skirmish with the Soviet forces in the 1980s. And bin Laden's low blood pressure and diabetic condition, which required periodic medical treatment, were widely known.[86]

Sayyid Qutb (1906–66), Islamic thinker and writer, Egypt.

Maulana Abul Ala Maududi (1903–79), Islamic thinker and writer, Pakistan.

The Temple of Queen Hatshepsut at Luxor, Egypt, on the eve of the massacre of foreign tourists on 17 November 1997.

Part of the Khobar Tower, an eight-story apartment block, at Khobar, Saudi Arabia, after a bomb explosion on 25 June 1996.

An Afghan Mujahedin guerrilla firing a US-made Stinger anti-aircraft missile, supplied by the CIA, during the Afghan jihad against the Moscow-backed regime in Kabul, 1987.

The corpses of Muhammad Najibullah (left) and his brother Shahpur Ahmadzai (right) hanging in Ariana Square, Kabul, on 27 September 1996.

The aftermath of the suicide truck bombing of the US Embassy in Nairobi on 7 August 1998.

Osama bin Laden, leader of Al Qaida, and Ayman Zawahiri, leader of Al Jihad.

Al Shifa Pharmaceutical factory, Khartoum, destroyed by US
missiles on 20–21 August 1998.

The World Trade Center
Towers, Manhattan, hit
by two hijacked planes on
September 11.

New Yorkers fleeing from the
burning WTC Towers.

The damaged Pentagon on September 11,
with the dome of the Capitol in
the background.

Mugshotsof 19 hijackers on September 11:
Khalid al Midhar; Majid Moqed; Nawaq
al Hamzi; Salem al Hamzi; Hani Hanjour;
Ahmad al Haznawi; Ahmad al Nami; Ziad
Samir Jarrah; Saeed al Ghamdi; Marwan
Yusuf al Shehhi; Fayez Rahsid al Qadi
Bani Hammad; Mohald al Shahri; Hamza
al Ghamdi; Ahmad al Ghamdi; Satam al
Suqami; Muhammad al Amir Awad al
Sayyid Atta; Abdul Aziz al Omari; Waleed
al Shahri; Wail al Shahri.

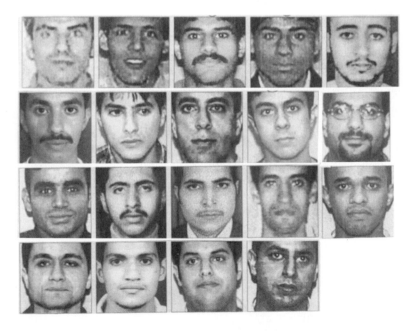

The War Cabinet of President George W. Bush, third on the left: (anti-clockwise, from left) Attorney-General John Ashcroft; Vice President Dick Cheney; Secretary of State Colin Powell; Secretary of Defense Donald Rumsfeld; Deputy Secretary of Defense Paul Wolfowitz; FBI Director Robert Mueller; Secretary of the Treasury Paul O'Neill; CIA Director George J. Tenet; White House Chief of Staff Andy Card; National Security Advisor Condoleezza Rice and Chairman of Joint Chiefs of Staff General Henry H. Shelton.

Mullah Muhammad Omar, Supreme Leader of the Taliban, Afghanistan.

The Pentagon's poster and leaflet showing Mullah Omar as a wanted fugitive, October 2001.

Chokar Karez hamlet, Afghanistan, hit by the American bombing on 22–23 October 2001.

Two dead Kashmiri terrorists on the steps of the Indian Parliament, New Delhi, 13 December 2001.

When Atwan referred to bin Laden's recent declaration of the jihad against America after the Al Khobar bombing, and the expectation of further such attacks by many, the Saudi fugitive replied,

> Military people are not unaware that preparations for major operations take a certain amount of time, unlike minor operations. If we wanted small actions, the matter would have been easily carried out immediately after the [August 1996] statement. [But] the nature of the battle calls for operations of a specific type that will make an impact on the enemy, and this of course calls for excellent preparations. We saw the Riyadh and al Khobar bombings as sufficient signal for people of intelligence among American decision-makers to avoid the real battle between the Islamic umma (worldwide community) and the American forces, but it seems they didn't understand the signal.[87]

The full implication of this statement would dawn on US policymakers and others in August 1998 and again in September 2001.

Bin Laden got a better worldwide forum to articulate his views in the form of an interview with Cable News Network (CNN) in early 1997, when he repeated his earlier call for attacks on American troops in the Arabian Peninsula.

Soon afterwards, a team of CIA operatives from its headquarters in Langley, Virginia, arrived in Peshawar to form a squad of Afghans and Pakistanis to help them abduct bin Laden. Though, in the end, the CIA did not proceed with the project, it hired 15 Afghan agents at $1,000 a month each to track bin Laden regularly. They did so often by breaking up into smaller units. Over the next four years the group would report firing on bin Laden's convoy, but to no avail. He followed no fixed pattern of travel or schedule, departing and arriving suddenly, and sometimes using a decoy convoy.[88]

The increased CIA activity in Peshawar helped persuade bin Laden to move to the safer confines of Kandahar, even though the security around him was very tight. "We [the CNN team] were called at our hotel [in Peshawar]," said Peter Jouvenal, the CNN cameraman who filmed the bin Laden interview.

> We were blindfolded and the car stopped on the mountain road. There we were body searched and a metal detector was passed over us three times. We were told to confess if we had any tracking devices. When we met bin Laden I was not allowed to use my camera. They had their own one, which worked. Bin Laden was surrounded by Arabs, fighters who had fought with him during the jihad against the Russians. He had no English but he was confident and relaxed. They know all about modern technology and they know what they're doing.[89]

Earlier, aware of the snooping on his telephone conversations by the American National Security Agency, bin Laden had stopped using his satellite telephone, a fact later confirmed by his mother, Hamida Alia Ghanoum.[90]

Bin Laden took up residence at the airport near Kandahar. The move went down well with Omar who reckoned that he would now be better able to control the Saudi mujahid. Actually, both men now became close friends. Engaging in night-long conversations, they came to share common views, politically and religiously, with Mullah Omar gradually turning against America and the West, and losing interest in gaining their recognition of his regime – especially after the Unocal-sponsored visit of a Taliban delegation in late 1997 to the US – first to the company's head-office in Houston and then to Washington where US officials, now pressured by the influential feminist lobby, held out little prospect of diplomatic recognition.[91] By strengthening the Taliban's combat power by lending them the services of his seasoned Afghan Arab fighters and by being generous to Taliban functionaries, bin Laden gained popularity with the Mullah Omar regime. "When bin Laden called on Taliban officials, he had wads of cash – $50,000, $100,000 – and distributed them freely," said Mullah Muhammad Khaksar, deputy interior minister of the Taliban. "He would just pull it out and give it to them. If the Taliban were planning an offensive against the Northern Alliance, bin Laden would have 50 trucks delivered to ferry fighters to the front."[92]

Having brought 70 percent of the country under his jurisdiction by early 1997, Mullah Omar resolved to expel the anti-Taliban forces from the rest of Afghanistan. The opposition's main bastion was Mazar-e Sharif, where President Rabbani had joined Gen. Dostum. Though situated in the Uzbek-majority area adjoining Uzbekistan, Mazar's population was multi-ethnic. The Taliban used their usual tactic of causing defection in the opposition camp through bribes. On 19 May 1997, when Dostum was abroad, his deputy, Gen. Abdul Malik Pahalwan, having received a reported sum of $1 million, mutinied and seized three of the five provinces under Dostum's jurisdiction. Calling Dostum "a bad Muslim" and "an obstacle to peace," Pahalwan claimed that he had defected for the sake of "national unity." He did not say that, in a typical Afghan feudal fashion, he had also acted to avenge the murder of his brother, Rasul, who had been murdered a year earlier, allegedly by Dostum's body-guards because he was beginning to rival Dostum.[93] Pahalwan's mutiny paved the way for the Taliban's march into Mazar five days later – forcing President Rabbani to fly out to Kulyab airport in Tajikistan. His exit from Afghanistan provided Pakistan with a rationale to formally recognize the Taliban regime. It did so on 26 May, and appealed to other countries to follow suit. But only Saudi Arabia and the United Arab Emirates did so.

The Taliban's capture of Mazar proved short-lived, though. Following their standard practice, they immediately began disarming all non-Taliban militias. The Hazara partisans of the Wahadat resisted, and were followed by the Uzbek fighters of Gen. Pahalwan as well. Together, they overwhelmed the Taliban, who suffered heavy losses. Some 300 Taliban perished in battle, and a majority of the 3,000 Taliban POWs died of suffocation when they were left unattended in sealed container trucks, while the rest were thrown into wells which were then blasted with grenades.[94]

Mazar's retrieval from the Taliban encouraged the opposition to gather under a single umbrella. The result was the formation of the United National Islamic Front for the Salvation of Afghanistan – United National Islamic Front (UNIF), for short – in early June in Mazar, now ruled by the Wahadat and the Pahalwan faction of the National Islamic Movement.[95] The UNIF replaced the earlier Supreme Coordination Council. Two months later, after Burhanuddin Rabbani had returned to Afghanistan, establishing his base in Taloqan, the UNIF reappointed him president.

However, this did not put an end to the intra-Uzbek violence between Pahalwan and Dostum. That enabled the Wahadat to become the sole ruler of Mazar in mid-September. Pahalwan escaped to Turkmenistan and Dostum was consigned to his home town of Shebarghan.

Continued violence within the ranks of the opposition buoyed the Taliban who consolidated their links with Saudi Arabia by sending a delegation to meet King Fahd. After the meeting, it declared that the monarch had pledged strong political and financial assistance to the Taliban regime. Meanwhile their Saudi guest in Kandahar, bin Laden, having established a cordial working relationship with Mullah Omar, was working on a plan to create a confederation of different extremist Islamist organizations in the Muslim world.

Bin Laden had by now revived two of the military training camps – Al Farouq and Al Badr – originally set up during the anti-Soviet jihad near Khost along the Afghan–Pakistan border, thus following the example of the Pakistani ISI and militant Islamic parties which had been training guerrillas to intensify Muslim separatist movement in Indian-administered Kashmir. Over time bin Laden's Al Qaida camps would increase to seven, and become sites for basic and advanced training, lasting six weeks and six months respectively, imparted to about 3,000 volunteers before their destruction in October 2001. In addition, some 8,000 others were trained in transferring cash, planning attacks, finding targets and safe houses, communicating surreptitiously and blending into a Western environment.[96]

Once a volunteer was accepted after an interview in a Pakistani city such as Karachi or Peshawar, he was asked to grow a beard and sent to Afghanistan along with an Afghan escort. There he met Abu Zubaidah (1970– ; aka Zain al Abidin Muhammad Hussein), a Saudi with Palestinian parentage, in overall charge of Al Qaida camps, for a final interview. If accepted, he took an oath of allegiance to Al Qaida and Shaikh Osama bin Laden, and joined a contingent of 50 to 100 Muslims from Sweden to Sudan. He spent a month each on small arms (from handguns to mini rocket launchers); bomb-making and sabotage (explosives, including dynamite, nitroglycerin, tri-nitro-toluene [TNT], ammonium nitrate, plastic explosives C3 and C4, HMDT and RDX); assembling a charge and blowing up civilian installations, military facilities, electric plants, airports and rail-roads; urban warfare tactics (operating in cities, how to block roads, assault buildings, etc.); assassinations (observing, survey-ing and monitoring a target and finding his vulnerabilities); deploying poison (potassium cyanide, ricin, sulfuric acid and lethal gases); and finally reviewing all aspects of the training and learning to integrate them.[97]

The funds for running these camps came from bin Laden's assets and his business activities as well as the donations he raised from affluent citizens in the oil-rich Gulf states and Islamic charities – a practice that went back to the early 1980s when the UAE-based Bank of Credit and Commerce International was used as a major conduit to finance the anti-Soviet jihad, with the knowledge of the CIA and the ISI, until its collapse in 1991.[98] Later bin Laden would reportedly get into drugs smuggling, content in the knowledge that heroin extracted from the Afghan opium was destined for the West, mostly populated by the Crusaders and their allies. With an expatriate population of 80 percent, the UAE remained an important link for bin Laden to transmit funds, often in US dollar notes and gold bars, with twice-weekly flights between Kabul and Dubai, a thriving port specializing in smuggling and the gold trade, which became crucial to the whole enterprise.[99] The UAE happened to be one of the two Gulf monarchies where the ruler, Shaikh Ziad ibn Sultan al Nahyan,[100] had publicly called for the lifting of UN sanctions against Iraq, imposed since 1990, to end the suffering of the Iraqi people, the full implication of which had not fully dawned on the public in the West, which was exposed mostly to Baghdad's failure to cooperate fully with UN weapons inspectors introduced after the Gulf War.

In the midst of a deepening Baghdad–Washington crisis in February 1998 regarding unfettered access for UN inspectors in Iraq, which resulted in the build-up of an American armada in the Gulf, a committee of like-minded Islamist leaders gathered in Afghanistan to assess the situation in the Middle East.

On 23 February 1998, under the aegis of the World Islamic Front for Jihad against Crusaders and Jews – World Islamic Front (WIF), for short – Shaikh Osama bin Laden, Ayman al Zawahiri (Al Jihad al Islami, Egypt), Abu Yasser Rifia Ahmad Taha[101] (Al Gamaat al Islamiya, Egypt), Shaikh Mir Hamza (Jamiat al Ulama, Pakistan) and Fazl ul Rahman (Harkat al Jihad, Bangladesh) issued a communiqué laced with the kind of language used earlier against the Soviets in Afghanistan.

For more than seven years America has been occupying the lands of Islam in the holiest of places, the Arabian Peninsula, plundering its riches, dictating to its rulers, humiliating its people, terrorizing its neighbors, and turning its bases in the Peninsula into a spearhead through which to fight the neighboring Muslim peoples. If some people in the past have argued about the fact of the occupation, all the people of the Peninsula have now acknowledged it. The most evident proof [of this] is the Americans' continuing aggression against the Iraqi people, using the Peninsula as the staging post, even though all its rulers are against their territories being used to that end, but they are helpless. Second, despite the great devastation inflicted on the Iraqi people by the Crusader–Zionist alliance, and despite the huge number of those killed, which has exceeded one million . . . the Americans are once again trying to repeat the horrific massacres as though they are not satisfied with the protracted blockade imposed after the ferocious war or the fragmentation and devastation [of Iraq]. So here they come to annihilate what is left of this people and to humiliate their Muslim neighbors. Third, though the Americans' objectives behind these wars are religious and economic, their aim is also to serve the Jews' petty state, and divert attention from its occupation of Al Quds (Jerusalem) and its murder of Muslims there. The most evident proof of this is their eagerness to destroy Iraq, the strongest neighboring Arab state, and their endeavor to fragment all the states of the region such as Iraq, Saudi Arabia, Egypt and Sudan into mini-states, and through their disunity and weakness to guarantee Israel's survival and the continuation of the brutal Crusader occupation of the Peninsula . . . All these crimes and sins committed by the Americans are a clear declaration of war on Allah, his Messenger (Prophet Muhammad) and Muslims.

Then came the fatwa:

The ruling to kill the Americans and their allies – civilians and military – is an individual duty for every Muslim who can do it in any country in which it is possible to do it, in order to liberate the Al Aqsa Mosque [in Jerusalem] and the Holy Mosque [in Mecca] from their grip, and in order for their armies to leave all the lands of Islam, defeated, and unable to threaten any Muslim [again]. This is in accordance with the words of Almighty God, "And fight the pagans all together as they fight you all together," and "Fight them until there is no more tumult or oppression, and there prevail justice and faith in God" . . . We also call upon Muslim ulama, faithful leaders, young believers and soldiers to launch raids on the American soldiers of Satan and their allies of the Devil, and to displace those who are behind them so that they may [also] learn a lesson.[102]

In mid-March, the 40-member Council of Senior Ulama of Afghanistan met to debate the presence of the American troops in the Arabian Peninsula, and decided that the WIF's call to jihad against America and Israel was in line with the Sharia.

Bin Laden's audacious call incensed Washington. It revived the earlier joint plan of the CIA and the Pentagon's Special Forces to abduct or kill bin Laden in the spring. But again, because of the high risk of many American and Afghan casualties, it was shelved.[103]

'We believe the biggest thieves in the world are the Americans and the biggest terrorists on earth are the Americans," said bin Laden in an interview with the American ABC-TV, broadcast on 10 June 1998. "The only way for us to [defend ourselves] against these assaults is by using similar means. We do not differentiate between those dressed in military uniforms and civilians. They are all targets in this fatwa . . . You will leave when the bodies of American soldiers and civilians are sent in wooden boxes and coffins."[104] Later that month, while not sharing the WIF's fatwa against the Americans, Shaikh Ali al Hudaybi, the imam of Prophet Muhammad's Mosque in Medina, called for the withdrawal of US troops from the Saudi kingdom, an act of considerable courage. The audio-cassettes of his speech were soon on sale not only in the Arabian Peninsula but also in Pakistan and elsewhere in the local languages.[105]

The public backing that Mullah Omar gave to the cause of bin Laden, being hounded by the Saudi Istikhabarat, did not seem to diminish the enthusiasm with which the desert kingdom's intelligence chief, Prince Turki, was assisting the Taliban's military plans. He arrived in Kandahar to provide Mullah Omar with cash and 400 Toyota pick-up trucks while the ISI finalized a $5 million worth logistical back-up for the Taliban, and thousands of madressa students signed up to participate in the upcoming battles.[106] By now, so overt was Pakistan's backing for the Taliban's military that foreign journalists and diplomats in Kabul had no difficulty spotting Pakistani intelligence agents and military advisors, conspicuous in their Western suits in the midst of Afghan men invariably wearing long shirts, baggy trousers and turbans.

As he had done before, bin Laden ordered several hundred of his experienced militia to fight alongside the Taliban. His fighters consisted of two categories of returnees: those veterans of the anti-Soviet jihad who, on returning home, had been intolerably harassed by their governments, and the post-1989 Mujahedin who, following the decline in the jihads in the Balkans, Chechnya and Kashmir, had returned to Afghanistan.

The Taliban's offensive against Shebarghan on 1 August put Dostum to flight because the (Pushtun) Hizb-e Islami of Hikmatyar, a nominal member of the opposition UNIF, had connived with the Taliban. On the other hand, Gen. Dostum's spokesman claimed that 12 Pakistani aircraft and some 1,500 Pakistani commandos had participated in attacks which led to the fall of his military base in Shebarghan.[107]

Further defections of the Hizb-e Islami's Pushtun fighters in the countryside to the Taliban prepared the ground for the latter to march into Mazar-e Sharif a week later. In retaliation for the killing of 3,300 Taliban fighters and POWs by ethnic Hazaras in 1997, they went on a rampage, massacring nearly 4,000 Hazaras.[108] In the ensuing mayhem, 10 diplomats and one journalist at the Iranian consulate in Mazar disappeared. Tehran claimed that the Taliban authorities were holding them hostage in Kandahar. They in turn said that either these diplomats were killed in the fighting or they departed along with the anti-Taliban opposition forces.[109]

Unlike the last time, the Taliban stayed in Mazar. Indeed, they followed up their success there with the seizure a few days later of Hariatan on the Afghan-Uzbek border to the west and Taloqan, the headquarters of President Rabbani, to the east, just as thousands of Afghani madressa students from Pakistan crossed the border to reinforce the Taliban positions.[110] With this, Mullah Omar's government extended its control over 85 percent of Afghanistan.

While these fast-moving military events gripped the local and regional populations, the world attention at large was turned to Nairobi and Dar as Salaam where huge bombs exploded on

7 August 1998 at the US embassies, killing 227 people. Washington held bin Laden responsible for the deadly blasts and called on the Taliban to hand him over. Mullah Omar refused, saying bin Laden was an honored guest not only of his government but of the people of Afghanistan.

With this, a new chapter opened in the relations between the Taliban regime and America – as also did a new chapter in the history of international terrorism.

Part III

Islamist terrorism and global response

7 Bombing of US embassies

A wake-up call

At 10.37 hours. on Friday 7 August 1998, Benson Bwaku, a private security guard manning the drop bar at the rear entrance to the five-story reinforced concrete building of the US embassy in downtown Nairobi, located at the roundabout junction of Haile Selassie Avenue and Arap Moi Avenue, near the bustling railway station, saw a 3.5 ton light-brown Nissan truck making an unexpected abrupt left turn off Selassie Avenue, bouncing over a raised curb and speeding towards the embassy's parking lot shared by Ufundi House, a five-story, non-reinforced structure housing a secretarial college. The truck lurched into its abrupt turn just as Bwaku had raised the drop barrier to allow a three-wheeled mail cart out of the parking lot behind the embassy's iron perimeter gate. Just as the truck steered into the narrow parking lot, a white sedan emerged from the underground parking garage beneath the bank in the 25-story reinforced concrete Cooperative Bank House and ended up nose to nose with the truck.

A slim, brown man of 21, with a rich thatch of black hair (later identified as Muhammad Rashed Daoud al Owhali), wearing a lightweight jacket, jumped out of the passenger side of the truck, leaving the door half shut. "Open the gate!" he shouted in English at Bwaku, who was too stunned to act. Owhali threw a stun grenade at Bwaku. "It passed over me and hit the ground at the back," Bwaku said later. "I heard an explosion." He ran like hell. Inside the truck, the driver (later identified simply as "Azzam," a Saudi national) pressed the dashboard switch connected to the truck batteries – and 530 lb (240 kg) of TNT (tri-nitro-toluene) mixed with aluminum nitrate exploded, rending the earth. It caused Ufundi House to collapse, floor by floor, crushing its occupants by the score. It wrecked the front of the Cooperative Bank House and reduced the rear-facing rooms of the US embassy to blackened shells. A thunderous bang, and then a thick plume of smoke rose hundreds of feet into the air. After momentary silence, glass and masonry rained down from the sky. The blast left 216 people dead, 12 of them American, and over 4,500 injured.[1]

Among the dead was "Azzam," but not Owhali. On his way to the embassy, Owhali, carrying three hand-made stun grenades taped to his belt and a pistol in his jacket pocket, had taken off his jacket and kept it on his seat, to make it easy for him to reach the grenades. But in his haste to jump off the truck at the embassy, he left his jacket and the pistol behind. Therefore the plan to threaten the guard at the drop barricade with a gun, then accompany the truck and be ready to open the rear of the truck and throw in a grenade at the assembled bomb – in case the dashboard switch failed – went awry. Instead he ended up throwing a stun grenade at the guard, who screamed "Bomb!" in his radio. Standing about 20 ft (7 m) away from Bwaku, Owhali decided not to commit suicide as had been planned. He ran. He returned to his room in the seedy 40–room Hilltop Lodge. He would be picked up five days later for not having proper identification papers, and confess to the FBI. Earlier, his co-conspirator, 33-year-old Jordanian Muhammad Sadiq Odeh, who had been running a fishing business in Mombasa, Kenya, for the past three years, was arrested at Karachi airport as he arrived there from Nairobi hours after the embassy blasts.[2]

Eight minutes after the blast in Nairobi, a 400 lb (180 kg) bomb, made up of TNT and an oxygen-acetylene cylinder aboard a refrigerator truck used for meat transport, went off out-side the US embassy in Dar as Salaam, located about 2 miles (3 km) from the city center and near the Indian Ocean. It deva-stated the front entrance to the embassy, blowing off the wall on the right side of the building and showering black debris around 20 damaged cars in the parking lot. Of the 11 people killed, none was American. Over 100 people were wounded.[3]

Unlike in Nairobi, 25-year-old Khalfan Kahmis Muhammad, the mate of the driver, Ahmad the German, an Egyptian national, had got off the truck just before it reached its destination. He would be arrested soon after, only one of the five surviving conspirators.[4]

Born into a poor peasant family on Zanzibar Island, Tanzania, Khalfan Muhammad moved to Dar as Salaam as a teenager to work in his brother's grocery. By 1994 he had saved enough to travel to Afghanistan to train for a jihad in Chechnya or Bosnia. However, after returning to Dar as Salaam in the following year, he started a fishing business, and traveled up and down the coast. In the spring of 1998 he was approached by "Hussein" who came from abroad, and he participated in assembling the bomb.

Unlike Khalfan Muhammad, who was not a sworn member of Al Qaida, Muhammad al Owhali, was. Born in Liverpool, UK, where his father had enrolled at the local university for a Master's degree, he was raised in an affluent home. He spent two years at Imam Muhammad ibn Saud Islamic University in Riyadh studying fiqh. In 1996, he went to Peshawar and then to al Khaldun camp in Afghanistan. He performed so well there that he was introduced to Osama bin Laden, and then given further training at another camp. He fought alongside the Taliban in their offensives in the north, and finished his training with a special course in surveying a targeted site with still and video cameras.

After the blasts in Nairobi and Dar as Salaam, in a telephone message to *Al Hayat* in London, the Army of Liberation of the Islamic Holy Lands claimed responsibility.

The only other time an American embassy had been so attacked was on 18 April 1983 in Beirut. That day a truck loaded with explosives rammed the embassy in West Beirut, destroying much of the building and killing 63 people, including 17 Americans, of whom 7 were CIA officers.[5] No group claimed responsibility, but the local Islamic Jihad was widely blamed.

Lebanon's Muslim militants were the first to resort to suicide bombing. They did so in the course of the 1975–90 civil war in which the US, France, Britain and Italy had intervened on behalf of the Lebanese Christians. They followed up the bombing of the American embassy with the truck-bombing of the US and French military headquarters in West Beirut which left 300 dead.[6] The person who killed him/herself in the process was regarded by radical Islamists as a martyr in the path of God, described in the Quran (Chapter 3, Verse 164) thus:

> Count not those who were slain in God's way as dead,
> but rather living with their Lord, by Him provided,
> rejoicing in the bounty that God has given them,
> and joyful in those who remain behind and have not joined
>   them,
> because no fear shall be on them, neither shall they sorrow,
> joyful in blessing and bounty from God,
> and that God leaves not to waste the wage of the believers.

The method of being killed in "God's way" varied. Since suicide committed by explosives either strapped to the body of a person or carried in a vehicle was a recent phenomenon it had caused debate in religious circles. "A Reading in the Islamic Law of Martyrdom" in a Cyprus-based Arabic weekly, *Al Islam wa Falastin*, in mid-1988, gave one exposition of the subject. The anonymous author wrote:

> Perhaps it is a blessing of God Almighty bestowed upon one mujahid or two mujahedin, enabling him or them to charge against the enemy's position, or against a concentration of enemy military forces on a martyrdom mission, assaulting with explosives, smashing down everything around them, inflicting the heaviest losses, breaking down the enemy's morale and determination in the face of this Islamic spirit of martyrdom which cannot be resisted. At the same time it increases fear of Muslims after a long period of weakness

and humiliation, and it increases the volunteers for martyr-dom who seek jihad in the way of God.[7]

Suicide bombing did not remain the monopoly of Muslim fundamentalists, however. By the beginning of the twenty-first century, it was adopted by 10 organizations, both religious and secular, and used 160 times in 13 countries, with Sri Lanka's Tamil rebels – Hindu by religion – fighting for an independent state, being the most frequent practitioners. Its unique effectiveness was explained by Rohan Gunaratna of the Center for Study of Terrorism at St. Andrews University, St. Andrews, Scotland, thus:

> Traditional concept of security is based on deterrence, where the terrorist is either killed or captured. The success of a suicide terrorist operation is based on the death of the terrorist. The certain death of the attacker prevents the captor extracting information. And it enables the group to undertake high quality operations while protecting the organization and its cadres.[8]

As a rule, the suicide bomber is supported by an operational cell which provides accommodation, transport, food, clothing and security until he/she reaches the target, this cell often consisting of "sleepers," legal residents of a country with jobs and families.

In the case of the Nairobi and Dar as Salaam explosions, this procedure was followed by those who planned the attacks – except that Owhali in Nairobi and Khalfan Muhammad in Dar as Salaam chose *not* to commit suicide. On top of that one of the bomb-makers, Odeh, got caught outside the targeted country.

Armed with the confessions of Owhali and Odeh, Washington blamed Osama bin Laden. To this Mullah Omar retorted, "How can a man living as a refugee in Afghanistan sponsor bomb explosions in distant Africa?"[9] Later he went on assure the world "100 percent" that bin Laden was not involved in any subversive activity.

This contrasted with the information that the FBI would gather by searching the house of Ali Muhammad (1952–), an Egyptian-American employed as a computer specialist at a music and video wholesaler, and his wife, Linda Sanchez, in Sacramento, California. It revealed documents on surveillance of government targets, assassination techniques, planning of terrorist acts and use of explosives. Following his arrest, he turned out to be the material on which popular Hollywood biopic movies are based. A multi-linguist, fluent in Hebrew, he was a tall, powerfully built man, who uncommonly combined physical prowess with outstanding intellect. While leading an active life, he found time and inclination to pursue a doctorate in Islamic studies. Born in Alexandria, Egypt, he enrolled at a military academy where he underwent paratrooper training, and rose to major before leaving the army when he was 32. During his military service he secretly joined Al Jihad. In 1980 he tried to ingratiate himself with the CIA in Egypt. Though rebuffed, he did not give up. Nor, it seems, did the CIA. For in 1986 he arrived in America with a visa waiver, a privilege that could only be conferred on a visitor with the blessing of the CIA or the State Department. He found a job as a security officer in Sunnyvale, California, and married Linda Sanchez, an American medical technician. In November 1986 he enlisted in the US army on a three-year contract and served as an army sergeant at the Special Forces headquarters at Fort Bragg, North Carolina. At the John F. Kennedy Special Warfare Center he was an assistant instructor. He assisted the seminar director to prepare classes on the history, politics, culture and armed forces of the Middle East. He was a frequent visitor at Al Khifa Refugee Center in Brooklyn. Indeed during his annual army leave he traveled to Afghanistan to fight there.[10] After an honorable discharge from the Pentagon, he started a leather import-export business. During his visits to New York, he started imparting weapons training to the Muslim militants attending Al Khifa Refugee Center. In 1993 he applied unsuccessfully for a translator's job at the FBI, telling his interviewers that bin Laden's group, then based in Sudan, planned to topple the regime in the Saudi kingdom. After the failed attempt on bin Laden's life in Sudan in 1994, Ali Muhammad retrained his bodyguards, a fact he reportedly conceded in an FBI interview in 1997,[11] the year he and his wife moved from Santa Clara to Sacramento. After his arrest he chose a plea bargain and turned a state witness in the US case against bin Laden. His own case was so sensitive that it was held in camera when it opened in late October 1998 in Manhattan.

In Washington the White House lawyers determined that the US could legitimately kill bin Laden and his lieutenants as that would be an act of war or national defense, and therefore legitimate under US and international law. In their view it would not contravene a ban on the assassination of foreigners first mandated by President Gerald Ford (r. 1974–6) in an executive order on 18 February 1976, and then confirmed by Presidents Carter (in 1977) and Reagan (on 4 December 1981).[12] President Clinton then issued a classified intelligence legal memorandum, which indicated that the executive orders banning assassination did not prevent the president from lawfully singling out a terrorist for death by covert means, and followed this up with three signed Highly Classified Notifications authorizing the killing, instead of capturing, of bin Laden, then placing several other Al Qaida leaders into bin Laden's category, and finally authorizing the shooting down of a private civilian aircraft believed to be carrying one or more of them. In addition, he ordered the stationing of two Los-Angeles-class attack submarines in the Arabian Sea on a permanent basis about 1,000 miles (1,600 km) from landlocked Afghanistan, thus enabling the Pentagon to hit any target in the country with Tomahawk cruise missiles within six hours of receiving the order. "Reluctant to risk lives, failure, or wrath of brittle allies in the Muslim world, Clinton confined planning for lethal force within two limits: US troops to use weapons from distance, and the enemy to be defined as individual terrorists, not those harboring them," reported Barton Gellman in the *Washington Post*.[13] Following the September 11 terrorist attacks, Clinton confirmed this. "We also trained commandos for a possible ground action, but we did not have the necessary intelligence to do it in the way we would have liked to do it then," he said. "Now we have the support of the people who would not have supported us then, and they give us many more tactical options than were available [in 1998]."[14]

Nonetheless, Clinton expanded his options by tapping into the northern neighbors of Afghanistan – Uzbekistan and Tajikistan – with whom his administration had been building up bilateral relations since the mid-1990s. This was particularly true of Uzbekistan. In 1995 the Pentagon began admitting Uzbek officers to its military academies. In August 1996 followed the next stage when US troops participated in joint military exercises in Uzbekistan. Two years later, after Mazar-e Sharif fell to the Taliban and the US embassies in East Africa were bombed, the Tashkent–Washington links tightened sharply against the background of the founding of the Islamic Movement of Uzbekistan (IMU) in Kabul by Jumaboi Namangan (1968– ; aka Jumaboi Ahmadjanovitch Khojayev) and Tahir Abduhalilovitch Yuldeshev, both of them from the Fergana Valley of Uzbekistan, to establish an Islamic state in their country by waging a jihad against the regime of President Islam Karimov.[15] In order to apprehend or kill bin Laden, the Pentagon sent 15-member US Marines Green Beret teams – part of the Special Forces – to train Uzbek soldiers in marksmanship, map reading and infantry patrolling. Soon joint American–Uzbek squads began making periodic forays into northern Afghanistan in search of bin Laden.[16]

The Clinton administration got the approval of the Tajik warlord Ahmad Shah Masoud to attach generously funded CIA operatives to the NSA technicians' team already based at his headquarters in the Panjshir valley to monitor all telephone calls in Afghanistan. Together they became extra vigilant in their monitoring of the telephone traffic in the Taliban-controlled area, while the National Reconnaissance Office (NRO), in charge of the spy satellites, increased the duration of its surveillance of the military training camps in Afghanistan, and the CIA's Afghan tracking group on the ground became more alert.[17] At the same time the CIA continued to lay much stress on human intelligence, in acquiring "assets." One of its successes would be to recruit, through Masoud, Mullah Muhammad Khaksar (1960–), deputy interior minister and former intelligence chief of the Taliban, and a close friend of Mullah Omar through Masoud. "CIA agents posing as journalists came two or three times to see me to collect information," he would reveal after the Taliban's overthrow. He provided insight into the workings of the regime, pointing out hardliners like his boss Abdul Razak and defense minister Obeid Ullah.[18]

In the immediate aftermath of the embassy bombings, Clinton was distracted by the sex and perjury scandal in which he had become mired and which crossed a threshold once he admitted on 17 August 1998 to the investigating grand jury an "inappropriate" relationship with Monica Lewinsky, a White House intern.

Three days later, having obtained reliable intelligence that bin Laden was at the al Badr camp in the Khost region to address 200–300 Al Qaida members around 23.00 hours local time, Clinton ordered strikes at six camps in Afghanistan, described by the Pentagon as the Zhawar Killi–al Badr complex, covering 60 buildings and 50 caves, and constituting training as well as base and support camps. As part of its Operation Infinite Reach, the Pentagon fired, from the *Abraham Lincoln* aircraft carrier in the Arabian Sea, 75 Tomahawk cruise missiles through Pakistani airspace at six camps. The strikes killed 26, all of them Pakistanis or Kashmiris. Bin Laden had left the al Badr camp a few hours before the missiles struck. Of the four training camps, the two near Khost were used for training Pakistanis and Kashmiris and were run by Harkat al Mujahedin, led by Fazl ur Rahman Khalil, and the other two – al Farouq and al Badr – were for Arab and other volunteers. Since the Zhawar Killi complex had originally been built by the CIA in the 1980s, the Pentagon knew its exact location.[19]

Explaining his action in a television address, Clinton said there was evidence that these terrorist groups in Afghanistan played a key role in bombing the US embassies, that they had staged terrorist acts against Americans earlier and were planning further attacks, and that they were attempting to acquire chemical and other dangerous weapons.[20] The last point provided Clinton with a rationale to direct seven Tomahawk missiles at Al Shifa pharmaceutical factory in Khartoum, causing damage of about $20 million. Washington's claim that samples taken from near the factory contained EMPTA, a precursor chemical used to make nerve gas VX, turned out to be false. Though it was conclusively established that Al Shifa was designed, built and commissioned by the Sudanese government for producing medicines and sold for $18 million in early 1998 to Salah Idris, a Sudanese businessman, who was not known to have any links with bin Laden,[21] the US administration did not offer to pay compensation or even apologize to Khartoum. Nonetheless, this blunder apparently taught Clinton to weigh very carefully the intelligence given to him before giving the final order to fire. Indeed, each of the three subsequent times he authorized preparation for missile launch, he aborted the mission when there were doubts about intelligence. Once the target – a leader in flowing robes, the type worn by bin Laden – turned out to be a UAE dignitary on a hunting trip in Afghanistan.[22]

For the present, the White House's messages were clear – there will be no sanctuary for terrorists anywhere in the world, and the US will retaliate, hoping that would act as a deterrent for the future. "This is going to be a long term battle against terrorists who have declared war on the United States," declared US secretary of state, Madeleine Albright.[23] The nature of the "long term battle" was explained by Brian Jenkins of Rand Corporation, an American think-tank, in terms that President George W. Bush would repeat three years later. "If we look at it as war, much of this war is going to be invisible," he said. "Rewards are offered, defectors are encouraged, sources are paid, diplomatic muscles are flexed, and as a consequence terrorist activities are thwarted."[24]

From then on, capturing or killing bin Laden became an obsession of the Clinton administration. "This [bin Laden problem] was a top priority for us over the past several years, and not a day went by when we didn't press as hard as we could," said Samuel

Berger, Clinton's national security adviser, after the September 11 attacks. "But this is a rough, rough problem."[25]

But there was a downside to this policy. The strikes inflicted only marginal physical damage but, in the words of a senior US counter-terrorism official, helped to make bin Laden a "revered figure" in the Muslim world. By attributing all terrorist acts, from the one in early 1993 at the World Trade Center in New York to the latest one, America had unwittingly consolidated his iconic status among wide swathes of the public in the Arab and Muslim world. Among those who criticized the American stance was Ghazi Salahuddin, Sudan's information minister. "I know the guy [bin Laden], he is not that mighty," he said. "He is being pumped up. I can understand that in the context of trying to personify terrorism. But [in the process] America has created a hero out of him."[26] Besides the expected defiant remarks by Mullah Omar and anti-American demonstrations in Afghanistan, came an official statement by Pakistan: "Prime Minister Nawaz Sharif told President Clinton that the unilateral US action constituted violation of the sovereignty and territorial integrity of independent states. This attack had caused anguish and indignation in Pakistan."[27] Nawaz Sharif was expressing a widely felt sentiment in his country. "When bin Laden speaks, he is reflecting the aspirations of the [Muslim] people," said Naseerullah Babar, a former interior minister of Pakistan. At Pakistan's oldest and largest madressa, Dar al Ulum Haqqania, at Akhora Khattak near Peshawar, large posters of bin Laden described him as Holy Warrior of Islam. "Osama is a hero," said Maulavi Sami al Haq, head of the madressa and leader of an Islamist group. "Every young man here wants to be like him."[28]

More disturbingly, for Washington, with the high profile gained by bin Laden as a result of the American strikes, many people in the Muslim world thought of helping him and his cause. While young zealots went to Afghanistan, a few affluent people in the Gulf region dipped into their pockets. They sent cash through couriers plying between Dubai and Kabul and contributed generously to scores of Islamic charities that existed in the region,[29] which diverted a portion of their collection to the bin Laden network. Modest contributors made use of the *hawala* (lit. trust), an informal money transfer system used since the days of the Silk Road to avoid being robbed. The sender gives cash to a hawala dealer for 1 percent commission, who gives him a code of one letter and four numbers. The sender then conveys the code to the recipient who calls on the agent of the hawala dealer based in the originating country, says the code, and gets the money. Both sides then tear up the records. It beats Western Union: the commission of 1 percent is low and no identification is required. In Pakistan $2–$5 billion are transferred through this system. And Pakistan, India and the Gulf form a thriving hawala triangle.[30] Given his entrepreneurial disposition, bin Laden took to raising money by trafficking in drugs originating in Afghanistan and smuggling consumer goods from Dubai and other Gulf ports to Iran, Pakistan and Central Asia.[31] Though Islam strictly forbids drugs, Mullah Omar and bin Laden had no qualms about dealing in narcotics, knowing well that their consumption by the Crusaders and Jews would damage them.

The missile attacks on Afghanistan came at a time when, during their summer offensives in July and August 1998, the Taliban had won control of five more provinces, centered around Mazar, routing Dostum's fighters. By then Kabul's tension with Tehran had built up to the point where the latter held military exercises by 70,000 soldiers of its ideologically committed Islamic Revolutionary Guard Corps (IRGC) near Torbat-e Jam, 25 miles (40 km) from the Afghan frontier, which Maj.-Gen. Yahya Safavi, the IRGC commander, described as "not without links to the new situation in Afghanistan." Responding to Iran's complaint to the United Nations regarding missing Iranian diplomats, the UN Security Council in its resolution on 28 August condemned the seizure of the Iranian consulate and diplomats in Mazar.

The latest confrontation between Iran and the Taliban was a reflection of deep ideological differences between them. Iranian leaders denounced many of the Taliban's actions, including its ban on female education and employment, as un-Islamic. "We are opposed to the Taliban's vision of Islam," Ali Akbar Hashemi

Rafsanjani, former president of Iran, said. "We are opposed to their ideology and their war mongering." Safavi denounced the Taliban as "a small group created by foreigners to serve their interests,"clearly referring to the Pakistanis.[32]

Part of the reason for the Iranian military build-up on the Afghan border was to dissuade the Taliban from launching a major offensive against the Shia-majority Bamiyan province by diverting Kabul's attention towards the Afghan-Iranian border. That ploy failed. In mid-September Bamiyan fell to the Taliban. With all but 10 percent of Afghanistan under its jurisdiction the morale of the Taliban rose.

Apparently Mullah Omar was in high spirits when Prince Turki called on him in Kandahar in late September. He arrived there with the evidence provided by Owhali, Odeh and Ali Muhammad to the FBI, linking the US embassy bombings to bin Laden, with a request that the Saudi fugitive be surrendered. But Mullah Omar was not convinced. When pressed, he blurted out an insult to the House of Saud. Prince Turki returned to Riyadh empty-handed. Saudi Arabia reduced its diplomatic relationship with the Taliban to the level of second secretary, asked the Taliban's chargé d'affaires in Riyadh to leave and recalled the head of its mission for Afghanistan, then operating from Islamabad.

Getting Saudi Arabia to secure bin Laden was one of several approaches that Clinton tried. He used the instrument of the UN Security Council to pressure the Taliban; he set up direct lines of communication, both overt (by the State Department) and covert (by the CIA). Between the embassy explosions and Clinton's departure from the White House 29 months later there would be 20 meetings between Taliban representatives and State Department officials in Bonn, Islamabad, Kandahar, Tashkent, New York and Washington. There were also satellite telephone conversations, one of them between Mullah Omar and Michael Malinowski, a middle-level State Department official. These conversations had a familiar pattern, with the Americans saying, "Give us bin Laden," and the Taliban officials replying, "Show us the evidence." Those insiders familiar with the talks said later that the American side was not serious enough. "We had no common language," said Milton Beardon, who supervised the CIA's covert operations in Afghanistan in the 1980s, "Ours was 'Give up Bin Laden.' They were saying 'Do something to help us give him up – *aabru*, dignity.'"[33]

Spurning the US demands to hand bin Laden over to Washington, the Taliban government proposed in early November that the evidence against him be passed on to it so that he could be tried in Afghanistan under the Sharia. Washington refused. When the deadline passed in late November, the Taliban's Supreme Court, having considered charges against bin Laden, concluded that America had failed to provide evidence of his guilt, and exonerated him. Later the Taliban would announce that bin Laden had promised in writing that he would not use Afghanistan as a staging area for terrorist attacks.[34]

4 November 1998 indictment against Bin Laden

On 4 November 1998 a US federal grand jury returned a 238-count indictment (covering 227 murders and 11 other charges) against Osama bin Laden and 16 others – including Muhammad Atef, Ayman Zawahiri and Khalid al Fawwaz – charging them with leading a terrorist conspiracy from 1989 to the present, working in concert with other terrorist groups to build weapons and attack American military installations. However, the indictment gave few details of the accused persons' alleged involvement in the US embassy bombings. The latest legal document superseded the June 1998 sealed indictment which was opened and found to center around bin Laden's activities in Somalia and Saudi Arabia. Washington announced a $5 million reward each for information leading to the arrest of bin Laden and Muhammad Atef, his deputy in charge of military operations.

"I was not involved in the [US embassy] bomb blasts," said bin Laden in an interview with ABC-TV's World News Tonight, aired on 23 December. "But I don't regret what happened . . . We are confident the Muslim nation [umma] will rid the Islamic countries of the Americans and the Jews." This was a brief excerpt from a long interview bin Laden had given to Rahimullah

Yusufzai, a Pakistani journalist on the staff of the Islamabad-based *News* daily, who was a stringer for *Time* and ABC-TV.

> The World Islamic Front for Jihad against America and Israel issued a clear cut fatwa calling on the Islamic umma (nation) to carry on jihad aimed at liberating the Holy Sites . . . If instigation for the jihad against the Jews and the Americans in order to liberate the Al Aqsa [Mosque] and the Holy Qaaba [in Mecca] is considered a crime, then I am a criminal. Our job is to instigate and . . . certain people responded to this instigation.[35]

On 25 December 1998, London-based *Asharq al Awsat* published an interview with bin Laden, conducted in Helmand province, in which he expressed "admiration and support for the Embassy bombers." He revealed that while the Taliban had banned him from carrying out attacks on foreign countries, he was continuing "to guide Muslims towards a jihad against Jews and Crusaders, which is a duty." He also revealed that he had survived an assassination plot ordered and financed by a Saudi prince. "They were offered large sums of money in return for assassinating me. But I was not hurt."

Earlier, during the Pentagon's Operation Desert Fox, on 16–19 December, the 100-hour blitzkrieg against Iraq by the US and the UK to punish Baghdad for its perceived obstruction of UN inspectors seeking evidence of weapons of mass destruction, raised temperatures in the Arab world. The bombing ended on the eve of the Muslim holy month of Ramadan. Bin Laden called on Muslims worldwide to "confront, fight and kill" Americans and Britons for "their support for their leaders' decision to attack Iraq," Referring to the Anglo-American air strikes, he said:

> The treacherous attack has confirmed that Britain and America are acting on behalf of Israel and the Jews, paving the way for the Jews to divide the Muslim world once again, enslave it and loot the rest of its wealth. A great part

of the force that carried out the attack came from certain Gulf countries that have lost their sovereignty.[36]

Taking bin Laden's threats seriously, Clinton named Richard Clarke, a member of the National Security Council since 1992, as Counter-terrorism Coordinator to "try to coordinate everything from the Pentagon down to local fire and police departments." Clarke's four secret presidential directives on terrorism helped expand the government's counter-terrorism cadres into an $11 billion a year enterprise.

He worked on the possibility of assault from nerve gas, bacteria and viruses to an electronic Pearl Harbor – when lights fail, phones stop ringing and trains don't move. He also had to guard against creating disproportionate fear.

In his meetings with Taliban and Pakistani officials in Islamabad in February, US deputy secretary of state, Strobe Talbott, demanded extradition of bin Laden from Afghanistan. The Taliban rejected the demand, saying bin Laden was "a guest of the Afghan nation," but agreed to impose restrictions on him. A few days later they said that the Saudi "guest" had gone missing. That was "officially" the case until July when a British journalist disclosed his hiding place – Farmada in the Nangarhar province near the Pakistani border. By then bin Laden was numbered among the FBI's "Ten Most Wanted Fugitives." On 6 July, invoking the International Emergency Economic Powers Act – which allows Washington to sever foreign governments and institutions from the US economy if they fail to act against a terrorists' financial network or cooperate in giving information on terrorist financing – Clinton signed executive orders banning trade with and investment in Afghanistan, and froze Taliban assets in America.[37]

By late June, however, world attention had turned to the fighting between the Indian military and the Pakistan-backed Kashmiri and Afghan insurgents in the Kargil region of Indian-administered Kashmir, which had continued since early May, raising the specter of an all-out war between India and Pakistan, both of whom had tested atomic bombs a year earlier. Alarmed by the prospect, President Clinton invited Indian Prime Minister Atal Behari Vajpayee and Pakistani Prime Minister Nawaz Sharif to Washington for talks in early July. Mentioning previous commitments, Vajpayee declined, aware that a tripartite meeting in the US would compromise the long-held Indian position that Kashmir was a bilateral, not an international, issue.

After their three-hour meeting at the White House on 4 July, American Independence Day, Sharif and Clinton issued a joint statement that steps would be taken to restore the UN-specified 460 mile (740 km) Line of Control, thus facilitating a ceasefire that would follow. There was of course no mention of the secret deal that was struck. In return for Clinton's easing of the US economic sanctions against Pakistan following the nuclear tests in May–June 1998, and his recommendation to the International Monetary Fund (IMF) not to withhold its next loan to Islamabad,[38] Nawaz Sharif agreed to call off the Kargil campaign and actively cooperate with Washington in apprehending bin Laden. Sharif's announcement of Pakistan's withdrawal of support for the Kargil campaign without consulting the armed forces high command incensed the military top brass, and paved the way for his eventual downfall.

On the night of 9–10 August 1999 two planeloads of special American teams arrived in Islamabad and Quetta to capture bin Laden. But the independent, Qatar-based Al Jazeera TV, an Arabic-language satellite channel, leaked the story – despite the pressure by the American ambassador in Doha not to do so – reportedly citing "freedom of speech." Breaking with its protocol of not commenting on intelligence operations, Washington strenuously denied the Al Jazeera story, which only made it more credible. It was presumed at the time that, due to the leakage, the Clinton administration aborted the US–Pakistani plan. This was not so. It later transpired that the American contingents entered Afghanistan. "Operatives of the CIA's Special Activities Division (SAD) made at least one clandestine entry into Afghanistan in 1999," reported Barton Gellman in December 2001. "They prepared a desert airstrip to extract bin Laden if captured, or evacuate US tribal allies, if cornered . . . And members of the

Special Collection Service (SCS), a joint project of the CIA and the NSA also slipped into Afghanistan to place listening devices within range of Al Qaida's tactical radios."[39]

On 24 August Kandahar was rocked by a massive explosion outside the home of Mullah Omar. It knocked out windows half a mile (1 km) away, and killed at least 10 people, including two bodyguards of the Taliban's supreme leader, and injured more than 40. No group or government claimed responsibility. But the blame could credibly be placed on either the US or Iran.

Shocking though the Kandahar bomb was, it had only momentary impact on the morale of the Taliban. Boosted by the retaking of the Bamiyan and three other central provinces in early May – followed by a three-day convention of a few thousand commanders and mullahs in Kandahar, where it was resolved to capture the remaining 10 percent of Afghanistan before autumn – the Taliban captured Taloqan, the headquarters of the Northern Alliance, on 25 September, with Ahmad Shah Masoud withdrawing further north, and dispatching his family to Dushanbe, Tajikistan. The prospect of the anti-Taliban forces being squeezed completely out of Afghanistan depressed the Clinton White House.

It accelerated its plans to seize bin Laden while seeking the active cooperation of Nawaz Sharif who in turn relied heavily on his family friend, Lt.-Gen. Khwaja Ziauddin, whom he had promoted to director-general of the Inter Services Intelligence a year earlier. Among other things Ziauddin had overseen the CIA train and equip 60 ISI commandos to seize or assassinate bin Laden.[40] Nawaz Sharif found it expedient to pressure Mullah Omar on the issue of the worsening Sunni–Shia violence in Pakistan, alleging that the Sunni extremists belonging to such organizations as Sipah-e Sahaba (Soldiers of the Companions [of Prophet Muhammad]) – responsible for the murder of 40 Shias over the past two months – had received training in the military camps in Afghanistan, and that these camps must be closed. He dispatched Ziauddin – freshly back from a trip to Washington to coordinate the next move to capture bin Laden – to Kandahar to pressure Mullah Omar. Soon Pakistani foreign minister, Sartaj

Aziz, claimed "concrete evidence" to show that Sunni terrorists had entered Pakistan from Afghanistan. The radical Islamist groups in Pakistan were alarmed. On 10 October 1999, Maulana Fazlur Rahman, leader of the fundamentalist Jamiat-e Ulama-e Islam (JIU, Association of Ulama) accused Nawaz Sharif of issuing "baseless, negative and irrational statements" against the Taliban regime in Afghanistan.[41] Apparently this was a pre-amble to the dispatch of Pakistani commandos into Afghanistan to shut down training camps and seize bin Laden. But the plans went awry.

On 12 October 1991, Gen. Pervez Musharraf (1946– ; r. 1999–), the army chief of staff, overthrew the government of Nawaz Sharif, who – it was said later – had planned to promote to army chief of staff his favorite, Ziauddin. Gen. Musharraf declared himself the chief executive and left in place President Rafiq Taroor. In the 52-year history of Pakistan, this was the fourth military coup.[42]

Two factors triggered the coup: Pakistan's involvement in the Muslim separatist insurgency in Indian-administered Kashmir, and the fate of bin Laden. "Sharif brought disgrace to the Pakistani army by bowing down before the US administration for an abrupt pullout from Kargil," a high military officer told the Islamabad-based *News* within hours of the coup. "In the aftermath of the Kargil crisis we went through almost a revolt situation in the army as the rank and file thought that the [Sharif] government had betrayed them."[43]

Then there was the issue of Islamabad's relations with the Taliban and its state guest, bin Laden. Kamran Khan, a Pakistani stringer for the *Washington Post*, wrote in the *News*:

> Military sources said that Sharif, on US insistence, had agreed to "compromise" Pakistan's long-standing strategic ties with Afghanistan's Taliban militia, a situation that could have created an internal security disaster in Pakistan because Taliban had deep roots in Pakistan's powerful and increasingly militant clergy . . . Twice in the past four days the Sharif administration surprised security observers here

by accusing the Taliban administration in Kabul of promoting sectarian [Sunni–Shia] terrorism in Pakistan and for operating terrorist training camps in Afghanistan.[44]

The European Union and the British Commonwealth condemned the Pakistani generals, with the latter suspending Pakistan from its membership until democracy had been restored. But Washington was muted in its criticism. It described Musharraf as "a modern thinker and religious moderate," despite the fact that, as the commander of Pakistan's Special Services Group, he had worked with extremist factions involved in the Kashmir insurgency, and that the three fundamentalist generals – Mahmoud Ahmad, Muhammad Aziz Khan and Muzaffar Usmani – had played a leading role in mounting the coup. Gen. Aziz Khan, chief of the general staff and head of the Sudhan clan dominant in the Poonch district of Pakistani-administered Kashmir, had masterminded the invasion in Kargil region, and during and after the 1980–9 Afghan War had supervised the establishment of the training camps for the radical Harkat al Ansar – renamed Harkat al Mujahedin after being listed as a terrorist organization by America in 1997. The rationale, explained US officials, was that Washington did not wish to alienate the new rulers of a country which possessed nuclear bombs. It emerged two years later that the Clinton administration wanted to keep Gen. Musharraf sweet so that he would continue the ISI's cooperation with the US to capture or kill bin Laden.[45] But he did not. He discontinued the CIA's involvement with the ISI commandos.

Clinton's public pressure on the Taliban continued unabated. At American instigation, on 15 October the UN Security Council passed Resolution 1267. It required the UN member-states to freeze the Taliban's assets abroad, and deny its airline landing rights if it failed to hand over bin Laden within a month to "appropriate authorities" to face the indictment filed against him in the US and ensure that its territory was not used for terrorist camps. An angry Mullah Omar, denouncing America as the "enemy of Islam," broke off talks with the US after it had rejected his proposal for a panel of ulama from Afghanistan, Saudi Arabia and a third Muslim country to consider the bin Laden case. "Tradition, culture and lack of extradition treaty with America make it impossible to hand over bin Laden," a Taliban official said. Until the Pentagon's attack in August 1998, the Taliban regime was interested in winning recognition from Washington and other Western capitals. Now the mood among the people and politicians had turned decidedly anti-American, and that helped bin Laden and his cause.

As 15 November approached, the Taliban became increasingly defiant. "We will never hand over Osama bin Laden, and we will not force him out," said Mullah Abdul Wakil Muttawakil, the newly appointed foreign minister. "He will remain free in defiance of America. We will not hand him to an infidel nation."[46] Anti-American demonstrations continued for several days in different cities, and were finally called off by Mullah Omar, who said Clinton lacked compassion for the suffering of Afghans. The end of flights to and from the UAE – where 80,000 Afghans found employment – which were Afghanistan's only direct outside link for post and medicines, caused much suffering in Afghanistan.

Just as the new millennium approached, there was much apprehension in the Western capitals that Islamist terrorists would strike to mar the essentially Christian festivities. There were also fears that computer failures due to the non-recognition by their operating systems of the arrival of the new millennium would result in catastrophe on airlines and power plants. The detention in mid-November of 13 suspected Islamist terrorists in Amman, Jordan, followed a month later by the arrest of 32-two-year-old Montreal-based Ahmad Ressam, a member of the Algerian Group Islamique Armée (GIA, Armed Islamic Group), at Port Angeles in Washington State, with the ingredients of a bomb in the boot of his hired car, on his way to Los Angeles International airport, confirmed the fears of the authorities. The alleged target of the Jordanian group was the Raddison Hotel, popular with foreign tourists.[47]

In the event, the millennium-end drama was provided by the hijacking of an Indian Airlines flight from Katmandu on Christmas eve by five Islamist militants who directed the plane to Kandahar, and insisted on the release of three Muslim extremists from Indian jails, including Maulana Masoud Azhar, secretary general of the Harkat al Mujahedin. After the hijackers had killed one of the 155 passengers, the Indian government conceded to the demands, with its foreign minister, Jaswant Singh, accompanying the released men to Kandahar airport and ending the week-long drama.[48] The Taliban condemned the hijacking and cooperated with Delhi. And yet the released men and the hijackers, riding cars, swiftly disappeared across the border into Pakistan, with India bitterly accusing Islamabad of complicity, which the latter denied.

This episode brought closer India and America, which had been flirting with each other. After a meeting in London in January, Jaswant Singh and Strobe Talbott agreed to establish a US–India Joint Working Group on Counter Terrorism. Aware of the fact that Pakistan had failed to apprehend the hijackers and the released Muslim militants, Washington publicly warned Pakistan on 27 January 2000 that it could be branded a state sponsor of terrorism if its army was found to have given direct support to the hijackers of the Indian Airlines jet. James Rubin, the State Department spokesman, said: "If secretary of state determines that a government has *repeatedly* provided support of international terrorism *directly*, then she would be prepared to designate that country as a state sponsor of terrorism."[49] Pakistan replied that while it was sympathetic to the secessionist uprising in Indian-controlled Kashmir, it was "firmly opposed to terrorism," and added it did not help "religious organizations" involved in the insurgency.[50]

In his interview with Pamela Constable of the *Washington Post*, Gen. Musharraf discussed two important aspects of political violence – distinction between terrorism and freedom struggle or national liberation, and the role of Islam – which would re-emerge as the major points of contention after the September 11 events. He distinguished sharply between terrorist crimes –

hijacking passengers, kidnapping – and the "Islamic freedom struggle" in Kashmir and other parts of the world. "Islam does not preach terrorism," he said. "But Islam believes in jihad, fight in the path of God. Wherever Muslims are being victimized or killed, Islam calls on all Muslims to come to their aid." The jihad that had started in Afghanistan with international support, had now shifted to Kashmir, he added. "It is a freedom struggle. To call all those activities terrorism in not correct."[51] A year earlier, in reply to a remark by a Muslim interviewer, "But there are many Muslims who do not agree with your kind of violence," bin Laden had replied, "We should fully understand our religion. Fighting is part of our religion and the Sharia. Those who love God and his Prophet and this religion [of Islam] cannot deny that. Whoever denies even a minor tenet of our religion commits the gravest sin in Islam."[52]

Little wonder that during his visit to South Asia in late March, Clinton spent four days in India and four hours in Pakistan, displeased as he was with Islamabad's refusal to ban the Harkat al Mujahedin, which his administration accused of terrorism, yet unwilling to pressure too hard, aware that if Musharraf faltered, it would precipitate a coup by fundamentalist generals who would further escalate the insurgency in Kashmir. In his television address to Pakistanis, Clinton said, "There is a danger that Pakistan will grow even more isolated, draining even more resources away from the need of the people, moving even closer to a conflict [with India] no one can win." Privately he urged Musharraf to act against terrorist groups and help him capture bin Laden.[53]

At the same time Clinton pursued vigorously his administration's own multi-faceted program for seizing bin Laden. In May 2000 the CIA's Special Activities Division (SAD) introduced into Afghanistan specialized case officers from its Near East division with knowledge of Persian, Dari and Pashto, and with previous clandestine contacts with the Northern Alliance stretching over years, with the purpose of recruiting local warlords and tribal leaders in southern Afghanistan with arms, ammunition, money and food, to create a network to subvert the Taliban.[54]

The first indication of the SAD activity was the report in mid-2000 of an unnamed Afghan group attempting to kill bin Laden by assaulting a convoy in which he was believed to be traveling. But he was not. This only added to bin Laden's stature, giving a boost inter alia to the sale of his taped speeches.[55]

Since entry of SAD units into southern Afghanistan, the bastion of the Taliban, was best gained through Pakistan, the pressure on the military regime in Islamabad to increase its co-operation with Washington grew. While Pakistan was strong in terms of its geostrategic assets, its economy was in a shambles, weighed down with huge foreign debts, low exports, a poor domestic tax collection record and massive expenditure on defense. It desperately needed periodic injections of loans from the International Monetary Fund if only to service its crippling foreign loans. In mid-2000, the IMF was undecided about the $2 billion package requested by Pakistan despite its failure to expand its tax-yielding base as promised.

"The military government is caught between competing pressures," said Zahid Hussein, editor of *Newsline* monthly in Islamabad. "On one hand it needed the West economically. On the other I doubt if it can afford to antagonize the religious groups that form its core political constituency."[56]

While the Pakistani Foreign Ministry informed the *New York Times* that it had asked the Taliban to shut down 18 training camps and extradite 25 Pakistanis sheltering in the country, the minister of religious affairs, Abdul Malik Kasi, told the *Washington Post*: "If we hit the [Pakistani] religious groups with a stick, they will hit us with a gun. We need to have a dialogue."[57] Little wonder that of the 40,000 madressas in Pakistan, the breeding ground of Islamic extremists, only 4,345 had registered with the military government. Those based in North West Frontier Province and the Baluchistan province almost invariably displayed posters of bin Laden.

This was also the case in the streets and news stalls of Sanaa, the capital of Yemen, the country of origin of the bin Ladens, with Osama's name and face scrawled on walls and printed on magazine covers, and the audio-cassettes of his speeches selling briskly in local bazaars. Yemen figured prominently on the radar of the US intelligence agencies when two suicide bombers maneuvered a harbor skiff – laden with lightweight C4 explosive encased in a metal housing (for maximum impact) – next to USS *Cole*, docked in Aden for refueling, and detonated the bomb at 11.18 hours on 12 October 2000, causing a huge hole at the destroyer's waterline, and killing 17 sailors and injuring 39.[58]

Washington demanded, and secured, cooperation from the Yemeni president, Ali Abdullah Salih (1942– ; r. 1978–), an elected general-turned-politician, who had moved steadily closer towards the US since the mid-1990s, culminating in the US navy starting to use Aden port for refueling in 1999.

But the task was fiendishly demanding. Unlike in the August 1998 bombings, when one of the conspirators decided not to commit suicide, both the bombers died, thus highlighting the effectiveness of such terrorist missions. It was more than a year before the US could name one of the two bombers as Hassan Said Awad al Khameri.[59]

At the same time, having quickly concluded that Al Qaida was involved in the latest attack, the Clinton administration seriously considered military strikes at the Taliban targets. After the Pakistani government had categorically stated that it would not permit the Pentagon to use its airspace for an attack on Afghanistan, the Pakistani media reported that Washington was planning a military reprisal against the Taliban, including bombing of its offices in Kandahar, from Tajikistan, and that it had sent its commando units to that country.[60]

In the end, Clinton refrained from taking action due to the risk of high American and Afghan casualties. Instead, he focused on isolating the Taliban diplomatically in conjunction with Russia, which maintained 25,000 soldiers in Tajikistan, four times as many as local troops.

On 19 December 2000, during the dying days of the Clinton administration, the UN Security Council adopted Resolution 1333, co-sponsored by America and Russia, by 13 votes to none (with China and Malaysia abstaining), describing "the Taliban-controlled Afghanistan" as "the world center of terrorism," demanding the extradition of bin Laden and the shutting down of military training camps for foreigners within a month, and having the closures monitored by the UN. Failure to do so, stated the resolution, would result in the Security Council prohibiting foreign travel by top Taliban officials, banning all Taliban international flights, closing Taliban offices abroad and freezing their assets, and imposing an arms embargo against the Taliban (while making no mention of the anti-Taliban forces).[61] As expected, the Taliban responded angrily, saying they would not expel bin Laden, and protesting that there was no ban on their enemy, the Northern Alliance, receiving arms. Increasing international isolation made Mullah Omar grow closer to bin Laden and his force of some 3,000 well trained non-Afghan fighters forming the 55th Brigade, who shared the view that the Taliban were running the purest Islamic state in the world. This perception had struck roots after Mullah Omar's ban on the growing of poppies in July 2000, which would result in a 91 percent drop in the output of a crop which had yielded 4,600 metric tons of raw opium in 1999, four-fifths of the global total, resulting in drugs trade worth $2 billion to the Afghani economy.[62] In return for this ban, strictly applied, Mullah Omar had expected assistance from the international community, not further isolation.

The assessment of some observers that the Security Council resolution was a preamble to a joint American–Russian military attack on the Taliban from the bases in Tajikistan and Uzbekistan to overthrow their regime was not too far off the mark, as later events would show.

Enter President George W. Bush

The administration of President George W. Bush carried on where Clinton's had left off. Indeed it wasted little time in devising a plan to overthrow the Taliban on its own, and replace them with the exiled King Muhammad Zahir Shah. With that aim it began financing and organizing the travel of several Northern Alliance leaders to Rome to meet the former monarch.

At home the American public was given a valuable insight into the workings of Al Qaida in Sudan during the public trial in February 2001 in New York of Wadi Hage, a 40-year-old Lebanese-American tire store manager in Arlington, Texas, one-time personal assistant to bin Laden; Khalfan Muhammad, a Tanzanian fisherman; Muhammad Sadiq Odeh, a Jordanian running a fishing business in Kenya; and Muhammad Rashed Daoud al Owhali, an unemployed Saudi. All, except Hage, were charged with conspiracy for bombing, with Muhammad and Owhali facing an additional charge of murder. Hage was accused of perjury in his earlier testimonies in the cases investigating bin Laden and the Al Qaida conspiracy to murder US citizens.[63]

Wadi Hage, a thin, feeble man with a withered right arm, had a bizarre background. Born into a Greek Catholic family in Lebanon, he embraced Islam before traveling to the US at 18 to pursue studies in urban planning at the University of Louisiana at Lafayette. He took eight years to obtain an undergraduate degree. In 1985, he married an American, April Ray, and together they moved to Quetta, Pakistan, where he worked for Abdullah Azzam's Maktab al Khidmat (Bureau of Service) for non-Afghan Mujahedin. In the course of this job, he visited Al Khifa Center in Brooklyn during 1987–90, and managed it in 1991 for a few months. Being a confidante of Azzam, he had the trust of bin Laden. And shortly after bin Laden had established himself in Khartoum, he joined the Saudi fugitive's entourage, rising up to become his personal assistant. Following bin Laden's departure for Afghanistan, Hage returned to the US and worked as the manager of a tire store in Arlington, Texas, where he set up a charity named Help Africa People, specializing in providing malaria vaccinations in the continent. This led to his periodic trips to Nairobi where he shared an apartment with Haroon Fazil, who would later be named as a participant in the attack on the American embassy in the Kenyan capital.

The prosecution's case was based on the testimony of Jamal Ahmad al Fadl, now given a new identity under the Federal Witness Protection program. He described the workings of Wadi al Aqiq, the holding company for several of bin Laden's commercial ventures in Sudan. As part of their remuneration, said Fadl, the employees reviewed a monthly bonus of "sugar, tea, vegetable oil and other stuff to help out the staff." Oddly, for someone who had arrived in the US in 1986 on a student visa and married an American, Fadl spoke poor English. "Sometimes they [Wadi al Aqiq employees] busy," he said, explaining the details of the monthly bonus. "They can't go shopping, and also because in Sudan sometimes hard to find sugar any time or oil and some stuff." Finding his monthly salary of $500 inadequate, he had resorted to taking kickbacks on contracts, pocketing $110,000. He was found out. But bin Laden did nothing more than ask him to return the money. Instead he absconded, and contacted the CIA at an unnamed American embassy in the region.[64]

The ongoing publicity given to the trial in New York enhanced bin Laden's status in the Muslim world, and that translated into him exercising greater influence over Mullah Omar, who hardened his stance further. This was manifested in his reversal of the policy on the massive 1,500-year-old statues of Buddha carved out of a giant rock face that dominated the Bamiyan valley. Having stated in mid-February that the statues would be protected so long as they were not worshiped – an almost impossible scenario – he now decreed their demolition. Despite appeals by many countries and the United Nations Educational, Scientific and Cultural Organization (UNESCO), the unique statues were destroyed by dynamite and tank fire on 10 March.[65]

Such state-sponsored vandalism further alienated the international community. To take advantage of the decline in the diplomatic fortunes of the Taliban, Ahmad Shah Masoud undertook a whirlwind tour of Europe in early April, and addressed the European Union parliament in Strasbourg, highlighting the dark side of the Taliban regime.

Working in conjunction with Washington, Turkey encouraged Gen. Abdul Rashid Dostum to return to Afghanistan and establish a base in the north. About the same time, aided by Iran, Ismail Khan, ensconced in the eastern Iranian city of Mashhad since his escape from a Taliban jail in March 2000, set up a base in Ghor province, thus opening a second front against the Taliban outside of the north-eastern enclave ruled by the Northern Alliance. Dostum and Ismail met Masoud in his bastion of the Panjshir valley in mid-April, and revived the old United National Islamic Front as National United Front (NUF).

Just then the death by cancer of 43-year-old Mullah Muhammad Rabbani, the nominal president of the Islamic Emirate of Afghanistan, and the second most powerful man in the Taliban, who favored talks with the opposition, destroyed any chance of rapprochement between the two camps, leaving the field free for the Taliban hardliners to escalate their anti-US struggle.

This suited the Bush administration. In the year that the CIA's Special Activities Division units had been active inside Afghanistan in the Pushtun areas, with wads of money, they had made progress in exploiting tribal and political differences between various commanders, nominally loyal to the Taliban, in Paktia and Kunar provinces, and also among the Murzai tribe in the Kandahar region.[66] This was good news for Washington. But the bad news – as pointed out in the US State Department's annual report on terrorism on 30 April 2001 – was that Islamabad was continuing to back the Taliban with cash, fuel, technical assistance and military advisors, with the New York-based Human Rights Watch pointing out in its report that by continuing to provide the Taliban with military equipment and manpower, Pakistan was in breach of the Security Council Resolution 1333.

So when, in mid-June, Gen. Musharraf removed President Taroor from office and appointed himself president, Washington was quick to condemn the move, and declared that the US sanctions would remain until Pakistan moved toward democracy. The American strictures had no impact on the ground in Afghanistan or Pakistan. Aided once more by the Pakistani ISI's material and technical support, in June the Taliban launched an offensive with 25,000 soldiers, including 10,000 non-Afghan troops made up partly of Al Qaida fighters and partly of Pakistani irregulars, in a determined attempt to seize Takhar province from the Northern

Alliance. But the Northern Alliance, aided by Russia, Iran and India, managed to hold on.

This encouraged America and Russia to return to the UN Security Council with a further resolution to restrict the Taliban's area of maneuver. On 31 July the Council unanimously adopted Resolution 1363. It specified posting of 15 UN officials in the neighboring countries, including Pakistan, to ensure the enforcement of the UN arms embargo against the Taliban.[67] The Taliban as well as the Taliban-supporting political parties in Pakistan threatened to kill any UN monitors posted on the Afghan-Pakistan border.

In reality, much of this was shadow-boxing so far as Washington was concerned. By then the National Security Council had finalized its policy paper on eliminating bin Laden and Al Qaida as well as overthrowing the Taliban regime, with the project cost put at $200 million. More specifically, in June a dry run of a plan to kill bin Laden by using a guided missile went well. A missile fired from a Predator drone flying 2 miles (3 km) high over the Nevada desert hit a mock structure of four rooms – modeled on the accommodation bin Laden used during his visit to the Tarnak Qila camp just outside Kandahar – with such a force that it pierced the wall, causing a crash that would have killed all those inside the targeted room. Unlike the six hours advance notice required to fire Tomahawk cruise missiles from a warship or submarine, an air-to-ground missiles from a drone could be fired within minutes of finding the quarry.[68]

At the UN-sponsored "Six+Two" (Afghanistan's six neighbors and Russia and America) quarterly meeting, held in Berlin from 17 to 22 July, and chaired by the UN's deputy special envoy, Francesc Vendrell, to discuss the current situation in Afghanistan, the American delegation, including Karl Inderfurth, until recently US assistant secretary of state for South Asia, told the chief Pakistani delegate, Niyaz Naik, former foreign secretary, the highest civil servant at the Foreign Ministry, "If the Taliban does not hand over bin Laden to us, and if Pakistan fails to persuade the Taliban to do so, then we will have no option but to take military action and overthrow the Taliban regime" from "the close vicinity of Afghanistan" – meaning thereby countries to the north – Uzbekistan and Tajikistan, where America already had its military, CIA and NSA personnel; and that "the action will be far more than what happened in August 1998."[69]

In August 2001 Senator Robert Graham and Representative Peter Goss, respectively heads of the Senate and House Intelligence Committees, arrived in Islamabad to promote better intelligence ties with Pakistan. Early the following month, Lt.-Gen. Mahmoud Ahmad, head of the ISI, visited Washington and met senior CIA officials as well as Richard Armitage, deputy secretary of state. The exchange of views was described by the American side as "extremely candid . . . one that left little room for misunderstanding. It is safe to say that the rules have changed." Shorn of diplomatic niceties, it meant that in their talks with Gen. Ahmad, US officials urged Pakistan to cut ties with the Taliban, or else face severe consequences.[70] On the positive side, Washington was building up support for the Rome-based King Zahir Shah by funding travel to the city by such exiled Afghan leaders as Hamid Karzai to meet the former monarch of Afghanistan.

Covert operations continued on both sides. In spring 2001, CIA operatives traveled to northern Afghanistan, and exchanged intelligence for cash and weapons.[71] As a result of increased co-operation between the intelligence services of Europe and America, during January to August, the authorities in Britain, Germany, Italy and Spain arrested 20 Algerians who were planning terrorist attacks in Europe. Between May and July 2001, the Western intelligence agencies managed to foil planned attacks on the US embassies in Sanaa and Paris and an American facility in Turkey. Earlier, Ahmad Ressam, an Algerian accused of planning to blow up Los Angeles international airport, was convicted; and Hage, Owhali, Odeh and Muhammad were found guilty as charged.[72]

On the other side, Ahmad Shah Masoud was assassinated at the Northern Alliance headquarters at Khwaja Bahuddin on 9 September. Two Moroccans, Karim Taizani and Kakem Bakkali, posing as journalists with Belgian passports, were taping an interview with Masoud, when Bakkali triggered explosives attached to the video-tape as well as to Taizani's body, resulting in the instant death of Taizani, and the killing of Bakkali by Masoud's bodyguards. With shrapnel lodged deep in his brain, Masoud died after a few hours. It would later transpire that the assassins had more ambitious plans. Abdul Rab Rasul Sayyaf, deputy chairman of the National Alliance's 40-member Leadership Council, said that the two Arab "journalists" wanted to photograph the meeting of the Council on 28 August at Dalan Sang at the mouth of the Panjshir valley to show the world that the Council was united, but the Council refused merely because they did not want to be disturbed.[73] The hand of bin Laden was suspected but he denied any involvement.

It seems he and his close aides were more interested in executing the most audacious attack against the US yet. Actually, the idea of using a plane to hit a target had occurred first to Ramzi Ahmad Yousef, a Pakistani who was raised in Kuwait and educated as an electrical engineer in Britain. Initially he considered the possibility of using a light aircraft piloted by a suicide bomber to hit the CIA headquarters at Langley, Virginia. Later he concluded that a long-haul passenger plane would be more effective as its jet fuel would turn it into a powerful flying bomb.[74] He did not pursue either of the ideas, but went on to mastermind the truck-bombing in the basement of the World Trade Center in February 1993. That explosion cost the attackers a mere $3,000, but it caused damage worth $500 million, and claimed six lives.[75]

Since the 1993 attack, the terrorist organizations affiliated to Al Qaida had kept pace with the rapid progress made in information technology, and taken to using computer files, electronic-mails and encryption to plan and further their operations. As most of the 19 conspirators of the September 11 attacks, who were merely told to prepare for a "martyrdom operation," were either close friends or blood-related Saudi nationals, and since the prospective hijacker-pilots came to know of their fellow conspirators only while walking towards the departure gate of the airport, they and their minders succeeded in keeping the project secret. The three primary plotters – Muhammad al Amir Awad al Sayyid Atta, Ziad Samir Jarrah (1975–2001) and Marwan al Shehhi (1972–2001) – were university students in Hamburg, Germany, and belonged to a radical Islamist group there. Later Atta and Shehhi shared a residence in Hollywood, Florida, and took flight lessons at Huffman Aviation International in Venice, Florida, for $27,300 each, finishing the training in January 2001.[76]

Their nurturing of a closely coordinated multi-team operation designed to cause maximum damage to the most prestigious symbols of American power in almost simultaneous attacks, requiring precise yet long-term planning of a complex nature, overlooked little, covering inter alia last-minute instructions – as was revealed by a four-page handwritten note in Arabic carried by each hijacker, which combined practical instructions with religious exhortation. "Check all your items – your bag, your clothes, knives, your will, your Identification Documents, your passport, all your papers," it said. "Make sure that nobody is following you." It warned against weakness in the face of the task ahead and asked for strength and guidance from God: "Remember the Battles of the Prophet . . . against the infidels as he went on building the Islamic state." On the night before the mission, "they must pray and fast, reciting the Quran and asking God for guidance." On the morning of the mission, "they should ensure that their shoes and clothes were clean, and that they had prayed with an open heart." The note stressed that "You have to be convinced that the hours left in your life are very few. From there on, you will begin to live the happy life, the infinite paradise. Be optimistic. The Prophet was always optimistic." The note ended with: "We are of God, and to God we return."

8 Eighty minutes that shook the world and global response

The preamble to the drama that would start unfolding on the East Coast of America at 09.03 hours Eastern Standard Time (EST) on Tuesday September 11, 2001, with the first strike against the North Tower of the World Trade Center (WTC) in Manhattan, New York, began an hour and a half earlier.

07.45 hours EST (for 07.59 hours take off) Arriving at Boston's Logan airport, Muhammad al Amir Awad al Sayyid Atta, an Egyptian with a Saudi passport, possessing 300 hours of flying experience, and "Abdul Aziz al Omari,"[1] a Saudi living in Hollywood, Florida, check into the business class of American Airlines Flight AA 11 for Los Angeles by Boeing 767, which will carry 81 passengers and 11 crew. Atta takes seat 8D next to al Omari.

Their three fellow conspirators, carrying razor-sharp cardboard cutters (also known as Stanley knives) take up seats in the economy class. They are Wail al Shahri, a Saudi teacher who had trained at Al Farouq camp in Afghanistan; his younger brother, Waleed al Shahri; and Satam al Suqami, a Saudi student at King Saud University who entered the US in May. Sons of Muhammad Ali al Shahri, a businessman in Khamis Mushayit in the Asir region, Wail and Waleed left home in December 2000 for Medina for treatment by a cleric for Wail's mental problems, never to return. The reason for splitting the hijackers into business and economy classes is to enable them to overwhelm the cabin crew at both ends as knife assaults lured the pilots from their cockpit.

07.58 hours EST (for 08.15 hours take off) Arriving at Boston's Logan airport, Marwan Yusuf al Shehhi, a Saudi national and trained pilot, living in Hollywood, Florida, and Fayez Rashid al Qadi Bani Hammad, a UAE national, check into the first class of the United Airlines Flight UA 175 bound for Los Angeles by Boeing 767, which will carry 56 passengers and 9 crew. Son of a high school headmaster, Fayez Rashid Bani Hammad had told his parents a year earlier that he was joining the International Islamic Relief Organization.

Their co-conspirators in the economy class are Mohald al Shahri, a Saudi from the Asir region, and a trained pilot; Ahmad al Ghamdi, a Saudi from Baha province, who had abandoned engineering studies at Mecca University at 19 to fight in Chechnya; and Hamza al Ghamdi, a Saudi, son of a prayer leader in Baljurshi in Baha province.

08.01 hours take off The business-class passenger list of the United Airlines Flight UA 93, carrying 38 passengers and 7 crew by Boeing 757 (filled with 30,000 lb [13,500 kg] of jet fuel) from Newark, bound for San Francisco, includes Saeed al Ghamdi (1976–2001), a Saudi pilot who trained with a flying school in Florida,[2] and Ziad Samir Jarrah, a Lebanese, who had joined Hamburg University of Applied Science in Hamburg, Germany, and taken flying lessons.[3]

Their fellow conspirators in the economy class are Ahmad al Haznawi, a Saudi originally from Baha province who was a student at King Khalid University's Sharia College in Abha, capital of Asir, now based in Florida; and Ahmad al Nami, a prayer leader at a mosque in Abha.[4]

08.05 hours (for 08.20 hours take off) Checking in the business class of the American Airlines Flight AA 77, which will carry 58 passengers and 6 crew by Boeing 757, from Dulles airport near Washington to Los Angeles, are Hani Hanjour (1976–2001), a Saudi, son of a wealthy businessman from Taif, with flying experience,[5] now based in San Diego, California; and Khalid al Midhar, a Yemeni with a pilot's license, member of both the Islamic Army of Yemen and Al Qaida, resident in Florida, who once shared an apartment with Nawaq al Hamzi in San Diego.[6]

Their co-conspirators in the economy class are Majid Moqed, a Saudi, son of the head of the Bani Auf tribe based near Medina, now based in New Jersey; Nawaq al Hamzi, a Saudi, son of the police chief in Jizan province, resident in San Diego; and his younger brother, Salem al Hamzi, who left home a year earlier, saying he was going to Chechnya.[7]

08.15–08.28 hours Terrorists hijack Flight AA 11 to Los Angeles. They attack cabin staff with cardboard cutters to lure the crew from the flight deck, and shout, "You won't get hurt. We have more planes." Some passengers call relatives on their mobile phones to raise the alarm. The flight is diverted and heads south towards New York City. Atta and Omari take control of the cockpit, turn off transponders to avoid tracking and make a coordinated descent into their target.

08.30 hours Terrorists hijack Flight UA 175 to Los Angeles.

08.46 hours Flight AA 11's Boeing 767, weighing 150 tons and carrying 15,000 gallons (68,000 litres) of jet fuel, strikes the 27-year-old, 1,368 ft (417 m) high, 110-floor North Tower (aka Tower 1), between the 87th and 92nd floors at 430–500 miles (670–800 km) per hour from the north.[8] A huge fireball results as fuel tanks explode. The Tower is the workplace of some 15,000 people.

08.55 hours Fire crews start arriving, and head for the stairwells.

09.03 hours Flight UA 175's Boeing 767, flown by hijackers who have turned off the transponders, slams into the 110-floor South Tower (aka Tower 2) between the 79th and 88th floors, from the south, at 540–590 miles (860–940 km) per hour.[9] A massive fireball results as fuel tanks explode.

09.05 hours Andrew Card, the president's chief of staff, informs George W. Bush of the WTC strikes, while he is reading to children at Emma Booker Elementary School, Sarasota, Florida.

09.21 hours First TV reports speak of 1,000 injured.

09.30 hours In his off-the-cuff remarks President Bush refers to the terrorists as "those folks" and "a faceless coward."

09.37 hours After being hijacked by four terrorists, Flight UA 93, bound for San Francisco, makes a U-turn.

09.36 hours Flight AA 77's Boeing 757 hits the west side of the Pentagon – a building with 2 ft (60 cm) thick walls – in Arlington, Virginia, across the Potomac, from the south-west, between Corridors 4 and 5, killing 126 of the Pentagon's 23,000 employees. This prompts a comment that in about an hour-and-a-half, "the enemies of America struck at its greatest symbols: the glittering spires of Mammon and the hulking head-quarters of its military might."[10]

09.40 hours All trading on the New York Stock Exchanges is suspended; and they will remain closed for the rest of the week.

09.45 hours The moment the Secret Service gets the word that one and possibly two hijacked planes are on their way to Washington, its agents literally pick up Vice President Dick Cheney from his seat in the White House and take him to an underground bunker.[11]

09.50 hours Unprecedentedly, the Federal Aviation Authority (FAA) shuts down all American airports and orders all flying aircraft to land at the nearest airport. Soon the Pentagon puts all US military in the United States and abroad on "Delta," meaning highest alert. For the first time since the Cuban missile crisis in October 1962, the North American Aerospace Defense (NORAD) Command orders round the clock anti-terror patrols by fighter aircraft over nine metropolitan areas with populations of 5 million or more, and puts its planes on alert at 30 bases. This is accompanied by random patrols over other metropolitan areas and key infrastructure such as 68 nuclear power stations and important bridges, which are provided extra protection. The operation uses 250 aircraft and engages 11,000 people.[12] In Washington military helicopters circle the White House and Capitol Hill. All oil and gas pipelines are put under heightened security and surveillance.

Admiral James Loy, commander of the Coast Guard, sends 50 cutters, 45 aircraft and hundreds of small boats to undertake port security duty and board every incoming commercial vessel, while all recreational boats are barred from within 100 yards (100 m) of any Navy ship – the biggest port security operation since World War II. He closes 12 ports, and will reopen them gradually to commercial and recreational traffic. He sends 16 of the Coast Guard's high- and medium-endurance cutters to prowl the Florida coast and the Caribbean, and another four cutters off the west coast of Mexico. Other cutters and aircraft patrol near major fishing areas. In contrast to transporting 186,000 passengers daily to and from Manhattan, the Coast Guard evacuates more than a million people by boat from the island, which is in a virtual lockdown state.

09.55 hours The White House, the State Department and US Treasury headquarters in Washington are evacuated.

09.59 hours The South Tower collapses even though it had been struck later because the plane hit it at a higher speed than the first plane did the North Tower. Each Tower, designed to withstand 150 miles (240 km) per hour hurricanes, took the impact of the jets without a shudder. But once the aircraft sliced through the building, the fuel explosion melted the steel. Unlike most skyscrapers, the strength of the WTC lay in its outer steel framework, not internal concrete supports. When the South Tower collapses, chaos ensues: about 350 firefighters go missing.

10.00 hours President Bush's jet, Air Force One, leaves Florida.

10.01 hours Fire crews are feverishly at work at the WTC.

10.06 hours Exactly 80 minutes after the first crash in Manhatten, Flight UA 93's Boeing 757 crashes at Stony Creek, 2 miles (3 km) from Somerset County airport (used for small aircraft), which is 2 miles (3 km) from Shanksville, Pennsylvania, 80 miles (130 km) south-east of Pittsburgh. Its target destination was the Camp David presidential retreat or probably one of the three nuclear power stations within a 5 miles (8 km) radius – Three Mile Island, Peach Bottom and Hope Beach, Salem. The recovered black boxes will show passengers voting to try and overpower the hijacker pilot, and a struggle ensuing, leading to a crash. This brings to 266 the total number of deaths due to the four plane crashes.

10.26 hours The North Tower collapses. By now eight federal emergency management agency task forces are working with the New York Fire Department on the disaster site. Army Corps of Engineers is assisting with debris removal.

10.55 hours US State Department evacuates all embassies worldwide.

11.40 hours Escorted by fighter aircraft, Bush arrives at Barksdale US Air Force base near Shreveport, Louisiana.

13.07 hours A Taliban spokesman says, "We condemn these attacks.'

13.10 hours The European Union condemns "cowardly attack on innocent civilians." North Atlantic Treaty Organization (Nato) general secretary, Lord Robertson, calls the attacks "an intolerable aggression against democracy."

13.15 hours Bush leaves for the Strategic Air Command base at Offcutt, near Omaha, Nebraska.

15.07 hours Bush arrives at Nebraska base, and holds video conference with his senior advisors. They decide to set up the federal "government in waiting" according to the Standing Directive of Continuity in Government (COG) Plan in the event of a disabling blow to Washington, first issued by President Dwight Eisenhower (r. 1952–60). The helicopters of the Military District of Washington, DC lift off with the first wave of evacuated officials who are senior career civil servants on their way to self-contained, fortified underground bunkers somewhere on the East Coast, who are to be joined by Dick Cheney two days later. With the terrorist threat persisting, this temporary arrangement will be extended, with the officials from all cabinet departments and independent agencies being rotated every 90 days. Cheney will remain incommunicado until late October.[13]

16.00 hours At the overland border crossings with Mexico and Canada, customs services are operating at Level 1 Alert. All incoming vehicles are checked thoroughly, causing a nine-hour wait at the commercial truck line at the Niagara Falls checkpoint.

19.00 hours Bush arrives at Andrews Air Base.

20.30 hours Bush addresses the nation on television, squinting nervously at the teleprompter and pausing in the wrong places, and fails to match the gravity of the occasion. Yet he offers the memorable phrase "the first war of the twenty-first century," and warns that "We will make no distinction between the terrorists who committed the crimes and those who harbored them."

Experts noticed that the hijackers acted only after the aircraft had reached cruising altitude and were put on autopilot, and that they had the navigational skills to find correct headings for their targets at that high altitude, which makes it difficult to calculate the aircraft's position by using visual landmarks on the ground, and that they flew the planes in the right direction and crashed straight into their targets.

This, and the scale of the attack, the choice of the targets – towering symbols of American economic and military power – and the meticulous planning and organization: all these shook not just Americans and fellow Westerners but also others worldwide. In about an hour and a half, 18 million sq. ft $(1.67$ million $m^2)$ of office space, yielding a monthly rent of \$900 million, was reduced to smoking rubble. Potential claims for loss of life, property and business with insurance and reinsurance companies, and reconstruction were put at \$70 billion, including the \$40 billion cost of clearing 1.2 million tons of rubble and rebuilding.[14]

Americans' feeling of safety at home was shattered as they discovered in the most gruesome manner that they were vulnerable en masse to foreign enemies, and that their government could not afford in future to act abroad with impunity with little or no fear of direct consequences on the US mainland.

President Bush formed a war cabinet, consisting of Cheney; Andrew Card; Secretary of State Colin Powell (1937–); National Security Advisor Condoleezza Rice; Defense Secretary Donald Rumsfeld (1932–); chairman of military joint chiefs of staff, General Henry H. Shelton; CIA director George J. Tenet; Attorney-General John Ashcroft; and FBI director Robert Mueller, who had immediately assigned 4,000 agents, a third of the total, 3,000 support staff and 400 forensic experts to the task of discovering the perpetrators of the ghastly aircraft-turned-missile bombing.

"The deliberate and deadly attacks, which were carried out yesterday against our country, were more than acts of terror; they were acts of war," said Bush on 12 September:

The American people need to know we are facing a different enemy than we have ever faced. This enemy hides in the shadows and has no regard for human life. This is an enemy who preys on innocent and unsuspecting people, then runs for cover. But it won't be able to run for cover for ever . . . This enemy attacked not just our people but all freedom loving people in the world . . . We will rally the world . . . This battle will take time and resolve but, make no mistake, we will win . . . The freedom-loving nations of the world stand by our side.[15]

That day, with the smoke from the WTC site – nicknamed Ground Zero – filling their nostrils, the members of the UN Security Council unanimously adopted Resolution 1368. It "unequivocally" condemned "in the strongest terms the horrifying terrorist attacks . . . in New York, Washington (DC) and Pennsylvania," regarded "such acts, like any act of international terrorism, as a threat to international peace and security," called on "all States to work together urgently to bring to justice the perpetrators, organizers and sponsors of the terrorist attacks," and stressed that "those responsible for aiding, supporting or harboring the perpetrators, organizers and sponsors of these acts will be held accountable."[16]

It was the first time that the Security Council had passed a resolution that applied not to a state or states but to individuals or groups. Resolution 1368 thus became a landmark document in international law. Yet it went largely unnoticed by the American media and commentators. And, in the coming days and weeks, despite its recognition of the inherent right of individual or collective self-defense under the UN Charter's Article 51, Security Council Resolution 1368 would not be invoked, or even mentioned in passing, by high US officials, including Powell, who set out to stitch together a worldwide coalition.[17]

Powell talked of a multi-faceted approach – diplomatic, military, intelligence, law enforcement and financial – aimed at assorted entities and sought to build a global alliance, the targets being terrorists as well as the organizations and states that provided haven to them. He visualized a broad-based coalition to be led by Washington. While pursuing this objective single-mindedly, he ignored Egyptian President Hosni Mubarak's call to organize immediately an international anti-terrorism convention that would become the basis of a common program of action for all UN member-states, which was endorsed by the Arab League.

The US Senate passed a resolution by 98 votes to none, authorizing the president to use "all appropriate and necessary force" against nations, organizations or individuals who were involved in the acts of terrorism against America or harbored people who were involved. In the House of Representatives the vote was 420 to 1, the dissenter being Barbara Lee, a California Democrat representing Berkeley and Oakland, who argued that military action "will not prevent further acts of international terrorism" against the US.[18] Remarkably, the resolution authorized the president to name any nations or organizations he thought fit, and stated no time limit. Both houses of Congress also approved $40 billion emergency appropriation to help strengthen the US fight against terrorism and pay the expenses incurred by the response teams at local, state and federal levels.[19] Bush immediately allocated $1 billion to the CIA, amounting to 30 percent of its annual budget, and called up 50,000 reservists out of 1.3 million, to be deployed in homeland defense, port operations and general security.

The military precision of the deadly operations, conducted simultaneously, pointed to bin Laden and Al Qaida. An aide of bin Laden informed Abu Dhabi TV's Jamal Ismail that "Osama got down on his knees and thanked Almighty Allah when he heard the news," and that he described the devastation in America as "a just punishment from Allah," adding that "He had no information or knowledge about the attacks ahead of time." In a hand-delivered letter to Hamid Mir, editor of *Ausaf* daily in Peshawar, bin Laden said, "I am not responsible for the 11 September bombing but I support it. It was a reaction of the oppressed to the tyranny of the tyrants." He also denied any involvement in the assassination of Ahmad Shah Masoud two days earlier.[20] Bin Laden was not alone in calling the mass murder a divine punishment. Jerry Falwell, a leading Christian fundamentalist in the US, described the attacks as God's vengeance on Americans for condoning homosexuality and feminism.[21]

From the information released by the FBI, it emerged that most of the suicide hijackers were well-educated, intelligent Saudis in their mid-twenties: three were law graduates, two were teachers, two were brothers of a provincial police chief, and one was a son of a rich businessman. In the coming days and weeks, much attention would turn on Muhammad Atta, who was believed to be the ring leader and the intermediary between the different teams: he had been a flat-mate of Marwan al Shehhi and Ziad Jarrah during their residence in Florida, and had bought the air ticket for Abdul Aziz al Omari.

Son of Muhammad al Amir Atta, a retired lawyer, originally from Kafr al Shaikh in the Nile Delta, Muhammad Jr. grew up in the Cairo suburb of Giza and graduated in 1990 with an architecture degree from Cairo University, whose engineering faculty was a bastion of the Muslim Brotherhood. He found work with a German firm in Cairo, then went to Hamburg Technical University in 1992 on a scholarship, pursued further studies while working part-time for a planning consultancy firm, and returned to Cairo in 1996 to be disappointed by the poor prospects there.[22] In November 1997, after he was laid off by the consultancy firm in Hamburg, he disappeared for about a year, probably undergoing training in Afghanistan. Back in Hamburg in early 1999, in August he submitted his thesis in which was judged "Excellent." Though still enrolled at the University, he was not to be seen in Hamburg. By early 2001 he had passed the US Federal Aviation Authority's pilot test. He then went abroad, and returned to the US in May to live in Hollywood, Florida.[23]

The thread of the Muslim Brotherhood could be detected in the case of most of his co-conspirators. Seven of the Saudi hijackers were from the south-western province of Asir, where many school teachers were Egyptian and members of the Brotherhood.[24]

In the Muslim world, there was much support for bin Laden at the street level, where he was seen either as someone defying the US which, in popular perception, imposed its will on their rulers, or as a pious man defending Islam against a combined Israel–American onslaught, who could not have been complicit in the deaths of so many innocent civilians. "As shown by the bearded portraits painted on the backs of trucks and gracing posters selling on the side walks, and the naming of new-born babies after him, bin Laden has developed a large network of followers in northern Pakistan, Afghanistan and parts of the Middle East," noted Farhan Bokhari from Peshawar in the *Financial Times*.[25]

Excepting Iraq, all Arab states condemned the attacks, including Sudan, Libya and Syria – as well as the Palestinian leader, Yasser Arafat, who described them as "terrible," "unbelievable" and "completely shocking." Embarrassed by the street dancing of some Palestinians in certain West Bank towns and the Palestinian refugee camps in Lebanon, he immediately banned all demonstrations. Later his police quelled a pro-bin Laden demonstration by firing, and killed two demonstrators. Abdul Ilah Khatib, foreign minister of Jordan, the current chairman of the Arab League, said, "We agree that this is an attack against us all." However, echoing the regional view that regards the Palestinian Hamas and Hizbollah as freedom fighters, he added, "We will need effort to draw lines between these issues – terrorism and the struggle for independence on the part of different people."[26]

Iraq went beyond its refusal to fly its flag half-mast at its UN mission in New York, a gesture in which it was joined by Libya as well as China. Declaring that "America is reaping the thorns planted by its rulers," its president, Saddam Hussein, advised Washington against using retaliatory force, and cited the example of Iraq where such force had failed. In an interview with a local weekly, Naji Sabri al Hadithi, Iraq's foreign minister, recalled American crimes against humanity – from Hiroshima, Japan, hit by an American atom bomb, to Vietnam, and Central America to Palestine – a bloody trail littered with millions of dead going back more than 50 years: "All Muslim and Arab people consider America the master of terrorism, the terrorist power number one."[27] In his address to the UN General Assembly, Iraqi ambassador Muhammad al Douri, said that Iraq had sent messages of condolences to individuals in America. "It would have been hypocritical to condemn the bombings, given the sanctions and bombings against Iraq."[28]

In contrast, Iran's President Muhammad Khatami condemned the attacks and called on the international community to "take measures to eradicate such crimes." Tehran's mayor, Murtaza Alviri, sent a message of condolences to his New York counterpart, Rudolph Giuliani: "Tehran's citizens express their deep hatred of this ominous and inhuman move, strongly condemn the culprits and express their sympathy with New Yorkers." Thanking Khatami, the Bush administration invited him to join the anti-terror campaign – by, say, sharing information on bin Laden and the Taliban with it. This was not on, at least not publicly, however much Tehran detested the Taliban. Addressing the Friday prayer congregation in Tehran, Leader Ayatollah Ali Khamenei said, "Mass killing is a catastrophe wherever it happens and whoever the perpetrators. It is condemned without distinction. But if, God forbid, a similar catastrophe is inflicted on Afghanistan, we will condemn that too."[29]

Admiral Ali Shamskhani, the defense minister of Iran, set out the official policy thus: "If strikes against terrorist bases took place within the framework of the international community, Iran would support it." That is, Tehran would participate in any UN-sponsored action against the perpetrators of the criminal act, well aware that Security Council Resolution 1368 provided the framework within which such action could be mandated by the international community.

Iran's position coincided with that of China, one of the Security Council's five permanent members. Its diplomats explained that cooperation needed to be channeled through a multilateral forum like the UN, not through retaliation by America or Nato, and that any US military action should be endorsed by the Security Council. Chinese leaders were aware of the anti-American feeling in their country. Many of their nationals – still reeling from the mid-air collision between an American spy plane and a Chinese fighter over the South China Sea in April, resulting in the death of a Chinese pilot – expressed satisfaction. "We have been bullied by America for too long," read a typical Internet comment. "Finally, someone helped us to vent a little." At one newspaper newsroom journalists cheered at the news, happy that for once America was facing a tragedy. Among all non-Muslim countries, China had established the warmest relations with the Taliban regime. It was trying to persuade the Taliban to close down camps training (Muslim) Uighur separatists in return for the renovation of Afghanistan's US-made power plant. Ink had hardly dried on the deal that China signed with the Taliban's mining minister, Mullah Muhammad Ishaq, on September 11 when the tragedy struck America.[30]

Expressing "deep shock, anger and indignation" at "this barbaric terrorist action," Russian President Vladimir Putin (r. 2000–) said that "such an inhuman act must not go unpunished." His government was as opposed to bin Laden as was Washington, and had a robust intelligence apparatus based in Tajikistan which shares a 720 mile (1,150 km) border with Afghanistan. But it did not want to be part of military strikes against bin Laden whose complicity in the attacks had yet to be proved.[31]

But once Bush had named Osama bin Laden as the prime suspect on 15 September, the die was cast. This started a series of debates between his hawkish and dovish senior advisors, the former led by defense secretary Donald Rumsfeld, and the latter by Colin Powell. Remarkably, in these discussions lasting several weeks, the top policymakers made scant reference to the root causes that led – in the words of Saudi foreign minister, Saud al Faisal – "terrorism's perpetrators to spread their ideology."[32]

The first debate was on whether the US should respond immediately and unilaterally, and hit Afghanistan on a much larger scale than Clinton had done in August 1998, or take time to cobble together an international coalition based on a common objective. It got so heated that the president's father, George Herbert Walker Bush, intervened publicly. "Just as

[Japan's attack on] Pearl Harbor awakened this country from the notion that we could somehow avoid the call to duty and defend freedom in Europe and Asia in World War II, so too should the most recent surprise attack erase the concept in some quarters that America can somehow go it alone in the fight against terrorism – or in anything else for that matter," he told an audience in Boston.[33] That settled the matter – at least for the time being – in favor of the doves.

They and President Bush had been heartened by the swift backing America had received from its Western allies. Comparing the attacks to a nuclear strike, Nato's Lord Robertson declared that they had changed the world "out of all recognition." The European Union foreign ministers promised full cooperation in helping to bring to justice those responsible for the horrific deed. "In the darkest hours of European history, America stood close with us," said European Commission president, Romano Prodi. "Today we stand close by America. We are ready to assist with every means at our disposal." German Chancellor Gerhard Schroeder (r. 1998–), who had opposed the 1991 Gulf War, said, "The attacks amounted to a declaration of war on the free world and on the civilized world. Germany will not let the values of the Western civilization be destroyed in the US, Europe or anywhere else. As for America, we pledge the unlimited solidarity of Germany." French President, Jacques Chirac (r. 1995–) would become the first foreign leader to visit Ground Zero in Manhattan. "It is a war," he declared. "It involves new means to battle . . . to be carried out on all fronts." He was in tune with public opinion in France where 73 percent backed retaliatory attacks.[34]

Mullah Omar argued that bin Laden could not have been responsible as he had no pilots: "In Afghanistan, there is no such possibility for the training [of pilots]." His government warned that if a neighboring country allowed its soil or air to be used for an attack against Afghanistan, "the possibility cannot be ruled out that we attack that country."[35]

Among Afghanistan's neighbors, Pakistan mattered most. For Washington, it was *the* key state in the way Saudi Arabia was after Iraq's invasion of Kuwait in August 1990. In the absence of land bases in an adjoining country sharing long borders with the targeted nation, the Pentagon's options would be severely limited and it would diminish the prospect of a short, successful campaign which, given the very real prospect of inflaming Muslim opinion worldwide, was essential.

The first signs were promising. In his television address on 13 September, Pakistan's military ruler, President General Pervez Musharraf, said: "I wish to assure President Bush and the US government of our fullest cooperation in the fight against terrorism." He immediately froze the assets of the Taliban regime in the State Bank of Pakistan and the accounts being used by various Pakistani organizations to fund the Taliban.[36] This was a swift and radical departure from his erstwhile policy of sustaining and aiding the Taliban while professing to have scant influence over them. It was a severe blow to the Taliban. Since its inception, Pakistan had been not only the chief provider of military supplies, fuel and food to its armed forces, but also the sole supplier of officers to act as its military planners. It had allowed 60,000 students, mainly from madressas, to participate in many Taliban offensives, at one time or another, and they had done so in the belief that they were battling Afghan Communists – the term invariably used by the Taliban to describe their opponents – and thus waging a jihad.[37]

Musharraf's statement set the stage for bargaining between the two sides. Washington demanded permission to use Pakistani air space for bombing targets in Afghanistan, full sharing of intelligence on the Taliban and bin Laden, an end to the flow of Pakistani fuel and supplies to the Taliban, and the sealing of the Afghan-Pakistan border.[38] Musharraf conceded all this – and more. He agreed, in strictest confidence, to sack the pro-Taliban Pakistani generals, specially Gen. Mahmoud Ahmad, who had refused to cooperate with an earlier CIA plan to subvert the Taliban by bribing local commanders to desert. Aware of Bush's declaration – "You are either with us or with the terrorists" – Musharraf knew that failure to meet all of America's demands would put Pakistan in the column of those who harbored terrorists. "If we don't opt for Washington then they will not only cut off economic funding, including that from the IMF, but also see us as a potential target," said a senior Pakistani official. With its foreign borrowings at $38 billion, half its GDP, and servicing them and domestic loans consuming 65 percent of government revenue, and another 25 percent going to the military – and the country's foreign reserves at $1.7 billion, barely enough for two months – Pakistan was in dire economic straits. So the talks that the two sides conducted behind closed doors were focused on working out the modalities of a graduated deal – the economic concessions to Islamabad moving up gradually from the lifting of the US sanctions imposed due to Pakistan's nuclear bomb testing in May–June 1998 to easier rescheduling of foreign loans, more bilateral and multilateral credits, and better access to the American market in return for Pakistan implementing the American requirements, culminating in the dismissal of the fundamentalist generals.[39] Regarding Afghanistan, Musharraf extracted a promise from Washington that it would not promote the Northern Alliance, which had been supported by Russia, Iran and India, an arch-rival of Pakistan, a pledge that would be broken.

On the domestic front, Musharraf faced opposition not only from the Islamist generals but also from the pro-Taliban civilian groups. What helped him overcome the jihadi generals' opposition was the Indian government's offer of the use of its soil for American military strikes against Afghanistan on 13 September, a decision kept secret by New Delhi so as not to inflame Muslim opinion at home.[40] Due to the lack of common borders with Afghanistan, India's offer could not match Pakistan's. Nevertheless, for the fundamentalist Pakistani generals, more anti-Indian than pro-Taliban, such a prospect was taboo. Reluctantly, they went along with Musharraf.

In the civilian sphere, the pro-Taliban groups formed the Afghan and Pakistan Defense Council. It included not just extremist groups but also the mainstream, 60-year-old Jamaat-e Islami (Islamic Group), which did not support the Taliban's puritanical brand of Islam and was led by a widely traveled cleric, Qazi Hussein Ahmad. "America has unwittingly turned bin Laden into a symbol of Muslim defiance against the West," he said. "Once you create a symbol, all those who are against you will try to associate themselves with it."[41] Though Musharraf dismissed such opposition as representing no more than 10–15 percent of the population, a later Gallup Poll would show 62 percent against Pakistan joining the US-led coalition.[42]

Having joined the coalition, Musharraf tried to persuade Mullah Omar to hand over bin Laden to Washington. During their eight-hour meeting in Kandahar, the Pakistani military delegates, led by the ISI chief, Gen. Mahmoud Ahmad, warned Omar that if his government did not turn over bin Laden it would face an attack by the US-led coalition. In return Omar told them that convincing evidence of bin Laden's involvement must be presented to the Taliban's Supreme Court or clerics of three Muslim states for judgment, his surrender must be approved by the Islamic Conference Organization, and if he was to be tried outside Afghanistan, then at least one of the judges must be Muslim.[43]

These conditions were unacceptable to the Pakistanis. As a compromise, therefore, Mullah Omar convened a conference of the Afghan ulama in Kabul to consider bin Laden's future. "Our Islamic state is the true Islamic state in the world," he said in his letter to the ulama:

> The enemies of our religion and our country . . . use different pretexts to try to finish it, including the one about the presence of bin Laden in Afghanistan . . . The question is: How did Osama tell the pilots, and which airports did they use, and whose planes were those? The answer is that it is [all in] America . . . We have taken away all resources from bin Laden and he cannot contact the outside world . . . Neither the Islamic Emirate of Afghanistan nor Osama is involved in the American events . . . But America does not listen. We have said, "If you have evidence against Osama, give it to the Afghan Supreme Court or ulama of three

Islamic countries, or have the Islamic Conference Organization observers keep an eye on Osama." But America rejected these one by one . . . And if America wants to use force we seek your guidance and fatwa on the issue in the light of the Islamic Sharia. Servant of Islam, Commander of the Faithful, Mullah Muhammad Omar Akhund.[44]

After meeting in Kabul on 20 September, about 700 members of the High Council of the Ulama expressed sadness over the deaths in America and demanded that the UN and the ICO should investigate the event. "To avoid the present tumult and also similar suspicion in the future, the High Council recommends to the Islamic Emirate of Afghanistan to persuade bin Laden to leave Afghanistan whenever possible." The statement concluded: "All books of our religious persuasion say that if infidels attack the soil of a Muslim country, jihad becomes an order for the Muslims of that country. If infidels invade an Islamic country and that country does not have the ability to defend itself, jihad becomes an obligation on all Muslims."[45]

There was no time limit on the Afghan authorities "persuading" bin Laden to leave. So Pakistan concluded that the game was up, and withdrew its embassy staff from Kabul. By now, the Musharraf government had allowed the US to use its air space for missile and air attacks on the Taliban regime, provided intelligence on the Taliban and bin Laden, and permitted the Pentagon's logistical and technical personnel to operate at Pakistani air bases, ports and "other locations."[46]

In his television broadcast of 19 September, Musharraf reiterated Bush's words that the battle was not against Muslims. "Nowhere have the words Islam or the Afghan nation been mentioned," he said. The campaign's target was "first and foremost Mr Bin Laden, then the Taliban, and thirdly, the war against international terrorism." He reminded his audience that he had backed the Taliban regime when the world was against it and still wanted to avoid inflicting suffering on the Taliban or ordinary Afghans. However, his "only priority" was "Pakistan and its defense," pointing out that "To be declared a terrorist nation by the US would harm Pakistan's strategic interests [i.e. nuclear and missile assets] and its support for Muslims in Kashmir." He asserted that the operation would be "short and sharp," and that it would not promote the Northern Alliance. At the same time, aware of the widespread skepticism in his country about the involvement of bin Laden and Al Qaida in the terrorist outrage in America, his foreign minister, Abdul Sattar, said, "The people of Pakistan expect that the evidence implicating bin Laden and the Al Qaida will be presented before the world opinion."[47] Powell promised to publish such a document, but this did not happen.

According to Representative Peter Goss, chair of the House Select Committee on Intelligence, the US administration could not present its full case without revealing some sources and methods that it would not like to reveal.[48] Secondly, the authorities had failed to acquire direct proof against bin Laden that would stand up in an American court. At the trial of the four accused of the 1998 US embassies bombings, the closest the prosecution got was the statement by Ali Muhammad, a former advisor to bin Laden turned state witness, that he had "scouted out" the American embassy in Nairobi at bin Laden's request. The other evidence was from Jamal Ahmad al Fadl, a defector from Al Qaida, who said that in 1993 in Sudan, bin Laden called on Al Qaida to wage a jihad against the US: "The snake is America . . . We have to cut the head and stop them."[49]

Forging a coalition

Having formally recruited Pakistan into the coalition, Bush turned to Central Asia, more specifically Uzbekistan and Tajikistan. Since the Clinton administration had already co-opted these states into its plans to seize bin Laden, it was now a matter of broadening and deepening the earlier ties. Given the special relationship existing between Tajikistan and Russia, Washington had to take into account Moscow's position. As it was, most of the 15,000-strong Russian 201st motorized infantry division, with air support units, normally based in the capital, Dushanbe, had been moved to the Tajik-Afghan frontier, and put on high alert. Russia had also upgraded its surveillance equipment along the border, and offered to sell the Pentagon its intelligence gathered at its fiber optic spy station.

On 18 September two large US Hercules transport planes landed secretly at Tashkent airport loaded with surveillance equipment to be installed along the Uzbek-Afghan border. Since the US planes could not fly over Iran they went through Turkmenistan's air space. In a flurry of telephone conversations with Bush, Uzbek President Islam Karimov and Tajik President Imamali Rahmanov struck deals to let the Pentagon use their air bases in return for increased financial aid and a freer hand to suppress their Islamists. Washington's annual grants to Uzbekistan were to rise threefold to $150 million.[50] In early October, Rumsfeld arrived in Tashkent with a letter from Bush to Karimov stressing the new relationship in view of the activities of the Islamic Movement of Uzbekistan (IMU). With 2–3,000 activists and a training camp at a former Soviet base near Mazar-e Sharif, Afghanistan, the IMU, well equipped with weapons and surveillance equipment, had been conducting hit and run assaults on police and political targets in the Fergana valley, straddling Uzbekistan, Kyrgyzstan and Tajikistan, since mid-1999, with the aim of establishing an Islamic state in the valley.[51]

With a CBS–*New York Times* poll showing 85 percent favoring military action against whoever was responsible, the national mood in America was hawkish. On 16 September, Bush warned the nation, "This *crusade*, this war on terrorism is going to take a while" – oblivious of the fact that bin Laden always referred to Christians as Crusaders. His statement raised protests by many Muslim leaders who accused him of conjuring up images of the worst conflict between Christians and Muslims: the Crusades were waged between the eleventh and the thirteenth centuries by west European Christians battling to recapture Palestine, the homeland of Jesus Christ. However, Bush was not alone in this deficiency. Having named their ensuing operation "Infinite Justice" – after "Infinite Reach" mounted by President

Clinton in August 1998 – the Pentagon altered the code name to "Enduring Freedom" within 48 hours when Muslim clerics pointed out that only God can dispense "infinite justice." [52]

Bush was, however, on firmer ground when it came to educating the American public on the unconventional nature of the forthcoming conflict. "I want to tell the world that this will be a different kind of battle – series of battles; that will be fought visibly sometimes, and sometimes we'll never see what may be taking place." [53] Since in all conventional wars, there are battles that are conducted unseen and unreported, there was nothing particularly unusual regarding Operation Enduring Freedom. Indeed, Rick Atkinson, an American military historian and the author of *Crusade: The Untold Story of the Persian Gulf War*, revealed that in that conventional war, the Pentagon had deployed 9,400 Special Forces servicemen to infiltrate enemy lines, hunt for sea mines, scout Kuwaiti beaches, conduct psychological warfare of diversionary feints and scattering of propaganda leaflets, and drop an occasional 15,000 lb (6,800 kg) gravity bomb – called a Daisy Cutter, after the vast swath it clears on impact. He disclosed further that two commando squadrons (800 men), one Army Ranger company and a helicopter unit, working in teams of 20 to 40, scoured the desert in western Iraq for Scud ground-to-ground missiles, but found none. [54]

Regarding the Taliban, as described in chapter 7, the Clinton administration had started the "unseen" war against it after August 1998, with a generously funded program of recruiting spies, offering cash bribes and fomenting defections, not to mention eavesdropping on the telephone traffic in Afghanistan and deploying spy satellites

Now, what this "unseen" element of war meant in practice was an above-average role for the Pentagon's Special Operations Forces and the CIA's Special Activities Division. The US Central Command (CENTCOM), based at MacDill air force base, near Tampa, Florida, charged with conducting warfare in the Middle East and Central and South Asia, had its own Special Forces Regiment (SFR), which drew its personnel from five different forces belonging to the army, navy, air force and Marines, totaling about 40,000, with the actual line units being about 12–15,000 strong.[55]

The Central Command's SFR drew 120 troops from the 160th Special Operations Aviation Regiment (SOAR, called Night Stalkers), based at Fort Campbell, Kentucky, and Hunter Army Field, Georgia, which flies helicopter night missions to provide air support to Special Force operations, and is equipped with specially adapted Black Hawk long-range helicopters with night vision and all-weather navigation; 800 men from the 2,500-strong Delta Force based at Fort Bragg, North Carolina, modeled on the British Special Air Service (SAS) regiment, specializing in close-quarter battle and reconnaissance and hostage rescue; 1,200 troops from the 5,000-strong Green Berets, based at Fort Bragg, acting as commandos specializing in explosives, communications, engineering and linguistics, and deployed for search and destroy missions; 600 men from the 1,800-strong 75th Ranger regiment, based at Fort Benning, Georgia, the army's highly mobile, rapid-deployment assault force; and 250 troops from the 2,200-strong SEALS (Sea, Air and Land), the navy counterpart to the Green Berets, specializing in snatch operations. The CENTCOM's SFR was to be assisted by Britain's 14th Intelligence Company (total strength, 120 men); Pathfinders (40 troops); Royal Marines (6,000); SAS (250); and Special Boat Squadron (100).[56]

Within a fortnight of the US Congress authorizing Bush to deploy "all appropriate and necessary force," a substantial proportion of at least 2,000 troops of the CENTCOM's SRF, already posted at the air bases at Dalbandin, Pasni, Jacobabad and Shamsi in Pakistan, Qarshi in Uzbekistan and Parkhar in Tajikistan, had infiltrated Afghanistan by helicopter in teams of 4 to 12, to hide during the day and at night use night vision equipment to pinpoint command posts, supply depots, training headquarters, etc.[57] They were supplemented by the CIA's SAD units, carrying inter alia bags of cash. Indeed, breaking with the protocol of never officially divulging the activities of secret services, Bush announced on 28 September that US Special Forces were already inside Afghanistan. As any moderately informed Westerner knows, even a conventional war begins with such operations behind enemy lines to obtain intelligence about potential targets. In Afghanistan, since intelligence was all the more difficult to gather due to the dearth of telephones,[58] implanting agents behind enemy lines was almost mandatory.

At home, President Bush tried to mobilize support for the war against terrorism. "Our grief has turned to anger, and anger to resolution," he told a joint session of the US Congress on 21 September. "Whether we bring our enemies to justice, or bring justice to our enemies, justice will be done." The evidence gathered so far pointed to a collection of loosely affiliated terrorist organizations called Al Qaida.

> Tonight the United States of America makes the following demands on the Taliban. Deliver to the United States authorities all of the leaders of Al Qaida who hide in your land . . . Protect foreign journalists, diplomats and aid workers in your country. Close immediately and permanently every terrorist training camp in Afghanistan. And hand over every terrorist and every person and their support structure to appropriate authorities. Give the United States full access to the training camps so we can make sure they are no longer operating.

After pointing out that the terrorists wanted "to overthrow existing governments in many Muslim countries such as Egypt, Saudi Arabia and Jordan. They want to drive out Israel from the Middle East," he referred to bin Laden's linkage to the Islamic (Al) Jihad (of Egypt) and the Islamic Movement of Uzbekistan. Promising to direct "every means of diplomacy, every tool of intelligence, every instrument of law enforcement, every financial influence, and every weapon of war to the destruction and the defeat of the global terror network," he declared: "Every nation in every region now has a decision to make: either you are with us or you are with the terrorists." Finally, he described the war on terrorism as "the fight of all who believe in progress and pluralism, tolerance and freedom."[59]

Eight out of 10 Americans watched the George W. Bush address to Congress on television, a record, and were impressed, resulting in his popularity rating soaring to 91 percent, the same as his father, George Bush Sr., achieved in the afterglow of the Gulf War a decade earlier. Over the past 10 days George Walker Bush had mutated from a diffident politician, prone to dyslexia, into a resolute leader with the nation solidly behind him.

Having won the presidency by one vote in the 541-strong electoral college while lagging behind his Democrat rival, Al Gore, by half a million in the popular vote in the 2000 presidential contest, George Walker Bush had considerable difficulty in overcoming his lack of gravitas, grasp of foreign affairs, and political experience at the federal level, something his father, George Herbert Walker Bush – having served as vice president for eight years and as director of the CIA and US ambassador to China before that – had in abundance. What he shared with his father were Phillips Academy in Andover, Massachusetts, and Yale University where he majored in history in 1968. He joined the Air National Guard in Texas, the base of his father's oil business, thus avoiding military service in Vietnam. After two years training he served as a part-time pilot until 1973 when he enrolled at Harvard University Business School, and graduated with a Master's degree in business administration. On his return to Midland, Texas, he set up an oil company. His first attempt to become a US Congressman in 1977 failed, and he focused on his oil business. When petroleum prices fell steeply in 1985 his company verged on collapse until it was acquired by a Dallas corporation which gave him a seat on the board of directors. In 1986, at 40, Bush, then given to excessive drinking, vowed never to touch alcohol again, and began attending Bible classes. He worked on his father's successful campaign for the presidency in 1988, then assembled a group of investors that bought the Texas Rangers Baseball franchise in 1989. After five years with the Rangers as managing general partner, he won the election for state governor with a narrow majority. In office he showed bipartisan spirit and was re-elected governor in 1998. As the Republican Party's nominee for president, he chose Dick

Cheney as his running mate. Cheney, who had served as defense secretary under Bush Sr., and commanded the Pentagon during the 1991 Gulf War, brought maturity, experience and gravitas – in which George W. Bush, nicknamed Dubya, was deficient – to the election campaign which focused on presenting the prime candidate as a "compassionate conservative," a deliberately vague phrase to entice centrist voters while appealing to the largely conservative electorate of the American hinterland by opposing abortion and gun control and favoring small government, tax cuts and strong military.

Now Osama bin Laden had inadvertently provided a convincing rationale to Bush to have the strong Pentagon he had promised to the electorate. Among those listening to his speech in the Congressional chamber were not only the members of his war cabinet but also British Prime Minister Tony Blair, the only foreign leader who was given full access to the Pentagon's detailed planning and intelligence for Operation Enduring Freedom.[60] This was Blair's reward for hurtling around the globe to help assemble the anti-terror coalition, particularly in the Muslim and Arab world, where Bush's unqualified support for Israel in the Israeli–Palestinian conflict was unpopular. Unhampered by a powerful pro-Israeli lobby in Britian, Blair was even-handed in calling for a "viable Palestinian state" and an Israel "existing within recognized and secure boundaries." Also his naturally preachy tone was tailor-made for inspirational calls on the international community. Furthermore, he was in tune with domestic public opinion, with polls showing 67–75 percent support for a military response.[61]

Bush was more domestically orientated than Blair. Indeed, in his address to the law-makers, he proposed an Office of Homeland Security at the cabinet level to coordinate 40 federal, state and local agencies in improving domestic defense against terrorism.[62] Besides the much-publicized, increased security at the airports, the Coast Guard had taken to boarding every incoming commercial vessel, and requiring incoming tankers carrying petroleum products or liquid natural gas to give 96 hours' notice, instead of the usual 24 hours, to give it ample time to check the crew and cargo manifest.[63] "It is going to change the way we go about our daily life here in the US," rued Colin Powell as he prepared for a foreign trip to forge as wide a coalition as he could.

As chairman of the military joint chiefs of staff under President Bush Sr., Powell had successfully argued for full mobilization of men and materials – and against incremental increases – before the US embarked on military action against Iraq. This time he applied this doctrine to diplomacy. Before undertaking an extensive foreign tour, he made it clear to his cabinet colleagues that his mission would proceed smoothly only if bin Laden and the Taliban remained Washington's sole targets. He opposed the idea of "eliminating" terrorism-sponsoring states, as espoused publicly by deputy defense secretary Paul Wolfowitz: "It is not just simply a matter of capturing people and holding them accountable, but removing the sanctuaries . . . ending states that sponsor terrorism."[64] Diplomatically, American actions should be multilateral – part of a broad, albeit fixed, global coalition encompassing Western allies and moderate Arab and Muslim countries, Powell argued. The hawks, led by Rumsfeld, advocated striking Afghanistan quickly, eliminating bin Laden and toppling the Taliban regime; then extending the war to Iraq to overthrow Saddam Hussein, and targeting the training bases operated by such non-Al Qaida terrorist factions as Hizbollah in Lebanon and Syria. Diplomatically, they argued, Washington should operate unilaterally when necessary, and as part of a revolving coalition – in which some nations help with certain operations and others with other operations – and eliminate the states harboring terrorists. Powell won this round partly because the hawks could not prove that groups such as Hizbollah had "a global reach," a qualification laid out by Bush in his key speech. The issues of Iraq and Hizbollah were put on the back burner.[65]

As it was, Powell had problems on hand. The presidents of Egypt and China argued that "hard evidence" should be the basis for any military action and that countries must not be punished for the actions of individuals. But, unlike during the

Kuwait crisis in 1990, this time Egypt did not matter much in geopolitical terms. And though Beijing was pacified by an economic bribe it agreed to do no more than exchange intelligence on terrorists. Over the weekend of 15–16 September, US trade representative Robert Zoellick helped finalize a deal for China to join the World Trade Organization at its November meeting. An economic carrot worked in the case of Jordan as well. The bill for free trade with Jordan that had been languishing in US Congress for three years was passed within three weeks by both houses. With this, Jordanian officials stopped talking about distinguishing between terrorism and national liberation. And, with IMF and World Bank loans of $1.7 billion for Turkey going through smoothly at Washington's behest, Ankara quietly allowed its air bases to be used as staging posts for attacks on Afghanistan.

In the case of Saudi Arabia the cash flow had been in the other direction for a long time. According to the Congressional Research Service, its foreign contracts for weapons and military construction since the 1979 Iranian revolution and the Soviet military intervention in Afghanistan had benefited American corporations to the tune of $50 billion. Immediately after the flying bomb attacks on the US, Saudi Crown Prince Abdullah instructed his oil minister, Ali Naimi, to renege on the agreement with the Organization for Petroleum Exporting Countries (OPEC) to slash output and instead increase production by 500,000 barrels per day (bpd) to counter the price rise expected in the aftermath of the terrorist acts. And, by shipping over 500,000 bpd in its own tankers to America, Riyadh succeeded in lowering the oil price from $28 to $20 in a few weeks. But so secretive is Saudi Arabia that this critical gesture by its de facto ruler, meant to cushion Western economies against the shock of the terrorist attacks, was leaked to the *Washington Post* four months after the event.[66]

Abdullah made this move as a quid pro quo for the encouraging letter he had received on 1 September from Bush concerning Israeli–Palestinian relations in response to his protest at the US policy. According to Adil Jubair, a foreign policy advisor to Abdullah, his boss was upset when, on 24 August 2001, he heard President Bush say at a press conference at his ranch in Crawford, Texas: "The Israelis will not negotiate under terrorist threat, simple as that. And if the Palestinians are interested in a dialogue, then I strongly urge Mr Arafat to put 100 percent effort into stopping the terrorist activity. And I believe he can do a better job of doing that." The crown prince telephoned the Saudi ambassador, Prince Bandar, then on vacation in Aspen, Colorado, to lodge a strong complaint. He delivered a strong message to Powell as well as Rice to the effect that

> We believe there has been a strategic decision by the US that its national interest in the Middle East is 100 percent based on Israeli Prime Minister Sharon. This was America's right, but Saudi Arabia could not accept the decision. Starting from today,"You are from Uruguay," as they say. You Americans go your way, we Saudis go our way. From now on, we will protect our national interests, regardless of where America's interests lie in the region.

Referring specifically to the Israeli–Palestinian violence, Abdullah said, "I reject the people who say when you kill a Palestinian, it is defense, and [that] when a Palestinian kills an Israeli, it is a terrorist act." The crown prince addressed a similar letter to President Bush in which he said that "failure to address the Israeli–Palestinian violence and adopting a more even-handed policy to Palestinians was putting the kingdom in an impossible position, and could damage mutual relations." This shook the Bush administration, particularly when Abdullah followed up the written messages with an order that the Saudi delegation should not attend the joint Saudi–American military planning meeting in early September. It also noticed the unceremonial sacking of the long-serving pro-American head of intelligence, Prince Turki, by Abdullah, and his replacement by the crown prince's 68-year-old half-brother, Prince Nawwaf, who had until then been a royal advisor on Gulf affairs. In his two-page letter, President Bush said that he endorsed the idea of a viable Palestinian state on the West Bank and Gaza, and expressed his willingness to work actively to revive the Israeli–Palestinian peace process. "I believe the blood of innocent people is the same – Palestinian, Israeli, Jewish, Christian or Muslim," he assured Abdullah.[67] With this, Abdullah declared himself satisfied even though it would be another month before Bush would publicly say, "I believe there ought to be a Palestinian state, the boundaries of which will be negotiated by the parties, so long as the Palestinian state recognizes the right of Israel to exist and will treat Israel with respect." In between, Abdullah had on his own initiative rushed extra supplies of oil to America after the September 11 attacks.

Of course there was not even a hint of this gesture by Abdullah in the official Saudi Press Agency report at the time, which quoted the crown prince telling President Bush over the telephone, "We in the kingdom of Saudi Arabia are fully prepared to cooperate with you in every way that may help identify and pursue the perpetrators of this criminal incident."[68]

In the afterglow of the exchange of Abdullah–Bush letters, Washington took this to mean that Riyadh would cooperate *fully* in its Operation Enduring Freedom. This was vital for political and technical reasons. If Saudi Arabia, the prime Islamic state, publicly cooperated with America militarily, that would underline the US argument that its campaign was against terrorists (who happened to be Muslims) and not against Islam or Muslims *per se* – a very significant distinction – and help it to secure the widespread backing of the Muslim world in its military campaign against Afghanistan. Secondly, some weeks earlier the Pentagon had finished constructing a state-of-the-art command center at the Prince Sultan air base, and it wanted to use this command post to direct its anti-Taliban air campaign, with its 170 warplanes stationed at the base (normally deployed to monitor the "no-fly" zone in southern Iraq) participating in it along with many others stationed elsewhere.

But when the Pentagon announced that Riyadh had agreed to let it use the newest command center at the Prince Sultan air base, the latter denied it. This troubled the White House as did Abdullah's failure to accept an invitation to meet the president after their exchange of letters. Bush had failed to accept Abdullah's repeated advice to invite Yasser Arafat to the White House to show an element of even-handedness between Israelis and Palestinians, since Bush had repeatedly held meetings with Sharon at the White House. Also, the timing of the invitation was awkward. Abdullah was wary of visiting the White House, reckoning, rightly, that if Bush launched a military campaign against Afghanistan soon after their meeting, it would appear that he had given his approval to the bombing of a fellow Muslim country, which would have damaged his standing at home. Finally, the crown prince could not have been unaware of the popularity bin Laden had come to enjoy in his kingdom, a phenomenon which would be substantiated later by a secret public opinion poll by the Interior Ministry. "If the government goes ahead with the Coalition [militarily], the gap between the people and the government will be very big," warned Shaikh Zaki Yamani, who ran Saudi Arabia's Oil Ministry for 26 years.[69] The subsequent jousting between Riyadh and Washington in private continued for so long that it resulted in the postponement of the US air campaign, scheduled to start on 2 October.

Then there was the issue of the war aim which troubled Pakistan. While secretly seeking the views of leading EU allies on "post-Taliban Afghanistan," the US in public talked of "punishing" the Taliban, not replacing it. This was done to pacify Islamabad, which openly opposed overthrowing the Taliban regime. "Knowing Afghans' fierce attachment to the independence of their country, we will not commit the blunder of trying to foist a government on the country," said Pakistani foreign minister, Abdul Sattar, on 25 September. "Any such move by foreign powers to give assistance to one side or other in Afghanistan is a recipe for greater suffering of the Afghan people."[70]

Pakistani officials could not afford to ignore the anti-American street protest which claimed three lives in Karachi when police fired on the demonstrators on 21 September. Bin Laden's comment on the event was aired on 23 September by

Al Jazeera TV, the most popular channel in the Arab world and the only foreign television channel allowed to function inside Afghanistan by the Taliban. Calling the three victims of the police firing "martyrs," bin Laden said:

> Just as Afghanistan was the first line of defense against the Russian invasion more than 20 years ago, now the Muslim nation in Pakistan is the first line of defense for Islam in this region. We call upon our Muslim brothers in Pakistan to deter with all their capabilities the American Crusaders from invading Pakistan and Afghanistan.[71]

While the Northern Alliance claimed that Islamabad's military advisors were still attached to the Taliban, and that 100 trucks carrying fuel and ammunition had traveled from Pakistan to Afghanistan, there were reports from the Pakistani side of hundreds of Pakistani Pushtuns crossing the border to bolster the Taliban ranks.[72] The Pakistani military officers that the Northern Alliance mentioned were most probably three to five mid-level ISI officers, serving and retired, who traveled on their own to Afghanistan to help the Taliban prepare their defenses against the US attack.[73] Accepting their expert advice, the Taliban dispersed their tanks and artillery around urban residential areas as well as rural areas to save them from American air strikes while some of their civilian leaders took refuge in mountain caves. At the same time, to create a strong buffer between them and the Northern Alliance, the Taliban deployed over 5,000 of their 45,000 troops in the plains north of Kabul around the Bagram air base. The Taliban military command assigned the members of the more than 3,000 strong 055 Brigade of Afghan Arabs such tasks as enforcing dusk to dawn curfews of cities and gathering counter-intelligence against America's Afghan allies attempting to build up anti-Taliban forces.

Musharraf made a last-minute attempt to avert armed confrontation by sending a delegation, comprising a top general and several militant Pakistani ulama, to Kabul on 28 September to urge the Taliban to surrender bin Laden, but in vain.[74] Though well-meaning, Musharraf's move was irrelevant as Washington was by now set to attack the Taliban no matter what it did or did not do. Niyaz Naik, head of the Pakistani delegation to the latest UN-sponsored "Six + Two" meeting in Berlin told the BBC World Service Radio of the American plan to capture or kill bin Laden and Mullah Omar with the wider aim of over-throwing the Taliban regime and replacing it with a transitional government of moderate Afghans, preferably led by former king Zahir Shah, with the operation to be launched from "north of Afghanistan" before winter snows in late October. "It is doubtful if Washington would drop its plan even if bin Laden were to be surrendered immediately by the Taliban," he said.[75]

Little wonder that Mullah Omar issued a defiant statement on 30 September on Radio Shariat. "The government may collapse but the result will be the same as the jihad against the Soviet Union," he said. "New fronts will be established, just like against the Communists. You [Americans] may capture the airports, the capital and the cities. But people will go to the mountains. God willing, America and its allies will only find the same destiny as the Communists."[76]

By then, the US-led coalition was well in place. The big break had come on 23 September as a result of an hour-long telephone conversation between Bush and Putin, which ended with the Russian president pledging cooperation "in the widest sense of the word." In return, Bush promised to forgive the Kremlin for its merciless war against the Chechens, and put its human rights violations in the Muslim-majority Chechnya on the back burner. In his television address the following day, Putin explained that the nature of cooperation in the international anti-terror campaign would depend on "the quality of our rela-tions" with other countries in the coalition, and would include "access to Russian airspace for humanitarian missions, participa-tion in some search and rescue operations, and weapons supplies to anti-Taliban forces" – not to mention sharing of intelligence. (Russian intelligence reckoned that Al Qaida with 3,000 fighters had a total of 55 facilities: training camps, safe houses, chemical

weapons laboratories, and houses for wives and children.[77])
Putin thus showed that he had come down on the side of the
"Westerners" in the Kremlin and against the military-security
establishment, which was opposed to the Pentagon's presence
in Russia's backyard. However, chief of military general staff
Gen. Anatoly Kvashnin ruled out participation in any military
strikes against the Taliban. Regarding the Central Asian republics, Russian foreign minister Igor Ivanov said that each state
must decide for itself about the presence of US troops on its soil.[78]

Actually, they had already done so – and long before the
September 11 atrocity, at least in the case of Uzbekistan, possessing 23 air bases. And, following the joint Uzbek–Nato military
exercises earlier in the year, the Pentagon had left its attack helicopter brigade behind at the Chirchik air base.

In the crucial Gulf region, the UAE severed diplomatic and
other links with the Taliban on 22 September after its efforts to
secure the hand-over of bin Laden got nowhere. The Emirate continued to host American and British forces on its air and naval
bases, as did neighboring Oman. And Bahrain remained the
headquarters of the US Fifth Fleet. Kuwait, storing US military
equipment, already hosted American air and naval attachments.
Qatar, a site of pre-positioned American military supplies, agreed
to allow the Pentagon use of its bases for support and logistics.[79]

On 25 September Saudi Arabia cut diplomatic ties with the
Taliban, regretting that the Taliban had used

> its high status gained due to the resistance to the Soviets not
> to build brotherly relations or set up high Islamic values, but
> to make the land a center to attract and train a number of
> misguided people to carry out criminal acts against the
> Sharia, to go on with terror operations, thus causing harm
> to Islam and spoiling the name of Muslims.[80]

Riyadh's words echoed the ones repeatedly used by Tehran
long before. Yet the Iranian leaders were unhappy at the
way they thought America was using the crisis to gain a foot-
hold in Central Asia while seeking assistance from Afghanistan's

neighbors, including Iran. "How can America that has tampered with Iran's interests, demand help from Iran to attack the suffering, oppressed and Muslim nation of Afghanistan?" Khamanei asked. "It is wrong to say that those who are not with us are with the terrorists. There are countries like Israel, side by side with America, whose leaders commit terrorist acts against Palestinians. No, we are not with you and we are not terrorists."[81] While opposing US military strikes against Afghanistan, Iran favored action against the Taliban under the aegis of the UN.

As it was, the UN Security Council remained cognizant of the crisis. On 28 September it unanimously passed the most comprehensive anti-terrorist resolution, 1373, under Chapter VII, which gave it the status of international law and authorized member-states to use force. Though drafted by America, all other Council members agreed to take ownership of the document, and they all voted without making any speeches. Resolution 1373 required all states (whether or not members of the UN[82]) to "prevent and suppress the financing of terrorist acts" and "freeze without delay funds and other financial assets or economic resources of persons who commit, or attempt to commit, terrorist acts." It required all states to "refrain from providing any form of support, active or passive, to entities or persons involved in terrorist acts" and "deny safe haven to those who finance, plan, support or commit terrorist acts, or provide safe havens." It called on all states to "cooperate, particularly through bilateral and multilateral arrangements and agreements, to prevent and suppress terrorist attacks and take action against perpetrators of such acts." It established a Committee of the Security Council, consisting of all Council members, to monitor its implementation, and called on all states to report within 90 days on "the steps they have taken to implement this resolution." Finally, it directed the Committee to "delineate its tasks, submit a work program within 30 days of the adoption of this resolution."[83] The passing of this resolution was expected to make many countries pass new immigration, asylum, prosecution and extradition laws.

The Security Council met a few days after Bush had frozen the assets of 11 political organizations, including Al Qaida, Al Jihad, the GIA and Harkat al Mujahedin; three charities, including Maktab al Khidmat and Al Khifah; 12 individuals, including Osama bin Laden, Ayman Zawahiri, Muhammad Atef and Abu Zubaidah.

Following a briefing to Nato in Brussels by a US counter-terrorism specialist, Frank Taylor, on 2 October, Lord Robertson said, "All roads lead to Al Qaida and pinpoint Osama bin Laden as being involved." This meant that the basis for activating Article 5 of the Nato Treaty – namely, that an attack on a member must originate abroad – had been satisfied, clearing the way for Nato to provide the US "unlimited use of its air space, base facilities, seaports, logistic support, early warning aircraft, extra security for US troops in Europe, and staging of a naval show of force in the Eastern Mediterranean."[84]

With this, the Pentagon was all set to stage its Operation Enduring Freedom the next day, using its state-of-the-art command center at the Prince Sultan air base in Saudi Arabia to coordinate the bombardment, making use of all its aircraft including those stationed at the Saudi base. But Crown Prince Abdullah refused to allow the deployment of the American war-planes stationed on Saudi soil against Afghanistan. Even inter-vention in person by Rumsfeld failed. Referring to the oblique statement made by Rumsfeld at a press conference after his meeting with his Saudi counterpart, Prince Sultan, in Riyadh, Michael Gordon of the *New York Times* said: "The comments suggested that the US might be able to use Saudi bases under which the Pentagon could direct bombing attacks [by planes based elsewhere] but could not conduct bombing missions from the Saudi territory."[85] (Also Uzbekistan refused to let its air bases be used for mounting aerial attacks against Afghanistan.) This led to a hurried, personal approach on 4 October by Rumsfeld to Oman's Sultan Qaboos, then camping in the desert at Sham Camp. The Sultan agreed – for a price. The Pentagon announced that it would sell Oman $1.2 billion worth of arms including 12 F16 fighter jets, air-to-air missiles and bombs.[86]

Rumsfeld then completed his whirlwind tour on 6 October after visiting Cairo, Tashkent and Dushanbe. While Rumsfeld was hurriedly concluding military deals, his fellow citizens in the US were alarmed by the death of an employee of a newspaper in Florida on 5 October, caused by anthrax, a deadly biological agent, sent to him anonymously in an envelope.

On 7 October, Musharraf delivered on one of his most secret promises to Washington. He forced the ISI's Gen. Mahmoud Ahmad, the second most powerful member of the ruling military junta, to resign. His replacement, moderate Gen. Ehansul Haq, former head of military intelligence, was expected to purge the ISI of the officers who had helped the Taliban in the past. He promoted Gen. Muhammad Aziz Khan, the fundamentalist corps commander of the Lahore region who had advocated military backing to the Taliban, to chairman of the joint chiefs of staff committee, a ceremonial job with no direct command of troops. By so doing, he dashed the hopes of deputy chief of army staff Gen. Muzaffar Usmani, a fundamentalist, who resigned in protest, and whose job then went to a moderate, Lt.-Gen. Muhammad Yusuf.[87]

Thus, the Taliban regime – a creation in essence of the Pakistani ISI – found itself orphaned, deprived of its god-fathers in Pakistan's military officer corps, and with its economic and political lifelines severed, as the Pentagon prepared to fire its first missiles.

Operation Enduring Freedom

The Pentagon had assembled four aircraft carriers in the Arabian Sea and the Gulf of Oman – *Carl Vinson*, *Enterprise*, *Theodore Roosevelt* and *Kitty Hawk* – the last one hosting US Special Forces commandos – equipped altogether with 400 strike air-craft; and Britain one carrier, HMS *Illustrious*. There were also American and British destroyers, frigates and submarines. Their task was to destroy 25 "high value" targets in Afghanistan. Strategically, their first priority was to control air space by disabling the Taliban's air defenses and command and control systems, and to make it safe for more American and British Special Forces units to infiltrate Afghanistan.

The US armory consisted of sea-launched Tomahawk cruise missiles (20 ft [6.4 m] long, 20 in [51 cm] diameter, 1,000 miles [1,600 km] range, and 550 miles [880 km] per hour speed), equipped with TERCOM (Terrain Contour Matching) computer, which reduces its height to 100 ft (32 m) before reaching land, maneuvers to avoid air defenses, compares ground contours over pre-selected terrain, finds the final position of and checks the target, before hitting; air-launched AGM-86c, air-to-ground cruise missiles; F14 Tomcat fighter bombers, launched from aircraft carriers, and loaded with air-to-air and air-to-ground missiles; F18 Hornet fighters launched from aircraft carriers, carrying missiles; land-based F15 E Strike Eagle ground-attack aircraft; Boeing B52 Stratofortress bombers, with a range of 10,000 miles (16,000 km), loaded with 25 cruise missiles, or 10 cluster bombs, or 18 bombs of 2,000 lb (90 kg), or 51 bombs of 750 lb (340 kg); Boeing B1 Lancer Stealth Bomber, with a range of 7,500 miles (12,000 km), carrying Joint Direct Attack Munitions (JDAM) gravity bombs, each weighing 2,500 lb (1,125 kg) – stationed at the British air base of Diego Garcia in the Indian Ocean and in the state of Missouri; North Grumman B2 Spirit all-weather Stealth Bomber, with a range of range 11,500 miles (18,400 km), loaded with 40,000 lb (18,000 kg) of satellite-guided bombs – either JDAM or conventional, cluster or deep penetration, each weighing 5,000 lb (2,250 kg) – also based at Diego Garcia and in Missouri.[88]

The day-to-day conduct of the war rested with Gen. Tommy Franks (1945–), commander-in-chief of the US Central Command – covering 25 countries, from Kenya to Kazakhstan in north-east Africa, the Middle East and Central Asia – who joined the army at 20 and won three Purple Hearts and a Bronze Star, but lacked imagination and was camera-shy. His British counterpart was Admiral Michael Boyce, chief of the defense staff. Daily Franks received a report from the CIA's Global Response Center which monitored intelligence and video. Twice a day Franks reported progress and proposed his next move to

Gen. Richard Myers (1942–), who had replaced Gen. Henry Shelton as chairman of the joint chiefs of staff on 1 October, and defense secretary Rumsfeld. Myers and Rumsfeld, working within the broad strategic decisions taken earlier by the National Security Council, provided Franks with guidance and direction. The American strategy was to hit first the Taliban's military infrastructure and then "targets of opportunity" such as tanks, followed by the dropping of cluster bombs to immobilize the enemy forces, and then target troop concentrations with AC-130 gun ships. Having thus degraded the Taliban and Al Qaida military, the planners aimed to introduce large contingents of US and UK Special Forces for (a) performing specific military tasks, and (b) providing leadership to the disparate elements of the Northern Alliance. However, following the stiff resistance the US Special Forces experienced in their first major undercover operation against the Taliban on 19–20 October, objective (a) would be dropped.

On the eve of the air strikes, Colin Powell telephoned 20 heads of government, including many Muslim and Arab countries, to notify them of the military action.

Week one

On Sunday 7 October, US–UK air raids on Afghanistan started at 20.45 local time (16.15 GMT) when 50 cruise missiles were launched from air and from four cruisers and one submarine of the US navy and one British submarine. They were joined by B1s and B2s from an air base in Missouri, US. President Bush addressed the nation on television, informing his audience that the 31 targets hit in Afghanistan included Al Qaida training camps and Taliban military installations in Kabul, Kandahar, Jalalabad, Mazar-e Sharif, Kunduz and Farah.

The triumphant Bush had hardly stepped out of his Oval Office when his aides told him that Al Jazeera TV had just broadcast a 20-minute statement by Osama bin Laden, with Ayman Zawahiri and Suleiman abu Ghaith, an Al Qaida spokesman, by his side. "Here is America, struck by God Almighty in one of its vital organs, so that its greatest buildings are destroyed," said bin Laden:

> [W]hat America is tasting now is only a copy of what . . . [o]ur Islamic *umma* (nation) has been tasting for 80 years – humiliation and disgrace, its sons killed and their blood spilled, its sanctities desecrated. God has blessed a group of vanguard Muslims . . . to destroy America . . . When they stood in defense of their weak children, their brothers and sisters in Palestine and other Muslim nations, the whole world went into an uproar, the infidels followed by the hypocrites.[89] We hear no denunciation . . . from the hereditary [Muslim] . . . rulers as Israeli tanks rampage across Palestine, in Ramallah, Rafah, Jenin and Beit Jala and many other parts of the Land of Islam, and we do not hear anyone raising his voice or reacting. But when the sword fell upon America after 80 years, hypocrisy [i.e. hypocrite Muslims] raised its head high bemoaning those [American] killers who toyed with the blood, honor and sanctities of Muslims. The least that can be said about those hypocrites is that they are apostates . . . Americans have been telling the world they are fighting terrorism. A million children [killed] in Iraq, to them this is not a clear issue.[90] But when a little over than 10 [Americans] were killed in Nairobi and Dar as Salaam, Afghanistan and Iraq were bombed, and hypocrites stood behind the head of international infidels, America and its allies . . . These events have divided the world into two camps, the camp of the faithful and the camp of the infidels . . . As to America, I say to it and its people a few words: I swear to Allah that those living in America will not live in security and safety until we live in peace and security in our lands and in Palestine, and all the army of infidels has departed from the Land of Muhammad, peace be upon him.[91]

Americans were already jittery, with the anthrax-related death in Florida setting off a nationwide alarm which became shriller when the FBI issued a general warning on 10 October, saying that "attacks may be carried out during the next week on US targets at home or abroad." This came as no surprise: according to a Gallup poll, 83 percent expected additional terrorist attacks, and 58 percent feared that someone in their family would become a victim. Since the WTC and Pentagon attacks, sales of firearms had increased by up to 30 percent in some states, and there had been a sharp rise in the sale of ammunition, bullet-proof jackets, gas masks and antibiotics to fight anthrax and smallpox. Security at sporting events and government buildings remained very tight. With fighter jets frequently scrambling over Washington on homeland defense missions, the mood in the nation's capital was hardly serene. The White House publicly pressured the US media to edit Al Qaida broadcasts on the ground that bin Laden interviews might be carrying hidden messages to Al Qaida members, and they did so.[92] Since most of the bin Laden tapes were 20 to 25 minues long, and the US broadcasting media showed only clips of one minute or less, the official argument was unconvincing.

The 23 targets that the Pentagon struck on the second day of the war, 8 October, included airfields and two UN offices in Kabul – one of them a demining agency, where four civilians died.[93] At the same time US aircraft started dropping food and medicine in certain areas of Afghanistan.[94]

On 9 October, the number of targets fell sharply to six, followed by seven the following day, highlighting the paucity of high value targets in Afghanistan. Confident that the Taliban's air defenses had been disabled, the Pentagon ordered day-light raids on targets, including the Taliban headquarters in Kandahar. Simultaneously, the US 4th Psychological Operations Group began transmitting propaganda broadcasts in Persian, interspersed with music from EC-130Es, equipped with radio and television transmitters. The message to the Taliban and Al Qaida was: "Attention: You are condemned. Did you know that? The instant the terrorists you support took over our planes, you sentenced yourself to death."[95]

On the ground, the pro-Iranian Gen. Ismail Khan, maintaining a base in Mashhad since his escape from a Taliban jail, claimed that his forces had captured Chakhcharan, the capital of Ghor province, and were proceeding to Qala-e Nau.

In Pakistan, with four airports – Dalbandin, Pasni, Jacobabad and Shamsi – handed over to the Pentagon, which set up helicopter bases to infiltrate and attack Afghan targets, protest became more vocal in the country. In the demonstrations in Karachi and Quetta, four protesters were killed by police firing.

In Kabul, the Taliban claimed that the US bombing had killed 76 civilians so far. On 11 October, the air strikes were the heaviest yet. Among others, they hit Khorum, a village near the Pakistani border, causing – according to the Taliban – 160 civilian deaths. Yet so untutored were the Taliban in public relations, it was only four days later that they invited Pakistan-based foreign journalist to the site. The reporters saw 18 fresh graves, some of them containing more than one corpse or parts of a corpse. Rumsfeld contested the dispatches, saying that the American warplanes had hit a nearby underground ammunition dump where the stored material was so abundant that it had caused a secondary explosion, followed by fires that lasted four hours.[96]

On Friday 12 October, there was a respite, with the Pentagon publicly deciding to respect Islam's weekly day of prayer. However, according to "Doctor" – the pseudonym for an English-speaking Afghan general practitioner from Kabul, who sought refuge in Peshawar after 16 days of bombing:

> [T]he Americans resumed attacks after the evening prayers [on 12 October], hitting a petrol storage depot. It was like an earthquake, the ground moved again. Then they hit a transport depot, old buses and trucks left behind by the Soviets in 1989. Next they hit the army barracks of the Baba Jan Battalion. The next target was a mile to the north of Kabul in a small valley where 015 Battalion looked after the food storage for the Taliban. The Americans bombed and destroyed all the stocks of food. They used six heavy bombs which exploded at short intervals.[97]

On 13 and 14 October the Pentagon deployed 25 strike aircraft and fired 15 Tomahawk missiles. It also began dropping 500,000 leaflets, saying strikes were directed against foreign terrorists and not Afghans. As part of its humanitarian effort, combined with its psychological warfare tactics, it started dropping tons of bright yellow tinfoil food parcels, containing precooked herbed rice and spicy bean salad along with peanut butter in a tube and strawberry jam, as well as plastic cutlery, with each package printed with an American flag and the words in English – "Humanitarian daily ration – Free gift from the People of America" – along with instructions in English on how to tear open the package and how to use cutlery.[98] Though well-meaning, the food parcels did not reach those in real need – children, old people, pregnant women. They ended up with the most able. Indeed, the Taliban soldiers from nearby front lines would rush to the scene on pick-up trucks and collect the packages.

Shielded from exposure to such ironies, the public in the West was solidly for the war. In Britain, for example, the backing for military strikes was 75 percent, 15 points behind the figure in America. In contrast, only 42 percent of Russians supported the military action, and about a third blamed the US for the conflict.[99]

There were of course no public opinion polls in the Middle East. However, the virtual absence of expression of support for the American bombing of Afghanistan at the popular and official levels in the Arab and Muslim world spoke for itself. Summing up the situation in the Arab world, the London-based *Al Hayat* – widely regarded as the *International Herald Tribune* of the Arabic-speaking region – wrote, "It is difficult for any Arab or Muslim country, however cooperative it is with the US, to mobilize people to support the war, as it is difficult for it to orchestrate internal media campaign to speak of the benefits of the US policy."[100]

Saudi Arabia remained at the center of the relationship between America and the Muslim world. While its rulers agreed with Washington's political objectives, they were also nervously aware of the popular anger caused in their kingdom by the Christian superpower's military strikes against the poor Muslim country of Afghanistan. Though the Council of Senior Ulama refrained from taking a position on the subject, the imam of the Grand Mosque of Mecca, the holiest shrine of Islam, Shaikh Salih bin Humaid, said, "This issue [of terrorism] calls for new policies [by America], not new wars." He warned that "an attack on Afghanistan could stir conflict between civilizations and religions."[101]

At the popular level there was much skepticism about bin Laden's guilt, which was shared by the Saudi political elite who blamed Washington's unabashed backing for Israel's suppression of Palestinians as the main reason driving young Saudis into the arms of Islamist extremists. They overlooked the fact that absence of political freedom in the kingdom had led many well-educated Saudis searching for a political cause to join the jihad in Bosnia or Chechnya after the victory of the anti-Soviet jihad in Afghanistan. They were the ones who now called bin Laden "the Conscience of Islam." As a senior (unnamed) Saudi lawyer in Jiddah told the visiting reporter of the *New York Times*, "What bin Laden says and what he does represents what most Muslims or Arabs want to say and can't. What he says, we agree with it."[102] This was borne out by a secret opinion survey conducted by the Interior Ministry: it showed 95 percent of educated Saudis in the 25–41 age group supporting "bin Laden's cause."[103] As for those in the lower age group, Dr. Mai Yamani, a Saudi Fellow at the Royal Institute for International Affairs, London, summed up the situation thus:

> The young have been exposed to satellite television and new ideas about the Palestinian intifada and sanctions against Iraq. The main issues are censorship and double standards. There is a rising demand to participate. Young men and women are saying, "We are the nation but we are never consulted." When Osama Bin Laden and others come up with alternatives, they cheer them.[104]

At the official level, differences arose between Riyadh and Washington on the question of freezing assets of organizations alleged to be funding terrorists. On 12 October Washington named 22 organizations and individuals whose assets needed to be frozen – throughout the world. They included Muwafaq Foundation, based in Saudi Arabia, and the Islamic Cultural Institute in Milan, Italy.[105] Riyadh refused to shut down the Muwafaq Foundation, an Islamic charity, partly because Islam enjoined charity, and the kingdom had affluent citizens in abundance, partly because the country lacked a supervisory body for banks, and partly because Washington had failed to prove that funds from any Saudi-based charity had gone to Al Qaida. The Bush administration then pressured Riyadh by leaking embarrassing information on the royal princes' moral and material corruption to the investigative journalist Seymour Hersh of the *New Yorker* weekly, implying further damaging revelations if Riyadh failed to meet its demands on freezing the assets of the US-named charities and providing full backgrounds of the 15 Saudi hijackers. After disclosing that the US National Security Agency had been monitoring the telephone conversations of the king, crown prince and several senior princes since the mid-1990s, Hersh referred to the intercept where the interior minister, Prince Nayif, instructed a subordinate to withhold from the police evidence of hiring of prostitute – a severe crime – "presumably by the members of the royal family," insisting that "the client list" must not be released "under any circumstances."[106] Though the ploy worked, with Riyadh freezing the assets of the Muwafaq Foundation within days of the Hersh article, the US unwittingly reinforced the anti-royalist argument of the bin Laden camp. Incensed, Riyadh denounced "the vicious campaign against the kingdom in the Western media" on 29 October. The White House spokesman said that Bush had telephoned Crown Prince Abdullah to say "I am very pleased with the kingdom's contribution to the war effort," and that the media citing differences between America and Saudi Arabia were "simply incorrect."[107] This was not enough. Throwing the customary Saudi discretion to the wind, the kingdom's foreign minister, Saud al Faisal, said, "Bush's failure to commit his personal prestige to forging the final peace settlement [between Israelis and Palestinians] makes a sane man go mad." All Bush had to do was to establish himself as an honest broker, continued al Faisal. "Bush cannot be an honest broker and meet only one side [Israeli Premier Ariel Sharon]."[108] Evidently he found unconvincing Bush's argument that Arafat had not done "enough" to lower the level of Palestinian violence and root out terrorists.

In any case, Saudi Arabia had not been the only one to refuse to toe the American line of freezing the assets of Washington-named parties, the others being Egypt, Jordan, Kuwait and Qatar.

Qatar had just finished chairing the conference of the foreign ministers of the 56-member Islamic Conference Organization in Doha. While declaring that the attacks on America contradicted "the teachings of all Semitic religions," the ministers called for the convening of an international conference by the UN to address the problem of international terrorism. Alluding to the complicity of bin Laden in the terrorist outrage, the presiding Qatari foreign minister, Hamad bin Jassem al Thani, said, "We [ICO members] have some evidence but we do not have sufficient evidence. We did not see anything concrete."[109] The ICO ministers failed to reach a consensus on America's Operation Enduring Freedom.

But Iraqi foreign minister, Naji Sabri al Hadithi, was in no doubt: "We are on the brink of a big war being launched against Islamic states and Muslim people, and there are threats against other Muslim countries and peoples." He was echoing the views of his president, Saddam Hussein. "The true believers cannot but condemn this act, not because it has been committed by America against a Muslim people but because it is an aggression committed outside international law," he said. "These methods will bring only greater instability and disorder in the world. The American aggression could spread to other countries."[110]

Across the border, Iran's supreme leader, Khamanei, condemned the American strikes. "How can you allow innocent civilians to be killed or injured?" he asked. "Terrorism is only an excuse. Why don't they announce their real intention – their motive for grabbing more power, for imperialism? Since when has it become a norm to send troops to another country and hit its cities with missiles and aerial bombardment because of so-called terrorism in that country?"[111]

In the Persian media as well as in the Arabic, there was much stress on the fate of Afghan civilians. "For the Arabs, the image of this war – that of a rich, strong superpower hitting a small country – does not lend itself to sympathy, and creates a gap that that cannot be bridged by propaganda," said Muhammad al Sayyid Said, an Arab media specialist in London.[112]

In Pakistan there was a gap between the official policy and the popular opinion, which remained opposed to the American campaign, with more and more shops doing brisk business selling T-shirts embossed with bin Laden's portrait, and even the English-speaking liberals criticizing America for mindlessly bombing an indigent Afghanistan. While Bush had all but declared that he would topple the Taliban no matter how long it took, Musharraf kept repeating: "I have got definite assurances that this operation will be short." Privately, the Pakistani leader assured Bush that the growing military pressure would lead to a split in the Taliban leadership between hardliners and moderates – such as foreign minister Wakil Ahmad Muttawakil and frontier affairs minister Jalaluddin Haqqani – who, being nationalist, disapproved of the presence of bin Laden and other Arabs in their country. Indeed Haqqani wanted the moderates to become part of the next broad-based Afghan government. With that view in mind, he dissuaded Bush from letting the Northern Alliance seize Kabul with the active assistance of the Pentagon. Accordingly, Washington dispatched emissaries to the Alliance to hold off an attack on the capital to give Islamabad time to assemble a multi-ethnic government.

Week two

Having destroyed the Taliban's air force of 12 aging Soviet war-planes and surface-to-air missiles, the Pentagon was now free to engage in daytime bombing. On 14 October, it hit Kabul's telephone exchange. During a secret visit to Pakistan, Muttawakil and Haqqani offered to surrender bin Laden to a third country without an advance presentation of evidence against him in return for stopping the bombing. Bush rejected the proposal, demanding that bin Laden's colleagues be handed over as well and all Al Qaida camps be shut and their closure verified by the US.[113]

The Pentagon refrained from attacking the Taliban north of Kabul partly because the two sides were too close to one another, and Alliance troops could have been hit. Attempts by Gen. Abdul Rashid Dostum, deploying 2,000 horses in the absence of tanks, to dislodge the Taliban from Mazar-e Sharif failed. Equally fruitless was the CIA's effort to establish a working relationship with Dostum, or to get him to coordinate his strategy with that of Gen. Ismail Khan or Muhammad Karim Khalili. And the CIA's continued failure to mobilize anti-Taliban forces in southern Afghanistan – a crucial ingredient in the White House's scenario of a successful Afghan campaign – added to Washington's problems.

So the stalemate continued on the front line north of Kabul, where the Northern Alliance's 3,000 to 5,000 troops near the Bagram airport faced 6,000 well-entrenched Taliban and Al Qaida fighters, who continued to defy the US bombing. With their command and control system decimated, the Taliban commanders resorted to sending messages by hand-carried notes.

On 16 October the Pentagon said that its bomb has mistakenly hit Red Cross warehouses in Kabul even though the buildings were clearly marked. The only television channel that broadcast this image was Al Jazeera whose bearded, Syrian-born correspondent in Kabul, Tayseer Aloumi, had become a fixture in the Arabic-speaking world, which was exposed daily to the images of US bombing and its after-effects. This further displeased American officials, already unhappy at the way they perceived the most popular satellite channel in the Arab world, claiming 35 million viewers in the Middle East, western Europe and North America, to be presenting their war on terror. During his visit to

Washington as chairman of the Islamic Conference Organization in early October, Qatari ruler Shaikh Hamad bin Khalifa al Thani was asked by Powell to "do more to rein in Al Jazeera" where stridently anti-American views were being expressed by many of its contributors. At the subsequent press conference Shaikh Hamad referred to the US request as "advice," and said that he would take no action against the channel because "parliamentary life requires that you have a free and credible media and that is what we are trying to do."[114]

Ever since its inception as a commercial channel in November 1996 at the behest of the Qatari government, its part-owner, Al Jazeera had followed its brief of being an independent 24-hours a day news and current affairs station, acting as the British Broadcasting Corporation does in Britain. Actually its reporting staff consisted almost wholly of BBC-trained journalists who, in April 1996, had lost their jobs when, angered by the BBC's interviews with Saudi dissident Muhammad al Masaari and a documentary on capital punishment in Saudi Arabia, the Rome-based Orbit TV, owned by Prince Khalid ibn Abdullah, canceled its contract with the BBC's Arabic Service to produce news for it. Al Jazeera's leading weekly features – "The Opposite Direction" and "The Other Opinion" – debate such controversial issues as religion and politics, Arab relations with Israel, and the role of monarchy in the Arab world. Little wonder that over the years the Qatari Foreign Ministry has received nearly 400 official complaints which it passes onto the Al Jazeera management with a note to the complainant: "If Al Jazeera has said something wrong, you always have the right to reply."[115] In a region where the rulers rigidly control broadcasting media, the arrival of Al Jazeera was greeted with the same enthusiasm as a traveler in a desert would greet an oasis. Little wonder it won plaudits from the US state department in its annual report on human rights in 2000 as a beacon of free speech in the Middle East. Within a week of the September 11 attacks, it interviewed Powell.

Now Al Jazeera's reporting of the consequences of US bombing on the Afghan people was turning the Arab public against America, a fact Middle Eastern rulers could not ignore. "We wish America had been able to flush out the terrorists in Afghanistan without resorting to the current action because this is killing innocent people," said Saudi interior minister, Prince Nayif. "We are not at all happy with the situation. This does not mean we are unwilling to counter terrorism."[116]

None of this had any impact on Washington, now more concerned about the anthrax cases at home, latterly in New York followed by an anthrax-containing letter addressed to the office of Senate majority leader, Tom Daschle, which would lead to the closure of the House of Representatives chamber for four days.[117]

The announcement by Rumsfeld on 16 October that the combat capacity of the Taliban had been "eviscerated" inaugurated the next phase of the campaign. The Pentagon began deploying its Oman-based, slow-moving cargo gun ships AC-130 with cannon and ultra-rapid machine-guns – 1,800 rounds a minute – to target individuals. At about the same time it started to arm the slow-moving RQ-1 Predator reconnaissance plane, deployed by the CIA's SAD units before the bombing campaign, with 10 lb (4.5 kg) missiles.[118]

Among the Afghans who noticed the arrival of aircraft with propellers, making "heavy sounds', over Kabul, was "Doctor," who provided a perspective on the US bombing from the other side. "When the first night of attacks came, we didn't know what to expect," he told Robert Fisk of the *Independent* in Peshawar:

> It was very sudden, but the bombs were on target. Later, the Americans started hitting civilians. Some were very badly wounded and were taken to the Jumhuriyat Hospital in the center of the city. But we were blocked from going to the hospital. We had no contacts [with the Taliban] . . . On the second night our neighbor's house was hit. People were buried when a wall collapsed but they were not killed . . . When military targets were attacked, the Taliban blocked us from going there just like they did [regarding] the hospitals. Then they announced that people were not to

come out of their houses . . . At the beginning 90 percent of the bombing was on target. But then the Americans started using 1,000 lbs bombs, and the areas [they hit] were badly damaged. When they hit the television transmitter towers, our houses shook and the earth moved, and we smelled a lot of smoke. Then Radio Shariat went off the air, but the next day I saw them reassembling a new antenna.[119] The Taliban always did this. Every time something was destroyed, they replaced it at once. They would go round and collect up all the wrecked equipment. The Taliban were very relaxed about it.

Referring to the pattern of bombing, he said, "Every night the Americans bombed around Kabul. But each night the circle of bombing got closer to the center – it got narrower and narrower."[120]

Then followed the Pentagon's next phase, requiring the deployment of the Special Forces for daring raids on specific sites. The first such operation, involving 100 Delta commandos, 200 troops from the 75th Rangers Regiment and AC-130 gun ships, was carried out on the night of 19–20 October. Once the Army Pathfinder forward troops had checked the Kandahar airstrip, the Rangers parachuted onto the site, but found nothing of value. Around 01.45 hours on 20 October, the Delta commandos raided Mian Koh near Mullah Omar's military compound with the aim of hauling all the documents – likely to incriminate the Taliban in the attacks on the US and reveal their war strategy. But the raiders faced heavy fire from the Taliban. It left 12 of them wounded, 3 seriously. After 30 minutes they began retreating. In the melee, an evacuating helicopter lost its undercarriage and had to make a forced landing. But the Pentagon, using the film footage of the Army Pathfinder unit performing smoothly, announced that the operation had been successful. This upset many insiders. Some Delta officers, unhappy at Gen. Franks' deployment of 300 troops and a squadron of AC-130 gun ships and helicopters – an unwise departure from the standard Delta practice of operating in small numbers with stealth and guile –

leaked the embarrassing facts to Seymour Hersh of the *New Yorker*, who published the true story. "The ferocity of the Taliban resistance scared the crap out of everyone," he wrote.[121]

As a result, Washington changed its strategy.

Week three

The Pentagon intensified air strikes on the Taliban front line north of Kabul, and decided to bolster the Alliance troops for ground operations. Intensified bombing resulted in increased civilian casualties. On the night of 22–23 October, around midnight, American AC-130 gun ships leveled every house in Chokar Karez, a tiny hamlet in an exposed, open desert 40 miles (64 km) east of Kandahar, leaving mounds of shattered mud bricks, reported Paul Rogers in *The Times*.

> Not a single house has been left intact. Debris, including pots and pans, a woman's plastic shoe and a can of infant formula lay scattered around. In one corner of the village compound, the smell of decomposing flesh was evident. We were allowed by our Taliban escorts to wander freely . . . There were several large bomb craters and many pieces of shrapnel. But evidence that this remote spot had ever been used for military or terrorist purposes was non-existent. The only machinery we found was farming implements and a smashed motor cycle.

Up to 90 people lost their lives, with Al Jazeera TV reporting a figure of 93. After interviewing the survivors in a hospital in the Pakistani city of Quetta, Catherine Philp reported:

> By the time the attack was over 18 members of the family [of Zamina Ahmad] were dead, killed by gunfire after running into the open. She was awakened by the warplanes roaring overhead and heard the deafening boom of a bomb dropping. Grabbing her five year old son, Sabir, she ran into the courtyard of the family compound, searching for a place to hide. As she sought shelter her daughter Shahida, 14, saw her

mother cut down by bullets fired from the circling gunships. Sabir, still in her arms, was injured by shrapnel.[122]

Civilian casualties in rural areas were particularly disquieting to Afghans: to avoid death or injury, the majority of the populations of Kabul, Jalalabad and Kandahar had fled to villages.

On 23 October the Taliban claimed that bombs has struck a hospital in Herat, but the Pentagon said an old people's home was hit. Two days later a guidance system malfunction resulted in two navy jets striking a residential area in Kabul and a Red Cross warehouse that had been bombed earlier. On 26 October a B52 bomber hit the same Red Cross complex again.[123] Belying the predictions of many Western experts on the Taliban, there had been virtually no defections from their ranks.

Indeed, the Taliban had withstood the punishing US bombing well so far. Having announced earlier that the Taliban's combat power had been "eviscerated," the Pentagon now expressed "surprise" at their ability to regroup, disperse and conceal troops and equipment while reorganizing resistance. US Rear Admiral John Stufflebeem, who on 17 October had said that "We are pulling away at the legs underneath the stool that Taliban leadership sits on," now conceded: "They [Taliban] are proving to be tough warriors."[124] His view was echoed by the American public. Only one out of four Americans, who had backed military action by nine to one, felt that the war was going well. The anthrax scare gripped the nation when spores were discovered at the center handling President Bush's mail on 23 October. It changed perceptions of security and attitudes toward federal administration in a country where distrust of government has been a political constant for a long time, with the easiest route for politicians to garner votes being to rail against Washington. A *New York Times*–Columbia Broadcasting Service poll showed 67 percent approval for US Congress, the highest since the question was first asked 30 years earlier.[125]

On 26 October Bush signed into law the Uniting and Strengthening of America by Providing Appropriate Tools Required to Intercept and Obstruct Terrorism (USA PATRIOT) Act, passed overwhelmingly by US Congress, which greatly enhanced the FBI's powers of search, wiretap and Internet eavesdropping. At the signing ceremony, Dick Cheney made his first public appearance since September 11.[126] Almost on cue, on 29 October, the FBI issued its second general warning – "attacks may be carried out during the next week on US targets at home or abroad" – since 10 October. That night Cheney was whisked away to an undisclosed location. A *Washington Post*–ABC News poll showed public confidence in the government to cope with terrorism at home declining from 66 percent on September 11 to 52 percent.[127]

By contrast what concerned the public in the Muslim and Arab world was the prospect of the bombing of Afghanistan during the holy month of Ramadan, beginning on 16 November. "The longer the war lasts the harder it will be for the US to maintain its coalition and be effective in the war for public opinion in the Muslim world," warned the *Washington Post*.[128] After his meeting with British premier Blair, Syrian President Bashar Assad (r. 2000–) said, "We cannot accept what we see on the screen everyday, hundreds of innocent [Afghan] civilians dying." He was obviously referring to television footage aired by many of the Arab world's channels, Al Jazeera being just one. In Riyadh, senior Saudi officials told Blair they backed the "global fight against terrorism" but wanted the US–UK air strikes against Afghanistan to end soon.[129]

But a break in bombardment, which would have allowed the Taliban to regroup, ran counter to the Pentagon's overarching strategy of wearing down the Taliban through relentless strikes. Meanwhile, to control the popular mood in the West, it became all the more important for the US Defense Department to continue to stage-manage news. It refused to permit any reporters onto USS *Kitty Hawk* from where Special Forces commandos were being dispatched to Afghanistan. There were no journalists in Oman where US Army Rangers and AC-130 gun ships were based. It was the same not only in Uzbekistan, keen to keep its military links with America secret, but also in British-controlled Diego Garcia. Overall, the access to the media was more limited than in the Kosovo air campaign in 1999 and the American intervention in Somalia in 1993. Quite simply, since the ground aspect of the war was being waged by US Special Forces, working in conjunction with the CIA's SAD units, the major sector of the conflict was out of bounds to the press. Unlike Gen. Norman Schwarzkopf who gave daily press conferences during the 1991 Gulf War, it was only on the fifteenth day of the present campaign that Gen. Franks faced the media.[130] "The bombing in Afghanistan has taken on a distant, numbing, lifeless sameness, punctuated occasionally by a Taliban report of civilian casualties," wrote Michael Getler, former executive editor of the *International Herald Tribune*, in the *Washington Post*.[131]

To break the morale of the Taliban and ensure that their units did not regroup, the US resorted to dropping 2,000 lb (900 kg) gravity cluster bombs from B52s on their front line positions as well as important road junctions and bridges. As a cluster bomb drops it releases many unexploded bomblets over an area of about 1 sq. mile (2.6 km^2). "Cluster bombs are being used on front line Al Qaida and Taliban troops to try to kill them," said Rumsfeld. "That is why we are using them, to be blunt about it." They were also comparatively cheaper. "Unguided bombs dropped by B-52s will be more cost effective than laser or satellite-guided weapons which are being used to hit relatively low value targets," said Robert Hewson, editor of *Jane's Air Launched Weapons*. "It is the only way to deal with dispersed troops out in the open."[132]

Week four

Up to 1 November, US warplanes had flown 2,000 sorties, or 80 a day. With a single Tomahawk missile costing $1 million, the war expense was running at $2 billion a month. Of the 50,000 American armed personnel assembled in the region – from the Red Sea to the Indian Ocean – 25,000 were aboard warships in the northern Arabian Sea, and the rest aboard warships in the Gulf and at the land bases in Saudi Arabia, Oman, Uzbekistan and Pakistan.[133] The Taliban's ranks had been swollen by the arrival of 12,000 fighters, sponsored by the Tahrik-e Nifaz-e

Shariat Muhammadi (Movement for the Establishment of Muhammad's Sharia) from the Pushtun tribal belt along the Afghanistan–Pakistan border, part of the autonomous Federally Administered Tribal Area (FATA), with a population of 5 million. "The Taliban brought justice and security to Afghanistan," explained a tribal elder in Batkhela.[134]

The Pentagon resorted to carpet bombing, using B52s loaded with 1,000 lb (450 kg) bombs, targeting the Taliban positions north of Kabul, with the objective of supporting Northern Alliance forces, which were being equipped with Russian weapons, including tanks, as well as ammunition and military uniforms and boots – all funded by the Pentagon. Most American pilots were now operating in "engagement zones," where they were permitted to hit targets of "opportunity" such as Taliban tanks rather than predetermined targets like airfields, air defense facilities, command and communications sites, ammunition dumps and fuel depots. For that purpose they used either a Joint Direct Attack Munitions gravity bomb, with an attachment to its tail section equipped with a satellite navigation kit, using the global positioning system (GPS), or a smartly guided bomb whose sensors pierced through darkness and clouds, or a Paveway bomb guided by a laser directed at the target. The laser-guided bomb went wrong only if the laser was obstructed by cloud or smoke whereas the satellite-guided bombs went off course due to bad weather or wrong coordinates being used, deliberately or inadvertently.

In his video-taped speech aired on Al Jazeera TV on 3 November, bin Laden called on the pro-Afghanistan demonstrators in the Muslim world to continue resisting "the strongest, most vicious and most dangerous crusade against Islam." He referred to Bush as the leader "carrying high the cross," and said that "Whoever stands behind Bush has committed an act that stands as annulment of their Islam." Describing the current battle as "in essence a religious war," he called on Muslims to "Rise in support of your religion." The issue, he asserted, was "a matter of beliefs and not, as portrayed by Bush, a war against terrorism."[135] Two days earlier an Al Jazeera anchorman read out a handwritten note from bin Laden in which he said, "Muslims in Afghanistan are being subjected to killing and the Pakistani government is standing beneath the Christian banner," and called on Pakistani Muslims to "stand in the face of a Christian crusade against Islam."[136]

Week five

There was much nervousness among Pakistani officials, the fear being that if American strikes continued into Ramadan and there was lack of progress on the ground, one or both of the two mainstream political parties – the Pakistan Muslim League and the Pakistan People's Party – would join the Islamist opposition and move the street protest from the border provinces of the North West Frontier and Baluchistan into the populous heartland of Panjab. Indeed, as soon as Maqdoum Javed Hashemi, the acting president of the Muslim League said that his party would join the anti-government strike on 9 November, he was arrested. On the eve of that strike the government ordered that mosques should bar sermons by extremists and that they should not use loudspeakers on minarets to stir public emotion. What alarmed the Pakistani authorities was the call by Jamaat-e Islami leader Qazi Hussain Ahmad for the overthrow of Musharraf's regime by the military. Musharraf arrested Ahmad as well as Maulana Fazlur Rahman of the Jamiat-e Ulama-e Islam, on 7 November, the day he left for the US in Paris and London – pledging to persuade Bush to stop, during Ramadan, the bombing which, according to the Taliban, had so far claimed some 1,500 civilian lives.[137]

While Musharraf was in London on 9 November, news reached him that Mazar-e Sharif had fallen to the Northern Alliance.

This happened only after the CIA's SAD units had finally succeeded in getting Atta Muhammad, an ethnic Tajik, and Hajji Muhammad Muhaqiq, an ethnic Hazara, belonging to the Hizb-e Wahadat (a nominal constituent of the Northern Alliance), to coordinate their strategies with Dostum, making full use of the CIA cash they had been carrying, with the going rate for a run-of-the-mill warlord to defect being $200,000.[138] They had also acted as the advance force for the Pentagon, entering northern Afghanistan on 27 September from Uzbekistan to set up a bridgehead for the US Special Forces that followed. Besides coordinating American air strikes with F18s and B52s on Taliban targets, they also taught different Alliance commanders how to do so. On the morning of 9 November heavy air strikes on Taliban defense lines around Mazar softened up the Taliban as the Hazara forces approached the city from the east and the Uzbek and Tajik troops from the south. Yet the ground fighting was fierce, lasting nine hours and resulting in 600 deaths. The hard-core Taliban troops withdrew, taking as many weapons and ammunition as they could.[139] The CIA's SAD unit reportedly secured a promise from the Northern Alliance leaders, particularly Dostum, not to massacre civilians on entering the city. Though Dostum kept his word regarding civilians, he ended up ordering the massacre of at least 180 Taliban and Al Qaida prisoners at the Qala Jangi fort near Mazar on 25–26 November following a prison riot.[140] In the immediate aftermath of the Taliban's defeat, some women in Mazar showed their faces in the street, and some men shaved off their beards. Perfume and vodka appeared in the bazaar, as did Iranian video cassettes, and pictures of Indian and Iranian movie stars. Cinemas reopened.

Over the next two days, the Alliance troops took over the adjoining provinces of Jozjawan, Faryab, Samangan and Sar-e Pul, including the strategic towns of Qala-e Nau and Pul-e Khumri close to the front line north of Kabul where the Pentagon had started deploying 7,500 lb (3,380 kg) bombs, called Daisy Cutters, for "psychological reasons" – that is, to demoralize the Taliban.

On Saturday 10 November at a joint press conference in New York, Bush and Musharraf called on the Northern Alliance not to march on Kabul. On the ground, though, the US Special Forces spearheaded Northern Alliance attacks near Bagram airport which forced the Taliban into concentrations in trenches. Then the Alliance troops called for US bombing of the Taliban trenches which lasted two hours on Monday afternoon, followed by an hour-long tank and infantry attack by Alliance forces. That resulted in the death of at least half of the 5,000 Taliban and 1,000 Al Qaida fighters. Another 1,300 Taliban troops surrendered as others fled and were attacked by American warplanes. The Taliban in Kabul started packing to leave as the Alliance troops advanced in their newly acquired Russian T-55 tanks within 4 miles (6 km) of Kabul later that day.[141]

Fall of Kabul

On the night of 12–13 November, the Taliban abandoned Kabul in an orderly manner, heading south to Kandahar. They took all the cash from the Central Bank as well as from 80 money-changers.[142]

At dawn on 13 November, finding the capital empty of the Taliban, looters attacked and ransacked the Pakistani embassy, throwing files and papers into the street. Some of the documents showed Pakistan trying to persuade Mullah Omar to desist from terrorist activities and the Taliban dismissing US warnings relayed through Islamabad. "The Taliban seemed addicted to 'international jihad' as a means of mobilizing support and a distraction from their own shortcomings," said Pakistani ambassador Arif Ayub in his memorandum to the Foreign Ministry in January 2001. In an unsigned report, another Pakistani diplomat referred to "hard core, moderate and neutral" Taliban, with the hard core under Mullah Omar being in full control. "They receive funds from drug smugglers and [Islamic] charity trusts."[143] That day the Taliban closed its embassy in Islamabad, which signified its final diplomatic demise, and it lost Herat to Gen. Ismail Khan, who led his 4,000 troops in a pincer movement.[144] As a sign of confidence in the future, the exchange rate of the local currency improved dramatically, from Afghanis 60,000 to 1 US dollar to Afghanis 25,000. In New York the stock markets, averse to uncertainty, rose sharply with the fall of Kabul, which signaled the virtual end of the Afghan war.

Fittingly, it was a woman newsreader, Jamila Mujahid, who on the evening of 13 November announced on Radio Kabul (formerly Radio Shariat) the arrival in the capital of the National Alliance – more specifically, its Jamiat-e Islami faction. Its leaders explained that they had no intention of marching on Kabul, but once the Taliban had fled they had no option but to move in to fill the vacuum. They did so with 6,000 troops which entered the Tajik sector of the city, where the cheering and waving crowds welcomed them with flowers – and treated the accompanying Western journalists as personal envoys of the American air force whose bombs had brought about the Taliban defeat. The Jamiat-e Islami soldiers – calling themselves Mujahedin – guarded government buildings, including the presidential palace, set up check points, and distributed leaflets in the market, saying "Everybody is forgiven, Taliban or not, as long as he does not resist the Mujahedin." Other Jamiat troops, armed with machine guns and anti-tank rockets, drove around in Jeeps. Kabul now had ministers of defense (Muhammad Qasim Fahim, former intelligence chief of Ahmad Shah Masoud), foreign affairs (Abdullah Abdullah) and interior (Yunus Qanuni) – all of them Tajiks from the Panjshir valley.

With the Taliban's religious police gone, many men trimmed their beards but few removed them altogether. Some women lifted their burqas for Western television crews, and then dropped them. Most women stuck to their all-enveloping shrouds. "When we are sure the Taliban will not come back and there is security in the country then we will decide whether to remove the burqa [and return to Western dress]," said Nabila Hashimi, a former teacher. "During the Taliban rule, we were not allowed to leave home without a male chaperon, that means we were in jail." Vendors did brisk business selling Iranian and Indian songs on cassettes as well as razor blades. On 14 November television returned to restaurants, as did family portraits and glossy Indian movie posters in shops. Music shops clustered in Farashgar Street were open again and filled with young customers while the air vibrated with a cacophony of Afghan, Indian and Western tunes. In Chicken Street, jewelers unpacked their goods – silver jewel boxes, brooches, necklaces, earrings and bangles. Since the Taliban left behind no posters or graphics or statues that the liberated Kabulis could tear up, deface or topple, the visiting Western photographers and television teams had a problem capturing the fall of the Taliban visually. The only visible signs that the Taliban rule left behind were slogans on the walls: "A Nation of Martyrs will never be subjugated to colonialism." There were even very few archives in public offices as most Taliban officials issued orders on walkie-talkies or on scraps of paper. They had replaced professional civil servants with mullahs who had little idea of finance, planning or public works – or official records and correspondence."[145]

Abroad, the White House spokesman described President Bush as "very pleased with the progress of the war and the latest developments." Both Bush and Blair were also relieved that Kabul fell to the Northern Alliance before Ramadan. There was relief too in Riyadh especially when, in his speech to the UN General Assembly on 10 November, President Bush had said, "We are working toward a day when two states, Israel and Palestine, live peacefully together."[146] Crown Prince Abdullah found a way of reciprocating in public. On the eve of Ramadan, addressing senior religious and judicial officials, Abdullah said, "I hope you appreciate your responsibility before God, your people and officials, so we do not land in an embarrassing situation . . . I urge you to examine with restraint every word that leaves our mouths [because] Allah has said in the Quran: 'We have made you a moderate nation' . . . I ask you not to be swept away by emotion or be incited by anyone. The government will handle foreign affairs judiciously and without hasty decisions." In reply, the minister for Islamic affairs, Shaikh Salih bin Muhammad al Luhaidan, said: "Our duty to our guardians [i.e. House of Saud] is to listen and obey properly within the limits imposed on us by God, and to hold our tongues properly except for that which brings benefits to our country and Islamic nation (umma)."[147]

In contrast, Pakistani President Musharraf was shocked by the "occupation" of Kabul by the National Alliance, and urged that an international force should occupy Kabul, not the Alliance.[148]

"I order you to obey your commanders and not scatter here and there," said Mullah Omar to his troops in Pashto on his wireless communications system. "Any person who does so is like a slaughtered chicken which falls and dies. You should regroup, resist and fight."[149] The Taliban were trying to regroup in the south but, according to Rumsfeld, the leadership was "having some communications difficulty."

With the Taliban's command and control system in tatters, Mullah Omar's orders had little impact on the battlefield. On 14 November, the Taliban withdrew from Jalalabad, the capital of Nangarhar province, after minimal resistance, with the city falling to the elderly Gen. Yunus Khalis who, having been part of the Taliban, had only recently placed himself halfway between them and the Northern Alliance. The rest of the province went to the former Mujahedin commanders, their leader being Hajji Abdul Qadir. In the adjoining Logar province, Gulbuddin Hikmatyar's followers took charge. Khalis, Qadir and 200 other local leaders set up the Eastern Shura Council for Nangarhar, Logar, Gardez and Asadabad, the last two provinces falling to local tribal elders and warlords. Their collective political position was summarized by Yunus Khalis's son, Mujahid, a minister without portfolio, thus: "Bin Laden is neither our friend nor our enemy."[150] Sporadic US bombing continued. In one such instance, the Pentagon claimed to have killed Muhammad Atef in an air strike near Gardez as he was fleeing to Kandahar from Kabul on the night of 15 November.[151]

As Bin Laden's Al Qaida soldiers and the Taliban in the north regrouped in the Pushtun-majority city of Kunduz on 16 November, the Taliban lost the area north of Kandahar, including Uruzgan, to their adversaries. With this, the Pentagon focused on setting up a forward base on a rough airstrip, later named Camp Rhino, 19 miles (30 km) south-west of Kandahar, manned by Marines and Special Forces detachments to thwart escape by the defeated Tailban. It seemed the Pentagon was following the policy of "take no prisoners." In the words of Rumsfeld, "It is becoming less and less hospitable for Al Qaida and Taliban to be around. The US forces are killing the Taliban that won't surrender and the Al Qaida that are trying to move from one place to another."[152] That explained why the Pentagon rejected the offer of unconditional surrender by Al Qaida members in eastern Afghanistan.

The arrival on 17 November of Dushanbe-based Burhanuddin Rabbani, Afghanistan's former president, in Kabul – plastered with posters of Ahmad Shah Masoud, his defense minister, in every conceivable spot – followed by his installation in the king's palace, put a formal stamp on the defeat of the Taliban.

To the surprise of many, including the Americans, the Taliban unraveled with astonishing speed, with their control of over 90 percent of Afghanistan reduced to 20 percent during 9–16 November – their rise over seven years undone in seven days.

The Pentagon's swift victory stemmed primarily from its success in marrying high-technology weaponry with conventional ways of gathering intelligence, while avoiding the deployment of ground troops on a large scale by which the Soviets and the British, at different times in the past, had exposed themselves to deadly ambushes. Instead, the Pentagon successfully coordinated its long-range air power, reliable tactical intelligence from the ground, and several hundred highly mobile Special Forces troops (some of them riding horses like nineteenth century warriors), operating with much firepower and covered by electronic support – such as Predator drones armed with missiles – to safeguard them from ambushes. While implementing this complex, multi-faceted strategy, the top US policymakers proved flexible enough to alter the strategy swiftly if it failed to deliver the expected result, as happened during the Special Forces' large-scale night raid on 19–20 October in Kandahar. No such nimbleness was shown by the Taliban strategists. Having never been exposed to the kind of heavy, almost non-stop air raids that the Pentagon inflicted on them, the Taliban behaved like the classic Afghan fighters: bluster one day and melt away the next. Those who survived went home and threw away their distinguishing black turbans, or changed sides for money. In any case, once

Pakistan, having cut its umbilical cord with the Taliban, turned against them, they were doomed: their collapse was only a matter of time.

Within hours of the fall of Kabul, American CIA and British MI6 agents began searching the safe houses and their backyards used by the non-Afghan recruits of Al Qaida, Harkat al Ansar (renamed Harkat al Mujahedin after 1997) and Islamic Movement of Uzbekistan in the former diplomatic Karte Parwan neighborhood in the city center and elsewhere – among them the Defense Ministry building – and were soon followed by Western journalists. During their visits to four such houses in Karte Parwan on 14–15 November they found maps on the walls inscribed with the logo of two crossed Kalishnikovs below the Quran with the motto, "Jihad is our way." One of the maps had all Muslim countries – excepting secular Turkey – colored dark green, and another showed power plants not only in Europe but also in Asia and Africa. A map of Saudi Arabia showed the kingdom surrounded by small US, UK and French flags, with American military bases marked in Arabic: "Occupation of the Holy Lands of Islam by the Crusaders." The published and handwritten material in Arabic, Urdu, Pashto, Dari, Tajik, Uzbek, Turkish, Russian, English and German included bomb-making instructions, "Microsoft Flight Simulator 98 Computer Program', which simulates the experience of flying a commercial jet (a copy was found in hijacker Muhamamd Atta's luggage left behind at Boston's Logan airport), a list of flight schools in America, a sheet torn out of *Flying* magazine, listing flight schools in Florida, and studies of rocket fuel, thrust capabilities and concept models of a missile with radar stealth capability and high load capacity to a speed of Mach 2.4. (Though unnerving to a lay person, these studies were in the public domain.) A 100-page notebook, written by a recruit in Turkish, described an Al Qaida cell, being divided into four units – intelligence, logistics, security and execution – the pattern followed in the August 1998 US embassy bombings. Another notebook focused on assassinating leading Western leaders. Altogether the documents pointed to a network involving Algerians, Americans,

Bangladeshis, Britons, Bosnians, Canadians, Chechens, Chinese, Dagestanis, Egyptians, Filipinos, Iraqis, Jordanians, Krygyzs, Kuwaitis, Libyans, Moroccans, Pakistanis, Saudis, Somalis, Sudanese, Syrian, Tajiks, Turks, Uzbeks and Yemenis.[153]

A similar exercise occurred in Jalalabad on 18 November but only undertaken by the aides of Hazrat Ali after his appointment as the provincial minister of law and order. It was in the course of that search that they found a bin Laden video-tape dated 9 November that would provide credible proof of bin Laden's complicity in the September 11 attacks.

In its last bombing raid on Kabul on 14 November at 01.30 hours US warplanes hit the Al Jazeera TV bureau in a residential area next to a mosque, clearly a vengeful act. With that ended its hitherto unique role of providing news and images from within Afghanistan. The American charge of giving bin Laden a propaganda forum was rebutted by Al Jazeera's managing director, Muhammad Jassim al Ali, who argued that the channel had aired only that material of bin Laden which had news value for its Arabic-speaking audience. "We have five or six propaganda bin Laden tapes before September 11, which we never broadcast because they were not newsworthy," he said. He provided a few examples. In one tape, addressing the Muslim audience, bin Laden said, "Your rulers, your princes, your kings, your presidents, they go groveling to the enemy. But they will never be respected, or trusted or believed." In another such tape, he averred, "This is the first time since the days of Prophet Muhammad that an armed Christian presence has dared to soil our Holy Land." In a clear reference to the Quranic verse that forbids the shedding of innocent blood, which his critics often cited against him, bin Laden argued, "The enemy has no regard for your lives. The Americans and the West kill our innocents. We should have no regard for the lives of their innocents." Alluding to the Western colonization of Muslim countries, he said, "As they [Westerners] have always done they want to subvert Islam and keep us as slaves . . . For us to win paradise we must use all means to liberate ourselves.

Every time they kill us, we must kill them. Jihad is the only way to paradise."[154]

Post-Taliban Afghanistan

With the ouster of the Taliban from Kabul, the Bush administration's main military focus turned to capturing Kandahar, the headquarters of Mullah Omar, and destroying the Al Qaida infrastructure in the Afghan-Pakistan border region, while its diplomats concentrated on installing an interim government in the capital that would include representatives of all ethnic groups in proportion to their size in the national population – the subject of a meeting of all anti-Taliban factions in early December in Bonn, Germany.

Much to America's annoyance, Iran became the first country to reopen its embassy in Kabul – within 10 days of the departure of the Taliban, bitterly detested by Tehran. And Russia became the first foreign state to send a delegation to Kabul, with the Russian defense minister, Sergei Ivanov, referring to the Northern Alliance as "the legitimate government" of Afghanistan. In its meeting with Burhanuddin Rabbani, the delegation secured his permission to establish a "humanitarian and diplomatic" presence in the city. By late November there were 88 Russians, including diplomats, construction crews and mine-clearing experts, working to get the Russian embassy functioning where the old Soviet embassy used to be. "This is a long term strategy about security for Russia," explained Yuri Barazhnikov, deputy minister for emergencies at the Defense Ministry, in Kabul. "We are very interested in building peace in the region and security on Russia's southern border."[155]

The intensive bombardment of the area around the Tora Bora (lit. Black Dust) cave complex, about 25 miles (40 km) south-west of Jalalabad, resulted in unintended bombing of civilian sites. The cave fortresses and uphill dug-in positions up to 11,000 ft (3,500 m) high in Tora Bora had been built in the mid-1980s with the assistance of the CIA. The eight-cave complex existed at two levels – the lower one used for accommodating fighters, with the terrain then rising up to the Maliwa valley on to the higher-level caves providing shelter and housing for the partisans' families. Over the weekend of 1–2 December, US bombs and missiles struck four villages within 10 miles (15 km) of Tora Bora, killing 80 people, and angering the Eastern Shura Council. Due to the strikes on 1 December all 15 houses in Madoo village were razed and 55 people killed. Hajji Muhammad Zaman, the locally appointed commander, claimed that "hundreds" had died. The high civilian death toll had occurred because the Pentagon had relied for intelligence on the Kabul-based National Alliance, which lacked local expertise.[156]

On the domestic front, once Rabbani had declared that individual Taliban members might be allowed to participate in the transitional government, Muhammad Khaksar, former deputy interior minister, became an intermediary between the new rulers in Kabul and the besieged Taliban leaders in Kandahar, which was bombed by US warplanes six or seven times a day, and where Mullah Omar had taken to moving from location to location at night after his compound had been hit. So Khaksar's effort proved sterile.

Ever since entering Afghanistan clandestinely on 21 October, Hamid Karzai had been hard at work to cause defections in the Taliban camp while playing down his links with the Americans, aware that Afghans had little respect for those allying with non-Muslims, but he had made scant progress. On 1 November he survived a Taliban attack on his party in Dera Wat district of Uruzgan province, and had to tread carefully. After the Taliban's flight from Kabul, he based himself at a camp 10 miles (16 km) north of Kandahar and tried to arrange the surrender of the Taliban leaders in Kandahar.[157]

At the UN-sponsored conference of four major groups of Afghans in Bonn, being held to assemble an interim government for Afghanistan, Karzai was a member of the Rome group loyal to former monarch Muhammad Zahir Shah. Guided by Lakhdar Brahimi and Francesc Vendrell, the Afghan representatives deliberated in public while the American delegation led by James Dobbins, and including Zalmay Khalizad, the Afghan-American director for Afghanistan at the National Security Council, worked behind the scene inter alia with the Iranian delegation to forge a compromise. It came on 5 December. The conferees agreed to a 30-member cabinet under chairman Hamid Karzai, with five deputy chairs, one each to important ethnic groups, and including three women, one of them, Sima Samar, a Hazara. Of the 30 seats, 11 went to Pushtuns, 8 to Tajiks, 5 to Hazars, 3 to Uzbeks, and the rest to others. The Northern Alliance, composed of 8 factions, got 17 ministries and the monarchist group 9.

Ironically, just as Karzai was elected leader of the interim government, a B52 mistakenly attacked his entourage and the US Special Forces unit assisting it, killing 3 US Special Forces soldiers and 5 Afghans, and wounding 18, including Karzai. He tried to belittle his injury, referring to it as a mere "scratch on my face."[158]

Born in Kandahar in the affluent household of Abdul Ahad Karzai, the leader of the Popalzai tribal confederation related to the Durrani ruling family, Hamid was the fourth of seven sons. He was seven when his father became a senator following the promulgation of the 1964 constitution, and the family moved to Kabul. After high school, his father sent him to Simla University in northern India where he obtained a post-graduate degree in international relations in 1982. He joined Sayyid Ahmad Gailani's National Liberation Front of Afghanistan, a moderate faction of the Afghan Mujahedin Alliance, based in Peshawar. There he ran a rest house for the NLFA jihadis. He spent much time visiting his brothers who ran a chain of restaurants in leading American cities. His tenure as deputy foreign minister under President Rabbani in 1992 did not last long as he insisted on greater representation for Pushtuns in the government. In 1993 he survived an assassination attempt in which his driver was killed. He welcomed the arrival of the Taliban in 1996, expecting them to pacify the country and end foreign intervention. Though peace was restored, the rising influence of Pakistan and Osama bin Laden troubled him. He left Kabul to join his father, then settled in Quetta, and got in touch with Zahir Shah in Rome. When his father was gunned down in 1999, most probably by Taliban agents, he was elected head of the Popalzai tribal federation. In a bold move, he took his father's corpse to Kandahar at the head of a convoy of 300 vehicles to bury it on the family plot, and the Taliban left him alone.

Now, within 36 hours of Karzai being chosen as chairman of the interim government, and exactly two months after the start of the US bombing – around 02.00 hours on 7 December – Taliban leaders fled Kandahar after their fighters had surrendered to Commander Naqib Ullah. The last sighting of Mullah Omar had him taking off on a motor cycle into the dark night several days after he had dispatched his family to an unknown destination.

Soon the forces of Naqib Ullah as well as those of pro-US Commander Gul Agha Sherzai converged on Kandahar. Their soldiers resorted to looting, and began fighting one another. In the resulting mayhem, about 280 Al Qaida fighters, who had been holding out at Kandahar airport, were massacred and their corpses bulldozed into a nearby mass grave.[159] Karzai, who moved into the sprawling residence of Mullah Omar, noted for the murals of waterfalls and pastoral scenes on the compound walls, tried to mediate between the warring factions. He succeeded.

With the final collapse of the Taliban, there was much relief and satisfaction in Washington and London, which was to a large extent shared by Islamabad: its fear of the post-Taliban regime in Afghanistan being dominated by Tajiks and other ethnic minorities at the expense of Pushtuns had proved misplaced. For the US and the UK, the scenario of Muslims worldwide venting their rage against them for pummeling a poor, underdeveloped Afghanistan with high-tech weaponry too did not materialize. The active involvement of the anti-Taliban Afghans in the US-led war, followed by the spontaneous jubilation of Kabulis at the flight of the Taliban, indicated to many, Muslims and non-Muslims alike, that the oppressive Taliban regime was widely unpopular, a point repeatedly reiterated four years earlier by the neighboring Islamic Republic of Iran.

While President Bush could claim that he had delivered on his declaration that those who harbored terrorists would share in their fate, a closer examination of his war aims showed that they had not been accomplished fully. He was completely successful in preventing Afghanistan from harboring and sustaining international terrorism in the future since the infrastructure of the training camps was totally destroyed and the country's leadership replaced. He had a great deal of success in preventing the much-weakened Al Qaida from posing a continued threat to the West. But his success in bringing bin Laden and other Al Qaida leaders to justice was partial. Only Muhammad Atef was confirmed dead so far.

Therefore Washington's military focus now turned almost exclusively to catching bin Laden and other leaders of Al Qaida who, along with some 1,000 fighters, were believed to have taken refuge in the Tora Bora cave complex. On 7 December the Pentagon intensified its strikes, dropping Daisy Cutter bombs at cave entrances, with the aim of unleashing fire and shards of metal over large areas, and demoralizing Al Qaida partisans. After a week of relentless bombing, guided by US Special Forces, 2,000 anti-Taliban militia men undertook a hunt for Al Qaida fighters. This went on for a week.[160]

On 18 December US bombs and missiles fell silent for the first time since the war began – except for a brief respite on 12 October, a Friday – with the Bush administration overthrowing the Taliban regime, harboring the prime suspect bin Laden, within 100 days of September 11 when three hijacked planes, exploding in 80 minutes, shook the world. By then the State Department had reopened the American embassy in Kabul, closed on the eve of the Soviet withdrawal from Afghanistan in February 1989,[161] the background to which had been closely studied by Gen. Franks.

His decision to rely on local anti-Taliban soldiers stemmed less from his concern for American casualties than from a resolve not to repeat the mistakes of the Soviet Union which, by committing large ground troops in Afghanistan, had emerged as an invader. Franks wanted to conduct further operations in a way that would not damage the trust and goodwill of Afghans and others in the Muslim world that his campaign had so far managed to gain.

But the local Pushtun militias, while working with the Americans, could not give up their traditional ways of making deals for money and would not jeopardize the lives of fellow Muslims if they could avoid it. As a result, hundreds of Al Qaida fighters and their families, possibly including Ayman Zawahiri, escaped with the help of local tribal leaders either to the Shah-e Kot area 45 miles (70 km) south-west of Gardez, or into Pakistan. While the Pakistani authorities arrested 95 Al Qaida partisans as they crossed into their country in early December, it was widely believed that most Taliban cabinet ministers and top army officers and their families were surreptitiously allowed to enter Pakistan.[162]

Pakistan was publicly accused by India of harboring the Harkat al Mujahedin and Jaish-e Muhammad (Army of Prophet Muhammad) which, it claimed, were responsible for a terrorist attack on the Indian parliament on 13 December in which 12 people were killed.

But, in the Western media, this outrage was overshadowed by the release of the latest video-tape of bin Laden by Washington after weeks of internal debate.[163] The hour-long amateurish video-recording, containing a long conversation between bin Laden and a visiting 38-year-old preacher from Jiddah, Shaikh Khalid al Harbi – a veteran of the jihads in Afghanistan, Bosnia and Chechnya, where he lost his legs in fighting – was apparently meant for internal usage, to be shown to bin Laden's followers as evidence of Al Qaida's progress.[164]

The claims that the tape was a forgery or had been tampered with could not be sustained due to the verification by journalist Abdel Bari Atwan, an earlier interviewer of bin Laden, that the video contained the Saudi fugitive's image and voice, and the tape's wayward structure and amateurish production. Footage of the interview seemed to have been recorded over images of bin Laden and some of his children visiting the site of a downed US helicopter, which took up the first 40 minutes. This accounted for the poor sound and image quality in part of the footage. The interview started where the previous footage ended, but when the tape ran out, it appeared to have automatically rewound to the beginning, with the ongoing meeting being recorded over the previously-recorded material.

However, the English translation released by the administration was flawed and incomplete due to the Pentagon's Arabic translators' unfamiliarity with Saudi accents. A more accurate version, produced by Ali al Ahmad, director of the Saudi Institute in McLean, Virginia, was aired by ABC-NEWS a week later.

While describing the current situation in the Saudi kingdom, Harbi mentioned Shaikh Hamoud al Shuabi from Buraidah, who was the first cleric in Saudi Arabia to condone the US bombings (and who had since then died a natural death), and Shaikh Suleiman Ulwan, who called the attacks acts of jihad and the hijackers martyrs, and described any support for America as "sinful." Referring to the hijackers, nine of whom bin Laden mentioned in the course of the conversation, he said, "They were asked to obtain visas to America and Europe and several other countries." He laughed.

> The brothers who conducted the operations, all they knew was that they have a martyrdom operation. We asked each of them to go to America, but they did not know anything about the operation, not even one letter. We did not reveal the operation to them until they were there [in America] and just before they boarded the plane . . . The [hijacking] pilots did not know their fellow martyrs until they were walking fast toward the airplane gate that the operation was to hit the building.

Regarding the anticipated damage to the World Trade Center, bin Laden said:

> We sat down to calculate the amount of losses within the enemy and we expected the number to be those inside the plane, and for the World Trade Center towers, the number

of people that the plane would actually hit. But I was the most optimistic of all because of my experience in this profession and in this business. I said the fuel on the plane would melt the iron and the iron would lose its properties. Therefore the building will be destroyed from the point of impact upward. What actually happened was a lot more than we expected.

Harbi told his interlocutor, "Everybody praises what you did, the great action you did, which was first and foremost by the grace of Allah. This is the guidance of Allah and the blessed fruit of the Jihad . . . God has prepared a great reward for you for your work." Bin Laden turned to the foot soldiers of the jihad. "They [the hijackers] made the whole world listen to them whether Arab or non-Arab or Africans or Chinese. Better than millions of books, tapes or booklets."[165]

If the Bush administration's purpose in making public the video-tape was to convince the Western public (in general) or Americans (in particular) of Bin Laden's guilt, the move was superfluous. Most of them already held him responsible for the outrages of September 11. It was the Arab and Muslim world where skepticism was the rule rather than exception. "People in the region will say that the Americans used carpet-bombing in Afghanistan even before they had evidence against Bin Laden," averred Atwan. "They passed judgment against him first, and now they are producing the evidence." In short, the timing was wrong. "If the video had come out at the beginning of the American bombing campaign, it would have made a bigger impact," said Muhammad Salah of *Al Hayat*. "Now nobody is really paying much attention any more."[166]

There was yet another video-tape of bin Laden, 33 minutes long, that surfaced, and was aired on Al Jazeera TV on 27 December though recorded earlier – in bin Laden's words, "three months after the blessed attack against the international infidels and their leaders, America [on September 11], and two months after the beginning of the vicious aggression against Islam [on 7 October]'. Looking haggard and hollow-eyed, and

wearing a graying beard, he said, "It is very important to concentrate on hitting the American economy with every available
tool, given that the economy is the base of its military power,
so America will be too busy [repairing it] to bother with Islamic
fighters . . . Our terrorism is blessed terrorism to prevent the
unjust person from committing injustice and to stop American
support for Israel, which kills our sons." He said that the US-
led bombardment of Afghanistan showed "indescribable hatred
of Islam" by the West and the US. "In Nairobi when the brothers
– may God take them as martyrs – used a 2,000-kilo bomb, the
US said this was terrorism. Now the US is using bombs, each
weighing 7,000 kilos."[167]

Familiarity with bin Laden's rhetoric had resulted in his words
losing much of their potency as far as the Bush administration
was concerned. Nonetheless, it was disappointed to discover
that he had not perished in the relentless bombing of the Tora
Bora complex or fallen into the hands of the anti-Taliban forces.

9   Ongoing war against terror

An uncharted territory

With the Taliban removed from power, US policymakers began discussing the second phase of the war on terror. As expected, the hawks advanced their case for attacking Iraq even though the intelligence agencies' in-depth investigation of Baghdad's complicity in the September 11 attacks, ordered earlier by Bush, had yet to be completed. The doves remained skeptical of the wisdom of an anti-Iraq military campaign to overthrow President Saddam Hussein's regime.

Anyway, the debate got sidetracked by a daring terrorist assault on the Indian parliament in Delhi on 13 December. Five gunmen carrying grenades, Kalishnikov rifles and explosives went past the perimeter entrance gate to the mammoth, circular Parliament House – built on a high platform with chambers for both houses of the federal legislature – in a white car with a red flashing beacon on the roof, used typically by parliamentarians. But when their car hit another in front of the entrance used by the members of the Upper House, they drew attention to themselves. As they rushed up the steps, firing, they wounded an unarmed sentry guarding the huge carved door. Despite his injury, the sentry managed to close the door and raise the alarm on his wireless. Swiftly the other 11 entrances to the building were shut tight. In the fire fight that ensued on the steps of the Parliament House, four of the assailants were shot dead while the fifth, carrying explosives, blew himself up, and five policemen and sentries lost their lives, as did two civilians. The terrorists had planned on entering the building and massacring many of the 800-odd Indian parliamentary deputies, with their focus on the front benches of the Lower House, occupied by cabinet ministers. It transpired later that, aside from the car accident and resulting mayhem, the terrorists' plan had gone awry due to the quintessentially Delhi experience of sudden power cuts. Electricity failure on that morning deprived Muhammad Afzal, the sixth co-conspirator arrested later, of his task of sitting at home to watch all-news television and inform the terrorist team by mobile phone of the arrival of cabinet ministers, including Prime Minister Atal Behari Vajpayee. So Afzal did not know that the Lower House had adjourned five minutes after opening (due to the continued noisy protest by the opposition over the Defense Ministry scam of paying excessive sums for soldiers' coffins) and that the prime minister had therefore decided to stay at his official residence. When Afzal told the terrorists' leader in the car of the lack of access to 24-hour television news, the latter got angry, and went ahead with the assault.[1]

The official statement by Delhi described the event as "an attack on not just the symbol, but the seat, of Indian democracy and on the sovereignty of the Indian people." The American embassy called it "an outrageous act of terrorism" and "a brutal assault on the heart of Indian democracy."[2]

India blamed the Lashkar-e Taiba (Army of the Pious) and Jaish-e Muhammad (Army of Prophet Muhammad), both based in Pakistan, for the audacious attack, accusing Lashkar's Hafiz Muhammad Saeed (1947–) of being the mastermind. It called on Gen. Pervez Musharraf to outlaw them and freeze their assets. Pakistan condemned the attack, claiming that it had never allowed its soil to be used for terrorism, and spurned the Indian demand. By contrast, Washington proved receptive, and went on to ban the two organizations which, according to later Pakistani briefings to the American reporters, had been responsible for 70 percent of the attacks in Indian Kashmir.[3]

The Lashkar-e Taiba, founded in 1986, was the military wing of the Markaz al Daawa (Center of Islamic Call), which ran health and education programs, including an Islamic University at Mureedke, 25 miles (40 km) west of Lahore. Its curriculum included science, English, Arabic, Quranic studies and Jihad, and it urged its students to wage jihad wherever Muslims were oppressed – from Xinjian in western China to Chechnya to Bosnia to Afghanistan and the Indian-administered Kashmir, thus subscribing to the pan-Islamic thesis, which bin Laden would later adopt, albeit independently. In Mureedke and elsewhere, mosques and bazaars displayed posters urging jihad under the Lashkar-e Taiba and other radical Islamist groups, a call that appealed to many poor, devout Muslims. In April 2000 the Islamic University campus was the site of a one-day conference of 1,200 Pakistani ulama, belonging to the Markaz al Daawa, Harkat al Mujahedin, Jamiat-e Ulama-e Islami and Jamaat-e Islami, which called for a jihad to liberate Kashmiri Muslims from the rule of the Indian government which, according to them, was perpetrating "terrorism in uniform" against them.[4] The Lashkar did not limit their activity to Indian-administered Kashmir. Indeed in December its activists attacked a military post at the historic Red Fort in Delhi, a sensational act. The following month its assault on the airport of the Kashmiri capital of Srinagar left six terrorists and four others dead.[5]

Younger but equally lethal was the Jaish-e Muhammad, whose establishment in 1995 was attributed by some to Pakistan's Inter Services Intelligence directorate, and which focused almost exclusively on the Indian-administered Kashmir. It claimed responsibility for an attack on the Kashmiri parliament in Srinagar on 1 October 2001, in which 39 people died. Delhi urged Washington to outlaw Jaish-e Muhammad and freeze its assets, but the latter failed to do so.[6]

The Kashmir dispute and pan-Islamic jihad

Since the Indian subcontinent's partition into predominantly Muslim Pakistan and Hindu-majority India in August 1947 on the eve of the end of the British rule, the princely state of Jammu and Kashmir – or Kashmir, for short – has been a bone of contention between India and Pakistan.

Established in 1901 within its present (legal) boundaries, this princely state enjoying local autonomy, with 77 percent Muslim population, was ruled by a Hindu king. Sharing common borders with Pakistan and India, Maharaja Hari Singh Dogra had the choice to join either. To pre-empt his options, the predominantly Muslim inhabitants of the Poonch-Mirpur region established an independent government, and sought help from contiguous Pakistan to liberate the rest of the state. On 25 October 1947, as armed Pakistani tribals approached Srinagar, the maharaja, in consultation with Shaikh Muhammad Abdullah (1905–82), leader of the secular National Conference, acceded to India, with the princely state ceding authority to Delhi only in defense, foreign affairs and communications. India's governor-general, Lord Mountbatten, added the proviso that "as soon as law and order have been restored in Jammu and Kashmir and its soil cleared of the invader, the question of the State's accession should be referred to the people." India lodged a complaint with the UN Security Council that Pakistan had armed and abetted the tribals from its territory to attack Kashmir, and that it should vacate the gains of its aggression. Fighting continued until January 1949 when the UN-brokered ceasefire came into effect, leaving Pakistan with 37 percent of the territory and as much of the population – later named Azad Kashmir (Free Kashmir), with its capital at Muzaffarabad.

Hari Singh Dogra abdicated in favor of his son, Karan Singh Dogra, while Shaikh Abdullah remained the state's executive head. A special provision in the secular Indian constitution of 1950 accorded Kashmir the right to have its own constitution. The popularly elected Constituent Assembly began drafting it. When the pro-Indian elements in the assembly insisted on India's right to impose presidential rule if the need arose, tensions mounted. Karan Singh arrested Abdullah in 1953 and kept him imprisoned for 11 years.

With Pakistan signing a Mutual Security Pact with Washington in 1954, the Kashmir issue got sucked into Cold War politics, with the Soviet Union calling it "an integral part" of India. In 1957, when the Kashmir issue was raised at the Security Council,

Moscow vetoed the discussion, describing it as India's internal problem.

Kashmir's own constitution was promulgated in 1956. The elections held in 1957 and 1962 were rigged, as the successors to Abdullah, hand picked by Delhi, lacked popularity. In late 1963, Kashmiri Prime Minister Bakshi Ghulam Muhammad was replaced by Ghulam Muhammad Sadiq. He ingratiated himself with Delhi by agreeing to dilute Kashmir's autonomy.

In early 1965, Abdullah, who had been free for a year, called for a plebiscite to decide the state's future, and set up the Plebiscite Front. In September Pakistan attacked India to seize Kashmir, but the three-week war ended in a stalemate. The Indian government decided to whittle down Kashmir's autonomy further. As a result, the National Conference was dissolved and resurrected as the state unit of the Indian National Congress (INC). Abdullah was re-arrested. The 1967 election was rigged by the invalidation of the nomination papers of the opposition – consisting of pro-independence and pro-Pakistani elements – with the INC winning 21 of the 54 seats unopposed.

Islamabad's defeat in the 1971 Indo-Pakistan War, resulting in the secession of Pakistan's eastern wing, disheartened the opposition in Kashmir. Yet the March 1972 poll too was marred by manipulation at the behest of Delhi. After his release later that year, Abdullah revived the Plebiscite Front under the name of the United Front. In local elections it won 70 percent of the popular vote.

Abdullah demanded that all steps taken to integrate Kashmir into India since his first arrest in 1953 must be annulled. But he settled for a compromise with Delhi. He became the chief minister of Kashmir after he had disbanded the Plebiscite Front and re-formed the National Conference. In a rare, fair election in 1977, his National Conference won a majority of seats. Following his death in 1982, his son Farouq took over his mantle. But he lacked the charisma and popularity of his father. So Delhi blatantly rigged the 1987 poll to keep him in power.

This energized the Jammu and Kashmir Liberation Front (JKLF), which wanted an independent sovereign state and which kept its focus strictly on self-determination of the people of the territory irrespective of their religious affiliation. But in the pan-Islamist environment created by the intensifying anti-Soviet jihad in Afghanistan, it lost ground to such pro-Pakistan, Islamist groups as the Kashmir-based Hizb al Mujahedin (Party of Mujahedin), and the Pakistan-based Lashkar-e Taiba and Harkat al Ansar (an extremist breakaway faction of the older Jamiat-e Ulama-e Islami) and Jaish-e Muhammad – especially after the capture of Kabul by the Afghan Mujahedin in 1992. They increasingly resorted to assassinations, car bombings and assaults on villages, causing many civilian casualties. This, combined with its failure to accommodate the aspirations of the new generation of Kashmiri Muslims that had grown up in the post-Shaikh Abdullah period, led India to become increasingly repressive, which further aided the militant separatist cause. Delhi kept the unpopular Farouq Abdullah in power through rigged elections while pouring military and border security troops, assisted by armed police, into the troubled territory, and repeating ad nauseam that Kashmir was an integral part of India.

In turn Pakistan's civilian and military leaders decided to escalate the insurgency to make it increasingly painful for India to hold on to its part of Kashmir, and to concede a plebiscite for all of Jammu and Kashmir, now populated by 13 million people (9 million on the Indian side, and the rest on the Pakistani side), confident that a majority would opt for Pakistan. However, if such a referendum was to be conducted under UN auspices, then the Security Council's preconditions – Pakistan's withdrawal from its portion of Kashmir and reduction of the Indian military presence to the pre-1948–9 war level, in that order – would have to be met. There was no sign of either Pakistan or India agreeing to this, with Islamabad reckoning that if it vacated its part of Kashmir it would never be allowed to return irrespective of the outcome of the plebiscite, and Delhi's unwillingness to loosen its military grip, afraid that the Muslim population would then stage a popular uprising.

In late 1996, after its capture of Kabul and the eastern provinces, the Taliban fell in with the Pakistani plan by handing over Al Badr training camp near Khost to Harkat al Ansar. Typical of those who trained there was "Ghulam," a Kashmiri Muslim, who signed a two-year contract for Pakistani rupees 400,000 ($8,400) and underwent three months' training.[7] It was noteworthy that all those killed in the American air strikes on Afghanistan in August 1998 were Kashmiris or Pakistanis.

In Kashmir, meanwhile, insurgency and counter-insurgency continued, claiming between 30,000 and 45,000 mostly civilian lives during the 1990s, with Delhi saturating the territory with 400,000 military troops and security personnel. As mentioned before, the fighting between the insurgents, bolstered by regular Pakistani troops, and the Indian soldiers in the Kargil region in the spring of 1999 became so intense that there was fear of full-scale war between the nuclear-armed neighbors.[8]

Now, in the winter of 2001–2, once more, tension rose, when India deployed nearly half of its 1.2 million regular troops along its 1,810 mile (2,900 km) border with Pakistan, and put them as well as the Kashmir-based armed forces on the highest alert.[9] It reduced its diplomatic staff in Pakistan and unilaterally suspended rail and bus links with its neighbor. It demanded that Pakistan hand over 20 wanted terrorists living in its territory, 6 of them Pakistani citizens, including Muhammad Ibrahim Azhar, one of the hijackers of the Indian Airlines plane two years earlier, whose brother Masoud was leader of the Jaish-e Muhammad. In the absence of an extradition treaty between the two countries, Islamabad refused to do so, calling on India to pass on the evidence against six Pakistani nationals to it for further action. "The Indians are just trying to exact maximum advantage out of this global campaign against terrorism," said retired Pakistani Gen. Ali Quli Khan. "The current military buildup has only political objectives."[10]

Delhi's strategy was directed as much at Islamabad as it was at Washington, well aware that, as the aggrieved party, it held a high moral ground. While the Bush administration, committed to eradicating terrorism worldwide, had no option but to go along with India, it could not afford to be seen to be too rough on Pakistan's Musharraf, who had played a pivotal role in the overthrow of the Taliban regime, and whose continued cooperation was essential to destroy the remnants of the Taliban and Al Qaida. On the other hand, it could not deflect the irrefutable argument Delhi advanced. Placing Pakistan's support for the Lashkar and Jaish in the same category as its backing for the Taliban – with the ISI's Kashmir and Afghan cells being the respective primary engines behind these groups – India reasoned that Islamabad could not wage war on terrorism on its western frontier (Afghanistan) while supporting it on its eastern border (Kashmir).

America had no option but to pressure Pakistan, albeit in private. As a consequence, on 29 December, Gen. Musharraf banned the Lashkar-e Taiba and Jaish-e Muhammad, froze their assets, and arrested 250 activists, including Hafiz Saeed and Maulana Masoud Azhar. The Lashkar and Jaish moved their offices from Pakistan proper to the Pakistan-administered Azad Kashmir.

Then, to the surprise and relief of all, on 1 January 2002, India and Pakistan exchanged top-secret information on each other's nuclear facilities – providing their exact locations and functions – thus continuing their earlier, agreed annual practice.[11] This was all the more remarkable in view of the authoritative report published in the *New Yorker* on 5 November by Seymour Hersh that India, as well as America and Israel, was planning pre-emptive strikes to prevent Pakistan's nuclear weapons falling into the hands of the fundamentalist generals if they succeeded in overthrowing Musharraf. On his part, fearful of US strikes, Musharraf began relocating critical nuclear components within 48 hours of the 11 September attacks, and stored them away from the air bases and air corridors to be used later by the Pentagon. On 7 October, while reshuffling top military posts, he established the Strategic Planning Division for nuclear arms, with its head, Gen. Khalid Kidwai, functioning directly under him.[12]

But the exchange of information on nuclear arms did not dispel the chance of a conventional war. India insisted on evidence that Musharraf was dismantling the infrastructure that supported "cross-border terrorism" in Kashmir. In response, Musharraf's aides told the *New York Times* that the president had ordered the dissolution of the ISI wing involved with the armed groups that Pakistan supported in Kashmir, and that in future Islamabad would limit its backing for the Kashmiri freedom struggle to the groups rooted in Kashmir – such as Hizb al Mujahedin – and rely on Kashmiris to conduct military operations on their own while getting from Pakistan only moral and political support.[13]

India found this insufficient, with its army chief of staff, Gen. Sunderajan Padamnabhan, declaring that his country was "fully ready" for war with Pakistan.[14] Islamabad had no choice but to improve its military readiness. This, it discovered, could only be done by moving the Pakistani air force into Jacobabad and Pasni air bases which had earlier been handed over to the Pentagon, by then in control of a third of the country's air space.[15] Also most of the 60,000 Pakistani troops deployed along the Pakistan-Afghan frontier to aid the American search for bin Laden and Al Qaida would have to be redeployed along the Indian border, its military planners concluded. Such a scenario would go down badly in Washington, reckoned India, and might jeopardize the prospects of its purchase of US-made weapons-locating radar, warplanes and jet engines that had been agreed in principle after the Indo-American Defense Policy Group meeting in Delhi in December had decided to work jointly to counter such threats as the spread of weapons of mass destruction (WMD), international terrorism, narcotics trafficking and piracy.[16] It therefore took Washington's advice to wait for an important speech by Musharraf on 12 January.

As a preamble to that speech, Musharraf appointed a National Commission on Kashmir to rally world opinion in favor of Pakistan's stand in order to emphasize to Pakistanis his commitment to the Kashmiri cause. In his hour-long television address, Musharraf denounced sectarianism – violence between Sunnis and Shias – as much as terrorism. "Terrorism and sectarianism must come to an end," he declared. Besides the Lashkar-e Taiba and Jaish-e Muhamamd, he banned the Sunni extremist

Sipah-e Sahaba (responsible for killing 400 Shias) and Tahrik-e Nifaz-e Shariat Muhamamdi (Movement for the Establishment of Muhammad's Sharia) as well as the Shia Tahrik-e Fiqh Jaafaria (Movement for Imam Jaafar's Jurisprudence). Criticizing madressas for producing "half-baked minds" and "Kalashnikov culture," he pointed out that only 6–8,000 of them, a minority, were doing social welfare by sheltering 700,000 mainly male children. He required all madressas to register, add courses in modern subjects and restrict foreign students and teachers. He threatened strong action if mosques were used for political activities.[17]

Musharraf reiterated his commitment to Kashmiri self-determination. "Kashmir is in our blood," he said. "No Pakistani can afford to sever links with Kashmir . . . We will continue to extend our moral, political and diplomatic support to Kashmiris." But, he added, "No organization will be allowed to indulge in terrorism in the name of Kashmir."[18] This was the key. While maintaining his backing for self-determination for Kashmiris – the principle which, when applied to Indian Muslims, had resulted in the creation of Pakistan in 1947 – Musharraf disengaged it from the pan-Islamist movement to which, influenced by bin Laden and Taliban, the Harkat al Mujahedin, Lashkar-e Taiba and Jaish-e Muhammad had linked it in the 1990s. So, now, having earlier done a U-turn on the Taliban, Musharraf did something similar on the Kashmir issue, removing it from the pan-Islamist agenda and returning it to a bilateral, territorial issue with India.

In Washington, Powell immediately hailed Musharraf's speech for creating "the basis for the resolution of tensions between India and Pakistan through diplomatic and peaceful means," as he prepared to travel to South Asia, mindful of the appeal Musharraf made to the international community, especially America, regarding Kashmir: "Now you must play an active role in solving the Kashmir dispute for the sake of lasting peace and harmony in the region."[19]

After brief equivocation, Delhi responded positively. It noted approvingly Musharraf's campaign against the outlawed factions leading to the closure of 390 of their offices, and the detention of about 1,500 of their activists under the Maintenance of Public Order Ordinance, which authorized the police to detain a suspect for 30 days without charge. That, however, did not mean any change of heart on the part of those who had been formulating India's stance on the disputed territory, summarized thus by Vinod Mehta, editor of the Delhi-based *Outlook* newsweekly:

> The simplistic and failed strategy – crush terrorism through force – continued to be the main policy instrument. The obvious linkage between cross-border terrorism (would "guest" militants be as effective as they are they are without local hospitality?) and popular alienation was largely ignored. The irony is that all our "experts" are aware that no military solution to terrorism is possible. Yet, folly persists.[20]

Apparently, Delhi had its version of Rumsfelds and Wolfowitzes.

For now, however, the defusing of the Indo-Pakistan crisis allowed US policymakers to focus fully on the next phase in the anti-terror war, which had yet to be defined, while reviewing what had been achieved in Afghanistan so far.

The Afghan front

Washington could claim, rightly, that sustained bombing of Afghanistan by its air force had reduced Al Qaida training camps to rubble, and that Al Qaida and Taliban leaders were dead or on the run, with thousands of their fighters either dead or imprisoned. As a consequence of the information that the CIA had communicated to foreign governments, they had arrested or detained 500 suspected Al Qaida members. Following the UN Security Council's adoption of Resolution 1373, the Council had notified UN members in late October that within three months they must inform its Committee on Counter-terrorism of the legislative and executive measures they had taken to bring terrorists to justice and to prevent terrorist actions, and show that their law enforcement agencies were trying to freeze the assets of terrorists.[21]

On the eve of the inauguration of the interim government in Kabul on 22 December, the Security Council unanimously passed a resolution authorizing the deployment of an International Security Assistance Force (ISAF) in Afghanistan. The swearing-in ceremony of the 30-member cabinet, led by Hamid Karzai, was conducted in Pashto, Persian, Dari and Uzbek. The three Tajik leaders – Muhammad Fahim, Abdullah Abdullah and Yunus Qanuni – retained their earlier ad hoc positions respectively of defense, foreign and interior ministers, disappointing inter alia Gen. Abdul Rashid Dostum, who later had to make do as deputy defense minister. Typically, none of the speakers uttered a word of thanks for America. Missing from the assembly of some 2,000 invited tribal leaders was a group of 65 from the Gardez region. On their way to the capital to witness the ceremony, they died when their convoy was bombed by US warplanes at Sato Kandua village for seven hours on 20–21 December.[22]

In another such incident on the night of 29 December, American aircraft hit the village of Qala-e Niyazi 3 miles (5 km) north of Gardez, killing 62 to 100 people, most of them wedding guests. The Pentagon claimed that the village was harboring Taliban and Al Qaida leaders while the locals said that after the installation of the interim government in Kabul the Taliban and Al Qaida men fled from the area.[23]

Three months into the war, the Pentagon was still staging 100 sorties a day, but most of these provided close air support to the anti-Taliban troops or US Special Forces, now getting ready to attack cave complexes. While Washington continued to follow its policy of "take no prisoners," Afghans stuck to their traditional ways as described by Jalal Khan, the spokesman for Gul Agha Sherzai, governor of Kandahar: "From the very start we said when they [Taliban and Al Qaida troops] surrender and give up their guns and cars, they will be given amnesty."[24] This was the case in most of the Pushtun belt, where cooperation with the Pentagon was patchy and would remain so. Indeed, a few weeks later the Pushtun leaders in three eastern provinces of Paktia, Paktika and Khost would refuse to cooperate with the Pentagon's search for the Taliban and Al Qaida fighters, weapons caches and intelligence. Elsewhere the Karzai government held 7,000 Taliban and Al Qaida POWs.[25]

The Pentagon started striking routes not only into Afghanistan but also in the countries to its north as well as Pakistan. Its 101st Airborne Division arrived at Kandahar airport to relieve 1,500 Marines and hold the territory for months, even years, by establishing permanent bases and extensive supply systems. They had already done so at Bagram air base in Afghanistan – just as 10th Mountain Division had done at Khanabad air base in Uzbekistan where runways, lighting, communications, storage and housing facilities had been improved.[26] Moreover, the Pentagon had started constructing the air base at Manas 20 miles (30 km) from the Kyrgyz capital of Bishkek, which would become America's transportation hub in the region, with 3,000 American soldiers and squadrons of warplanes and support aircraft stationed there. The four Pakistani air bases under US control too were being upgraded at the Pentagon's expense. Along with this construction activity went the Pentagon's much expanded technical support and training exercises with its regional counterparts. "The bases and [military] exercises will send a message to all in the region that we have the capacity to come back, and we will come back, if need be," said Paul Wolfowitz.[27]

In mid-January, the Pentagon claimed that its week-long bombing of the Zhawar Killi complex of 50 caves and 60 buildings east of Khost had been a success. Following his visit to the bombed cave sites, Jon Swain of the *Sunday Times* wrote:

> I dropped down into a tunnel leading to the center of the mountain. New passageways opened to the left and right, each with rooms of varying sizes and significance. One was a storeroom filled with hundreds of new Russian helmets. Another contained rows of empty desks. There were tin trunks bulging with files and identity cards of Commander Jalaluddin Haqqani's fighters during his anti-Soviet war.

Among the material piled on shelves were land mines, detonators, mortar bombs and anti-aircraft barrels.

During the 1980s war, Zhawar Killi was the headquarters of Haqqani, who later became the Taliban's minister for tribal and frontier affairs.[28]

Against the background of the Afghan campaign, the debate among American policymakers on the next target(s) in the war against terrorism continued, with 45 countries harboring, according to the State Department, cells of Al Qaida and affiliated groups, being the candidates.

Future targets and the "axis of evil"

Of the countries on the State Department list, most attention was paid to Singapore, Malaysia, the Philippines, Indonesia, Somalia, Yemen and Iraq.

The police in Singapore claimed to have discovered an Al Qaida cell with possible links with individuals living in Muslim-majority Malaysia. The militant Abu Sayyaf group, active in Muslim-majority Mindanao and Basilan islands of the Philippines since the early 1990s, had grabbed international media headlines by abducting Western tourists from 2000 onwards. Given the close historic Filipino-American ties, it did not require much persuasion on Washington's part to have Manila accept its contingent of 600 Special Forces personnel to assist the Philippines in its campaign against the Abu Sayyaf group. But Indonesia, with the largest Muslim population in the world, was a different story. Though it was home to radical Islamist groups like Lashkar Jihad and Jamaah Islamiya, whose leader, Hambali, publicly admired bin Laden, the Bush administration shied away from putting them on the banned list in order to avoid implicit criticism of the government of President Megawati Seokarnoputri (r. 2001–). She had told Bush during her visit to Washington soon after 9/11 that the presence of US troops on her soil would destabilize her government.[29]

Somalia appeared on the Bush administration's terrorist radar because it lacked an effective central government and there were rumors of the country hosting training camps for terrorists. In Yemen though the central authority had emerged stronger after the 1994 civil war, it had failed to subdue fully the tribal chiefs in the distant mountainous regions who complained that their areas were being deprived of economic development. Yemen's mountainous terrain was seen as ideal for setting up training camps; and it also had the distinction of being the homeland of the bin Ladens and being contiguous with the Asir region of Saudi Arabia from where several of the 9/11 hijackers had come.

Finally there was Iraq. The swift victory in Afghanistan encouraged the hawks in Washington to turn to Iraq with renewed vigor. Baghdad was the particular obsession of Wolfowitz and Richard Perle, chairman of the 18-member Defense Policy Board, a bipartisan body of national security experts that advised the Pentagon.[30] Before the hawks could get into full swing, Colin Powell issued a word of caution. In an interview with the *Washington Post*, he said, "Iraq and Afghanistan are two different countries with two different regimes and two different military capabilities. They are so significantly different that you cannot take the Afghan model and immediately apply it to Iraq."[31]

Unlike Afghanistan, where the state barely impinged on the lives of most people living in villages, Iraq has been a strong centralized state ever since the overthrow of the monarchy in 1958. It has been ruled by the secular Baathist Party since 1968, and governed by the same leader, Saddam Hussein (1937– ; r. 1979–), since 1979. At the end of its eight-year war with Iran in the 1980s, its armed forces were more than a million strong. And within a few years of the humiliating defeat in the 1991 Gulf War, Saddam Hussein built up the shattered military to 350,000 troops. Furthermore, unlike Afghanistan, Iraq is part of the Arab world, where most political-diplomatic issues revolved around the Israeli–Palestinian conflict. So Washington's policy toward Iraq could not be devised in isolation from the latest state of play between Israelis and Palestinians. This simple axiom seemed to have escaped those presidential advisors who won the latest argument, which Bush, still maintaining an approval rating of more than 80 percent,[32] reflected in his State of the Union address to the US Congress on 29 January:

> My hope is that all nations will . . . eliminate the terrorist parasites who threaten their countries and our own. Our second goal is to prevent regimes that sponsor terror from threatening America or our friends and allies with weapons of mass destruction . . . North Korea is a regime arming with missiles and weapons of mass destruction, while starving its citizens. Iran aggressively pursues these weapons and exports terror . . . Iraq continues to flaunt its hostility toward America and to support terror . . . This is a regime that has something to hide from the civilized world. States like these, and their terrorist allies, constitute an axis of evil, arming to threaten the peace of the world.[33]

Bush's remarks about an "axis of evil" evoked largely adverse comments not only from Europeans but also many Americans, including Bill Clinton. "They may all be trouble, but they are different," he said. Support for sanctions against Iraq had fallen apart. "Iran has two governments now, progressive elements that the US can work with and hard-liners whose every move must be watched." On North Korea, he added, "I have a totally different take . . . I was ready to go to Pyongyang to close a deal on North Korea's missile program but had to stay in Washington on a last-minute Middle East peace initiative which fell apart."[34]

The "axis of evil" was not a coherent description of the perils facing America, said the *New York Observer*. Comparing Iraq, Iran and North Korea to the fascist axis of World War II was facile as these regimes had signed no pact of aggression against the West. Indeed, Iran and Iraq fought a protracted war not very long ago. Bush's "Divisive Bluster" has actually aggravated dangers facing America by provoking contempt among our closest allies such as the European Union with its policy of constructive engagement toward Iran[35] – a country which had only a week earlier promised $500 million aid to the Karzai government over the next five years at an international donors' conference on Afghanistan in Tokyo.[36]

In an interview with Radio France International, French foreign minister, Hubert Vedrine, said, "Today we are threatened by a new simplistic approach that reduces all the problems in the world to the struggle against terrorism." He urged Europeans to speak out more as they faced an America that "acts unilaterally, without consulting others, taking decisions based on its own view of the world and its own interests."[37] Rumsfeld's address to Nato defense ministers in December was a perfect example of wrapping up everything in terrorism's garb. Unveiling the military doctrine for "defense against terrorism," he urged fellow defense ministers to develop plans on how "to defend against cyber attacks, attacks on space assets and information networks, advanced conventional weapons . . . cruise missiles, ballistic missiles and nuclear, chemical and biological weapons of mass destruction."[38] With the advancement of computers and their growing indispensability to Western life, civilian and military, it had become imperative for Western authorities to devise ways of safeguarding their computer systems against virus and cyber assaults, long before the terrorist outrages against US embassies in East Africa in 1998. The successful attacks that many whizz-kid American hackers had mounted against the Pentagon's computer systems – as well as high-profile American corporations – since and before 1998 had nothing to do with terrorism and everything to do with hi-tech one-up-manship.

In any case, Vedrine's views were echoed by Chris Patten, the European Commissioner for international relations. In an interview with the *Guardian*, he attacked America for its "absolutist and simplistic" approach, and said, "There is more to be said for trying to engage and to draw these societies [of the 'axis of evil'] into the international communities than to cut them off." He called on EU leaders to raise their voices before Washington went into "unilateralist overdrive."[39]

But the one to speak up was the seniormost American Democrat senator, Tom Daschle, Senate majority leader. In a television interview, he cautioned against military action against Iraq and urged Bush to continue hunting for Al Qaida leaders. He sharply criticized Bush on his "axis of evil" statement, chided his administration for its incautious rhetoric, and warned against alienating allies and friends.[40]

Daschle's caution on Iraq had a constitutional ramification. Though the Congressional resolution on the terrorist attacks on America on 14 September 2001 gave wide powers to President Bush, constitutionally, only Congress could declare war – something it had done only five times: 1812 (against Britain), 1845 (against Mexico), 1898 (against Spain), 1916 (World War I) and 1941 (World War II).[41] The Senate majority leader was aware that after a long, exhaustive investigation, the US intelligence agencies had concluded that Iraq was not involved in the September 11 terrorist attacks – a conclusion that would be confirmed by a report of John Scarlett, chairman of Britain's Joint Intelligence Committee.[42] According to the long-time Saudi intelligence chief, Prince Turki, who possessed volumes of intelligence on Iraq and on bin Laden, "Iraq does not come very high in the estimations of bin Laden. He thinks of Saddam Hussein as an apostate, an infidel or someone who is not worthy of being a fellow Muslim."[43] Jamal al Fadl, the Al Qaida defector, repeatedly testified to the US authorities that bin Laden criticized Saddam Hussein "sometimes for attacking Muslims and killing women and children, but most importantly for not believing in 'most of Islam', and for setting up his own political party, the Baath."[44]

But Bush and his hawkish advisors were intransigent, aware that opinion polls showed 88 percent supporting military action against Iraq, up from the previous 78 percent. They argued that in his "axis of evil" remarks, Bush had set out markers for the future. "All the three countries I mentioned are now on notice that we intend to take their development of weapons of mass destruction very seriously," reiterated Bush. Later administration officials went on to explain that the US had to plan the prevention of the possibility of a terrorist group obtaining weapons of mass destruction from Iraq which retained the possibility (even probability) of acquiring them. This threat, built on two pre-conditions, was presented as something new. But it was not. The Clinton administration had considered this eventuality and appointed an advisory panel, called the Gilmore Commission, to examine the problem. In its report published in December 1999, it concluded: "The rogue states would hesitate to entrust such weapons to terrorists because of the likelihood that such a group's action might be unpredictable even to the point of using the weapon against its sponsor." Regarding the rogue states themselves, they would be reluctant to use such weapons due to "the prospect of significant reprisals."[45] What those "significant reprisals" would mean became perfectly clear by the end of 2001 in Taliban-administered Afghanistan, and also by the rigorous regime that the UN Security Council's Committee on Counter-terrorism was in the process of setting up in accordance with Resolution 1373. Under the circumstances, no leader of Iraq or any other member of the "axis of evil" would be foolhardy enough to pass on its weapons of mass destruction if and when he comes to possess them.

However, behind these essentially exaggerated statements lay an unexpressed plan to advance the neoconservative agenda of Bush and his coterie of hawks: increased spending on defense in the name of enhancing national security, the argument used during the four-and-a-half decade long Cold War. Sure enough, the $2,130 billion federal budget for October 2002–September 2003 that Bush presented to Congress on 4 February showed a 13.7 percent increase in defense expenditure – rising to to $379 billion – compared with 2 percent for education,[46] a subject he had stressed heavily in his election campaign. Most of the extra funding for the Pentagon was meant for developing and producing advanced conventional and nuclear weapons. How such weaponry would aid the fight against terrorists engaged, by and large, in guerrilla attacks often on property rather than persons remained unclear.

The State Department's breakdown of 304 incidents of "international terrorism" in 1997, in its *Patterns of Global Terrorism*, for example, showed that most attacks were directed against

commercial targets. Only about a third of these were aimed at
American targets, most of them being low-level bombings of
American corporation's oil pipelines in Colombia by members
of the left-wing Fuerzas Armadas Revolucionarias de Colombia
(FARC).[47]

The direction that President Bush had given to the battle
against terrorism, and its continued vagueness, worried not just
America's European and Arab allies, but also such senior
Congressional leaders as Senators Daschle and Robert C. Byrd
(Democrat, West Virginia).

'How will we win this war?" Byrd asked. "What are the costs?
What are the objectives? What are the standards by which we
measure victory? How long will we be in Afghanistan? Where
else will we go?" He pointed out that though the president was
the commander-in-chief, it was Congress that had the authority
to "provide for the common defense and general welfare, to
raise and support armies, and to declare war," and therefore it
had "a constitutional responsibility to weigh in on war-related
policy decisions."[48]

Byrd was critical of the way Bush had sidelined the law-makers
in the new war. Congress had been left to learn about "major war-
related decisions through newspaper articles," he complained.
"One day . . . advisors are heading for the Philippines. Another
day . . . into Georgia. The next day . . . into Yemen . . . We
also learn from the media that we have a shadow government
in our own backyard, composed of unknown bureaucrats, up
and running at undisclosed locations, for an indeterminate
length of time."[49]

In short, the uncharted territory into which Bush had led the
anti-terror war in the first six months caused concern and
worry both inside America and outside. Even the most unilateralist US president could not afford to ignore criticism leveled at
him by high-level American politicians for long.

10 Summary and conclusions

Two conclusions are self-evident in Part I of this book. Revival and reform have been recurring phenomena in Islamic history. And they manifest themselves differently in different circumstances.

Closely related to Islamic revival is the movement to return to the fundamental scriptures of the faith: the Quran and the practices of Prophet Muhammad as recorded in the Hadiths, which together form the Sharia (Islamic law). When it comes to applying the Sharia to the everyday life of Muslims, the choice is between taqlid – that is, dependence on or imitation of the opinions and interpretations of the ulama of the past – and ijtihad (independent interpretation), an ongoing process. By and large Islamic reformers, unlike the religious establishment, have reiterated the believer's right to practice ijtihad. This applies more to Sunnis than Shias: unlike Sunnism, Shiaism almost always kept the gates of ijtihad open. But irrespective of their sectarian persuasion, fundamentalist reformers have been unanimous that what the Quran offers is final, unique and most authentic, and that in Islam there is no room whatsoever for synthesizing the Quranic message with any non-Islamic doctrine or practice.

Thus fundamentalist reform means returning to the Sharia, creative interpretation of the Islamic law in the context of changing circumstances, and rejection of non-Islamic accretions to Islam.

The dynamic of fundamentalism derives from the conflict that exists between the egalitarian message of the Quran and the exploitation and iniquity of the real world, between the demands of virtuous existence made on the believer by the Sharia and the actuality of life surrounded by temptation and vice.

It was their commitment to the Quran and pious living that drove the Shia Ali, followers of Imam Ali, to struggle against his enemies. In that sense Shias were the first fundamentalists. Later, the rise of the pragmatic, yet despotic, Ummayyads was seen by true believers to be an affront to the teachings of Islam, and to bring about their downfall became the prime objective of the fundamentalists. They succeeded.

In subsequent centuries the Islamic community became vast and complex due to the spread of the faith throughout much of Asia, Africa and Europe, the firming up of the Sunni–Shia divide, the codification of the Sharia into four Sunni schools and one Shia, and the emergence of Sufism as a prime agent of popularizing Islam. Sufism included the heterodoxy of Al Hussein ibn Mansour al Hallaj as well as the orthodoxy of Abu Hamid Muhammad al Ghazali, who attempted to fit the mystical experience within the limits of the Sharia – a stance which has been consistently maintained by such Sufi orders as the Naqshbandi.

There was creative tension between popular Islam, as represented by Sufi brotherhoods, and establishment Islam, as represented by the ulama. Sufism itself had an uneasy existence between pure and syncretic versions of Islam. When the Mogul emperor Akbar, who was close to the Chisti Sufi order, launched Din Illahi in the late sixteenth century, it was an example of someone offering the world syncretic Islam, a development which elicited a frontal attack from Khwaja Abu al Muayyid al Baqibillah, a Naqshbandi leader: a position vehemently maintained by his disciple Shaikh Ahmad Sirhindi. He reaffirmed the Sufi orthodoxy that a true believer's mystical experiences had to adapt themselves to the Sharia. It was left to another Naqshbandi personality, Shah Waliullah, to combine an assault on syncretic Islam with one on establishment Islam by calling for perpetual ijtihad to cope with contemporary problems.

However, the credit for mounting simultaneous attacks on popular Islam, syncretic Islam and establishment Islam went to Muhammad ibn Abdul Wahhab in the mid-eighteenth century. He condemned Sufism as well as pre-Islamic practices and beliefs of the tribes in Najd, and upheld the believer's right to ijtihad. His uncompromising stance was molded by the social and geographical conditions of Najd. He functioned in a tribal society in an underpopulated central Arabian desert where Islam did not have to compete against any other well-developed religious creed – an environment vastly different from the populous Indian subcontinent with a long-established pantheistic Hindu civilization.

Abdul Wahhab and the Islamic reformers in India were grappling with doctrinal and other problems of the faith in an environment where Islam was either the only organized religion (as in Najd) or the dominant political-administrative force (as in India). But beginning in the mid-eighteenth century, as the Muslim world became increasingly subservient to the West and exposed to Western secular ideas, practices and political models, the situation changed substantially. Now fundamentalist reform acquired the twin task of releasing Islam from the legal-scholastic tradition of fossilized jurisprudence and purging it of the secular concepts which had penetrated Islam under the cloak of modernism.

The credit for conceiving Islam's global predicament and offering solutions must rest with Jamaluddin Afghani, the father of the modern Islamic reformist movement. Having lived in all the important countries of the Muslim world – as well as Britain, France and Russia – he acquired an unrivaled breadth of understanding. He propagated pan-Islamic ideas and called for a jihad against Britain and Russia, the leading European imperialists of the age. He advocated opening up the long-shut doors of ijtihad, and went on to pronounce the parliamentary system as being in line with basic Islamic tenets. He urged Muslims to study science and scientific method. Since he preached his gospel during a period of irreversible decline of the Ottoman empire, the seat of the caliphate, his message fell on receptive ears. In 1876 the Ottoman emperor became the first Muslim ruler in Islamic history to adopt a written constitution, albeit under political pressure from a powerful group called the Young Ottomans.

Muhammad Abdu, one of Afghani's disciples, interpreted the Islamic concept of shura (consultation) as parliamentary democracy, ijma (consensus) as public opinion and maslah (choosing that interpretation of the Sharia which causes maximum good) as utilitarianism. Finally Muhammad Rashid Rida, a disciple of Abdu, offered a blueprint of the modern Islamic state. Only a mujtahid, chosen by representatives of all Islamic sects, was qualified to rule this state. He needed the assistance of popular representatives to legislate, where the Sharia had to be supplemented by civil and administrative law (qanun), which was in tune with the spirit of broad Islamic teachings. The believers must obey the ruler so long as his actions were in line with Islamic precepts and served the common weal. When his decisions seemed to contravene Islamic principles or the public interest, the popular representatives must exercise their religious right to challenge him. Here was an outline of Islamic democracy well suited to the temper of the times.

Once Islamic reformers had offered political and other interpretations of the Sharia which took into account contemporary circumstances, it was only a matter of time before the tools of propagation and implementation of ideas employed by them too followed suit.

Hassan al Banna, for instance, went beyond pamphleteering and soliciting the support of the elites in Muslim countries, the techniques used by Afghani and Abdu. In tune with the times of mass participation in political movements, he engaged the attention and energies of ordinary Muslims and created in the late 1920s the Muslim Brotherhood, a popular party with a slogan which included the Quran, Prophet Muhammad, God, constitutional government and martyrdom. The timing was right too. The Muslim masses were feeling disheartened and bewildered at the disappearance of the thirteen-centuries-old caliphate, and the message disseminated by the Muslim Brotherhood gave them succor and hope. It also provided a countervailing force to the tide of secularism sweeping Egypt not only from the West but also from the post-caliphate Turkey of Mustafa Kemal Ataturk.

But Banna did more than found a mass party. By insisting that every branch of the Brotherhood should have its own mosque, center, school and club or home industry, he gave flesh to the idea that Islam is all-pervasive. By so doing, he also offered an institution which helped its predominantly poor and lower-middle-class membership to overcome the spiritual and social alienation it felt in an environment dominated by secular, Westernized classes.

Since then as economic development has accelerated in Muslim countries in the wake of political independence after World War II, and a dramatic rise in the mid-1970s in the price of oil – a mineral found in many Muslim states – cities have attracted vast numbers of migrants from villages. They feel lost and rootless in their new environment. This reservoir of alienated masses packed into the poor quarters of urban centers provides a ready audience and recruiting ground for radical and revolutionary groups, secular and religious.

Muslim fundamentalists try to rally the alienated and under-privileged on the basis of Islam, if they are allowed to function openly. They present it as a religion of justice and equity and decry the current ruling elite as unjust, un-Islamic and corrupt, deserving to be overthrown, or at the very least replaced non-violently, by true believers. The tactics used to achieve this objective vary: from setting up secret cells to addressing large congregations inside a mosque or outside, from bloody confrontations with the security forces to peaceful participation in elections, from carrying out terrorist actions to holding non-violent demonstrations, from subverting official institutions through infiltration to total withdrawal from society, from waging open warfare against an infidel state to conducting intelligent debate with secular adversaries.

As a rule large organizations tend to function openly and small ones clandestinely. One could argue that because certain bodies are not allowed to operate openly they remain small. On the other hand, a popular party such as the Muslim Brotherhood in Egypt had an underground apparatus even when it was permitted to function legally. But whatever the size and structure of a fundamentalist organization, or the intensity of its commitment to the cause, its ultimate goal remains to install a regime in the country that derives all its laws from the Sharia, allowing for different interpretations.

One way to accomplish this is by transforming social protest into a revolutionary movement, in stages, using Islamic symbols, language, customs and festivals. This is what happened in Iran, except that there was no Islamic party like the Muslim Brotherhood functioning there – instead, more significantly, there was a general body of Shia ulama with its own independent economic base and widespread network. Another path to the goal of installing an Islamic regime is for a fundamentalist group to assassinate the ruler (like Muhammad Anwar Sadat in Egypt) or capture an important holy shrine (such as the Grand Mosque in Mecca), hoping that the incident will trigger an uprising against the state, enabling the fundamentalist forces to seize power.

But whatever method is used the key element is the loyalty or otherwise of the military. The regimes in Egypt and Saudi Arabia survived the severe blows struck by radical fundamentalists because they continued to retain that loyalty.

Yet the corruption and oppression that drove the dissidents to violent actions remain in both Egypt and Saudi Arabia. Instead of allowing the moderate Muslim Brotherhood to participate in parliamentary politics by issuing it the required official license – a course recommended to President Hosni Mubarak inter alia by the Clinton administration – thus aiding it to mellow, as invariably happens when a radical group gets co-opted into the established order, the Egyptian leader continued to suppress it, using military courts and summary trials. The Brotherhood's militant offshoots, Gamaat al Islamiya and Al Jihad, were so severely repressed by the security forces and military courts that their activists sought refuge abroad. So, while Mubarak seemingly solved the problem of Islamist militancy at home, he exported it to other countries of the Mediterranean and beyond – thereby, inadvertently, aiding Al Qaida, a comparative latecomer on the Islamist scene, to set up an international network by merging with Al Jihad in 1998.

It was the corruption of the *nouveaux riches*, created by the economic liberalization introduced by Sadat, that so disgusted educated young men like Muhammad Atta that they were driven into the arms of extremist organizations like Al Jihad.

Corruption is not unique to Egypt or the Arab world. But if Egypt or Saudi Arabia were a multi-party democracy, the subject would be high on the agenda of competing political parties, as is the case now in the emerging democracies in the former Soviet bloc countries. By suppressing freedom of expression, the rulers of these leading Arab states – which for different reasons are *also* important players in the field of Islam as a political ideology – have driven underground the disaffection that exists among their nationals.

In material terms, though, Egypt, a poor, overpopulated country, and Saudi Arabia, sparsely populated and endowed with the globe's largest oil deposits, stand poles apart. In the post-monarchical era, Egyptian leaders have managed to cope with the poverty of their people either by raising popular, emotive slogans such as "Egypt as the leader of pan-Arabism" or by exporting their skilled manpower to oil-rich Arab states. In Saudi Arabia, on the other hand, to the alarm of its royal rulers, the per capita annual income has plummeted from $28,000 (on a par with America) to $7,000 within two decades.[1] In a country where unemployment among nationals was unknown a generation ago, the official figure now is 18 percent. Each year 100,000 Saudis are entering the job market which is creating only half as many jobs.[2] What the princes envisaged as long-term problems have already cropped up. Yet they persist in their mistaken belief that any political reform at the expense of their monopoly of power and privilege would result in them losing all – to commoners.

The House of Saud has frittered away several of its assets, material and otherwise. With the country possessing a quarter of the world's oil reserves, it had enough material resources to co-opt whatever opposition arose, whether among technocrats or dissident tribal leaders at home, or even opposition leaders in exile. Being the custodians of the holy shrines in Mecca and Medina gave it a unique status among Muslims throughout the globe. This also aided it in securing and maintaining the loyalty of the ulama who enjoyed higher rank and material well-being in its kingdom than anywhere else in the Sunni world. Following the shock of the 1979 Mecca insurrection by the revived Ikhwan, now preaching the (republican) salafiya doctrine, the kingdom sharpened and deepened its instruments of intelligence and coercion. It also managed to blunt the republican message from revolutionary Tehran by stressing the fact that those who ruled Iran were Shia, a sect held in low esteem by most Saudi Sunnis, by tightening up the enforcement of Islamic injunctions in the kingdom and by increasing religious input into education.

Though, by the early twenty-first century, the halcyon days of rocketing oil prices were long gone, the venal arrogance of princes remained undiminished. When asked about the widespread corruption of the Saudi royals by an interviewer on an American Public Broadcasting Service program, Prince Bandar replied that the royal family had spent nearly $400 billion to develop the kingdom. "If you tell me that while building this whole country . . . we misused or got corrupted with $50 billion, I'll tell you 'Yes' . . . So what? We did not invent corruption nor did those dissidents, who are so genius, discover it." [3] Actually, some dissidents reckon that the House of Saud has siphoned off 40 percent of the oil income, or about $160 billion. Since King Fahd alone is reportedly worth $18 billion,[4] this estimate is hardly exaggerated. Given the attitude encapsulated in Bandar's remark, it is not surprising that the efforts of Crown Prince Abdullah – the de facto ruler since King Fahd's severe illness in late 1995 – to get the royal princes, now numbering nearly 7,000, to refrain from dipping into public coffers through commissions on contracts etc., have met with little success.

While the material corruption of the Saudi royal house is by now an open secret at home and abroad, the kingdom's military links with America remain under wraps not only in Riyadh but also in Washington, where only a few top officials are in the know. "Military relationship with Saudi Arabia does not work when it gets a lot of attention," said Gen. Anthony Zinni, former commander-in-chief of the US Central Command. "It has to be quiet."[5]

It was the continued presence of US troops on Saudi soil *after* the 1991 Gulf War that was the starting point of the disaffection of Osama bin Laden, until then an integral part of Saudi Arabia's affluent commercial establishment, which a decade later would culminate in the most devastating attack on the American mainland in history. In a democratic Saudi Arabia, this contentious issue would have become an important part of the public debate, with rival political parties taking different positions. And even under the royal autocracy that exists in Saudi Arabia, allowing newspapers or marketing experts to conduct and publish public opinion polls would have revealed how much, or how little, support there was for American troops in Saudi territory.

With US troops, warplanes and other military hardware stationed in all the Gulf Arab monarchies, and the Fifth Fleet based in the island state of Bahrain, why does the Pentagon need to maintain military presence on Saudi soil?

The purpose(s) of this force need to be explained to Saudis as well as Americans at large. When King Fahd invited US troops to his kingdom on 6 August 1990, it was to bolster the Saudi defenses against the threat of an Iraqi invasion following Baghdad's occupation of Kuwait. Once the US-led coalition had expelled the Iraqis from Kuwait by March 1991, this mission was accomplished.

Not so, according to an unnamed Pentagon official, "who has worked with Saudi Arabia" and who talked to the *Washington Post* in mid-January 2002 against the background of continuing Riyadh–Washington bickering caused by the Saudi origins of most of the September 11 hijackers. Claiming that the US had promised to withdraw its contingent from the Saudi kingdom "when the job is done," the Pentagon official said: "Saudis interpreted that to mean the job of expelling Iraq from Kuwait [in 1990–1], but many US officials think the job remains undone as long as Saddam Hussein is in power in Baghdad."[6] In the case of such a dispute, it goes without saying that the host's interpretation must override the guest's.

The unofficial explanation offered by the State Department and the Pentagon for years has been that the purpose of the US warplanes stationed in Saudi Arabia, Kuwait and Bahrain – and the American troops required to operate and maintain them – was to conduct Operation Southern Watch, to enforce the air exclusion zone (for the Iraqi regime) in southern Iraq.

This rationale is flawed on three counts. One, since Washington has publicly acknowledged defense agreements with Kuwait and Bahrain, why not limit the stationing of US warplanes and troops to these countries, and exclude Saudi Arabia because of its special religious significance to Muslims worldwide? Two, the southern no-fly zone in Iraq was not imposed until August 1992 – 17 months *after* the end of the Gulf War – ostensibly to prevent the Iraqi government from persecuting the Shias of the region. So this could not have been the reason American aircraft were stationed in Saudi Arabia before that time. Finally, with one or two aircraft carriers of the US Fifth Fleet permanently plying in the Gulf, is there really a need to station US warplanes, including tank-killers, on Saudi soil?

For monitoring southern Iraq, the land-based planes only complement the ones parked on US aircraft carriers. There is no military reason why the Pentagon cannot shift the responsibility for monitoring the no-fly zone in southern Iraq exclusively to the aircraft carriers.

This makes one turn to examining seriously the explanation offered by those defense experts who claim inside knowledge of the joint Washington–Riyadh strategy devised and implemented after the armed uprising in Mecca in November 1979, which seriously threatened the Saudi royal family. In the case of an anti-royalist coup, they say, America would need 72 hours to marshal its full military might to reverse the coup. For many

years the Saudi Defense Ministry has been purchasing sophisticated weapons systems chiefly from America to bolster its
defenses. But the Pentagon was alarmed by a report by General
Norman Schwarzkopf, the commander of the US-led coalition
forces in the Gulf War, that the Saudi military, especially air
force, was incapable of operating the sophisticated weaponry it
possessed. Washington therefore considered it essential to base
its warplanes on Saudi soil for use in case of a national emergency
within the kingdom, these experts say. The presence of US
military officials at key Saudi defense facilities, often in civilian
clothes, too is regarded as indispensable in order to ensure swift
coordination and secure communications in such an emergency.[7]

Unexpectedly, the above explanation seemed more or less in
accord with what Colin Powell told Fox TV on 20 January
2002: "US military presence in Saudi Arabia might end only
when the world turned into the kind of place we dreamed of.
They [US forces] serve a useful purpose there as a deterrent to
Saddam Hussein, but beyond that as a symbol of American
presence and influence."[8]

Yet the days of the US troops on Saudi soil seemed numbered
in the aftermath of unprecedentedly bitter public exchanges
between Saudi princes and US officials, who leaked damaging
information to the American media, thus destroying the strict
confidentiality on which the Riyadh–Washington relationship
was built since 1932 when the Saudi kingdom was founded.
"Since September 11, America has lost the Saudi people," said
Dr. Abdul Rahman Al Zamil, chairman of the al Zamil business
group, to the *Sunday Times* in January 2002. "America tried to
convince people that they are here to protect the [Saudi] regime,
and that is garbage. Their presence is a liability to the Saudi
government."[9] The airing of such a view by an affluent businessman, who was also a member of the Consultative Council
appointed by the monarch, could only have happened with the
connivance of the royal family. Perceiving widespread opposition
to the presence of the American troops on the kingdom's soil,
Crown Prince Abdullah seemed to have decided to raise the
previously taboo issue in public, if only to signal to his subjects

that their views were being taken into account. On the other side, it finally dawned on Washington that any military advantage it had in operating warplanes from Saudi soil was heavily outweighed by the political cost. "Much of our presence is destabilizing to the [Saudi] government," admitted a senior commander in March. "The best thing we can do is to make a measured decrease in our presence. The dilemma we face now is that if we leave now, it looks like we are caving to Osama bin Laden's demands."[10] But bin Laden happened to be voicing a view held by many, if not most, Saudis who were denied the freedom of expression.

'Saudi Arabia's autocratic system, while convenient for negotiating arms and oil deals, is itself one of the root causes of Islamic extremism," noted the *Washington Post* on 12 November 2001 – which happened to be the day the Taliban fled Kabul, the capital of Afghanistan, where a sustained struggle by the fundamentalists to overthrow a secular regime succeeded primarily due to the immense military and financial backing that the Washington–Riyadh–Islamabad alliance provided it.

There were several reasons for the Afghan fundamentalists' lack of success on their own. Fundamentalism did not flower as a movement of protest against the repressive autocracy and corruption of the regimes of King Zahir Shah and President Daoud Khan, vaguely labeling themselves Islamic, but grew in reaction to an attempt by leftist military officers and intellectuals to transform the April 1978 military coup into a fully fledged Marxist revolution. Just as the leftist regime in Kabul found its powerful northern neighbor(s) – first the Soviet Union, then Uzbekistan and Tajikistan – indispensable to its survival so did the fundamentalist and traditional Islamic groups become deeply dependent on the Muslim neighbors of their country – Pakistan and Iran – as well as America and Saudi Arabia for their sustenance and growth. In short, Islamist leaders were not full masters of their movement.

Having created propitious conditions for the growth of Islamic fundamentalism by its extreme actions during the first 20 months of the 1978 revolution under the duo of Nur Muhammad Taraki and Hafizullah Amin, the leftist regime under Babrak Karmal and later Muhammad Najibullah retreated on socio-economic reform and secularization of society. Its policies activated previously dormant sections of society – urban illiterates, women and landless peasants – and this strengthened its hand. At the same time it did much to end the alienation that the ulama felt during the early months of the revolution. Being the paymaster of the ulama gave an advantage to the government, which it tried to use in winning tacit approval for its much-moderated policies. It succeeded at least partially in presenting itself as a genuine peace-seeker to an increasingly war-weary people without slackening in its counterinsurgency activities, including the bribing of border tribes along the Afghan-Pakistani frontier. It thus managed to hold on to the urban centers for three years after the withdrawal of Soviet troops in early 1989. In the end, it fell more due to the traditional Afghan traits of intrigue and sudden, dramatic switches than something politically or materially tangible.

The anti-Soviet jihad in Afghanistan turned Pakistan into a front-line state in the Cold War. Its military dictator, Gen. Muhammad Zia al Haq, lacking a popular base, encouraged the Islamization of state and society to build up a constituency for himself, and created a military–mullah nexus, which survived his assassination in 1988.

Just as the Soviet military intervention in Afghanistan in December 1979 was a turning point in the politics of the region, so were the Egyptian–Israeli accords at Camp David, brokered by US President Jimmy Carter, in September 1978 in the Middle East, the heartland of Islam. The bilateral peace treaty that President Sadat and Israeli Prime Minister Menachem Begin signed in March 1979 broke the unity that the members of the Arab League had maintained since the 1948–9 Arab–Israeli War, and violated the League's cardinal principle that Arabs would engage only in multilateral talks with Israel. This dealt a blow not only to the cause of Arabs in general and Palestinians in particular but also to Egypt's status as the fountainhead of Arab nationalism that President Gamal Abdul Nasser had carved out for it.

What made it worse was the blatant manner in which Sadat manipulated the state machinery and state-run media to produce a popular endorsement of his sudden turnaround on Israel.[11] When, following the signing of the peace treaty with Israel, Egypt was suspended from not only the Arab League but also the Islamic Conference Organization, Sadat dissolved parliament two years short of its normal tenure. Outside parliament the treaty was opposed by Islamists, represented in the main by the Muslim Brotherhood, as well as leftists. Inside parliament whatever the deputies said against the treaty went unreported in the state-controlled media. Having won parliamentary approval, Sadat put the issue before the electorate along with a string of such disparate subjects as a Bill of Rights etc., in a referendum, with the voter required to respond to all the questions with a single yes or no. On 19 April 1978, 99.1 percent of those voting said yes. In June Sadat blatantly rigged the first multi-party election in Egypt since the 1952 coup, with his National Democratic Party securing 83 percent of the seats.[12] In a free and fair election, open to the Brotherhood, it would have beaten Sadat's NDP. The depth and persistence of popular disapproval of Egypt's bilateral peace with Israel is illustrated by the fact that nearly a quarter century after the treaty, peace between the two neighbors remained cold and had not trickled down even to the level of academics and intellectuals.

Sadat's betrayal of the Arab cause and negation of the popular will marked the germination of Islamist militancy and terrorism which resulted in his assassination and much greater violence and bloodshed later as Muslim extremists from Egypt and elsewhere acquired lethal terrorist skills by joining the anti-Soviet jihad in Afghanistan in the 1980s – a campaign in which America, the strategic ally of Israel, played a pivotal role, hailing such jihadis as freedom fighters. With Riyadh, allied closely with Washington, combining its financial and other backing for the anti-Moscow campaign with active encouragement to Saudi individuals and non-governmental organizations to do so, the process of gradual "privatization" of the jihad got started, a process that would culminate in the founding of Al Qaida network and terrorist attacks on America, with the Taliban-ruled Afghanistan turning into an incubator of Islamist terrorists worldwide.

In the 1980s the training imparted to the jihadis by Pakistan's Inter Services Intelligence, working in conjunction with the CIA, included both military skills and political education, which emphasized Islam and nationalism, and was directed against Soviet imperialism. On their return home to Egypt or Saudi Arabia, the non-Afghan veterans of the victorious anti-Soviet jihad, possessing heightened political consciousness, soon concluded that their countries were dominated by America to the extent of being its client states. And so they turned their terrorist skills, acquired at the expense of the ISI–CIA, against their own rulers in their struggle against (what to them seemed) American imperialism.

This happened in the aftermath of the collapse of the Soviet Union in 1991, which inter alia changed the parameters of the Washington–Riyadh relationship. During the Cold War, America co-opted religion and religious groups in both the Christian and Muslim worlds in its battle against Soviet Communism. One of the earliest tasks that the CIA, established in 1947, performed was to co-opt the Pope and the Catholic hierarchy in its successful campaign to defeat the Communists in Italy's 1948 general election. So, as the oldest Islamic fundamentalist state in the world, Saudi Arabia, also staunchly anti-Communist, had an important part to play in America's global strategy. Free from the constraints of accountability, and checks and balances, of a democratic polity that exist in America, the House of Saud did what it liked, funding pro-American groups not only in the Muslim world but also in Angola, Mozambique and Nicaragua.

In ideological terms, though, the Soviet Union's demise meant that Islamic fundamentalism ceased to be an important tool in the armory of the US.

With this, the contradiction between Riyadh, staunchly anti-Zionist, and Washington, the underwriter of Israel, that had existed all along could no longer be ignored, especially when it was imperative for the House of Saud to keep on board the Wahhabi religious establishment which underscores its legitimacy. So long as the Palestine Liberation Organization and Israel were pursuing the path of peace opened up by the 1993 Oslo Accords, the Saudi royals had little difficulty in maintaining close economic, military and intelligence ties with Washington. But the second Palestinian intifada (uprising) that erupted in September 2000, in which the US, particularly after George W. Bush's election as president, increasingly sided with Israel as the Israeli–Palestinian conflict escalated, meant that they found themselves in an invidious position both at home and in the Arab world.

Riyadh–Washington relations soured after 9/11, when 15 of the 19 hijackers turned out to be Saudi nationals. News reports and comments in the US print media, often inspired by off-the-record briefings by US officials, held that Saudi Arabia had been complicit in terrorism, that it paid "protection" money to bin Laden supporters, and that the Saudi educational system had too much religion, which inter alia taught hatred of non-Muslims. This reached a point when even the most pro-American senior prince, Sultan ibn Abdul Aziz, defense minister since 1964 and next in line for the throne after Abdullah, fulminated in public. "The media blitz [in America] against the kingdom is not in the interests of the United States," he said in December 2001. He surmised that it was the result of Riyadh's support for the Palestinians, voiced by Abdullah in his letter to Bush in late August to which Bush's response had been "rational." The more recent moves by his administration to back the Israeli government of Ariel Sharon (1928– ; r. 2001–), he added, had been influenced by Zionist pressure. "International Zionism will never become our friend in any way unless we become our own enemy."[13]

The next month, in his interview with the *Washington Post*, Crown Prince Abdullah focused on the Israeli–Palestinian conflict. "We see [Palestinian] children being shot at, buildings being destroyed, trees uprooted, people encircled, territories closed and women killed, unborn babies being delivered at checkpoints', he said. "These are very painful images. And when we worry about the future, and we worry about the causes that lead people to become violent, the reasons that lead people to become suicide bombers, these are the reasons they do so."[14]

Abdullah thus became the latest Arab leader to advise US policymakers to examine the root causes of terrorism, implying that they should pay as much attention to tackling the causes as they do to eradicating the symptoms. The counsel was overdue. European reporters based in America had noticed the almost total absence of serious discussion there of poverty, bad governance in the Muslim and Arab world, the Israeli–Palestinian issue, the suffering inflicted on Iraqis by economic sanctions, or the presence of American troops in Saudi Arabia as the causes of Islamist terrorism. "You will find more opinion pieces on airport X-ray machines and new check-in procedures than about global injustice," noted Jonathan Freedland of the *Guardian*.[15]

Since Europe had been plagued with terrorism for more than 30 years – emanating primarily from radical nationalist groups such as ETA (Euskadi Ta Akalasuna, Freedom for Basque Homeland) in Spain, and the IRA (Irish Republican Army) in the United Kingdom, or extreme leftists such as Brigate Rosse (Red Brigade) in Italy – Europeans had long experience in tackling it by combining suppression with a political resolution of the root cause.[16] By successfully redressing the grievances of the Catholic minority suffering discrimination by the Protestant majority, the British government had succeeded in co-opting Sinn Fein, the political wing of the IRA, in running the province of Northern Ireland in coalition with its Protestant adversaries.

European leaders were swift in offering sympathy and help to the American people and government after the devastating attacks of 9/11. Several European members of Nato offered military assistance to the US in its planned strikes against Afghanistan, but Washington took on board only Britain.

Most Europeans expected that the traumatic experience would lead the Bush administration to adopt a multilateralist policy in world affairs, and scrap its unilateralist stance, as signaled by its refusal to mediate peace talks between Israelis and Palestinians; its abandoning of the Kyoto treaty on global warming and the Comprehensive Test Ban Treaty (CTBT) on nuclear weapons; its walking-out of the negotiations to outlaw biological weapons; and its decision to forge ahead with its National Missile Defense (NMD) program despite opposition from its allies as well as rivals. But they were soon to be disappointed.

France and Germany discovered that the anti-terror coalition they had joined had not turned out to be a discussion forum of equal voices. Instead, it had proved to be more like a meeting hall where Washington assigned exact tasks to each of the coalition members, taking care not to ask too much of most of its allies, and even hurting some by not asking anything at all. Washington had treated the United Nations in a similar fashion too. Having secured a unanimous Security Council Resolution 1368 on the September 11 attacks, Washington never mentioned it before, during or after its Afghan war. In the words of the Munich-based *Sueddeutsche Zeitung* (South German Newspaper): "America the world power has rediscovered the United Nations system, but is following the raisin-in-the-cake theory of picking out what looks good and tossing most of the rest aside."[17]

Even within the 19-member North Atlantic Treaty Organization, which offered sympathy and cooperation to the US in the immediate aftermath of the tragedy of September 11, questions were being asked about America's conversion to multilateralism

The gap between Europe and America widened when, having trounced the Taliban, Bush looked around for fresh targets, with his officials leaking plans for a military campaign against Iraq, involving 200,000 US ground troops, to overthrow Saddam Hussein's regime. As Iraq had no proven connection with the September 11 attacks, and as the UN Security Council had been dealing with it before and since the 1991 Gulf War, this saber-rattling by Washington unsettled many European leaders.

'The stunning and unexpectedly rapid success of the military campaign in Afghanistan was a tribute to American capacity," wrote Chris Patten, the European Commissioner for international relations, in the *Financial Times*. "But it has reinforced some dangerous instincts: that the projection of military power is the only basis of security; that the US can rely on no one but itself; and that the allies may be useful as an Optional Extra."[18] The French foreign minister, Hubert Vedrine, was more forthright. "Washington's single minded drive to broaden the war against terrorism was wrong headed because it failed to consider the root of terrorism," he said. "You have to tackle the root causes, the [political] situations, the poverty."[19]

It seemed the Bush administration was rushing to fill in the threat vacuum, created by the Soviet Union's demise, with terrorism – and in the process furthering the neoconservative agenda of increased expense on defense and the revival of the national security state. In the case of fighting the Soviet bloc, there was a group of independent, sovereign states committed to the ideology of Marxism–Leninism, which had to be defeated.

Now, by contrast, there was no bloc of independent, sovereign states run according to the ideology of terrorism. Unlike fascism, capitalism or socialism, terrorism is not an ideology. It is a method which is open for deployment not only by individuals or groups but also by governments. Indeed the term entered political vocabulary two centuries ago as part of the "Reign of Terror" (1793–4), unleashed by the government of the Republic of France, established a year earlier by the French revolutionaries, when about 12,000 people were executed as counter-revolutionaries.

Yet, those being briefed by President Bush at his Oval Office in the White House on 18 October 2001 heard him say: "So long as anybody is terrorizing established governments, there needs to be a war."[20] This is a recipe for war without end. America or India or China can defeat particular enemies practicing terrorism without necessarily removing the cause(s) that brought them into existence. And, by tightening national laws and increasing international cooperation, UN members can discourage terrorism. But terrorism as a tactical – or even strategic – tool to gain personal, social or political ends can never be eliminated.

While Bush and his cabinet officials were making sweeping statements about war on terror, none of them had offered a universally accepted definition of terrorism. Indeed, had Bush asked for a briefing on the subject he would have discovered three different definitions. According to the Defense Department, "Terrorism is the calculated use of violence or the threat of violence to inculcate fear, intended to coerce or intimidate governments or societies as to the pursuit of goals that are generally political, religious or ideological." According to the State Department, "Terrorism is premeditated, politically motivated violence perpetrated against non-combatant targets by subnational groups or clandestine agents, usually intended to influence an audience." Finally, according to the Justice Department's FBI, "Terrorism is the unlawful use of force or violence against persons or property to intimidate or coerce a government, the civilian population, or any segment thereof, in furtherance of political or social objectives." None of these matched the definition used by the British government in the Prevention of Terrorism Act 2000: "The use or threat, for the purpose of advancing a political, religious or ideological cause of action which involves serious violence against any person or property, endangers the life of any person or creates a serious risk to the health or safety of the public or section of the public."[21] Britain's definition is very wide. But its sovereign government has the right to define and apply it anyway it likes.

But since terrorism is an international phenomenon and since countries like India have been victims of "cross-border" terrorism, a globally accepted definition is the first step that the United Nations must take, daunting though it may be. After three days of intense debate in April 2002, the foreign ministers of the 57-member Islamic Conference Organization meeting in Kuala Lumpur failed to agree on "what amounts to an act of terror, what amounts to terrorism." Their final communiqué, however, called for an internationally agreed definition of terrorism that differentiated it from "the resistance of people under colonial or foreign occupation." It specifically rejected "any attempt to link terrorism to the struggle of the Palestinian people in the exercise of their right to establish their independent state."[22]

This was the nub of the problem, the wide gap that existed between the Muslim world, as represented by ICO, the pan-Islamic institution of intergovernmental cooperation, and America, on the relationship, if any, between terrorism and resistance to military or colonial occupation. On the one hand there was US national security advisor Condoleezza Rice saying, "You cannot help us with Al Qaida and hug Hizbollah [of Lebanon] or [Palestinian] Hamas."[23] On the other hand, there was Lebanon's finance minister, Fuad Siniora, stating, "Lebanon's stance is that there is a difference between defining terrorism and the groups that seek to liberate their countries."[24] He therefore refused to freeze the assets of Hizbollah which was included in the US list of 22 terrorist organizations on 2 November 2001. Hizbollah had 13 members in parliament, and ran 12 schools and 4 hospitals and many small health clinics. During his visit to the country as a member of a US Congressional delegation, Darrell Issa, a Lebanese-American, said, "You must differentiate between any organization working here [in Lebanon] from other organizations that might have a global reach."[25] It turned out that US officials had raked up Hizbollah's alleged misdeeds in the mid-1980s, following the group's establishment to end Israel's occupation of south Lebanon in the wake of its invasion of Lebanon in June 1982.

In that case it would be fair to examine not just the general US policy in the 1980s of fostering terrorist insurgency in Afghanistan or Nicaragua, but the specific instance of running the School of Americas (SOA) – nicknamed "School of Assassins" by its critics – for training military officers from Latin America at Fort Gulick in the Panama Canal Zone from 1946 to 1984, and then transferred to Fort Benning, near Columbus, Georgia. "More than 500 soldiers who had received training at the academy have since been held responsible for some of the most hideous atrocities carried out in countries in the region during the years they were racked by civil wars and since," reported Christine Toomey in the *Sunday Times Magazine* in November 2001. They included such dictators as Manuel Noreiga and Omar Torrijos (Panama), Anastasio Somoza (Nicaragua), Leopoldo Galtieri (Argentina), Gens. Hector Gramajo and Manuel Antonio Callejas (Guatemala), and Hugo Banzar Suarez (Bolivia) – as well as Roberto D'Aubisson, leader of right-wing death squads (El Salvador).[26]

Following a brief reference, in a 1996 government report to an earlier Pentagon investigation into CIA operations in Central America, to "improper instruction material" used to train Latin American officers from 1982 to 1991, Congressman Joseph Kennedy managed under the Freedom of Information Act to have seven manuals, written in Spanish, released. Called "torture manuals," used for counterintelligence instructions, they described the most effective ways of recruiting and controlling informants – arresting and beating their relatives, if necessary, extortion, blackmail, false imprisonment, administering truth serum intravenously, and so on – as well as "neutralizing" – a euphemism for killing – an opponent. These training manuals were distributed widely throughout Latin America by mobile teams of US intelligence advisors. "They were teaching this stuff for 35 years at the SOA," said Retd. Maj. Joseph Blair, who gave Toomey a six-hour exposition of the series of abuses that occurred at the SOA.[27] Much of the text in these manuals was derived from the training manuals used for US counterintelligence instruction in South Vietnam (1963–1975), where the national liberation movement of the Vietnamese people had started with their struggle against their French colonial masters after World War II.

It was to the French Resistance during the Nazi occupation of France – held legitimate by international law – that Syrian President Bashar Assad referred at his joint press conference with British Premier Tony Blair in Damascus in October 2001. "Resisting occupation is an international right," he said. "An act of resistance is different from an act of terrorism."[28]

Arabs were not the only ones to point out that Nelson Mandela, engaged in the liberation of non-whites from the apartheid regime in South Africa (1948–94), was described as a "terrorist" not only by his government but also by those of Britain and America. Then there was Gen. Pervez Musharraf of Pakistan who, while playing a pivotal role in the downfall and eradication of Al Qaida and the Taliban, remained steadfast in securing the right of self-determination for Kashmiris, although not by violent means.

There was also a substantial body of opinion in the Arab and Muslim world which shared bin Laden's views on terrorism. Referring to the September 11 attacks in a video-taped interview, he said, "It is what we instigated, for a while, in self-defense . . . And it was in revenge for our people killed in Palestine and Iraq . . . So if avenging the killing of our people is terrorism, let history be a witness that we are terrorists . . . Every time they kill us, we kill them, so the balance of terror is achieved."[29] By "we," he meant Muslims, and by "them," he meant Christians and Jews, or the West.

During a visit to Berlin in late September 2001, Italian Prime Minister Silvio Berlusconi (r. 2001–) told an on-the-record press conference,

> We should be confident of the superiority of our civilization, which consists of a value system that has given people widespread prosperity in those countries that embrace it, and guarantees respect for human rights and religion. This respect certainly does not exist in Islamic countries. [Therefore] the West is bound to occidentalize [the rest of the world] and conquer new people. It has [already] done it with the Communist world and part of the Islamic world, but unfortunately part of the Islamic world is 1,400 years behind. From that point of view, we must be conscious of the strength and force of our civilization.

He then suggested that "Europe must reconstitute itself on the basis of its Christian roots."[30]

This led to a storm of protest from the Muslim and Arab world as well as many European leaders. "His remarks are lacking in logic, and he has much to learn about Islamic civilization," said Amr Mousa, secretary-general of the Arab League. "His remarks are indecent and racist, and we expect apologies from the Italian government." Belgian Prime Minister Guy Verhofstadt, the European Union's current chairman, averred that, "Affirmations like these can dangerously enhance a feeling of humiliation that could lead to the division between the two worlds." And the president of the European Commission, Romano Prodi, an Italian, declared: "We are equal, we have the same rights, the same history, and we have given the same contribution to humanity, especially in the Mediterranean area, where dialogue is founded on peace and cooperation."[31]

Facing the flak, Berlusconi told the Italian Senate, "I am sorry that some of the words dragged out of the general context, interpreted wrongly, could have offended my Arab and Muslim friends." But there was no "wrong interpretation" whatsoever. It emerged later that at the closed-door EU summit on 21 September, Berlusconi had launched "a tirade against Muslims," saying, "We must protect our civilization and spread the message of its advantages." Little wonder that, after expressing sorrow to the Senate, he added: "I will continue to want to be sincere . . . saying what I think and what the great Italian public think."[32]

The net result of this incident was that a frank – and ultimately fruitful – debate on the vital subject of Western (Judeo-Christian) and Islamic civilizations was squashed because of the timing: Washington was frantically trying to assemble a coalition in which such Muslim countries as Pakistan, Uzbekistan, Tajikistan and Saudi Arabia had important military and intelligence roles to play.

On both sides of the religious divide, moderate leaders tried to gain the initiative. Referring to the specific circumstances under which the 9/11 attacks occurred, Prince Nayif, the Saudi interior minister, said, "Those who are now in caves and burrows [in Afghanistan], they are the ones who do harm to the [Saudi] kingdom, and unfortunately Muslims are being held accountable for them though Islam is innocent." And, speaking in generalities, General Pervez Musharraf would declare, "Islam teaches tolerance, not hatred; universal brotherhood, not enmity; peace, not violence."[33]

President Bush made a point of visiting an Islamic center in Washington soon after the September 11 attacks, and inviting the ambassadors of 50 Muslim countries to the breaking the fast ceremony at the White House on the eve of Ramadan. Such gestures, however, failed to remedy the disjunction that existed (and still does) between America in particular and the West in general and the Muslim masses abroad. A measure of the distance between these two worlds was provided by the Gallup poll in nine Muslim countries in February 2002 which found 74 percent refusing to believe that Arabs had perpetrated the September 11 attacks.[34] On the other side, there is reluctance among Americans to examine whether these strikes were related to the policies their government had been following in the Muslim and Arab world. There was a sharp divergence of perception between Americans and others, including Europeans, regarding the main cause of these attacks. In a survey by the *International Herald Tribune* and the Pew Research Center for the People and the Press in November–December 2001, 275 influential people in politics, media, business, culture and government in 24 countries, including 40 in America, were asked: "Do many or most ordinary people (in your country) consider American policies to be a 'major cause' of the September 11 attacks?" Whereas three out of five non-US respondents replied yes, less than one in five US respondents did so, giving a 3:1 proportion.[35]

Washington and the capitals of other Christian countries have a daunting task ahead to dispel the prevalent view in the Islamic world which sees Muslims as victims in Bosnia, Chechnya, Iraq and the Palestinian Territories. Mouthing such sentiments as Islam being the religion of peace which has been hijacked by the likes of bin Laden – as Blair frequently does – is not going to help bridge the dangerous gap that has developed between the two civilizations.

There was a need for moderate ulama to speak out. And they did. Four months before 9/11, Abdul Aziz ibn Abdullah al Shaikh, the grand mufti of Saudi Arabia, declared that those who killed themselves in attacks did not die as martyrs but as suicides, and suicide was prohibited in Islam. The Quran says (2:187): "And fight in the way of God those who fight you, but transgress not: God loves not the transgressors." Referring to Muhammad al Tabari, the ninth-century scholar, Roy Mottahdeh, an American specialist on Islam, wrote that Tabari had cited with approval the interpretation ascribed to Prophet Muhammad, who "understood the verse to mean one should never fight women, children, the elderly or the one who offers peace and restrains his hand." Also, noted Mottahdeh, in war both the Sharia and tradition prohibit any damage to property.[36] In December 2001, Muhammad al Sabil, the imam of the Grand Mosque of Mecca, denounced the suicide killing of civilians as against the Sharia.[37]

However, these arguments mean little to radical Islamists. When reminded that the Al Azhar's rector in Cairo had issued a fatwa that "the views and beliefs of Osama bin Laden have nothing to do with Islam', bin Laden replied: "The fatwa of any official religious-legal scholar (*alim*) has no value for me. History is full of such ulama who justify usury, who justify the occupation of Palestine by the Jews, who justify the presence of American troops around the Noble Holy Places."[38] In general, he could have easily justified his jihad against Christians and Jews by citing the Quran (5:82): "Cursed were the Unbelievers of the Children of Israel by the tongue of David, and Jesus, Mary's son; that, for their rebelling and their transgression,/ They forbade not one another any dishonor that they committed; surely evil were the things they did."

The simple fact is that, unlike Roman Catholics, but like Jews, the world's 1.25 billion Muslims do not recognize any central authority either in doctrine or in the ordaining of preachers or ulama. Most theological colleges, training young Muslims in Islam and its jurisprudence, exist as independent entities. Within a particular Islamic legal school, how they interpret the Sharia is their privilege. While the madressas, inspired by Dar ul Ulum in Deoband, India, came to spawn some of the most virulent mullahs in Pakistan and Afghanistan, including Mullah Muhammad Omar, Dar ul Ulum's vice-chancellor, Shaikh Marghbur Rahman, told a *New York Times* reporter, "You won't even find a stick on our premises."[39] So it is hard to delineate heterodoxy and heresy from orthodoxy in Islam.

Also, Islam lacks a central authority – such as the Pope at the Vatican for the world's one billion Roman Catholics – to ordain ulama. So any alim can issue a fatwa – just as anybody nowadays can set up a website on the Internet after paying a fee. How many Muslims follow that fatwa or take steps to implement it depends on the standing of the alim.

Nonetheless, fundamentalist of the three major monotheistic faiths share certain traits. Fundamentalist Christians who bomb abortion clinics in America claim to derive their inspiration from the Bible and base their calls for support from fellow Christians on the biblical text. They and other staunch Christians offer a crusading interpretation of their religion. "The same temptation exists in Judaism today as one can see in the more radical branches of the Israeli settlers movement, which is fired by the eschatological belief that reclaiming the land will hasten the coming of the Messiah," notes Mark Lilla, an American expert on monotheism.[40]

While Islam has certain features in common with Christianity and Judaism, in one regard its stands apart from these faiths as well as others. Its founder, Muhammad ibn Abdullah al Hashim, was not only a prophet, who conveyed the Word of Allah to humanity in the form of the Quran, but also a commander, governor, tax collector and judge, and handled a great variety of situations. Revelations made to him in Mecca, where he was persecuted, and in Medina, where he was the ruler, are different in tone and content, the earlier ones being more imaginative and the latter more mundane, full of legal and moral guidelines. Since the Sharia is composed of both the Quran and the Hadith, the Words and Deeds of Prophet Muhammad, the interpretation of the Sharia has kept tens of thousands of senior ulama busy over the past fourteen centuries, creating a vast body of religious literature. Therefore it is impossible to make a particular interpretation of the Sharia stick with all Muslims worldwide.

A major controversy rages on the interpretation of jihad. Literally, jihad means effort or struggle, which is waged in various forms and degrees, war being the most extreme. Historically, the term has been used to describe an armed struggle by

Muslims against unbelievers in their mission to advance Islam or counter danger to it. Among the several verses in the Quran that require believers to mount a religious war on unbelievers is (9:5): "Then, when the sacred months are away,/slay the idolators wherever you find them,/and take them, and confine them, and lie in wait/for them at every place of ambush. But if they/ repent, and perform the prayer, and pay the alms, then/let them go their way." According to the *sunna* (lit. custom or path), jihad is to be launched only after unbelievers have turned down the offer to embrace Islam or become *dhimmis* (lit. people of dhimma, contract between Muslims and non-Muslims).[41]

When a Muslim community is ruled by non-Muslims, a jihad can be justified only if Islam is suppressed. But as mentioned before, radical Islamist ideologues like Faraj Foda have ruled that jihad is the sixth pillar of Islam,[42] and that Muslims have a religious duty to join a jihad to end the injustice that their fellow religionists may be suffering anywhere in the world. The latter was the driving force behind the non-Afghan volunteers for the anti-Soviet jihad in the 1980s.

Washington was so deeply involved in that jihad that one could convincingly say that American democracy was in alliance with Islamic fundamentalism for a whole decade in Afghanistan. Nobody could have foreseen then that the self-same Afghanistan would turn into an American nemesis. When it did, with Afghanistan-based bin Laden masterminding devastating attacks on the icons of American military and economic powers, Bush described them as assaults on all civilized nations. Other Western leaders agreed. But having said so, they all reverted back to the notion that 9/11 was above all an attack on the West, and took to pleading with Muslim nations that the retaliation they were planning was not directed at Islam. Yet when the parliament of India – a Hindu-majority nation – became the target of terrorist assault in December, neither Bush nor any other Western leader seized the opportunity to highlight the fact that India was not a Christian-majority country or part of Western civilization.

The main reason for overlooking this facet of the war on terrorism was not to upset Pakistan, the rival of India, and was informed by the same opportunism that had shaped Washington's Afghan policy more than two decades ago.

Now, by continuing to turn a deaf ear to the plea of the Arab and Muslim leaders, starting with President Mubarak, a loyal ally of Washington, and ending with the ICO in April 2001, to convene an international conference under the UN auspices to formulate "a joint organized response of the international community to terrorism in all its forms and manifestations,"[43] the Bush administration is failing to live up to the expectations of people around the world that America, the sole superpower, would spearhead a multilateral campaign against the scourge of terrorism based on a commonly agreed platform, and stop indulging in unilateralist interpretations and actions to fight terror, which would set it on an inexorable course of war without end.

Epilogue

As elucidated in chapter 10, the rise of Islamist terrorism in the Middle East can be traced to the Egyptian President Sadat's breach of the Arab solidarity by signing a bilateral peace treaty with Israel in 1979. A generation later, Arab–Israeli relations, as defined by Palestinians, remain at the core of the problem of terrorism in the region and elsewhere.

The escalating violence between Israelis and Palestinians in March–April 2002 brought into focus the contentious issue of the relationship between terrorism and resistance to military or colonial occupation. While the Muslim world maintained that the two were separate, the Bush administration – divided between the hawks, who regarded Yasser Arafat as a sponsor of terrorism and thus unfit to be a peace partner; and the doves, who advocated an even-handed stance toward Israeli Prime Minister Ariel Sharon and the popularly elected Arafat – failed to make up its mind.

As it was, the second Palestinian intifada (uprising) against the Israeli occupation, that erupted in September 2001, had moved from mass protest, with stones hurled at Israel Defense Force (IDF) troops, to armed assaults on Israeli soldiers and settlers soon after the election in February 2001 of hardline Sharon as Israel's prime minister. Under his rule Israel escalated its response from dispersing the protesters by army firings to besieging Palestinian enclaves to making military incursions into the Palestinian territories under the jurisdiction of the autonomous Palestinian Authority (PA), and resorting to assassinating suspected terrorists.

By ordering IDF tanks and helicopter gunships on 28 February 2002 into the Palestinian refugee camp of Balata, near Nablus, and into the Jenin refugee camp to hit the terrorist network and arrest wanted culprits, Sharon crossed a red line. The Israeli incursion left 30 Palestinians dead and 200 injured, most of them seriously. This opened a new chapter in the Israeli–Palestinian conflict which would reach a peak a month later.

When a lone Palestinian sniper shot dead seven Israeli soldiers and three settlers in the West Bank on 4 March, the IDF killed 16 Palestinians. "If you declare war against the Palestinians, thinking you can solve the problem by seeing how many Palestinians can be killed, I don't know that that leads us anywhere," Colin Powell told a Congressional subcommittee three days later. "Israel is only fighting back against the terrorist organization in the context of its right to self-defense," replied Sharon. The ratio of the dead since the start of the intifada was running at 10 Palestinians to three Israelis.[1]

Sharon mounted Operation Vital Security, sending 20,000 troops and scores of tanks and armored personnel carriers (APCs) as well as helicopter gunships into and around Palestinian towns and refugee camps in the West Bank, while gunboats fired at targets in the Gaza Strip. More than 150 tanks and APCs descended on Ramallah and the nearby Amari and Qadura refugee camps. For the first time the Palestinian Authority publicly called on the Palestinians to "confront the invaders."[2] The calls by the US and the European Union for a halt to Israel's military action were ignored by Sharon.

The Israeli action shocked and upset not only the Arab and Muslim public and their leaders but also the UN Secretary-General Kofi Annan. In his letter to Sharon on 12 March, Annan referred to the IDF "waging what looked like an all out conventional war – judging by the F16 fighter bombers, helicopter and naval gun ships, missiles and bombs of heavy tonnage – on Palestinian civilians" with "disturbing patterns" such as mistreatment of civilians by the IDF, and "failure to protect and respect ambulances and medical personnel." He added that Israel was "fully entitled to defend itself against terror," but that right did not exempt it from "its obligation to respect the fundamental principles and rules of international humanitarian law and the law of armed conflict with respect to the treatment and protection of civilians in occupied territories." On the same day, speaking at the UN Security Council, Annan condemned the Palestinian attacks on Israeli civilians as "morally repugnant," and noted that the Palestinians had "played their full part in the escalating cycle of violence, counter-violence and revenge." He called on Israel to end "the illegal occupation." Later that day the Security Council adopted the US-sponsored Resolution 1397 by 14 votes to none, affirming "a vision of a region where two states, Israel and Palestine, live side by side with secure and recognized borders." [3]

Soon after Sharon had ended his week-long military incursion into the West Bank, his aides let it be known that the IDF had prepared an assault on Palestinian cities, towns and refugee camps that would be broader and deeper than any of the offensives undertaken earlier.

The IDF implemented this plan, code-named Operation Defensive Wall, after a particularly gruesome suicide bombing by Abdul Baset Odeh, a member of Hamas's Al Qassam brigade, at the Park Hotel in Netanya at the Passover dinner on 27 March, killing 27 Israeli Jews – the worst Palestinian attack during the second intifada. The objective of Israel's four-week-long offensive, launched on 29 March, was to confiscate illegal weapons, arrest known terrorist suspects, and uproot their network. That day Ayat Akhras, a female teenager, blew herself up outside a West Jerusalem supermarket, killing two and injuring 20. The following day another suicide bomber, Shadi Tobasi, killed 14 Israelis in Haifa.

During the next fortnight, the IDF completed its re-conquest of six of the eight Palestinian cities: Ramallah, Bethlehem, Tulkarm and Qalqilya on 2 April – the day the UN Security Council passed Resolution 1402, calling for an Israeli withdrawal from the Palestinian areas – followed by Nablus and its two refugee camps and Jenin on 3–4 April. Within a week it demolished the Nablus casbah with 30,000 residents and the Jenin refugee camp housing 13,000. It destroyed Arafat's headquarters in

Ramallah, and confined him and his bodyguards to two unlit rooms. Offered the chance to go into exile, Arafat declared, "I will not leave. I will die as a martyr, martyr, martyr."[4]

Sharon described the military offensive as part of the global war on terrorism, a resolute response to the suicide bombings carried out by Palestinian extremists directed by Arafat. "Yasser Arafat is the head of the coalition of terrorism," he declared. To the rest of the world, however, Arafat remained the elected president of the Palestinian Authority. Even British Foreign Secretary Jack Straw refused to accept that the Israeli drive into the West Bank was part of "the global war on terrorism."[5]

"The problem with equating Israel's campaign against terrorism with that of the US, as Sharon and some of his American supporters do, is that it overlooks this contest for territory and sovereignty underlying the Israeli–Palestinian bloodshed," noted the *Washington Post*:

> Though it has been contaminated by suicide bombings and other acts of terrorism, the Palestinian national cause and its goals are recognized as legitimate by the Bush administration and the UN, and they were accepted by Israel when it signed the Oslo accords of 1993. Sharon and most of the rest of his government, however, never accepted these.[6]

The problem at the White House was that, having calmed the nerves of distraught Americans in the aftermath of 9/11 by adopting the simple, indisputable doctrine that terrorism was evil which had to be confronted firmly by the civilized world, Bush had failed to realize that this doctrine was not on a par with democracy or human rights or the free market, which deserved to underwrite most of his international policies.

Arab leaders, meeting at the Arab League summit in Beirut on 27–28 March discussed the subjects of terrorism and foreign occupation. "It is not a question of terrorism," said Amr Mousa, the League's Secretary-General. "It's a question of occupation of the Arab land, which necessarily leads to legitimate resistance." While reaffirming the League's condemnation of the September 11 attacks, and recommitting themselves to contributing to every UN effort in the war against terrorism, the League members in their final communiqué reasserted the right of the Palestinian, Syrian and Lebanese peoples to resist Israeli occupation and aggression; and re-emphasized the difference between terrorism and the legitimate right of the people to resist foreign occupation. It praised the Palestinian intifada, and pledged $330 million aid to the Palestinians.[7]

In the first three weeks of Operation Defensive Wall, the IDF killed at least 250 Palestinians, arrested 1,500 and detained nearly 3,000, and intercepted 10 suicide bomb volunteers who had made farewell videos in Jenin.[8] But that failed to dispel the fear that had gripped Israelis following a series of suicide bombs in cafés, pizza parlors, supermarkets and hotels – not to mention buses and bus stops. "Central Jerusalem is a vacant shell with absences: empty shops, shuttered eateries, bored soldiers milling about, submachine guns at the ready," noted Noga Tarnopolsky of the *Ha'aretz* (The Land). "Signs read, 'Due to the security situation, we are obliged to close the seating area and provide only take-away service'." Armed security guards checked bags and faces outside stores and restaurants. "The fear is nationwide," reported Glenn Frankel. "In the northern port city of Haifa, Mayor Amram Mitzna ordered the annual children's arts festival shut down."[9]

Undoubtedly, Osama bin Laden (if still alive) would have relished such reports. In his videotape broadcast on 7 October 2001, he had warned that Israelis and Americans would not live in security and safety until "we live in peace and security in our lands and in Palestine, and all the army of infidels has departed from the Land of Muhammad, peace be upon him."[10]

Actually, the departure of the American troops from Saudi Arabia was in the offing, despite the oblique way Washington and Riyadh had tried to present it. The Pentagon had started moving out its warplanes from the Saudi kingdom to Qatar.[11]

In that tape bin Laden had also attacked the Arab leaders for not denouncing Israel for its actions. However, this time, during the Israeli invasion of the West Bank, the leaders of both Egypt and Saudi Arabia were vehement in their denunciation of the Sharon government. President Hosni Mubarak used the twentieth anniversary of the "Liberation of Sinai" – being in reality Israel's final, phased withdrawal from Sinai as part of the Egyptian–Israeli peace treaty – on 25 April to lambaste Sharon. "Israel has overstepped all boundaries this time by laying siege on the Holy Church of Nativity and perpetrating horrific human rights abuses in all Palestinian towns and villages, particularly the Jenin town and refugee camp," he said in his television address to the nation:

> It has also tried to cover up those violations by preventing relief agencies and media from entering those towns, villages and refugee camps until the horrific crimes committed by the Israeli Defense Force under the pretext of combating terrorism had been concealed. It relies on interpretations seeking to equate the legitimate Palestinian resistance against occupation with terrorism on one hand, and to avoid branding [of] horrific Israeli practices as state terrorism on the other."[12]

On that day, Saudi Crown Prince Abdullah, accompanied by his foreign minister, Prince Saud al Faisal, had five hours of often tense meetings with George W. Bush, Colin Powell and Condoleezza Rice at Bush's ranch in Crawford, Texas. He, in essence, told them in person what his letters to top US officials had said six months earlier,[13] and which his foreign policy adviser Adil Jubair had articulated in his briefing to American journalists on the eve of the Crawford meeting:

> The Bush administration's alliance with Israel has become so thorough that the stability of friendly governments is in question, with US allies struggling to justify their stands, and radical groups and governments contending that confrontation is inevitable because of the American–Israeli alliance . . . Israeli attacks in the West Bank have fed the region's most vivid fears about the Jewish–Muslim conflict. While Bush calls on Arab states to show "real leadership" by cracking down

on terrorist attacks and pressuring Arafat to do the same, Prince Abdullah will ask that the US must prove its good intentions by cracking down on Israel. Failure to do so will speed a decline in US prestige and credibility in the Gulf and throughout the Arab world.[14]

As the world's largest oil producer, and the second largest foreign supplier of oil (at 1.64 million bpd) to America, Saudi Arabia was the only Arab country with a certain leverage over Washington. Also having won unanimous backing for his peace plan at the Arab summit, offering total peace for total Israeli withdrawal from all Arab lands and a "just solution" for Palestinian refugees, Abdullah had enhanced his regional standing.

Unlike in the past, the regimes in the Arab world were unable to control and manipulate information to their citizens due to the proliferation of satellite television channels. "As network coverage of Vietnam shocked Americans with the immediacy of a far off war, satellite television's insistent, graphic imagery of the intifada has taken this bloody drama into millions of Arab households," wrote Cairo-based Max Rodenbeck of the *Economist* in the *New York Times*:

> The drama generates not weariness with war but a thirst for justice, for sacrifice and revenge . . . Some Palestinian casualties have become household names from Morocco to Muscat – Muhammad Dura, the 12-year-old boy from Gaza whose father could not shield him from a hail of Israeli gunfire, or Wafa Idris and Ayat Akhras, the first female suicide bombers.

Yet, argued Rodenbeck:

> Arab coverage of the conflict is not really much more one-sided than, say, America's gung-ho coverage of the Gulf War. Or, for that matter, Israeli reporting on the intifada. It does not require subtle manipulation to frame the ongoing tragedy as an epic struggle of the weak against the strong.

The imagery saturating Arab screens of tanks crushing ambulances and helicopters rocketing refugee camps is, alas, all too real.[15]

It was not just Arab television. Two weeks into Israel's offensive, Serge Schmemann of the *New York Times* reported that:

The uprooting inflicted by Sharon's tanks, bulldozers, helicopters and sappers has created a landscape of devastation from Bethlehem to Jenin. The images are indelible: piles of concrete and twisted metal in the ancient casbah of Nablus, husks of savaged computers littering ministries in Ramallah, rows of storefronts sheared by passing tanks in Tulkarm, broken pipes gushing precious water, flattened cars in fields of shattered glass and garbage, electricity poles snapped like twigs, tilting walls where homes used to stand, gaping holes where rockets pierced office buildings.[16]

These images had made such an impact on Europeans that on 10 April, by 269 to 208 votes, the EU Parliament called on the member states to impose political and trade sanctions against Israel due to its violation of international and humanitarian law in its offensive against the Palestinians.[17]

As expected, the impact of such images in the Arab world was more pronounced. In an open letter published in the Saudi kingdom, 126 Saudi ulama and writers said, "We consider America and its administration a first class sponsor of international terrorism, and it along with Israel forms an axis of terrorism and evil in the world." Aware of the depth of popular feelings, the authorities allowed a march by 5,000 protesters to the US consulate in Khobar.[18]

But, unprecedently, Saudis and other Arabs went beyond shouting slogans. They resorted to boycotting American goods and brand names. "We are deleting everything that relates to America," said Samir Nasier, a Jiddah-based fast-food king. "We share the same outraged feelings of the Saudi public toward the attitude of the American administration [toward Israel]."

The American fast-food outlets in the Arab world registered a decline of 20 to 30 percent in sales. When the Al Montazah supermarket chain in Bahrain replaced about 1,000 American products with alternatives, its sales rose. The state-run print media backed the boycott, often initiated by student organizations and other NGOs. Such bodies, explained Kamal Hamdan, a Lebanese economist, were planning "detailed programs against specific [American] goods and services that might involve banking, insurance and financial markets," and that would have a real economic impact. Shaikha Fatima Nahyan, wife of the ruler of the Ajman Emirate in the UAE urged a woman's group: "Start by boycotting all make-up and clothes made by the enemies [America and Israel] and prevent your children from buying their products too." The web site of Shaikh Yusuf Qaradawi, the vastly popular cleric on Al Jazeera TV displayed a blinking banner: "BOYCOTT AMERICA, FROM PEPSI CANS TO BOEING."[19]

In Egypt, echoing Syrian President Bashar Assad's argument that since all of Israel was "an armed camp," the Palestinian "fighters" were not obliged to differentiate between military and civilian targets in their attacks,[20] Al Azhar's rector, Muhammad Sayyid Tantawi said, "All Israelis – men, women and children – are forces of occupation. Therefore martyrdom operations are the highest form of jihad operations." He added, "A suicide attack is an Islamic commandment until the people of Palestine regain their land and cause the cruel Israeli aggressor to retreat." By so doing, Tantawi reversed his earlier stance against such attacks on civilians. Supporting his view, Grand Mufti Ahmad Tayyib declared: "The solution to the Israeli terror lies in a proliferation of suicide attacks that strike horror into the hearts of the enemies of Allah. The Islamic countries, people and rulers alike must support these martyrdom attacks."[21]

About then, Ghazi Algasoibi, a Saudi diplomat whose powerful anti-Saddam Hussein poems before and during the 1991 Gulf War had resulted in his promotion to his country's ambassador to Britain, published a poem, entitled "Martyrs" and dedicated to Ayat Akhras, on the front page of *Al Hayat*:

Say to those who composed fatwas: Hold on!/
It might be a fatwa that makes the sky rumble./
When jihad calls, ink falls silent/
and shows respect, as do books, and jurisprudents./
When jihad calls, there is no referendum./
The fatwas, on the day of jihad, are blood.[22]

Algasoibi captured the popular feeling prevalent among Arabs about the impotence of their leaders thus:

You committed suicide?
We [too] committed suicide by living like the dead.
O People, we died!
Let's hear your obituaries of us . . .
We complained to the Tyrant of the White/
House whose heart is filled with darkness;
We kissed the shoes of Sharon until/
He shouted, "Stop! You're spoiling my shoes!"
O People, we died!
But the dust refused to inter us.[23]

Such vehemence and unanimity of opinion in the Arab world contrasted with the confusion prevailing at the higher echelons of the US administration. On 4 April Bush coupled his criticism of Arafat who, in his view, had "missed his opportunities, and thereby betrayed the hopes of the people he's supposed to lead," with a call to Sharon: "Enough is enough. I ask Israel to halt." Consistent with the George Mitchell plan, he added, "Israeli settlement activity in the West Bank must stop. And the occupation must end through withdrawal to secure and recognized boundaries consistent with UN Resolutions 242 and 338."[24] Sharon paid no heed, and continued his offensive. He went on to ignore a second call by Bush on 8 April to pull out "without delay," thus making the American chief executive appear ineffective and eroding his standing in the world. Then, three days later Bush's spokesman, Ari Fleischer, said, "The President believes Sharon is a man of peace."[25] On top of that, Bush went on to reward Sharon for his defiance by inviting him to the White House yet again. After 15 months in office, Bush had failed to demonstrate an assured grasp of foreign affairs, especially in the Middle East. Instead of continuing the practice of the Clinton presidency of limiting Middle East policy making to the White House and the State Department, he had also brought in the Defense Department, dominated by hawkish Donald Rumsfeld, Paul Wolfowitz and Douglas Feith, undersecretary for defense policy. Perceiving the Israeli campaign against the Palestinians as a legitimate war on terrorism, they successfully urged giving Sharon a free rein – without realizing the full implications of this stance. "To back the Israeli invasion, as the Bush administration has done, is not just to back the cause of counter terrorism," the *Washington Post* wrote editorially:

> It is also to abet Sharon's drive to suppress Palestinian national rights . . . [If] counter terrorism is to remain an effective cause, the administration must discriminate between terrorism and the sometimes legitimate political causes it is used for; and it must also differentiate between legitimate defenses against terrorism and attempts to use counter terrorism to justify unacceptable aims.[26]

This was also the position of the State Department officials, from Powell down, much concerned about the medium- and long-term consequences of Israel's disproportionate responses. They worried that the unprecedented Israeli offensive was fostering greater Palestinian hatred and destroying their ability to govern themselves, and that despite his many faults, Arafat remained central to any peace settlement. This view was shared not only by such moderate Arab leaders as King Abdullah II of Jordan,[27] but also by the *Ha'aretz*, the prestigious Israeli daily. "Israel's military operation . . . has succeeded in landing a considerable blow on the Palestinian terrorist framework, but it cannot uproot terror or eliminate the ground on which it grows," it said. "On the contrary, the deeper and longer the operation, the more its inherent contradictions are exposed."[28]

The respite that Israel gained from its Operation Defensive Wall lasted a mere fortnight. On 26 April, two Palestinians dressed in IDF uniform killed four Jewish settlers near Hebron. And just as Sharon sat down to talk with Bush on 7 May in Washington, a Palestinian suicide bomber killed 16 Israelis in Rishon Le Tzion, south of Tel Aviv. Arab officials argued that the latest bombing underlined the need for Washington to pressure Israel to resume political talks with the Palestinians for a final peace settlement. But, with the central committee of the Likud party (led by Sharon) voting almost unanimously for the resolution, "There will be no Palestinian state west of the River Jordan," on 12 May,[29] the chances of such negotiations were slim.

Those US policy makers who advocated backing Sharon unequivocally in the name of fighting terrorism also wanted to attack Iraq and overthrow Saddam, unaware that if they started equating the Palestinians with Al Qaida, they would lose all their support for whatever they want to accomplish in Iraq and elsewhere in the Middle East. They had not drawn the right lesson from the failure of Dick Cheney to muster support for action against Baghdad. When asked whether Bahrain would back an anti-Iraq military campaign (at a joint press conference with Cheney), Bahraini Foreign Minister Salman ibn Hamad al Khalifa said,

> In the Arab world the threat is perceived quite differently. The people who are dying today on the streets are not a result of any Iraqi action. The people are dying as a result of an Israeli action. And likewise people in Israel are dying as a result of action taken in response [by the Palestinians].[30]

This position was formalized at the Arab summit which decided to "reject exploitation of war on terrorism to threaten any Arab country and reject use of force against Iraq." At this meeting Iraq signed a document recognizing Kuwait's sovereignty and security; and Iraq's Izzat Ibrahim and Kuwait's Sabah al Ahmad al Sabah shook hands for the first time in 12 years.[31] The leader most responsible for bringing about this reconciliation was Saudi Crown Prince Abdullah. By mediating successfully on this long-running issue, Abdullah won the backing of Iraq, the most anti-Zionist state in the Arab world, for his peace plan. The other consideration that motivated the Saudi leader was to counter the criticism that if Arabs failed to get along with one another how could they do so with Israel.

Overall, of the three issues of deep concern to the Arab and Muslim world – the stationing of US military in Saudi Arabia, the Palestinian–Israeli conflict and the fate of Iraq – only the first one had been virtually resolved, with the remaining two continuing to be running sores, spawning terrorism.

Notes

Prologue

1 *Sunday Times*, 10 March 2002.
2 *Vanity Fair*, March 2002, p. 75.
3 *Sunday Times*, 10 March 2002.
4 *Middle East International*, 28 September 2001, p. 32. All told 343 firefighters and 23 police officers lost their lives.
5 *Independent*, 27 October 2001.
6 *New York Times*, 30 October 2001.
7 *Ibid.*, 31 December 2001.
8 *The Times*, 25 September 2001.
9 Associated Press, 4 October 2001.
10 *New York Times*, 1 October 2001.
11 Associated Press, 4 October 2001; *Financial Times*, 11 October 2001.
12 *New York Times*, 5 November 2001. The CIA is one of 13 intelligence
   agencies functioning under cabinet departments and the Executive
   Office of the President. The others are the Defense Intelligence
   Agency, US Army Intelligence Center, Office of Naval Intelligence,
   Marine Corps Intelligence Activity, and Air Intelligence Agency
   (Defense Department); Non-Proliferation and National Security
   (Energy Department); National Security Agency, National Recon-
   naissance Office, and National Imagery and Mapping Agency
   (Executive Office of the President); Federal Bureau of Investiga-
   tion (Justice Department); Bureau of Intelligence and Research
   (State Department); and Office of Intelligence Support (Treasury
   Department).
13 *New York Times*, 1 October 2001.
14 *International Herald Tribune*, 9 January 2002.
15 *Washington Post*, 15 November 2001.

16 The *New York Times* puts the total of the dead at 2,950 and the Associated Press at 2,612.
17 Of the non-US opinion leaders, 67 applaud America for its technical and scientific advances. *International Herald Tribune*, 20 December 2001.
18 *International Herald Tribune*, 28 December 2001.
19 *Observer*, 10 March 2002.
20 *Ibid.*, 6 January 2002.

1   The rise of Islam: Sunnis and Shias

1 "The 'Presence' said to Muhammad, 'Read.' Muhammad replied, 'What shall I read?' The 'Presence' shook him and crushed him until he felt drained of all strength. Twice this happened. Finally the words came to him. Later these appeared as the opening of Chapter 96:
   Recite: In the name of thy Lord who created,
   Created man of a blood clot.
   Recite: And thy Lord is the Most Generous,
   Who taught by the pen,
   Taught man that he knew not."
   Arthur J. Arberry (trans.), *The Koran Interpreted*, Oxford University Press, Oxford and New York, 1964, 96:1–5.
2 *Ibid.*, 5:49.
3 *Ibid.*, 4:3.
4 *Ibid.*, 4:19.
5 W. Montgomery Watt, *Islamic Political Thought: The Basic Concepts* Edinburgh University Press, Edinburgh, 1968, pp. 5 and 132.
6 Cited in David K. Shipler, *Arab and Jew: Wounded Spirits in a Promised Land*, Times Books, New York, 1986, p. 141. Since Jews and Christians are mentioned in the Quran, they are known in Islam as "People of the Book."
7 Of these obligations, prayers, charity and fasting during Ramadan are mentioned in the Quran, the rest in the Hadiths.
8 Arberry, *op. cit.*, 9:60. The 2.5 percent rate applies to the believer's cash and ornaments of precious metals. The rates for cattle and agricultural and mineral output vary. Ghulam Sarwar, *Islam: Beliefs and Teachings*, Muslim Educational Trust, London, 1982, p. 75.
9 One of the several verses on resurrection in the Quran reads:
   "Say: 'God gives you life, then makes you die,
   Then He shall gather you to the Day
   Of Resurrection, wherein is no doubt,
   But most men do not know.'"
   Arberry, *op. cit.*, 45:25.

10 Malise Ruthven, *Islam in the World*, Penguin Books, Harmondsworth, 1984, p. 97.
11 *Ibid.*, p. 98.
12 The first four Shia Imams are Ali, Hassan, Hussein and Zain al Abidin.
13 The first six Shia Imams, according to Twelvers, are Ali, Hassan, Hussein, Zain al Abidin, Muhammad al Baqir and Jaafar al Sadi.
14 The rest of the twelve Imams are Musa al Kazim, Ali al Rida (Reza, in Persian), Muhammad al Taqi Javad, Ali al Naqi, Hassan al Askari and Muhammad al Muntazar.

2 Orthodox Islam and Sufism

1 Muhammad Asad, *The Principles of State and Government in Islam*, Dar als Andalus, Gibraltar, 1980, pp. 48 and 106.
2 Malise Ruthven, *op. cit.*, p. 160.

3 Islam in modern times

1 Cited in N. A. Ziadeh, *Sanusiyah*, E. J. Brill, Leiden, 1958, pp. 41–4.
2 In contemporary Iran he is known as Jamaluddin Asadabadi.
3 Wilfred Cantwell Smith, *Islam in Modern History*, Princeton University Press, Princeton, NJ, 1957, p. 49.
4 Edward Mortimer, *Faith and Power: The Politics of Islam*, Faber & Faber, London, Holt, Rinehart, New York, 1982, p. 115.
5 See Hamid Enayat, *Modern Islamic Political Thought*, Macmillan, London, 1982, pp. 70–83.
6 Mortimer, *op. cit.*, p. 250.

4 The Muslim Brotherhood in Egypt and its offshoots

1 Richard P. Mitchell, *The Society of Muslim Brothers*, Oxford University Press, Oxford and New York, 1969, p. 4.
2 Zakariyya Sulaiman Bayyumi, *The Muslim Brothers* (in Arabic), Wahhab Library, Cairo, 1979, p. 90.
3 Mitchell, *op. cit.*, p. 14.
4 Said Ismail Ali, *Al Azhar: A Participant in Egyptian Politics* (in Arabic), Dar al Thaqafa, Cairo, 1974, p. 104.
5 *Ibid.*, p. 299.
6 Muhammad Ghazali, *Our Beginning in Wisdom* (trans. Ismail el Faruqi), American Council of Learned Societies, Washington, DC, 1953, pp. 30–1.
7 *New York Times*, 24 January 2002.

8 Cited in Judith Miller, *God Has Ninety-Nine Names: Reporting from a Militant Middle East*, Simon & Schuster, New York, 1996, pp. 62–3.

9 Cited in Fouad Ajami, "In the Pharoah's Shadow: Religion and Authority in Egypt," in James Piscatori (ed.), *Islam in the Political Process*, Cambridge University Press, Cambridge and New York, 1983, p. 25.

10 *Majallat al Azhar*, February and October 1968.

11 Ghali Shoukri, *Egypt: Portrait of a President, 1971–81*, Zed Press, London, 1981, p. 296.

12 *Ibid.*, pp. 292–3.

13 Dilip Hiro, *Inside the Middle East*, Routledge & Kegan Paul, London, and McGraw-Hill, New York, 1982, p. 112.

14 Shoukri, *op. cit.*, p. 201.

15 *The Times*, 16 November 1978.

16 R. Hrair Dekmejian, *Islam in Revolution: Fundamentalism in the Arab World*, Syracuse University Press, Syracuse, NY, 1985, p. 105.

17 *Al Ahram*, 10 May 1979.

18 Cited in *8 Days*, 25 July 1981.

19 Cited in Gilles Kepel, *Muslim Extremism in Egypt*, University of California Press, Berkeley, CA, 1993, p. 192.

20 *Washington Post*, 27 September 2001.

21 This was all the more striking in contrast to the death of Nasser which had led to unprecedented scenes of public grief.

22 Dekmejian, *op. cit.*, p. 106.

23 Dilip Hiro, *Dictionary of the Middle East*, Macmillan, Basingstoke, and St Martin's Press, New York, 1996, pp. 151–2.

24 *Ibid.*, pp. 4–5.

25 *Washington Post*, 4 July 2000.

26 Assad Abdul Rahman would be killed in a US air raid in Afghanistan in November 2001, and Ahmad captured near Mazar-e Sharif. *Los Angeles Times*, 29 November 2001.

27 A later inquiry revealed that the computers at the US embassy in Khartoum were down on the day when Shaikh Omar Abdul Rahman's tourist visa application was being processed. It is widely believed that the CIA smoothed his way into America for the services he had rendered to the anti-Soviet jihad in Afghanistan.

28 Judith Miller, *God Has Ninety-Nine Names: Reporting from a Militant Middle East*, Simon & Schuster, New York, 1996, p. 25.

29 *Middle East International*, 26 October 2001, p. 27.

30 Miller, *op. cit.*, p. 68.

31 *Daily Telegraph*, 23 August 1993.

32 *Sunday Times*, 28 March 1993. Later Prime Minister Atef Sidqi banned the local media from writing about the scandal.

33 *Guardian*, 3 February 1994.

34 By the end of 1993 foreign tourists were down by about a half. *The Times*, 26 November 1993.

35 *Sunday Times*, 21 March 1993.

36 *Observer*, 7 February 1993.

37 Interview in October 1993. Miller, *op. cit.*, p. 43.

38 Cited in Miller, *op. cit.*, p. 42.

39 *Independent*, 31 August 1993, citing a report in the Cairo-based *Al Arabi*, an opposition left-wing weekly.

40 *Sunday Times*, 22 August 1993.

41 *Daily Telegraph*, 16 August 1993; *Guardian*, 19 August 1993.

42 "Behind Closed Doors: Torture and Detention in Egypt," Human Rights Watch/Middle East, New York, July 1992; and "Egypt: Ten Years of Torture," Amnesty International, London, October 1991.

43 *Independent*, 1 April 1993; *Sunday Times*, 22 August 1993.

44 *Guardian*, 28 November 1993.

45 Cited in Miller, *op. cit.*, p. 28.

46 *The Times*, 26 November 1993.

47 *Independent*, 13 December 1997.

48 *Observer*, 13 February 1994.

49 *Middle East International*, 20 January 1995, pp. 16–17.

50 *Sunday Times*, 20 February 1994.

51 Deaths in police custody continued to occur. The Egyptian Organization for Human Rights reported 20 such deaths in the first nine months of 1995. *The Middle East and North Africa 2001*, Europa Publications, London and New York, p. 441.

52 *The Middle East and North Africa 2001*, p. 440.

53 *Middle East International*, 4 November 1994, p. 19.

54 *Observer*, 7 February 1993; and *Sunday Times*, 22 August 1993. Mustafa Mashhour, a Muslim Brotherhood leader, told *Al Hayat* on 15 July 1995 that his organization received considerable funds from its offices in Germany, Britain and America. Miller, *op. cit.*, p. 483, note 51.

55 Issam al Aryan, a most effective Brotherhood organizer, received a five-year jail sentence with hard labor. *Middle East International*, 1 December 1995, p. 9.

56 In a further move to block a revival of the Muslim Brotherhood, in December 1996 the parliament outlawed speeches in mosques not registered with the Ministry of Religious Trusts.

57 Cited in the *Guardian*, 25 November 1995.

58 *Middle East International*, 15 December 1995, p. 11.

59 The Al Khifa Refugee Center, known as the Al Jihad Center, funded the departure of 200 American volunteers to Afghanistan. Peter L.

Bergen, *Holy War, Inc.: Inside the Secret World of Osama bin Laden*, Weidenfeld & Nicolson, London, 2001/ The Free Press, New York, 2001, p. 143. Among those who had visited the Al Jihad Center in the early 1990s to raise funds for the widows and orphans of the dead Mujahedin was Ayman Zawahiri, traveling under a false name. *The Times*, 25 September 2001.

60 *Independent*, 6 December 1995; *The Middle East and North Africa 2001*, p. 444.

61 Dilip Hiro, *Sharing the Promised Land*, Hodder & Stoughton, London, 1995, p. 200–1/ Interlink, New York, 1999, pp. 100–1.

62 Cited in *Guardian*, 31 March 1993.

63 Among those sentenced to death in absentia was Ahmad Ibrahim Sayyid Najjar. Arrested later in Albania, he would provide crucial information about Osama bin Laden and Al Qaida.

64 *Independent*, 19 September 1997.

65 *Ibid.*, 18 and 19 November 1997.

66 *The Middle East and North Africa 2001*, p. 442.

67 *Sunday Times*, 11 November 2001.

68 *New York Times*, 22 November 2001; *Sunday Times*, 25 November 2001. On 6 August 1998, Muhammad Salah, the Cairo correspondent of *Al Hayat*, received a fax from Al Jihad saying it would attack American interests everywhere (to avenge the torturing of its members). The next day the US embassies in Nairobi and Dar as Salaam were hit. *Observer*, 16 August 1998.

69 *New York Times*, 22 November 2001. Ahmad Najjar was hanged in February 2000.

70 *The Middle East and North Africa 2001*, p. 445.

71 *Guardian*, 3 February 1994.

72 *International Herald Tribune*, 20 September 2001; *Observer*, 23 September 2001.

73 *Middle East International*, 24 November 2001, pp 14–15.

5 Saudi Arabia: the oldest fundamentalist state

1 Taqi al Din Ibn Taimiya, *Politics of Legitimacy* (in Arabic), Dar al Kutub al Arabiya, Beirut, 1966, p. 106.

2 Cited in Edward Mortimer, *Faith and Power: The Politics of Islam*, Faber & Faber, London, and Holt, Rinehart, New York, 1982, p. 166.

3 Christine Moss Helms, *The Cohesion of Saudi Arabia: Evolution of Political Identity*, Croom Helm, London, 1981, p. 137.

4 Arthur J. Arberry, (trans.), *The Koran Interpreted*, Oxford University Press, Oxford and New York, 1964, 3:153.

5 *Arab World File*, No. 100, 16 October 1974.

6 King Faisal disbanded the Royal Guard, incorporated part of it into the National Guard, and part of it into the forces of the Interior Ministry, which had its Frontier Guard, Coastal Guard as well as the Department of Public Security and the much dreaded General Investigation (*Mabahith al Amaa*). By 1969 the Interior Ministry's security services had been reorganized, expanded and trained by American specialists and given generous budgets. Sandra Mackey, *The Saudis: Inside the Desert Kingdom*, Houghton, Mifflin, Boston; and Harrap, London, 1987, p. 299; Mordechai Abir, *Saudi Arabia: Government, Society and the Gulf Crisis*, Routledge, London and New York, 1993, p. 58; and Miller, *op. cit.*, p. 101.

7 Cited in James P. Piscatori, "The Roles of Islam in Saudi Arabia's Political Development', in John L. Esposito (ed.), *Islam and Development: Religion and Socio-political Change*, Syracuse University Press, Syracuse, NY, 1980, p. 134.

8 *Al Hayat*, 7 November 1964.

9 Sandra Mackey, *op. cit.*, p. 210.

10 Dilip Hiro, *Inside the Middle East*, Routledge & Kegan Paul, London, and McGraw-Hill, New York, 1982, p. 341.

11 Dilip Hiro, *Dictionary of the Middle East*, Macmillan Press, Basingstoke, and St. Martin's Press, New York, 1996, pp. 232–3.

12 Abir, *op. cit.*, p. 34.

13 Dilip Hiro, *Inside the Middle East*, p. 342.

14 Sandra Mackey, *op .cit.*, pp. 210–11; *Newsweek*, 3 March 1980, p. 22.

15 *Time*, 29 May 1978, p. 20.

16 *Observer*, 19 December 1976, cited in Dilip Hiro, *Inside the Middle East*, p. 342.

17 Dilip Hiro, *Inside the Middle East*, p. 342.

18 Sayyid Abul Ala Maududi, *A Short History of the Revivalist Movements in Islam*, Islamic Publications, Lahore, 1963, p. 33.

19 M. T. Houtsma, A. J. Wensinck, E. Levi-Provencal, H. A. R. Gibb and W. Heffering (eds.), *The Encyclopaedia of Islam, Vol. III*, E. J. Brill, Leiden, 1936, p. 115.

20 Dekmejian, *op. cit.*, p. 142.

21 Cited in David Holden and Richard Johns, *The House of Saud*, Sidgwick & Jackson, London, 1981, p. 522.

22 Dilip Hiro, *Inside the Middle East*, p. 395, note 31. This arrangement ended in 1986 when Pakistan's military ruler, Muhammad Zia al Haq, refused to exclude Shias from the brigades to be assigned to the Saudi kingdom, as demanded by Riyadh.

23 Sandra Mackey, *op. cit.*, p. 310.

24 *Observer*, 28 October 2001.

25 Interview with Yeslam bin Laden, who supervises the foreign business of the Saudi Binladin Group in Geneva, Switzerland, in the *Sunday Times*, 16 December 2001.

26 Cited in Mortimer, *op. cit.*, p. 174.

27 Cited in Yvonne Y. Haddad, "The Arab–Israeli Wars, Nasserism and Islamic Identity', in John L. Esposito (ed.), *Islam and Development*, p. 239, note 23.

28 *Guardian*, 26 January 1981.

29 Sayyid Qutb, *Conflict between Islam and Capitalism* (in Arabic), Dar al Shuruq, Beirut, 1975, p. 25.

30 *Wall Street Journal*, 1 May 1981. A well-researched update on corruption in the kingdom is provided by the Committee Against Corruption in Saudi Arabia at http://www.saudhouse.com.

31 *Newsweek*, 3 March 1980, p. 22. There was also money to be made through currency transactions by those princes who had inside information from the Saudi Arabian Monetary Agency (SAMA), which controlled the value of the Saudi riyal. Sandra Mackey, *op. cit.*, p. 212.

32 *Ibid.*, p. 223.

33 Ruh Allah Khumayni (trans. Hamid Algar), *Islam and Revolution*, Mizan Press, Berkeley, CA, 1981, p. 202.

34 *Sunday Times*, 30 December 1979.

35 Sporadic demonstrations and rioting continued for two months, and resulted in 6,000 arrests. Dilip Hiro, *Inside the Middle East*, p. 87.

36 *Daily Telegraph*, 4 February 1981.

37 *The Middle East*, February 1982, p. 14.

38 *Financial Times*, 12 May 1984. Dilip Hiro, *The Longest War*, Grafton Books, London, 1989, and Routledge, New York, 1991, p. 96.

39 *Ibid.*, p. 107.

40 Riyadh Radio, 24 July 1983.

41 Dilip Hiro, *Between Marx and Muhammad: The Changing Face of Central Asia*, HarperCollins, London and New York, 1994, p. 251, note 18.

42 Sandra Mackey, *op. cit.*, p. 378.

43 Judith Miller, *op. cit.*, p. 102.

44 Of these, 85 were Saudi nationals, the rest pilgrims, 275 of them Iranian. Dilip Hiro, *Holy Wars: The Rise of Islamic Fundamentalism*, Routledge, New York, 1989, p. 218 (originally published as *Islamic Fundamentalism*, Paladin Books/HarperCollins, London, 1988).

45 Dilip Hiro, *Desert Shield to Desert Storm*, HarperCollins, London, and Routledge, New York, 1992, pp. 224–5.

46 Dilip Hiro, *Between Marx and Muhammad*, p. 253.
47 Dilip Hiro, *Desert Shield to Desert Storm*, p. 111.
48 Dilip Hiro, *Inside the Middle East*, p. 339; and Mordechai Abir, *op. cit.*, p. 31.
49 Mordechai Abir, *op. cit.*, p. 41.
50 *Observer*, 15 July 1979.
51 Cited in Dilip Hiro, *Desert Shield to Desert Storm*, p. 288.
52 *Independent*, 15 September 1990.
53 *Observer*, 28 October 2001.
54 Dilip Hiro, *Desert Shield to Desert Storm*, p. 128. When finally an endorsement came from COSU as a body, it was based on the concept of "necessity," not the text of the Sharia. Jane's Intelligence Review, *Saudi Arabia: The Threat from Within*, Special Report 12, December 1996, p. 16.
55 Jane's Intelligence Review, *op. cit.*, p. 17.
56 Judith Miller, *op. cit.*, p.125.
57 *Independent*, 25 May 1991. In late February, 43 pro-Western liberals had petitioned King Fahd for democratic reform, proposing a change-over to constitutional monarchy with a multi-party political system, votes for women, and freedom of expression and the press. Dilip Hiro, *Desert Shield to Desert Storm*, p. 498, note 65.
58 *The Middle East and North Africa 2001*, p. 1012.
59 Cited in *The Middle East*, July 1991, p. 8.
60 *New York Times*, 30 March 1992.
61 Jane's Intelligence Review, *op. cit.*, p. 20.
62 See further Dilip Hiro, *Dictionary of the Middle East*, pp. 283–4.
63 Cited in *London Review of Books*, 22 November 1993, p. 8.
64 This classified fact would be leaked by the George W. Bush administration in October 2001 to pressure the Saudi rulers. See p. 343.
65 *Los Angeles Times*, 12 February 2001; *Guardian*, 17 February 2001.
66 *Boston Globe*, 26 August 2001.
67 Cited in Peter L. Bergen, *op. cit.*, p. 97.
68 *New York Times*, 8 April 1994; *Newsday*, 26 August 1998; *Sunday Times*, 16 December 2001.
69 Mamoun Fandy, *Saudi Arabia and the Politics of Dissent*, Palgrave, New York, 2001, pp. 181–2. "We [CAR] were there [in Saudi Arabia], working secretly since the early 1980s," Khalid al Fawwaz told Fandy. "But because we did not want the government to find out about our activities, we delayed the declaration of the organization." *Ibid.*, p. 181. If so, Osama bin Laden, then barely 25 and very much part of the Saudi establishment, could not have been one of the founders.
70 *Sunday Times*, 7 February 1999.

71 *The Economist*, 5 December 1992, pp. 39–40; *Wall Street Journal*, 15–16 January 1993.

72 Giving financial assistance to the needy or for an Islamic cause is a religious requirement for Muslims.

73 *Guardian*, 17 August 1993.

74 *Wall Street Journal*,15–16 January 1993. The following joke about the consultative council was doing the rounds. A veiled woman riding a donkey loaded with a lot of cash arrived at a Saudi border post. Unsure of how to handle the situation, the guards phoned their superiors who in turn called further up until the question was put to King Fahd. "Hand over the woman to the Interior Ministry, and the cash to the Finance Ministry," he ordered. "And the donkey, Your Excellency?" asked the timorous official. "Send him to the consultative council."

75 *Guardian*, 29 December 1993.

76 *Middle East International*, 7 October 1994, p. 12.

77 Cited in the *Guardian*, 24 March 1995.

78 *Guardian*, 22 February 1996.

79 *The Middle East and North Africa 2001*, p. 1013.

80 *Guardian*, 7 July 1995.

81 Miller, *op. cit.*, p. 491, note 54. It was only after Saudi Arabia's order for advanced US weapons in 1986 was curtailed from $3,000 million to $260 million due to the opposition by the Israeli-influenced Congress, that it turned to Britain for its fighter-bombers, helicopters, trainer aircraft and mine sweepers. *The Middle East and North Africa 2001*, p. 1010.

82 *Washington Post*, 26 May 1996.

83 Mamoun Fandy, *op. cit.*, pp. 2–3.

84 *Independent*, 27 June 1996.

85 Sandra Mackey, *op. cit.*, p. 100.

86 *International Herald Tribune*, 24 August 1998.

87 Saudi interior minister, Prince Nayif, said that Osama bin Laden did not mastermind the 1995 and 1996 bomb attacks in the kingdom. Reuters, 13 December 1998.

88 *Washington Post*, 3 October 2001. The move was organized by one of his principal aides, Ali Muhammad, a former Egyptian-American military officer.

89 *Sunday Times*, 16 September 2001.

90 *Independent*, 27 June 1996; *Middle East International*, 5 July 1996, pp. 7–8.

91 *Independent*, 27 June 1996; and author's interview with a Gulf specialist at Royal United Services Institute, London, January 2000.

92 *Boston Globe*, 26 August 2001.

93 In 1993 and 1994 the Saudi Binladin Group gave two $1 million gifts to Harvard University for research on Islamic law and Islamic architecture. *Sunday Times*, 7 October 2001.
94 Xinhua News Agency, 2 November 1998.
95 *Wall Street Journal*, 15–16 January 1993.
96 In December 1995, while Crown Prince Abdullah was attending the Gulf Cooperation Council summit in Muscat, Prince Sultan summoned the Council of Senior Ulama to seek its support in his bid for the throne. The Council denied him the endorsement. On his return Abdullah traveled to the Qasim province, the base of the Shammar tribal confederation, to participate in ceremonial tribal dancing despite a rumored plot against his life. This show of defiance and courage secured him the loyalty of the tribes and decisively shifted the balance of power from Sultan to him. *Daily Telegraph*, 2 November 2001.
97 Peter L. Bergen, *op. cit.*, p 109.
98 *Daily Telegraph*, 10 December 1997.
99 Reuters, 11 December 1997.
100 *Middle East International*, 13 February 1998, p. 4.

6 Afghanistan: fundamentalism victorious, with American backing

1 Derivative of *hazar* (1,000), being the number of Mongol soldiers that Jenghiz Khan left behind after ravaging Afghanistan. Their descendants are known as Hazaras.
2 Attended by 3,500 male students, it is now run by 86-year-old Vice-Chancellor Shaikh Marghbur Rahman. It is the second oldest Islamic university in the world, after Al Azhar. *New York Times*, 26 February 2002.
3 Louis Dupree, *Afghanistan*, Princeton University Press, Princeton, NJ and Guildford, 1980, pp. 126–7.
4 *Al Falah*, Seventh Year, No. 7, pp. 62–3.
5 Arberry, *op. cit.*, 24:31.
6 Of the 113,000 tourists in Afghanistan in 1971, more than half were Western. Dupree, *op. cit.*, p. 656.
7 In 1974 the Pakistani parliament declared the Ahmadiya sect heretical and its followers non-Muslim. In late 1978 Abul Ala Maududi traveled to America for medical treatment and died there a few months later.
8 Sayyid Abul Ala Maududi, *Purdah and the Status of Women in Islam*, Islamic Publications, Lahore, 1979, p. 23.
9 *Ibid.*, pp. 197–8.
10 Olivier Roy, *Islam and Resistance in Afghanistan*, Cambridge University Press, Cambridge and New York, 1986, p. 83.

11 *The Area Handbook of Afghanistan*, Kabul, 1973, p. 36.
12 Anthony Hyman, *Afghanistan under Soviet Domination, 1964–83*, Macmillan, London, 1984, p. 90.
13 *Kabul Times*, 9 December 1978.
14 Dilip Hiro, *Between Marx and Muhammad*, p. 240; *Washington Post*, 17 November 2001.
15 *Washington Post*, 11 October 1979.
16 *Kabul New Times*, 1 January 1980. After the Soviet intervention the *Kabul Times* became the *Kabul New Times*.
17 Cited in Mark Urban, *War in Afghanistan*, Macmillan, London, 1988, p. 56.
18 Bahauddin Majrooh was assassinated by gunmen in early 1988 at his house in Peshawar. David B. Edwards, *Before Taliban: Genealogies of the Afghan Jihad*, University of California Press, Berkeley, CA, and London, 2002, p. 83.
19 Cited in Kurt Lohbeck, *Holy Wars, Unholy Victory: Eyewitness to the CIA's Secret War in Afghanistan*, Regency Gateway, Washington, D.C., 1993, p. 4.
20 *Observer*, 21 May 1988.
21 Tahir Amin, *Afghanistan Crisis: Implications and Options for Muslim World, Iran and Pakistan*, Institute of Policy Studies, Lahore, 1982, pp. 96–7.
22 See chapter 4, p. 78–9.
23 About twice that number of Islamic radicals studied at the madressas that cropped up along the Afghan-Pakistan border, funded by the Pakistani government, thus raising the number of non-Afghan Muslims who participated in the anti-Soviet jihad, or were exposed to it, to over 100,000. Ahmed Rashid, *Taliban: Islam, Oil and the New Great Game in Central Asia*, I. B. Tauris, London, 2001, and Yale University Press, New Haven, CT, 2001, p. 130.
24 *Washington Post*, 16 October 2001.
25 Dilip Hiro, *Between Marx and Muhammad*, p. 158.
26 Anthony Hyman, *op. cit.*, pp. 203 and 204.
27 *Ibid.*, p. 204.
28 Anthony Arnold, *Afghanistan: The Soviet Invasion in Perspective*, Hoover Institution Press, Stanford, CA, 1985, p. 100
29 *Sunday Times*, 23 Septembr 2001.
30 Peter L. Bergen, *Holy War, Inc.*, p. 60.
31 Agence France Presse, 27 August 1998.
32 This information is based on the revelations made by the former Soviet archivist at the KGB, Vasili Mitrokhin, who defected to Britain in 1992. *Washington Post*, 24 February 2002.
33 Dilip Hiro, *Holy Wars*, p. 264.

34 Babrak Karmal went into voluntary exile in Moscow.

35 *Sunday Times*, 8 February 1987.

36 Ahmed Rashid, *Taliban*, p. 130; *Sunday Times*, 20 January 2002.

37 Peter L. Bergen, *op. cit.*, pp. 61–2. Describing another battle encounter, Osama bin Laden said, "Once I was only 30 meters from the Russians, and they were trying to capture me. I was under bombardment but I was so peaceful in my heart that I fell asleep." Cited in Mamoun Fandy, *Saudi Arabia and the Politics of Dissent*, Palgrave, New York, p. 192.

38 *Observer*, 28 October 2001.

39 *Washington Times*, 23 April 1987. This attack so pleased CIA director William Casey that during his next secret trip to Pakistan he crossed the Afghan border with Gen. Zia al Haq to review the Hizb-e Islami units. Ahmed Rashid, *Taliban*, p. 129.

40 In any given year, the aggregate strength of all the Mujahedin factions ranged between 175,000 and 250,000. Mark Urban, *op. cit.*, p. 60. The estimate of the guerrillas active on any day varied between 35,000 to 100,000. These figures excluded the Iranian-backed insurgents.

41 *Observer*, 9 May 1987.

42 *Ibid.*, 15 May 1988.

43 *The Times*, 15 February 1989; *Guardian*, 16 February 1989. The figure of 70,000 was the approximate mean of the estimated 35,000 to 100,000 guerrillas active on any day. See above note 40. The loyalty of many of the 45–50,000 men in Afghanistan's army and air force to the Najibullah government was questionable.

44 Dilip Hiro, *Between Marx and Muhammad*, p. 255.

45 *Observer*, 28 October 2001.

46 *The Economist*, 1 February 1992, p. 66.

47 *Far Eastern Economic Review*, 2 April 1992, p. 18.

48 Dilip Hiro, *Between Marx and Muhammad*, p. 262. The publicly acknowledged figures were only part of the total. Further larger sums came from the US Defense Department's secret budget. During the 1980s the Pentagon's annual secret budget quadrupled to $36 billion, and the Afghan operation, involving procurement of arms and ammunition for the Mujahedin, was an important item on the list. John K. Cooley, *Unholy Wars: Afghanistan, America and International Terrorism*, Pluto Press, London and Sterling, VA, 2000, p. 109.

49 Dilip Hiro, *Between Marx and Muhammad*, p. 262.

50 *Ibid.*, p. 265. Mujahedin leaders often mentioned a figure of 2 million dead, with no breakdown into direct and indirect deaths.

51 *Guardian*, 26 February 1993.

52 *Sunday Times*, 16 September 2001. A copy was found in the home of a Al Qaida activist in Manchester, UK, and was used as evidence in the trial of four suspects in the 1993 World Trade Center bombing. *New York Times*, 28 October 2001.
53 John K. Cooley, *op. cit.*, p. 121; Peter L. Bergen, *op. cit.*, pp. 87–8.
54 *Far Eastern Economic Review*, 18 February 1993, p. 20; *Middle East International*, 28 May 1993, p. 18.
55 Latifa, *My Forbidden Face: Growing up under the Taliban, a Young Woman's Story* (trans. Lisa Appignanesi), Virago, London, 2002, pp. 123–4.
56 *Middle East International*, 7 January 1994, pp. 13–14; *Guardian*, 9 March 1994.
57 *News* (Islamabad), 2 February 1995.
58 *Observer*, 9 March 1997.
59 *New York Times*, 11 December 1996.
60 Ahmed Rashid, *Taliban*, pp. 28–9.
61 Punishment for long hair was a hair cut and/or two days in jail. Later, at Kabul University dormitories, the officials of the Department of Propagating Virtue and Preventing Vice would wake students in the middle of the night to measure their beards and hair. *New York Times*, 16 January 2002.
62 *Middle East International*, 14 April 1995, pp. 13–14.
63 *Ibid.*, 14 April 1995, p. 12.
64 *Ibid.*, 16 February 1996, p. 14.
65 Ahmed Rashid, *Taliban*, p. 42. Since the Saudi king, even though not wearing Prophet Muhammad's cloak, too is called Emir al Muminin, this interpretation is not strictly correct.
66 *Ibid.*, p. 45.
67 In late 1995, in a secret meeting between American and Sudanese officials in Europe, the Americans listed eviction of bin Laden as one of the conditions for helping Sudan gain "international legitimacy." *New York Times*, 6 September 1998.
68 *Observer*, 28 October 2001.
69 *New York Times*, 6 September 1998.
70 The names of the country where Jamal al Fadl contacted the CIA and his birthplace in Sudan remain classified.
71 Cited in *The Nation*, 15 February 1999, p. 19, and Peter L. Bergen, *op. cit.*, p. 103.
72 Ahmed Rashid, *Taliban*, p. 48.
73 *Observer*, 29 September 1996.
74 Muhamamd Najibullah spurned the offer of President Burhanuddin Rabbani to leave the city with him, seeing in such a move a betrayal of his Pushtun ethnicity.

75 Mullah Muhammad Rabbani would later be promoted to President of the Islamic Emirate of Afghanistan.

76 Cited in Latifa, *op. cit.*, pp. 31–2 and 36.

77 *The Times*, 22 July 1997.

78 Cited in *Middle East International*, 25 October 1996, p. 16.

79 *Financial Times*, 29–30 September 2001.

80 Cited in *Middle East International*, 25 October 1996, p. 16.

81 Ahmed Rashid, *Taliban*, p. 176.

82 Inter Press Service, 8 October 1996.

83 Following an attack by the Afghanistan-based insurgents of the Islamic Renaissance Party of Tajikistan in July 1993 on the border area, resulting in the deaths of 25 Russian border guards and 200 Tajik rebels, Russian President Boris Yeltsin had declared: "The Oxus river is Russia's border as well as Tajikistan's." Inter Press Service, 5 August 1993

84 *Observer*, 28 October 2001.

85 *Guardian*, 12 November 2001; Peter L. Bergen, *op. cit.*, p. 102.

86 Osama bin Laden's diabetes was not severe enough to require a daily insulin injection.

87 *Guardian*, 12 November 2001, which published the English translation of Abdel Bari Atwan's interview with Osama bin Laden, which originally appeared in *Al Quds al Arabi* in December 1996.

88 *Washington Post*, 24 December 2001. The code name of the Afghan tracking group remains classified.

89 *Observer*, 30 August 1998.

90 "I have not spoken to Osama for six years," Hamida Alia Ghanoum told Khalid Batarfi, editor of *Al Medina*. "He used to telephone regularly from Sudan, but stopped calling [from Afghanistan] when he realized the Americans were monitoring his calls." *Sunday Times*, 23 December 2001.

91 *Washington Post*, 5 November 2001.

92 *Ibid.*, 1 December 2001; *Daily Telegraph*, 1 December 2001.

93 *Independent*, 21 May 1997.

94 *Sunday Times*, 11 November 2001. Later Mullah Omar would put the number of the Taliban POWs killed at 3,500.

95 Associated Press, 3 June 1997.

96 The camps that Al Qaida was believed to run near Khost were Al Badr, Abu Bakr al Sadiq, Darunta, Al Farouq, Jihad Ali, al Khaldun and Khalid ibn Walid. Of these only Al Farouq would be directly linked to the 2001 terrorist attacks on the US. Peter L. Bergen, *op. cit.*, p. 97; *New York Times*, 24 September 2000; *Observer*, 30 September 2001.

97 This description was based on the testimony by Ahmad Ressam, a Montreal-based Algerian, arrested in November 1999 as he crossed

into the Washington state of the US with a plan to attack Los Angeles airport. *Sunday Times*, 7 October 2001.
98 John K. Cooley, *op. cit.*, pp. 116–17.
99 *New York Times*, 23 September 2001; *Washington Post*, 18 February 2002.
100 The other state was Qatar.
101 Abu Yasser Rifia Ahmad Taha was given a five-year jail sentence for his role in President Sadat's assassination in 1981.
102 *The Nation*, 15 February 1999, p. 20; Peter L. Bergen, *op. cit.*, pp. 104–5; and Fred Halliday, *Two Hours that Shook the World: September 11, 2001, Causes and Consequences*, Saqi Books, London, 2002, pp. 217–19.
103 *New York Times*, 6 September 1998.
104 Cited in *Middle East International*, 4 September 1998, p. 3.
105 Peter L. Bergen, *op. cit.*, p. 109.
106 Ahmad Rashid, *Taliban*, p. 72.
107 *Middle East International*, 21 August 1998, pp. 13–14.
108 The figure of 4,000 was given by the United Nations on 7 November 1998.
109 Inter Press Service, 31 August 1998.
110 In the Pakistani border district of Mardan alone, about 1,000 of the 6,000 students enrolled in the seven local madressas departed for the front lines. *Middle East International*, 21 August 1998, pp. 13–14.

7 Bombing of US embassies: a wake-up call

1 *Washington Post*, 14 August 2001; *Observer Magazine*, 5 August 2001, pp. 21–23. The CIA claimed later that in 1997 its operatives had foiled two attacks on US embassies, one of them being in Tirana, Albania, in advanced stages of planning, and disrupted three incipient plots by infiltrating cells and monitoring and intercepting communications. *Washington Post*, 11 August 1998.
2 A clean-shaven Muhammad Odeh was carrying a Yemeni passport with a picture of a bearded man. The suspicious immigration officer at Karachi airport, having heard of the bombing in Nairobi over the BBC, passed him on to the security officers. He confessed, saying he was a follower of bin Laden, and had been based in Pakistan before setting up a business in Kenya. He had stayed at the same Hilltop Lodge as Owhali, and had helped to assemble the bomb in Nairobi. Peter L. Bergen, *op. cit.*, pp. 124–5.
3 *Independent*, 8 August 1998; *Middle East International*, 15 January 1999, p. 16; Peter L. Bergen, *op. cit.*, pp. 120–2.

4 Another suspect, Ahmad Salim Swedan, a Kenyan, would be arrested by the Kenyan authorities at the border with Somalia in December 2001. Associated Press, 10 December 2001. That left free three remaining suspects: Mustafa Muhammad Fadl, an Egyptian, and Ahmad Khlafan Ghailani and Fahd Muhammad Ali Msalam, both Kenyan. *New York Times*, 25 December 1998.

5 Dilip Hiro, *Sharing the Promised Land*, Hodder & Stoughton, London, 1996, Interlink Publishing Group, New York, 1999, p. 266.

6 *Ibid.*, p. 266.

7 *Al Islam wa Falastin*, 5 June 1988, p. 14.

8 *Financial Times*, 13 September 2001; *Sunday Times*, 16 September 2001. In early 1996 a suicide truck-bombing in front of the Central Bank of Sri Lanka in downtown Colombo killed 72 people and devastated a large area.

9 *Observer*, 16 August 2001.

10 As a serving US soldier he should have sought permission to do what he did. He returned with a Soviet tactical map and a belt of a Spetsnaz (Soviet Special Forces) soldier whom he claimed to have killed. Peter L. Bergen, *op. cit.*, p. 142.

11 *Ibid.*, p. 145.

12 The Senate Select Committee on Intelligence under Senator Frank Church reported on 20 November 1975 that it had found five US plots against foreign leaders under Presidents Dwight Eisenhower (r. 1952–60), John Kennedy (r. 1961–3) and Richard Nixon (r. 1969–74). *Washington Post*, 28 October 2001. The foreign leaders were Ahmad Seokarno (r. 1949–67) of Indonesia, Fidel Castro (r. 1959–) of Cuba, Patrice Lumumba (r. 1960) of Congo, Ngo Din Diem (r. 1954–63) of South Vietnam, and François Duvalier (r. 1957–71) of Haiti. Lumumba and Dien were assassinated, Seokarno and Duvalier died naturally, and Castro is still in power.

13 President Clinton declined to authorize a large-scale operation, necessitating deployment of ground forces, that Gen. Henry Shelton, Chairman of the Joint Chiefs of Staff, said would be required. *Washington Post*, 19 December 2001.

14 *New York Times*, 23 September 2001.

15 Ahmed Rashid, *Jihad: The Rise of Militant Islam in Central Asia*, Yale University Press, New Haven, CT, and London, pp. 148–9.

16 *Washington Post*, 15 October, 2001.

17 *International Herald Tribune*, 17 September 2001.

18 *Daily Telegraph*, 1 December 2001; *Washington Post*, 1 December 2001. Muhammad Khaksar remained in Kabul while other Taliban leaders fled in November 2001, and lived in his earlier spacious residence unmolested.

19 *Financial Times*, 22–3 August 1998; *International Herald Tribune*, 27 August 1998; *Observer*, 30 August 1998.
20 Associated Press, 20 August 1998. Clinton's statements were based on a sealed indictment against bin Laden from a New York grand jury charging him with terrorist crimes, based on the testimony of Jamal Ahmad al Fadl. *New York Times*, 6 September 1998.
21 *Observer*, 30 August 1998; *International Herald Tribune*, 31 August 2001.
22 *Washington Post*, 19 December 2001. Inside Afghanistan, the hired tribal allies of the CIA twice skirmished with bin Laden forces, but they inflicted no verifiable damage.
23 *International Herald Tribune*, 22–3 August 1998.
24 *News International*, Islamabad, Pakistan, 19 February 1999.
25 *Washington Post*, 30 September 2001.
26 *New York Times*, 8 February 1999.
27 Cited in *Financial Times*, 22–3 August 1998. Whether the Pentagon had secured permission to use Pakistani airspace was left deliberately obscure by both sides.
28 *New York Times*, 8 February 1999.
29 There were 6,000 Islamic charities worldwide. Three years later 30 of these would be scrutinized by the US.
30 *New York Times*, 3 October 2001. Some of the biggest family-based hawala dealers are based in London. *Financial Times*, 24 September 2001.
31 *Daily Telegraph*, 15 September 2001.
32 Inter Press Service, 31 August 1998.
33 *Washington Post*, 29 October 2001; *International Herald Tribune*, 30 October 2001.
34 *The Nation*, 15 February 1999, pp. 19–20; Associated Press, 15 December 1998.
35 *Time*, 11 January 1999, pp. 34–5.
36 *The Nation*, 15 February 1999, pp. 19–20; *Time*, 11 January 1999, pp. 34–5.
37 On 10 August 1999 the Clinton administration froze the assets of Afghan Ariana Airline in the US because of its links with bin Laden.
38 Washington cut off direct aid to Islamabad in 1990 when President George Bush determined that Pakistan was developing nuclear weapons. *New York Times*, 28 January 2000.
39 *Washington Post*, 20 December 2001.
40 *Middle East International*, 3 September 1999, p. 16; *Washington Post*, 3 October 2001.
41 *Middle East International*, 12 October 2001, p. 31.

42 The country had been governed by the military for 27 years. Popular confidence in politicians was so low that only 37 percent voted in the 1996 parliamentary poll.

43 *Middle East International*, 12 October 2001, p. 31.

44 *Ibid.*

45 *Washington Post*, 3 October 2001.

46 *Ibid.*, 15 November 1999.

47 Reuters, 15 November 1999; *Sunday Times*, 19 December 1999.

48 *Observer*, 2 January 2000.

49 Author's italics. *New York Times*, 28 January 2000. The ill-defined word "repeatedly" gave the US much leeway.

50 Associated Press, 30 January 2000.

51 *Washington Post*, 5 February 2000.

52 *Time*, 11 January 1999, p. 35.

53 *Sunday Times*, 26 March 2000.

54 SAD units were run by the deputy director in charge of the CIA's operations. *Washington Post*, 19 November 2001.

55 By the summer of 1999, an estimated quarter million audio-tapes of Osama bin Laden's speeches had been sold. *Sunday Times Book Review*, 26 September 1999, p. 7.

56 Cited in *New York Times*, 12 June 2000.

57 *Ibid.*; *Washington Post*, 23 June 2000.

58 *Ibid.*, 16 November 2000.

59 *New York Times*, 8 December 2000.

60 *Washington Post*, 2 November 2000.

61 *Middle East International*, 26 January 2001, p. 17.

62 The direct gain to the Taliban treasury was modest, $25–50 million in taxes on poppies and opium production. *New York Times*, 26 September and 6 October 2001; *Observer*, 18 November 2001.

63 Peter L. Bergen, *op. cit.*, pp. 147–8.

64 *Los Angeles Times*, 12 February 2001; *Guardian*, 17 February 2001.

65 About a year earlier Mullah Qudratullah Jamal, information and culture minister, and Aghajan Motasem, finance minister, examined each object at the National Museum in Kabul to determine if it depicted a living being. If it did, it was smashed with axes forthwith. *Los Angeles Times*, 24 November 2001.

66 *Observer*, 4 November 2001.

67 *Middle East International*, 10 August 2001, p. 21.

68 *Washington Post*, 20 January 2002.

69 "As the chief Pakistani delegate at the Berlin conference, I informed my government," said Niyaz Naik. Telephone interview with Niyaz Naik in Islamabad, January 2002. Both the Taliban and the Northern Alliance were invited to the meeting; but only the Northern Alliance's Abdullah Abdullah turned up.

70 *Daily Telegraph*, 14 September 2001; *Sunday Telegraph*, 23 September 2001.
71 *Washington Post*, 20 January 2002.
72 They would all later receive life sentences.
73 *Middle East International*, 14 September 2001, p. 21; *Sunday Times*, 23 September 2001; *Washington Post*, 7 November 2001.
74 *Sunday Times*, 16 September 2001.
75 Peter L. Bergen, *op. cit.*, p. 113.
76 *International Herald Tribune*, 14 March 2002.
77 *Washington Post*, 28 September 2001; *Financial Times*, 29–30 September 2001.

8 Eighty minutes that shook the world and global response

1 The real Abdul Aziz al Omari was an electrical engineer in Saudi Arabia, whose passport was stolen in a burglary in 1996 when he was a university student in Denver, Colorado.
2 Another Saeed al Ghamdi, a pilot with Saudi Airlines, was in Tunis on that day, having been based there for the past 10 months to learn to fly Airbus A320.
3 Ziad Jarrah left Hamburg in June 2000. On 10 September 2001, he wrote a four-page letter to his Turkish-German girlfriend, Ayse Sengun, a medical student at Bochum University at Karlsruhe, Germany. "I did what I had to do and you should be very proud of me," he said. "It is a great honor, and you will see the result, and everyone will be celebrating." Jarrah posted the letter with a mistake in the address, so the German Post Office returned it, stamped "Address Unknown," to the US where it was intercepted, and opened, by the FBI, in mid-November. In Germany Jarrah visited Sengun regularly and stayed in her flat. *Observer*, 18 November 2001.
4 Another Ahmad al Nami, aged 33, was an administrative supervisor with Saudi Airlines, who had not lost his passport.
5 Six weeks before the hijackings, Hani Hanjour flew over the Washington area three times.
6 On 23 August 2001, the CIA had put Hani Hanjour on its banned list due to his confirmed membership of Al Qaida.
7 Another Salem al Hamzi, aged 26, worked at a petrochemical plant in Yanbo, Saudi Arabia: his passport was stolen by a pickpocket in 1998 in Cairo.
8 *New York Times*, 24 February 2002.
9 *Ibid*. The World Trade Center Complex of seven buildings in Lower Manhattan was built by the Port Authority of New York and New Jersey in 1974 and then leased.

10 *Sunday Times*, 16 September 2001.
11 The reports that the authorities believed that one or more hijacked planes were heading for the White House had to be treated with caution. Had such an aircraft approached the White House, it would have most probably been shot down by the Secret Service equipped with shoulder-held Stinger missiles.
12 Associated Press, 14 January 2002.
13 *Daily Telegraph*, 27 October 2001; *Washington Post*, 2 March 2002.
14 *New York Times*, 22–23 September 2001; *Independent on Sunday, 30 September 2001; Guardian*, 17 October 2001.
15 *International Herald Tribune*, 13 September 2001. By the night of 13 September, a *Washington Post*–American Broadcasting Corporation poll showed Bush enjoying 86 percent approval rating, up from 55 percent over the weekend. *Financial Times*, 15–16 September 2001.
16 See Appendix I.
17 However, the US Congress promptly paid up its long-standing arrears to the UN.
18 *International Herald Tribune*, 17 September 2001.
19 *Financial Times*, 15–16 September 2001.
20 *Daily Telegraph*, 13 September 2001; *Independent*, 13 September 2001; BBC News, 13 September 2001.
21 Peter L. Bergen, *op. cit.*, p. 242. He later apologized for his remarks and withdrew them.
22 See p. 111.
23 *International Herald Tribune*, 20 September 2001; *Observer*, 23 September 2001. His father Muhammad al Amir Atta insisted that his son was murdered and his identity stolen.
24 *Washington Post*, 25 September 2001. Abha happened to be the home town of the radical Saudi cleric Safar al Hawali.
25 *Financial Times*, 13 September 2001.
26 *Independent*, 13 September 2001; *Washington Post*, 14 September 2001.
27 *International Herald Tribune*, 17 September 2001; *Daily Telegraph*, 23 September 2001.
28 *New York Times*, 10 October 2001.
29 *International Herald Tribune*, 13 and 17 September; *Sunday Telegraph*, 23 September 2001; *Washington Post*, 25 September 2001.
30 *International Herald Tribune*, 13 and 14 September 2001; *Independent*, 14 September 2001; *Financial Times*, 24 September 2001. China had kept the reporting on the September 11 attacks "modest and factual" in contrast to the "extensive or emotional" coverage in the West, reported the Beijing correspondent of the *New York Times*, 1 October 2001.

31 *Independent*, 13 September 2001; *Washington Post*, 15 September 2001.

32 Reuters, 26 September 2001.

33 *International Herald Tribune*, 20 September 2001.

34 *Ibid.*, 13 and 20 September 2001; *Independent*, 13, 14 and 20 September 2001.

35 *Observer*, 16 September 2001.

36 *Independent*, 14 September 2001; *Washington Post*, 14 September 2001.

37 In September 2001, some 4,000 madressa students were engaged in fighting alongside the Taliban in their anti-Northern Alliance offensives.

38 As a result of the Afghan Transit Trade Agreement with Pakistan – stemming from the transit facility for landlocked countries mandated by the UN Charter – about half of Afghanistan's imports came through Pakistan. This facility led to misuse. In 2000, for instance, Afghanistan imported a large number of television sets despite the Taliban's ban on television, as well as 1 million telephone sets when there were only 35,000 telephones in operation. As a result, goods worth $1 billion are smuggled across the border, losing Pakistan $400 million in customs and tax revenue annually. *Financial Times*, 27–28 October 2001.

39 In 2000, Pakistan's domestic debt was $38 billion. In October the Paris Club of lenders agreed to reschedule $12 billion in loans to Islamabad, and the EU rushed through trade concessions to Pakistan worth $1.35 billion. Besides rescheduling a $1 billion loan to Pakistan, Japan and America authorized $90 million in aid. At their behest, the IMF gave Islamabad debt relief and relaxed its conditions governing its loan of $1 billion. *Washington Post*, 3 October 2001; *Guardian*, 20 October 2001; *New York Times*, 31 October; *Financial Times*, 31 October 2001; *International Herald Tribune*, 20 December 2001.

40 *New York Times*, 18 September 2001. The Indian government's caution was justified. Sayyid Ahmad Bukhari, the imam of Delhi's historic Jama Masjid, backed the Taliban and denounced the American strikes on Afghanistan as attacks on Islam. Associated Press, 9 November 2001.

41 *International Herald Tribune*, 18 September 2001. "Bin Laden has become a symbol of defiance in the face of American arrogance," said a journalist in Saudi Arabia to Neil MacFarquhar of the *New York Times*, 6 October 2001.

42 *Financial Times*, 21 September 2001.

43 *International Herald Tribune*, 18 and 19 September 2001; *Washington Post*, 20 September 2001.

44 *Independent*, 20 September 2001.

45 *Guardian*, 21 September 2001.

46 *International Herald Tribune*, 17 September 2001.

47 *Independent*, 20 September 2001; *Financial Times*, 21 September 2001.

48 In an internal debate regarding declassifying some secret information within the Bush administration, the decision to publish evidence against bin Laden was postponed indefinitely. *New York Times*, 27 September 2001. In the end, different versions would be shown privately to different parties, from Pakistan to Egypt to Nato, with Britain publishing a sanitized version with the connivance of Washington in early October.

49 *New York Times*, 27 September 2001. The Pakistan Foreign Ministry spokesman said that the 21-page evidence, linking Al Qaida also to the 1998 bombings, given to them by Washington on 2 October was convincing: "This material certainly provides sufficient basis for indictment in court of law." *Guardian*, 5 October 2000. Later, on BBC television, foreign minister Abdul Sattar explained that "Indictment is not the same as conviction. It is up to a court to convict bin Laden or not.'

50 This was a substantial amount for Uzbekistan with per capita annual income of $2,400.

51 *International Herald Tribune*, 11 October 2001.

52 *Sunday Telegraph*, 23 September 2001. In December, at the height of tension between India and Pakistan, President Bush referred to "Indians and Pakis," unaware that "Paki," a pejorative term for "Pakistani," is used by white racists.

53 *International Herald Tribune*, 20 September 2001.

54 *Washington Post*, 6 October 2001. Retd. Maj.-Gen. Wayne Downing, who commanded these units in the Gulf War, was appointed Director of Counter-terrorism at the National Security Council.

55 *New York Times*, 27 January 2002.

56 *Sunday Times*, 23 September 2001; *Independent on Sunday*, 30 September 2001.

57 *International Herald Tribune*, 29–30 September 2001.

58 Afghanistan had only 35,000 telephones. *Financial Times*, 27–28 October 2001.

59 *Ibid.*, 22–23 September 2001.

60 Though five European nations – Britain, France, Germany, Italy and Spain – offered military support, the US accepted only Britain's. *Financial Times*, 24 September 2001.

61 *Independent*, 20 September 2001.

62 A day earlier President Bush had appointed Tom Ridge, governor of Pennsylvania, director of the Office of Homeland Security, as a presidential advisor. *Financial Times*, 21 September 2001.

63 *Washington Post*, 26 November 2001.

64 Cited in *Financial Times*, 17 September 2001.

65 Actually, the idea of "revolving coalitions" was first aired by Richard Haas in his book *The Reluctant Sheriff*, published in 2000. In it he proposed a form of ad hoc multilateralism based on "coalitions of the willing," with the US acting as the reluctant sheriff, to deal with the unpredictable crises thrown up by the deregulated post-Cold War world. He had since then been appointed head of the policy planning section at the State Department.

66 *Washington Post*, 12 February 2002. This happened in the midst of a Riyadh–Washington spat once it emerged that 15 of the 19 suicide hijackers were from Saudi Arabia.

67 *Washington Post*, 30 September 2001; *Financial Times*, 13–14 and 29 October 2001; *International Herald Tribune*, 10–11 November 2001; *New York Times*, 9 November 2001; *Washington Post*, 10 February 2002.

68 *New York Times*, 17 September 2001.

69 *Observer*, 30 September 2001.

70 *New York Times*, 27 September 2001.

71 *The Times*, 25 September 2001.

72 The mountainous Afghan-Pakistan border had 300 crossings, very few of which were staffed. So there was free flow of traffic after dark. Fuel supplies also got into Afghanistan from Iran and Turkmenistan, both of them being oil-producing countries.

73 *Daily Telegraph*, 9 and 10 October 2001.

74 Associated Press, 28 September 2001.

75 http://news.bbc.co.uk/hi/english/world/south_asia/newid_1550000/1550366.stm.

76 *New York Times*, 2 October 2001.

77 *Observer*, 9 December 2001.

78 *Financial Times*, 24 September 2001; *International Herald Tribune*, 25 September 2001; *Washington Post*, 27 September 2001.

79 The discreet presence of American troops and military hardware in Qatar would become public knowledge in early November when a gunman would fire at Qatari and American troops at al Udaid air base 20 miles (32 km) from Doha. The Qatari–American military cooperation agreement signed in 2000 allowed the Pentagon the use of the Qatari air base in "times of need." *New York Times*, 8 November 2001.

80 *Washington Post*, 26 September 2001.

81 *New York Times*, 27 September 2001. On the eve of the US bombing on 7 October, Bush sent a confidential memorandum to Iran through the Swiss embassy assuring it that the Pentagon would not use Iranian air space. The next day Iran replied that it would rescue any US personnel in distress in its territory, thus implying its *de facto* membership of the coalition. That day the Bush administration petitioned a federal judge to throw out a $10 billion suit against Iran by the 1979 American hostages. *New York Times*, 16 October 2001; *Guardian*, 19 October 2001. It later transpired that Iran had allowed 165,000 tons of US food aid for the Afghan people to be unloaded at an Iranian airport and shipped through their territory into Afghanistan.

82 For example, Switzerland was then not a member of the United Nations.

83 *Financial Times*, 29–30 September 2001. There were already 11 UN Conventions on terrorism, some of them concerning its specific aspects such as hijacking, piracy, bombing and diplomatic security. Within a fortnight, 111 countries informed the UN that they had modified their banking laws to crack down on terrorists.

84 *International Herald Tribune*, 3 and 5 October 2001.

85 *New York Times*, 4 October 2001; *Observer*, 7 October 2001.

86 *Guardian*, 5 October 2001.

87 Gen. Musharraf extended his term as army chief of staff indefinitely. *Daily Telegraph*, 9 and 10 October 2001.

88 *Daily Telegraph*, 8 October 2001; Agence France Press, 9 October 2001; Associated Press, 9 October 2001; Reuters, 9 October 2001; *New York Times*, 9 October 2001; *Washington Post*, 9 October 2001; *The Times*, 9 October 2001.

89 Hypocrite (*munafiq*) is the one who claims to be Muslim but is not because of his failure to follow Islamic requirements in his life. According to the Quran (4:144), "Surely the hypocrites will be in the lowest reaches of the Fire [of Hell]; you will not find for them any helper.'

90 The estimates given by the World Health Organization in March 1996 were "500,000 dead during 1990–94," and by Unicef in July 2000, "500,000 dead during 1991–98'. *Guardian*, 10 October 2001.

91 Reuters, 7 October 2001; *Daily Telegraph*, 8 October 2001. Ayman Zawahiri pointed out that America had lost in Vietnam, fled from Lebanon and Sudan, and was attacked in Yemen. And, addressing Muslims worldwide, Suleiman abu Ghaith said: "Either you are on the side of believers or you are on the side of infidels." *Financial Times*, 8 October 2001.

92 *Financial Times*, 11 October 2001.

93 According to "Doctor" from Kabul, "The four Afghan demining officials at the UN premise got killed because their office was rented from Radio Shariat'; and they died during an operation designed to destroy transmission towers. *Independent*, 27 October 2001.

94 *International Herald Tribune*, 9 October 2001.

95 *Guardian*, 20 October 2001.

96 *Financial Times*, 16 October 2001; *International Herald Tribune*, 17 October 2001.

97 *Independent*, 27 October 2001.

98 *The Times*, 15 October 2001; *Financial Times*, 16 October 2001.

99 *International Herald Tribune*, 26 September 2001; *Guardian*, 10 October 2001; *Observer*, 14 October 2001.

100 *Al Hayat*, 12 October 2001.

101 *Washington Post*, 8 October 2001. On 7 October a bomb in Khobar killed one American and injured several more.

102 *New York Times*, 6 October 2001.

103 This figure was leaked to the *New York Times* by a US intelligence source, and was published on 28 January 2002.

104 *Sunday Times*, 21 October 2001.

105 Established in 1988, the Islamic Cultural Institute in Milan, described by Washington as "the main Al Qaida station house in Europe," turned out to be a rundown, two-story warehouse off a gray, polluted road, with a badly lit counter serving food and a small grocery on the ground floor, and a prayer room, a shop selling videos and the Quran, and a television room. Its 54-year-old Libyan-Italian director, Shari Abdul Hamid, said that the donations collected at Friday prayers and income from the restaurant and grocery paid the $2,275 monthly rent and supported the family of Imad, jailed in 1995 for six months along with 63 Egyptians suspected of being members of a terrorist organization, all of whom were released for lack of evidence. *Financial Times*, 13–14 October 2001.

106 *Washington Post*, 11 and 26 October 2001. *New Yorker*, 22 October 2001, pp. 13–25. The issue was on sale on 17 October. However, with 6 million expatriate workers in Saudi Arabia sending home $15 billion a year – some of it through the illegal hawala system – and tens of thousands of Saudi nationals holding foreign assets, it was impossible to block off money to Al Qaida from Saudi sources.

107 *Washington Post*, 4 November 2001.

108 *New York Times*, 9 November 2001.

109 Foreign ministers of Egypt, Pakistan and Saudi Arabia said they were satisfied that bin Laden was responsible. *Financial Times*, 11 October 2001.

110 Reuters, 8 October 2001; *The Times*, 8 October 2001.

111 *Guardian*, 9 October 2001.

112 *Financial Times*, 13–14 October 2001.

113 *Ibid.*, 15 October 2001; *Guardian*, 20 October 2001.

114 *Financial Times*, 6–7 October 2001. Protesting against the US pressure on Al Jazeera, the Paris-based Reporters Sans Frontières said in its letter to Powell: "The United States is joining the many authoritarian regimes in the Middle East, who have little respect for freedom of the press, in their criticism of the channel. Informational pluralism must be respected in all circumstances." Reuters, 12 October 2001.

115 Al Jazeera TV was funded by a Qatari state subsidy, advertising revenue and its contracts with such broadcasting organizations as the BBC, CNN and Sky TV.

116 *International Herald Tribune*, 16 October 2001.

117 *Ibid.*, 19 October 2001.

118 Once airborne, the control of the Predator was taken over by the US air force.

119 'We follow the Voice of America in Pashto at 7 p.m., then we turn to the Pashto service of the BBC," said "Doctor." "The best program is on the BBC Dari Service: *Majaliya Asiayeh Miona (Central Asian Magazine)* which knows what is happening in Afghanistan." *Independent*, 27 October 2001.

120 *Ibid.*, 27 October 2001.

121 *Sunday Times*, 21 October and 4 November 2001; *Independent*, 26 October 2001; *Guardian*, 6 November 2001.

122 *The Times*, 2 November 2001; *Financial Times*, 3–4 November 2001.

123 *Financial Times*, 3–4 November 2001.

124 *Observer*, 28 October 2001.

125 *New York Times*, 30 October 2001.

126 Even in normal times US president and vice president tend not to appear together in public. But now Bush's personal team of Karl Rove, Joe Allbaugh and Karen Hughes decided to keep Cheney in the shadows to ensure that Americans or others did not think Cheney was pulling the strings of a less-assured Bush whose image of a confident, resolute leader had to be cultivated and maintained.

127 *Washington Post*, 10 November 2001.

128 *Ibid.*, 23 October 2001.

129 Agence France Presse, 31 October 2001; Associated Press, 31 October 2001; Reuters, 31 October 2001.
130 *New York Times*, 21 October 2001.
131 *Washington Post*, 5 November 2001.
132 *Financial Times*, 3–4 November 2001.
133 *International Herald Tribune*, 2 and 9 November 2001.
134 *Washington Post*, 7 November 2001; Agence France Presse, 12 January 2002.
135 Al Jazeera TV used bin Laden's 20-minute tape as an introduction to a discussion in which Chris Ross, former US ambassador to Syria and Algeria, speaking in Arabic, answered each of bin Laden's points. *Observer*, 4 November 2001; *New York Times*, 4 November 2001.
136 *Guardian*, 2 November 2001.
137 *Ibid.*; *New York Times*, 9 November 2001. The anti-government demonstrations in Pakistan on 9 November claimed three more lives.
138 The CIA spent $7 million to bribe 35 warlords to change sides. *Washington Times*, 7 February 2002.
139 *Sunday Times*, 11 November 2001; *Observer*, 11 November 2001; *Middle East International*, 23 November 2001, pp. 6–7.
140 *Ibid.*, 21 December 2001, p. 16.
141 That day Bamiyan in central Afghanistan fell to the Wahadat.
142 On 16 October, Mullah Omar's emissary withdrew $5 million in US dollars and Pakistani rupees from the Central Bank in Kabul. On the night of 12 November, senior Taliban leaders took away $6 million. *Washington Post*, 9 January 2002.
143 *Observer*, 18 November 2001.
144 Typically, at a press conference, pro-Tehran Ismail Khan did not thank the US, merely saying, "American bombing was useful in some places." *Washington Post*, 17 November 2001.
145 *New York Times*, 14 November 2001; *Washington Post*, 14 and 26 November 2001; *The Times*, 17 November 2001.
146 "But," Bush added, "peace will only come when all have sworn off forever violence, incitement and terror." *Sunday Times*, 11 November 2001.
147 Associated Press, 16 November 2001; Reuters, 16 November 2001; *New York Times*, 12 December 2001.
148 *International Herald Tribune*, 14 November 2001.
149 *Guardian*, 14 November 2001. On the eve of Ramadan, Bush had "saluted" Islam, and pledged $320 million to buy 500,000 tons of food for Afghans.
150 *The Times*, 15 November 2001.
151 *Sunday Times*, 18 November 2001.

152 *The Times*, 17 November 2001.

153 Associated Press, 15 November 2001; *The Times*, 15 November 2001; *New York Times*, 16 November 2001; *Observer*, 18 November 2001. David Rohde and other reporters of the *New York Times* collected more than 5,000 pages of documents from abandoned safe houses in Kabul, Mazar-e Sharif and Kandahar as well as the destroyed training camps, which were later translated into English. The documents included training manuals – such as *TM 31–210 Improvised Munitions Handbook*, published by the Department of US Army in 1969 – references books, course curriculums, instructor lesson notes and student notebooks. *New York Times*, 17 and 18 March 2002

154 *The Times*, 15 November 2001. Nothing underscored Al Jazeera's professionalism better than its readiness to let Israeli Prime Minister Ariel Sharon use the channel to deliver his threatening message to Yasser Arafat and the Palestinian Authority following the suicide bomb on Passover, 27 March 2002, which killed 27 Israeli Jews. Al Jazeera's cameras were all ready to roll when Sharon canceled the arrangement. *International Herald Tribune*, 29 March 2002.

155 *Middle East International*, 7 December 2001, pp. 16–17.

156 *New York Times*, 3 and 17 December 2001; *Sunday Times*, 20 January 2002.

157 *International Herald Tribune*, 8 November and 6 December 2001.

158 *Washington Post*, 7 December 2001. A subsequent Pentagon inquiry blamed the mishap on a US Special Forces air controller replacing a dead battery in the midst of providing target coordinates to B52 bombers. *Ibid.*, 25 March 2002.

159 *Middle East International*, 21 December 2001, p. 16.

160 *New York Times*, 12 December 2001; *Washington Post*, 24 December 2001.

161 Following the murder of US ambassador Adolph Dubs in his room at the Intercontinental Hotel in Kabul in December 1979, the State Department reduced the embassy staff to the absolute minimum.

162 *Middle East International*, 21 December 2001, p. 16.

163 After viewings by the lower echelons of the State Department and Pentagon, the video-tape traveled up to cabinet members and finally reached Bush on 29 November when he watched it. Those opposed to the release of the tape argued that it would help the defense of Zacarias Moussaoui, a French-Moroccan trainee pilot arrested in the US before September 11 and facing trial on charges of complicity in the attacks, on the ground that since he did not make the journey to any airport on September 11 he could not have known what the operation was.

164 *New York Times*, 17 December 2001. The Saudi government said that Khalid al Harbi had departed from the kingdom around 21 September.

165 *Washington Post*, 14 and 21 December 2001; *Daily Telegraph*, 22 December 2001; *International Herald Tribune*, 31 January 2002.

166 *Washington Post*, 14 December 2001; *Middle East International*, 21 December 2001, pp. 15–17. Skeptics noted that in the long bin Laden–Harbi conversation, there was no mention of the target of the fourth hijacked jet, which crashed in Pennsylvania. If bin Laden, apparently speaking in a triumphant mood, had stated the intended destination of that plane, his guilt would have been established, they argued.

167 Agence France Presse, 27 December 2001; Associated Press, 27 December 2001; Reuters, 27 December 2001.

9 Ongoing war against terror: an uncharted territory

1 *New York Times*, 13, 14 and 15 December 2001. The opposition protest at the Defense Ministry's payment of $2,500 each for 500 coffins for dead soldiers in the Kargil region of Kashmir led to three straight days of noisy protest and adjournment of the Lower House.

2 *New York Times*, 14 December 2001.

3 *Ibid.*, 3 January 2002.

4 Associated Press, 27 April 2000.

5 *The Times*, 17 January 2001.

6 *International Herald Tribune*, 2 and 4 October 2001.

7 *Sunday Times*, 4 October 1998.

8 See pp. 282–3.

9 The Indian military was equipped with 5,000 tanks and 700 combat aircraft while Pakistan's 600,000 soldiers were armed with 2,300 tanks and 350 warplanes. *Washington Post*, 2 January 2002.

10 *Ibid.*, 29 December 2001.

11 *Ibid.*, 2 January 2002.

12 Pakistan possessed enough material for 30–40 atomic bombs.

13 *New York Times*, 3 January 2002.

14 *International Herald Tribune*, 12–13 January 2002. On the eve of its Republic day, India tested a missile with 440 miles (700 km) range, capable of carrying nuclear weapons.

15 Over 35,000 Pakistani soldiers protected the US troops and military hardware at four air bases, at the annual cost of $400 million. *Washington Post*, 29 December 2001.

16 *New York Times*, 6 December 2001.

17 Agence France Presse, 12 January 2002.

18 *Ibid.*, 12 January 2002; *Sunday Times*, 13 January 2002.

19 Associated Press, 12 January 2002.

20 *Outlook*, 14 January 2002, p. 160.

21 This was to be the preamble to the Council deciding as to which UN members had complied with the requirements of Resolution 1373 and which ones had not, with the latter category to be penalized by sanctions to be decided by the Council. *New York Times*, 11 October 2001; *Financial Times*, 27–28 October 2001.

22 *Washington Post*, 22 December 2001.

23 *Ibid.*, 10 January 2002.

24 Reuters, 9 January 2002.

25 *Washington Post*, 22 December 2001.

26 The Pentagon's earlier such missions had dragged on. Its 5,400 troops had been in Kosovo since 1999, and 3,100 soldiers in Bosnia since 1995. *New York Times*, 9 January 2002.

27 *Ibid.*, 9 January 2002.

28 *Sunday Times*, 20 January 2002.

29 *International Herald Tribune*, 23–24 November 2001.

30 The Defense Policy Board's members included Dan Quayle, former vice president; Henry Kissinger, former secretary of state; James Schlesinger and Harold Brown, both former defense secretaries; Newt Gingrich, former House Speaker of the House of Representatives; Admiral David Jeremiah, former deputy chairman of joint chiefs of staff; and James Woolsey, former CIA director.

31 Cited in *Daily Telegraph*, 22 December 2001.

32 *Washington Post*, 11 February 2002.

33 Cited at http://www.whitehouse.gov/news/2002/01/20020129-11.html.

34 *New York Times*, 4 February 2002. In a television interview, Madeleine Albright said that Bush had made "a big mistake" by lumping together Iran, Iraq and North Korea. The Clinton administration had a "potentially verifiable agreement" with North Korea to stop the export of missile technology. Reuters, 1 February 2002. North Korea said that the US had staged 150 U-2 spy plane reconnaissance flights during past 30 days in readiness for an attack. There were 37,000 US troops in South Korea. *Sunday Times*, 3 February 2002.

35 Summarized in *This Week*, 23 February 2002, p. 13.

36 *New York Times*, 23 January 2002.

37 *Ibid.*, 7 February 2002.

38 *Financial Times*, 19 December 2001.

39 *Guardian*, 10 February 2002.

40 *Financial Times*, 15 February 2002.

41 However, US presidents have dispatched troops abroad 120 to 200 times. Congress passed the War Powers Act in 1973, requiring the

president to notify Congress in a timely fashion when troops are sent abroad. The troops must be withdrawn within 90 days unless Congress approves the mission. President George Bush Sr. sought and won Congressional approval for military operations against Iraq in January 1991, with the Senate voting 50:47.

42 The British report said that there was no evidence to link Iraq with the 9/11 attacks or to the Al Qaida network. *Sunday Times*, 10 March 2002.

43 *International Herald Tribune*, 22 November 2001.

44 *Washington Post*, 30 September 2001.

45 *Ibid.*, 21 February 2001.

46 *International Herald Tribune*, 2–3, 5 and 6 February 2002.

47 Cited in *Middle East International*, 22 May 1998, pp. 10–11.

48 *New York Times*, 12 March 2002.

49 *Ibid.*

10 Summary and conclusions

1 Both figures are in terms of the purchasing power of the US dollar in 1981.

2 *New York Times*, 27 August 2001.

3 Cited in *New Yorker*, 22 October 2001, p. 21.

4 See p. 162.

5 *New York Times*, 11 March 2002.

6 *Washington Post*, 18 January 2002.

7 *Observer*, 23 September 2001. See also pp. 157–9.

8 *International Herald Tribune*, 21 January 2002.

9 *Sunday Times*, 27 January 2002.

10 *New York Times*, 11 March 2002.

11 The persistent rumors that Anwar Sadat was recruited by the CIA during his 1966 assignment to secure peace in North Yemen's civil war through his contacts with the Saudi intelligence chief remain uninvestigated by scholars in America despite the access to CIA documents allowed under the Freedom of Information Act, 1974.

12 *Middle East International*, 23 April 1999, p. 21.

13 *New York Times*, 21 December 2001.

14 *Washington Post*, 30 January 2002.

15 *Guardian*, 14 November 2001.

16 By 2001, terrorism by ETA, which started in 1968, had claimed 835 lives. Terrorism by the Catholic IRA, seeking unification of Northern Ireland with the Republic of Ireland, and its Protestant adversary, the Unionist Volunteer Force, committed to maintaining the present division of the island, had resulted in 3,500 deaths by 2001.

17 *Sueddeutsche Zeitung*, 2 October 2001.

18 *Financial Times*, 15 February 2002.
19 *New York Times*, 7 February 2002.
20 *International Herald Tribune*, 19 October 2001.
21 David J. Whittaker, *The Terrorism Reader*, Routledge, London and New York, 2001, pp. 3 and 245. Even the USA PATRIOT Act 2001 has two different definitions of terrorism – in Sections 802 and 808.
22 *International Herald Tribune*, 3 April 2002.
23 *New York Times*, 9 November 2001.
24 Associated Press, 6 November 2001.
25 *Financial Times*, 26 November 2001.
26 *Sunday Times Magazine*, 18 November 2001, p. 26.
27 *Ibid.*, pp. 26, 29 and 31.
28 Agence France Presse, 31 October 2001.
29 *The Times*, 15 November 2001.
30 *New York Times*, 27 September 2001.
31 *Washington Post*, 28 September 2001.
32 *Financial Times*, 29–30 September 2001; *International Herald Tribune*, 29–30 September 2001.
33 Associated Press, 18 October 2001; Agence France Presse, 12 January 2002.
34 Reuters, 26 February 2002.
35 *International Herald Tribune*, 20 December 2001.
36 *New York Times*, 30 September 2001.
37 *Ibid.*, 12 December 2001.
38 *Dawn*, 10 November 2001.
39 *New York Times*, 26 February 2002.
40 *Ibid.*, 7 October 2001.
41 Dilip Hiro, *Dictionary of the Middle East*, p. 151.
42 See pp. 78–9.
43 *International Herald Tribune*, 3 April 2002.

Epilogue

1 *New York Times*, 8 March 2002.
2 *International Herald Tribune*, 9–10 March 2002; *Middle East International*, 22 March 2002, p. 11.
3 *Washington Post*, 13 March 2002; *New York Times*, 19 March 2002. A poll by the mass circulation Hebrew daily *Ma'ariv* showed 71 percent support for the Israeli offensive.
4 *Middle East International*, 19 April, pp. 4–12.
5 *Washington Post*, 1 April 2002; *International Herald Tribune*, 3 April 2002.

6 *Washington Post*, 24 April. Sharon's view, shared by many Congressional leaders, was summarized by Representative Henry Hyde (Republican, Illinois), chairman of the International Relations Committee, thus: "The Israelis have had many September 11ths in their country nearly every day with these suicide bombings. Sharon has a duty to protect his country and his people."

7 *Independent*, 29 March 2002; *International Herald Tribune*, 29 March 2002.

8 *Washington Post*, 25 April 2002. The damage to the Palestinians from the Israeli offensive was officially put at $360 million. *New York Times*, 16 May 2002.

9 *Washington Post*, 25 March 2002; *International Herald Tribune*, 26 March 2002.

10 See p. 338.

11 *Washington Post*, 7 April 2002.

12 BBC News, 25 April 2002.

13 See p. 327.

14 *Washington Post*, 25 April 2002.

15 *New York Times*, 17 April 2002.

16 *Ibid.*, 12 April 2002.

17 *International Herald Tribune*, 11 April 2002. Whereas an opinion poll in Britain showed 28 percent being pro-Palestinian and 17 percent pro-Israeli, the figures in the US – according to a *Washington Post*-ABC NEWS poll – were: pro-Palestinian 14 percent, and pro-Israeli 49 percent.

18 *Washington Post*, 25 April 2002. Smaller demonstrations against America and Israel were held in Hasa, Qatif, and Safwa.

19 *New York Times*, 11 May 2002.

20 *Washington Post*, 28 March 2002.

21 *New York Times*, 15 April 2002.

22 *Al Hayat*, 13 April 2002.

23 *Ibid.*, 13 April 2002.

24 *International Herald Tribune*, 5 April 2002.

25 *Ibid.*, 5 April 2002; *Observer*, 14 April 2002.

26 *Washington Post*, 24 April 2002.

27 In an interview with the (Jordanian) Petra News Agency, King Abdullah II said, "I told the Israelis that for each Palestinian they kill or injure, a hundred others will be born, ready to seek revenge." *New York Times*, 9 May 2002.

28 Cited in *International Herald Tribune*, 19 April 2002. As a result of the escalating violence, the already low annual GDP of the Palestinians had declined by 53 percent.

29 After deciding by 669 votes to 465 to vote on the resolution on a Palestinian state in defiance of Sharon's stand, the Likud party's

central committee adopted it by a show of hands. BBC News, 12 May 2002.

30 *International Herald Tribune*, 18 March 2002.
31 *Independent*, 29 March 2002; *Financial Times*, 30–31 March 2002.

Abbreviations

9/11	September 11, 2001/ 11 September 2001
ABC	American Broadcasting Company
AH	after hijra (migration of Prophet Muhammad from Mecca to Medina)
aka	also known as
AIG	Armed Islamic Group
ASU	Arab Socialist Union
AWACS	Airborne Warning and Control Systems
BBC	British Broadcasting Corporation
bpd	barrels per day
CAR	Committee for Advice and Reform
CBS	Columbia Broadcasting Service
CDLR	Committee for the Defense of Legitimate Rights
CENTCOM	Central Command
CIA	Central Intelligence Agency
CNN	Cable News Network
CNR	Commission for National Reconciliation
COG	Continuity in Government
COSU	Supreme Council of Senior Ulama
CSF	Central Security Forces
EOHR	Egyptian Organization for Human Rights
EU	European Union
FAA	Federal Aviation Authority
FARC	Fuerzas Armadas Revolucionarias de Colombia (Revolutionary Armed Forces of Colombia)

FATA	Federally Administered Tribal Area
FBI	Federal Bureau of Investigation
FIS	Front du Islamique Salvation (Front of Islamic Salvation)
GCC	Gulf Cooperation Council
GDP	Gross Domestic Product
GIA	Group Islamique Armée (Armed Islamic Group)
GMT	Greenwich Mean Time
GPS	Global Positioning System
IAAM	Islamic Alliance of Afghan Mujahedin
IAEA	International Atomic Energy Agency
ICO	Islamic Conference Organization
IJC	Islamic Jihad Council
IJG	International Justice Group
IMF	International Monetary Fund
IMU	Islamic Movement of Uzbekistan
INC	Indian National Congress
INS	Immigration and Naturalization Service
IRA	Irish Republican Army
IRGC	Islamic Revolutionary Guard Corps
IRM	Islamic Revolutionary Movement
ISAF	International Security Assistance Force
ISI	Inter-Services Intelligence
JDAM	Joint Direct Attack Munitions
JIU	Jamiat-e Ulama-e Islami
JKFL	Jammu and Kashmir Liberation Front
KGB	Komitet Gosudarstevenoy Bezopasnosti (Committee for State Security)
Khad	Khidmat-e Amniyat-e Dawlati (Service of State Security)
MI5	Military Intelligence 5
MI6	Military Intelligence 6
MP	Member of Parliament
Nato	North Atlantic Treaty Organization
NDP	National Democratic Party
NGO	Non-Governmental Organization
NIF	National Islamic Front

NIM	National Islamic Movement
NIMA	National Imaging and Mapping Agency
NORAD	North American Aerospace Defense
NRO	National Reconnaissance Office
NSA	National Security Agency
NSC	National Security Council
NUF	National United Front
OAU	Organization of African Unity
OPEC	Organization of Oil Exporting Countries
OSS	Office of Strategic Surveys
PDPA	People's Democratic Party of Afghanistan
PLO	Palestine Liberation Organization
POW	Prisoner of War
SAD	Special Activities Division
SAS	Special Air Service
SBG	Saudi Binladin Group
SCRG	Supreme Council of Judges
SCS	Special Collection Service
SFR	Special Forces Regiment
SSI	State Securuity Investigation
TERCOM	Terrain Contour Matching Computer
TNT	tri-nitro-toluene
UAE	United Arab Emirates
UK	United Kingdom (of Great Britain and Northern Ireland)
UN	United Nations
UNESCO	United Nations Educational, Scientific and Cultural Organization
UNIF	United National Islamic Front
US/USA	United States of America
USAF	United States Air Force
WIF	World Islamic Front
WMD	weapons of mass destruction
WML	World Muslim League
WTC	Word Trade Center

Glossary of foreign terms

aabru: dignity
aal: of a family or tribe
abu: father
adha: sacrifice
adil/adila: just
ahl: people
ahram: pyramids
akbar: great
akhbar: report, news
al/el/ol/ul: the
alamiya: international, world
alim (pl. ulama): religious-legal scholar
amaa: general, public
aminyat: security
amn: security
amr: command
ansar: helper (of Prophet Muhammad)
awsat: middle
ayatollah: sign or token of Allah
azhar: resplendent
bayat: oath of allegiance
beduin (sing. bedu): nomads
beit/bait: house
bida: innovation
bin: son

bint: daughter
bismillah: in the name of Allah
burqa: all enveloping shroud
daawa: call (of Islam)
dar: house or realm
dawlat: state or nation
dawlati: state or national
dhimmi: (lit.) one who has singed a dhimma, contract between
    Muslims and non-Muslims; (fig.) non-Muslims living in a
    Muslim state
din: religion
-e: of
eid: festival
emir/amir: one who gives amr (command); commander
faqih (pl. fuquha): one who practices fiqh; religious jurist
fatwa: religious ruling
fiqh: (lit.) knowledge; (fig.) Islamic jurisprudence
fitna: sedition or civil strife
fitr: breaking the fast
gamaat: group, society
hadd: (lit.) boundary; (fig.) punishments contained in the Sharia
hadith: (lit.) narrative; (fig.) action or speech of Prophet
    Muhammad or a (Shia) imam
hajj: (lit.) setting out; (fig.) pilgrimage (to Mecca)
hajji: one who has performed hajj
haram: religiously forbidden
harb: war
harkat: movement
hawala: trust
hayat: life
hijab: cover or screen
hijra: migration or flight
hizb: party
hizbollah: Party of Allah
-i: of
ibn: son
ihtisab: observance of religious morality

ijma: consensus
ijtihad: interpretative reasoning
ikhwan: brotherhood or brethren
illahi: divine
imam: (lit.) one who leads prayers in a mosque; (fig.) religious
   leader
intifada: (lit.) shaking off; (fig.) uprising
irhab: terror or terrorism
irhabi: terrorist
islam: state or act of submission (to the will of Allah)
isma: impeccability (of Shia imam)
istikhabarat: intelligence
jahiliya: (lit.) period of ignorance; (fig.) pre-Islamic era
jaish: army
jamaah/jameh: association
jamaat: group, society
jamiat: association
jihad: (lit.) effort; (fig.) holy war
jihadi: supporter of jihad
jirga: assembly
jizya: tribute
khalifa: caliph or deputy
khalq: people
kharaji: outsider or seceder
khidmat: service
khifa: struggle
khirqa: (lit.) used cloth; (fig.) cloak
khums: one-fifth (of gains)
koran/quran: recitation or discourse
lashkar: army
loya: national
mabahidth/mubahas: investigation
madhhab: (lit.) adopted policy; (fig.) a school of jurisprudence
madressa: religious school
mahdi: one who is guided by Allah
mahrim: (lit.) a man barred from marrying a particular woman;
   (fig.) male escort

majallat: review
majlis: assembly
maktab: bureau
manar: tower
maruf: virtue
maulana: cleric or preacher
maulavi: cleric or preacher
marja: source
markaz: center
maslah: beneficial
mawali (sing. mawla): clients or associates
medina: city
millat: nation
mubarak: blessed
mufti: one who delivers fatwas
muhammad: praiseworthy or blessed
mujahedin (sing. mujahid): those who conduct jihad
mujtahid: one who practices ijtihad (interpretative reasoning)
mukhabarat: intelligence
mullah: cleric or preacher
muminin: believers
munafiq: (lit.) hypocrite; (fig.) a deviant Muslim
munazamat: organization
munkar: vice
muqawama: resistance
musavat: unity
muttawin (sing. muttawi): (lit.) one who enforces compliance;
    (fig.) religious police
muwahhidin (sing. muwahhid): unitarians
nawruz: new year
nifaz: establishment
parcham: flag
qadi/qazi: judge
qaida: base
qanun: positive law (subordinate to the Sharia)
qisas: retribution
qiyas: analogy

quds: holy
quran/koran: recitation or discourse
rasul: messenger
riba: usury
salaf: (lit.) roots; (fig.) ancestor
salafiya: ideology of following the precedents of the first
　generation of Muslims
salat: prayers
salih: pious
sawm: fasting during Ramadan
sayyid: (lit.) lord or prince; (fig.) a hereditary title applied to a
　male descendants of Prophet Muhammad
shaab: people
shah: king
shahada: (lit.) act of witness; (fig.) central precept (of Islam)
shaikh (pl. shuyukh): (lit.) old man; (fig.) a title accorded to a
　senior man of power
Sharia/Shariat: (lit.) path or road; (fig.) sacred law of Islam
sharif: noble
shia/shiat: partisans or followers
shirk: idolatry
shura: consultation
suf: wool
Sufi: follower of Sufism, the Islamic mystic path
sultan: ruler
sunna: tradition or beaten path
Sunni: one who follows sunna (of Prophet Muhammad)
tahrik: movement
takfir: denunciation or repentance
talfiq: synthesis of rulings of different schools of law
taliban: (sing. talib) students of religion
tanzimat: reorganization
taqlid: imitation or emulation
tariq/tariqa: road
ulama (sing. alim): body of religious-legal scholars
ulum: knowledge
umm: mother

umma: community of all Muslims
umra: short hajj
va: and or by
vali: guardian
vilayat: rule
wa: and or by
wahadat: unity
waqf: (lit.) prevent: (fig.) religious endowment
watan: homeland or nation
wolesi: people
-ye: of
yom: day
zakat: der. of zakaa, to be pure: (fig.) alms or charity

Appendix I

United Nations Security Council Resolution 1368, 12 September 2001 (adopted unanimously)

The Security Council,

Reaffirming the principles and purposes of the Charter of the United Nations,

Determined to combat by all means threats to international peace and security caused by terrorist acts,

Recognizing the inherent right of individual or collective self-dence in accordance with the Charter,

1. Unequivocally condemns in the strongest terms the horrifying terrorist attacks which took place on 11 September 2001 in New York, Washington (DC) and Pennsylvania and regards such acts, like any act of international terrorism, as a threat to international peace and security;

2. Expresses its deepest sympathy and condolences to the victims and their families and to the People and Government of the United States of America;

3. Calls on all States to work together urgently to bring to justice the perpetrators, organizers and sponsors of these terrorist attacks and stresses that those responsible for aiding, supporting or harbouring the perpetrators, organizers and sponsors of these acts will be held accountable;

4. Calls also on the international community to redouble their efforts to prevent and suppress terrorist acts including by increased coooperation and full implementation of the relevant international anti-terrorist conventions and

Security Council resolutions, in particular resolution 1269 of 19 October 1999;

5. Expresses its readiness to take all necessary steps to respond to the terrorist attacks of 11 September 2001, and to combat all forms of terrorism, in accordance with its responsibilities under the Charter of the United Nations;

6. Decides to remain seized of the matter.

Appendix II

United Nations Security Council Resolution 1373, 28 September 2001 (adopted unanimously)

The Security Council,

Reaffirming its resolutions 1269 (1999) of 19 October 1999 and 1368 (2001) of 12 September 2001,

Reaffirming also its unequivocal condemnation of the terrorist attacks which took place in New York, Washington, DC, and Pennsylvania on 11 September 2001, and expressing its determination to prevent all such acts,

Reaffirming further that such acts, like any act of international terrorism, constitute a threat to international peace and security,

Reaffirming the inherent right of individual or collective self-defence as recognized by the Charter of the United Nations as reiterated in resolution 1368 (2001),

Reaffirming the need to combat by all means, in accordance with the Charter of the United Nations, threats to international peace and security caused by terrorist acts,

Deeply concerned by the increase, in various regions of the world, of acts of terrorism motivated by intolerance or extremism,

Calling on States to work together urgently to prevent and suppress terrorist acts, including through increased cooperation and full implementation of the relevant international conventions relating to terrorism,

Recognizing the need for States to complement international cooperation by taking additional measures to prevent and suppress, in their territories through all lawful means, the financing and preparation of any acts of terrorism,

Reaffirming the principle established by the General Assembly in its declaration of October 1970 (resolution 2625 (XXV)) and reiterated by the Security Council in its resolution 1189 (1998) of 13 August 1998, namely that every State has the duty to refrain from organizing, instigating, assisting or participating in terrorist acts in another state or acquiescing in organized activities within its territory directed towards the commission of such acts,

Acting under Chapter VII of the Charter of the United Nations,

1. *Decides* that all States shall:
    (a) Prevent and suppress the financing of terrorist acts;
    (b) Criminalize the wilful provision or collection, by any means, directly or indirectly, of funds by their nationals or in their territories with the intention that the funds should be used, or in the knowledge that they are to be used, in order to carry out terrorist acts;
    (c) Freeze without delay funds and other financial assets or economic resources of persons who commit, or attempt to commit, terrorist acts or participate in or facilitate the commission of terrorist acts; of entities owned or controlled directly or indirectly by such persons; and of persons and entities acting on behalf of, or at the direction of such persons and entities, including funds derived or generated from property owned or controlled directly or indirectly by such persons and associated persons and entities;
    (d) Prohibit their nationals or any persons and entities within their territories from making any funds, financial assets or economic resources or financial or other related services available, directly or indirectly, for the benefit of persons who commit or attempt to commit or facilitate or participate in the commission of terrorist acts, of entities owned or controlled, directly or indirectly, by such persons and of persons and entities acting on behalf of or at the direction of such persons;

2. *Decides also* that all States shall:
    (a) Refrain from providing any form of support, active or passive, to entities or persons involved in terrorist

acts, including by suppressing recruitment of members of terrorist groups and eliminating the supply of weapons to terrorists;

(b) Take the necessary steps to prevent the commission of terrorist acts, including by provision of early warning to other States by exchange of information;

(c) Deny safe haven to those who finance, plan, support, or commit terrorist acts, or provide safe havens;

(d) Prevent those who finance, plan, facilitate or commit terrorist acts from using their respective territories for those purposes against other States or their citizens;

(e) Ensure that any person who participates in the financing, planning, preparation or perpetration of terrorist acts or in supporting terrorist acts is brought to justice and ensure that, in addition to any other measures against them, such terrorist acts are established as serious criminal offences in domestic laws and regulations and that the punishment duly reflects the seriousness of such terrorist acts;

(f) Afford one another the greatest measure of assistance in connection with criminal investigations or criminal proceedings relating to the financing or support of terrorist acts, including assistance in obtaining evidence in their possession necessary for the proceedings;

(g) Prevent the movement of terrorists or terrorist groups by effective border controls and controls on issuance of identity papers and travel documents, and through measures for preventing counterfeiting, forgery or fraudulent use of identity papers and travel documents;

3. *Calls upon* all States to:

(a) Find ways of intensifying and accelerating the exchange of operational information, especially regarding actions or movements of terrorist persons or networks; forged or falsified travel documents; traffic in arms, explosives or sensitive materials; use of communications technologies by terrorist groups; and the threat posed by the possession of weapons of mass destruction by terrorist groups;

(b) Exchange information in accordance with international and domestic law and cooperate on administrative and judicial matters to prevent the commission of terrorist acts;

(c) Cooperate, particularly through bilateral and multilateral arrangements and agreements, to prevent and suppress terrorist attacks and take action against perpetrators of such acts;

(d) Become parties as soon as possible to the relevant international conventions and protocols relating to terrorism, including the International Convention for the Suppression of the Financing of Terrorism of 9 December 1999;

(e) Increase cooperation and fully implement the relevant international conventions and protocols relating to terrorism and Security Council resolutions 1269 (1999) and 1368 (2001);

(f) Take appropriate measures in conformity with the relevant provisions of national and international law, including international standards of human rights, before granting refugee status, for the purpose of ensuring that the asylum seeker has not planned, facilitated or participated in the commission of terrorist acts;

(g) Ensure, in conformity with international law, that refugee status is not abused by the perpetrators, organizers or facilitators of terrorist acts, and that claims of political motivation are not recognized as grounds for refusing requests for the extradition of alleged terrorists;

4. *Notes* with concern the close connection between international terrorism and transnational organized crime, illicit drugs, money-laundering, illegal arms-trafficking, and illegal movement of nuclear, chemical, biological and other potentially deadly materials, and in this regard *emphasizes* the need to enhance coordination of efforts on national, subregional, regional and international levels in order to

strengthen a global response to this serious challenge and threat to international security;

5. *Declares* that acts, methods, and practices of terrorism are contrary to the purposes and principles of the United Nations and that knowingly financing, planning and inciting terrorist acts are also contrary to the purposes and principles of the United Nations;

6. *Decides* to establish, in accordance with rule 28 of its provisional rules of procedure, a Committee of the Security Council, consisting of all the members of the Council, to monitor implementation of this resolution, with the assistance of appropriate expertise, and *calls upon* all States to report to the Committee, no later than 90 days from the date of adoption of this resolution and thereafter according to a timetable to be proposed by the Committee, on the steps they have taken to implement this resolution;

7. *Directs* the Committee to delineate its tasks, submit a work programme within 30 days of the adoption of this resolution, and to consider the support it requires, in consultation with the Secretary-General;

8. *Expresses* its determination to take all necessary steps in order to ensure the full implementation of this resolution, in accordance with its responsibilities under the Charter;

9. *Decides* to remain seized of this matter.

Select bibliography

Abdo, Geneive, *No God But God: Egypt and the Triumph of Islam*, Oxford University Press, Oxford and New York, 2001.

Abir, Mordechai, *Government, Society and the Gulf Crisis*, Routledge, London and New York, 1993.

Aburish, Said K., *The Rise, Corruption and the Coming Fall of the House of Saud*, Bloomsbury, London, 1995; St. Martin's Press, New York, 1996.

Amin, Tahir, *Afghanistan Crisis: Implications and Options for Muslim World, Iran and Pakistan*, Institute of Policy Studies, Lahore, 1982.

Arberry, Arthur J. (trans.), *The Koran Interpreted*, Oxford University Press, Oxford and New York, 1964.

Arney, George, *Afghanistan*, Mandarin/Random House, London, 1990.

Arnold, Anthony, *Afghanistan: The Soviet Invasion in Perspective*, Hoover Institution Press, Stanford, CA, 1985.

Beling, Willard (ed.), *King Faisal and Modernisation of Saudi Arabia*, Westview Press, Boulder, CO, 1980.

Bergen, Peter L., *Holy War, Inc.: Inside the Secret World of Osama bin Laden*, Weidenfeld & Nicolson, London and The Free Press, New York, 2001.

Cooley, John K., *Unholy Wars: Afghanistan, America and International Terrorism*, Pluto Press, London and Sterling, VA, 2000.

Dekmejian, R. Hrair, *Islam in Revolution: Fundamentalism in the Arab World*, Syracuse University Press, Syracuse, NY, 1985.

Dupree, Louis, *Afghanistan*, Princeton University Press, Princeton, NJ, and Guildford 1980.

Enayat, Hamid, *Modern Islamic Political Thought*, Macmillan, London, 1982.

Esposito, John L., *Islam and Politics*, Syracuse University Press, Syracuse, NY, 1984.

Fandy, Mamoun, *Saudi Arabia and the Politics of Dissent*, Palgrave, New York, 2001.

Ganguly, Sumit, *The Crisis in Kashmir: Portents of War, Hopes of Peace*, Cambridge University Press, Cambridge and New York:, 1999.

Ghazali, Muhammad, *Our Beginning in Wisdom* (trans. Ismail el Faruqi), American Council of Learned Societies, Washington, DC, 1953.

Halliday, Fred, *Two Hours that Shook the World: September 11, 2001, Causes and Consequences*, Saqi Books, London, 2002.

Heikal, Mohamed, *Autumn of Fury: The Assassination of Sadat*, André Deutsch, London, 1983.

Helms, Christine Moss, *The Cohesion of Saudi Arabia: Evolution of Political Identity*, Croom Helm, London, 1981.

Hiro, Dilip, *Inside the Middle East*, Routledge & Kegan Paul, London and McGraw-Hill, New York, 1982.

Hiro, Dilip, *Holy Wars: The Rise of Islamic Fundamentalism*, Routledge, New York 1989 (originally published as *Islamic Fundamentalism*, Paladin Books/HarperCollins, London, 1988).

Hiro, Dilip, *Between Marx and Muhammad: The Changing Face of Central Asia*, HarperCollins, London and New York, 1994.

Hiro, Dilip, *Dictionary of the Middle East*, Macmillan Press, Basingstoke, and St Martin's Press, New York, 1996.

Holden, David and Richard Johns, *The House of Saud*, Sidgwick & Jackson, London, 1981.

Hyman, Anthony, *Afghanistan Under Soviet Domination, 1964–83*, Macmillan, London, 1984.

Keddie, Nikki R., *Sayyid Jamal al Din "al Afghani': A Political Biography*, University of California Press, Los Angeles and Berkeley, CA, 1972.

Keddie, Nikki R. (ed.). *Scholars, Saints and Sufis: Muslim Religious Institutions since 1500*, University of California Press, Los Angeles and Berkeley, CA, 1972.

Kepel, Gilles, *The Revenge of God: The Resurgence of Islam, Christianity and Judaism in the Modern World*, Polity Press, Cambridge, 1994.

Kerr, Malcolm H., *Islamic Reform: The Political and Legal Theories of Muhammad Abduh and Rashid Rida*, University of California Press, Los Angeles and Berkeley, CA, 1972.

Latifa, *My Forbidden Face: Growing up under the Taliban, a Young Woman's Story* (trans. Lisa Appignanesi), Virago, London, 2002.

Lohbeck, Kurt, *Holy Wars, Unholy Victory: Eyewitness to the CIA's Secret War in Afghanistan*, Regency Gateway, Washington, DC, 1993.

Long, David E., *The United States and Saudi Arabia: Ambivalent Allies*, Westview Press, Boulder, CO, 1985.

Mackey, Sandra, *The Saudis: Inside the Desert Kingdom*, Houghton Miflin, Boston and Harrap, London, 1987.

Malley, William (ed.), *Fundamentalism Reborn? Afghanistan and the Taliban*, C. Hurst, London, 1998

Marsden, Peter, *The Taliban: War, Religion and the New Order in Afghanistan*, Oxford University Press, Karachi, and Zed Press, London and New York, 1998.

Martin, David C. and John Wolcott, *The Best Laid Plans: The Inside Story of America's War against Terrorism*, Harper & Row, New York, 1988

Maududi, Sayyid Abul Ala, *Towards Understanding Islam*, Islamic Publications, Lahore, 1960.

Maududi, Sayyid Abul Ala, *A Short History of the Revivalist Movements in Islam*, Islamic Publications, Lahore, 1963.

The Middle East and North Africa 2001, Europa Publications, London and New York, 2001.

Miller, Judith, *God Has Ninety-Nine Names: Reporting from a Militant Middle East*, Simon & Schuster, New York, 1996.

Mitchell, Richard P., *The Society of Muslim Brothers*, Oxford University Press, Oxford and New York, 1969.

Mortimer, Edward, *Faith and Power: The Politics of Islam*, Faber & Faber, London, and Holt, Rinehart, New York, 1982.

Piscatori, James P. (ed.), *Islam in the Political Process*, Cambridge University Press, Cambridge and New York, 1983.

Qutab, Sayyid (trans. William, E. Sgepard), *Sayyid Qutab and Islamic Activism: A Translation and Critical Analysis of Social Justice in Islam*, Brill Academic Publishers, Leiden, 1996.

Qutb, Sayyid, *Islam: The Religion of the Future*, New Era Publishers, Kuwait, 1977.

Qutb, Sayyid, *Milestones*, American Trust Publications, Chicago, IL, 1991.

Qutb, Sayyid, *Social Justice in Islam* (trans. Hamid Algar), Islamic Publications International, Berkeley, CA, Revised Edition, 2000.

Rashid, Ahmed, *Taliban: Islam, Oil and the New Great Game in Central Asia*, I. B. Tauris, London, 2000; and Yale University Press, New Haven, CT, 2001.

Rashid, Ahmed, *Jihad: The Rise of Militant Islam in Central Asia*, Yale University Press, London and New Haven, CT, 2002.

Roy, Olivier, *Islam and Resistance in Afghanistan*, Cambridge University Press, Cambridge and New York, 1986.

Roy, Olivier, *Afghanistan, from Holy War to Civil War*, Princeton University Press, Guildford, and Princeton, NJ, 1995.

Ruthven, Malise, *Islam in the World*, Penguin Books, Harmondsworth, 1984.

Tamimi, Azzam (ed.), *Power-Sharing Islam?*, Liberty for Muslim World Publications, London, 1993.

Trimingham, J. Spencer, *The Sufi Orders in Islam*, Oxford University Press, Oxford and New York, 1971.

Wendell, Charles (ed.) *Five Tracts of Hassan al Banna (1906–49)*, University of California Press, Los Angeles and Berkeley, CA, 1978.

Whittaker, David J., *The Terrorism Reader*, Routledge, London and New York, 2001.

Wirsing, Robert G., *India, Pakistan and the Kashmir Dispute*, Macmillan Press, Basingstoke and St. Martin's Press, New York, 1994.

News agencies, newspapers and periodicals

Agence France Presse
Asharq al Awsat (London)
Associated Press
BBC News (London)
Boston Globe (Boston)
Daily Telegraph (London)
Dawn (Karachi)
Economist (London)
Financial Times (London and New York)
Guardian (London)
Al Hayat (London)
Independent (London)
Independent on Sunday (London)
Inter Press Service (Rome)
International Herald Tribune (Paris)
Los Angeles Times (Los Angeles)
Middle East International (London and Arlington)
Nation (New York)
New York Times (New York)

New Yorker (New York)
Observer (London)
Observer Magazine (London)
Outlook (Delhi)
Reuters
Sunday Times (London)
Sunday Times Magazine (London)
This Week (London)
Time (New York and London)
The Times (London)
The Wall Street Journal (New York)
Washington Post (Washington)

Index

For a name starting with "Al" or "The/the" see its first part. For a surname starting with "al" see its second part. A person's religious or secular title has been omitted.

502 *Index*